THE BATTLE OF THE SELLE

This book is firstly dedicated to my mother, Norma Hodgkinson, who sadly died as the manuscript was being completed. The support that she and my father, engineer and author, Allan Hodgkinson, gave me throughout their lives was steadfast.

It is further dedicated to three soldiers of the Great War. My grandfather, Private Peter Rimmer, 168093 ASC (27 Motorised Ambulance Convoy), ended his war on the Selle battlefield, at Forest in November 1918. Also my great-uncle, Private William Robert Moxey, 206165 ASC; and my great-uncle, Corporal Henry John Boyd, 14004 and 113481, 12th Battalion 'Bristol's Own' Gloucestershire Regiment and RE (Special Brigade). Without these men's stories in my childhood, my passion for the Great War would have been the less.

The Battle of the Selle

Fourth Army Operations on the Western Front in the Hundred Days 9-24 October 1918

Peter E. Hodgkinson

Helion & Company Limited

Helion & Company Limited
Unit 8 Amherst Business Centre
Budbrooke Road
Warwick
CV34 5WE
England
Tel. 01926 499 619
Email: info@helion.co.uk
Website: www.helion.co.uk
Twitter: @helionbooks
Visit our blog at blog.helion.co.uk

Published by Helion & Company 2017. Reprinted in paperback 2022
Designed and typeset by Mach 3 Solutions Ltd (www.mach3solutions.co.uk)
Cover designed by Paul Hewitt, Battlefield Design (www.battlefield-design.co.uk)

ISBN 978-1-80451-048-3

British Library Cataloguing-in-Publication Data.
A catalogue record for this book is available from the British Library.

Contents

List of Illustrations

List of Tables

List of Maps

In colour section

Acknowledgements

My thanks firstly go to Professors John Bourne and Peter Simkins, and Dr Trevor Harvey, for reading the first draft of this book and proffering their comments. John and Peter deserve particular thanks for their close consideration of the British generals at the Selle; and John, in addition, allowed free use of his database of generals. Secondly, acknowledgement must be made to the work of Mark Whisler in his 2001 dissertation, 'Der Tommy Kommt', in respect of his research in German records concerning the German units present on the Selle. Chapters Four and Five would be much the poorer lacking Mark's knowledge of the enemy side of the line. Lastly, I am grateful for the help of Geoff Clarke, who sadly died before his own PhD could be submitted, in the issue of railways.

Further thanks are due to the Imperial War Museum for access; and the Documents Collection and individual copyright holders for permission to quote from Fourth Army papers and the private papers etc. of R.G. Dixon and A. Caseby. Every effort has been made to contact the copyright holders of the papers of R. Cude, K. Earle, and F.J. Rice. The author and the Imperial War Museum would be grateful for any information which might help to trace these whose identities or addresses are not currently known.

Abbreviations

AA&QMG	Assistant Adjutant & Quartermaster General
ADOS	Assistant Director of Ordnance Services
AEF	American Expeditionary Force
AFA	Australian Field Artillery
AFC	Australian Flying Corps
AQMG	Assistant Quartermaster General
ASC	Army Service Corps
ATC	Australian Tunnelling Company
AWM	Australian War Memorial
BEF	British Expeditionary Force
BGGS	Brigadier General General Staff
BGRA	Brigadier General Royal Artillery
CB	Companion of the Order of the Bath
CBE	Commander of the Order of the British Empire
C-in-C	Commander in Chief
CGS	Chief General Staff
CIE	Companion of the Order of the Indian Empire
CMG	Companion of the Most Distinguished Oder of St Michael and St George
CO	Commanding Officer
CRA	Commander Royal Artillery
CRE	Commander Royal Engineers
CSM	Company sergeant major
CVO	Commander of the Royal Victorian Order
CWGC	Commonwealth War Graves Commission
DAC	Divisional Ammunition Column
DCM	Distinguished Conduct Medal
DDOS	Deputy Director Ordnance Services
DFC	Distinguished Flying Cross
DHQ	Divisional headquarters
DL	Doctor of Literature
DLI	Durham Light Infantry
DSO	Distinguished Service Order
EA	Enemy aircraft
FOO	Forward Observation Officer
FR	Fusilier Regiment
FSR	Field Service Regulations

GCB	Knight Grand Cross of the Most Honourable Order of the Bath
GCSI	Knight Grand Commander of the Most Exalted Order of the Star of India
GCVO	Knight Grand Cross of the Royal Victorian Order
GHQ	General Headquarters
GOC	General Officer Commanding
GOCRA	General Officer Commanding Royal Artillery
GSO	General Staff Officer (1,2 or 3)
HE	High explosive
HQ	Headquarters
HT	Horse transport
HWL	*Hauptwiderstandline* (line of resistance)
IR	Infantry Regiment
IWM	Imperial War Museum
KBE	Commander of the Most Excellent Order of the British Empire
KCB	Commander of the Most Honourable Order of the Bath
KCMG	Knight Commander of the Most Distinguished Order of St Michael and St George
KCVO	Knight Commander of the Royal Victorian Order
KOYLI	Kings Own Yorkshire Light Infantry
KPM	King's Police Medal
KRRC	Kings Royal Rifle Corps
LR	Light railway
LSH	Lord Strathcona's Horse
LTM	Light trench mortar
MC	Military Cross
MG	Machine-gun
MGC	Machine Gun Corps
MGGS	Major-General General Staff
MM	Military Medal
mm	Millimetre
MT	Motor transport
NAA	National Archives of Australia
NCO	Non-Commissioned Officer
OB	Order of Burma
OH	Official History
OHL	Oberste Heeresleitung (German Supreme Army Command)
OR	Other ranks
RAF	Royal Air Force
RE	Royal Engineers
RFA	Royal Field Artillery
RGA	Royal Garrison Artillery
RIR	Reserve Infantry Regiment
RSJ	Rolled steel joist
SAA	Small arms ammunition
SMTO	Senior Mechanical Transport Officer
TNA	The National Archives (UK)
USAWW	*United States Army in the World War*
VC	Victoria Cross

Introduction

During the centenary years 2014-2018, the topic of the First World War will have reached the zenith of its popularity. There will never have been so many books concerning it published in such a short period, never so many dramas presented on radio or television, and never so many documentary series aired. Yet only a few of these have embraced the scholarship of the so-called 'revisionist' historians who over the past 30 years have painstakingly put the bricks in the wall of understanding the nature of the effort the British state, people and its army invested in the defeat of Germany in 1918, based on weight of fact rather than burden of sentiment.

As Professor Gary Sheffield has argued: 'The last few years has made clear that … the "futility/'lions led by donkeys'" narrative of Britain's involvement in the conflict is very much with us'. He continued:

> The ideas that there were no great issues at stake during the First World War, that a million men died for nothing and, in an accompanying myth, the lives of soldiers were routinely thrown away by criminally incompetent generals has been rebutted over and over again, but display remarkable longevity.[1]

Sheffield draws our attention to the so-called 'Luvvie's Letter', published in the *Guardian* newspaper on 21 May 2013 protesting the centenary commemoration of the war. This declared that: 'Far from being a "war to end all wars" or a "victory for democracy", this was a military disaster and a human catastrophe'.[2] He further flags Dr Jessica Meyer's response which notes 'the apparent belief that those engaged professionally with and in the arts (as the majority of the signatories are) have a particular authority to speak about the horror of war'.[3] The signatories to the letter, however, only represent the eloquent tip of an attitudinal iceberg that this author has described elsewhere.[4] Volume of death has become the defining feature of the war, the soldier's experiences viewed through a filter of sentimentality, misplaced psychological analysis, and modern pacifism.

The distortion that this sentiment has brought to our vision of the war and the men who fought it is no better demonstrated than in the British government's decision to commemorate the defeat at Gallipoli and the terrible first day on the Somme rather than the Hundred Days campaign which brought the war to an end. Sheffield describes this omission as 'historical illiteracy', citing

1 G. Sheffield, 'A Once in a Century Opportunity?', p.3.
2 http://www.theguardian.com/world/2013/may/21/remembering-war-to-promote-peace
3 Jessica Meyer, http://armsandthemedicalman.wordpress.com/2013/05/22/possibly-an-angry-post/
4 P. Hodgkinson, *Glum Heroes*, pp.xii-xiii.

Professor Peter Simkins' incisive analogy that this is 'akin to commemorating the Second World War by marking the Fall of Singapore but ignoring D-Day'.[5] Any nationalistic celebration of victory in a Europe that has attempted to bury its plethora of hatchets in the European Union would be anathema. It is surely, however, as inappropriate to ignore the nation's skilled effort in the Hundred Days as it is to concentrate solely on the supposed victimhood of those who fought. It is as if effort is only indicated by the uniform gravestones of the Commonwealth War Graves Commission that follow the line of the Western Front. Failure to commemorate this skilled effort is the ultimate disrespect, as demonstrated by the *Guardian* letter writers who see only 'military disaster' rather than the final achievement – the most remarkable series of victories ever achieved by a British army.

Historians were late in reducing the vacuum of knowledge concerning the final victory, the turgid volumes of the *Official History* which dealt with the Hundred Days lying unread on most bookshelves. John Terraine was the first modern historian to subject the year 1918 to analysis in his book *To Win a War: 1918 – The Year of Victory*, published in 1978. Gregory Blaxland explored the opening British contribution to the final campaign in *Amiens 1918*, published in 1981. The initial book that addressed the whole campaign exclusively, *Amiens to the Armistice*, by Paul Harris and Niall Barr, appeared in 1998, 80 years after the events described. Two years earlier Peter Simkins had begun to erode the myth of the poor tactical performance of the British army in comparison with the Canadian and Australian corps in his statistical analysis of 'British Divisions in the "Hundred Days"'.[6] The first historian to drill down exclusively into the experience of one of the five British armies during the final offensive was Jonathan Boff in his *Winning and Losing on the Western Front: The British Third Army and the Defeat of Germany in 1918*, published as recently as 2012. The works of Terraine and Boff are notable for their titles – they contain the words 'victory', 'defeat', 'winning' and 'losing'. We live in an era where internationalism means that such words are largely restricted to sporting events.[7] But defeated the German Army was, and its commanders and the politicians of the neonate republic knew it. It was not defeated in detail, but it was defeated in spirit and purpose. As Paul Harris observes: 'Except for rear-guards, the German Armies on the Western Front had virtually ceased fighting by 5 November'.[8] This defeat came through no 'stab in the back', the *Dolchstoßlegende*.[9] It was delivered militarily through multiple stabs to the front, specifically the Western Front. Yet even in the war's aftermath, as James Diehl succinctly notes, 'it was easy in 1918 for Germans to imagine that they were still undefeated', there being no fighting on German soil.[10] Such a view involved effortless sleight of mouth to spin. Chancellor Friedrich Ebert, who had actually authorised the signing of the Armistice, declared to the returning troops at the Brandenburg Gate on 10 December 1918 that 'no enemy overcame you', and that they were returning 'undefeated from the battlefield'.[11]

5 Sheffield, op. cit., p.6.
6 P. Simkins, 'Co-Stars or Supporting Cast? British Divisions in the "Hundred Days", 1918', in P. Griffith (ed.) *British Fighting Methods in the Great War*, p.52.
7 Similarly, the question of responsibility or war guilt which preoccupied the Paris Peace Conference has mutated from 'who' caused the war to 'what were the causes' of the war.
8 J.P. Harris & N. Barr, *Amiens to the Armistice*, pp.287-8.
9 The term appears to stem from its use in a centrist political meeting in the Munich Löwenbräu-Keller on 2 November 1918, by Ernst Müller-Meiningen, a member of the Progressive coalition in the Reichstag.
10 J.M Diehl, 'Germany in Defeat, 1918 and 1945: Some Comparisons and Contrasts', p.397.
11 *The Times*, 12 December 1918. Ebert was seeking to bind the army to his government, as *The Times* headline put it, with an 'Oath of Fealty'.

Inability to win is not quite the same as defeat. The point where can it be said that Germany would be unable to be victorious in the First World War probably dates to the end of the First Battle of the Marne (5-12 September 1914). When the German retreat began on 9 September it was an acknowledgement that the Schlieffen Plan (and its revisions) were a conceptual and practical failure. A short war was henceforth impossible, and Germany was condemned to fighting on two fronts. A further nail in the coffin of winability was the struggle on the Somme from July to November 1916, where the extent of the effort that the British intended to put into eventual victory became clear. The key date that heralded the death of any remaining German hopes was 6 April 1917, when the United States of America declared war on Germany. At a point of dwindling manpower, the might of the USA promised a battering ram that would at some point break the defences of the German armies in the west.

The series of strategically, operationally and logistically ill-conceived offensives beginning on March 21 1918 drained the German Army to a large extent of the capability for further offensive action. But the German army did not defeat itself as a result of the effort it had thus expended. It had been ground down by the great attritional battles of 1916 and 1917. As Nick Lloyd observes, in late 1918 it 'was not the great, cohesive and professional force it had been.' Yet attrition applied to the Allied forces as well. As Lloyd continues, if the enemy was diminished, 'then the same, equally, could be said for both the British and the French'. The French were 'a pale, gaunt shadow of their former selves' after the grind of Verdun and operational catastrophe followed by unrest in the army in 1917. The British army, though far from stripped of its experienced NCOs and officers, was beginning to be reinforced with young conscripts. These two forces, however, coupled with the inexperienced American army, were now the possessors of the mass of ordnance that industries committed to total war could provide. The trio, and the BEF in particular, would storm 'some of the toughest defensive positions ever constructed' and continually force their opponents back towards their own frontier.[12]

The true unification of allied purpose came on 26 March 1918, when Ferdinand Foch, who had risen from command of the French *Ninth Army* in 1914 to chief of the French General Staff in 1917, was appointed to coordinate the allied effort on the Western Front. This role was later glorified with the title General-in-Chief of the Allied Armies, although Sir Douglas Haig,[13] the French Commander-in-Chief Philippe Pétain,[14] and the American General John Pershing,[15] retained tactical control of the three main national armies. Foch was a man 'renowned for his energy, decision and aggression',[16] who had allegedly declared in September 1914: 'My centre is yielding. My right is retreating. Situation excellent. I am attacking'. Yet he was no proponent of 'huroosh' – already in 1916 he was writing of 'la bataille profonde et de longue durée', deep and long battle. Foch would direct the 'first truly modern operational offensive, which he dubbed "bataille

12 N. Lloyd, *Hundred Days – The End of the Great War*, p.275.

13 Field-Marshall Sir Douglas Haig (1861-1928) was commander of I Corps in August 1914, promoted to command First Army on Boxing Day 1914, and then became Commander-in-Chief of the BEF on 19 December 1915.

14 Philippe Pétain (1856-1951) was a brigade commander in August 1914, promoted to command *6th Division* at the Battle of the Marne, and *XXXIII Corps* in October 1914. Commanding *Second Army* at the opening of the Battle of Verdun in 1916, he became Commander of *Army Group Centre* and subsequently Commander-in-Chief in 1917.

15 John Joseph Pershing (1860-1948) had fought in the Spanish and Philippine wars, and led the less than successful Pancho Villa expedition in 1916. He was given command of the United States armies immediately after the USA entered the war.

16 Lloyd, op. cit., p.21.

generale", sequencing battles on the scale of earlier limited offensives in a co-ordinated high-tempo attritional campaign'.[17] This would, however, have to wait until the summer to be unleashed.

The date that German defeat was set in motion was 18 July 1918, the day of the allied counterattack known as the Second Battle of the Marne. The enemy had attacked east and west of Reims along a 65 mile front. The Allies were expecting them, and within two days the attack had been halted and a vulnerable salient created. A well-prepared counterattack was then sprung. The jaws comprised a large American force with the French on the west side of the salient, and two French corps (with an Italian presence) to the east. The attack, supported by hundreds of tanks, mounted behind a massive creeping barrage that began without any previous bombardment, netted nearly 12,000 prisoners on the first day alone. From that day, the German armies on the Western Front were on the back foot, constantly driven to the rear. There were 117 days to go to the Armistice.

On 24 July, Foch convened a conference with Haig, Pétain and Pershing at his headquarters, Château de Bombon at Melun. Here, his Chief of Staff, Maxime Weygand, read out a memorandum which he had written but which expressed Foch's intention.[18] There would be a 'series of movements' which would inflict a 'succession of blows' upon the enemy.[19] These would, as Haig noted, 'regain the initiative' and 'clear the main railway lines, with a view to further operations'. The Paris-Avricourt railway would be freed where the enemy sat astride it at Château Thierry, interdiction of the same line would be relieved at Saint-Mihiel, and by attacking at Amiens the threat to rail communications would be removed there as well. The second aim was the restoration of 'the free use of the western part of the northern coalfield, of which the output was essential for the prosecution of the war'.[20] Haig described dismissively how at the meeting, 'nothing startling happened',[21] yet the following day all three national commanders signed up to Foch's plan. The startling thing, in truth, was that for the first time there would be truly co-ordinated military action on the Western Front. On 28 September Sir Henry Rawlinson wrote, anticipating the result of the assault on the Hindenburg Line on the morrow: 'Under Foch's tuition and the lessons of over four years war we are really learning and the synchronisation of the various attacks has been admirable'.[22] From the operational point of view, these co-ordinated attacks on multiple axes 'undermined German defence in depth doctrine by leaving individual corps with weak intervention formations, by thinning army and army group level reserves, and by forcing the commitment of virtually all *OHL* reserves'.[23] This was attrition in its wider sense.

The British Hundred Days campaign (which in fact lasted 95 days) opened on 8 August with the first of the 'series of movements', the Battle of Amiens. Planned in great secrecy as part of the general allied strategy, Fourth Army assembled the Canadian and Australian Corps in secret. Together with the British III Corps, these deeply skilled formations utilised the same tactics employed at Second Marne, attacking conjointly with the French *First Army*. They assaulted poor

17 W. Philpott, https://rusi.org/commentary/beyond-learning-curve-british-armys-military-transformation-first-world-war.
18 Maxine Weygand (1867-1965) served as a staff officer to Foch for most of the war. He was commanding the French armies when an armistice was sought in 1940.
19 F. Foch, *The Memoirs of Marshal Foch*, pp.425-449.
20 A.M. Henniker, *Transportation on the Western Front*, p.421.
21 D. Haig, letter dated 24 July 1918 to Sir Henry Wilson, G. Sheffield and J. Bourne, *Douglas Haig – War Diaries and Letters 1914-1918*, p.434.
22 Sir H. Rawlinson, War Journal, 28 September 1918, Churchill College RWLN 1/11.
23 M. Whisler, 'Der Tommy Kommt', p.33. Oberste Heeresleitung was the German Supreme Army Command.

defences, on flat ground that would be ideal for tank action. There was no preliminary bombardment, and at Zero some 700 field guns opened a creeping barrage whilst two-thirds of 670 heavy guns performed counterbattery work. The locations of 95 per cent of the enemy artillery had previously been identified. In the skies, RAF bombers attacked German aerodromes and fighters were directed at enemy planes and ground targets. Around 450 tanks went forward with the infantry. Ludendorff's 'black day for the German army' led to an eight mile advance. The vital rail-hub of Amiens was now beyond German threat. Fifteen thousand prisoners were taken and 9,000 of the enemy killed or wounded. Although progress was made on the next three days, there were diminishing returns as German resistance stiffened, and the offensive was ended.[24] This was to be a feature of the British approach – closing down an offensive when it had ceased to be productive and delivering another blow elsewhere. Operationally this represented forces at the peak of their powers. Being rich in artillery resources the BEF was now able to strike with all its five armies, something it had previously been unable to achieve.

The 'series of movements' would be executed by the British in the area between Ypres and the Somme, in conjunction with French in the Oise-Aisne sector. The American effort further south would be directed at reducing the Saint-Mihiel salient. The next British step was an offensive by the Third Army across the old Somme battlefield, commencing on 21 August. General Byng's attack lacked vigour,[25] and whilst the enemy was pushed back, it fell well short of the spectacular success achieved at Amiens. Haig, somewhat frustrated by Byng's effort but with the bit now between his teeth, sent a telegram to all his army commanders on the 22nd noting that: 'Risks which a month ago would have been criminal to incur, ought now to be incurred as a duty'. The caution of trench warfare had now to be abandoned:

> It is no longer necessary to advance in regular lines and step by step. On the contrary, each division should be given a distant objective which must be reached independently of its neighbour, and even if one's flank is thereby exposed for the time being.[26]

The warfare for whose direction he had overseen the crafting of *Field Service Regulations* in 1909, he hoped, was back. From 24 to 29 August Third and Fourth Armies, particularly the Australian Corps of the latter, drove the enemy back. The *Second* and *Eighteenth German Armies* were formally ordered to retreat on 26 August to the *Wotan Stellung* or Drocourt-Quéant Line, the northern extension of the *Siegfried Stellung* (Hindenburg Line). From the 26th, First Army joined in to the north in the Battle of the Scarpe, pushing across the old Arras battlefield. At the end of the month the Australian Corps, which had reached the banks of the Somme, crossed to take Mont St Quentin and Péronne.

On 27 August Haig, now seeing the war as winnable by the autumn, suggested to Foch, who still saw victory as only achievable in 1919, a 'concentric movement being begun without delay on Cambrai, on St Quentin, & from the south on Mézières', realigning the American attack from Saint-Mihiel.[27] Moving from protecting the Allies' rail centres to targeting those of the enemy would threaten the enemy's 'decisive points that allowed him to use his strength.' Intercepting the

24 See R. Prior & T. Wilson, *Command on the Western Front*, pp.301-336; Harris & Barr, op. cit., pp.59-117; and C. Messenger, *The Day we Won the War*.
25 Julian Byng (1862-1935) was a cavalry officer who successively commanded the Cavalry, IX and XVII Corps until promoted to command Third Army in June 1917.
26 War Diary, HQ Fourth Army, GHQ Order, OAD 911, 22 August 1918, TNA WO158/241.
27 D. Haig, letter to Sir Henry Wilson 27 August 1918, Sheffield & Bourne, op. cit., p.450.

north-south rail links would fatally disrupt the movement of German reserves. This would 'break the German front into isolated sectors, and force a general retreat'.[28] Whilst this attack could not begin immediately, in the meanwhile, the BEF pressed on. On 2 September the Canadian Corps of Third Army broke the Drocourt-Quéant Line and the Fourth Army attacked north of Péronne. The German Winter Position, based on the Canal du Nord and the Somme, which *OHL* had ordered prepared on 8 August was thus rendered untenable. Between 3 and 9 September the enemy withdrew towards the *Siegfried Stellung*. Haig, however, who had received a telegram from Sir Henry Wilson, Chief of the Imperial General Staff, warning him against 'incurring heavy losses in attacks on the Hindenburg Line',[29] now became more cautious. On 3 September he informed his Army commanders: 'The principle on which Army commanders will now operate will be to press the enemy with advanced guards with the object of driving in the enemy's rearguards and outposts, and ascertaining his dispositions'.[30] Fourth Army steadily pushed its way towards the Hindenburg Line.

It was now possible for the general offensive to begin. On 26 September the French and American armies would attack between the Meuse and Reims towards Mézières. The following day the First and Third British armies would assault north of Cambrai and cross the Canal du Nord. On the 28th the Belgian, French and British Second Armies would attack in Flanders across the old Ypres battlefield, whilst on the 29th Fourth Army would penetrate the Hindenburg Line. The success of these operations was such that on 28 September, when the Bulgarians sought a separate peace, Ludendorff and Hindenburg decided that they must advise the Kaiser that Germany had no alternative but to seek an armistice.[31] The two commanders hoped that this breathing space would allow their armies a chance to regroup. On the day they met Wilhelm at Spa, the Hindenburg Line was breached, and five days later the German government asked President Wilson of the United States for an armistice based on his 'Fourteen Points'.[32]

The wings of the general offensive were, meanwhile, bogged down. The Americans in the Argonne-Meuse sector had achieved less than remarkable success, and their logistics had collapsed. The Belgian-British effort in Flanders had ground to a slithery halt because of heavy rain. To the south of the British, the actions of the French Armies during the campaign have often been seen as being half-hearted. On 29 September, for instance, General Debeney's *First Army* only supported the attack of the British Fourth Army with artillery fire, and Foch had to encourage Debeney forward to take St Quentin.[33] Yet the French casualty rates of 171,000 in August, 100,900 in September and 133,000 in October,[34] stand in comparison with the British total of 363,000 for the Hundred Days campaign. They offer reminder that the French were indeed fighting, even if their major contribution was during the summer rather than the autumn. The BEF at the Armistice was the smallest of the three armies, and held the shortest line. Yet, as Harris and Barr conclude: 'There

28 Whisler, op. cit., p.12, after D.F. Trask, *The AEF & Coalition Warmaking 1917-1918*.
29 Sheffield & Bourne, op. cit., p.453.
30 War Diary, HQ First Army, GHQ Order, OAD 915, 3 September 1918, TNA WO158/191.
31 Paul von Hindenburg (1847-1934) had commanded German armies in Russia before being promoted to Chief of the General Staff on the Western Front in August 1916. Erich Ludendorff (1865-1937) had also commanded on the Eastern Front before being appointed Quartermaster General to Hindenburg.
32 Woodrow Wilson's 'Fourteen Points', a statement of principles for world peace that was to be used in negotiations to end the Great War, were published on 8 January 1918.
33 Marie-Eugène Debeney (1864-1943) was Chief of Staff of the French *First Army* in August 1914, and after divisional command and the command of *XXXII Corps*, he served as Petain's Chief of Staff before returning to command *First Army* in December 1917.
34 A. Clayton, *Paths of Glory*, p.162.

can … be very little doubt that on 11 November 1918 the British Armies represented by far the largest share of the combat power of the forces ranged against the Germans'. And as the general offensive stalled, the British centre had to bear the burden of pushing on.

As October opened, the Beaurevoir-Fonsomme Line, or Hindenburg Support Line, represented the very last prepared German defences. The German infantry had been told to 'hold the Beaurevoir Line at all costs',[35] but could not. A set-piece battle on the first day of the month was required to rupture it, carried out in Fourth Army by three divisions of IX Corps; one of the Australian Corps; and one of XIII Corps. The enemy resisted strongly, counter-attacking and recovering the villages of Beaurevoir and Montbrehain on the opening day, and fighting continued until the evening of 6 October. V Corps of Third Army, immediately to the north, finally took their section of the Beaurevoir Line on the 8th as part of what Haig had hoped would be a concerted push by the British First, Third and Fourth Armies in conjunction with the French *First Army*. That would indeed happen on 9 October, but on the 8th the assault was made by the Third and Fourth Armies alone.

Fourth Army attacked that day with the IX, II American and XIII Corps. The Americans, commanded by Major-General George Read,[36] had come into the BEF's line to replace the exhausted Australian Corps during the night of 5-6 October after they had recaptured Montbrehain. The corps was unique in terms of the history of the American forces in the First World War in that it spent all of its period of service in the British sector. Originally composed of ten divisions, General Pershing had removed eight, leaving only the 27th and 30th, albeit comprising over 50,000 troops.[37] The three corps followed a 'deep, dense creeping barrage', supported by 53 tanks.[38] Success was such that the Army commander, Sir Henry Rawlinson, issued orders at 12.35 that day to continue the advance beyond the line of exploitation, but 'without fuller artillery support the infantry brigadiers were disinclined to go further'.[39] The combined attack by Third and Fourth Armies was so successful, however, that by the evening Cambrai could no longer be held. The German *Second Army* recorded that: 'The penetration of the enemy had progressed so that it became impossible to hold the enemy in this line for any length of time … the right flank of the army seemed seriously threatened. It was necessary to withdraw into the HERMANN position'. This had been hastily prepared behind the River Selle. At 23.00 'the main body of the divisions in line started to move; the rearguards followed at 2:30 A.M. Posts remained in contact with the enemy'.[40] To hold the

35 According to prisoners taken from the German *241st Division* (Harris & Barr, op. cit., p.234).

36 George Windle Read (1860-1934), a cavalryman, had served in Cuba, New Mexico and the Philippines. A lieutenant-colonel in 1914, he had been given command of 30th American Division in April 1918, and II American Corps in June.

37 Pershing had insisted on maintaining an independent army, but had sent the ten divisions to the British sector for training as II American Corps, beginning in June 1918 for the 27th and 30th Divisions. They were assigned to Second Army in July, and took part in the Ypres-Lys offensive 18 August to 1 September. Withdrawn into reserve, they were transferred to Fourth Army on 20 September and took part in the assault on the Hindenburg Line on 29 September.

38 25 Mark V and 28 Medium Mark A tanks. The most advanced make of British heavy tank, the Mark V had made its combat debut at the Battle of Hamel on 4 July 1918. The Medium Mark A, a light tank known as the Whippet, sported 4 machine-guns in a turret, but despite its name, only had a speed of 8 mph, even if this was twice the speed of the Mark V.

39 J.E. Edmonds & R. Maxwell-Hyslop, *Military Operations France and Belgium 1918 Vol. V*, p.197. Sir Henry Seymour Rawlinson GCB GCSI GCVO KCMG (1864-1925) was commissioned into the King's Royal Rifle Corps in 1884. During the Great War he commanded successively 4th Division, IV Corps and Fourth Army.

40 War Diary, HQ German *Second Army*, 8 October 1918, *United States Army in the World War Vol. 7*, p.890.

British on 9 October, 'strong rearguards, well provided with artillery and machine-guns', were to 'be left behind on the line; BEAUVAIS-en-Cambresis, west of MONTIGNY, east of MARETZ, rail triangle west of BUSIGNY, standard gauge railway west of BOHAIN'.[41] The stage was set for the pursuit to and battle of the River Selle. Rawlinson wrote hopefully on 8 October: 'I have given objectives for another 10,000 yard advance and may quite likely pull it off'.[42]

Harris and Barr noted in 1998 that 'almost no-one has now heard of the Battle of the Selle' which 'seems never to have entered British national consciousness'. Yet, in their view, 'objectively ... it must be regarded as one of the greatest military victories in the nation's history'.[43] Gary Sheffield, in noting that the battle involved the retaking of the town of Le Cateau, scene of the historic stand of II Corps on 26 August 1914, wrote: 'The capture of (this) landmark of 1914 ... went virtually unnoticed'.[44] Simon Justice asserts that the reason for the lack of acknowledgement of British victory on the Selle rests on 'the tendency of British and Commonwealth historians to search for the decisive, victorious moment in a war of indecision'.[45] In seeking such they focus on the Battle of Amiens and on the breaking of the Hindenburg Line. These were stellar achievements in the context of the war, but are far from being the whole story of the Hundred Days. Outside of the account given in Volume V of the *Official History* covering 1918,[46] and that of Archibald Montgomery, Major-General General Staff of Fourth Army in his description of Fourth Army operations in the Hundred Days,[47] there is no detailed modern reflective account of the battle that has been published. American Mark Whisler completed a master's dissertation on the battle of 17-18 October in 2001.[48] This work is remarkable for its depth of study of the German side of the battle. The account of the Fourth Army is handicapped, however, by reliance (below Army level) on secondary sources. Similarly, Simon Justice, in another master's dissertation, has considered various aspects of Fourth Army 9-19 October, particularly drawing attention to the preparation for the cavalry operations.[49] Robin Prior and Trevor Wilson in their examination of the war career of Sir Henry Rawlinson, award the Selle operations only two and half pages of examination,[50] and make a number of errors. They attribute success to the artillery and counter-battery fire in particular, and underestimate the ferociousness of German resistance, stating that 'rarely could the enemy gather enough troops even to attempt a counter-attack'.[51] Neither of these assertions is true. Harris and Barr, in their nine page account,[52] indicate much more the essence of the battle, writing that 'much depended that day on the morale, initiative and determination of Fourth Army's infantry'. They note the intelligence failure that underestimated the strength of the enemy defence, and the fact that the defending enemy, despite their lack of cover, not only survived the artillery preparation,

41 Order, HQ German *Second Army*, 'Withdrawal of Front', 8 October 1918, *USAWW Vol. 7*, p.891.
42 Rawlinson, op. cit., 8 October 1918.
43 Harris & Barr, op. cit., p.262.
44 G. D. Sheffield, *Forgotten Victory : The First World War : Myths and Realities*, p.256.
45 S. M. Justice, 'Means to an End: The Experience of 1918 and its influence on the British Fourth Army's Performance on the Selle', p.2.
46 Edmonds & Maxwell-Hyslop, op. cit., pp.212-385.
47 A. Montgomery, *The Story of the Fourth Army in the Battles of the Hundred Days*, pp.192-238.
48 Whisler, op. cit.
49 Justice, op. cit., See also S.M Justice, 'Behind the Lines: Sir Douglas Haig and the Cavalry Corps', in G. Sheffield & P. Gray (eds), *Changing War.*
50 Prior & Wilson, op. cit., pp.382-386.
51 Prior & Wilson, op. cit., p.385.
52 Harris & Barr, op. cit., pp.246-263.

but 'did so in a condition to fight back hard'.[53] Beneath that statement lies a suggestion that the BEF's artillery was less than effective.

This book seeks to increase the volume of knowledge about the Hundred Days. It aims to examine the skilled effort of the nation in the final four weeks of the war by understanding the performance of the British Fourth Army at the Selle. From Amiens to the Hindenburg Line, this force had been the spearhead of the British advance. Three periods of fighting will be described and reviewed. First, the three days of the Pursuit to the Selle (9-11 October 1918). Second, the Battle of the Selle itself, when the river and associated German defences were forced (17-18 October). Third, Fourth Army's role in the final stage of the battle (23-4 October), supporting Third and First Armies' Battle of the Selle, as the BEF pushed towards the Sambre-Oise canal. (See Map 1.) Not simply will the fighting be covered – it is also necessary to grasp the engineering and logistical effort that made the fighting possible. And not least, Fourth Army's way of war, both in semi-mobile and set-piece warfare, will be a principal focus of examination, as will the expertise of its infantry.

53 Harris & Barr, op. cit., p.250.

1

'The Germans Appear to Have Vanished'.[1] Pursuit to the Selle: 9 to 11 October 1918

If they could have seen through the heavy mist at dawn on 9 October 1918 the units of Fourth Army would have looked out on a landscape that for a distance of some three miles was almost completely devoid of the German Army. Overnight, the German *Eighteenth, Second,* and *Seventeenth Armies* had retired on the fronts of the left of the French *First Army* and the Fourth, Third and right of the First British Armies. Fourth Army faced elements of the exhausted *Second Army*, commanded by General von Carlowitz;[2] and the *Eighteenth Army*, commanded by General von Hutier.[3] Their rearguards were stretched out along features from Seboncourt (to the south in the French sector) to Bohain, Busigny and Gattigny Wood on Fourth Army's northern flank. The brief period of movement that followed from 9 to 11 October was awarded the stirring title 'The Pursuit to the Selle' by the Battles Nomenclature Committee.[4] Major-General Sir Archibald Montgomery, Major-General General Staff of the Fourth Army, described a wider period less grandiosely as: 'The Advance to Le Cateau, October 6th to 16th',[5] whilst most of the units involved viewed the central period of action as 8 to 11 October 1918.

On 9 October Fourth Army held a front 17,000 yards long from east of Sequehart in the south to west of Elincourt in the north. From the right to the left, the line was composed of IX Corps, commanded by Lieutenant-General Sir Walter Braithwaite;[6] II American Corps, commanded by

1 Sir Douglas Haig, diary entry 9 October 1918, G. Sheffield & J. Bourne (eds), *Douglas Haig – War Diaries and Letters 1914-1918*, p.471.

2 Adolph von Carlowitz (1858-1928) had replaced Johannes Georg van der Marwitz in command of *Second Army* on 22 September 1918. He had previously commanded *XIX Army Corps*.

3 Oskar von Hutier (1857-1934), had commanded *Eighth Army* on the Eastern Front, notably in the siege of Riga, and was transferred to the Western Front in 1918 to command the *Eighteenth Army* which played a prominent role in the offensive of 21 March 1918.

4 The Battles Nomenclature Committee, under Major-General Sir J.E. Headlam began its meetings in August 1919, categorizing events as battles, actions and miscellaneous incidents. It reported in May 1921.

5 A. Montgomery, *The Story of the Fourth Army in the Battles of the Hundred Days*, pp.192-208. Sir Archibald Armar Montgomery-Massingberd GCB GCVO KCMG DL (1871-1947) was commissioned in the Royal Artillery in 1891. A major and GSO2 at the Staff College, Camberley in August 1914, he became Chief of Staff of IV Corps and then Fourth Army.

6 Sir Walter Pipon Braithwaite GCB (1865-1945), commandant of the Staff College at Quetta at the outbreak of war, had commanded 62nd Division from December 1915 to August 1918, and had only been appointed to command IX Corps on 13 September 1918.

Major-General George Read; and XIII Corps, commanded by Lieutenant-General Sir Thomas Morland.[7] There were no more elaborate trench systems, dugouts or concrete emplacements. There was only open country. The landscape over which the Pursuit was to be conducted comprised rolling farmland of big fields, with gentle valleys and rises. It was, however, dotted with woods, some of them large; and was criss-crossed by the well-developed Le Cateau-St Quentin railway system, enhanced by the Germans, with its branch lines, cuttings and embankments. There was little in the way of obstruction caused by waterways until the Selle itself was reached. The villages of the area were, and still are, long straggling affairs that offered limited defensive value, there being only one sizeable town, Bohain. Le Cateau itself, built in the valley of the Selle, remained hidden until the high ground to its west was passed. The first question facing Fourth Army was how the enemy would use topography, especially the BEF's old bogey of woods, to resist. The second question concerned the enemy's morale – the will to resist – although the belief was that this was crumbling. Sir Henry Rawlinson was hopeful that 'if our victory were followed up at once, the cavalry might be given the opportunity, denied to them on the 8th, of completing the rout of the enemy'.[8] Indeed, Sir Douglas Haig had temporarily ceded control of the Cavalry Corps to him for just this purpose. On 29 September Rawlinson had received GHQ's orders that he should pass the corps 'through the Fourth Army as soon as the enemy's defences on the line MONTBREHAIN-BEAUREVIOR have been captured', yet on 8 October they had failed.[9]

The Pursuit – Day One: Wednesday 9 October 1918

Fourth Army issued orders for the attack to resume at 05.20 on the 9th, with all infantry corps having two objectives, the first being on average 4,500 yards ahead, with exploitation to a second objective, a further 2,500 yards on. This comprised a line east of Fresnoy, Bohain, Busigny, Honnechy, and Maurois. The Cavalry Corps was set the objective of pushing into Le Cateau and then exploiting north and north-east 'with a view to working against the flank and rear of the enemy opposing the Third and First Armies, and, if possible, to cut the enemy's communications about Valenciennes'.[10] The extent of the optimism is indicated by the fact that this distant objective was over 20 miles away.

IX Corps

The first objective of IX Corps was the railway line between Fresnoy-le-Grand and Bohain. Bohain itself was the second objective (see Map 2). On the extreme right of the BEF's line 138 Brigade of the 46th Division was deployed. The division was commanded by Major-General Gerald Boyd,[11]

7 Sir Thomas Lethbridge Napier Morland KCB KCMG DSO (1865-1925) commanded 5th Division from October 1914, and X Corps from July 1915. He was transferred to command XIII Corps on 14 April 1918.

8 Montgomery, op. cit., p.197.

9 War Diary, HQ Cavalry Corps, OAD 928, 'Directive to GOCs First, Second, Third, Fourth, Fifth Armies, Cavalry Corps, 29 September 1918', TNA WO 95/575.

10 War Diary, HQ Fourth Army, 9 October 1918, TNA WO95/439.

11 Gerald Farrell Boyd KCB CMG DSO DCM (1877-1930), a commissioned ranker, was a captain of the Leinster Regiment at the outbreak of war. He had been brigade-major, 11 Brigade, until February 1915, then spent two months as GSO2 in 1st Division and 16 months as GSO1 of 6th Division. He then served as BGGS V Corps until July 1918, when he was given command of 170 Brigade, 70 Division. He assumed command of 46th Division on 5 September 1918.

and 138 Brigade by Brigadier-General Frank Rowley.[12] The brigade was lucky to get into position by 05.20. The adoption of part of the line held by 6th Division on their left had only been ordered after 22.00 the previous evening. Battalion commanders had little idea where the 'front line' actually was, and units were shelled continually with gas and high explosive (HE) shells. Three battalions were employed over a front of some 3,000 yards, supported by 230 Brigade Royal Field Artillery (RFA) as advanced guard. Attached to both the 46th and 6th Divisions were the 5th Tank Battalion with 12 Mark V tanks and one company of Whippets, but although six tanks moved up to near Mericourt overnight, they would not see action. There had been no time for written orders – General Rowley, like many that day, gave his orders to his battalion commanders verbally. 1/5th Leicestershire, commanded by its adjutant, Captain Jack Hills,[13] were on the brigade's right, abutting the French. The adjacent posts 'fraternized vigorously', the French producing 'Jimmy Blink' despite the early hour. Beyond the concrete machine-gun emplacements of the Fonsomme line at Sequehart, surrounded by the fog which would enshroud operations for another three hours, Hills stood 'with a map in one hand and a slice of bread in the other' contemplating whether the enemy had indeed vacated the hamlet of Mericourt to his front, as he had been told.[14] Moving without the protection of a barrage, patrols of C and D companies pushed forward down the gentle valley at the head of which stood Mericourt, to find the enemy indeed gone. As if to offer further confirmation, a mounted officer of the Staffordshire regiment mysteriously appeared and rode into the village unharmed. Mericourt was duly occupied, and from the ridge beyond the larger village of Fresnoy-le-Grand could be observed. The orders of IX Corps were that if Fresnoy was strongly held, a set-piece attack should be prepared,[15] but no enemy could be seen. At this point allies appeared, the Leicesters being joined by a liaison platoon of the French *55e Régiment d'Infantrie*. Rowley, keeping close touch with his units, rode up and reconnoitred himself from the furthest position occupied by C Company. He ordered its commander, Captain Godwin Banwell,[16] to proceed down into Fresnoy, stating a little prematurely that 'the enemy is retiring along a wide front offering no opposition'.[17] Banwell met the first resistance of the morning, however, having to advance under heavy machine-gun fire emanating from the railway cutting and station on the eastern side of the town and from Etaves Wood just to its south (which would hold up the French advance that day).[18] Banwell found Fresnoy's main street blown in two places, dotted with the rotting carcasses of long

12 Frank George Mathias Rowley CB CMG DSO (1866-1949) commanded 1st Middlesex for two periods from October 1914 to June 1916, and was then promoted to command 56 and 107 Brigades. He was GOC 138 Brigade from 16 June 1917.

13 The CO, Lieutenant-Colonel James Llewellyn Griffiths DSO, had been wounded by shellfire on 3 October 1918. Captain John David Hills MC and bar, was commissioned in 1/5th Leicestershire on 14 September 1914. He served as brigade intelligence officer and as adjutant to his unit from 5 April 1917.

14 J. D. Hills, *The Fifth Leicestershire*, p.331. Mericourt had, according to other accounts, been taken the day before, but the Leicesters seemed not to have progressed that far in their relief.

15 War Diary, HQ IX Corps, Order No.144, 8 October 1918, TNA WO95/837.

16 Godwin Edward Banwell CBE MC & bar KPM was commissioned in January 1916 and was posted to France in May that year. Wounded at Gommecourt on 1 July 1916, he was wounded a further five times. Recommended at least once for the Victoria Cross, he became Chief Constable of both the East Riding and Cheshire.

17 War Diary, HQ 138 Infantry Brigade, 9 October 1918, TNA WO95/2689.

18 Indeed, Fourth Army was highly conscious of its flank with the French – orders to the 5th Tank Battalion and heavy artillery all concerned Bois D'Etaves and Seboncourt in the French sector War Diary. (HQ 46th Infantry Division, Message from Sender G.191, 9 October 1918, TNA WO95/2665).

dead horses. Here he was joined by Captain John Nichols and A Company of 1/5th Lincolnshire.[19] The Lincolns were the centre battalion of 46th Division and had moved off at dawn also to find the enemy gone, and had pushed into the western outskirts of the town. At 11.00 138 Brigade HQ moved to Mericourt, keeping on the heels of progress, but the movements had been well observed. As soon as all were ensconced, enemy shelling of Fresnoy and Mericourt and the country in between commenced, comprising gas and high explosive. 5th South Staffordshire, moving up later in the day, were diverted from Mericourt 'because G.O.C. Division ... considered the village itself untenable' due to the gas, and even west of the village it was 'often very uncomfortable owing to the gas drifting towards us and causing practically all to sneeze most energetically'.[20]

Suffering no casualties despite the heavy fire, Banwell and his men turned north from Fresnoy attempting to outflank the enemy in the railway cutting, but were halted. There was no artillery support immediately available, but 46th Battalion Machine Gun Corps (MGC) moved the guns of B and C Companies up and put down a barrage on the railway. Hills then sent Lieutenant Alfred Hawley of D Company with two platoons and ten French soldiers to work along the railway from the south.[21] Hawley ordered one platoon under Sergeant Thomas Marston to encircle and bomb the enemy from the rear,[22] and the station was captured by 16.30. Twenty Germans escaped, but five were made prisoner and three machine-guns taken. The 5th Leicesters had advanced some 6,000 yards for the loss of one killed and seven wounded. 1/5th Lincolnshire had similarly pushed on towards the railway, also without artillery support. Like the Leicesters, they had become held up by machine-gun fire from the embankment. In another piece of infantry initiative, Private George Briggs identified the machine-gun chiefly responsible for delaying the advance. Leading his section forward on a flank, he succeeded in knocking it out with Lewis gun fire, and then 'by skilful handling of his gun succeeded in neutralising another enemy machine-gun, which was holding up the company on his flank'.[23] The Lincolns suffered twelve casualties, one fatal, in arriving on their objective.

Meanwhile, 1/4th Leicestershire had advanced to the north of Fresnoy and had enjoyed the most comfortable progress of the three units that day, having met little opposition.[24] They suffered

19 John Sebastian 'Strafing Henry' or 'Crasher' Nichols DSO and bar, MC and bar was commissioned in September 1914. He became a regular officer with the Border Regiment after the war and commanded 1st Essex 1940-1 and variously 114, 151 & 182 Brigades. He was briefly GOC 10th Indian Division before commanding 50th Division at the Battle of El Alamein. 1/5th Lincolnshire were commanded by Lieutenant-Colonel Harold Wilson, a captain of 5th Lincolnshire in August 1914, who was CO from July 1918.

20 War Diary, 1/5th Battalion South Staffordshire Regiment, 9 October 1918, TNA WO95/2686.

21 Alfred Ernest Hawley MC was a pre-war ranker commissioned in October 1914.

22 Thomas Marston won one of the two bars to his Military Medal for both this action and his subsequent work two days later at Riquerval Wood. The citation reads: 'This N.C.O. was platoon sergeant. He led a small party round the flank of the enemy's position in spite of machine-gun fire from high ground on the east side of the railway line. Here by bombing the enemy's machine-gun position he enabled it to be attacked from the front. During the attack on Riquerval Wood on 11th October 1918, he was in charge of a flank platoon working with the next position. He showed complete indifference to the enemy's machine-gun fire, which was exceptionally heavy, and more than once, by his promptness ... enabled the advance to continue. He set the finest possible example throughout'. (*London Gazette*, 23 July 1919, p.9340). He died in 1922 of 'war gases'.

23 T.E Sandall, *A History of the 5th Batt. The Lincolnshire Regiment*, p.182. Briggs was awarded the Military Medal.

24 1/4th Leicestershire Regiment were commanded by Major Geoffrey Reid Arnott Beckett MC, a lieutenant of the Gloucestershire Regiment in August 1914. He was commanding in place of Lieutenant-Colonel F.W. Foster who had been wounded on 29 September.

The railway embankment north of Fresnoy station which halted the advance of 138 Brigade on 9 October 1918.

no fatalities, and ended the day on the railway line on the left of 138 Brigade's line. No further progress by the brigade was possible – the German rearguard had effectively fulfilled its mission. Heavy shelling of Fresnoy and the whole of the railway line position continued until 20.00 and some 200 French residents who had just been liberated thus had an 'exceedingly bad time'.[25] The conditions were marked by confusion – in the swirls of gas and darkness, Banwell and Hills of 5th Leicestershire wandered about looking for C and D companies, it being hours before they were located. Despite these problems, 5th Lincolnshire managed to take over the whole of the brigade front by the end of the day.

The 6th Division, commanded by Major-General Thomas Marden,[26] employed 16 and 71 Brigades, right and left, both 'very tired' from recent fighting. The two brigades had to cede part of their front to the 46th Division and in turn take over part of the front of the 30th American Division. These 'almost impossible' orders were successfully carried out in the pitch dark.[27] 6th Division's two brigades of field artillery and four brigades of IX Corps artillery fired a creeping barrage remaining for ten minutes on the start line, with 100 yard lifts every three minutes. The

25 War Diary, 1/5th Battalion Leicestershire Regiment, 9 October 1918, TNA WO95/2690.

26 Sir Thomas Owen Marden KBE CB CMG (1866-1951) was commanding 1st Welsh at the outbreak of war until his wounding at Second Ypres in May 1915. He led 114 Brigade, 38th Division, from November 1915 until his promotion to command 6th Division on 21 August 1917, a post he retained until the end of the war.

27 T.O. Marden, *A Short History of the Sixth Division*, p.68.

whole barrage lasted 71 minutes, whereupon six brigades of field artillery moved forward in consultation with the GOCs of the infantry brigades.[28] Although the French to the right of IX Corps would only begin their attack at 10.00, and 46th Division had proceeded without much regard to the French keeping up, 6th Division was instructed that it was 'particularly important that the left flank of the Corps keep level with the advance of the II American Corps' on the left.[29]

In 16 Brigade, commanded by Brigadier-General Henry Walker,[30] a depleted 1st King's Shropshire Light Infantry received their orders to lead the attack at midnight. They had been in action the previous day losing nine officers and 110 other ranks, and must have considered it desirable to spend the 9th reorganising.[31] Like the 5th Leicesters, they were in position only just in time but arrived at their objective, Jonnecourt Farm, some 4,000 yards away 40 minutes later, despite the fog, sending back three prisoners. They then pushed on to the railway in line with 1/4th Leicestershire on their right, where at 10.00 they began to be subject to erratic shelling.[32] There they remained, with four other ranks killed, but with another officer wounded,[33] their leadership was in a sorry state of depletion, as only six officers remained.[34] When it became evident that 71 Brigade on their left had pushed on into Bohain, 16 Brigade was ordered to exploit further, but darkness precluded this.

71 Brigade, commanded by Brigadier-General Percy Brown,[35] fielded 1st Leicestershire and 9th Norfolk, right and left. Orders were received only at 01.40 on 9 October and the brigade found the assembly 'exceedingly difficult', having to carry out a relief involving taking over part of the American front on a 'very black night' across a 'considerable tract of unknown country'.[36] Both battalions advanced with one section of field artillery attached. The regular Leicester unit,[37] progressing behind the creeping barrage, reached Jonnecourt Farm without loss, capturing one anti-tank gun. After they had passed through, two explosions, likely booby traps, occurred. They pressed on to the railway, but like the other units, were met with heavy machine-gun fire. C

28 War Diary, Commander Royal Artillery 6th Division, Operation Order, 8 October 1918, TNA WO95/1591. Edmonds and Maxwell-Hyslop, op. cit., p.213. 6th Division were supported by two RFA brigades of 6th Division, and four Army brigades.

29 War Diary, HQ IX Corps, Order No.144, 8 October 1918, TNA WO95/837.

30 Henry Alexander Walker CB CMG DSO (1874-1953) was a major of the Royal Fusiliers at the outbreak of war. He served successively as brigade-major to the Dehra Dun Brigade, GSO2 8th Division and GSO1 165th Division before being promoted to command 16 Brigade from 26 October 1917 until his wounding on 16 October, the day before the opening of the Battle of the Selle.

31 1st King's Shropshire Light Infantry were commanded by Lieutenant-Colonel Godfrey Meynell CMG, a regular major of the Shropshire Light Infantry in August 1914 who had served as a brigade-major, GSO2 and AA&QMG. He had also commanded 6th King's Own Yorkshire Light Infantry between November 1915 and July 1917, commanding the 1st Battalion of his own regiment from 3 April 1918. On the evening of the 9th he received news he was promoted to command 171 Brigade.

32 War Diary, HQ 16 Infantry Brigade, 9 October 1918, TNA WO95/1607.

33 Captain John Malcolm Lawrence Grover, commissioned in December 1914.

34 The unit would attack again on 17 October, but whilst the war diary does not report reinforcement in terms of other ranks, Captain A.B. Rogers returned from leave on the 12th, and the unit was loaned two second-lieutenants from 1st Buffs, and two from 2nd York & Lancaster. They received a glut of 14 officers on the 19th.

35 Percy Wilson Brown DSO was a regular captain of the Gordon Highlanders at the outbreak of war. He had a remarkable five infantry battalion commands between April 1915 and August 1917. He commanded 71 Brigade from 19 August 1917 until the end of the war.

36 War Diary, HQ 71 Infantry Brigade, 'Narrative of Operations – 8th to 11th October 1918', TNA WO95/1620.

37 The unit began the month of October with 30 officers and 741 other ranks.

Company, under the personal command of the CO Lieutenant-Colonel Francis Latham,[38] attempted to outflank the enemy with a captured light machine-gun from the north, whilst the second-in-command, Major John Herring-Cooper, with a Lewis gun section, moved to outflank them from the south.[39] Having a covered line of retreat, approximately 100 of the enemy were able to flee. Although by 18.00 the operation had been successful, it had not been without cost. The adjutant, Second-Lieutenant Douglas Sims, was mortally wounded whilst drafting orders for A Company to join the manoeuvre.[40] Remaining in position on the railway at the end of the day, the unit had lost two officers killed, with 20 casualties in the ranks, of whom five were fatalities.[41] They had further captured two heavy and three light machine-guns, as well as a 'dart machine',[42] and more than ten prisoners.

As per Rawlinson's wishes, 5th Cavalry Brigade, attached to the division, had sought to make progress. 12th Lancers moved up to Jonnecourt Farm behind 1st Leicesters, and reconnaissances were made, with much loss of direction in the fog, to see if the railway line could be turned from the north in the American Corps area. Being met with strong machine-gun fire, the patrols turned back. Just after midday a wildly optimistic order was received from Fourth Army for IX Corps to seize the Bellevue spur, at least 7,500 yards ahead of the position it had reached, with the cavalry to exploit to Wassigny a further 5,500 yards beyond. This being impossible, some four hours later a further order was received to 'turn Bohain' from the north in the American area. This was known from the morning patrols to be impossible, and the cavalry hence made no further progress.[43]. The logic of the first order was impeccable. In seizing the Bellevue spur, the Selle position would be turned. The fact was that at that moment Fourth Army HQ was out of touch with the effectiveness of the enemy rearguards. Sent at 11.45, Montgomery, had written: 'Little opposition is being met with on 4th Army front and a rapid advance has been made … corps will continue to advance forthwith'.[44]

It was 9th Norfolk who would take Bohain that day. Commanded by Lieutenant-Colonel Francis Day, their front lay on the far left of IX Corps.[45] The orders to take over part of the line from the 118th American Infantry Regiment were some of the last to arrive. Despite a task which was very difficult in the dark and mist, they somehow managed to start on time. The unit advanced uneventfully behind the barrage to high ground to the north of Jonnecourt Farm and, working round to the north, sent out a patrol which at 13.00 found Bohain, the largest town on the west bank of the Selle, which lay just to the east of the railway, to be seemingly empty. The Norfolks pushed on in the spirit of Rawlinson's midday orders, but matters were not straightforward. It was

38 Lieutenant-Colonel Francis Latham DSO and bar served in the Second Boer War with 4th Yorkshire, transferred to the West India Regiment in 1904, and to the 2nd Battalion Leicestershire Regiment in 1907. He was shot through the heart in June 1916, but amazingly survived to command 9th Suffolk and 1st Leicestershire from February 1918.

39 Major John Gustavus Herring-Cooper, an Irish hockey international, served in 3rd Queen's Own Royal West Kent and had been commissioned in the Leicestershire Regiment in 1911.

40 Second-Lieutenant Douglas Henry Sims MC had commissioned from private in August 1917.

41 In addition to Sims, the unit lost Second-Lieutenant Albert Edward Brown, who had been commissioned from lance-corporal in July 1917.

42 War Diary, 1st Battalion Leicestershire Regiment, 9 October 1918, TNA WO95/1622.

43 War Diary, HQ 5th Cavalry Brigade, 9 October 1918, TNA WO95/1138.

44 War Diary, HQ Fourth Army, Message G.319, 9 October 1918, TNA WO95/439.

45 Francis Reginald Day DSO, a regular captain of the Norfolk Regiment in August 1914, commanded successively from January 1917, 8th Norfolk, 12th Royal Fusiliers, and 9th Norfolk whom he took over on 1 April 1918.

not until 18.00 that they had finally managed to drive the enemy rearguard from the town and secure the eastern edges. The unit had advanced nearly 6,000 yards and captured 15 prisoners, one light trench mortar and a 4.2 inch howitzer for the loss of five other ranks killed. The Norfolks had also liberated 4,500 French inhabitants, being 'mobbed by an hysterical crowd of men, women and children, almost delirious in their joy',[46] some of whom had been without food for three days.[47] Although 'little wilful destruction' had been carried out, at every cross-roads in Bohain a mine had been blown, stretching across the street from side to side, 'while the houses on either side had collapsed'.[48]

In respect of Rawlinson's high hopes of midday, the Bellevue spur remained unreachable in the distance. Little progress had been made beyond the rearguard line the enemy had held during the morning, with one exception, the capture of Bohain. A discontinuity remained in the line that night. 2nd Sherwood Foresters of 16 Brigade, who had relieved 9th Norfolk, controlled Bohain, whilst on their right flank, units of both 16 and 138 Brigades remained on the railway, some 1,500 yards to the rear. The Germans had put up stout resistance based on a machine-gun defence, and it had taken much longer to master this than had been expected, even if the infantry tactics used were effective.

II American Corps

In the centre of Fourth Army's attack, the objectives set for the American Corps were firstly the railway line between Bohain and Busigny Station, which was to the west of Busigny itself; and a line of exploitation running east of Busigny to Bohain (see Map 3). The attack was conducted by the 30th 'Old Hickory' Division, commanded by Major-General Edward Lewis.[49] It was supported by the Australian Corps artillery. The 2nd, 4th and 5th Australian Artillery Divisions fired a barrage of 18 pounder field guns, with 4.5 inch howitzers engaging selected points. The field gun barrage, which included smoke that only added to the visibility issues, remained on the start line for four minutes with 100 yard lifts every four minutes. The Americans were thus allowed more time to overcome resistance, the line of howitzer fire progressing 200 yards in advance until the first objective. One brigade from each of the two artillery groups then followed the infantry.[50] The advance was also supported by the 4th Tank Battalion,[51] whose approach was masked by the noise of low-flying aircraft from 3rd Squadron Australian Flying Corps. This battalion had only five battle-worthy machines, and borrowed a further six from the 8th and 13th Battalions. Their march to the fighting of the 9th indicates the problems tanks experienced with mechanical reliability. Of the eleven machines that moved up from Bellicourt to Wiancourt on the 8th, only nine arrived, one having dropped out with engine and one with track trouble. On the 4,000 yard march from Wiancourt into action on the subsequent night, a further three developed engine trouble, and hence only six were able to start. Their orders were to keep the 'closest touch' with the infantry, but if they 'went ahead to deal with opposition they were to wait for the Infantry until they came up'. Particular attention was to be paid to the substantial Butry and la Sablière woods that lay in

46 R.E. Priestley, *Breaking the Hindenburg Line – The Story of the 46th (North Midland) Division,* p.130.
47 Montgomery, op. cit., p.197.
48 Priestley, op. cit., p.130.
49 Edward Mann Lewis (1863-1949) had served in Cuba and the Philippines.
50 War Diary, HQ 2nd Australian Divisional Artillery, Operation Order 9 October 1918, AWM Item No. 13/11/32 Part 1.
51 The 301st American Tank Battalion and two companies of Whippets were also attached but did not see action during the pursuit.

front of the American advance. Further, the tanks were instructed 'not to go ahead until all hostile machine-gun fire had been silenced' i.e. they were not to expose themselves to risk or allow pockets of resistance to remain undealt with.[52] There had, of course, been no reconnaissance, and time had allowed no liaison with the infantry beforehand.

59 American Infantry Brigade, commanded by Brigadier-General Lawrence Tyson,[53] was tasked with taking the first objective, a distance of some 4,000 to 5,000 yards. 60 American Brigade, commanded by Brigadier-General Samuel Faison,[54] would then leapfrog their fellows to reach the line of exploitation 2,000 yards beyond. Tyson described how: 'At a late hour at night, I was directed to proceed to General Faison's headquarters at the head of the canal near Bellicourt' to receive his orders for the attack. He and his brigade-major and operations officers of the 117th and 118th Infantry only got back to his HQ at 01.00. It was hence 'very, very late' before the operations officers could assemble the six battalion commanders 'owing to the distance they had to go and the darkness' of the moonless night. The jump-off time was 'finally accomplished in a most extraordinary manner',[55] made more uncomfortable by the enemy bombing of forward areas and shelling of back areas. In 59 Brigade, advancing on a 5,000 yard front from Brancourt to Prémont, the 118th Infantry Regiment,[56] on the right, attacked with three battalions, the 117th on the left, with one. The leapfrogging 60 Brigade followed 800 yards behind, 120th Infantry Regiment on the right, 119th on the left.[57] The 2nd Battalion of the 118th, in support to the leading 1st Battalion, set off on empty stomachs, no food having been brought up. They lost not only their breakfast – difficulties in forming up meant that the barrage was lost as well. Leapfrogging the 1st Battalion at the railway, their first haul was 300 enemy bicycles in a barn. Reaching the road beyond, three German couriers on bicycles were surprised and killed. The German speakers in the battalion translated their despatches which indicated that there were seven battalions of infantry in Bohain to their right and 'this information caused considerable excitement for a time'.[58] Seven battalions or not, the rapid progress came to an end as the regiment ran into fire from the town. The American units were followed by the 43rd Battery of the 11th Brigade Australian Field Artillery, who now came into action against 77-millimetre guns and parties of enemy troops. Reflecting the Americans' inexperience, the Australians reported being 'handicapped in not being able to obtain any definite information as to the situation at the front', but kept up harassing fire or roads, woods and valleys in the enemy's rear.[59] 5th Brigade Australian Field Artillery was one of the exploiting brigades, and found itself in a better position. The 14th Battery 'moved forward in close touch' with the infantry and 'dealt with machine-gun nests as they appeared'. Officers went forward with the infantry on

52 War Diary, 4th Tank Battalion, 'Report upon Action of Tanks with 30th American Div. East of Prémont October 9th 1918', TNA WO95/110/5.
53 Lawrence Davis Tyson (1861-1929), politician and textile manufacturer, had seen action in the Apache Wars in the 1880s, and had been a regimental commander in the Spanish-American War.
54 Samuel Lane Faison (1860-1940), had served in the Apache Wars and the Geronimo Campaign, and in the Philippines.
55 Quoted in E.A. Murphy & R.S. Thomas, *The Thirtieth Division in the World War*, p.112.
56 American Infantry Regiments had three infantry battalions, technically 3,770 combatants. The 118th was commanded by Colonel Orrin R. Wolfe, the 117th by Colonel Cary F. Spence.
57 The 120th was commanded by Colonel Sidney W. Minor, the 119th by Colonel John Van Bokkelen Metts.
58 P.H. Fike, *History of Company F, 118th Infantry*, p.27.
59 War Diary, HQ 11th Brigade Australian Field Artillery, 9 October 1918, AWM Item No. 13/38/33.

reconnaissance, and at the end of the day, acting on the evidence gleaned, 'put down a protective barrage S.O.S. for the hours of darkness'.[60]

On the left of the 'Old Hickory' Division's advance, the 117th and then the 119th Infantry (the latter of 60 Brigade which was to leapfrog the 117th) similarly met with opposition from machine-guns on the downhill slope approaching the woods which blocked their way to Busigny. Here they were quite exposed, and despite the attached artillery, waited for assistance from tanks in order to progress. Two of the 4th Tank Battalion's machines had progressed to the north of Prémont to attack Butry Wood, the most northerly of the two woods that faced the American left. They strayed further north towards Maretz, getting in front of the infantry of 25th Division in the XIII Corps area. (The battalion commander, Lieutenant-Colonel Louis Henshall, glorified the loss of direction in the aftermath by describing that he had met a company commander from 25th Division who said that 'the unexpected sight of two Tanks forging ahead of his Company gave them great moral support'.)[61] Turning south towards Butry Wood, they found the Americans stalled. One tank was sent along the north side of the wood, the other along the west, dealing with the machine-gun nests along the edge of the trees. Moving on towards the first objective, the two tanks encountered further machine-guns on the railway line beyond the woods, one tank being put out of action. The other four tanks operating to the south patrolled west of la Sablière Wood, responding to calls from the infantry to assist them. Tank commanders later reported that the American infantry were prone to call for help at the 'slightest opposition', imagining enemy machine-guns, as 'when the Tanks approached the places they found nothing there at all there'. Indeed, the reported opposition at one location proved to be none other than occupying American infantry. Once opposition had been overcome and 'the enemy was in full retreat … the infantry followed easily'. The slightly scathing view of the tank crews was that 'the Infantry should have carried all before them without Tanks', there being too much waiting for tanks to arrive to deal with opposition that well-practiced infantry tactics should have easily overcome. In dealing with obstructions, real or not, the six tanks fired 75 6-pound shells, and 1,200 machine-gun rounds.[62] In essence, the Tank Corps was hinting that the 30th Division was 'sticky', and in light of the events of 17-18 October, their comments are interesting.

Eventually freed from the impasse at the woods, the 117th Infantry arrived at Busigny station at 12.30, where two hours prior to their arrival the railway had been blown up. The leapfrogging 119th passed through, liberating Busigny's 1,800 residents at 16.30 and capturing a mass of matériel, including a battery of 5.9 inch guns and several field pieces. Even before the enemy 'had been driven entirely out, the civilians were in the streets offering the soldiers hot coffee'.[63] To the right, the 120th Infantry should have passed through the 118th at 10.00, but due to that unit having been held up by the fire from Bohain, were only able to do so much later, arriving on the objective at 16.00. A party of the 3rd Battalion was detailed to assist in overcoming resistance on the northern edge of Bohain. Proving that the British did not hold a monopoly on eccentricity, 'the Commanding Officer of G Company, as usual, went in with a sword in one hand and a spade in the other – close on his heels came his orderly, Turner, with an SOS rocket, which neither one

60 War Diary, HQ 5th Brigade Australian Field Artillery, 9 October 1918, AWM Item No. 13/33/35.

61 Louis Sydney Henshall DSO was an architect and territorial lieutenant of the South Lancashire Regiment in August 1914.

62 War Diary, HQ 4th Tank Battalion, 'Report upon Action of Tanks with 30th American Div. East of Prémont October 9th 1918', TNA WO95/110/5.

63 Anonymous, *History 119th Infantry, 60th Brigade, 30th Division, U.S.A.*, p.50.

knew how to use'.[64] The Americans, who had advanced 11,500 yards, concluded that the enemy was 'fighting a rearguard action, depending in the main upon skilfully placed and rapidly manoeuvred machine-guns'. The Germans, it appeared to them, were 'very definitely "on the run" but fighting desperately every inch of the way'. They 'held high ground against us' giving them 'long fields of fire' the sources of which were hidden in 'large patches of woods'.[65] The Americans finished the day on a line east of Busigny holding Bois de Busigny and Bois de Proyart. Orders had been given by Rawlinson at around midday for the corps to push on to Molain, but had subsequently been cancelled. The Americans had thus achieved their objectives, but the morning had proved difficult, and would foreshadow difficulties to be experienced by the 30th Division during the Battle of the Selle itself. However, they had achieved no less than any British division that day. In front of the Americans lay the villages of Vaux-Andigny and La Haie Menneresse. These would prove a much harder nut to crack.

In the air above the Americans, the supporting 3rd Squadron Australian Flying Corps had 'a fine day for operations'. The squadron clocked-up 32 flying hours on 9 October, in 13 sorties. There were three contacts with enemy machines, in groups of one, five and seven aircraft. Without loss, encountering little anti-aircraft and practically no machine-gun fire from the ground, they dropped phosphorous bombs to form a smoke screen in front of the advance, and bombed transport and troops on the Roman road to Le Cateau. A panorama of conflagration in various towns and villages could be observed from the air, many the fires of burning stores. The infantry indicated their positions to contact patrols by lighting red ground flares and waving white patches sewn on the inside of box respirators. A typical patrol was flown by Lieutenants William Palstra and Wallace Macdougall in an R.E.8 reconnaissance and bomber bi-plane.[66] They took off at 07.30 and landed at 10.00. They watched the Americans advancing and mopping up in Butry and la Sablière Woods, and holding the railway line in front. In another example of air-ground cooperation, they then observed a counterattack developing from Busigny, dropped a parachute flare, and sent an SOS to which the 'art[iller]y responded with barrage'. They demonstrated the emphasis on ground attack, engaging the advancing Germans with machine-gun fire, with 'many casualties inflicted'. They then flew south over Bohain, where they saw a multitude of fires burning, another large fire in St Souplet, some 7,000 yards in front of the advancing troops, and observed a large explosion in Bertry, in Third Army's area to the north. For Palstra, it was one of 23 sorties flown during October, eight of them with MacDougall.[67]

64 J.O. Walker, W.A. Graham & T. Fauntleroy, *Official History the 12th Infantry, 3rd North Carolina, 30th Division*, p.29. The 117th had seven fatalities, the 118th and the 119th two each, and the 120th four.

65 Murphy & Thomas, op. cit., pp.114-5.

66 William Palstra MC was born in Holland in 1892, to British parents. He had served in Transvaal Scottish Cadets for four years, and, as an accountancy clerk resident in Melbourne, had enlisted in January 1916, 39th Battalion Australian Imperial Force. Promoted to sergeant, he was commissioned in March 1917, and awarded the MC in August 1917. He was seconded for training with the AFC in December 1917, but only proceeded to France on 11 September 1918, where he was credited with six kills (National Archives of Australia, Series B2455, Palstra, William). He was killed in the wreck of British airship R.101 in 1930, a squadron leader acting as RAAF Air Liaison Officer to the British Air Ministry. Wallace Andrew Macdougall, born in 1891, was an engineer who had had served in the Scottish Rifles for three years. He enlisted in November 1916 and was sent to a light trench mortar battery, but was commissioned and attended aviation school between January and July 1917. He was only sent to France on 22 September 1918. (National Archives of Australia, Series B2455, Macdougall, W.A.).

67 Squadron Record Book, 3rd Squadron AFC, October 1918, AWM, Item no. 8/6/22 Part 1.

XIII Corps

XIII Corps suffered a communications blackout during the evening of the 8th, caused not only by shelling but also by the enemy bombing the area continuously and cutting telephone wires. Major Frederick Rice, a battery commander in 82 Brigade RFA noted that: 'The Boche seemed to have detailed every aeroplane in his army to drop bombs on the advancing XIIIth Corps'.[68] Motor cars and cycles had to 'move without lights, and at a very restricted pace', leaving wireless and runners as the main communication assets. 'Had it not been for the wholehearted co-operation of subordinate commanders it seems doubtful whether the advance could have been continued up to time on the 9th'.[69] With its depth of experience, the corps had anticipated what would be required of the following day.

The objectives set for XIII Corps were firstly the village of Maretz, with exploitation to Honnechy and Maurois along the Roman road (see Map 4). The corps had the longest distance of the three to travel 'due to the long flank which the IX Corps was compelled to maintain in consequence of the difficulty experienced by the French in advancing north-east of St Quentin'.[70] 25th Division was deployed on the right and 66th Division on the left. The barrage involved three brigades of field artillery covering the advance of each division, with two 60-pounder and two 6-inch howitzer batteries, the barrage advancing at a rate of 100 yards every three minutes. In addition, 'a few Heavy How[itzer]s were able to assist, but most of them became out of range soon after the commencement'.[71]

25th Division, commanded by Major-General Ronald Charles,[72] could not issue definite orders until the early hours of the morning because of the communications blackout. Their attack was spearheaded by 75 Brigade, commanded by Brigadier-General Charles Frizzell, who had only been at the helm of his formation for eight days.[73] 1/8th Royal Warwickshire and 1/5th Gloucestershire, tasked with obtaining the first objective, advanced in artillery formation on a 3,000 yard front, two companies leading for each unit, followed by 110 Brigade RFA. The Warwicks progressed from Serain and arrived at Maretz at 06.30.[74] Whilst the Warwicks' war diary makes no mention, the Glosters on the left had had a torrid time, entering the western outskirts of Maretz and being caught by friendly artillery fire. This fell behind the leading companies, their support and reserve companies suffering casualties. The Glosters' war diary was specific, stating clearly that they believed this was 66th Division's barrage 'overlapping our sector', which, they claimed, started late at 05.45.[75] Their forward companies had to withdraw from the village. 25th Division and XIII Corps in turn attributed this mishap to their fast progress – 'the rapidity of their advance in the fog.'[76] It appeared

68 F.J. Rice, Private Papers, IWM Docs 7197. Frederick Joseph Rice MC joined the Royal Field Artillery in October 1914 from the Special Reserve of the Royal Garrison Artillery.

69 'XIII Corps Narratives', IWM Docs 20537, Fourth Army Papers, Vol. 64.

70 Montgomery, op. cit., p.197.

71 War Diary, Commander Royal Artillery XIII Corps, 9 October 1918, TNA WO95/902.

72 James Ronald Edmonston 'Don Carlos' Charles KCB CMG DSO (1875-1955) was commissioned into the Royal Engineers in 1894, and served in the Second Boer War and on the North-West Frontier in 1908. He was employed as a GSO2 then a GSO1 until July 1915 in the Indian Corps, and as BGGS with the Indian then XVII Corps until July 1918, taking command of 25th Division on 4 August 1918.

73 Charles William Frizzell DSO MC (1888-1951), had been commissioned into the Royal Berkshire Regiment in 1907, and was a lieutenant at the outbreak of war. He commanded 10th Essex from September 1916 until his elevation to command 75 Brigade on 1 October 1918.

74 1/8th Warwickshire were commanded by Lieutenant-Colonel Philip Henry Whitehouse DSO, a captain of the battalion in August 1914, and he had commanded since December 1917.

75 War Diary, 1/5th Battalion Gloucestershire Regiment, 9 October 1918, TNS WO95/2251.

76 M. Kincaid-Smith, *The 25th Division in France and Flanders*, p.326.

to the Glosters, however, that their own barrage had by this time lifted. The view of the support battalion, 1/8th Worcestershire, was that 'our barrage was falling short', and one of their companies suffered five casualties from 'the shells of one 4.5 How[itzer] and one 18 p[ounde]r gun bursting very short'.[77] The left hand unit of 198 Brigade in neighbouring 66th Division reported the same experience (i.e. *not* the unit abutting the Glosters). Curiously, the war diary of 66th Division is explicit that 'no artillery barrage was put down',[78] but 198 Brigade's orders for 9 October detail that whilst 'the operation must be in the nature of open warfare' a barrage would open 300 yards in front of the infantry progressing 100 yards in three minutes for the first 1,000 yards and 100 yards every four minutes from 1,000 yards to the objective, with specific shelling of Elincourt.[79] The war diary of the supporting artillery of 18th Division is similarly clear that a barrage was fired. It seems highly unlikely the barrage would have started nearly half an hour late, and if the Glosters' account of following the barrage lift into Maretz is correct, the infantry did not progress too quickly. No units suggested that this was a German counter-barrage. If the units on the ground were correct, then either the artillery did not fire to plan, or there was clear inaccuracy in the firing of the creeping barrage or the guns which were seeking out specific targets on the left of the XIII Corps attack. 75 Brigade noted on the day both that their units suffered casualties by 'running into our own barrage in the morning mist', but also that British artillery failed 'to lift according to time table'.[80] In the report on operations the brigade again concluded that the artillery 'continued to fire' after troops had entered Maretz, and that 'there was a great deal of short shooting by our artillery, which caused many casualties to our troops'.[81] The cause will not finally be known, lost in the fog of war, but the root cause was almost certainly the hastiness of arranging the attack of 9 October.

When the 'friendly' shelling stopped, the two leading units pushed on again into Maretz, liberating many civilians. 66th Division lagging, Lieutenant-Colonel Dudley Lewis of the Glosters ordered the formation of a defensive flank to the left and pushed on,[82] his unit meeting resistance from both machine-guns and snipers on the eastern outskirts of the village, which he consolidated under heavy fire. The Glosters lost eleven other ranks killed and two missing, with two officers and 33 other ranks wounded. The Warwicks suffered eleven killed, 35 wounded (including two officers), with two missing. Initiative and skilled and courageous junior leadership showed itself in the attack. Sergeant Stone of 1/8th Warwickshire set 'a fine example in rushing a German post and capturing three prisoners'.[83] In 1/5th Gloucestershire, Private Granville Cobb won the Distinguished Conduct Medal for his actions in 'rushing a house near Maretz, and capturing, single-

77 War Diary, 1/8th Battalion Worcestershire Regiment, 'Narrative of Operations 9 October 1918', TNA WO95/2251.

78 War Diary, HQ 66th Infantry Division, 'Narrative of Operations 66th Division 8th to 10th Oct. 1918', TNA WO95/1918.

79 War Diary, HQ 198 Infantry Brigade, Order No. 116, 8 October 1918, TNA WO95/3139. 199 Brigade's orders contain similar references.

80 War Diary, HQ 75 Infantry Brigade, 9 October 1918, TNA WO95/2249.

81 War Diary, HQ 75 Infantry Brigade, 'Operation Report for 9 October 1918', TNA WO95/2249.

82 Dudley Lewis DSO and bar MC was commissioned in October 1914. The award of the bar to his MC was partly for his work at Maretz. The citation reads: 'For gallant leadership and devotion to duty during the period 5th/10th October, 1918. He was called upon suddenly to organise and carry out the attack on Beaurevoir. This he did with the greatest skill. His battalion took all their objectives splendidly, thereby making the next big attack possible. On the 9th inst., he successfully attacked Maretz, clearing the village and taking about thirty prisoners. Throughout he showed great courage and ability to command'. (*London Gazette*, 4 October 1919, p.12216).

83 Kincaid-Smith, op. cit., p.327.

handed, a German officer with a machine-gun and about 15 other prisoners'.[84] Lance-Corporal Percy Ireland similarly won the Military Medal (MM) for leading 'parties against machine-gun posts in Maretz and alone attacked and captured three snipers'. Sergeant William Stephens also won the MM when he and 'two Lewis Gunners rushed a house and captured 16 Germans'.[85] The division's accounts of individual courageous initiative often refer to the skilled use of Lewis guns.

Following the capture of Maretz, 74 Brigade, commanded by Brigadier-General Hugh Craigie-Halkett,[86] came into line to the right of 75 Brigade. The formation had marched eleven miles during the night and came into action without rest or food. All its three units were weak in numbers. On 8 October 13th Durham Light Infantry had seven officers and 200 other ranks; 11th Sherwood Foresters had nine officers and 250 ORs; and 9th Yorkshire had seven officers and 320 ORs.[87] Supported by 86 Brigade RFA, the Sherwoods were the leading battalion. They too had been subject to hurried arrangements – on arrival at the jump-off position there had been 'barely time available for the issue of verbal orders' to company commanders.[88] Their objective was in a north-easterly direction, where the Busigny-Le Cateau road cut the railway at a bridge by the station south-east of Honnechy. This bridge would become notable for a variety of reasons. They advanced at 08.00 on a frontage of 1,200 yards opening out to 1,700 yards. Encountering machine-gun fire coming from Honnechy they were forced to occupy the railway cutting to their right, just north of the Busigny-Maretz road at le Trou aux Soldats where the enemy had built a detraining point. The bridge across the railway a few hundred yards ahead of them was blown up as they approached. 9th Yorkshire moved up in close support in artillery formation and joined them.[89] The enemy was forced out of the cutting and could be seen retiring about 400 yards away, but with the Lewis gun carts to the rear, their retreat could not be harassed. Further advance was not possible due to 1/8th Worcestershire advancing only slowly from Maretz, and no information was available as to the progress of the Americans on the right. Their position was uncomfortable, being enfiladed on both sides. The support battalion, 13th Durham Light Infantry,[90] arrived before long and formed a defensive flank to the right, all three units crowded into the cutting.

84 Granville Douglas Cobb would be killed on 18 October.

85 Kincaid-Smith, op. cit., p.327. On 5 October 1/5th Gloucestershire had a ration strength of 562. During the period 9-11 October the battalion suffered 13 fatalities in the other ranks, with six officers and 66 wounded/missing.

86 Hugh Marjoribanks Craigie-Halkett CMG DSO (1880-1952) was commissioned into the Highland Light Infantry in 1900, and was a captain at the outbreak of war. He commanded the 2nd Battalion briefly in July 1916, then 2nd South Lancashire and 9th North Lancashire from January 1917 to March 1918, being appointed to the command of 74 Brigade on 1 April 1918.

87 War Diary, HQ 74 Infantry Brigade, 'Report of Operations from October 3rd to October 11th 1918', TNA WO95/2245.

88 War Diary, 11th Battalion Sherwood Foresters, 9 October 1918, TNA WO95/2247. The battalion was commanded by Lieutenant-Colonel Herbert Nugent Young DSO, a regular captain of the Royal Irish Fusiliers in August 1914. He had commanded 7th Royal Inniskilling Fusiliers for periods between February 1916 and November 1917 (a stretch disrupted by his being severely wounded by a sniper in September 1916). He formally took over command of 11th Sherwoods on 29 September 1918 but would be killed on 25 October.

89 9th Yorkshire were commanded by Lieutenant-Colonel Reginald Seton Hart DSO, a regular captain of the Sherwood Foresters at the outbreak of war.

90 13th Durham Light Infantry were commanded by Major Leonard Montague Greenwood DSO MC & bar, who had led the battalion since 5 October when Lieutenant-Colonel D.H. Clarke was badly wounded. He had been commissioned in December 1914. He had served since August 1915 in France

The objective of 1/8th Worcestershire, advancing on the left flank of the stalled battalions of 74 Brigade, was Honnechy, some 5,000 yards further on from Maretz. The St Quentin-Le Cateau railway line, which had been an objective for the units of the two corps further south, ran to their right (where the units of 74 Brigade had taken shelter) and then passed to the battalion's front. Here it branched to the west to Cambrai, crossing the Roman road in a deep cutting south-west of Maurois, with the other line continuing north to Le Cateau. The enemy had created a railway triangle with the addition of a spur where the railway branched. The Worcesters were subject to machine-gun fire from the railway embankment to their right, Gattigny Wood to their left and houses in Honnechy ahead. Lieutenant Archibald Watson and a platoon of C Company drove off the machine-guns on the railway to their right (thus probably dispersing the guns that that had opposed 74 Brigade), but the guns to the left and front of their advance continued to give trouble.[91] By 'skilful use of cover afforded by undulating ground',[92] the battalion worked its way forward to a quarry in front of the railway triangle, at which point, at about 11.00, the cavalry arrived.

It was on this part of the battlefield that the Cavalry Corps would attempt to fulfil Haig's and Rawlinson's vision of penetration and mayhem behind the enemy lines. The corps was ordered to move towards Le Cateau and Busigny and 'occupy the railway junctions', and then to 'operate against the flank and rear' of the enemy facing Third and Fourth Armies, proceeding to 'cut the Enemy's communications at Valenciennes'. Lieutenant-General Charles 'Black Jack' Kavanagh had received these orders directly from Haig on 29 September, and understood that he was to 'have his head', i.e. the moment of launching was his decision, and 'left fully confident that there is a great opportunity offering for the cavalry'.[93] The corps had been in action the previous day but had been presented with no opportunity to break through. Now they would seemingly have their chance. Lieutenant John Bickersteth, 1st Royal Dragoons, recorded how that morning 'the men had hardly managed to get some hot tea (it now being light) when the order to move forward came – and it was whispered that the Boches had gone'.[94] 3rd Cavalry Division, commanded by Major-General 'Jake' Harman,[95] was keeping close touch with the progress of the infantry. As Simon Justice notes, three weeks previously it 'had been practising, semi-successfully, against machine guns represented by chalk arrows and football rattles'.[96] Soon the division would be facing them for real. Passing through Maretz, Bickersteth described 'the inhabitants crowding to the doors and waving flowers and shouting good wishes'.[97] At 08.45 Harman had learnt that 'touch with retreating enemy had been temporarily lost', and ordered 6th Cavalry Brigade, commanded by Brigadier-General Ewing

and Italy. Gassed at St Benin, and ill with influenza, he remained at duty until the 13th, dying of pneumonia on the 17th aged 25.

91 Archibald René Watson had been commissioned from sergeant in September 1915.

92 War Diary 1/8th Battalion Worcestershire Regiment, 9 October 1918, TNA WO95/2251.

93 D. Haig, diary entry 29 September 1918, Sheffield and Bourne, op. cit., p.467. Charles Toler McMurrough Kavanagh had been commanding 7th Cavalry Brigade in August 1914, and commanded successively 2nd and 5th Cavalry Divisions before the Cavalry Corps itself to which he was promoted in 1917.

94 J. Bickersteth, *The Bickersteth Diaries 1914-1918*, pp.282-3.

95 Anthony Ernest Wentworth 'Jake' Harman KCB DSO (1872-1961) was commissioned in 1894 into the Dragoon Guards. A major in August 1914, he commanded 18th Hussars from June 1915 until promoted to command 6th Cavalry Brigade in May 1916.

96 S.M. Justice, 'Means to an End: The Experience of 1918 and its influence on the British Fourth Army's Performance on the Selle', p.39. See Chapter Three.

97 J. Bickersteth, op. cit., p.283.

Paterson,[98] to advance south of the road in 25th Division's area. The Canadian Cavalry Brigade, commanded by the unrelated Brigadier-General Robert Paterson,[99] was to advance to the north, in 66th Division's area. The Canadians would come into action, successfully (if bloodily), at 11.00, and at 11.45 Kavanagh received orders to 'push forward as rapidly as possible on LE CATEAU and after reaching that place…carry out mission already allotted…by the C-in-C'.[100] To achieve this, the matter of the enemy resistance at Honnechy had to be dealt with.

C Squadron of 6th Brigade arrived near Honnechy first, and Lieutenant John Houstoun-Boswall led a party of scouts to the quarry where the advance elements of 1/8th Worcestershire were lodged,[101] having 'come under pretty heavy MG fire getting there'.[102] Bickersteth joined them and a party went on to the railway, scrambling up the embankment and running a 'gauntlet of bullets' to a railwayman's house in the triangle.[103] Looking through a window covered with corrugated iron and straw Bickersteth could see the enemy with machine-guns occupying hedges and orchards on the edge of the town, which was well wired. The enemy were also visible on high ground to the south towards Busigny, where the Americans would not arrive for another hour or so. Ewing Paterson made his own reconnaissance, and encountered the brigade-major of 75 Brigade who told him that 'the infantry were exhausted and that in view of the strong forces opposed to them, it was not intended to advance further that day'.[104] This was not what the cavalry wished to hear. Within the hour, Harman and his two brigade commanders had decided to attempt to take Honnechy and then Reumont, the latter beyond the second objective line of exploitation, to maintain the momentum of the attack. The high ground to the west of Le Cateau could then be seized. From his position in the front line in the quarry, the Worcesters' CO, Lieutenant-Colonel Hubert Clarke,[105] took a lead in coordinating the infantry element. In conjunction with the CO of 21st Manchester (7 Brigade, 25th Division),[106] Lieutenant-Colonel Cyril Lomax,[107] whose battalion had been pushed forward to fill a gap that had opened between 75 Brigade and 74 Brigade on the right, he planned a direct assault on Honnechy. Assuming the authority of the 'man on the spot' he sent a message to the CO of the 2nd South African Infantry of 66th Division, on the other side of the Roman road, requesting co-operation. A five minute barrage on the village was arranged with the assault to follow at 14.00.

98 Ewing Paterson DSO (1873-1950) had been a major of 6th Dragoons, and commanded from August 1915 until his appointment to command 6th Cavalry Brigade on 2 September 1918.
99 Robert Walter Paterson DSO (1876-1936) had previously commanded the Fort Garry Horse.
100 War Diary, HQ Fourth Army, Urgent Operation Order G. 319, 9 October 1918, 11:45, TNA WO 95/439.
101 John Francis Houstoun-Boswall rose to the rank of major and was aide-de-camp to the Governor of South Australia between 1920 and 1922.
102 J. Bickersteth, op. cit., p.283.
103 J. Bicketsteth, op. cit., p.283.
104 J.B. Bickersteth, *History of the 6th Cavalry Brigade*, p.112.
105 Hubert Thomas Clarke DSO was a captain in August 1914 and had commanded 1/8th Worcestershire since October 1917.
106 The strength of 21st Manchester was 18 officers and 442 other ranks, and between 4 and 11 October it suffered 10 officer and 266 other rank casualties. Second-Lieutenant John Harold Webb MC (commissioned from corporal in June 1917) was killed on the 9th and Second-Lieutenant Richard Arthur Tresise (commissioned from sergeant in August 1917) on the 12th.
107 Cyril Ernest Napier Lomax CB CBE DSO and two bars MC was a regular lieutenant of the Welsh Regiment in August 1914. He had commanded 21st Manchester since June 1917. In the Second World War he commanded 16 Infantry Brigade and the Indian 26th Infantry Division in Burma for two years.

Houstoun-Boswall's reconnaissance demonstrated to the cavalry that the heavy presence of the enemy faced by the Worcesters, coupled with heavy wire, made a direct frontal attack on Honnechy unfeasible. The only approach possible was from the road from Busigny in the south or the Roman road from Maretz to the west. The Royal Dragoons with the 10th Hussars in support would therefore come from the west whilst the 3rd Dragoon Guards would attack from the south supported by the Inniskilling Dragoons (see Map 5). They would be further supported by C Battery Royal Horse Artillery and the 6th Machine Gun Squadron. This machine-gun unit would engage in various tasks that day which included firing 'with great effect' on a retiring enemy convoy, driving off enemy aircraft, and covering the flank of the cavalry attack.[108] The Horse Artillery similarly supported the attack, firing on Honnechy and targeting enemy batteries.

To confuse the picture, at 13.15 reports arrived that armoured cars had been through Maurois and Honnechy which were free of enemy, but these were correctly dismissed. Whilst one car had indeed made the journey, those places had been full of the enemy, as the units on the ground could see. As the cavalry advanced from the south-west, heavy HE shelling and machine-gun fire opened on them, gas shells making all the riders sneeze, and 'the air became black with Boche aeroplanes'.[109] Strafed by a low-level air attack with machine-gun and bomb, the Royals galloped on, only to be frustrated by the railway cutting to their front which was not on their maps. This forced them on a detour round Maurois to the north and they arrived on the Roman road between that village and Reumont. Initially they were opposed by machine-gun fire from Reumont, and took casualties, but when they occupied the high ground to the south-east of the village, the enemy retired. Meanwhile the 3rd Dragoons, their attack protected by armoured cars on one flank, galloped towards Honnechy from the south, across the front of 74 Brigade. They jumped the numerous ditches enfiladed by machine-gun fire from Escaufort and Bois Proyart on their right flank, as well as being bombed and machine-gunned from the air. The history of the 6th Cavalry Brigade claimed that as the cavalry passed though the infantry, 'the latter rose as a man and advanced with a great cheer'.[110] They particularly sustained casualties funnelling through the bridge under the railway (the objective of 74 Brigade) to the east of the railway triangle. Three of the attached armoured cars held the bridge as a mobile strong point until the infantry arrived. Shelled whilst consolidating the orchards beyond, their commander, Lieutenant-Colonel Charles Rome, became a casualty.[111]

The enemy had, however, begun to withdraw from Honnechy about ten minutes before the barrage was due to fall, and the perception of Lieutenant-Colonel Clarke was that in the ensuing wait for the shelling to be countermanded, they escaped. At 14.00 8th Worcestershire occupied the railway line and then the village. Many civilians were liberated in Honnechy, 'who spoke in praise of the rapidity of the British advance, which they said had prevented the evacuation of the women and children'.[112] The Worcesters' losses had been heavy, however, including five other ranks killed and 71 men wounded, including three officers. Again, initiative and junior leadership amongst the other ranks was evident. Corporal Charles Prince was awarded a bar to his MM for his work in establishing communication with his flanks and 'though wounded, still carrying on in charge of the

108 War Diary, 6th Machine Gun Squadron, 9 October 1918, TNA WO95/1152.
109 J. Bickersteth, op. cit., p.294.
110 J.B. Bickersteth, op. cit., p.114.
111 Charles Leslie Rome DSO, an Australian, had been commissioned in the 11th Hussars in 1898, and had served as military secretary to the Governor-General of Australia 1910-11. He had been a captain at the outbreak of war.
112 Kincaid-Smith, op. cit., p.327.

The approach of the Royal Dragoons of 6th Cavalry Brigade to the railway bridge at Honnechy on 9 October 1918.

leading wave of the attacking troops'. Private Arthur Ruggles similarly won the MM as when the advance was held up, he 'went forward alone, killed a German officer and came back with useful information as to the whereabouts of the German machine-gun posts'.[113]

The units of 74 Brigade also renewed their advance at 14.00, 9th Yorkshire to the left, 11th Sherwood Foresters to the right. In pressing on to Honnechy, Second-Lieutenant Coleman Sallmayer of the Sherwood Foresters won a bar to his MC as when coming under heavy machine-gun fire south of the village he rallied his men and led them on.[114] Sergeant Beechcroft and Private Ainsworth went unrewarded when they 'pushed forward alone and captured a machine-gun and its crew which was holding up the advance'; and it was a practical norm that Sergeant Wilkes should take command of his company when its commander, Captain Bartlett, was killed. He also went unrewarded. In 9th Yorkshire, six other ranks are mentioned in the divisional history for various

113 Kincaid-Smith, op. cit., p.327.

114 Coleman Leonard James Maurice Sallmeyer was commissioned in August 1917. The citation for his MC reads: 'During the advance from Le Catelet to Le Cateau from 5th/10th October 1918, inclusive, he displayed marked gallantry and devotion to duty. During the attack south of Honnechy the leading line came under heavy machine-gun fire and began to waver. He collected the remainder of his men and led them to the successful capture of the final objective. His example was mainly instrumental in rallying the men at a critical time and thus ensuring the success of the operation'. (*Edinburgh Gazette*, 8 October 1919, p.3224).

acts including reconnaissance and bringing in the wounded under fire.[115] After a total advance of some 3,500 yards, the units reached the railway bridge, the Sherwoods recording the capture of a light field gun that had been firing over open sights and a motor lorry. The station and railway line yielded 'a great deal of rolling stock and railway material'.[116] The battalion had lost one officer and twelve other ranks killed, with 67 wounded and one missing.[117] 13th Durham Light Infantry also lost an officer killed,[118] as well as 15 other ranks, whilst 9th Yorkshire had suffered least, losing seven other ranks killed.

Meanwhile, moving on in front of the infantry, the cavalry continued to sustain casualties on the road between Honnechy and Reumont. Bickersteth lodged himself in a farm where he could see up the main street of Reumont, with a mixture of South African Infantry from 66th Division and civilians. 'An old man with a grey beard had picked up one of our rifles and was peering cautiously out of the yard gateway to get a shot if he could see a "Sale Boche".'[119] Reaching the crest of any rise, of which there were a number on this road approaching the high ground to the west of Le Cateau, the advancing cavalry attracted heavy fire. The enemy were visible on the higher ground above Le Cateau with a line of machine and field guns. The cavalry, however, galloped to the sight and sound of the artillery, shelled the while with HE and Blue Cross shells,[120] an aircraft dropping two bombs. The enemy withdrew.

The armoured cars that had allegedly declared Honnechy free of the enemy belonged to 17th Armoured Car Battalion. Of its nine cars, seven were attached to the 3rd Cavalry Division, three to the 6th Cavalry Brigade, and four to the 7th. It was the cars attached to the 7th which had held the railway bridge at Honnechy station after the execution done to the cavalry there,[121] a bridge which a car attached to the 6th Brigade had played a crucial role in preserving. The 6th had sent their vehicles, under Lieutenant Alfred Ridlington,[122] forward at 09.00 to report on progress at Maretz. On encountering a large crater on the Roman road at the Serain-Prémont crossroads, the vehicles had to be hauled through a field, where one bent an axle. The remaining duo proceeded

115 Kincaid-Smith, op. cit., pp.327-8.
116 Kincaid-Smith, op. cit., p.326.
117 The officer casualty was 26 year-old Captain Cyril Ward Bartlett MC, killed by shellfire whilst consolidating the final objective. He had been commissioned from the ranks in March 1915. His men brought his body back and buried it on the start line at Le Trou aux Soldats, but it was subsequently lost and he is commemorated on the Vis-en-Artois memorial.
118 Captain Isaac Bewley MC had been commissioned in August 1915.
119 J. Bickersteth, op. cit., p.284.
120 Blue Cross shells dispensed a particulate which irritated the nose. Its use was intended to make the soldier remove his gas mask, making him vulnerable to more toxic gasses.
121 The two sections comprising four cars were commanded by Lieutenant Thomas Edwin McKinney (commissioned in August 1914); and Second-Lieutenant David Wighton Herd MC (commissioned into the Tank Corps in December 1917 from a gunner sergeant in the Motor Machine Gun Service which comprised motorcycle/sidecar combinations carrying a Vickers gun).
122 Lieutenant Alfred Charles Ridlington MC was commissioned from corporal in March 1917. His MC was awarded for this action. 'On the Le Cateau-Maretz Road on October 9th, 1918, he displayed marked gallantry and skill when in charge of a section of armoured cars. He first attacked a Machine Gun post which was holding up our advance, and in conjunction with the infantry successfully cleared it and captured the guns. In proceeding forward with two cars, a bridge was blown up behind him by the enemy, separating him from the second car and from our troops. With one car, however, he went forward through Maurois and Honnechy, which were both strongly held by the enemy, of whom he killed five in one spot in the latter village. His prompt action prevented the railway bridge from being blown up by the enemy'. (*London Gazette*, 30 July 1919, p.9768).

up the Roman road to Gattigny Wood. At the crossroads at the corner of the wood they found the South African Scottish of 66th Division held up by about 30 of the enemy. Passing though the machine-gun fire, they outflanked the position, capturing ten machine-guns and two mortars, killing four of the gunners. They then headed further up the road towards Maurois and in conjunction with the South Africans, attacked the enemy in the railway cutting north of where the railway crossed the road. The two cars were 50 yards apart, and the bridge over the cutting was promptly blown behind Ridlington in the leading vehicle as he pushed on. Undaunted, Ridlington proceeded through Maurois to Honnechy, under fire in both villages, but took a wrong turn up a by-road near Honnechy church. Germans emerged from a nearby house to investigate and one of the gunners swiftly killed five of them in the doorway. Reversing and proceeding towards the station, the car surprised a group of the enemy about to blow the bridge, who promptly fled leaving the bridge intact. The vehicle then continued its journey south to Busigny and took on a party of 20 of the enemy going up the road with four trench mortars from the rear, killing five. Driving back to the Roman road at Gattigny Wood where the exciting three mile odyssey had begun, Ridlington's car was rejoined by its companion cut off at Maurois, and returned to XIII Corps HQ with its intelligence. It had fired 2,500 rounds from its machine-guns.[123]

The front of 66th Division, commanded by Major-General Hugh 'Beetle' Bethell,[124] lay to the north of the Roman road. The division initially deployed 199 Brigade on the right and 198 Brigade on the left. 25th Battalion MGC attached one company to each brigade, as well as to the South African Brigade which was to advance with one brigade of Royal Field Artillery and one company of Royal Engineers and leapfrog its two fellows. Support from 1st Tank Battalion was requested by the division, then cancelled. 199 Brigade, commanded by Brigadier-General Guy Williams,[125] advanced with 18th King's Liverpool in front,[126] and 1/9th Manchester in support.[127] The Manchester unit should have been relieved but 5th Connaught Rangers could not be assembled in time to achieve this, another casualty of hasty organisation on a dark night. Setting off at 05.20, the fog was such that little could be seen before 07.00. Passing Avelu and Maretz, leaving the Manchesters to mop up, the Liverpool battalion had reached L'Epinette when machine-guns from Gattigny Wood (which lay to the west of Honnechy) opened up down the valley and their advance was stalled. The unit suffered six other ranks killed, and three officers and 31 other ranks wounded. 1/9th Manchester, although in support, did not escape without loss. Attacked by a

123 Montgomery, op. cit., pp.199-200; Anon, *Operations of the 17th (Armoured Car) Tank Battalion during the Battle of 1918*, pp.42-4.

124 Hugh Keppel Bethell OB CMG CVO DSO (1882-1947) had been commissioned in the Royal Garrison Artillery, and served with the 7th Gurkha Rifles, being subsequently transferred to the 7th Hussars in February 1914. After spending most of 1915 as a staff captain and brigade-major, he commanded 1st Northamptonshire for ten months from December 1915 when he was promoted to command 74 Brigade. He commanded 66th Division from 31 March 1918.

125 Sir Guy Charles Williams KCB CMG DSO (1881-1959) was commissioned into the Royal Engineers. Never having commanded an infantry battalion, he commanded 199 Brigade from 16 March 1918.

126 18th Liverpool were commanded by Major Richard Owen Wynne DSO and bar, an Australian who was commissioned in the Bedfordshire Regiment in August 1914. He commanded 2nd Bedfordshire from February to May 1918, but had had brief spells in temporary command of both 17th and 19th Liverpool. He was given command of 18th Liverpool on 29 September 1918 when Lieutenant-Colonel George Rollo was promoted to command 150 Infantry Brigade.

127 1/9th Manchester were commanded by Lieutenant-Colonel John Frederic Baker Morrell DSO, a regular lieutenant of the Royal Lancaster Regiment in August 1914. He had previously commanded 2nd East Yorkshire, 7th Berkshire and 13th Manchester, taking over 1/9th Manchester when the 13th was merged with it in August 1918.

squadron of enemy planes they suffered four casualties. In 198 Brigade, commanded by Brigadier-General Alan Hunter,[128] 1/6th Lancashire Fusiliers advanced towards Elincourt,[129] and like the units of 75 Brigade fell victim to friendly artillery fire.[130] Hampered by both this and the fog, at 06.00 they paused for an hour and a quarter, resuming to clear the east of the village. The support battalion, 5th Royal Inniskilling Fusiliers,[131] and the reserve battalion, 6th Royal Dublin Fusiliers,[132] converged on Elincourt to mop up, capturing 12 prisoners. The 'hurried departure' of the enemy was clear from uneaten meals 'found on the tables in some houses'.[133] The village was searched for mines and booby traps, and the attached Royal Engineers found one such at the village railway crossing. Advancing to the north-east of Elincourt the Irish units met more resistance. Meanwhile, the Lancashire Fusiliers to the south pressed on and occupied the first objective, Bois de Pinon, at 08.45, and their second, the Maretz-Clary Road, at 10.50. Three of their number were dead, one was wounded, and nine missing. Here, however, they faced Gattigny Wood.

The South African Brigade, commanded by Brigadier-General William Tanner,[134] followed both brigades, advancing with the 2nd Battalion South African Infantry on the right and the 4th Battalion on the left. The 2nd Battalion only received orders to follow 198 Brigade at 05.30, and had to forgo their rations, 'the men realising the urgency of a quick move cooperated in a splendid manner'.[135] On empty stomachs they progressed beyond Maretz under both heavy machine-gun fire from the hedges and undergrowth ahead, and accurate enemy shelling. Pausing to allow the 4th Battalion to catch up, the enemy machine-guns which were 'well placed tactically and at points from which oblique fire could be directed',[136] were overcome one by one. The South Africans then leapfrogged both 198 and 199 Brigades only to find, as had the other two battalions, that further progress was blocked by the machine-guns and snipers in Gattigny Wood. Here the second part of the cavalry action was played out.

At 11.00 the Canadian Cavalry Brigade appeared with two armoured cars. Under covering fire from the Royal Canadian Horse Artillery Brigade and the Machine Gun Squadron, the Fort Garry

128 Alan John Hunter KCVO CB CMG DSO MC (1881-1942) was commissioned into the King's Royal Rifle Corps. Having spent most of the war in staff posts, and never having commanded an infantry battalion, he was given command of 198 Brigade from 17 April 1917.

129 1/6th Lancashire Fusiliers were commanded by Lieutenant-Colonel Robert Ferguson Gross DSO. A regular captain of the South Wales Borderers in August 1914, he had served as a GSO3, GSO2, and GSO1, before commanding 12th Lancashire Fusiliers from January to August 1918. He moved on 13 August to command the 1/6th Battalion.

130 The battalion described this as the barrage being late. (War Diary, 1/6th Lancashire Fusiliers, 9 October 1918, TNA WO95/3140).

131 5th Royal Inniskilling Fusiliers were commanded by Lieutenant-Colonel Arthur William Sibbald Paterson DSO. A regular captain of the Somerset Light Infantry in August 1914, he had commanded 6th Royal Irish Fusiliers from January to November 1916, when he was moved to command 5th Inniskilling Fusiliers.

132 6th Royal Dublin Fusiliers were commanded by Lieutenant-Colonel William Benjamin Little DSO. A horticultural instructor in August 1914, he was commissioned in the 6th Durham Light Infantry in October 1914, and commanded 1/5th Border Regiment from October 1917, taking command of 6th Dublin Fusiliers at the end of August 1918.

133 War Diary, 6th Battalion Royal Dublin Fusiliers, 'Operations 7-11 October 1918', TNA WO95/3140.

134 William Ernest Collins Tanner (1875-1943) was commissioned in the Natal Carbineers in 1899, later transferring to the Scottish Horse and Natal Militia. He commanded the 2nd South African Infantry on the Western Front until 15 October 1917 when he was promoted GOC 8 Infantry Brigade, commanding the South African Brigade from 3 April 1918.

135 War Diary, 2nd South African Infantry, 9 October 1918, TNA WO95/3147.

136 War Diary, 2nd South African Infantry, 9 October 1918, TNA WO95/3147.

The western edge of Gattigny Wood attacked by the Canadian Cavalry Brigade on 9 October 1918.

Horse attacked Gattigny Wood. Lieutenant James Dunwoody, with the 3rd Troop of B Squadron, was ordered to attack the enemy machine-guns on the right flank, four of the Canadian machine-guns providing overhead fire, whilst Major Edward Middlemast with A Squadron attacked the left (see Map 5). Dunwoody's seemingly suicidal mission, galloping over 2,000 yards in the teeth of frontal fire, predictably resulted in himself and most of the troop becoming casualties, although the Machine Gun Squadron believed their covering fire had 'caused the enemy's fire to practically cease'. In the violence of the attack, a number of the enemy were killed and the remainder driven off, abandoning their guns,[137] the Canadian machine-guns 'preventing the enemy escaping on spare horses of the LSH that were wandering about'.[138] On the left flank, Middlemast and his squadron attacked wielding the *arme blanche*, capturing some 200 of the enemy. Meanwhile, Lord Strathcona's Horse were working round from the north, and Lieutenant Harry Finnigan and a troop from B Squadron 'galloped it',[139] taking 30 prisoners.[140] The additional bag from the wood included

137 James Moore Dunwoody was awarded the DSO for this action. Born in Belfast in 1892 he was an accountant in Manitoba, Canada, in August 1914.

138 War Diary, Machine-Gun Squadron Canadian Cavalry Brigade, 'Narrative of Operations 9th and 10th October 1918', Library and Archives Canada, RG 9 III-D-1, Vol. 4686, folder 36, file 6, http://data4.collectionscanada.ca

139 Harry Finnigan was awarded the MC for his part in this action, for 'cool leadership', his citation noting that he 'assisted in the capture by the squadron of a further 43 prisoners'. (*London Gazette*, 30 July 1919, p.9791).

140 War Diary, Lord Strathcona's Horse, 9 October 1918, Library and Archives Canada, RG 9 III-D-3, vol.4955, folder 494 http://data4.collectionscanada.ca

one 5.9-inch howitzer, two field guns and forty machine-guns. Pushing on, Middlemast and his squadron saw the enemy abandoning the village of Bertry, north-west of Honnechy, but becoming scattered in pursuit, he and many of his troopers became casualties. Once his wounds were dressed, Middlemast pressed on.[141] The remainder of B Squadron Fort Garry Horse proceeded to the east, capturing Maurois, driving the enemy out of the eastern edge of the village.[142] Forty-two of the enemy were taken prisoner, along with five machine-guns.

At about noon, Rawlinson ordered XIII Corps to capture Le Cateau. The wood having been cleared, 2nd South African Infantry pushed on, but beyond the railway line again met stiff resistance which held the battalion up for half an hour before it was subdued. To their right the villages of Maurois and Honnechy could be seen, many house displaying white flags. Out of touch on both flanks, the battalion occupied Maurois in the wake of the cavalry attack from 25th Division's area, and moved beyond. With the arrival of a party of the Fort Garry Horse about 35 strong, the South African CO, Major Leslie Francis Sprenger, borrowed one of the horses and rode into Reumont, the next village, demonstrating the sort of aggressive spirit in tune with Rawlinson's orders.[143] He found a group of the enemy escaping on bicycles, and in attempting to pull up to them had his horse shot from under him by a sniper for his pains. Guns firing over open sights were observed on the ridge beyond the village, protecting the enemy fleeing on horseback and in all sorts of vehicles. The South African Brigade's machine-gunners, however, had not advanced sufficiently fast to be in position to do execution. More cavalry appeared, but in the view of the South Africans, 'much manoeuvring took place to no particular object' other than the sustaining of casualties.[144] They were more complimentary to the RAF, noting 'our aeroplanes in dozens dominated the air' (arriving too late, it seems, to protect the cavalry during their charge), one dropping the message 'all clear ahead'.[145] Despite the South African sarcasm, C Squadron of the Fort Garry Horse, under Major Richard Mills (also wounded that day),[146] swung north around Reumont, charged, and captured 42 prisoners and six machine-guns. With the assistance of B Squadron, the machine-gun section, and the Royal Canadian Horse Artillery, the town was secured. For 'moderate' casualties, 2nd South African Infantry had captured 150 prisoners, about twenty machine-guns and some anti-tank weapons, as well as a staff motor car. The reserve unit of the Canadian Cavalry Brigade, the Royal Canadian Dragoons, C Squadron of which had participated in capturing Reumont, was now ordered to take the high ground north-west of Le Cateau. As Lieutenant-Colonel Charles Van

141 Edward Liddell Middlemast was born in Northumberland in 1884, and was a manager of a printing press in Regina, Saskatchewan, Canada in August 1914. He was awarded the DSO for this action: 'On the morning of October 9th, 1918, he was in charge of advanced guard squadron of the regiment, and located the enemy with many machine-guns in the Bois-du-Mont Aux-Yilles and Bois-de-Gattigny. After successfully sizing up the situation and timing himself with the advancing infantry, he charged the wood with the sword around the enemy's right flank, killing large numbers and capturing approximately 200 prisoners and 20 machine-guns. Although wounded in this charge, he, after having his wound dressed, resumed command of his squadron and did valuable work during the remainder of the day. He did splendid work'. (*London Gazette*, 30 July 1919, p.9685)

142 War Diary, Fort Garry Horse, 9 October 1918, Library and Archives Canada, RG 9 III-D-3, Vol. 4956, folder 496, http://data4.collectionscanada.ca

143 Leslie Francis Sprenger DSO MC was educated at RMC Sandhurst and served with the Witwatersrand Rifles as a sniper, and as an officer with the Transvaal Light Infantry.

144 War Diary, 2nd South African Infantry, 9 October 1918, TNA WO95/3147.

145 War Diary, 2nd South African Infantry, 9 October 1918, TNA WO95/3147.

146 A Canadian-born law student, Richard Burkett Mills MC rose from trooper to major. His wound on the 9th terminated his war service. He finished his career as a barrister then judge in Saskatoon, Canada.

Straubenzee was forming his regiment up on the north side of the Roman road, he learnt that C Squadron was being counterattacked. He left dismounted troopers of B Squadron to help hold the attacking Germans, but whilst returning from reconnoitring was killed by a shell. The securing of the high ground was subsequently achieved in conjunction with Lord Strathcona's Horse with an encircling movement.[147]

On the extreme left of 66th Division's attack, the 4th South African Infantry, commanded by Lieutenant-Colonel Donald Macleod,[148] made a flanking movement around the northern edge of Gattigny Wood as the cavalry cleared it, a move which drew them towards the village of Bertry. They were following in the wake of Major Middlemast and his troopers who galloped thither, reaching it just after 12.00. Bertry was not part of the unit's objectives – indeed, it was in the area of V Corps, Third Army. The 4th Battalion's justification for its decision to assault it was that as units of V Corps had yet to appear, 'it would not have been possible to have taken and held Maurois if the enemy had still been in possession of Bertry'.[149] Indeed, the village is on higher ground than Maurois, and enfiladed progress along the Roman road there. Bertry was captured at 14.45, with the assistance of the two armoured cars which had been held in reserve and which dealt with obstructive machine-guns in the railway cutting. When the 1st Scottish Rifles (19 Brigade, 33rd Division) reached the village a short time later, however, they found it only 'roughly cleared'.[150] Meeting some 'slight opposition' still,[151] they liberated 1,500 civilians. The 4th South African Infantry suffered one officer and 23 other ranks killed, with four officers and 71 other ranks wounded. Their detour had, however, caused a gap to open up between the 2nd and 4th Battalions, and the 1st South African Infantry was moved up, indicating General Tanner's good grip on what was happening to his units, but in the end they saw no action. The brigade casualties for the day included one officer and 23 ORs killed in action, with four officers and 71 other ranks wounded.

By the end of the day, the cavalry had secured the high ground to the west of Le Cateau, and the infantry eventually caught up. The artillery moved up in support, 66 lorries of field gun and howitzer ammunition being sent up during the day, and 6-inch guns were moved up to shell Le Cateau and roads east.[152] All the Army's first objectives set the previous night had been achieved, with the exception of the longed-for cavalry breakthrough, although there had been exploitation in both IX and XIII Corps areas. Indeed, most progress had been made in the area of the latter, the corps that had the longest distance to travel. 66th Division congratulated itself on having 'again had a most successful day', succeeding in advancing its line to a maximum depth of 12,000 yards on a front of 2,500 yards. 'The physical fitness of all ranks, and the way in which units made efficient arrangements and carried out at comparatively short notice was satisfactory'.[153] The same might have been said of all the divisions that fought that day. Ninety-five German officers and 2,593 other ranks had

147 War Diary, Royal Canadian Dragoons, 9 October 1918, Library and Archives Canada RG 9 III-D-3, vol.4956, folder 495. Charles Turner Van Straubenzee enlisted in September 1914, having previously served with the Canadian Dragoons in South Africa. He does not appear to have been popular. Trooper Colin Greener described him as 'a man most heartily detested' who 'cared more for spit and polish that he did for his men'. When he was killed Greener alleged: 'Many cheered and few were sorry at the event'. http://elinorflorence.com/blog/canadian-cavalry.

148 Lieutenant-Colonel Donald McLeay Macleod DSO MC DCM had commanded the battalion since April 1917.

149 War Diary, 4th South African Infantry, 9 October 1918, TNA WO95/3147.

150 Edmonds and Maxwell-Hyslop, op. cit., p.220.

151 War Diary, 1st Battalion Scottish Rifles, 9 October 1918, TNA WO95/2422.

152 War Diary, Commander Royal Artillery XIII Corps, 9 October 1918, TNA WO95/902.

153 Operational Order, War Diary, HQ 66th Infantry Division, 9 October 1918, TNA WO95/3122.

been taken prisoner. The Cavalry Corps, too, had had its most exciting day since the opening of the Battle of Amiens, albeit without ultimate success. The cost had, however, been considerable. Three hundred and ninety five casualties were sustained on 9 October – 338 wounded, with four officers and 53 ORs killed.[154] This heavy loss was not just in manpower. 6th Cavalry Brigade sustained 16 dead and 145 wounded, but the loss of horses totalled 235. The Canadian Brigade lost 30 killed and 11 wounded, with 171 horses becoming casualties.[155] Rawlinson's concluding comment – 'The Cav[alry] were rather sticky today and did not get through'[156] – was perhaps not a fair epitaph for their efforts.

Above the battlefield, as the South Africans had stated, the RAF largely dominated the skies, one omission being the failure to protect the cavalry. 5 Brigade RAF provided the 22nd Army and 15th Corps Wings.[157] The tasks of the squadrons of a Corps Wing were the control of artillery fire and tactical reconnaissance; the squadrons of an Army Wing comprised fighter-reconnaissance, fighters and bombers, 'whose task it was to take the battle beyond the front line to both protect the Corps Wing from the German Air Force and attack targets in depth'.[158] Both IX and XIII Corps also had a squadron assigned.[159] On 9 October, a day described as 'fair but misty', in the air above Fourth Army, 268 pilots clocked-up 778 hours of flying, including 39 contact patrols and 244 offensive flights.[160] Eighteen reconnaissances were carried out, including eight photographic flights, whilst 19 artillery patrols made 49 zone calls, i.e. directing counter-battery fire on a particular zone of the map, claiming eleven enemy batteries neutralised. Enemy opposition in the air was 'slight', but there were 19 combats, five of which were decisive, along with the destruction of six observation balloons. Bombing included dropping some 28 112-pound bombs on Wassigny, a junction of railway lines over 6,000 yards beyond the Selle. Every available machine was put to the task of ground-strafing the retreating enemy, 30,670 rounds being fired at ground targets. Patrols of 24 Squadron alone dropped 44 25-pound bombs from a height of 200 feet, and fired 5,250 rounds at ground targets. Troops, transports and a train in Busigny also became targets. It was believed that 'considerable confusion and casualties were caused among retreating troops and transport'.[161] A good example of the degree of co-operation between air and ground is provided by the actions of 'ace' Captain Walter Longton of 24 Squadron. Flying a patrol in his single-seater S.E.5a fighter late in the afternoon, Longton was observing troops and transport going north-east from Le Cateau to Forest and was above cavalry who were being harassed by a machine-gun. He

154 War Diary, HQ Cavalry Corps, 'Cavalry Corps Narrative of Operations 8th to 10th October 1918', TNA WO 95/575.
155 War Diary, HQ 3rd Cavalry Division, 'Narrative of Operations, Oct 8th-11th 1918', TNA WO95/1142.
156 Sir H. Rawlinson, War Journal, 9 October 1918, Churchill College RWLN 1/11.
157 22nd Army Wing had eight squadrons of single-seater scouts for fighting, balloon destruction and low attack (23, 24, 46, 80, 84, 85, 92 and 208 Squadrons, flying Sopwith Dolphin, S.E.5 and Sopwith Camel aircraft); and two squadrons of two-seaters (20 and 205 Squadrons, flying Bristol Fighters and D.H.9s) for fighting, bombing, reconnaissance and photography. 15th Corps Wing contained 8 Squadron, flying F.K.8s; and 73 Squadron, flying Sopwith Camel single-seater bi-plane fighters. Both were attached to the Tank Corps.
158 A. McCluskey, 'The Battle of Amiens and the Development of British Air-Land Battle, 1918-45', in G. Sheffield and P. Gray, *Changing War*, pp.232-3.
159 XI Corps had 9 Squadron attached, flying R.E.8 two seat bi-planes, the standard British reconnaissance and artillery spotting aircraft. XIII Corps had 35 Squadron attached which was equipped with Bristol F.2 Fighters, a two-seater biplane fighter and reconnaissance aircraft useful in a low-level role.
160 War Diary, HQ Fourth Army, 9 October 1918, TNA WO95/439.
161 War Diary, HQ Fourth Army, 9 October 1918, TNA WO95/439.

landed his plane and gave them the location of the nest, the cavalry informing the attached artillery. Longton then 'rose and attacked the enemy who scattered as soon as our gunners engaged them'.[162] He had already that day shot down an enemy balloon with 100 rounds of Buckingham incendiary ammunition. Although enemy opposition was slight, the Germans were not absent from the air, as the cavalry had discovered. Lieutenant Howard Heintzman of 35 Squadron,[163] with his observer, Second-Lieutenant Howard, were performing an artillery patrol near Bertry in their Bristol Fighter when six Fokker bi-planes dived on them from the sun. Howard returned fire, but his Lewis gun jammed, but on firing a red Very light six Sopwith Camels joined them, surprising the German machines, one Fokker being sent crashing in flames near Honnechy.[164]

To the south, IX Corps had ended the day in a highly optimistic fashion. The 'large fires and explosions' which had been 'observed all day' indicated that the enemy were 'retiring on an extensive scale'. Indeed, as darkness fell the hubristic view was adopted that 'the hostile retirement had developed into the nature of a rout'.[165] Inescapably, however, the 'further objectives that Sir Henry Rawlinson had ordered to be taken during the day had … not been secured'.[166] The Bellevue spur, St Souplet and Le Cateau itself were still in enemy hands. In the wider context, whilst Third Army, to the north, had kept pace on the army boundary, the French, who had met more severe resistance, were stalled in front of Etaves Wood on Fourth Army's southern boundary, just to the south-east of Fresnoy. Rawlinson declared with some irritation that Debeney's *First Army* were 'gradually coming up into line but it was the devil getting them to start'.[167] The enemy, however, experienced being 'pursued vigorously on the entire front'. They had always intended to move their rearguards back on the night of 9 October, and 'the movement was continued, beginning at 10 p.m. with the main body of the infantry; the rearguards followed at 12.30 a.m'.[168] Whilst the Official History states that according to the regimental accounts consulted, 'the German rear guards were considerably mauled on the 9th October',[169] their action had been really quite effective, slowing Fourth Army's progress so that the idea of 'rout' was largely illusory.

162 War Diary, 5 Brigade RAF, Annexe to Summary 9 October 1918, TNA AIR 1/2225/209/40/26. Walter Hunt 'Scruffy' Longton DFC & two bars, AFC (1892-1927) was a private in the Queen's Own Worcestershire Hussars Yeomanry, and had fought on Gallipoli. He was commissioned into the RFC in April 1916. His first aerial victory was on 7 July 1918, and he soon became an 'ace', downing 11 enemy machines before the end of October 1918. He was awarded a bar to his DFC for his actions on 9 October: 'Between 29th September and 9th October this officer carried out twelve tactical reconnaissances, bringing back most valuable information; he also displayed great gallantry in attacking enemy troops on the ground. On 9th October, when on a low patrol, he observed a machine-gun nest which appeared to be the sole obstacle to our cavalry advance. Having informed the cavalry and field artillery of the situation, he co-operated with the former in their attack, and, after the enemy had been driven out, pursued them with machine-gun fire as they retreated'. (*London Gazette*, 31170, p.2033). He was killed in a flying accident at Bournemouth in 1927.

163 Howard Crichton Heintzman, a piano manufacturer, was commissioned lieutenant in the Canadian Field Artillery but was seconded to the RAF in February 1918.

164 War Diary, HQ 5 Brigade RAF, Combat Reports 9 October 1918, TNA AIR 1/2225/209/40/26.

165 War Diary, HQ IX Corps, 9 October 1918, TNA WO95/837.

166 Montgomery, op. cit., p.200.

167 Sir H. Rawlinson, War Journal, 9 October 1918, Churchill College RWLN 1/11.

168 War Diary, HQ German *Second Army*, 9 October 1918, *USAWW Vol.* 7, pp.893-5.

169 Edmonds & Maxwell-Hyslop, op. cit., p.229.

The Pursuit – Day Two: Thursday 10 October 1918

Fourth Army issued orders at 19.30 on the 9th for IX Corps to secure the high ground north and south of Andigny-les-Fermes on the Bellevue spur; for XIII Corps to take Le Cateau; and for the American II Corps to take St Benin, St Souplet and Molain and 'push forward advanced troops across the Selle in order to cover the passages of that river'.[170] The Official Historian noted in relation to this optimism that the British were 'uncertain, of course, whether the enemy was holding' their new position on the eastern bank 'merely by rearguards or was meaning to stand'.[171] On the morning of the 10th mist and rain unhelpfully 'prevented any observation of the enemy's movements',[172] and in particular no aeroplane observation was possible before midday which might have shed light on the German intentions.

IX Corps

On the right of the British line, 138 Brigade of the 46th Division continued the attack. With the 'probability of the enemy retiring for some distance', both the 46th and 6th Divisions 'were re-organised into an advanced guard formation with one Inf[antry] B[riga]de in the line and two in support', with one mixed brigade of artillery allotted to each division in the line.[173] The mobile brigade of heavy artillery comprised two 60-pounder and two 6-inch howitzer batteries.[174] At 05.45 1/5th Lincolnshire, who had held the line overnight, found Landricourt Wood in their front to be clear. In an act of across army co-operation, they informed the French who were able to attack Bois d'Etaves from this direction.[175] The brigade had received a troop of Royal Scots Greys the previous afternoon to be used in patrol work, and they advanced through the infantry to the Bohain-Seboncourt road, which the Lincolns then secured. 5th Tank Battalion moved ten tanks up to Landricourt Wood, two developing engine trouble during the march, but, again, none would see action. 1/4th Leicestershire then leapfrogged the Lincolns towards the next thoroughfare which crossed their front, the Bohain-Aisonville road, which they secured by midday. They pushed on towards Riquerval Wood but, with a taste of what was to come, met the enemy heavily defending its edge with machine-guns. The corps cyclists, attached to the brigade, reconnoitred the road to the north of the wood from Bohain, and reported encountering the enemy at Regnicourt.[176] At 18.00 1/5th Leicestershire, now commanded by Major Richard Dyer-Bennet who had taken over from Captain Hills,[177] were ordered to take over and push on into the wood. Dyer-Bennet's orders were that his unit would assault it at 02.00 the following morning without the protection of a barrage. His plan was as follows – C and D Companies would flank the wood to the left on the same route that the corps cyclists had taken and then turn south into the trees, whilst A Company would keep touch with the French at Retheuil Farm and advance up a ride into the wood to the

170 War Diary, HQ Fourth Army, Message G.322 10 October 1918, TNA WO95/439.
171 Edmonds and Maxwell-Hyslop, op. cit., p.234.
172 Montgomery, op. cit., p.200.
173 War Diary, HQ IX Corps, 9 October 1918, TNA WO95/837.
174 Montgomery, op. cit., p.201.
175 Sandall, op. cit., p.183.
176 1/4th Leicestershire did not record their casualties. CWGC records indicate three fatalities in the other ranks 9-10 October.
177 Richard Stewart Dyer-Bennet was commissioned into the 1st Battalion Leicestershire Regiment in November 1905, and after serving as machine-gun officer, was appointed adjutant of the 4th Battalion in 1913.

right. B Company drew one of what would prove to be three short straws, assigned to tackle the centre of the wood. On arrival at the road, and after some excitement evacuating the cellar used as battalion HQ when a ticking clock was mistaken for a booby trap,[178] Dyer-Bennett discovered that 1st Leicestershire on his left had orders to attack at 05.15 on the following day, the 11th. Looking up at the absence of a moon, he decided that the dangers of losing direction were great, and secured permission to attack in conjunction with the flanking unit.

To the north of Riquerval Wood, 6th Division rested 16 Brigade and continued with 71 Brigade, which had D Company 6th Battalion MGC attached. 1st Leicestershire attacked on the right, with 2nd Sherwood Foresters on the left.[179] There was no covering barrage, but 24 Brigade RFA bombarded houses, copses and sunken roads that might contain resistance. Little was met by either unit. Having taken eight prisoners, 1st Leicestershire, due to the lack of progress at Riquerval Wood, formed a defensive flank along the Bohain to Regnicourt road, a route which would pose 1/5th Leicestershire considerable problems the following day. 5th Cavalry Brigade again sent the 12th Lancers forward, and they pushed patrols forward beyond the infantry to Vallée Hasard and Vaux-Andigny, whilst the Sherwood Foresters on the left covered some 5,000 yards, arriving at Vaux-Andigny somewhat later than the Americans on their left, delays having been caused by collecting patrols that had been sent into Bohain. They noted that 'the country was practically untouched and the farms were still occupied by civilians and the country in cultivation'.[180] For the Sherwoods, 'the long-hoped-for open warfare had begun'.[181]

As has been noted, no flying was possible before 12.00 on 10 October because of low cloud and rain. Overall in the skies above Fourth Army, 194 pilots flew 321 hours of missions, less than half that of the previous day. Two photographic flights and eight reconnaissances were achieved, with 147 offensive missions. There were 16 combats in the air of which three were decisive, the enemy planes being destroyed with no British losses.[182] Fewer German aircraft were seen, it being thought that the poor weather accounted for this, although a strong flight of 31 enemy machines was seen over Reumont, and the Americans reported that enemy aircraft were surveying their forward area all afternoon. In 5 Brigade RAF, six artillery patrols were flown with 29 zone calls. The emphasis on ground attack continued, and 618 25-pound bombs were dropped, with 48,370 rounds fired at troops and transports. Major Arthur Coningham of 208 Squadron in a Sopwith Camel attacked two trains and destroyed a rocket battery.[183] Captain James Robb of 92 Squadron in an S.E.5a attacked horse transport and silenced a 'Flaming Onion' battery.[184] 'Ace' amongst aces

178 Hills, op. cit., p.339.
179 2nd Sherwood Foresters were commanded by Lieutenant-Colonel Charles Edward Hudson DSO, who had taken over at the end of September. A civilian and a piano dealer in August 1914, commissioned in November that year, Hudson had previously commanded 11th Sherwood Foresters from November 1917 to June 1918.
180 War Diary, 2nd Battalion Sherwood Foresters, 10 October 1918, TNA WO95/1624.
181 H.C. Wylly, *The First and Second Battalions The Sherwood Foresters (Nottinghamshire and Derbyshire Regiment) in the Great War*, p.181.
182 War Diary, 5 Brigade RAF, Daily Report 10 October 1918, TNA AIR 1/2225/209/40/26
183 A future Air Chief Marshal, Arthur 'Mary' Coningham DSO MC DFC AFC had fought with the New Zealanders at Gallipoli. Invalided unfit for military service, he journeyed to Britain at his own expense to join the RFC, going to the Western Front in December 1916. In 11 months he conducted 176 patrols, with 16 victories and three shared victories to his name. He commanded the Western Desert Air Force in 1941 and died in a commercial airliner accident in 1948.
184 A 'Flaming Onion' was a 37-mm five revolving barrel anti-aircraft gun. All five round were discharged as swiftly as possible giving the 'string of flaming onions' effect. A future Air Chief Marshal, Sir James

Captain Tom Hazell of 24 Squadron, also in an S.E.5a, bombed sidings in Wassigny.[185] Captain Carl Falkenburg in his S.E.5a carried out a low-level reconnaissance of Le Cateau and Bohain.[186] At 12.30 he could see the enemy 'retreating rapidly', noting that most transport and guns had been moved in the night. The enemy appeared present only in small bodies of 20-30. He estimated that 'there is a space of 2 or 5 miles between our troops and the enemy', with villages such as Neuvilly and St Souplet 'deserted'.[187] Later in the day when visibility allowed a clearer view, 'Scruffy' Longton flew the length of the *Hermann Stellung I* on the east bank of the Selle at 16.30, bringing back a report of its route.

II American Corps

On this second day of the Pursuit, the advance of the American 30th Division to secure crossings of the Selle again received artillery support, 2nd Australian Divisional Artillery firing a similar barrage to the previous day.[188] The 120th Infantry (60 Brigade) advanced on the right of the corps attack, their final objective being the village of Molain, on the river. They were followed by one section of the 41st Battery Australian Field Artillery, who engaged moving targets and machine-guns, opportunistically manning a captured battery of German 5.9-inch guns and firing 100 rounds into Bois l'Évêque to the north-east between Le Cateau and Landrecies, where enemy artillery was located.[189] The 43rd Battery kept up a constant fire on targets around the Selle. Approaching downhill towards Vaux-Andigny the 120th came under fire from the houses there, and both machine-gun and artillery fire from Bellevue Farm on the high ground of the spur of the same name to the south-east. They suffered significant casualties. With heavy fighting the 120th cleared the village, but their right flank was nearly 3,000 yards in the air. After waiting under heavy shellfire for the arrival of the support regiment, the 118th (59 Brigade), the regiment had to withdraw to the western edge of the town and form a defensive line on the railway south of the village. The 118th had been following 1,000 yards behind, but passing though the 120th was unable to advance more than a further 200 yards. The enemy resistance was again proving effective. By the evening, a line was established just to the east of Vaux-Andigny, 1,000 yards short of Molain. On their right flank, the 2nd Sherwood Foresters were at Vallée Hasard, some 1,000 yards to the rear, the ground to their front dominated by the Bellevue spur. The 118th closed the gap but according to reconnaissance carried out for the Australian artillery the enemy exploited the situation and penetrated the line to within 2,000 yards of the artillery that had been pushed forward.[190]

Milne Robb GCB KBE DSO DFC AFC (1895-1968) was commissioned in October 1914 into the Northumberland Fusiliers. He had seven kills to his name, but Arthur Coningham took the view that he was 'largely responsible for the destruction of a further 25'. (V. Orange, *Coningham – A Biography of Air Marshal Sir Arthur Coningham*, p.31).

185 Thomas Falcon Hazell DSO MC DFC (1892-1946) was commissioned in October 1914 into the Royal Inniskilling Fusiliers. Appointed Flying Officer in June 1917, he was the fifth most successful 'ace' of the war with 43 kills.

186 Carl Frederick Falkenburg DFC was the Canadian-born grandson of Baron Andreas Falkenburg, the Swedish consul. Wounded fighting for the Canadian infantry he was commissioned into the RFC in June 1917. He had 17 kills to his name.

187 War Diary, 5 Brigade RAF, Annexe to Daily Summary 9 October 1918, TNA AIR 1/2225/209/40/26.

188 Operation Order, HQ 2nd Australian Divisional Artillery, 10 October 1918, AWM Item No. 13/11/32 Part 1.

189 War Diary, HQ 11th Brigade Australian Field Artillery, 10 October 1918, AWM, Item No. 13/38/33.

190 War Diary, HQ 5th Brigade Australian Field Artillery, 10 October 1918, AWM Item No. 13/33/35.

On the left of the American II Corps, a runner from 60 Brigade only reached the 119th regimental HQ at 04.30 with information that the advance was to be continued and that the barrage to be followed would open at 05.00. In fact, the barrage was timed for 05.30, which if the orders had not been late and led to delay 'might have caused disastrous results'.[191] It was an example of the sort of poor staff work that would dog the American Corps in its operations at the Selle. The objective, over-optimistic as it would be discovered, was the heights 500 yards east of the River Selle, from which the enemy had an excellent view of the allied advance, and which were also believed to be strongly held. Mishap being avoided by luck, and meeting little resistance, Escaufort was reached at about 10.00. Whilst the left of the advance was held up by fire from the east bank of the river, the right fought its way forward and downhill into St Souplet, which was clearly not deserted as the RAF had reported. After a 'brisk fight cleaning out German machine-gun nests in the cemetery' there,[192] the battalion arrived on the river by 13.00, and was in full possession of the village by 15.00. Even so, they were not comfortable, as they were enfiladed from St Benin to the north. Half an hour later, however, this had been taken by 25th Division, and by 17.00 the 119th had pushed up to occupy the heights above the river to the south of that village, linking with the British 74 Brigade. From the other side of the Selle there was a steady heavy barrage of machine-gun and artillery fire, and it became lethal to attempt to cross the valley. It was claimed that 'repeated efforts were made to cross the River, and at a few points were successful',[193] but 'the Germans held splendid positions on high ground from which they poured terrific fire into out troops'.[194] Eventually the 119th Regiment settled for digging in on the west bank. They had advanced 4,000 yards that day, liberating 706 French civilians from three villages, and had captured several field artillery pieces and large amounts of ammunition. They were, however, 1,000 yards in advance of the American units on their right flank, and a gap existed between the two brigades that was never closed. Overall, there were 26 American fatalities that day, but the 120th Infantry had suffered particularly. Supporting them in the sky, the 3rd Squadron Australian Flying Corps mounted another 17 flights totalling 29 hours. Only one flight of five enemy planes was seen, and four of the missions were to carry out bombing. Two were directed at road transport, one at a train, and one at a railway siding and road junction.[195]

It was the view of the 5th Brigade Australian Field Artillery that if the fortified railway embankment on the other side of the river had 'been rushed immediately on arrival of the infantry our position would have been strong', and it was hinted that by adhering too closely to precise orders, and waiting for the artillery to come up and provide a barrage, the opportunity for exploitation had been missed.[196] Indeed, the Americans were the only forces likely to have been able to rush the positions on the east bank, but to do so they would have had to have crossed the Selle without bridging. Like the British tanks the previous day, the Australian artillery was suggesting that 30th Division was at best overcautious, without actually describing it as 'sticky'. The inexperienced leadership of the infantry units was unlikely to have been able to make the decision. At the end of the day, Molain had not been secured and the Selle had not been crossed, but in comparison the units of IX Corps had made possibly less progress.

191 *History 119th Infantry*, p.50.
192 Murphy & Thomas, op. cit., p.115.
193 *History 119th Infantry*, p.51.
194 Murphy & Thomas, op. cit., p.116.
195 Squadron Record Book, 3rd Squadron AFC, 10 October 1918, AWM, Item no. 8/6/22 Part 1.
196 War Diary, HQ 5th Brigade Australian Field Artillery, 9 October 1918, AWM Item No. 13/33/35.

XIII Corps

25th Division, the southern formation of the XIII corps attack, again used 74 and 75 Brigades, their joint objective being the high ground to the east of Le Cateau, i.e. it was hoped that the river would be crossed and the town itself taken. The attack at 05.30 was carried out without a barrage, as cavalry reconnaissance had indicated there would be little opposition, but in 74 Brigade on the right, 86 Brigade RFA was attached to deal with any local opposition, although this 'did not materialise'.[197] The 100th Battalion MGC protected the right of the advance. Opposition was, however, met at 08.30 when the brigade reached St Benin which was on high ground at the confluence of the Rivers Selle and Essarts. Very heavy machine-gun fire from the north-east across the Selle and from the south-west where the Americans had yet to take St Souplet halted progress. At 12.30 the brigade received orders to assault the village, and at 14.30 a creeping barrage was put down. Whilst 9th Yorkshire guarded the right flank from the high ground to the south of the village, the much under-strength 13th Durham Light Infantry went through a heavy hostile barrage and captured the village within an hour 'with great dash'[198] after hand-to-hand fighting. Sergeant Arthur Sledge MM won the DCM in this action, taking command when his company commander was killed. He 'led them to their objective under great difficulties. Although wounded several times he refused to leave the line, and, after having his wounds dressed, again took command'.[199] Private soldiers also demonstrated leadership. Privates Horne and Dyer, 'when all their N.C.Os. had been wounded, collected parties of men and successfully carried on the attack'.[200] The enemy, being driven across the river, retaliated with heavy gas shelling. 9th Yorkshire had nine wounded, and, given the severity of the combat, the DLI had a surprisingly small total of seven other rank fatalities amongst their casualties.

75 Brigade on the left crossed country that was 'open and undulating and afforded little cover',[201] supported by 110 Brigade RFA. 1/8th Warwickshire, jumping-off to the north of Honnechy, advanced after 'heavy fighting' to the southern outskirts of Le Cateau, where the slow progress on their right meant that they had to dig in.[202] 1/5th Gloucestershire followed, with 1/8th Worcestershire 800 yards to their rear.[203] Even with the support of 100th Battalion MGC putting down a barrage on the railway cutting south of Le Cateau, where the enemy was concentrated, the leading battalion stalled. B Company of the Glosters was 'gallantly lead thru' the Warwicks by Captain Rupert Rogers but being 'heavily infiladed (sic) by M.G. fire having lost all its officers wounded and many of its N.C.O.(s) … was forced to fall back'.[204] The battalion received two orders to attack during the afternoon, but both were mercifully cancelled. Heavy machine-guns and artillery were firing at 'point blank range', and as further advance would have been across a 'series of

197 War Diary, 9th Battalion Yorkshire Regiment, 10 October 1918, TNA WO95/2247.
198 Montgomery, op. cit., p.201.
199 Arthur Sledge had arrived on the Western Front in August 1915. His DCM was awarded on 2 December 1919.
200 Kincaid-Smith, op. cit., p.330.
201 War Diary, HQ 75 Infantry Brigade, 10 October 1918, TNA WO95/2249.
202 1/8th Warwickshire suffered one officer and 24 other ranks killed and 5 officers and 168 other ranks wounded in the period 8-11 October,
203 Over their two days in action 1/8th Worcestershire had three officers and 68 ORs wounded, with five ORs killed.
204 War Diary, 1/5th Battalion Gloucestershire Regiment, 10 October 1918, TNA WO95/2251. Claude Rupert de Warenne Rogers, originally commissioned into the Leinster Regiment, won the DSO for his part in the attack on Beaurevoir Line and for this action, which he carried out despite having been wounded the previous day.

re-entrants enfiladed by the positions held by the enemy on the high ground E[ast] and N[orth] of St Benin', division ordered the brigade to dig in on a frontage of 1,500 yards west of St Benin.[205]

In the north of the corps area 7th Cavalry Brigade pushed forward at 06.00 through the infantry outposts to the north of the Roman road, its ever-optimistic objectives being the villages of Forest and Amerval on high ground on the eastern bank of the Selle, and in a northerly direction reconnoitered as far north as Neuvilly and Briastre on the river. The horsemen soon encountered heavy shelling and machine-gun fire, the river crossings being found to be strongly held. One brigade of artillery from 33rd Division and three armoured cars went forward to assist them, but by 09.00 they were ordered to withdraw. Frustratingly, the enemy could be seen retiring along the Roman road on the spur of high ground on the other side of the river through Forest, but out of range of field artillery.[206] German resistance, it was concluded (if it had not been obvious on the preceding day): 'Had now obviously become too strong to be overcome by cavalry action'. Indeed, the whole of the Cavalry Corps was now withdrawn.[207] The reconnaissance had been costly – 7th Cavalry Brigade, which had taken part in none of the major attacks the previous day, lost 11 killed, and 82 wounded.[208]

66th Division attacked in the wake of the cavalry with 199 Brigade leading and 198 in support, each brigade having attached a troop of Northumberland Hussars and one section of corps cyclists for reconnaissance, with their right protected by the 100th Battalion MGC. A brigade of field artillery followed. Gunner Major Frederick Rice progressed through Bertry and Troisvilles. 'The former was populated by old men, women and children. The men lifted their caps to us as they had been made to do to the Boche'. Rice found it moving that 'all the civilians waved or cheered or cried, and lots of houses had French flags flying'. Of all the deaths he must have seen during the war he described how in Troisvilles 'a Boche shell crashed through the wall of a house' just in front of them, and 'an old man came out wringing his hands which were covered in blood', two soldiers carrying out a 'girl who was apparently badly hit'.[209] Rice no doubt had a sense of the bitter irony of a death on the cusp of liberation. The division's general objective was, as for 25th Division, the high ground to the east of Le Cateau. 199 Brigade's initial objective was the undulating plateau of high ground to the west of the Roman road near its cross with the Le Cateau-Cambrai road. 18th King's Liverpool were in the lead. Advancing in relative safety on the reverse slope beyond their first objective to the highest point north-west of Le Cateau looking down on the village on Montay, matters altered radically as they proceeded on to the forward slope. Here they encountered strong machine-gun fire and were pounded by 5.9-inch guns sited on the equally high ground on the east bank. At 12.50 18th Division's artillery and heavy guns responded by shelling the area of the Forest spur. The centre and right companies of the Liverpool unit dropped down the slope into the north-west corner of Le Cateau under 'whizz bang' fire from German field artillery firing over open sights. Even though they were able to enter the outskirts of the town, the attack stalled under this resistance. 198 Brigade had meanwhile followed 45 minutes later with 1/6th Lancashire Fusiliers leading. The brigade was supported by a troop of yeomanry, three sections of cyclists, a brigade of artillery and machine-guns. The Fusiliers, with one section of machine-guns, advanced with three companies in line in artillery formation. They encountered shellfire as they reached the

205 War Diary, HQ 75 Infantry Brigade, 10 October 1918, TNA WO95/2249.
206 War Diary, HQ 3rd Cavalry Division, 'Narrative of Operations, Oct 8th-11th 1918', TNA WO95/1142.
207 Montgomery, op. cit., p.200.
208 War Diary, HQ 7th Cavalry Brigade, 10 October 1918, TNA WO95/1154.
209 F.J. Rice, Private Papers, IWM Docs 7197.

high ground over which the Liverpool unit had passed, enemy heavy artillery firing at them over open sights from the high ground beyond Montay, just as their predecessors had been treated. They could see that the eastern bank beyond was heavily held along the line of the railway, and at midday the brigade noted: 'It became evident that a further advance without more artillery support and without counter-battery work would be difficult'.[210] Brigadier-General Williams of 199 Brigade was similarly clear that the 'attack could not succeed unless a simultaneous attack took place on the right against the high ground east of the Selle'. He further thought it 'advisable to carry attack out of this nature at dawn under an artillery barrage', as many casualties would be sustained 'approaching in daylight before the town was reached'.[211] He proceeded to divisional HQ at 16.00, where in the effort to maintain tempo he was only granted half of his wishes. At 16.30 66th Division issued verbal orders for an assault in conjunction with the 25th Division from the south to take place at 17.30, with a barrage to commence at 17.00, the optimistic goals again being the high ground to the east of Le Cateau and the Forest spur.

Verbal orders for the attack were passed to battalion commanders only 15 minutes before the barrage was due at 17.00. The 25th Division, unable to complete its arrangements due to the short notice, cancelled their part in the assault just before the barrage was put down, noting 'the weakness and tiredness of the battalions'.[212] The attacking troops of the 66th could not, however, be contacted in time. The very thing that General Williams had sought to avoid was about to happen. At 17.30 the 1/6th Lancashire Fusiliers pushed on down into Montay with two companies of the support battalion, 5th Royal Inniskilling Fusiliers, under enfilade artillery fire on their right flank. They found the banks of the river wired and could not cross. 18th Liverpool similarly found the hedges to the south of Montay heavily wired, and the Selle impassable – the bridges were down and the river unfordable. The expedition was costly. The Lancashire Fusiliers lost five subalterns, including one killed;[213] whilst 59 other ranks were wounded and 68 missing.[214] The Inniskilling Fusiliers had nine other ranks killed, whilst 18th Liverpool had suffered 23 fatalities within the other ranks.

The 5th Connaught Rangers of 199 Brigade, in support to 18th Liverpool, had been shelled whilst stationary outside Le Cateau. Their CO, Lieutenant-Colonel Vincent Scully, was wounded, but remained at his post.[215] Two parties of B Company who were sent into the town on reconnaissance were also shelled, but encountered none of the enemy. Orders were received 12 minutes before the barrage came down for the whole battalion to attack the town at 17.30 with two companies of 1/9th Manchester, and capture the fortified railway that ran to the east. When the barrage lifted, B, C and D companies advanced through the town, their attack resisted by machine-guns. Pushing right through the eastern suburbs, battalion HQ was set up at the north corner of the bastion that was the railway triangle, and the line of the railway to the north was taken. Indeed, some of the Connaughts penetrated as far as the higher ground beyond 'as was proved by their corpses found

210 War Diary, HQ 198 Infantry Brigade, 10 October 1918, TNA WO95/3139.
211 War Diary, HQ 199 Infantry Brigade, 'Narrative', October 1918, TNA WO95/3143.
212 War Diary, HQ 25 Infantry Brigade, 10 October 1918, TNA WO95/2227.
213 Second-Lieutenant Charles Jackson was the officer killed. Second-Lieutenants James Rupert Smith-Saville (commissioned September 1917), H.H. Smith, T.C. Marriott (commissioned in April 1918 from private), and Percival Baker (commissioned from private in February 1917) were wounded.
214 CWGC records indicate that 23 ORs were killed.
215 Vincent Marcus Barron Scully DSO was a captain in the Special Reserve of the Border Regiment in August 1914, and he had commanded 5th Connaughts since June 1916. He was invalided on the 11th, Captain J.H.R. Dickson taking over.

lying there on the 20th when the ground was finally captured'.[216] The unit had, of course, pushed into an exposed position, its predicament due to the high ground untaken by the 25th Division to the south, and 198 Brigade's inability to cross the river to the north. At 22.50 Colonel Scully sent back the imploring message that he was consolidating the railway line near the corner of the railway triangle, 'with about 1½ companies Manchesters and 1 platoon 5 Connaught Rangers. Remainder appear to have lost their way. Please support me when possible. Objective lightly held I think but it's a difficult situation sniping being all around'. The Irish were enfiladed from both sides, and at 01.05 the order was issued: 'As both your flanks are in the air you must withdraw at once and consolidate on original line W[est] of the village'.[217] They had suffered one officer killed,[218] one missing and seven wounded; with four dead and twelve missing amongst the other ranks,[219] with 98 wounded and 19 affected by Blue Cross gas. Their achievement would frustrate stronger forces seven days later, when the attack would be re-attempted.

Colonel Scully was able to provide a detailed and useful report to brigade HQ that the enemy held no ground on the west bank of the Selle, but around the church on the higher ground in the east of the town centre had deployed 'a few machine-guns'. The houses to the east of the railway bridge on the Le Cateau-Bazuel road were similarly occupied by machine-guns. From the prisoners the unit had taken he concluded that: 'The enemy obviously intends to withdraw from his present line and is carrying on a systematic destruction of the town'. He reported the railway station purposely set alight with the enemy 'burning many of the chief buildings in the town'. The main bridge across the Selle was intact but guarded, all other bridges having been destroyed, although a bridge in the southern part of the town was both partially intact and unguarded, usable by infantry as the handrails were still in position. However, the enemy's main position in the railway cutting was 'very deep and steep', forming 'a very considerable obstacle to infantry and is impassable to anything else'. The outpost line varied from 100 to 300 yards in front of this, where there were 'many barbed wire fences (not entanglements) both in front and in rear of the outpost line'. Although the railway line was held by 'gun positions', those in front of Scully's exposed position during the night had been seen to be withdrawing. The prisoners taken were from *27th Reserve Infantry Regiment* who stated that there were two other infantry regiments in the town as well as a pioneer regiment carrying out demolitions. Scully concluded on a high note: 'The prisoners surrendered willingly, did much to assist us, and altogether had from the enemy's point of view, very bad morale. One said that he was a Pole and all were very frightened of shells'.[220]

At 21.00 that night, Major Wynne commanding 18th Liverpool sent a message to his brigade HQ, which began with the bald statement: 'Everything here seems very obscure'. He had lost two of his companies, did not know where his right flank was, and his intelligence officer had just reported that the enemy had re-crossed the river and returned to Montay. He had encountered Lieutenant O'Connor of the Connaughts with 50 of his men, who reported how 'the Germans pretended to surrender then fired' as his men came to take them prisoner. Wynne had also encountered men of both the Inniskilling Fusiliers and Lancashire Fusiliers (198 Brigade) – units were

216 War Diary, HQ 66th Infantry Division, 'Narrative of Operations 66th Division 8th to 10th October 1918', TNA WO95/3122.
217 War Diary, HQ 199 Infantry Brigade, 'Narrative', October 1918, Appendix 14, TNA WO95/3143.
218 Second-Lieutenant Charles James Waites, who had been on the Western Front since December 1915, originally with the Mounted Military Police, had been commissioned in June 1917.
219 Regimental Sergeant-Major Thomas Gallagher MSM, who had been on active service since July 1915, was amongst the dead.
220 War Diary, HQ 199 Infantry Brigade, 'Narrative', 10 October 1918, Appendix 16, TNA WO95/3143.

clearly intermingled. His message ended plaintively: 'Will you please let me have further instructions'.[221] Unsurprisingly, although orders were issued by division twice during the night to advance again on the 11th, these were cancelled.

The German view of the day, as revealed in a captured document of *17th Reserve Division*, as presented to its troops, was bolstered with a certain amount of spin. 199 Brigade had 'succeeded in nearing the town, but further progress was held up by strong German artillery fire'. British losses 'were considerable'. The 17.30 attack had only succeeded in penetrating 'one portion of the town. Losses were again heavy. Many men lost touch with their units in the streets and thus got taken prisoner'. The German division's orders were that 'in case of an enemy attack on a large scale' (an attack that they were obviously aware was bound to be made), the outposts that Colonel Scully had reported 'should retire, in order to leave a clear field of fire for the main line of resistance'.[222]

If to Wynne the situation was obscure, to Montgomery writing a year later, 'considerable progress had been made' on the 10th. Not only had 'numerous villages been captured', but 'with the exception of a few posts on the western bank the enemy had been driven across the Selle'.[223] Twenty-one German officers and 1,616 other ranks had been taken prisoner. Yet German resistance had been strong enough to prevent the objectives both across the river and on the western bank in the south being taken, and these latter would have to be attempted on the following day. In particular, the artillery on the high ground to the east could fire on any ground the BEF chose to advance across. Fourth Army HQ recorded the stiffening resistance being 'much too vigorous to allow the cavalry to get through', with artillery activity increasing 'considerably in the vicinity of St Souplet and in the valley of La Selle River'.[224] Rawlinson acknowledged in his journal that although his army had advanced, 'today we have been unable to penetrate the line anywhere'.[225] Yet Fourth Army's progress was no less and no more than any other that day. To the north, Third Army had secured Neuvilly north of Le Cateau on the river, and to the south the French *First Army* had pushed on to the edge of the Andigny Forest, of which Riquerval Wood (which had frustrated the 46th Division) was an outcrop.

The Pursuit – Day Three: Friday 11 October 1918

The objectives set by Fourth Army at 20.30 on the 10th were again the high ground to the east of the Selle that covered the passages over the river for the XIII and American Corps; and in XI Corps area, Andigny-les-Fermes on the Bellevue spur and the looming bulk of Riquerval Wood.[226]

IX Corps

On the right of the British line, in 138 Brigade of 46th Division, 1/5th Leicestershire formed up along the Bohain-Aisonville road in the dawn light, and 'in absolute silence and without a barrage … started to climb the rise towards the edge of the wood'.[227] Riquerval Wood formed the western portion of the larger Andigny Forest. It had been exploited by the enemy for wood, and whilst there

221 War Diary, HQ 199 Infantry Brigade, Appendix 13, 10 October 1918, TNA WO95/3143.
222 War Diary, HQ 199 Infantry Brigade, Order of *17th Reserve Division* 14 October 1918, TNA WO95/3143.
223 Montgomery, op. cit., p.202.
224 War Diary, HQ Fourth Army, 10 October 1918, TNA WO95/439.
225 Sir H. Rawlinson, War Journal, 10 October 1918, Churchill College RWLN 1/11.
226 War Diary, HQ Fourth Army, Message G.340 10 October 1918, TNA WO95/439.
227 Hills, op. cit., p.340.

were therefore clearings, these were filled with scrub that obscured its defenders. 'Filled as it was with machine-gun nests and strongly organized networks of trenches and strong-points, it posed a serious obstacle in the path of our advance'.[228] Memories of High Wood in 1916 and Bourlon in 1917 might have sent a shudder down the spine of a man who had met those particular 'obstacles'.

As per Major Dyer-Bennet's plan, C and D companies proceeded east along the road that bounded the northern side of the forest, along which 1st Leicestershire held a defensive flank, towards Regnicourt. They came under fire from a group of houses ahead on a small hill. In the belief that that the cyclists had found the village unoccupied the previous day, they assumed this to be a lightly held outpost. Lieutenant Hawley, who had practiced his outflanking techniques at Fresnoy on the first day of the Pursuit, worked his way with D Company up the hill using cover, and took the machine-gun and killed its operator. Beyond the houses was a dip, however, and on the next rise lay Regnicourt proper, which to their surprise was held in force. The corps cyclists had clearly mistaken the first small group of houses (Colombier Fountain) for Regnicourt itself. D Company, deployed on both sides of the road, walked into a death trap on the forward slope, and fell flat. Those who took shelter in a ditch were enfiladed – in half an hour, ten were killed, 14 injured and one taken prisoner. The toll of the action was heavy on NCO leadership. Lance-Sergeant Cecil Bradshaw was killed,[229] as was Sergeant William Dimmocks,[230] with Sergeant H. Foster being wounded. Captain Banwell, the captor of Fresnoy, then arrived with C Company. Despite spreading out into the woods, they could not advance more than 400 yards further, nor could they make contact with any of their fellows whom they believed to be advancing through the wood itself. There they remained until relieved.

B Company, attacking the wood head on, had an even worse time, finding themselves trapped on a forward slope in front of the wood. After taking casualties, the troops grouped together for shelter in two German practice trenches, unable to progress. A Company on the right made even less progress. Attempting to cross the 150 yards of slightly uphill open ground as dawn broke, they were pinned down by machine-gun fire from a 'chateau' on the corner of the ride and the wood, which commanded the country in front of it. Dyer-Bennet himself came up with his headquarters, and the French interpreter, Henri Letu, went on reconnaissance and found a platoon of 10 French *poilus* with two machine-guns, and a Lewis gun team of the 4th Leicesters. Number one platoon of A Company were also discovered, and Dyer-Bennet decided to attack the chateau, an imposing three-storied building with tall chimneys and gable windows in the roof, surrounded by walls and with a walled courtyard giving on to the ride. In order to complete an outflanking manoeuvre, he sent both his Lewis gun team and the French platoon through the woods to the rear. After skirmishing, which left one Leicester soldier dead, the enemy fled and the rest of A Company came up and occupied the edge of the wood. This progress did not, however, last. The French on the right were counter-attacked, and at 10.00 the bulk of A Company were pressed back towards their starting point. Dyer-Bennet held on, he and his motley band maintaining their position in their little fort.

Perhaps unaware how comprehensively 1/5th Leicestershire were pinned down, division now determined that they were to be relieved by the 1/5th South Staffordshire of 137 Brigade.[231]

228 Priestley, op. cit., p.132.
229 Cecil Bradshaw had enlisted in August 1914.
230 William Edgar Dimmocks of Hinckley, Leicestershire, was aged 20 on his death.
231 5th South Staffordshire were commanded by Lieutenant-Colonel Alfred White DSO, a captain of 4th East Surrey in August 1914. He had commanded 19th Manchester from September 1916 to April 1917, and took command of 5th South Staffords on 1 September 1918.

On the left, this was completed with effort by 11.30, C and D Companies of the Leicester unit crawling back over the exposed hill under fire; but on the right, the relief proved far more difficult. Lieutenant-Colonel Alfred White of the South Staffords, with his adjutant and company commanders, spent several hours on horseback attempting to find Dyer-Bennet. 'They had frequently to go to ground to avoid hostile machine-gun fire',[232] and eventually had to give up. By midday the missing Dyer-Bennet and his HQ group feared being surrounded. Indeed, the house was soon recaptured by the enemy and the group fell back and dug in out in the open. Now knowing where the relief had to made, the Staffords did not find it easy. A Company of their battalion moved to relieve Dyer-Bennet's beleaguered group and suffered 'fairly heavy casualties'.[233] Communication was at times only possible by use of a Lucas lamp.[234] For a while, Leicesters and Staffordshires were mixed, awaiting a renewed attack to be made at 16.00.

5th Tank Battalion recorded that 'tanks allotted to 46th Division were not required by them', the division probably taking the view based on past experience that tanks could not effectively penetrate woods. The two machines that appeared to support the 16.00 attack had been 'lent to the French to take Retheuil Farm', from whence the Leicesters and Staffords were being enfiladed. As Dyer-Bennet could see from the 'two blazing heaps',[235] both were soon knocked out, receiving direct hits, and 'only two of the crew of one of the tanks returned'.[236] (Colonel White reported that another tank operating a little to the north 'broke down and could not move till the enemy shelled and it went home').[237] The trench system in the wood was bombarded by 16th Royal Horse Artillery under Colonel White's direction, whereupon the enemy retaliated with an hour's bombardment with gas and high explosives and then counter-attacked. The British attack collapsed. Dyer-Bennet was forced to withdraw to the road, his starting point, digging a line of pits and ordering B Company back from its position in front of the centre of the wood. 1/5th Leicesters finally left their position at 20.00. The day had gone badly for them. Nineteen of their number had been killed, including their medical officer, Captain William Jack.[238] Withdrawing the brigade's troops further, 46th Division's guns carried out a concentrated bombardment of trench systems and strong points, not to mention the much fought-over chateau recently vacated. The division concluded that 'it was now quite plain that the enemy's rearguard intended to make as prolonged a stand as possible' at Riquerval Wood,[239] and the Germans, in confirmation, kept up heavy machine-gun fire on the Staffords all night.

In 6th Division, 71 Brigade advanced without a barrage, fire being directed only on centres of likely opposition. The Americans on the left being more advanced, the brigade front was extended, and all three units were employed. 1st Leicestershire were on the right, 9th Norfolk were in the centre, with 2nd Sherwood Foresters on the left. 'It was soon discovered however that the enemy's

232 Priestley, op. cit., p.134.
233 War Diary, 5th Battalion South Staffordshire Regiment, 11 October 1918, WO95/2686.
234 The Lucas Signalling Lamp was a powerful electrical handheld device with an orange filter, which was used for transmitting Morse code.
235 Hills, op. cit., p.350.
236 War Diary, HQ 5th Battalion Tank Corps, 11 October 1918, WO95/111/1.
237 War Diary, 1/5th Battalion South Staffordshire Regiment, October 1918 Appendix XXI, TNA WO95/2686.
238 William Boyd Jack MC, a Lake District GP, was Honorary Medical Officer to the Westmorland County Hospital, a police surgeon, and the public vaccinator for Greyrigg. He had only joined the RAMC in March 1917, and had been gassed in May 1918. Jack went to tend to a wounded stretcher bearer and was 'badly hit in the body', and died in an ambulance that evening. (Hills, op. cit., p.347).
239 Priestley, op. cit., p.135.

The southern edge of Riquerval Wood and the 'chateau' attacked by A Company 1/5th Leicestershire on 11 October 1918 as seen from their jump-off position.

The 'chateau' at Riquerval Wood defended by Major Dyer-Bennett of 1/5th Leicestershire on 11 October 1918.

resistance had very much stiffened',[240] the brigade encountering some trenches and wire on the northern aspect of Riquerval Wood and on the ridge that barred the approach to the Bellevue spur south-east of Vaux-Andigny. As the 2nd Sherwoods noted, whilst the German line had been located by patrols the previously night, 'it was not known that the enemy had a continuous and very skilfully concealed entrenched and wired position on the ridge, or that he meant to hold it with all his energy'.[241]

1st Leicestershire had one section of field artillery, two sections of machine-guns, and one section of Stokes mortars attached. Despite this support they were only able to advance some 400 yards before having to dig in due to heavy machine-gun fire. The battalion lost two officers,[242] and ended the day with a trench strength of only 12 officers and 356 other ranks. 5th Tank Battalion had made nine tanks available to 6th Division and sent five. Two had mechanical trouble, one long before it reached the line, another breaking down coming back. They operated towards Riquerval Wood, one venturing south of the road into 46th Division's area (the machine observed by Colonel White), but were soon spotted by enemy observation balloons and heavily shelled, one tank receiving a direct hit, and were unable to progress the infantry assault.[243] In the centre, 9th Norfolk had received their orders to attack at 05.30 only at 03.15, and after a hastily called conference the battalion was guided over the unfamiliar ground at 04.15. Attacking at 05.30, they soon met machine-gun fire and became aware that the flanking battalions were held up. Their advance was halted whilst artillery fire was brought to bear on the offending machine-guns. At 12.50 orders were issued to continue towards the farm on the Bellevue spur in conjunction with the Sherwood Foresters, and two tanks having arrived ten minutes later, these were sent forward to deal with any machine-gun nests. Infantry followed the tanks, but the barrage called to support the advance fell short, and they were forced to retire to their original line, where they remained.[244] On the left, 2nd Sherwood Foresters recorded that the enemy was 'evidently expecting' the advance,[245] and whilst forming up they were subjected to an artillery barrage. The delay caused by this enemy counter-barrage meant that the attacking troops had to cross the exposed shallow valley in front of the ridge in daylight. Battalion HQ, with two 18-pounder guns attached, had followed up the two attacking companies, B and D. The artillery observer, situated on higher ground, only now became aware of the strength of the enemy position, in front of which the Sherwoods were about to debouch, completely unaware of their danger. D Company was recalled, but B could not be reached. The unsuspecting troops, in two waves, walked into withering fire. To the observing battalion HQ, 'the Company seemed to melt away'. Many of the soldiers were hit and fell, 'the rest, unable to face the hail of bullets, lay down'. The enemy thereafter 'contented himself with only firing if any attempted to crawl forward of back'.[246] It was clearly impossible to cross the 500 yards of valley. The companies

240 War Diary, HQ 71 Infantry Brigade, 'Narrative of Operations – 8th to 11th October 1918', TNA WO95/1620.
241 Wylly, op. cit., p.181.
242 One was a fatality, Captain Duncan Vere Webb MC, who died of wounds on 16 October. Second-Lieutenant T. Pollard was wounded. During the month of October the battalion lost two officers and 36 other ranks killed, and 12 officers and 228 other ranks wounded, with 12 missing.
243 War Diary, HQ 5th Tank Battalion, 11 October 1918, TNA WO95/111/1. It is interesting that the 'Report of Operations of 11th October' in War Diary of 3rd Tank Brigade (TNA WO95/105), written on 13 October, mentions neither of the tank casualties at Retheuil Farm, and describes the tanks assisting 71 Brigade as having been 'unmolested'. This does not accord with other evidence.
244 Lieutenant S.W. Clarke was wounded during these operations.
245 War Diary, 2nd Battalion Sherwood Foresters, 11 October 1918, TNA WO95/1624.
246 Wylly, op. cit., p.182.

on the right attempted to assist the Norfolks, but could make no progress. The support company was transferred to the left on reports that the Americans had taken Vaux-Andigny, and it was planned to outflank the Bellevue spur in conjunction with them. The report proved false. At the end of the day the Sherwoods remained in a sunken road on top of the small ridge, a position they viewed as a 'death trap' due to continuing German artillery and machine-gun fire. 'Darkness soon gave the longed for cover, and rations and water could be sent up to the troops at last'.[247] Between 6 and 11 October 2nd Sherwood Foresters had lost two officers and 47 other ranks killed, with seven officers and 145 other ranks wounded with nine other ranks missing. At nightfall on the 11th 'two companies were commanded by second-lieutenants who had never been in action before, and one by a lieutenant who had practically no experience'.[248] It had been a deeply frustrating day – at the furthest extent, 6th Division had advanced 1,500 yards. IX Corps acknowledged that progress had been 'very slow … as the enemy had reinforced his line with a fresh Division which had been resting for a month'.[249]

The weather had been poor for flying on the 11th, with low clouds and rain. In the air over Fourth Army, 448 hours had been flown by 225 pilots. Only eleven reconnaissances, with three photographic flights were possible. Sixteen artillery and 23 contact patrols had been undertaken, with 25 zone calls sent down, seven enemy batteries being neutralised. 179 offensive patrols were flown with 14 indecisive combats, one British machine being lost. 'Scruffy' Longton again flew the length of the *Hermann Stellung I*, noting now that the British troops were in touch with the enemy along its length. Four hundred 25-pound bombs were dropped and 29,705 rounds fired at troops and transport.[250] Lieutenant James Gascoyne of 92 Squadron, for instance, attacked a column of guns and limbers passing through Molain, shooting down the leading horses, and flew round until another limber attempted to pass, attacking again and blocking the road. The enemy guns now had to go across fields, and Gascoyne fired on them repeatedly. Gascoyne would later describe that: 'If you could shoot up transport and block the road that was a fine thing, you stopped the whole lot. So personally I used to try and attack them from the front'.[251] He went on from this mayhem to attack trenches running between Le Cateau and St Benin, and, in another example of close air-ground cooperation, observing eight enemy machine-guns lying in wait for cavalry, fired his guns in their direction to alert the horsemen.[252]

II American Corps and XIII Corps

The task allotted to the 30th American Division on 11 October was to reach the River Selle, whose source lay just between Vaux-Andigny and Molain, along its whole front, and cross it to reach the high ground beyond. The Australian artillery gave the same barrage protection as it had on

247 Wylly, op. cit., p.182.
248 Wylly, op. cit., p.182.
249 War Diary, HQ IX Corps, 9 October 1918, TNA WO95/837.
250 War Diary, 5 Brigade RAF, Daily Summary 11 October 1918, TNA AIR 1/2225/209/40/26.
251 Orange, op. cit., p.30.
252 War Diary, 5 Brigade RAF, Annexe to Summary 11 October 1918, TNA AIR 1/2225/209/40/26. James Victor Gascoyne DFC had served in the RFC since 1913, as a driver in the Transport Section of 3 Squadron, and a mechanic with 9 Squadron. He was commissioned from an NCO in 1917, his DFC citation stating: 'During the months of October and November this officer has accounted for five enemy machines, and during recent operations he has displayed splendid daring and great skill in attacking enemy troops, etc. On 9th November, although he was wounded in the head early in the attack and his machine was badly shot about, 2nd Lieut. Gascoyne made a most successful attack on the enemy from a height of 100 feet, obtaining three direct hits and inflicting heavy casualties'. (*London Gazette*, 31170, p.2039).

the previous two days. The 118th Infantry would attack and straighten the line, whilst the 119th, already on the river, would provide fire only, and would not cross the river until the 118th reached it. Their position was exposed, and they were under enemy artillery fire from the eastern bank. The 118th attempted to advance with all its three battalions, and with one battalion of the 120th. On the left, the small village of La Haie Menneresse, directly north of Vaux-Andigny but still over 1,500 yards from the river, was taken. On the right, however, they were unable to progress beyond the eastern edge of Vaux-Andigny, encountering a newly dug practice trench system between there and Molain, situated on high ground. This system could not be overcome as it was 'alive with machine-guns, minenwerfers and light artillery, all of which poured murderous fire into our lines',[253] even with quickly arranged artillery support. This was provided by 5th Brigade Australian Field Artillery who 'harassed the railway and high ground East of it during the night and day'. 11th Brigade Australian Field Artillery similarly carried out 'concentrated shoots' on trenches beyond Vaux-Andigny. The 118th Infantry had gone no further than 200 yards. Despite each battalion having attached one 37-mm gun and two trench mortars, as well as 'one pounder cannon', they had found that either the rapidity of the advance prevented them from being brought up and brought into action, or once they were, the enemy on higher ground brought fire swiftly to bear upon them. Two companies of the 115th Machine Gun Battalion were ordered forward but had six guns knocked out whilst getting into position. The Australians noted that whilst the enemy did 'not appear to be in force', they were 'well supplied with machine-guns which [they] used to considerable advantage'.[254] Digging in, the American units were subject to a bombardment, particularly with gas around Escaufort. Despite the shelling, French inhabitants were able to be evacuated, the Australians noting that they were 'wonderful in the brave show they made in the face of so many and so great dangers', suffering 'excruciatingly painful eyes and throats' from the gas.

In XIII Corps, as with the American left, on the fronts of 25th and 66th Divisions there was no movement, none being attempted. 25th Division's artillery, however, shelled the fortified railway held by the enemy on the eastern bank of the Selle with both field and heavy artillery, day and night. Patrols had been sent out on the night of 10/11 October to ascertain the enemy's dispositions. 18th Liverpool, for instance, pushed patrols into Le Cateau, the north-west and west of which was in British hands, 'and came across about 200 Bosche in the square, busily engaged in loading motor lorries. The party immediately opened up a strong fire with the Lewis gun and rifles putting out over 50 Bosche'.[255] 66th Division were similarly able to discover that whilst there were no Germans west of the Selle, across the river there were a series of trenches and rifle pits in the vicinity of the railway, with outposts in a sugar factory and petroleum refinery close to the river. According to prisoners and released civilians, the main positions were heavily wired.

253 Murphy & Thomas, op. cit., p.117.

254 War Diary, HQ 5th Brigade Australian Field Artillery, 11 October 1918, AWM, Item No. 13/33/35.

255 War Diary, 18th Battalion King's Liverpool Regiment, 12 October 1918, TNA WO95/3144. During these three days of actions the battalion had lost two officers killed – Lieutenant Francis Egerton Sanders MC (commissioned from private in October 1916); and Second-Lieutenant Leo John Hayes (commissioned from private in July 1917). In addition the unit lost 19 ORs, including Sergeants Stephen Thompson and George Robbins, both who had been in France since September 1915. 115 ORs were wounded and one officer and 16 ORS were missing. Six officers were wounded: Captains Henry McEwen, William McKnight Docharty MC (commissioned in December 1914), and James Walter Greville Edmonds (commissioned in February 1915), and Second-Lieutenants Eric Andrew Raynold Gill (commissioned in March 1918), William Owen Williams (commissioned in July 1917) and T. Moreland.

It had been a dispiriting day. As it ended, Fourth Army recorded that 'the enemy's opposition strengthened along the whole Army front'.[256] The lack of progress was reflected in the much decreased number of prisoners, only two officers and 215 other ranks being taken. As Archibald Montgomery later noted, the 'result of the day's fighting proved conclusively that the Germans meant to make a stand behind the Selle'.[257] The Official Historian, imbued with the power of hindsight, suggested that even on the evening of the second day of the Pursuit: 'It was by now evident that the Germans were holding the line of the Selle in strength' with 'heavy artillery in position' and from the prisoners taken from the *5th Reserve Division* (brought from rest near Laon) and the *17th Reserve Division*, (arrived from Lorraine), learned that the enemy had been reinforced. 'Further advance without good artillery support and counter-battery work would be costly'.[258]

Stalemate – Saturday 12 October 1918

Despite having observed that the enemy was clearly making a stand, on 12 October Fourth Army made two attempts to improve its position on its right flank in front of IX Corps. It is interesting that Montgomery, in his history of Fourth Army, neglects to mention these attempts. Both are reminiscent of small unit actions on the Somme in late July 1916, where a position unable to be taken by a stronger force on one day was attacked by a weaker force the next. Both were predictably abortive. In IX Corps, 138 Brigade of 46th Division had been relieved by the 137th, commanded by Brigadier-General John Campbell.[259] Despite the complete failure of the previous day, 1/5th South Staffordshire (in conjunction with the *55th Regiment* of the French *First Army*) were tasked with taking the whole of Riquerval Wood. They were to advance at noon under a creeping barrage progressing at the standard rate of 100 yards every three minutes (a rate far too fast given the likely resistance that would be offered from within the trees), Regnicourt being bombarded by howitzers. The left of the Staffords' attack was unable to move despite the barrage, and the right was immediately held up by machine-gun fire, the obstacle of Retheuil Farm still eluding capture by the French, thus enfilading the British attack. The centre companies, despite being caught by the German counter-barrage before reaching the wood, penetrated the enemy trenches in the wood, and advanced to a depth of 150-200 yards before machine-gun, trench mortar and artillery fire, followed by counter-attack, drove them back to their starting point. Over the two days 11-12 October the 5th South Staffords had suffered five officer and 82 other rank casualties.[260] They had been given an 'impossible task', and 'never during the German retreat did their machine-gunners fight better, or more stubbornly, than in those days when Riquerval Wood held up the Division'.[261]

256 War Diary, HQ Fourth Army, 11 October 1918, TNA WO95/439.
257 Montgomery, op. cit., p.202.
258 Edmonds and Maxwell-Hyslop, op. cit., pp.237-8.
259 John Vaughan Campbell VC CMG DSO (1876-1944) was commissioned in the Coldstream Guards in 1896, and had reached the rank of major in August 1914. He was promoted to command 3rd Coldstream Guards from July 1915 to November 1916, when on the 17th of that month he was elevated to command 137 Brigade, being transferred five days before the Armistice to command 3 Guards Brigade.
260 War Diary 1/5th Battalion South Staffordshire Regiment, 12 October 1918 TNA WO95/2686. Over the two days of action the officer casualties included two fatalities: Second-Lieutenant Cyril Stuart Embrey MC (a 20 year old Cambridge undergraduate commissioned in November 1917), and Second-Lieutenant Victor Craddock commissioned in July 1917). Three officers were wounded. Nineteen ORs were killed with nine missing, and 54 wounded.
261 Priestley, op. cit., p.138.

In the adjacent 6th Division, 18 Brigade, commanded by Brigadier-General Standish Craufurd,[262] which had not taken part in the Pursuit, was brought into the line. Their task was to advance, particularly on the left, and pull level with the Americans in Vaux-Andigny. As the brigade war diary noted, their line was 'very much dominated by a minor spur running North for about 1,500 yards from REGINCOURT (sic)'.[263] This spur, which had been impossible to attain the previous day, formed the western edge of the valley that lay between the attacking units and the dominating Bellevue spur. It was the objective of an attack carried out at 16.30 on the 12th by 2nd Durham Light Infantry on the left and 11th Essex on the right. The Essex unit had a trench strength of 16 officers and 401 other ranks, the DLI being better off having 28 officers and 631 other ranks. The danger posed by the ridge was clearly known – 2nd Sherwood Foresters had come to grief there 24 hours previously. An artillery barrage therefore concentrated on the wire and trenches on this ridge for 15 minutes before moving 100 yards every four minutes in four lifts with 25 per cent smoke, resting as a protector barrage for 30 minutes. By this time it would be dusk and the ridge could be consolidated in darkness. Meanwhile, heavy artillery was to pound the Bellevue spur to the rear, with machine-guns firing in enfilade from Vaux-Andigny.

The DLI attacked with only one company.[264] They attained the ridge but ran into their own barrage, were pushed to the right by it and even so, could not locate 11th Essex who had failed to penetrate the wire. They were driven back by machine-gun fire and bombing.[265] As 18 Brigade reported, in front of the Essex battalion: 'The wire was hidden from view, and unfortunately it was found that the barrage had been placed too far back, and had thus missed the wire'. Despite the unusual jump-off time, the enemy counter-barrage came down as soon as the British barrage lifted, just in front of the start line. The units of 18 Brigade were jumping-off into the unknown: 'The maps of this area were most indifferent, and many copses existed which were not shown'.[266] In addition to being uncut, the wire itself was much stronger than expected, consisting of 'two formidable and strongly constructed belts'.[267] The enemy was also found to have dug a series of trenches in front.[268] In an event horribly reminiscent of much earlier operations, after they had overcome the enemy outposts in front of the wire, one platoon tried to force its way through the gap cut by the Germans for access, on which machine-guns were naturally trained.[269] 2nd DLI suffered one officer and 47 other rank casualties,[270] 11th Essex lost three officers and 65 other ranks.[271] The enemy reported the

262 Sir George Standish Gage Craufurd CB CMG CIE DSO (1872-1957) was a major of the Gordon Highlanders in August 1914. He commanded the 1st Battalion for a year from December 1915, when he was promoted to command 3 Brigade on 19 November 1916 until March 1917, taking command of 18 Brigade on 14 September 1917.

263 War Diary, HQ 18 Infantry Brigade, 12 October 1918, TNA WO95/1615.

264 2nd Durham Light Infantry were commanded by Lieutenant-Colonel Robert Villiers Turner DSO. A captain of the battalion in August 1914, he had commanded 13th DLI for two months in 1916, and the 2nd Battalion from 13 July 1918.

265 War Diary 2nd Battalion Durham Light Infantry, 12 October 1918, TNA WO95/1617.

266 Marden, op. cit., p.69.

267 War Diary, HQ 18 Infantry Brigade, 'Account of Minor Operation, 12 October 1918', TNA WO95/1615.

268 Marden, op. cit., p.69.

269 War Diary, 11th Battalion Essex Regiment, 'Preliminary Report on Operations, 12 October 1918', TNA WO95/1616.

270 One officer was wounded, with 42 ORs wounded, four killed and one missing.

271 In 11th Essex, Second-Lieutenant Horace James Widgery, who had only been commissioned on 31 July 1918, was taken prisoner whilst on patrol. Second-Lieutenant Donald William Wiley (commissioned April 1917) was killed, as were 13 ORs, and Second-Lieutenant Frederick James Thomas Clabon

disaster thus: 'A strong enemy attack against the 1st Bavarian Corps ... on Oct 12th was broken with heavy loss'.[272] Major Alistair Saunders, commanding the Essex unit,[273] was the only CO who attacked that day who lodged anything approaching critical observations. He wrote, underlining his remarks three times: 'It is essential that the Division on our right progresses before we advance in this sector. Otherwise enemy can shoot right up valley. This will be readily realised by seeing the ground as the maps are very inaccurate'.[274]

In recognising failure, IX Corps noted that 46th Division had captured prisoners of 'a new and fresh Division', so that 'over the last few days three fresh Divisions had come into the line opposite the Corps front'.[275] The failure was not, however, simply due to enemy reinforcement, but also to the old problem of single battalion attacks on a narrow front.

Meanwhile, in the north, the South African Brigade's attempts to establish bridgeheads across the Selle were rebuffed and then deemed impossible. It was now perfectly clear that only another set piece battle would shift the enemy. The enemy, however, had little to promote cheer. *17th Reserve Division* trumpeted the following day that: 'Lieut. Rux and Corpl. Eckert of the 9th Coy 76 R.I.R. surprised an enemy post and captured the garrison – 1 Corporal and 8 men of the 1st South African Infantry Regt.'[276] This meagre news probably did little to boost morale, even if the pair won the appreciation of the divisional commander, General von Mutius.[277] All knew a storm was coming.

(commissioned from private in June 1918) was wounded. Forty-seven ORs were wounded and five missing.

272 War Diary, HQ 199 Infantry Brigade, Order of *17th Reserve Division* 14 October 1918, TNA WO95/3143.

273 Alistair Grant Saunders, commissioned in October 1914, was commanding in the absence of Lieutenant-Colonel C. Dumbell, the latter having gone to brigade HQ to assist General Craufurd who had been injured in a dump explosion.

274 War Diary, 11th Battalion Essex Regiment, 'Preliminary Report on Operations, 12 October 1918', TNA WO95/1616.

275 War Diary, HQ IX Corps, 12 October 1918, TNA WO95/837.

276 War Diary, HQ 199 Infantry Brigade, Order *17th Reserve Division*, 14 October 1918, TNA WO95/3143.

277 Louis von Mutius (1862-1937) had commanded *17th Reserve Division* since April 1917, and was regarded as having handled his command well in the defensive battles of August 1918.

2

'All Pursuing Troops Should Act With the Greatest Boldness'.[1] The BEF in Semi-Open Warfare: October 1918

> Dear Tommy. You are welcome to all that we are leaving. When we stop, we shall stop, and stop you in a manner you won't appreciate. Fritz.[2]

Guy Chapman, an officer in the Royal Fusiliers, was one of the few who later wrote of the period 8-10 October. At the time he believed that the war had another year to run and described of his own condition: 'Probably I was more fatigued than I knew'. No doubt many of his fellow infantrymen felt much the same – the cycle of set-piece battle and advance over distance was physically demanding. His memories of the time were a set of 'disconnected pictures' yet they conjure up the autumn weather of mist, fine rain and early morning attacks. He recalled a 'group of us sitting back to back shivering and nodding with sleep at three o'clock in the morning' – winter clothing, and even a second blanket had yet to be issued. Up ahead he could see the *HWL I*, the German line of resistance on the eastern bank of the Selle. This was marked by 'a line of railway being methodically shelled blown into clouds of pink smoke', with troops working their way forward 'against a sweeping flail of machine guns, invisible in the roofs of a distant town'. On the Roman road between Cambrai and Le Cateau, near Caudry, he observed 'the flash of a troop of cavalry, tearing up the road'. On this occasion there was no cheering. The gallop to the east was followed by 'the horrid chuckle of firearms, the check, and the riderless horses galloping back'. In a flash of sardonic wisdom Chapman recorded: '"The bloody fools", remarks the twenty-year-old veteran at my elbow'. Chapman's experience of pursuit was devoid of excitement or glamour.

The advance was made over ground little marked by any British assault, yet which appeared scoured as if by locusts and covered in the detritus of flight. 46th Division noted that the enemy 'had managed to remove most of his munitions of war' leaving only 'ammunition, both S.A.A. and shells, with occasional dumps of signal stores'. Booty had been jettisoned – there were 'small heaps of brass copper and iron utensils' plundered from French homes lying about, whilst the fields had been stripped of anything edible.[3] Chapman described Caudry itself as 'pillaged so thoroughly that even the covers of the chairs have been ripped out', with houses 'defiled' with excrement. It was

1 War Office, *Field Service Regulations, Part I, Operations 1909* (amendments 1912), p.153.
2 Notice found in the old German front line at Richebourg by 5th Leicesters. War Diary, 1/5th Battalion Leicestershire Regiment, 4 September 1918, TNA WO95/2690.
3 R.E. Priestley, *Breaking the Hindenburg Line*, p.127.

difficult for him to comprehend: 'We wonder, having no knowledge of the agony of defeat, that such hatred should still exist, and that it should find expression in so childish an offence'.[4]

The pace of pursuit for the artillery is reflected in the comments of Alexander Caseby of the Royal Field Artillery. He wrote of the advance on the north side of the Cambrai-Le Cateau road: 'Our infantry had advanced and taken Ouisey before we had arrived … In broad daylight we rushed our guns forward to St Aubert and came into action immediately'. He described this new kind of warfare: 'Our methods now were swift, lightning, daring attacks preceded by a short, sharp bombardment'. Caseby recorded the marked resistance, the enemy 'fighting a last great defensive movement and all his artillery was thrown into the fray'. He was clear, however, that his fellow soldiers' tails were up: 'We had the great consolation that victory for us was now a positive fact. This filled us with high spirited hopes even although the task in front was severe'.[5] Captain Kenneth Earle, Machine Gun Corps, disliked the relentlessness of the attacks but recognised that 'it was obvious that at all costs we must keep the Bosch on the run till we had him absolutely beaten'.[6] Guy Chapman clearly did not have the energy to share in this enthusiasm. From a more elevated position, Brigadier-General Henry 'Harry' Walker of 16 Brigade, 6th Division, writing on 14 October, regarded the approximation to open warfare as the 'most satisfactory' action 'during my period of command'.[7] (Two days later he may have revised his view when his arm was blown off on the evening before the Selle crossing). Brigadier-General Frank Rowley of 138 Brigade, 46th Division, recorded with pride his formation's performance during the pursuit as 'most successful'. The methods of 'open warfare that the Brigade had been practised in were found to have been well assimilated by both officers and men'.[8]

Yet the very notion of 'pursuit' is deceptive. The so-called Pursuit to the Selle more closely approximated to what the suddenly more cautious Sir Douglas Haig set out for his army commanders on 3 September when he instructed them to 'press the enemy with advanced guards with the object of driving in the enemy's rearguards and outposts, and ascertaining his dispositions'.[9] Jonathan Boff suggests that operations such as 9 October 'more closely resembled a reconnaissance in force'.[10] The units of the BEF advanced to contact on 9 October, and the opposition that they met did not prove quick to master. The enemy described being 'pursued vigorously', and acknowledged that on the 9th their rearguards were driven in more quickly than had been wished.[11] Over the next three days, however, there was a process of diminishing returns which bore no relation to pursuit. The German rearguards, taking good advantage of topography, proved highly successful in *not* being driven in particularly swiftly, mounting their defence with a plethora of machine-guns. The British Official History in its review of German regimental histories describes the enemy infantry at this point as 'absolutely "played out"', with the Bavarian official account going as far as to portray its units as 'burnt to cinders'.[12] The enemy retreating to the Selle in front of Fourth Army was, however, not quite played-out yet.

4 G. Chapman, *A Passionate Prodigality*, pp.208-9.
5 A. Caseby, 'War Memoirs of a Gunner in the Royal Field Artillery', IWM Docs 70861, p.49.
6 K. Earle, Private Papers, IWM Docs 3233.
7 War Diary, HQ 16 Infantry Brigade, 14 October 1918, WO95/1607.
8 War Diary, HQ 138 Infantry Brigade, 'Report on Operations on Mericourt, Fresnoy-le-Grand, Riquerval Wood, Regnicourt & Andigny-les-Fermes', 21 October 1918, WO95/2689.
9 GHQ Order, OAD 915, 3 September 1918, TNA WO158/191.
10 J. Boff, 'Command Culture and Complexity', in G. Sheffield & P. Gray, *Changing War*, p.25.
11 War Diary, *Second Army*, 9 October 1918, *United States Army in the World War Vol. 7*, p.893-5.
12 J.E. Edmonds & R. Maxwell-Hyslop, *Military Operations – France and Belgium 1918, Vol V*, pp.210-211.

Field Service Regulations (FSR) had anticipated the process of pursuit correctly. Firstly, tempo was emphasised. Infantry and artillery, once an enemy was either fleeing in the aftermath of defeat or withdrawing after breaking off a battle, 'must follow him up and continue to press him to the utmost'. It was warned, however, that 'exhaustion, both of *personnel* and of stores, at the end of a protracted battle, makes such a pursuit only temporary, and it will rarely lead to decisive results'. As would happen in front of the Selle position, 'it will usually be necessary to re-form a part of the force at least, and to replenish ammunition and supplies'. Pursuit should therefore 'be taken up by as large a body of mounted troops as possible, so that the enemy may be allowed no respite while this is being done'. A small body of cavalry was to keep in touch with the enemy whilst the main force, both cavalry and horse artillery, 'should aim at the enemy's flanks'. The role of the main body of infantry and other artillery was to 'assist that body of cavalry which is directed against the flank of the enemy's main force'. Not only was there an emphasis on tempo, there was a premium placed on boldness: 'All pursuing troops should act with the greatest boldness, and be prepared to accept risks which would not be justifiable at other times'. Given that the German Army did not present a flank to attack, what therefore happened on 9 October was an adaptation of tactics enshrined within the BEF's loose pre-war 'doctrine'.[13]

Cavalry

Both traditionally and within the context of *FSR*, the cavalry was the spearhead of pursuit and exploitation. The Official Historians, however, took the view of its efforts on 9 October that 'the cavalry had done nothing that the infantry, with artillery support and cyclists, could not have done for itself at less cost'. They focussed on the cost to benefit ratio, claiming 'the supply of the large force of horses with water and forage had gravely interfered with the sending up of ammunition and the rations for the other arms, and with the allotment of the limited water facilities'.[14] Whilst the burden of beasts was always heavy, there is little in the record to substantiate the logistic claim in relation to the cavalry alone.[15] As will be seen subsequently, Fourth Army at the Selle successfully managed its logistics, with effort, on a 'just in time' basis. Simon Justice, however, claims completely the reverse: 'The Corps … proved to be the formation uniquely equipped to spearhead and facilitate the considerable gains of the "Pursuit to the Selle"'. He goes even further to suggest that: 'Indeed, they came close to pulling off the war-shortening coup that the Commander-in-Chief, Sir Douglas Haig, desired (albeit not in the way he envisaged)'.[16] This proves to be an over-enthusiastic interpretation of events.

Justice draws our attention, correctly, to the Cavalry Corps training exercise of 17 September 1918. The corps, as Gary Sheffield notes, was 'a shadow of its former self' after the start of September, when it was reduced to just two divisions (1st and 3rd). However reduced, Haig 'continued to plan to use the Cavalry Corps as a strategic asset directly answerable to him',[17] operating only when the

13 War Office, *Field Service Regulations, Part I, Operations 1909* (amendments 1912), pp.152-3. Italics in original.
14 Edmonds & Maxwell-Hyslop, op. cit., p.235.
15 S. Badsey, 'Cavalry and the Breakthrough Doctrine', in P. Griffith (ed.), *British Fighting Methods in the Great War*, pp.141-2. A relatively small proportion of the fodder shipped was for cavalry horses. (See also Badsey, *Doctrine and Reform in the British Cavalry 1880-1918).*
16 S.M. Justice, 'Means to an End: The Experience of 1918 and its influence on the British Fourth Army's Performance on the Selle', p.10.
17 G. Sheffield, *The Chief*, p.321.

conditions of the pursuit of the enemy in retreat existed.[18] Once the Hindenburg support system had been breached by Fourth Army, the Cavalry Corps would be passed through to the rear of the *Second* and *Eighteenth Armies* and the enemy's communications around Valenciennes would be severed. Haig met with Ivor Maxse (Inspector General of Training) and the GOC Cavalry Corps, Charles Kavanagh, on 6 September 1918 to discuss the matter of 'training infantry divisions to co-operate with the Cavalry Corps in pursuit'.[19] He personally issued a training plan on the same day.[20] The details of this plan and exercise are worth examining as they illuminate how the Army's senior officers were conceiving pursuit.[21] That the Selle area was the target rehearsed for is indicated in the stated key objectives, namely: 'forcing the passage of a river',[22] seizing high ground beyond and holding it until the arrival of infantry, 'dealing with hostile machine gun nests … attacking villages and woods' and 'destroying a railway centre'.[23] Haig had ordered the creation of an expanded mobile force 22 days previously: 'I directed CGS to augment Cavalry Corps by the addition of good infantry brigade in buses, and extra machine gun batteries in motors'.[24] In the exercise, the 1st and 3rd Cavalry Divisions, five motor machine-gun batteries together with the Household Machine Gun Brigade, and 17th Armoured Car Battalion were involved, as were No. 6 Squadron RAF,[25] corps cyclists, horse artillery and a mobile 34 Infantry Brigade in busses. It was thus an all-arms rehearsal, leaving out only the tanks. Even the ammunition column, field ambulances and signal sections took part, as well as the Royal Engineers, practising throwing bridges and demolition. The umpired exercise (the umpires with the cavalry were largely from XIII Corps, with whom they would be deployed on 9 October) was subject to rigorous criticism. The two most heinous errors noted were, firstly, repeated attempts to take machine-gun posts at the gallop which 'failed, with what would have proved in action severe loss.' This was part of a pervasive over-reliance on 'shock action' to overcome machine-guns. Secondly, 'artillery support for attacks on infantry posts was the exception rather than the rule'. Similarly, at one point the infantry brigade and Household Machine Gun Brigade were over 12 miles to the rear of the cavalry they were supposed to be supporting. There was one example noted, however, when a position was fixed from the front and 'galloped from a flank'.[26] In the ensuing discussion,[27] a series of points concerning pursuit were flagged. These included, firstly, the matter of communications. The importance of getting information to the rear via motor cyclists, to enable decisions to be taken swiftly, was reinforced. Secondly, even in pursuit, objectives needed to be allocated with boundaries with other units regarded as

18 As per *Field Service Regulations 1909 (Amended Edition), Part I (Operations)* (1914), Chapter VII, Section 112.
19 Sheffield, op. cit., p.317.
20 War Diary, HQ Cavalry Corps, D. Haig, Memorandum: Instructions to Kavanagh and Maxse, 6 September 1918, TNA WO95/575.
21 It was carried out between Blangy and St. Pol.
22 There were two involved, the Rivers Canche and Authie – unlike the Selle, the exercise involved the capture of intact bridges.
23 War Diary, HQ Cavalry Corps, Cavalry Manoeuvres, Appendix D Cavalry Corps Special Instructions, 16 September 1918, TNA WO95/575.
24 G. Sheffield & J. Bourne, *Douglas Haig – War Diaries and Letters*, 25 August 1918, p.49. 4th (Guards) Brigade was employed.
25 The weather, as at the Selle, was not favourable on the day.
26 War Diary, HQ Cavalry Corps, 'Narrative and Criticism of Cavalry Corps Exercise', 17 September 1918 (n.d.), TNA WO95/575.
27 War Diary, HQ Cavalry Corps, Conference held at Headquarters Cavalry Corps, 19 September 1918, TNA WO95/575.

flexible in achieving them. Thirdly, there had to be the 'closest cooperation between Armoured Cars and Cavalry'. Lastly, in relation to further training, there would be a focus on 'dealing with M.Gs. by fire and movement'. The action of the cavalry on 9 October should therefore be seen within the context of a plan for all-arms pursuit – the focus of historians on the well-trod theme of 'Haig and the cavalry' obscures the broader vision of what was intended. The rehearsal had been the trial of a 'mobile column', an idea that was certainly not new to the British Army, if previously with a smaller range of weaponry, and not entirely new in the context of the Great War. Such had been assembled for the Canadian attack on the Drocourt-Quèant Line on 2 September (two motor machine gun brigades, an artillery battery, a cyclist battalion, trench mortars in lorries and two regiments of cavalry) but never used. The model would be employed again in the last days of the war.[28]

As seen in Chapter One, the Canadian Cavalry Brigade attacked Gattigny Wood entirely in accordance with the principles identified from the exercise of 17 September, from the flanks both north and south, and under the supporting fire of artillery and machine guns.[29] That the flanks were as well defended as the centre was an unfortunate demonstration of the friction of war. They 'galloped it', but in the case of Lieutenant Dunwoody's attack at least, the action amounted to a frontal charge against machine-guns. The Canadian Brigade was thus forced to rely on exactly what the exercise had dictated it should not, i.e. 'shock action', which indeed resulted in 'severe loss'. It was, however, in tune with Haig's slightly contradictory remarks on the operation, 'that a sudden fierce attack by mounted troops promises far-reaching results'. Haig still believed in the 'moral effect of cavalry', albeit 'combined with the fire of its horse artillery and machine guns'.[30] Similarly, the attack of 6th Cavalry Brigade against Honnechy was an affair planned with the principle of flanking in mind. The village was attacked on either side and not frontally where the infantry were held up, well supported by artillery and machine-guns, and even with armoured cars. It was again bloody, however, due to the funnelling under the railway bridge, another example of friction. The expensive reconnaissance of 7th Cavalry Brigade the following morning, however, showed that the idea that the cavalry could have operated crossing the river against the *Hermann Stellung I*, was fantasy. In mitigation, the defences that would be faced were not understood when the original orders for the cavalry had been issued. As will be seen in Chapter Three, it was only on 9 October that the nature of the *Hermann Stellung* came more clearly into focus, with more knowledge gained on the 14th.

Simon Justice claims that: 'The Cavalry Corps had *pulled* the infantry of 66th and 33rd Divisions *five miles* through the rearguard zone'.[31] This is not strictly true – 66th Division had made it through nearly four miles to Gattigny Wood and Honnechy under its own steam. There they had indeed stalled, and it would undoubtedly have taken the bringing up of artillery additional to the mobile batteries attached to the advance to get them unstuck. David Kenyon suggests that it is no coincidence that the range of an 18-pound field gun is approximately four miles – the infantry had simply advanced to the limit of their barrage. This is not the whole story. Rather, the infantry had come up against the next layer of effectively placed enemy rearguards – the barrage on 9 October in this area hardly facilitated their advance at all. The Canadian cavalry, however, undoubtedly got

28 D. Kenyon, 'British Cavalry on the Western Front', op. cit., p.266.
29 The Canadian Cavalry Brigade had not actually taken part in the 17 September exercise.
30 War Diary, HQ Cavalry Corps, 'Remarks by the Commander-in-Chief on the Cavalry Exercise', TNA WO95/575.
31 Justice, op. cit., p.46.

66th Division moving at Gattigny Wood through the rearguards. Their counterparts across the road, however, had decided to withdraw from Honnechy before the cavalry attack of 6th Cavalry Brigade went in (although it could clearly be argued that the presence of the cavalry hastened the withdrawal). It is a fact that beyond Honnechy and Maurois the infantry were advancing in the wake of the cavalry, but the German infantry were withdrawing into Le Cateau, and not offering opposition (even if their artillery were). Kenyon's proposition, however, that: 'The presence of the cavalry was … arguably an important element that could "add value" to an attack by increasing the gains made beyond what was possible with infantry alone',[32] is undoubtedly correct.

Justice alleges that after the attacks on Gattigny Wood and Honnechy, 'the Cavalry Corps made an error of strategic importance'. This was to probe north-east 'into, demonstrably, the most heavily defended localities and higher troop concentrations which had been bottled up by the severing of the main road into Le Cateau'. In doing so, of course, they were following the direction indicated in their orders. Justice believes that it was a failure not to consider advancing south-east. 'This potentially open two-and-a-half mile stretch of the River Selle may have revealed a crossing point'. Further, 'more importantly, in the middle of the "gap" was St. Benin and its viaduct, probably not demolished until midday on 10 October at the earliest'. In reality, however, there was no gap. Not to mention having to cross exposed ground to the south-west of Le Cateau similar to that to the north-west, both areas being swept by enemy artillery, there were no bridges to cross, the river was dammed and ground on either side was flooded. Further, the *HWL I* was a garrisoned and more than effective barrier all along the west bank. The St Benin viaduct that carried the railway on the east bank of the Selle into Le Cateau station would have delivered the cavalry into the arms of a raft of machine-gun strongpoints on the *HWL I*, which would have enfiladed what would have had to have been a careful progress across. Beyond the *HWL I* were rifle pits and machine gun nests on the rising ground. At the top of the slope the fortified point of the brickworks had a direct line of fire on where the cavalry would have debouched from the viaduct. These positions made an effective defence, as will be seen, on 17 October. It would also be mistaken to think that the viaduct was not already mined, ready to be blown as the cavalry was crossing it, as had been the case with the bridge crossed by Ridlington's armoured car. David Kenyon concludes that 'while ultimate "breakthrough" was never at issue, a five-mile gain could be converted into a ten-mile gain by the well timed intervention of mounted troops'.[33] The cavalry indeed got the infantry nearer to the Selle quicker on 9 October than would otherwise have been the case in the area of XIII Corps. In the event, however, this had no operational significance. The nature of the Selle defences meant that they would have to be forced by a set-piece attack, and this was not clear when the horses and their sword-wielding riders bore down on Gattigny Wood.

Simon Justice concludes: 'Haig had prepared, as best he could, the only arm of exploitation he had, to make the most of the opportunity before the Selle'. This is a fair judgement, and nothing less would have been expected of the commander-in-chief. And in attempting to weld together an all-arms mobile force, he did his very best with the totality of what was available to him. The cavalry would, of course, have spearheaded this – undoubtedly, they were the fastest thing on the battlefield in October 1918. But there was never a real chance of their generating a 'war shortening coup'. The action of the cavalry at the Selle brings into question (again) the whole issue of cavalry on a battlefield dominated by the killing machines of machine-gun, artillery, and aircraft. The action in the pursuit was bloody, as the exercise of 17 September had forewarned. Between 8-10 October the

32 Kenyon, op. cit., p.277.
33 Kenyon, op. cit., p.278.

Cavalry Corps sustained 605 casualties, 84 fatal. Horses suffered even more, about 1,300 falling, some eight per cent of 'the combined horseflesh of the two cavalry divisions'.[34] The meeting of cavalry, machine-guns and artillery was always going to end in favour of the weaponry in terms of the butcher's bill. Stephen Badsey dismisses the idea of the cavalry suffering its casualties charging machine-guns as an 'old cliché' which 'vanishes like smoke when attempts are made to pin down cases of it actually happening'.[35] Gattigny Wood was one such occasion, however, although enemy artillery largely accounted for those who did not fall to the machine-gun, as it did during the rest of the war. David Kenyon has argued that 'the battlefield became more "cavalry-friendly" as the war evolved'.[36] By this he means the increasing adoption by the Germans of defence in depth, 'a deeper and more porous defensive system'. This offered 'ready-made gaps for the cavalry to exploit, by not riding on to capture railheads deep in the rear, rather by outflanking and attacking positions within the fighting zones themselves',[37] seizing them and defending them with their attached machine-guns until the infantry caught up. He concludes that: 'There is little evidence that (Haig) ever truly recognised the tactical function of cavalry *within* the German defensive systems, and in co-operation with other arms, preferring still to see them as an independent exploitation force'.[38] The first part of this claim is possibly correct – the latter part ignores the evidence of the training exercise of 17 September. Gary Sheffield observes that the achievements of the Cavalry Corps 'fell well short of Haig's grandiose vision of its use in a strategic "breakthrough" role, it did vindicate his cherished operational concept'. The cavalry 'was able to extend and widen the infantry's "bite"'.[39] The Official Historians were therefore both wrong and right in their assessment. The cavalry achieved more than the infantry could on its own on 9 October, but the infantry could have achieved the same on the 10th. The Selle defences, in all likelihood, could not have been pierced by the cavalry, and the ground and time made up by their sacrifice, sadly, made no difference.

Armoured Cars

Mobile armour was, of course, a development of the war. Tanks, however, did not take part in the training exercise of the 17th, the first reality being that those which were operational were engaged in fighting. The second and paramount reality was that the Mark V tank was not a weapon of mobile warfare with a speed of five mph. Even the top speed of the Whippet was only 8.3 mph, although Stephen Badsey draws attention to the fact that at the Battle of Amiens whilst Whippets could not keep up with the cavalry in the advance, they 'tended to surge ahead on their own when under fire'. In terms of cooperation on the battlefield, it is fair to say that as arms, cavalry and tank did not share a close relationship, a reflection of the difficulty of 'how to co-ordinate other arms with armour'.[40] As had been demonstrated, tanks played little useful part in the Pursuit. The Tank Corps itself described the 'battle of movement' as possessing an 'interesting problem and a new experience', i.e. constantly moving machines forward to be near the battlefield if required. As plans were often only settled late in the evening 'it was well-nigh impossible to think of getting Tanks up

34 Justice, op. cit., p.38 (footnote 189). War Diary, HQ Cavalry Corps, 'Narrative of Operations – 8th to 10th October 1918', 20 October 1918, TNA WO 95/575.
35 Badsey, op. cit., p.140.
36 Kenyon, op. cit., p.294.
37 Kenyon, op. cit., p.295.
38 Kenyon, op. cit., p.279.
39 Sheffield, op. cit., p.327.
40 Badsey, op. cit., p.163.

by dawn to precede the Infantry attack'. Tanks, the corps itself believed, should only be used 'sparingly', playing 'catch up', and used tactically to 'help the infantry when held up in the later stages of their advance'. The Tank Corps felt that infantry corps commanders simply did not understand that machines could not be used two days running, as crews need 48 hours recovery.[41] The tank was thus a very limited weapon, one that could 'barely keep up with the relatively hectic pace of operations in which the infantry were engaged'.[42]

Their faster distant cousins, the armoured cars, did take part in the September training and played a very small, if dramatic, role in the events of 9 October, at least for one car. Such vehicles had been quickly developed and deployed to France in December 1914. The Royal Naval Air Service were the first to be equipped, expanding to six squadrons of 12 vehicles, initially using the Rolls Royce 'Silver Ghost' chassis with an armoured body and a rotating turret carrying a Vickers gun. They did not cope well with the muddy conditions of France and Flanders, and some were deployed elsewhere, two squadrons seeing action in Gallipoli and the Middle East, where they excelled in desert patrols. On the Western Front, the cars were taken over by the army in 1915 and incorporated into the Machine Gun Corps. In the search for new weapons with the capacity for exploitation, a new type of armoured car originally ordered by the Russian government from Austin Motors was therefore taken over after the Bolshevik Revolution and sixteen were sent to the Western Front, forming the 17th Tank Battalion.[43]

The car itself was an Austin Colonial chassis with paired rear wheels, powered by a 35/40 hp four cylinder engine giving a top speed of 35 mph, although it was generally driven at no more than 30 mph. It weighed over five tons, had twin rotating turrets carrying two Hotchkiss machine guns, and was manned by a crew of four or five. Its armour was solid, and combined with speed, only four penetrations were recorded by German armour-piercing rounds. The battalion had been in action seven times before its outing on 9 October. The first three actions were with the French Army,[44] the subsequent four were with the BEF. The battalion had fought at Amiens on 8 August and on 21 August on the Somme at Achiet-le-Grand and Bucquoy. It had then assisted the Canadians in forcing the Drocourt-Quéant line on 2 September, and on 29 September had supported the Australian and II American Corps in the breaking of the Hindenburg Line.

At the Battle of Amiens, four cars had been ear-marked for long-distance reconnaissance with the Australian Corps, whilst twelve were to exploit breakthrough. They carried out reconnaissance in front of the Canadians, fired on withdrawing troops, captured a train, brought down telegraph poles, destroyed transport, shot up a German staff car and captured another, and captured maps and documents from an enemy corps HQ. Operating sometimes 5-6 kilometres in front of the infantry, it has been claimed that they 'created an atmosphere of alarm and confusion in the German ranks out of all proportion to their numbers'.[45] In reality, the armoured cars had been little more than a surprise nuisance to the enemy. The battalion itself, predictably, believed that with sufficient numbers the cars might have unlimited possibilities. In fact, their tactical use was quite

41 War Diary, HQ 4th Tank Brigade, 'Report on Operations 4th Tank Brigade September 27th to October 17th 1918', TNA WO95/108/5.
42 J.P. Harris, 'The Rise of Armour', in Griffith, op cit. p.133.
43 http://bef-battles.org.uk/ (accessed 28 January 2016). Twenty-four were sent to Mesopotamia and subsequently used by Dunsterforce in its excursions in Persia.
44 June 11 1918 at Ravenel, with the *10th French Army*; 18 July with General Fayolle's *Army Group Reserve* at the Second Battle of the Marne; and on 28 July at the River Ourcq with the French *5th Cavalry* and the First American Army.
45 C. Messenger, *The Day We Won The War*, pp.126-130.

limited. Aggressive exploitation relied heavily on the men in the turrets, these gunners requiring more initiative than the tank gunner as they were isolated from the rest of the crew. They needed to seize fleeting opportunities to engage the enemy. In terms of all-arms cooperation, training had been carried out with the cavalry, as has been mentioned, but given their numbers, only limited training had been carried out with the infantry, who were much more familiar with the role of tanks. The view of the battalion, in retrospect, was that from the tactical point of view they should ideally attack and pass though the infantry when the latter were 75 per cent of the way to the target when the enemy were fully preoccupied in repelling them, and should attempt to turn a flank. They correctly recognised their particular value in reconnaissance.

As a weapon of war, however, like the tank, they were firstly limited by their mechanical unreliability. Their chassis was regarded by those who operated them as too weak for purpose, and often up to 50 per cent were out of action with mechanical problems. The axles, as was demonstrated on 9 October, were particularly vulnerable. Rough ground or debris on the road surface could be an insuperable obstacle to the weak chassis, and the Germans were experts in blowing obstructive craters in roads. Even farm tracks sometimes proved impossible. During the Pursuit the cars were sent straight down the Roman road, and Lieutenant Ridlington's deeds of derring-do were all performed on metalled surfaces.[46] Secondly, whilst their armour and speed resulted in few penetrations by armoured piercing bullets, an artillery round could wreak havoc. At the attack on the Drocourt-Quéant line only the intervention of ground-strafing RAF planes had allowed the car crews to return to the British lines, four out of six cars having being put out of action by artillery (four cars were similarly destroyed by shellfire at the Hindenburg Line). At Achiet-le-Grand/Bucquoy cars had frequently to be pulled out of ditches by Whippet tanks. They were therefore reliant at times on the other components of the weapons system. To avoid being hit by shellfire, constant swift movement was the key, hence the importance of a self-reliant, opportunistic, fast-thinking gunner.[47]

The armoured car was, therefore, an under-developed weapon of mobile warfare deployed in the last stages of a war that had been marked by unprecedented lack of mobility. There had been no time or impetus for its refinement, whereas the tank, designed to break positional warfare and of no use in pursuit, had undergone two years of development. The armoured car's main potential use from August 1918 was therefore reconnaissance and opportunistic harassment, as achieved by Lieutenant Ridlington. Whilst, as happened that day, some machine gun posts were neutralised either by flanking or swift moving attack, there was only a limited if any role for the car (as there was similarly no role for the cavalry) in an attack against a position such as the *Hermann Stellung.* The destruction of the cars at the Hindenburg Line had been due to the infantry being held up – indeed, there was no doctrine concerning infantry-car cooperation. They did not exist in sufficient numbers to have merited developing thought as to how they should be integrated into the weapons system.[48] That the cars protected the flank of the cavalry attack on Honnechy reflected the one area where there had been training, yet with a part of the weapons system on the cusp of vanishing from modern warfare. Those who wrote a history of its operations in 1919 acknowledged 'the imperfections in a new untried machine, and the experience of the crews in handling it'. In forming a 'just

46 At the Battle of Amiens, tanks towed a pair of cars into action, the rear wheels sitting comfortably in the tracks made by the tanks, and they carried bridges for crossing trenches.

47 'War Experiences and Tactical Notes of the 17th Armoured Car Tank Battalion', IWM Docs 10076.

48 After the war the battalion suggested three cars should work with an infantry or cavalry battalion, and 40 with a group of three tank brigades.

estimation of the potentialities' of the armoured car, 'the undue optimism of its supporters' had to be balanced against the 'initial surprise effected upon the enemy, who, presumably, will not yet have provided himself with an adequate reply'.[49] The weapons of *blitzkreig* just over 20 years later no doubt reflected the enemy's judgement.

Infantry

If the cavalry hoped to be the rapier of the Pursuit, the 'queen of the battlefield' were the bludgeon. The infantry of the BEF had learnt about mobile warfare in the German spring offensives, even if they were moving in the wrong direction, and they prepared for it. In the light of Frank Rowley's comments it is worth looking at the training of 138 Brigade, 46th Division in 1918. They had an extended period of training from 11-25 February, the nature of which is not specified. Between 15 and 23 April the brigade notes: 'Battalions training in open warfare. Defence and attack. Much use made of ranges'. There were further short periods of training 25-6 April and 28-30 July, and between 14 and 16 September there was 'special training in attacking with tanks' with a 'tactical exercise for officers' the following day.[50] The open warfare training reflected itself in the orders issued by the division for pursuit in anticipation of the enemy retiring from the St Venant salient on 7 August 1918. Units were instructed to constantly probe the enemy lines and to have, for each company in line, a 'battle patrol' ready to seize vacated tactical points. Whilst brigades were to advance under the direction of division, with a general line of objective, such was 'not intended to tie down Brigades if there is better ground a short distance forward or back'. After initial advance, the reserve brigade would then push though. Forward machine-guns were to be sent up to cover any advance, and routes were identified for pushing forward field artillery.[51] Further orders issued 12 days later clarified tactical issues. The enemy would 'delay our advance … by every possible means', holding outposts with a minimal number of troops 'skilfully handled so as to deceive us as to his strength'. It was held to be 'undesirable to be held up by a few isolated machine gun or rifle posts', and that 'the capture of one or more of such posts is a sufficient inducement for the whole outpost line to retire to its next position'. Further, 'in such minor attacks, every advantage will be taken of artillery, Machine Gun, and Light Trench Mortar support'.[52] The infantry tactics of the Pursuit to the Selle are thus clearly pre-figured.

In terms of the other divisions in IX Corps, 6th Division had extensive periods of training in 1918, but the details have not survived. 1st Division underwent much less training, but 1 Brigade had a three week period from 19 August 1918, of which it was stated: 'This opportunity will be taken not only to improve the standard of training of all Units in <u>open warfare</u> but also to get the troops as fresh and fit as possible, both mentally and physically'.[53] 'Special attention' was to be paid in the open warfare training to: 'Protection on the march; positions of assembly under cover; protection after assault and during consolidation; re-organisation after the assault; movement and handling of limbers and supply of ammunition; communication between platoons and co[mpanie]s; [and] tactical handling of Lewis guns'. On 26 August there was a 'brigade group tactical exercise without troops for 1st Inf[antry] Brigade and detachments of other arms', an exercise repeated two days

49 Anonymous, *Operations of the 17th (Armoured Car) Tank Battalion During the Battle of 1918*, p.vi.
50 War Diary, HQ 138 Infantry Brigade, February-September 1918, TNA WO95/1607. The brigade therefore spent one month in nine in 1918 training.
51 War Diary, HQ 46th Infantry Division, Order No. G. 106/4, 7 August 1918, TNA WO95/2665.
52 War Diary, HQ 46th Infantry Division, Order No. G. 106/32, 19 August 1918, TNA WO95/2665.
53 Underlining in original.

later and attended by the GOCs of the other two brigades and battalion COs. This was followed by a third period of training where units were 'to take advantage of the situations and lessons' of the tactical exercise 'in carrying out battalion, field co[mpany], and M.G. co[mpany] schemes'.[54] Clearly, despite unevenness across divisions, training was indeed taking place for open warfare, and was being carried out on a (partial) all-arms basis.

During the Pursuit, infantry were never carried in motorised transport, as in the exercise of 17 September – the operational need never arose. Despite IX Corps deciding somewhat optimistically on 7 October that 2 Infantry Brigade would be used as a 'mobile striking force … to be carried in lorries ready at 3 hours notice',[55] this never happened, the line having become fixed again by the time 1st Division was used. Over the period 9-11 October, the BEF's infantry divisions advanced on foot with two brigades leading and one leapfrogging after a certain distance. Simon Peaple describes this pushing forward of fresher units as 'an interesting facet of open warfare which is beginning to emerge in the studies of the North West Europe campaign in the Second World War'.[56] This echeloned approach helped maintain the impetus of attack. Units advanced with little fear of open flanks, although always ready to string out a defensive flank. Most accounts refer to them advancing in 'artillery formation', the purpose of this arrangement being to reduce the incidence of casualties from shellbursts. The advancing unit would divide into four sub-units (platoon of four sections, or company of four platoons). One sub-unit would lead, two more following slightly behind, one on each side, with the fourth following to the rear in the track of the first, making a diamond formation overall. Each sub-unit proceeded in single or double file in the direction of advance. Machine-gun sections as well as light trench mortars were embedded in the advancing infantry units, both arms sometimes deployed on flanks for protection. Sometimes, however, the infantry advanced much faster than the heavy machine-guns. Opportunities for execution, such as of the enemy fleeing in front of the South Africans on 9 October, could not be taken advantage of. Units were sometimes accompanied by Royal Engineers, when the turning of a captured position for defence was required. Lastly, sections of field artillery accompanied, under the direction of the infantry battalion commander. This indicates a high level of devolved command, and the movements of infantry brigade commanders, where documented, often shows them close to the front line.

As noted in the examples given during the Pursuit, platoon actions were common where NCOs or private soldiers showed a firm grasp of fire and movement, pinning down and outflanking enemy positions such a machine gun nests. These were the tactics actively taught in the training of platoons. *SS143*, first published in February 1917, established the vision of the self-contained platoon comprising a small HQ and four sections of specialists. By February 1918, when the pamphlet was reissued, Lewis guns were more plentiful and the notion of specialist sections was dispensed with. In open warfare, it was the matter of 'tactical points' that required attention. In dealing with these: 'If held up, open covering fire to assist a movement to envelop one or both flanks'. Rapid movement was deemed best under the covering fire of Lewis guns placed frontally (and as will be seen in a later chapter, Lewis gun training had a high premium placed on it in October). Movement forward was the most desirable thing: 'More may often be accomplished by reinforcing a platoon which is not held up than by directly supporting one which is'.[57] These were exactly the methods seen, for

54 War Diary, HQ 1st Infantry Brigade, Order No. G. 470/2, 19 August 1918, TNA WO95/1262.
55 War Diary, IX Corps Senior Motor Transport Officer, 7 October 1918, TNA WO95/846.
56 S. Peaple, *Mud, Blood and Determination*, p.188.
57 General Staff, *[SS143] The Training and Employment of Platoons 1918.*

instance, in tackling the machine-guns on the railway at Fresnoy on 9 October. Infantry tactics of pursuit at the Selle, however, did not differ in any particular way to the set piece operations of 17 or 23 October. Indeed, *SS143* set out that the same methods were applicable in trench-to-trench as in open warfare.

Artillery

Mindful of the struggles around Cambrai and the Beaurevoir-Fonsomme line, on 8 October 'without fuller artillery support the infantry brigadiers were disinclined to go further'.[58] The barrage fired the following morning (which as Table 2.1 shows, had a quarter of the weight of those fired on 8 August and 29 September), fell largely on unoccupied ground, however. This, of course, reflected nothing other than a failure to be prescient concerning the enemy's movements at the time orders were issued.

Table 2.1 Artillery ammunition expenditure during the Pursuit in comparison with set-piece battles[59]

	Amiens	Hindenburg Line	Pursuit to the Selle		
	8 August 1918	**29 September 1918**	**9 October 1918**	**10 October 1918**	**11 October 1918**
Guns					
13 pdr. AA	305	534	997	1,029	1,273
13 pdr. RHA		6,231	2,261	492	1,262
18 pdr.	281,697	244,502	65,563	8,694	19,749
60 pdr.	27,627	23,801	6,629	3,550	2,990
6 inch	3,936	2,404	627	118	497
12 inch	26	42			
14 inch		26			
Howitzers					
4.5 inch	60,500	67,656	13,621	3,219	4,220
6 inch	57,329	63,271	10,601	3,800	3,316
8 inch	10,576	9,764	1,012		319
9.2 inch	6,553	7,768	1,032		70
12 inch	369	805			

There are grounds to question the effectiveness of the artillery during the Pursuit. Brigadier-General 'Harry' Walker, whilst judging the Pursuit as 'most satisfactory' complained about artillery barrages not being up to 'the high standard to which we have become accustomed'.[60] The artillery were, of course, constantly being pushed forward, receiving their orders late at night and having to position themselves in the dark. Standard rates of fire and lifts (100 yards every three minutes) had been introduced to reduce the need for repeat orders. That there was raggedness in their performance, as on the front of XIII Corps on the morning of 9 October, is thus not surprising. Similarly,

58 Edmonds & Maxwell-Hyslop, op. cit., p.197.
59 Abstracted from A. Montgomery, *The Story of the Fourth Army in the Battles of the Hundred Days*, Appendix G.
60 War Diary, 16 Infantry Brigade Headquarters, 14 October 1918, WO95/1607.

lack of intelligence other than in broad brushstrokes reduced effectiveness when having to fire on a very specific location, as happened with the failure to destroy the wire in front of the Bellevue spur for the disastrous attack of 12 October. Further, in terms of infantry pushing forward quickly, good quality information as to where they were was crucial. The 2nd Australian Divisional Artillery noted that 'considerable difficulties' had been experienced due to the 'apparent inability of the American Infantry to locate their position'. The only way that the Australians could obtain the information necessary to give accurate supporting fire was through artillery officer patrols sent forward at frequent intervals to find where the front line was.[61]

In most respects, however, the barrage of the set-piece action had a very limited place in a pursuit, and on 10-11 October the contribution of heavy artillery dropped significantly, mostly firing on targets well beyond the infantry. Artillery support in this semi-mobile warfare had to be moving support. Sections of field guns moved up in close support of the infantry to deal with local issues as they arose, although this was not consistently achieved. Thus 138 Brigade, pushing forward towards Fresnoy on 9 October, attacked the railway line with no artillery support, relying on a machine-gun barrage instead. Alternatively, 139 Brigade on 17 October were able to completely destroy a counter-attack at Regnicourt with the assistance of the mobile field guns, as will be seen. 46th Division were particularly complimentary about this mobile support describing how the guns were used to deal with strongpoints, 'firing over open sights and from behind hedges, brushwood or any slight cover', the crews taking 'great risks' and suffering 'comparatively severe casualties'.[62] As Paul Strong and Sanders Marble describe: 'Typically a field battery moved forwards with each infantry brigade headquarters to provide on-call indirect fire, while the leading battalions could have a section (two guns) pushed forwards to blast machine gun nests'.[63] Thus, HQ 46th Division artillery issued an order on 9 October directing 230th Brigade RFA 'to form Artillery of the 46th Division Advanced Guard under General F.G.M. Rowley',[64] i.e. under the command of the 'man on the spot'. This brigade followed up and supported at Riquerval Wood on 10 October, its role as advanced guard being taken by the 231st Brigade on the 11th, which supported the unsuccessful attack on the wood on 12 October. Mobile warfare, however, requires quick action. Thus Lieutenant-Colonel Clarke found on 9 October that he could not move forward at Honnechy to attack and capture the withdrawing enemy because he had to wait for the bombardment he had been at least partially responsible for organising to be cancelled. The current communications technology did not allow a swifter decision to be implemented. The enemy, however, described the British forward movements of artillery to support an advance the following day as being conducted with 'astonishing speed'.[65]

Air-power

Sir Douglas Haig questioned Major-General John Salmond on 7 October 'as to whether he was ready to support the Cavalry Corps with large numbers of low flying machines'.[66] Whilst Salmond

61 War Diary, Headquarters 2nd Australian Divisional Artillery, 11 October 1918, AWM Item No. 13/11/32 Part 1
62 Priestley, op. cit., p.151.
63 P. Strong & S. Marble, *Artillery in the Great War*, p.188.
64 War Diary, HQ 46th Division Royal Horse Artillery and Royal Field Artillery, 9 October 1918, TNA WO95/2669.
65 War Diary, German *Second Army*, 10 October 1918, *USAWW Vol.* 7, p.898.
66 Sheffield & Bourne, op. cit., diary entry 7 October 1918, p.470.

had the machines, they did not effectively protect the cavalry on 9 October. There appears to have been little or no documented liaison between cavalry and RAF on 9 October. Thus when German machines appeared in the sky above the charging horses, the RAF was not there to drive them off. There was again no effective means of asking them quickly to do so. This element of the full all-arms practice of 17 September did not transfer into full all-arms action that day.

Following an enemy who was retiring was a relative novelty for the RAF until the Battle of Amiens on 8 October. Reconnaissance was a key activity. In these days of movement, identifying where the infantry of both sides were was crucial. On 9 October 39 contact patrols were carried out, none on the 10th due to poor weather, but 23 on the 11th. Secondly, as Simon Coningham notes: 'The highest profile form of air-ground co-operation, the provision of ground support, was the last to appear'. Low-flying ground attacks, however, 'despite their proven effectiveness against troops in the open, were unpopular with pilots, who regarded them as requiring no special skill and therefore arbitrarily dangerous'.[67] On 9 October, however, 5 Brigade RAF wrote that: 'The chief feature of today's operations has been the engagements of Ground Targets'. That afternoon, 'signs of a considerable withdrawal were noticed and every machine available was put on ground straffing'. Ground attack, from pilots' reports, was an opportunistic matter, but continued over the next two days. Further, there was bombing of groups of enemy, trains etc. The RAF dropped an average 508 25-pound bombs 9-11 October and fired an average 36,248 rounds, 10 October being the busiest day, when 618 bombs were dropped and 48,370 rounds fired.[68]

Communications in mobile warfare

Effective communication of information is the *sine qua non* of effective command and control. As Captain Wyn Griffiths, a staff captain with 115 Infantry Brigade wrote: 'A general without a telephone was to all practical purposes impotent – a lay figure dressed in uniform, deprived of eyes, arms and ears'.[69] Captain Charles Clayton, in a similar role with 2 Brigade, was Brigadier George Kelly's eyes, arms and ears on 17-18 October, constantly active in obtaining information. On the 17th, brigade staff had 'a wild morning trying to find out what has happened'. Kelly accepted that 'fighting troops cannot be expected to send back messages while they are actually on the move and fighting', but was constantly anxious. On the morning of the 18th, Kelly, his brigade HQ in a dug-out in a quarry near Vaux-Andigny, had 'heard by runner that the positions are correctly taken up', but was 'not satisfied'. Clayton had to proceed on Kelly's horse through shellfire 3,000 yards to ascertain that the battalions were in the correct position in terms of the barrage, which indeed they were.

In positional warfare prior to 1918, the BEF had relied on deep buried cable networks for communication. The German spring offensive had shaken the comfortable reliance on this, and as early as the end of April 1918 GHQ had formed the view that as telephone communication 'cannot be extensively maintained in warfare of movement ... units must accustom themselves to rely entirely upon other methods of communication'.[70] 46th Division produced two and half sides of closely typed

67 S. Coningham, 'The Battle of Amiens', in Sheffield & Gray, op. cit., pp.213-4.
68 Forty-four 128-pound bombs were dropped during these three days.
69 W. Griffith, *Up to Mametz*, p.185.
70 NARA, RG120, Entry 403, NM-91, Box #1, Miscellaneous Summaries of Information, 1917-19, General Headquarters, General Staff, G-5 Schools, Langres, Army Signal School, 'Notes on Recent Fighting No. 8. Issued by the British General Staff, April 28, 1918', 30 April 1918. (Cited in B.N. Hall, 'The British Expeditionary Force and Communications on the Western Front 1914-1918', p.286).

instructions concerning communication at the end of September/start of October 1918. One of the pages was taken up with the matter of laying one central trunk route of cable, and indeed, telephone and telegraph would always remain the BEF's main means of communication. This was a challenge of effort in rapid forward movement. 25th Division regarded the cable work carried out by its signal engineers in October as 'the most difficult work that the Signal Co[mpan]y had been called upon to perform during the war'.[71] The remaining one and a half sides dealt with alternatives. The first main technological standby was wireless. One Wilson set was established at advanced divisional HQ (where one trench set was kept in reserve); one trench set was at a central point in relation to brigade headquarters; and the third, with means of transport, was with the Divisional Observation Officer. Wireless transmission was in its infancy at the outbreak of war, and with their spark transmitters, sets 'were very unselective and were highly prone to mutual interference and jamming'.[72] The Wilson set with its higher number of sparks gave 'a musical note at the headphones, thereby making the Morse signal more easy to hear through interference'.[73] In addition, its higher power gave it a range of 9,000 yards from its 30 foot mast. BF Trench sets had a range of 4,000 yards, but even the 12-foot mast in a forward position was something of a give-away to the enemy. Technically carried by three men, it actually required a further six to move it and its associated equipment forward.[74] 46th Division further allocated loop sets as the situation demanded. The loop set was lighter, more compact and its one yard square aerial could be mounted on a rifle bayonet, but its range was only 2,000 yards and it was particularly prone to interference. Such were issued, on occasions, to battalions (none at the Selle make mention of this, however), but the limited range meant that a swiftly moving battalion might easily pass out of effective contact. In the latter stages of the advance, 46th Division took to leapfrogging radio sets. Further, the technical skill in operating the sets was high, and messages took a good deal of time to encode/decode.[75] II American Corps appears to have had a trench set based with each of the front-line regiments,[76] but made no mention of loop sets with battalions. As will be noted, American signallers were busy running traditional (and vulnerable) wire up to Arbre de Guise under fire on 17 October. Wireless was used more during the Hundred Days than ever before, but remained a very imperfect means of communication. It was of limited use in front of brigade, yet to the rear continuous wave sets were found very useful by the artillery.

With these limitations to technology, visual signals, mounted orderlies, despatch riders, pigeons, and aeroplane signalling using Popham Panels (a dark cloth laid on the ground with a 'T' in white fabric on it, additional flaps being folded open or closed to create symbols that had known meanings) were also listed in 46th Division's resumé. Visual signalling (a Lucas lamp was used in front of Riquerval Wood on 11 October) sometimes proved effective, yet by and large, terrain, early morning starts which created light issues, and the ever present fog at the Selle limited the effectiveness of such activity. 46th Division noted in early October that: 'A complete visual scheme, on which a great deal of energy had been expended, was rendered useless by the fog'.[77] Carrier pigeons were a generally slow means of communication. As Captain Clayton found, therefore, the human

71 M. Kincaid-Smith, *The 25th Division in France and Flanders*, p.346.
72 Hall, op. cit., p.100.
73 K.R. Thrower, 'Army Communication in the Great War', p.6.
74 Hall, op. cit., p.101.
75 Due to inexperience, messages were often over-long, and took 40 minutes to arrive compared with 55 minutes by pigeon. (Boff, op. cit., p.18).
76 War Diary, II Corps AEF, Operations Instructions Series B No. 8, Signal Instructions, 16 October 1918, *USAWW Vol. 7*, pp.613-5.
77 R.E. Priestley, *Breaking the Hindenburg Line*, p.62.

being on foot, horse, bicycle or motorbike was often the only effective carrier of information. Yet again, however, this was not necessarily quick – the condition of the roads and fog created problems for despatch riders. The RAF could, of course, provide broad brush strokes of communication. Contact patrols were able to report to corps the progress of its forward units. II American Corps, for instance, scheduled seven contact patrols by 3rd Squadron Australian Flying Corps on 17 October to spot flares sent up by troops as they reached each objective, with a last patrol at dusk to locate final dispositions. Similarly, there would be a counterattack patrol up continuously throughout the day, dropping white parachute lights immediately over counterattacking troops.[78] The testament to success is the breaking up of all enemy counterattacks.

There were, manifestly, no easy solutions to communication issues in mobile warfare. This lack directly influenced one matter – devolved command. As Sir Charles Fergusson, commanding XVII Corps wrote: 'Divisional, brigade and battalion commanders must be right up where they can see the fluctuations of the battle and command. To command by the telephone – basing action on the reports of junior commanders – is a crime. It is better to be cut off from communication with the rear than to be out of direct touch with the front'.[79] Thus, on 9 October, Brigadier Frank Rowley of 138 Brigade was up with his leading battalion in Mericourt, observing from the furthest forward position himself before issuing further orders. Rowley almost certainly kept so close to the action due to his perception that a central problem that his units faced was communication. Messages from front line companies were 'taking at least 3 and 4 hours to come back to Brigade Headquarters'. In his view visual communications were 'not sufficiently practised', units relying on runners, 'who are as a rule very slow'.[80] 50th Division at the Selle took the view that battalion HQs should move forward with their reserve company, and that COs should not remain at report centres as they could not take charge when needed. Brigade HQs were ordered to move forward to keep in touch with battalions, progressing in bounds two or three times a day.[81] As brigades pushed their HQs forwards behind their battalions, responsibility then lay with divisions to play catch-up. 50th Division recommended daily moves. In the IX Corps area, 6th Division Advanced HQ moved four times in the first half of October, being at the Hindenburg Line on the first day of the Pursuit, and moving to Preselles Farm on the Beaurevoir-Fonsomme Line on the second. It was thus some 7-8,000 yards behind the front line of its units' actions on the first day, but over 10,000 yards on the second day (moving closer on the third day).[82] 71 Brigade, which spearheaded the division's advance on both of the first two days of the Pursuit, had its HQ at Ramicourt on the morning of 9 October, 3,000 yards behind its units' start line, moving to Doon Mill Copse that afternoon, some 6,000 yards behind. It caught up the following day by moving twice, first to Brancaucourt farm and then to Bohain, some 3,000 yards behind the front.[83] In the XIII Corps area, 25th Division HQ moved six times during the same period, being at Ponchaux on the morning of 9 October and Le Trou aux Soldats on the 10th, on both occasions 5,000 yards from its units' jump-off positions.[84] 75

78 27th Division AEF, 227-32.1: Order, Plan for Aircraft, 16 October 1918, *USAWW Vol. 7*, p.620.
79 War Diary, HQ XVII Corps, 'Lessons Learnt During the Operations From 21st August to 7th September, September 1918', TNA WO95/837, cited in Hall, op. cit., p.322.
80 War Diary 138 Infantry Brigade Headquarters, 'Report on Operations on Mericourt, Fresnoy-le-Grand, Riquerval Wood, Regnicourt & Andigny-les-Fermes, 21 October 1918', WO95/2689.
81 War Diary, HQ 50th Infantry Division, 'Lessons Learnt During Recent Operations, November 1918', TNA WO95/2812.
82 War Diary, HQ 46th Infantry Division, October 1918, TNA WO95/2666.
83 War Diary, 25 Infantry Brigade, 9-10 October 1918, TNA WO95/1620.
84 War Diary, HQ 25th Infantry Division, October 1918, TNA WO95/2227.

Brigade, spearheading the advance on 9 October, 'moved to Sonia Wood before commencement of operations with forward report centre at Serain Farm' (the distance between the two being 2,000 yards, Serain Farm being close to the start line), and then 'moved forward to Maretz early in the afternoon, and billeted there the night in cellars'. On the 10th brigade HQ moved shortly after zero to Honnechy Station.[85] Here it was some 3,000 yards behind its leads units and 3,500 yards in front of divisional HQ. In II American Corps, where there was more need to spell things out, Major-General Lewis of 30th Division sent orders to 59th Brigade on 9 October that 'moving warfare … require(s) your regimental commanders to move their headquarters as the advance progresses'. Brigade HQs were instructed to 'keep within 2,500 yards of regimental headquarters'.[86]

More varied means of communication were used in the Hundred Days then previously, and there was greater use of wireless. Communication at the sharp end, however, fell increasingly into a technological vacuum. There was more reliance on individuals to transport information over the 3,000 or so yards between battalion and brigade, a distance that would expand with progress and then contract. Devolved command was the only solution to the essential maintenance of tempo in the face of slow progress of information to the rear. The men at the sharp end, often the battalion commander and sometimes the brigade commander, had the most detailed knowledge of the specific locality of any unit's advance (but in the fog at the Selle, sometimes not). There was little realistic alternative, therefore, to them having control of the mobile weaponry attached. All the formal bases of communication and command and control could do was to push forward as swiftly as they could.

Conclusion

Historians have alternately used the words 'open', 'semi-open' and 'mobile' to describe the warfare of the Hundred Days. Any image of mobile warfare in the Great War is sandwiched between two visions of movement. One stems from the Victorian era where massed cavalry could supposedly smash into the flank of an enemy army, speed into its rear and cause havoc with its communications. The other stems from the *blitzkrieg* of 1940 where armour and motorised infantry, concentrated at a specific point, the *schwerpunkt*, could rupture defences and proceed to pursuit.[87] Both visions contain idealisations of speed and effectiveness. The reality of 1918 was somewhat different. The enemy, although in retreat, never presented a flank to turn. Similarly, the whole history of warfare on the Western Front is of the acceptance that a decisive *schwerpunkt* leading to successful breakthrough was not achievable in the face of the opposing defences. The BEF in the Hundred Days did not change their view of this acceptance, switching the locus of a series of set-piece attacks which kept its enemy off balance and prevented any effective placement of reserves. Mobile warfare for the BEF fell between two technological stools. The cavalry was an arm about to leave the 20th Century battlefield in the face of rapid development of firepower; armour and communications were not sufficiently developed to achieve what in another 22 years would be the shape of mobile warfare. At best, the BEF could only achieve semi-mobility in warfare that was semi-open, the word 'semi' being used in its true meaning of 'half'. This, however, does not mean that the BEF lacked an effective formula.

85 War Diary, HQ 75 Infantry Brigade, 9-10 October 1918, TNA WO95/2249.
86 G-3, AEF, 30th Div: Fldr. 3: Message, *USAWW Vol.* 7, p.457.
87 The most heavily used tank (Panzer II) of the forces that drove a wedge between French forces and Lord Gort's BEF in fact had a speed of just 25 mph, one which was far from 'lightning'.

The so-called Pursuit to the Selle of 9 October 1918 was one of the most extensive displays of all-arms warfare in motion in the whole of the Great War. Infantry, mobile artillery, machine-guns and light trench mortars, cyclists, tanks and aircraft were used across the whole front to drive in the enemy's rearguards. In XIII Corps area, cavalry and attached armoured cars attempted to achieve Haig's longed-for breakthrough, whilst in the air the RAF pursued ground-attack. The reasons for the failure of the combination to set in motion a true pursuit was largely down to the degree and nature of the enemy resistance. Well-chosen rearguard positions effectively held up the infantry, as the will to resist of key aspects of the enemy's defences was not yet broken. Machine-gun and artillery fire held up the cavalry thrust, and the *Hermann Stellung* to which the rearguards were ushered by Fourth Army's advance was sufficient, even if the cavalry had reached it, to have led to that arm's decimation. The cavalry attack was launched at what appeared to be the right time, but in lack of full realisation of what lay just ahead. Further, although it was supported by many of the arms employed in the exercise of 17 September, the thrust lacked a powerful dedicated contribution from the RAF. It was, sadly, not the best day for flying on 9 October, and whilst one squadron of 5 Brigade RAF was attached to the cavalry for reconnaissance, the brigade records reveal no planned attempt to provide an offensive spearhead above the cavalry. The contribution of the RAF in ground attack during the Pursuit is difficult to assess in its own right. The planned use of a mobile striking force as rehearsed on 17 September therefore went off slightly half-cocked, uncoordinated with both air support and infantry. The sad reality was that the point both in time and geographically at which the action carried out on 9 October could have had a chance of success was beyond the Sambre-Oise canal, breached on 4 November, by which time it would have been irrelevant. The infantry proved the true weapon of the Pursuit to the Selle, with their mobile supporting companions in arms. Yet they could be stopped by determined machine-gun defence judiciously using topography. The enemy was determined to control their withdrawal, and successfully protected much of their matériel, notably their ordnance. The BEF deployed semi-mobile or semi-open warfare at the Selle only to the extent that the enemy allowed them to do so. Hoping for rout, these three days demonstrated the truth of von Moltke's maxim that in operations 'one will soon encounter the independent will of the enemy'.[88] And in attempting to overcome the enemy's independent will, effective communication, essential in quick decision making in this type of warfare, was increasingly reliant on primitive means. Command and control was inevitably hampered.

On 9 November 1918, 66th Division was ordered to form the Fourth Army Advanced Guard, a 'mobile column …to act in advance of the Outpost Line', to keep in touch with the retreating enemy. On the night of 8/9 November, intelligence suggested that the enemy would now retire east of the River Meuse. The problem of following them, however, was now a matter of logistics. 'Owing to continued rain and to the delays which were being caused by the explosions of delayed action mines far in rear', the state of communications 'was at this time causing considerable anxiety'.[89] Despite curtailing transport and ammunition supply to a minimum, the problem with supplying troops with food was 'becoming exceedingly difficult'. A halt for three or four days was ordered, and 'Bethell's Force' was substituted for a general advance. It was not, it should be noted, formed in response to a perceived tactical need for a fast moving column. Rather, in response to the straightened circumstances surrounding supply which meant that the whole of Fourth Army could not proceed, it served in lieu of a more powerful force. As Table 2.2 shows, its composition

88 H. von Moltke (the elder), 'On Strategy', translated in D. Hughes, *Moltke on the Art of War: Selected Writings.*
89 War Diary, HQ Infantry 66th Division, 'Narrative of Operations 4th November 1918 to 11th November 1918', TNA WO95/3122.

in terms of arms reflected very much the experience of the Pursuit to the Selle.[90] On 10 November, Bethell's Force set off, less 5 Cavalry Brigade (although 12th Lancers were present, pushing ahead in reconnaissance with the RAF acting as eyes in the sky), the Royal Engineers creating diversions around craters which could 'pass all transport, except motor vehicles' (thus the armoured cars were stymied). The Divisional Signal Company laid lines to the rear of the advance, there being no mention of the use of radio. The infantry soon encountered the enemy holding high ground along the Belgian frontier, and essentially made little progress until the Armistice was declared at 11.00 the following morning.[91] In many ways, much the same problems as at the Selle were encountered – a mobile force could advance as far as an enemy armed with a phalanx of machine-guns situated in advantageous topography would allow. Sandwiched between the mobile warfare of a cavalry attack on a relatively small army with open flanks, and the mobile warfare of the faster moving armour of a world war yet to come, semi-mobile or semi-open warfare at the end of the Hundred Days was something of a deliberate progress. It was governed by the speed of its main element, the infantry, and the time it took them to overcome temporary resistance.

Table 2.2 Composition of 'Bethell's Force' 10 November 1918

South African Infantry Brigade
5 Cavalry Brigade
Two batteries 18-pounder guns, RFA
Two sections 4.5-inch howitzers
One section AA guns
1 Company, 100th Battalion MGC
17th Armoured Car Battalion
Three Field Companies RE (with bridging equipment)
One company Pioneers (9th Gloucestershire)
Eight light ambulances
Two squadrons RAF
66th Division Signal Company
IX & XIII Corps Cyclist Battalion

90 War Diary, HQ 66th Infantry Division, Order No. 120, TNA WO95/3122.

91 War Diary, HQ 66th Infantry Division, 'Narrative of Operations 4th November 1918 to 11th November 1918', TNA WO95/3122.

3

Preparing for Battle: 11-16 October 1918

Fourth Army had been clear by the evening of 11 October that as the 'enemy's resistance is stiffening … Corps will make preparations to carry out a concerted attack under barrage … on 14th or 15th Oct … as much art[iller]y as ammunition supply permits will be brought up to assist in this operation'.[1] The plan of attack itself would be dictated by the ground and the nature of the German defences, whilst the date the plan could be enacted would be dependent on logistics. Indeed, Sir Henry Rawlinson noted on 13 October, the day he met with his corps commanders: 'I … put off the attack until the 17th so as to get all the artillery and ammunition up and make sure of penetrating the line, for we must not have a failure at this juncture'.[2]

Topography

The enemy had for the most part retired to the east bank of the River Selle. This was a river widely used for industrial purposes, powering more than 50 factories. The river was not, however, a barrier across the front of the whole of Fourth Army – it had its source between the villages of Vaux-Andigny and Molain, and hence was no impediment to IX Corps. This corps faced different topographical challenges. Below the source of the Selle, and in the north of IX Corps area, lay the dominating Bellvue spur, whereas the southernmost part of the front of this corps faced a different sort of challenge, Riquerval and Hennechies woods and the rest of the Andigny Forest on their right. IX Corps had already fallen foul of both. If the forest was not cleared, the Germans who had so far stoutly defended it would enfilade the army's right flank.

To the north, as Sir Archibald Montgomery noted, 'it seemed from the map' that the Selle 'could be crossed without much difficulty anywhere from its source near Vaux-Andigny as far as St. Benin'. Between there and Solesmes to the north of Le Cateau, 'it appeared probable that a crossing could only be effected at the fords or by bridges'.[3] Near its source at Molain, the river was 10 feet wide and two foot deep. From St Souplet to Le Cateau it was normally 15 to 18 feet wide, and only three to four feet deep, with water meadows stretching some 100 to 200 yards on either side. The banks were three feet high, and in peaceful times a pleasant sight adorned with poplars, alders

1 War Diary, HQ Fourth Army, Message G.356 21.40 11 October 1918, TNA WO95/439.
2 Sir H. Rawlinson, diary entry 13 October 1918, Churchill College GBR/0014/RWLN
3 A. Montgomery, *The Story of Fourth Army in the Battles of the Hundred Days*, p.192. At its mouth at Denain, west of Valenciennes, it was nearly 50 feet wide and over six feet deep.

and willows. There was, however, more water in the river than usual. At Marsh Mill, just north of St Martin Rivière it was slightly under 20 feet wide and three foot three inches deep. There had been road bridges at Molain and St Souplet, and three small bridges at St. Martin-Rivière, but the enemy had blown all of them. In Le Cateau itself the river's span was 20 feet between brick banks. Unfortunately, reference to the map alone was not sufficient. Reconnaissance revealed that recent rain and the enemy's damming of the river in three places at its southern exit from Le Cateau, and at St. Benin and St. Crepin (between St. Benin and St Souplet), had created an expanding and deepening flood.[4] The British could take heart, however, from the fact that 'most efforts made to cross a river which is being defended have proved successful',[5] Fourth Army's previous efforts in the Hundred Days campaign standing testament to this.

The river itself was not the only topographical problem. It lay in a valley just over half a mile wide, 'bounded on either side by slopes which rise steeply to undulating country some 200 feet' above the river itself.[6] Having advanced over country that was gently undulating, largely devoid of hedges and dotted with only small, scattered woods, the army now had to advance down a slope without cover and up the other side of the valley. This eastern slope was 'more abrupt in nature',[7] rising into plateaued country which was 'covered with small pastures and plantations surrounded by thick thorn hedges', with 'many scattered farms and houses with orchards, many ditches and irrigation channels'.[8] In short, it was perfect for a fighting withdrawal, with view restricted and movement difficult. To add to the difficulties, a number of small valleys cleave the eastern slope. From Le Cateau one such runs south-east towards Le Quennelet Farm. To the south, another runs south-east from St. Benin towards l'Arbre de Guise, and after two smaller valleys, another that contained a railway runs in a similar direction from Molain, dominated on its southern side by the Bellevue Ridge. All these valleys lay in an oblique direction to the general direction of attack.

Le Cateau itself, a sizeable town with a population of 10-11,000, presented all the difficulties that urban fighting might entail – cellars to shelter in during bombardment and to hide in and emerge from in the rear of those clearing. There was a network of railways in the area, whose cuttings and embankments had already been used to good effect to delay the British advance. One such ran north-south on the east bank of the Selle, through the town itself. Le Cateau station lay outside the town, and with its buildings, was 'a little fortress'.[9] A short distance to its north, where the railway line diverged, a 'railway triangle' had been created through the addition of a third line to allow trains coming from the east to run north. Finally, a further problem which lay outside Fourth Army's area was the ridge of high ground north-east of Le Cateau climbing from Montay on the river towards Forest. From here the entire river valley and the plateau to the south-east over which Fourth Army would advance could be enfiladed.

German preparation for defence

Speaking at the Royal United Services Institute in 1925, Colonel Denis Bernard noted that the 'value of rivers as obstacles is a debatable point'. He continued that history demonstrated that 'in many cases a river line has proved to be a snare and a delusion to those who have placed undue

4 Montgomery, op. cit., p.204.
5 D.J.C.K. Bernard, 'The Crossing of Rivers in Warfare', p.423.
6 Montgomery, op. cit., p.192.
7 Montgomery, op. cit., p.204.
8 Fourth Army Intelligence Summary No. 299, 13 October 1918, TNA WO157/199.
9 J.E. Edmonds & R. Maxwell-Hyslop, *Military Operations France and Belgium 1918 Vol. V*, p.297.

reliance in its power to hold up the enemy's advance'. A river is not a defence in itself, rather an adjunct to defence.[10] Thus, along the railway line on the eastern bank of the Selle, facing Fourth Army, lay the *Hermann Stellung I*.[11] This was, however, a defensive system more impressive in name than in practice. Works to the rear of the *Siegfried Stellung* (Hindenburg Line) had actually begun in 1917, and in 1918 the dissolution of German divisions released staff officers who were used as Chief Construction Staffs.[12] On 12 September, evidently not trusting the durability of the Hindenburg Line, parts of which were in disrepair, orders were given for the construction of the *Hermann Stellungen I and II* and other works including the *Hunding*, *Brunhild* and *Kreimhild Stellungen*.[13] On 30 September further orders were given by OHL for the construction of the *Antwerpen-Maas Stellung*, from Antwerp to the River Meuse, and on 8 November for a position even further to the rear, the *M-Stellung*, running along the Meuse from Liège to Namur.[14] The plethora of construction projects was hardly realistic. The Hindenburg Line had taken the Germans some four months and the effort of 65,000 men.[15] As Jonathan Boff notes, *Second Army* had only '8,865 pioneers and civilians, plus 1,500 prisoners of war and five railway construction companies working on the Hermann Line from mid-September on'.[16] What could be achieved would likely be very limited.

The German assessment of the Selle position noted the virtues of 'the railroad embankment which is piled up high in many places (and) affords good cover (dugouts, trench mortar emplacements), and constitutes a tank obstacle to some extent'. It also noted that the 'small undulations of the terrain on the hill slopes offer a good opportunity for the construction of concealed machine gun nests and strong points, and for assembly areas for counterattack'. Direct artillery observation of the British would, however, be impossible from the plateau to the rear of what would be the main battle zone. In assessing the advantages for Fourth Army, it was considered that the villages such as St. Benin and St Souplet offered good opportunity for cover, but that the western banks of the river were steeper than the defended side, and afforded little cover. The Germans concluded: 'The position is usable but not especially favourable'.[17] The order went out on 12 September to begin the construction of the defences. Reconnaissance for the work was to commence immediately, and steps were to be taken for the 'destruction of all important installations in the enemy territory, which may be of value to the enemy infantry or artillery'.[18] Hindenburg informed *Army Group Boehn* on the day after the *Siegfried Stellung* which it had been defending was smashed open: 'No more reserves can be expected from the High Command. Nevertheless, an enemy breakthrough must under all circumstances be prevented'.[19] Without betraying any longer-term strategy other than 'to gain

10 Bernard, op. cit., p.418-9.
11 Originally called *Siegfried IV*.
12 H. Cron, *Imperial German Army 1914-18: Organisation, Structure, Orders of Battle*, p.104.
13 *Hermann Stellung II* was to run east of the Sambre-Oise Canal. The *Kreimhild Stellung* was an extension of the Hindenburg Line facing the American attack on the St. Mihiel salient and the French Fourth Army. The *Hunding* and *Brunhild Stellungen* ran in a south-easterly direction from *Hermann Stellung I*, partly along the line of the Aisne.
14 J. Boff, *Winning and Losing on the Western Front*, p.227.
15 G.C. Wynn, *If Germany Attacks*, pp.135-6.
16 Boff, op. cit., p.227.
17 *Group of Armies Boehn*, Report of Operations, 11 September 1918, *United States Army in the World War Vol. 7*, pp.824-5.
18 German *Eighteenth Army*, Order: Army to Begin Organization of Hermann Position Immediately, 12 September 1918, *USAWW Vol. 7*, p.826.
19 *Army Group Boehn* (*2nd, 9th and 18th Armies*) existed between 12 August 1918 and 8 October 1918, under the command of Max von Boehn, its purpose being the defence of the *Siegfried Stellung*.

time', he set out the tactics: 'Inflict heavy losses on the enemy, constitute fresh reserves, remove our artillery to the rear, and to destroy the railway and telephone installations completely'. Aware of the demands on his armies, all he could do was to insist: 'The firm resolve to repel the enemy onset and not yield too hastily is enjoined upon all'.[20] His words indicate that he recognised it was inevitable that his armies would yield, whatever.

After a few days on the ground *Second Army* reported more favourably that: 'The SELLE position is particularly suited to being organised for a stubborn defence'.[21] Fifteen days later it reported that work had begun on the *Hermann Stellung* defences on 3 October (i.e. 14 days before it would be attacked), and that it had selected the main line of resistance and largely chosen its battery positions. The army had, in addition, begun clearing fields of fire and organising outposts, and had dammed the Selle. Dugouts were being installed at 50 yard intervals along the main line of resistance, which was to be constructed first, and wire was being placed. *Second Army* promised to have finished selecting artillery and anti-tank gun positions by the 7th, and to have begun the construction of artillery command posts. By 11 October dugouts would be three yards deep and machine gun nests two yards deep, with half the communication trenches dug, with dugouts and other firing positions, and the signalling system complete.[22]

Fusilier Regiment 122 of *243rd Infantry Division*, positioned south of Le Cateau, recorded on 14 October the limitations of their defensive position. 'Our men lay, with the exception of our knee deep trench and our initial machine guns nests, in fox holes … or behind available hedges'. From the main resistance line on the railway, however, fields of fire were 'mostly good', whilst on the ridge to the east were 'our initial machine gun nests' which could sweep the ground downhill to the main resistance line, and which could also 'work with indirect fire in the outpost zone'. A third line of resistance was on another ridge on the plateau to the east (the Mazinghien-la Jonquière farm ridge). The regiment took the view that 'the sector is quite suitable for defence … the natural conditions for a tough sector wide defence are also present'.[23] The Germans were thus attempting to construct a variation on their usual defence in depth system. There was an outpost zone, largely consisting of machine gun nests, which with the addition of troops in buildings (e.g. in Le Cateau and St Benin) had a depth of up to 750 yards in places (although in others, much less). There was then the main resistance line or *Hauptwiderstandline* (*HWL I*), sited along the railway embankment/cutting east of the river and cutting across the Bellevue Ridge towards Riquerval Wood. Some 500 to 750 yards to the east was the *HWL II* or *Zwischenstellung* (Intermediate Position), which largely consisted of machine gun nests and rifle pits. The artillery protection line lay between 1,750 and 2,500 yards behind this position.[24]

Roads, bridges and the work of the Royal Engineers

It would have been impossible to reach the Selle and attack the *Hermann Stellung* without the work of the Royal Engineers (RE) repairing the infrastructure and facilitating the logistic imperative – the movement of men, ordnance, ammunition and supplies. In addition to the damage caused by the fighting, the enemy (as ordered by Hindenburg) deliberately destroyed as much of the transport

20 Order of Hindenburg to Group of Armies Boehn, 30 September 1918, *USAWW Vol. 7*, pp.849-850.
21 German *Second Army*, Memorandum: Study of Defence Positions, 18 September 1918, *USAWW Vol. 7*, p.830.
22 Operations Section *Second Army* to *Army Group Boehn*, 3 October 1918, *USAWW Vol. 7*, pp.864-5.
23 War Diary, *Fueselier Regiment 122*, 14 October 1918, quoted in M. Whisler, 'Der Tommy Kommt', p.215.
24 Whisler, op. cit., p.163.

infrastructure as they could to delay the Allied advance. As 1st Australian Tunnelling Company (ATC), at work on the west bank of the river, stated: 'Owing to our continual advance and the systematic destruction by the enemy of railways, roads and bridges, road communication became a matter of vital importance'.[25] There were five principal thrusts to the engineers' work – road maintenance, bridging, water supply, billets and fieldworks, although there was little call for the latter on the Selle. Reconnaissance was an important precursor to engineering role. This was demonstrated 'not only in the examination of forward roads and railways … for the purpose of locating and destroying enemy mines and traps, but also to ascertain the condition of the roads and what labour and material would be required to make same immediately fit for traffic'.[26] Of the strength of 24 officers and 563 other ranks of 1st ATC, one officer and 20 ORs were used for reconnaissance. That this was not a safe pursuit was found by officers of 430 Field Company RE. On 12 October Captain Henri de Panet and Lieutenant Hugh Davies set out to meet Major Stanley Morgan, acting Commander RE 66th Division,[27] to reconnoitre for bridges across the Selle, when a shell fell on them in the ravine behind the high ground north-west of Le Cateau. Davies was killed, as were Driver Harold Hayes and three horses, Panet being wounded.

The role of the engineering effort in the Hundred Days was extraordinary. On 24 October, essentially at the end of the Fourth Army's Selle operations, the Chief Engineer of IX Corps, Brigadier-General George Cartwright,[28] reported on the achievement of his units.[29] Since the start of the offensive in August, 19 pumping stations had been erected; six miles of pipe had been laid and nine repaired; two bore-holes had been sunk and seven recovered. In terms of water supplied, 431,400 gallons of horse water and 446,045 gallons of drinking water had been carried by motor transport across the road network maintained by the corps. Sixty miles of dry weather tracks, and 65 miles of horse transport and 100 of motor transport road had been opened and kept up. In achieving this, at least 40 large craters had been filled in, including 13 in Bohain. Sixty-nine bridges had been erected – 23 for horse transport and 27 for lorry transport. Fifteen could take all loads except tanks (including one bridge of 85 foot span) and four were capable of use by tanks (including five bridges with 60 foot spans).[30] It was also estimated that six tons of explosives had been removed from mines and booby traps.

The pattern of moving forward was that the divisions, the lowest formation that had RE Field Companies attached, took first responsibility for engineering issues, with corps resources moving as quickly as possible in their rear to relieve them, enabling them to move on. Army moved in the corps rear, relieving them in turn. In the matter of bridging, for instance, divisions would build initial structures, whilst heavier bridges would follow constructed by corps. Thus, in the first days of October, as the three corps were pushing on to the Beaurevoir-Fonsomme line, IX Corps engineers were bridging the St Quentin Canal, taken on 29 September, replacing initial structures.

25 War Diary, 1st Australian Tunnelling Company, October 1918, AWM4 RCDIG1006531.
26 War Diary, 1st Australian Tunnelling Company, October 1918, AWM4 RCDIG1006531.
27 Henri de Lotbinière Panet was a Canadian, commissioned in January 1915. Serving throughout WW2 he became Director of Fortifications and Works at the War Office as a Brigadier-General in 1947. Hugh Mercer Davies was commissioned in September 1917. Stanley Herbert Morgan, a pre-war surveyor's assistant, had been commissioned from private in July 1915.
28 George Strachan Cartwright CB CMG (1866-1959) was a Canadian commissioned in the Royal Engineers in 1885. He served as Chief Engineer VIII Corps from March 1916 to September 1917 and with IX Corps from March 1918.
29 War Diary, HQ Chief Engineer IX Corps, E.3082, 24 October 1918, TNA WO95/844.
30 The major waterways obstructing the advance of Fourth Army had been the River Somme and the Somme Canal; the St Quentin Canal, and then the Selle.

An Inglis heavy bridge was completed at Bellenglise on 1 October,[31] and a second steel bridge was brought up two days later.[32] XIII Corps were erecting an Inglis bridge on the canal on 6 October at Vendhuille, and a second bridge on 7th. Otherwise stiffening and widening of other bridges was being carried out, and roads repaired and maintained as the corps advanced though the Beaurevoir-Fonsomme Line. By 8 October, the IX Corps road boundary had been advanced to a position about 1,000 yards behind the jump-off line for 9 October. Even small watercourses could absorb time and effort. On 11 October XIII Corps engineers were still completing bridges over the stream at Le Catelet that could take a 17 ton axle load, over 8,000 yards to the rear of the 9 October start line. Immediately before the Pursuit began, corps engineers were taken off bridging work and put to establishing forward water supply. A forward horse watering supply was, for instance, established at Levergies on 8 October, a thousand yards to the west of Sequehart, on the eastern side of which at 05.20 the following morning Captain Hills of 1/5th Leicestershire would stand, bread and butter in hand, contemplating setting off on the Pursuit. This watering point was fed by 18 lorries with tarpaulin tanks; and on 9 October a second water point was established and an extra 26 lorries fitted for water carrying. The previous day XIII Corps had started laying water pipes up to Beaurevoir, some 4,000 yards behind the start line.

At a divisional level, from 10-16 October, 46th Division's three RE companies were involved in 'repairing forward roads, improving billeting accommodation, water supplies, destroying German "booby traps" etc.' The repair and maintenance of the roads was crucial. 465 Field Company RE marched to Fresnoy on the 10th and the following day was cutting a roadway through the railway embankment on the Fresnoy-Bohain road, where the bridge crossing the road had been blown.[33] Sections of all three of the division's companies were engaged on this task for two days.[34] The next day sections of 468 Company were further working on a diversion round a road crater on the same road in the outskirts of Bohain, and over the following days worked backwards, first clearing roads in Fresnoy, and then filling two craters on the same road further back between Mericourt and Fresnoy, which were 30 feet wide and ten deep. This road was a crucial part of 46th Division's transport artery for the attack on the 17th. They were joined by 409 Field Company from 1st Division who from 13-15 October worked in Fresnoy 'cutting out & filling potholes, drainage, scraping and relaying pavé'.[35] 1st Monmouthshire were the 46th Division Pioneers, the difference between this role and the engineers being skill-based – all engineers had a trade, the role of pioneer having been introduced in 1912 to compensate for insufficient numbers of skilled individuals. For some five days prior to the Pursuit the Monmouths had been used in both defence and attack, and

31 Charles Edward Inglis (pronounced Ingles) was an engineer from Kings College, Cambridge, who by 1918 was responsible for all military bridging in the BEF as a captain. The Inglis Bridge (Mark 1) was able to carry a 17 ton axle load over gaps up to 96 feet and had been a modification of an earlier design re-engineered with tanks in mind. Its sides comprised a series of Warren trusses, equilateral triangles. Forty sappers could erect the 60 foot version in 12 hours.

32 These were dismantled on 26-7 October for re-use at the Sambre-Oise Canal. Removal of bridges from back areas was important due to the 'small reserve of stock spans'. These were in fact moved to the German pioneer park at Bohain, which remained the advanced army depot until the Armistice. (Anon. *The Work of the Royal Engineers in the European War 1914-19 – Bridging*, Section 22).

33 War Diary 465 Company Royal Engineers, 11 October 1918, TNA WO95/2676.

34 War Diary, 468 Company Royal Engineers, 12 October 1918, TNA WO95/2678. Reflecting another aspect of the engineers' role, on the same day other sections of 465 Company were repairing baths in Fresnoy, whilst sections of 468 Company improved the hospital at Fresnoy for accommodation and salvaged fuel to heat water for the baths.

35 War Diary, 409 Field Company Royal Engineers, TNA WO95/1254.

had lost their CO, Lieutenant-Colonel John Jenkins, died of wounds.[36] With little time to recover from fighting, they were thrown into the work on the Bohain road and in clearing Fresnoy.[37] The October rain added to the engineers' grief – on 12 October: 'Light rain cause[d] great havoc with the roads. Large parties put on to scrape mud'.[38] This hampered the use of farmers' dry-weather tracks which were taken into service to ease road congestion.

Multiply-cratered Bohain fell in the area of 6th Division. The enemy had singled out Bohain for destructive attention as literally all main roads in the area converged on this town. It was essential that through-traffic be achieved. The RE Field Companies of the division arrived there on 10 October, and began clearing the roads and filling craters, a task which took some six days. Traffic having to move all the time, a deviation around a crater was created first, the crater itself filled second. 509 Field Company began the creation of deviations in Bohain on the 10th, and 12 Company joined them on the 12th,[39] whilst other sections of 509 Company removed an unexploded mine from the railway west of Bohain.[40] 12 Company then began filling in craters on the roads to the west of the town, where they were joined by the divisional pioneers, 11th Leicestershire. Water also remained a priority, and after filling the site of an undetonated mine in the centre of Bohain, 459 Company were ordered to the sucrerie to work on a water point, building a brick culvert and repairing the sail cloth water banks.[41] 509 Company meanwhile worked on restoring the town's wells.

1st ATC assisted with work in the II American Corps area. They had been attached because of the 'urgency' of freeing the flow of transport, and because 'the American engineer units engaged were more or less new to the work under war conditions'. The American engineers had identified potential hazards, but had not dealt with them. They had 'left notices and warnings, such as "Mines Beware", "Danger do not touch" in all places on railways, in railway station yards, dugouts, and billets, which appeared to them to be suspicious'. The Australians had to investigate each case and deal with it as appropriate. Delayed action devices were everywhere in crucial locations. 46th Division noted that: 'At every cross-roads mines had been buried – some of them timed to explode a few hours after the enemy had left, others a few days, some even after a delay of several weeks'.[42] 6th Division set up their HQ at Brancaucourt Farm, between Brancourt and Bohain, as the battle moved on. The railway bridge opposite had been blown, and the engineers repairing the line had removed many bombs. 'Three days after the arrival of D.H.Q. a delay-action mine went off on the railway at 7.30pm, and two days later again at 7 a.m.'[43] Fortunately only nearby staff cars suffered damage. The mines had a psychological effect. The detonation of one such on the railway crossing at the railhead of Roisel, east of Péronne, '50 days after the enemy had been driven out, caused a good deal of uneasiness with regard to the safety of bridges etc. further forward which had not already been blown'.[44] The Australians also participated in the general engineering. In the week up to the

36 John Jenkins had progressed from RSM in the Kings Royal Rifle Corps to honorary lieutenant and quartermaster. He had commanded 20th KRRC for two months in 1917, and 1st Monmouthshire from 20 May 1918.
37 They were 'working four hours only in view of likelihood of strenuous times in the near future'. (War Diary, 1st Battalion Monmouthshire Regiment, 14 October 1918, TNA WO95/2679).
38 War Diary, HQ Chief Engineer IX Corps, 13 October 1918, TNA WO95/844.
39 War Diary, 12 Field Company Royal Engineers, 11-15 October 1918, TNA WO95/1599.
40 War Diary, 509 Field Company Royal Engineers, 10-15 October 1918, TNA WO95/1600.
41 War Diary, 459 Field Company Royal Engineers, 11-15 October 1918, TNA WO95/1599.
42 R.E. Priestley, *Breaking the Hindenburg Line*, pp.127-8.
43 T.O. Marden, *A Short History of the Sixth Division*, p.68.
44 War Diary, 1st Australian Tunnelling Company, October 1918, AWM4 RCDIG1006531.

commencement of the Pursuit, they worked on the roads in the area behind the American front.[45] The following week, prior to the assault on 17 October, they dealt with the blown road bridge on the railway crossing the Bohain-Busigny road, clearing the debris and constructing a 'metalled detour road, fit for double motor traffic across railway line', as well as a horse deviation track. They similarly worked on a crater in the centre of Busigny. It was a case of all hands to the pump.

The strength of the American 105th Engineers who preceded the Australians on the 30th American Division front was 38 officers and 1,475 other ranks as of 7 October 1918, organised into two battalions. The regiment has left detail that is instructive about the nature and size of the engineering task. Lieutenant Hill of D Company, 2nd Battalion, investigated the minefield at the railway triangle south-west of Busigny on 10 October. Listing the mines, he found '22 on one fork V14 to V20, 18 in another fork V14 central to V21 a 3.7. Bridge at V14 d 6.4 blown from underneath but will hold'. He identified how the Germans had mined this structure: 'From evidence in side ditches, the enemy used from 8 to 10 6-inch trench howitzer bombs, placed in a shaft two feet by two feet by 15 feet deep with one kilo blocks picric compound which looks to be spring munition'.[46] The Americans cut the wires to the mines and disabled the time fuses. The following day Company A of the 1st Battalion was working on a crater on the Prémont-Bohain road, near the detraining point where the three battalions of 74 Brigade had taken shelter two days before. Thirty men worked for 10 hours to create a detour suitable for motor transport. In terms of the filling in of the crater the reporting officer suggested that: '100 men be employed. It will take them about four days to complete the filling in ... if only picks and shovels are used. Twenty tons of road metal will be needed for surfacing the crater and it will need repairs from time to time for a month or two'.[47] In fact, the work took only three days with a different immediate solution. Four thousand sandbags filled with dirt were placed in three layers on top of the crater fill. Wire netting was placed on the sandbags, and rather than placing a metalled surface, a plank road was established on the top, three lorries being required to transport the timber.[48] The plank surface was in contrast to the perilous expedient the 2nd Battalion found British lorry drivers to have been using in filling ruts on the road into Vaux-Andigny, namely live 6-inch shells.

To the north in the XIII Corps area the RE companies of 25th Division had predictable tasks. During the Pursuit and up to the 17th, 130 Field Company RE worked on the water supply in Honnechy, renovated billets and searched for enemy mines in Busigny and Le Trou aux Soldats. The company also prepared a hospital in Serain for 78th Field Ambulance.[49] 106 Company established water supply in Maretz, Prémont and Serain, as well as working on billets.[50] 105 Company similarly filled craters and assisted with the water supply at Prémont.[51] On 16 October 430 Company's efforts were directed at baths and a splinter-proof shelter for the South African Brigade HQ in the ravine where their own Lieutenant Morgan had been killed.[52] 431 Company had been preparing strongpoints on a reverse slope west of Le Cateau and Montay on the three

45 As did 2nd Australian Tunnelling Company up to 13 October.
46 W.P. Sullivan & H. Tucker, *The History of the 105th Regiment of Engineers*, p.184. Picric acid is a nitrate compound similar to TNT.
47 Sullivan & Tucker, op. cit., p.188.
48 Sullivan & Tucker, op. cit., p.193.
49 War Diary, 130 Field Company Royal Engineers, 10-15 October 1918, TNA WO95/2237.
50 War Diary, 106 Field Company Royal Engineers, 9-10 October 1918, TNA WO95/2235.
51 War Diary, 105 Field Company Royal Engineers, 'Narrative of Operations 3-31 October 1918', TNA WO95/2235.
52 War Diary, 430 Field Company Royal Engineers, 16 October 1918, TNA WO95/3129.

days prior to this. Other than this, there was very little need for the construction of fieldworks. 66th Division employed 182 Tunnelling Company on the whole of the divisional front to identify and remove mines and booby-traps. They were not sufficient for the size of the task, for on 9 October 431 Field Company RE had to remove three land mines from the Serain-Elicourt road, and the next day dealt with a mine in a culvert under the Cambrai-Le Cateau road. Similarly, 432 Company had to deploy their whole strength in removing three explosive charges between Elincourt and Maretz, whilst filling two craters. Not all mines and booby-traps were in structures. On 8 October it was noted: 'Bomb traps have been recently found under the bodies of dead Germans'. The bomb would be placed 'under the head or neck in such a manner that when the body is lifted for burial the bomb explodes'.[53] Ropes were supplied to tie to the feet of corpses to drag them before lifting. Similarly, the roads and tracks were found to be strewn with nails in the hope that they would be driven into the hooves of the army's animals. 'Pick up Nails' notices were erected with boxes for their collection. The three RE Field Companies of 66th Division all worked on opening one of the most important communication arteries, the Roman road. The bridge over the railway south-west of Maurois which carried this, and which had been blown behind Lieutenant Ridlington's armoured car, first had a diversion created around it, work beginning on 11 October. On the 12th, a large crater that had been blown in the same road 2,000 yards beyond Reumont was filled and the route opened to lorries, which were able to use the Maurois diversion and get close to the limit of the army's advance. On 15 October, a new bridge was under construction across the railway at Maurois, 30 foot in span and using trestles and girders, although this was only complete on the 19th.

The location of the work of the field companies of all three corps reflected the need for Fourth Army to have two-way transport routes open in a north-easterly direction following the direction of the army's attack (see Map 6). Limitations on what could be achieved were three-fold. First, there was the issue of whether the road was metalled or not. In the American area, as far as the outskirts of Prémont, the road was wide and well metalled, and allowed two-way traffic. Second, many of the other roads were not wide. Such roads would inevitably not be metalled or only thinly so, and could not carry heavy motor traffic in wet weather. Third, there was the matter of damage. Although much effort was put into by-passing craters, this inevitably allowed only a one-way route, and caused traffic congestion.[54] By 16 October there were two two-way routes open, the Roman road through Maurois for XIII Corps, and the route Sequehart-Fresnoy-Bohain for IX Corps. In the American area one north-easterly route was open, Ramicourt-Brancourt-Bohain, but this was one-way only, return being via one of a series of north-south routes which had been restored. To the rear was a route Beaurevoir-Montbrehain to a point on the Sequehart-Mericourt road; and in the centre there had been opened two routes Fresnoy-Brancourt-Serain and Bohain-Prémont-Serain. Lastly, there was a forward route, Bohain-Busigny-Maretz. All of these were one-way only apart from the routes Bohain-Busigny and Bohain-Serain. Within seven days of the start of the pursuit the enemy sabotage of the road system had been undone sufficiently to allow Fourth Army a network of lateral and transverse routes open in their immediate line of communications.

The main difference for the engineering thrust of XIII Corps and II American Corps was the matter of crossing the River Selle. The history of the Royal Engineers' bridging activities states that at the Selle: 'The work of the divisional field companies was very arduous and dangerous' due

53 War Diary, Assistant Quartermaster General IX Corps, Memo 8 October 1918, TNA WO95/840.
54 182-42.2: Fldr. 1: Report, Operations II Corps Engineers, *USAWW Vol. 7*, pp.802.

to the areas of construction being overlooked by the enemy, but added: 'The heavy bridging, which consisted almost entirely of short spans, was of no particular interest'.[55] Three types of bridging activities were necessary. First, footbridges were needed to get the infantry swiftly across. Second, artillery bridges were necessary to get guns across to support the advance as soon as possible. Third, more substantial structures such as the Inglis bridges were needed to get the heaviest transport across.

On 13 October 50th Division, who had taken over the line from 25th Division, reconnoitred the Selle for both bridging and the demolition of the enemy's dams. This reconnaissance revealed a broken bridge just south of St. Benin, the Fassiaux bridge, with a dam and trees felled across the river just to the south, all of which were good for crossing by infantry. No other crossing survived in 50th Division's area, however. The infantry crossing points chosen reflected the areas where it was narrowest and easiest to do so. Such bridging needed to be conducted swiftly in the face of the enemy, and the Germans were holding outposts in the form of machine-gun nests in the area between the *HWL I* and the river. The river was between 12 and 20 feet wide and four to five feet deep at St Souplet, making a straightforward portable duckboard a possibility. At St Benin it was 20 to 26 feet wide and three to four feet deep, which would necessitate a floating bridge which would take up to 15 minutes to assemble in situ. The first phase of the attack of 17 October would, therefore, use the more swiftly installable crossings in the north of St Souplet. Here 12 bridges of the duckboard type were built from timber from a German dump near Honnechy, adding as 'stools' some shorter bridges which had been constructed before the exact width of the river was known. These took 16 carpenters seven hours to build, and were tested 'at the dump by crowding as many men on to them as possible'.[56] RE field companies transported the bridges to about 1,300 yards from the crossings during the afternoon of 16 October, and carried them to within 500 yards of the river by 22.30 that day. Eight bridges were positioned, two for each of the leading infantry platoons of the three battalions, with two spare. One bridging group was responsible for each battalion, consisting of an RE and Pioneer officer, 17 sappers and 50 pioneers, each bridge being attended by two sappers and six pioneers. From 01.00 on the 17th the groups worked their way forward cutting gaps in hedges, followed by the infantry. Five minutes before zero, five of the bridges had already been put in place, the area chosen at St Souplet being one where there were a few houses and trees on the river bank which gave cover. When the barrage lifted on to the *HWL I*, the remaining three bridges were placed within a minute. For the second phase of the attack, bridging was placed at St Benin. Four bridges with floating piers were secured from Army Park and taken to within 500 yards of the crossing point, and 'quietly carried forward and carefully concealed about 50 yards from the sites of this bridges'.[57] This feat was completed by 00.30 on 17 October. The footbridges were placed in pairs on each side of the damaged Fassiaux road bridge, and on the day took ten minutes to carry, assemble and place in position, eight sappers per bridge, the infantry crossing after seven minutes. From the engineering view, it almost a complete success. 102nd Engineers, attached to the 27th American Division, also had to prepare similar constructions, but on the day 'severe losses' were sustained by the engineers whilst placing footbridges across the river.[58]

55 Anon. *Royal Engineers – Bridging*, Section 22.
56 War Diary, Commander Royal Engineers 50th Division, 'Bridging of River Selle in Connection with the Operations of 17th October 1918', 26 October 1918, TNA WO95/2816.
57 War Diary, Commander Royal Engineers 50th Division, 'Bridging of River Selle in Connection with the Operations of 17th October 1918', 26 October 1918, TNA WO95/2816.
58 J.F. O'Ryan, *The Story of the 27th Division*, p.373.

North of Le Cateau in 66th Division's area, the Selle was 20 feet wide and five feet deep, with steep grassy banks. 432 Field Company RE put two bridges across near Montay as early as 13 October, after a dusk reconnaissance by no lesser personages than the 66th Division CRE and the company commander, Major Robert Gracey. Their task was more successful than the disaster that had befallen 430 Company on the same mission the previous day.[59] 431 Company attempted to reconnoitre potential crossing sites further south two days later, but were deterred by the enemy presence on the eastern bank. On the night of 16/17 October, a party 100-strong from 431 and 432 Companies, assisted by 9th Gloucestershire (Pioneers), erected four footbridges comprising two rafts each made from 30 petrol cans with trussed duckboards, ten feet long.[60] These were placed in the valley between Baillon Farm and the northern edge of Le Cateau, finishing by 02.00, a feat achieved under fire without a casualty.

Logistics

Along the reconstructed arteries the life-blood that would fuel Fourth Army's attack flowed. Reviewing land transportation in the war, Colonel M. G. Taylor, Assistant Director of Movements, concluded: 'Transportation was the cause of our greater difficulties – not fighting power, leadership, or the more active side of military training'.[61] In 1916 it had been calculated that the tonnage per mile of front on a day of intensive fighting which had to be removed from railheads was 1,934 tons.[62] Even before the Hundred Days campaign began, when GHQ became aware that the German offensives had petered out and an enemy withdrawal to the Hindenburg Line seemed possible, the Quartermaster General stated: 'The problem of effective pursuit will largely be one of supplies and transport'.[63] Although such a retirement did not happen, the QMG had correctly foreseen a central issue for the rate of any future advance. Railways, both standard gauge and light, would have to be pushed forward, and roads and bridges onwards from the railheads reconstructed as rapidly as possible. Ian Brown suggests that: 'The BEF showed a far better grasp of the operational limitations of logistics at this time than did the German Army'. The British had learnt much about mobile logistics whilst being pushed back earlier in the year, the corresponding German advance being logistically naïve. The BEF, successfully supporting the advance and massive demands of all its five armies at once, 'settled on the less glamorous, but more logistically feasible, limited-objective set-piece attack – the correct choice at the time'.[64]

The BEF's logistics system had grown on an ad hoc basis. As the army expanded, the officers of the departments of the Quartermaster General and Inspector General Communications pragmatically responded to the increased demand. The collapse of that system on the Somme in 1916 had led to the appointment of Sir Eric Geddes, civilian railwayman turned Director-General of Transportation, who remodelled logistic procedures. He had begun with the railways, on which the whole imperative relied. The BEF's front was always many miles from it ports and 30 miles was 'the maximum that could be reasonably be expected from motorized and horse-drawn supply

59 Robert Lloyd Gracey MC had been commissioned as a Territorial engineer in March 1914.
60 War Diary, 431 Field Company Royal Engineers, 15 October 1918, TNA WO95/3129. Enough material had been provided for thirty bridges.
61 M.G. Taylor, 'Land Transportation in the Late War', p.700
62 A.M Henniker, *Transportation on the Western Front*, p.157.
63 War Diary, QMG Branch, 'Explanatory Review July 1918', TNA WO95/39.
64 I. M. Brown, *British Logistics on the Western Front 1914-1919*, p.198-202.

columns'.[65] GHQ further pushed the use of light railways to save on both motor transport and rail transport of road stone, and in 1918 these were shifting over 200,000 tons per week onwards from the railheads.[66] Despite proving vulnerable to interdiction by artillery at Third Ypres (just as standard gauge proved similarly vulnerable during the German spring offensives of 1918), light railway had numerous economical features. Firstly, its track came in sections and required less specialist engineering to lay, and being lighter ostensibly required less earthwork and less robust bridges. Secondly, like standard gauge railway, it could haul goods that would take many lorry loads. Thirdly, it required fewer personnel than motor transport in terms of volume of goods shifted. Lastly, in the Hundred Days advance, light railway could be easily linked to any German system left undamaged. The downsides were that their loads were limited to around 30 tons, and ten light trains would be required to shift the contents of one standard gauge train. The heavy use thus required robust construction, which negated the original proposition that they required less construction effort. Repaired rail systems of both light and standard gauge were less vulnerable to interdiction in late 1918 as the enemy retreated, however. Motor transport, though rapidly expanding, would only ever be an adjunct to the railway system. Some 150 lorries were required to shift the load of one train.[67] Lorries were, however, the crucial link between railhead and the fighting, especially as the distance between the two expanded late in the Hundred Days. It was, therefore, prescient that in the winter of 1917-18 both the vehicles and organisation of motor transport were overhauled. Firstly: 'Every M.T. vehicle which could be spared from units' was taken into GHQ reserve and reconditioned, more reliance being placed on light railways during this period. Secondly, 'general purpose M.T. companies' were formed from the reconditioned vehicles and kept in GHQ reserve for allocation to where they were most needed.[68] During the railway crisis caused by the German spring offensives on early 1918, motor transport proved crucial.

Amiens was the rail hub of central importance to the southern line of communication on which British logistics relied, hence its defence in the German spring offensives had been essential. In October 1918, the BEF had 1,398 locomotives and 48,186 wagons capable of carrying over 600,000 tons.[69] Sir Henry Rawlinson was anxious about rail supply for Fourth Army as the Hundred Days campaign progressed. It was not capacity that troubled him, rather reconstruction. On 5 September he first confided to his journal: 'My chief anxiety is to get the railways through in time' – in that case for the attack on the Hindenburg Line – describing them as the 'governing factor'.[70] In the aftermath of its breach, on 8 October a single-track standard gauge line from Amiens was open across the old Somme battlefield west to east,[71] then turning to run south parallel to the line of Fourth Army's advance from Epehy, through Villers-Faucon to Roisel and Montigny Farm to Vermand (see Map 7). A double-track railway ran south of the Somme from Amiens, into Péronne and then on to Roisel. From Roisel a single-track railway ran to Hargicourt, three miles behind the Hindenburg Line. A single-track line operating both up and down had a theoretical capacity of 48 trains per day, 24 in each direction. Double track offered 72 train paths each way, assuming that the destination railhead had the capacity for them. Single-track rail was a risky option – if

65 Brown, op. cit., p.143.
66 W.J.K. Davies, *Light Railways of the First World War*, cited in Brown op. cit., p.145.
67 R. Bonham-Smith, 'Railway Transport Arrangements in France', p.48.
68 Taylor, op. cit., p.708.
69 War Office, *Statistics 1914-1920*, p.607.
70 Sir H. Rawlinson, War Journal, 5 & 6 September 1918, Churchill College RWLN 1/11.
71 Another route was open running south to Péronne. War Diary, Assistant Quartermaster General Fourth Army, Army Administrative Situation Map 8 October 1918, TNA WO95/445.

the service became disrupted by sabotage, derailment or track repair, the even procession of trains would be significantly affected. Lost time remained lost, however, especially when the arrival window was constrained by matters such as hours of darkness per day, increasing as the Hundred Days progressed.[72] A light 'Decauville' railway ran from Hargicourt to Bellicourt on the canal and thence on to Joncourt. The supply column of 25th Division believed, however, that 'a great waste of time and labour … and considerable losses' were incurred using this route 'from pilfering and … trucks overturning'.[73] The meeting of standard gauge and light railway staff was also not always one of mutual co-operation. On the day of the attack of 17 October, Fourth Army's Deputy Director Ordnance Service (DDOS) noted that light railway officers would not supply trucks until the number needed was known. The reality was, however, that it was impossible to know how many would be required until the standard gauge train had arrived and what was aboard could be assessed. Light trains were departing before stores could be loaded.[74] Stores and ammunition were not the only things carried by rail, of course. Troop movements were a significant element, and by the start of October 16 divisions had been moved to Fourth Army, and ten from it.[75]

Table 3.1 XI Corps railheads for 9 October 1918 (LR = light railway, HT = horse transport)

	6 October			17 October
	Railhead	**LR to**	**Onwards**	**Railhead**
Corps	Montigny Farm		HT	Essigny (from 18th)
1st Division	Péronne	Marteville	HT	Essigny (from 18th)
6th Division	Montigny Farm		HT	Roisel
46th Division	Montigny Farm		HT	Essigny (from 18th)

The railheads for most of the IX Corps divisions were approximately a minimum ten miles as the crow flies behind the start line for 9 October (with the exception of 1st Division, whose railhead was Péronne, divisional packs and ammunition being brought on via another light railway to Marteville, just south of Vermand). From these points bringing supplies forward relied on horse transport, there being no light railway system behind IX Corps. The situation had not improved by 17 October. An alternative route via St Quentin was by this time open, however, a railhead being established on the 18th at Essigny le Petit, just south of Fresnoy, but within the French area. This was still twelve miles in a straight line from the Selle, but on 17 October 1st Division's railhead was still some 20 miles in the rear of its jump-off.

In early September GHQ set out a railway policy. Outside of a few main feeder lines from base ports to army zones, within those zones there would be a main lateral line with the development of systems connected depending on the circumstances. There would be lines deemed temporary and permanent, but even the main lateral lines might have to be taken up and relayed ahead to economize on steel.[76] Fourth Army was concentrating on pushing its railheads forward for the

72 G. Clarke, personal communication, email dated 27 July 2016.
73 War Diary, 25th Division Supply Column, October 1918, TNA WO95/908.
74 War Diary, Deputy Director Ordnance Service Fourth Army, 17 October 1918, TNA WO95/452.
75 Henniker, op. cit., p.425. This slackened from the start of October onwards as armies kept the same composition.
76 Henniker, op. cit., p.437.

bound across the Selle rather than developing too many intermediate railheads which would soon (hopefully) be left behind. From experience of the German retreat of early 1917, the BEF knew that repairing the infrastructure damage would require large numbers of personnel and materials. Colonel Taylor observed that: 'Where the enemy have had time to destroy railway works, even though the destruction be confined to cutting the bridges, and demolishing signal equipment, electrical communications, and engine water supply installations, the possible rate of advance is very slow indeed'.[77] Embankments had to be rebuilt, bridges restored, new rails laid, and detraining points created – the Essigny railhead beyond St Quentin was established with six lines. Whilst the railway yard at St Quentin had been found nearly intact, the bridge over the canal that delivered trains to it had been blown. This was opened on 15 October, having taken eleven days work by 2nd Battalion Canadian Railway Troops to repair. The 56 foot girders weighing five tons requiring replacement to span the stream posed particular problems. A 35-ton steam crane proved to have too short a boom, and manually operated winches had to be used. Canadian relationships with their French engineer counterparts were sometimes tetchy. On 28 October the Canadians were called to a bridge just beyond Essigny at Fonsommes which the French were concerned was not safe. The Canadians were irritated to find that their allies had undermined the structure themselves whilst clearing debris, and had to replace the rails and shore up the bridge abutments at each embankment.[78]

From the start of October the 1st Battalion Canadian Railway Troops had been working on the section of railway from Roisel to Marcoing, just south of Cambrai. Brief snapshots of their work indicate the difficulties faced. 'Most of this track had been badly destroyed by the enemy, the rails and sleepers had been forced from the roadbed and there were many bad craters'. The double-track bridge at Epehy on this route had been completely destroyed and required rebuilding. Infuriatingly, further north near Villers-Plouich 'a delayed-action mine exploded after both tracks were complete', although 'traffic was resumed within eight hours of the explosion', the company nearby having begun work within five minutes of the blast. At one point a grave marked 'unknown German soldier' was located suspiciously between two tracks near Caudry and on investigation proved to be a mine.[79] On 24 October a delayed-action mine blew up at the Roisel railhead causing more disruption to supplies.[80] Nor were the enemy the only source of mishap. On 13 October at 02.00 a long troop train ran into the back of an ambulance train just outside Montigny Farm, causing the deaths of 13 with 30 injured. The line was, however, cleared by 'early daylight'.[81] The railway work was complex. Not only were there general labouring jobs such as building embankments and filling craters, there was the more specialist requirement of laying the steel, and the technical engineering needed for bridge repair. Further, there was the necessity for electrical and mechanical engineers not only to repair signals (telegraph engineers

77 Taylor, op. cit., p.709.

78 War Diary, 2nd Battalion Canadian Railway Troops, 28 October 1918, RG9 Militia and Defence, Series III-D-3, Volume 5012, Reel T-10861.

79 On October 31st a mine exploded at 03.00 on the line running south-west through the Cambrai suburbs actually half-way long a 34 car train operated by the Canadian Railway Troops. The crater was 40 feet wide and 25 deep, but trains were running again within 7 hours.

80 Many mines remained undetected. On the St Quentin-Busigny line 13 mines exploded 2-14 November, eight being at Bohain, and over the following six days five more exploded there. (Henniker, op. cit., p.440).

81 War Diary, 2nd Battalion Canadian Railway Troops, 13 October 1918, RG9 Militia and Defence, Series III-D-3, Volume 5012, Reel T-10861.

being needed as well to install station-to-station communication), but also to re-establish water supply. Every standard gauge steam locomotive required 2-4,000 gallons of water 'at intervals varying from about thirty miles in easy country to ten miles on very heavy grades', where each train might require four locomotives.[82]

In the XIII Corps area the railheads for the two divisions that would take part in the pursuit, the 25th and 66th, were at Roisel, approximately the same distance from the start of the pursuit as those of IX Corps. The railheads for 18th and 50th Divisions remained in Amiens (Poulainville) and only moved up as those divisions were required for action. The 25th and 66th Divisions both had the onward use of light railway, from whence the carry was by horse transport, a situation which had improved further for the attack on 17 October when the light railhead was at Joncourt. Onward transport to here was now largely by lorry, and whilst the distance was about 17 miles as the crow flies from the Selle for 66th Division in the north, in practice it was 29 miles by road via Bellicourt. II American Corps were supplied via the same railheads and light railway system. Progress in supply was beginning to limit tempo. Anticipating that the enemy would stand on a line east of the Selle, Rawlinson wrote in his journal on 9 October: 'I shall have to wait a day or two to get railways forward and guns up to bombard the line'.[83] The next day he seemed even more worried: 'We are getting a long way from our rail heads and must call a halt until we get our railways through'.[84] On the third day of the Pursuit his view of the logistic problem became even more negative. Driving himself around the forward areas he saw with his own eyes: 'The damage done to the railway at Bohain is serious and very complete so it will greatly delay us'. He declared himself 'not satisfied with the progress made by our railways', and, fair or not, he took his irritation out on handy scapegoats: 'I told the transport people what I thought of them this evening'.[85]

Divisional requirements were predictable due to the 'divisional pack' system adopted early in the war. One 'Geddes' train of divisional pack per two divisions was approximately 25 per cent of overall requirement for cargo per day, total rail demand being made most variable by ammunition trains, the need for which would fluctuate as the battle progressed or not. Ammunition was not usually handled in the same place as other stores, yet had to be in the same vicinity. A railhead such as Roisel needed to cope with about 12 trains per day in the vicinity.[86] On 15 October the strength of the divisional pack for 66th Division delivered there was 10,797 all ranks and 2,247 animals. However, an additional burden was liberated French citizens. On the 11th, the division distributed 1,536 sets of rations to the citizens of Avelu, Maretz, Elincourt and Serain, with double rations for invalids and infants. The next day 2,464 rations were similarly distributed at which point, no doubt to 66th Division's relief, XIII Corps took over responsibility. This respite was short, however, for on 18 October the 1,000 civilians liberated in Le Cateau were deemed to 'urgently require bread, meat, cheese, jam and tea'. It was decided by the division that 'liberal issues' of these commodities were to be made 'irrespective of any scale'.[87] (The plight of the residents of Le Cateau had been identified as early as 13 October as 'starving'. 35 Squadron RAF described how 'our machines went up repeatedly and dropped food into the town; seventeen trips being made during

82 E.P. Anderson, 'The Railway Organization of an Army in War', p.505.
83 Sir H. Rawlinson, War Journal, 9 October 1918, Churchill College RWLN 1/11.
84 Sir H. Rawlinson, War Journal, 10 October 1918, Churchill College RWLN 1/11.
85 Sir H. Rawlinson, War Journal, 11 October 1918, Churchill College RWLN 1/11.
86 G. Clarke, personal communication, email dated 27 July 2016.
87 War Diary, 66th Divisional Train ASC, 11-18 October 1918, TNA WO95/3133.

Table 3.2 XIII and II American Corps railheads for 9 October 1918 (LR = light railway, HT = horse transport, MT = motor transport)

	9 October			17 October		
	Railhead	**LR to**	**Onwards**	**Railhead**	**LR to**	**Onwards**
XIII Corps troops	Epehy		HT & MT	Epehy		MT
18th Division artillery	Poulainville/		HT & MT	Poulainville/		MT
	Quinconce		HT	Epehy		MT
25th Division artillery	Roisel	Bellicourt	HT	Roisel	Joncourt	HT & MT
				Roisel	Joncourt	MT
50th Division artillery	Quinconce	Villers-Faucon	HT	Epehy		MT
				Epehy		MT
66th Division	Roisel	Bellicourt	HT	Roisel		MT
27th (Am) Division	Roisel	Bellicourt	HT	Roisel		MT
30th (Am) Division	Roisel	Bellicourt	HT	Roisel	Joncourt	MT

the afternoon on this mission'.)[88] The Assistant Director Ordnance Services (ADOS) of IX Corps reported, however, that during the period 6-16 October 'very few req[uirements] of troops [were] beyond ordinary scale'.[89]

It was undoubtedly a blessing for the logistics system that the BEF had largely moved away from lengthy bombardments prior to attacks. This reduced the demand for artillery ammunition by about a third in comparison with 1916.[90] At the height of demand on the Western Front, the artillery requirement for battle reached one train load of ammunition per quarter-mile of front.[91] In contrast with 1916, however, the location of dumps for the artillery were constantly changing. There was also criticism that such dumps were 'not well laid out or sited', this due to 'the difficulties of moving warfare, labour shortage and unpunctuality of trains'.[92] Corps artillery dumps were very congested and separation of ammunition was 'almost impossible to do satisfactorily owing to enormous turnover'.[93] This situation continued and on 21 October it was noted that there were 'great delays in arrival of trains', which made 'conditions very trying for ordnance officers owing to large numbers of trucks to be off-loaded and late working hours'.[94] Similarly, 18th Division's Ammunition Column (DAC) recorded that: 'Being continually on the move enforced much hard work on men and horses – the latter standing the extra work extremely well'.[95] One further task that fell on DACs was the need to collect ammunition from gun positions abandoned in the swift advance. During the period 1-18 October the DAC of 66th Division salved 8,700 18-pounder and 3,000 4.5-inch rounds from vacated gun positions now in the divisional rear. Over the same period

88 'Historical data concerning No. 35 Squadron Royal Air Force', TNA AIR1/173/15/164/1.
89 War Diary, Assistant Director Ordnance Services IX Corps, October 1918, TNA WO95/844.
90 Boff, op. cit., location 2746.
91 Anderson, op. cit., p.503.
92 War Diary Assistant Director Ordnance Services IX Corps, 6-16 October 1918 TNA WO95/844.
93 War Diary Assistant Director Ordnance Services IX Corps, 22-31 October 1918 TNA WO95/844.
94 War Diary Assistant Director Ordnance Services IX Corps, 17-21 October 1918 TNA WO95/844.
95 War Diary, 18th Division Ammunition Column October 1918, TNA WO95/2026.

8,000 18-pounder and 2,800 4.5-inch rounds were received and 16,000 18-pounder and 3,500 4.5-inch rounds were transported onwards to the divisional artillery. [96]

The demands on motor transport were many and various.[97] Ammunition was still a major component of load. Amidst this heavy demand, random burdens would drop on motor transport without warning. As noted in the previous chapter, on 7 October IX Corps decided that 2 Infantry Brigade would be used as a 'mobile striking force … to be carried in lorries ready at 3 hours' notice'.[98] The Senior Mechanical Transport Officer (SMTO) no doubt received this order with a glum face as 120 lorries would be required, to be found by taking 30 from each Divisional Motor Transport Company. (The same sudden demands could happen on the railways. The order that captured guns be sent to rear was assessed on 18 October as requiring 300 trucks out of a system already short of rolling stock).[99] On the 13th the mood of the SMTO of IX Corps mood would have darkened further during an inspection with the Corps AQMG of forward areas. 'The condition of the roads as affecting Mechanical Transport has become very serious', he recorded, as indeed the supply of roadstone was dwindling.[100] He continued: 'A large number of lorries are becoming ditched all along the roads, so lessening our carrying capacity'.[101] Roadstone, of course, had to come by train. And it was not simply a deficiency in lorries, but also personnel that was a challenge. On 19 October concern was raised over the fact that 'E' Siege Park was 179 men deficient – 'Owing to the heavy pressure of work it is more than one man's capabilities to look after a 3-ton lorry, in consequence the mechanical efficiency is bound to deteriorate'.[102] Illness was of course one reason for understaffing. 66th Divisional Train noted on 20 October the 'prevalence of disease in the re-occupied areas from Serain to Le Cateau', and had started to issue two tablets of quinine a day to its troops. It was particularly handicapped by the so-called Spanish Flu with a large 'number of men in hospital with that disease, which has been aggravated by the wet weather and lack of accommodation, the men more frequently sleeping in the open than under shelter'.[103]

Despite these problems, supply of ammunition for the fighting on 17 October went well. In the days before the attack, the Supply Column of 6th Division was deploying 30 lorries daily to divisional supplies, up to about 40 on ammunition, and 20-25 on other carries.[104] 1st Division in contrast over the same days used up to 30 lorries on supplies, but had probably 25 fewer lorries than 6th Division and was carrying little ammunition.[105] On the 17th itself, 96 lorries stood by to carry ammunition to the divisional artillery that would fire the second barrage on IX Corps front, moving up the Bohain to Vaux-Andigny road as soon as the infantry attack went in. The scale of the carry required is indicated by the fact that the divisional guns fired up to 12.00 that morning: '18-p[ounde]r – 66,000 rounds. 60-p[ounde]r – 4,170 rounds. 4.5-inch How[itzer] – 10,400 rounds. 6-inch How[itzer] – 14,100 rounds. 6-inch gun – 390 rounds. 8-inch How[itzer] – 1,400 rounds.

96 War Diary, 66th Division Ammunition Column October 1918, TNA WO95/3128.
97 In November 1918 the BEF had 26,809 lorries operating on the Western Front. (*Statistics*, p.595).
98 War Diary, IX Corps Senior Motor Transport Officer, 7 October 1918, TNA WO95/846.
99 War Diary, Deputy Director Ordnance Services Fourth Army, 18 October 1918, TNA WO95/452. The BEF actually had provided enough rolling stock for its own needs, but pooling meant that it was making up the shortfall experienced by the French and Americans. (Henniker, op. cit., pp.424-5).
100 To construct a railhead and its associated hardstanding, 20 train-loads of stone were needed. (Henniker, op. cit., p.167.
101 War Diary, IX Corps Senior Motor Transport Officer, 13 October 1918, TNA WO95/846.
102 War Diary, IX Corps Senior Motor Transport Officer, 19 October 1918, TNA WO95/846.
103 War Diary, 66th Divisional Train ASC, 20 October 1918, TNA WO95/3133.
104 War Diary, 6th Division Supply Column, October 1918, TNA WO95/848.
105 War Diary, 1st Division Supply Column, October 1918, TNA WO95/847.

9.2-inch How[itzer] 1,530 rounds, 13-p[ounder]r – 3,245 rounds'.[106] In XIII Corps, 73 lorries were engaged in moving ammunition on 8 October, and 168 were involved in carrying shells to forward dumps on the 13th, including 100 loaned from Fourth Army. One hundred and fifty of Fourth Army's lorries were similarly engaged drawing ammunition from Tincourt and Epehy on 18 October and delivering them to divisional ammunition refilling points, the same the next day. Motor transport itself, of course, created further supply issues – the 3-ton lorries of 25th Division supply column consumed 16,716 gallons of petrol in October and the 30-cwt lorries 1,624.[107] On top of illness the stress was immense – lorries were in continual movement and on 15 October 25th Division's Supply Column noted: 'The weather is bad and this combined with the very long hours men are working occasions a very great strain on all'. Eight miles per hour was the maximum, and often not more than five was achieved. A driver would likely spend twelve hours behind the wheel plus two hours unloading.[108] It was, however, stated: 'The morale of the men is excellent'.[109] It is fortunate that the RAF had achieved as much local command of the skies as it had – if not, logistics near the front would have been a slower and bloody experience. As it was, the efforts of the German artillery caused problems during the Pursuit. Gunner Alexander Caseby, just across the Cambrai-Le Cateau road in Third Army's area, described how: 'We experienced difficulty in bringing up ammunition as our rear areas were being heavily shelled'.[110]

Sir Henry Rawlinson had delayed the start of the attack from 14/15 October because of the need to amass ammunition – indeed, his remarks imply that the number of guns available would be dependent on the amount of ammunition brought up. (There does not seem to have been much concern about the guns themselves. Fourth Army noted that repairs were 'well maintained' but there were a 'large number of condemnations from wear and scoring'.)[111] Moving the guns, although part of the logistic effort, was similarly not really an issue, although it took time. The artillery had their own transport. A battery of field artillery had almost as many drivers for the horse teams (70) as it had gunners (75). At the other end of the scale, a siege battery of four 9.2-inch howitzers had 66 drivers for lorries and 12 for caterpillars to pull the guns. How quickly, however, was the artillery brought up for the attack on 17 October? The heavy artillery of IX Corps was in action on 9 October. The following day it moved, the mobile 21 Brigade following 6th Division, the mixed 83 Brigade following 46th Division, with the mixed 79 Brigade under the Corps BGRA. 21 Brigade came into action east of Fresnoy, and 83 Brigade north of Bohain, later on 10 October. The 8-inch howitzer 12 and 14 Brigades were in action on the 12th, and the long-range 8-inch guns and 9.2-inch howitzers were brought up that day. On 14 October a 'slow bombardment' opened, and during the night of 14/15 October the 9.2-inch howitzers of 69 and 98 brigades were brought into action. The bombardment continued during 15-16 October. From the beginning of the move it thus took three days to get the bulk of heavy artillery of IX Corps into place, and a day or so longer for concerted action for the set-piece attack.[112] XIII Corps used both field and heavy artillery on 9 October, and notes that both divisional artilleries moved that day, as well as heavy artillery. The mixed 76 Brigade positioned itself near Maretz and the 6-inch guns were sited to the north of Prémont. Sixty-six lorries of field gun ammunition were sent up during the day, and

106 War Diary, IX Corps Senior Motor Transport Officer, 17 October 1918, TNA WO95/846.
107 War Diary, 25th Division Supply Column, October 1918, TNA WO95/908.
108 G. Clarke, personal communication, email dated 27 July 2016.
109 War Diary, 25th Division Supply Column, 15 October 1918, TNA WO95/908.
110 A. Caseby, 'War Memoirs of a Gunner in the Royal Field Artillery', IWM Docs 70861, p.49.
111 War Diary, Deputy Director Ordnance Service Fourth Army, October 1918, TNA WO95/452.
112 War Diary, HQ Heavy Artillery IX Corps, 9-16 October 1918, TNA WO95/842.

later, more heavy artillery was ordered to move forward. On 10 October the field artillery moved again, and by the following day a full range of heavy artillery was in action harassing the enemy, the '48 hours bombardment' commencing on the 15th.[113] From the beginning of the move it took three days to get a full range of the heavy artillery of IX Corps into action. As the Australian Corps artillery noted, it was always able to support the advances closely, but 'the huge supply of ammunition required by the guns at each stage of the advance has entailed a great amount of labour by men, horses and lorries'. Gratifyingly, however: 'Very little difficulty has been experienced in maintaining an adequate supply'.[114]

There may have been no problem with artillery, but the heavy reliance on automated small arms fire was being to become an issue. By 9 October DDOS Fourth Army was concerned about the supply of Lewis guns. Only 56 complete and 26 incomplete guns were in stock. Ten days later the situation was that only 262 were 'available and due', 250 more being requested.[115] The urgency of the shortage is indicated by the fact that in October 50th Division alone had to supply 66 Lewis guns to its battalions to replace those lost in action.[116]

Fourth Army Planning

Fourth Army's attack on the Selle would take place within the wider allied theatre strategy. Sir Douglas Haig had met with Marshal Foch at Mouchy le Châtel on 10 October, and Foch had produced a new 'Directive'. This reiterated 'three convergent operations'. The first was in Belgium (the Flanders Group of French, British and Belgian Armies); secondly in the Solesmes-Wassigny area (British); and thirdly the Aisne-Meuse (French and American). The first and the third struggling, the 'most profitable to exploit' was the Solesmes-Wassigny thrust. Haig noted proudly in his dairy that 'the success of the British Armies is to be exploited to the full', and that Debeney's *First Army*, which lay to the right flank of Fourth Army, would be reinforced to assist, this 'covering my right'.[117] GHQ issued orders for a resumption of the general offensive, and Haig continued in his diary on the 12th: 'At 11 am I held a conference with Army Commanders and General Kavanagh, Commanding Cavalry Corps … I explained Foch's *general plan* and told them how I proposed to operate with the British Army'.[118] The first important matter was logistics – to 'complete our railway communications on the Cambrai-Le Cateau front'. These were 'being pushed on very satisfactorily' (it is not clear whether Rawlinson, given his privately recorded concerns, openly disagreed). 'As soon as these enabled adequate ammunition to be brought up', Haig continued: '*our main advance* will be made between the Scheldt and the Sambre Rivers', then 'joining hands with our Second Army and cutting off the Lille salient'.[119] Fourth Army was 'to establish itself on the general line Wassigny-Le Cateau, and, in co-operation with the French *First Army*, was to push forward strong advance guards to the line of the Sambre and Oise Canal'.[120] Haig was highly optimistic. On 12

113 War Diary, HQ Royal Artillery XIII Corps, 9-15 October 1918, TNA WO95/902.
114 War Diary, HQ GOCRA 1st Anzac Corps, 6 October 1918, AWM4 Item No. 13/4/17.
115 War Diary, Deputy Director Ordnance Service Fourth Army, October 1918, TNA WO95/452.
116 War Diary, Deputy Assistant Director Ordnance Service, 50th Division, October 1918, TNA WO95/2816.
117 G. Sheffield & J. Bourne (eds), *Douglas Haig – War Diaries and Letters*, p.472.
118 Montgomery states this conference occurred on the 11th.
119 Sheffield & Bourne, op. cit., p.473.
120 Montgomery, op. cit., p.203. Whilst the Fourth Army was thereby to cross the Selle, Third Army to the north was to establish itself on the river and secure passages, whilst First Army would protect its flank.

October he had written: 'The Enemy is in such a state that we can run all kinds of risks without any chance of Enemy hitting back in any force'.[121] On Fourth Army's front, however, Archibald Montgomery was clear that due care would take the place of 'all kinds of risks'. It was 'evident' that the German position on the Selle 'was too strong to be rushed, and that it could only be taken by an organised attack, adequately supported by artillery'.[122] Having met his army commanders, Haig visited General Cameron Shute of V Corps, Third Army, which had suffered a recent repulse, and his risk-tolerant view mellowed in line with Mongomery's, recognising that 'we seem to be in presence of a hostile rear guard', but that 'as soon as we organise an attack with adequate artillery support the Enemy will fall back'.[123]

On the Fourth Army front, it was clearly important to maintain tempo, but it was soon realised that the hopes of the 11th that the major operation could take place on 14 or 15 October could not be fulfilled. Rawlinson met with the three corps commanders on 13 October at his HQ at Eterdigny ('after church', it being Sunday), and Fourth Army began to issue orders, firstly in the form of artillery instructions. As Andrew Simpson has described, by this stage of the war Army would issue general instructions, particularly concerning artillery, and Corps would then produce detailed plans, devolving varying degrees of responsibility down to their divisions.[124] Fourth Army's artillery instructions occupied two pages.[125] This specified 'vigorous counter battery work', the bombardment by heavy howitzers of 'important localities to be selected by Corps', and 'normal harassing fire' on the enemy's communications, approaches to villages, and important cross roads. Army specified several roads/railways on the east bank of the Selle in each corps area that should be 'engaged in enfilade'. Six-inch guns were to be positioned 'well forward' to deal with the villages on the west bank of the Sambre-Oise canal, and the railways.[126] Army was, therefore, issuing instructions that operationalised GHQ's instructions to push advanced guards to the canal.

The following day, Fourth Army indicated the date of the attack (set now for 17 October) verbally to corps commanders, and specified the objectives, simply drawn as lines on a map.[127] Both British corps, for topographical reasons, would take over parts of the line of II American Corps. The orders of 14 October became more prescriptive concerning the artillery. Given that surprise in terms of whether an attack was coming or not could not be achieved, only the date and time could be kept secret. A two-day bombardment was ordered, continuing until zero, in which 'free use should be made of Gas shells'.[128] The start line bombardment supporting the main attack would be 200 yards in front of the infantry for the 18-pounder and 400 yards for the 4.5-inch howitzer barrages, and the distance and timing of lifts were also set (100 yards per three minutes).[129] Corps were left to decide the matter of protective barrages on the Red line (first objective), but the time for departure

121 Sheffield & Bourne, op. cit., p.472.
122 Montgomery, op. cit., p.203.
123 Sheffield & Bourne, op. cit., p.473.
124 A. Simpson, 'The Operational Role of British Corps Command on the Western Front', (see also Simpson, *Directing Operations: British Corps Command on the Western Front 1914-18.*)
125 War Diary, HQ Fourth Army, Order No. 20/39(G), 13 October 1918, TNA WO95/439.
126 Corps were authorised to maintain the following number of rounds per gun. 18-pounder & 4.5-inch howitzer (400); 60-pounder & 6-inch howitzer (300); 8 & 9.2-inch howitzer, and 6-inch gun (200); and 12-inch howitzer (100).
127 War Diary, HQ Fourth Army, Order No. 20/40(G), 14 October 1918, TNA WO95/439.
128 War Diary, HQ Fourth Army, Order No. 20/41(G), 14 October 1918, TNA WO95/439.
129 Army set the types of shells to be used. Shrapnel/HE with 106 fuzes in the barrage; 101 fuzes without delay in the bombardment; and shrapnel or HE with 106 fuzes in harassing fire. (War Diary, HQ Fourth Army, Order No. 20/41(G), 14 October 1918, TNA WO95/439).

from this line was set for zero+336 minutes. Tanks were allotted, and 5 Brigade RAF was ordered to liaise directly with corps concerning covering the advance of the tanks to the start line. The timing of the customary 05.20 zero hour was set on 16 October,[130] a matter which should have been no surprise to the enemy.

General Braithwaite of IX Corps met with his divisional commanders at Magny-la-Fosse on both 13 and 14 October. On the 13th, 14th and 15th three sets of artillery orders were issued. The first two released artillery from corps reserve to the divisions, stating that the command of all heavy artillery would remain with the BGRA, i.e. at corps level.[131] After the conference of 14 October a second artillery order was issued, concerning the distribution of guns to the divisions.[132] 6th Division were to command the guns of 1st, 6th, & 32nd Divisions (24 batteries of 18-pounder guns, and 8 of 4.5-inch howitzers); 46th Division had three 13-pounder and 16 18-pounder batteries, and three 4.5-inch howitzer batteries. The composition of the heavy artillery was 36 60-pounder guns, 74 6-inch howitzers, 24 8-inch and 18 9.2-inch howitzers, and 8 6-inch guns. In addition there were also four of each of following captured guns: 77, 105 and 150-mm, these being ordered to shell Hennechies Wood southeast of Regnicourt with Yellow Cross (mustard) gas shells.[133] Divisions were given the responsibility for the siting of the guns and preparing barrage maps, but it was specified that as 1st Division passed through the 6th, CRA 1st Division would assume command of the artillery, three brigades being detailed to 'move forward in close support of the advance of the 1st Division.[134] The orders issued on 15 October concerned rate of fire and types of shell, and the artillery moves to support the advance from the first to second objective. On the same day, the orders for the machine gun barrage (coordinated by the Corps Machine Gun Officer, but devised by the divisional machine gun officers), cavalry and tanks were issued.[135]

The 46th Division attack on the right was given a final objective, whilst 6th Division attacking on the left would secure an intermediate objective, where 1st Division, which had last seen action 13 days previously, would pass through. The objective of 46th Division was to secure a flank to Riquerval and Hennechies Woods on the Bohain to Andigny-les-Fermes road which passed through Regnicourt, preventing counterattack from that direction. The left of the division's attack would breach the *HWL I* which ran in wired trenches south from Vaux-Andigny station across the Bellevue spur. The right of the division's attack would take the section that ran south-west from the base of the spur across the valley and then south again to the west of Regnicourt, the portion which had been ineffectively attacked by 11th Essex on 12 October.[136] The objective of 6th Division was the forcing of the *HWL I* and the taking of the Bellevue spur and the ground to the north. A line would then be reached between Andigny-les-Fermes and the ground in front of la Vallée Mulâtre (Blue Line). The *HWL II* positions would be overcome and la Vallée Mulâtre itself secured by 1st Division who would proceed to capture Wassigny and exploit towards the Sambre-Oise Canal. Riquerval and Hennechies woods, and indeed, the whole Andigny Forest would be pinched out by

130 War Diary, HQ Fourth Army, Order No. 20/42(G), 16 October 1918, TNA WO95/439.
131 War Diary, HQ IX Corps, 12 & 13 October 1918, Orders No. 34 & 35 TNA WO95/837.
132 War Diary, HQ IX Corps, 14 October 1918, TNA WO95/837.
133 Mark Whisler states the barrage was fired by 330 field guns and howitzers, and 192 heavy guns and howitzers, as well as 128 Vickers machine-guns. (Whisler, op. cit., p.242).
134 These were the two brigades RFA of 1st Division (15 & 29); and 298th Army Brigade RFA.
135 War Diary, HQ IX Corps, Oder No. 145, 15 October 1918, TNS WO95/837.
136 The map of the division's attack suggests that in front of 139 Brigade this was not a continuous line of trenches but a series of positions at various angles to each other. (War Diary, HQ 46th Infantry Division, October 1918, TNA WO95/2666).

the end of the day, the French *15th Corps* attacking on its southern side between the forest and the Sambre-Oise Canal, shaking hands with 1st Division on its far side near Wassigny. The threat of envelopment from this pincer movement would force a German withdrawal from the forest. These objectives were to prove highly optimistic to achieve in one day.

The plan, however, reflected two learning points from the abortive actions of 12 October. The first was that the attack at zero would not include a frontal assault on Riquerval Wood. The second was that there was similarly to be no frontal assault to take the Bellevue spur. Braithwaite directed that the ridge was to be taken in a south-easterly direction, along its length. This must have been discussed at the conference at Army HQ on the 13th, and communicated to the divisional commanders on the same day. To facilitate this, Army ordered the corps to take over 2,000 yards of the II American Corps line to the north, so that the attack could start at Vaux-Andigny. The order for this move was given on 14 October, to take place on the night of the 14th/15th.[137] The 6th Division regarded the change to a south-easterly axis of attack as a 'very pretty tactical move', a manoeuvre in which a 'great deal of enfilade fire' would be brought to bear.[138] The first part of the scheme had the threefold advantage of pinning the infantry in the woods to a location where an immediate attack was not being made; dissipating the strength of the enemy counter-barrage; and avoiding strong defensive features. The scheme as a whole also delivered the maximum force of the infantry attack in a relatively small area, whilst major attacks were undertaken on either side.

XIII Corps issued its first artillery instructions on 13 October, specifying objectives (based on the lines on the map issued by Army) and the artillery units that would be employed.[139] The following day there was a corps conference,[140] after which further instructions about the barrage were issued, passing on Army's specific instructions. It was added: 'The bombardment would be spread over 48 hours previous to the attack and will be accompanied by strong harassing fire. There will be no hurricane bombardment immediately preceding the assault'. Unlike IX Corps, half of the two-page order was taken up with instructions to the attached 35 Squadron RAF concerning contact patrols, and the smoke bombing of the left edge of the battle area adjacent to V Corps, Third Army.[141] On 15 October, when the 'Army Commander called in (the) afternoon' on 66th Division,[142] another set of orders was produced which unlike those of IX Corps nearly exclusively referred to the bombardment of specific locations by heavy artillery.[143] Although there was a reference under 'Counter Preparation' to CRAs liaising with divisional commanders, there was more prescription of the activities of divisional artillery in the XIII Corps barrage.[144] 25th Divisional artillery with three army brigades RFA would support 50th Division, 18th Divisional artillery with two army brigades RFA would support 66th Division. The surviving corps orders do not refer to the pushing forward of artillery following the attack, presumably due to the issue of the bridging of the Selle.

137 War Diary, HQ Fourth Army, Order No. 20/40(G), 14 October 1918, TNA WO95/439.
138 T.O. Marden, *A Short History of the Sixth Division*, p.70.
139 War Diary, HQ XIII Corps, Instructions No. 2 Series B, 13 October 1918, TNA WO95/897.
140 War Diary, HQ 66th Division, 14 October 1918, TNA WO95/3122.
141 War Diary, HQ XIII Corps, Instructions No. 3 Series B, 14 October 1918, TNA WO95/897.
142 War Diary, HQ 66th Division, 15 October 1918, TNA WO95/3122.
143 The following points were to be targeted by heavy howitzers: the brickworks, railway triangle, railway from Le Cateau station to St Benin, petroleum factory, sugar factory, Bazuel, Le Roux farm, Le Quennelet farm, various sunken roads, and targets in the Richemont valley.
144 War Diary, HQ XIII Corps, Instructions No. 5 Series B, 15 October 1918, TNA WO95/897. Further artillery instructions were issued the following day.

Because of the inundations south of Le Cateau, which prevented the crossing of the river in a number of locations, the front of XIII Corps was also lengthened in the south by taking over 2,000 yards of the line of II American Corps, also on the night of 14/15 October. The infantry attack was to be made by the 50th Division on the right, and 66th Division on the left. The corps occupied an 8,000 yard front from St Souplet to Montay, but would only attack in two areas. 50th Division would make its crossings of the Selle between St Souplet and St Benin, where as noted footbridges were to be placed; 66th Division would cross north of Le Cateau and clear the town itself. This had the unfortunate effect of reducing the power of the XIII Corps attack, the two divisions being unable to support each other. The assault would also be unsupported on its left flank, as Third Army would not be attempting to cross the river until 02.00 on the 20th. It would, however, curtain off the enemy's observation of Fourth Army from the Forest ridge north-east of Montay with smoke, and mount a 'Chinese attack' in the form of a creeping barrage and the shelling of specific points. The intermediate objective for 50th Division (Red dotted line) was the Wassigny-Le Cateau road; the first objective proper (Red line) was the Mazinghien-la Jonquière farm ridge; the second objective (Blue line) was Bazuel and the high ground above the Richemont valley for 66th Division. When Rawlinson visited XIII Corps HQ on 15 October, he 'found 50 Div[ision] rather full of the difficulties of their attack, Jackson pointing out that he had only 800 yards on which he could start and that it was difficult to get his Div[ision] through so small a hole'. Rawlinson acknowledged his difficulty, writing: 'I admit there are risks'.[145] On the day before the battle opened he added: 'XIII Corps is my only anxiety'.[146]

II American Corps, with its line reduced on both flanks, also began to issue artillery instructions on 13 October,[147] and on the 14th issued a series of three sets of instructions.[148] The artillery support for II American Corps would again be provided by ten Australian artillery brigades.[149] There were approximately 90 18-pound field guns and 30 4.5-inch howitzers, and the heavy artillery comprised 24 60-pounder guns, 60 6-inch howitzers, and up to 12 9.2-inch howitzers.[150] The corps orders are largely indistinguishable from the British corps instructions, although they were issued in a more piecemeal fashion. At a divisional level, however, perhaps reflecting the anxiety concerning level of skill, 30th Division circulated a document entitled 'Tactical Instructions' on 14 October. This was based on extracts from 'a report of a brigade commander in our First Army', and stated that 'commanding officers of all grades will find many valuable points worthy of careful study'. The advice, all of it sound, ranged from the more sophisticated, e.g. the differential allocation of Stokes mortars and 37-mm guns between leading and second battalions; to the more standard issue of envelopment of machine gun nests; and to the rather banal statement: 'Rifle fire was used to its utmost; the men had been taught to fire as they advanced ... This was found to be of great

145 Sir H. Rawlinson, War Journal, 15 October 1918, Churchill College RWLN 1/11.

146 Sir H. Rawlinson, War Journal, 16 October 1918, Churchill College RWLN 1/11.

147 182-33.3 No. 3: Artillery Instructions, (Heavy artillery), 13 October 1918, *USAWW Vol. 7*, p.533.

148 II Corps AEF Instructions Series B, Nos. 1, 2 & Artillery Instructions No. 2, 14 October 1918, *USAWW Vol. 7*, pp.553-557.

149 4th Australian Artillery Division, supporting the 27th American Division, commanded the 5th & 4th (Left Group), 14th & 7th (Right Group) Brigades, with the 12th Army Brigade as mobile reserve, superimposed, advancing to just west of St Souplet at 06.38, sweeping the St Maurice valley. 5th Australian Artillery Division, supporting the 30th American Division, commanded the 13th & 8th (Right Group), and 10th & 11th (Left Group) Brigades, and 6th Army Brigade.

150 'Operations II Corps Artillery', 15 October 1918, *USAWW Vol. 7*, pp.579-580; Whisler, op. cit., p.242.

use'.[151] It is not that the instructions were inappropriate, far from it; it is the fact that it was thought necessary to issue them that is of note. Similarly, 27th Division issued 'Combat Instructions' the following day (one marked by a flurry of artillery orders).[152] Again, there were perfectly appropriate instructions therein concerning open warfare, but it was a different document to 30th Division's. Again, it is notable that 27th Division felt it necessary to issue them. It is also striking that whilst there was seemingly a clear awareness of the need for tactical improvement, this was centred at a divisional level, and II Corps was not involved. 27th Division also issued 'Instructions for Brigade Commanders'.[153] This 18 point document concluded with Major-General O'Ryan stating: 'The foregoing are suggested and are not intended as specific directions which might hamper those charged with carrying on the local operations'. However, with comments such as: 'I know from observation the tendency is toward insufficient elasticity of movement in such operations', it is clear that in terms of the slow movement of American forces during the Pursuit, O'Ryan was anxious about the performance of his brigade commanders. All the documents are evidence of the need for learning in a still novice corps. Finally, on 16 October, II Corps sent out orders concerning contact patrols to be operated by 3rd Squadron Australian Flying Corps, a document very similar to that issued by XIII Corps. In terms of its preparatory orders over the four days prior to the attack, given the difficulties that would arise over the next two days for the corps, those emanating from corps HQ cannot be faulted.

The American advance, the most straightforward on paper that day, would be in an east-north-easterly direction, with the attacks of the two British corps fanning out on either side. Unlike IX Corps, the Americans had the headwaters of the Selle in front of them, although it only constituted a real obstacle in the northern area of their attack. After crossing the river the intermediate objective on the ground rising away from the river included the hamlet of l'Arbre de Guise on the Wassigny-Le Cateau road (Red dotted line – the intermediate objective) some 2,500-3,000 yards from the river.[154] In achieving this, both *HWL I* and *HWL II* would have been taken. From reconnaissance of the ground it was clear that this attack would be 'arduous'.[155] The first objective proper was a line some 1,000 yards further, on a second low ridge to the east of Jonc de Mer farm (Red line). The Wassigny-Le Cateau road that was the intermediate objective lay on the top of the first ridge in the British sector to the north, whereas in the American sector the road lay on the shoulder of the ridge. Not to progress beyond there would leave the enemy still on the higher ground. The final objective was some 2,500 yards further on including the villages of Mazinghien and Ribeauville (Brown Line). This was on another ridge with a view over Catillon and the Sambre-Oise Canal, towards which there was to be exploitation. Hopefulness, misplaced as events showed, was implied by the specific instruction that this exploitation was to start at 6 hours and three minutes after zero.

151 230-32.15: Memorandum, 'Tactical Instructions' 30th Division AEF, 14 October 1918, *USAWW Vol. 7*, pp.560-562.
152 182-33.3 No.3: Memorandum, 'Combat Instructions' 27th Division AEF, 15 October 1918, *USAWW Vol. 7*, pp.587-589.
153 182-33.3 No.3: Memorandum, 'Instructions for Brigade Commanders', 15 October 1918, *USAWW Vol. 7*, pp.590-593.
154 This hamlet stood at crossroads on either side of the road that ran downhill to the Selle. The American War Department later claimed that the name Arbre Guernon, appearing on British maps, was an error, and the real name of the location was Arbre de Guise. 'Arbre Guernon is a large and conspicuous tree', the monograph noted haughtily. (*Operations of the 2nd American Corps in the Somme Offensive*, p.30). On modern maps Arbre Guernon denotes the area sloping up from the river to the hamlet.
155 Montgomery, op. cit., p.216.

The dividing line between the two divisions at St Martin Rivière left 30th Division with a greater problem. The boundary between 27th Division and XIII Corps now lay in the northern part of St Souplet and whilst the enemy still held the eastern outskirts of the village, 27th Division's frontage was close to the Selle. From near St Martin (the village itself was actually on the east bank) the American line ran in a loop south–west away from the river uphill to la Haie Menneresse. This meant that not only were the Germans in possession of all of Molain and the west bank to Vaux-Andigny to the south, at the furthest point 30th Division had to cross 2,000 yards of ground before reaching the river at Molain. Recognizing the likelihood that the attack would be heavily contested, as part of the barrage, the 113th and 115th Machine Gun Battalions were to fire for 21 minutes after zero on the eastern edge of St Souplet, Molain and the road in between them. On the other side of the river both divisions also faced the fortified railway embankment that was the *HWL I*, much closer to the start line in 27th Division's area, which was of varying height. At the railway bridge beyond St Souplet in the path of 27th Division's attack, for instance, the ground rose steeply from the river and where the road to l'Arbre de Guise passed under the railway, the *HWL I* was on embankments 20 feet above the road. Each division would attack on a 2,000 yard front with two battalions of both its regiments, one battalion being in support.

The planning of the battle, therefore, followed the process outlined by Andrew Simpson. Army set the date and time of the attack, and sent out instructions that set guidelines for the coordination of the artillery of the three corps yet also included specific targets. Corps incorporated these in enhanced instructions sent out to its divisions, who planned both their barrages and specific targets based on local knowledge, and their infantry attacks. From the meeting of Rawlinson with his corps commanders, the planning and preparation time was only four days. In comparison, the planning for Fourth Army's attack on the St Quentin Canal had taken 11 days, and the planning for the Battle of the Sambre would take six.[156] The fact that a set-piece attack could take place so quickly is a testimony to the efforts of the engineers, the railways and motor transport. The objectives were ambitious, but Rawlinson had 'no doubt things will go well even if we do not reach all the objectives right up to the Canal'.[157]

Intelligence

Over the days between 8 and 16 October, Fourth Army attempted to build up a picture of the enemy's intentions. This included: (i) the defences being prepared against them; (ii) who might be opposing them; and (iii) what shape they were in. The intelligence was compiled from the interrogation of German prisoners, the reports of French citizens, aerial reconnaissance, and infantry patrols, each of varying utility. As will be seen, aerial observation and photography were rendered very difficult by adverse weather, whilst infantry patrols faced the difficulty of being under constant observation from the heights on the eastern bank.

On 8 October Fourth Army's intelligence summary recorded that French prisoners of war who had escaped on the 6th stated that the enemy had begun 'a line of trenches in the area E. of BOHAIN – REGNICOURT – VAUX-ANDIGNY', 2.8 metres broad and one deep, with a belt of wire in front'. This was clearly the nascent *Hermann Stellung I*. Army noted that: 'The work had not progressed sufficiently to appear on the latest photographs available', although a photograph from 5 October, whilst being 'indistinct shows what appears to be a new line of defence consisting

156 Simpson, op. cit., p.220.
157 Sir H. Rawlinson, War Journal, 15 October 1918, Churchill College RWLN 1/11.

of artificial shell-holes' east of Le Cateau station, these being rifle pits or machine gun nests of the *HWL II*.[158] On 9 October,[159] more escaped French prisoners were reported as adding that in Riquerval Wood 'the trees are felled to make an abbatis' and that there was wire 4-5 metres wide. The acquisition of this information makes the decision to assault the wood the following day with only one battalion less explicable. Air photography, however indistinct, began to show the *HWL I* taking shape in the form of perceptible trench lines. 'These indications seem to point to a line of defence along the LE CATEAU – ST SOUPLET railway and then past VAUX-ANDIGNY to the BOIS de RIQUERVAL'.[160] On 10 October, air reports suggested that 'the enemy are retiring in apparent confusion and many of the villages and roads leading east are blocked with troops and transport'. Information as to where the retirement might stop was confusing. Many prisoners suggested 'a general report was current that they were to retire to a line near VALENCIENNES'. Other captured on the 9th near Caudry were more accurate, stating that 'it was the intention of the Germans to withdraw to a line about 10 kilometres east of CAUDRY'. The trenches at Vaux-Andigny had been confirmed 'in detail' by air photographs on 9 October, but at the same time field guns and infantry were seen heading east through Wassigny, i.e. behind and away from the *Hermann Stellung I*. Fourth Army concluded that the Germans intended 'only to make a temporary stand on the VALLENCIENNES – LE CATEAU line'. On the same day, Army HQ published extracts from GHQ Summary No.646 dated two days previously. This circulated a captured German order of *119th Infantry Division* dated 29 August. Whilst it referred to the defence of the Somme valley, it was no doubt published in terms of its relevance as to how the enemy would defend the Selle valley. The defence would be based on infantry and machine-gun fire, single machine guns, both light and heavy pushed forward to have 'undisputed command' of the river, especially at 'favourable crossing places'. These would be permanently manned – 'shell-proof emplacements are not necessary; the chief requisite is adequate concealment'. Further, 'skilful patrolling' was to prevent any British reconnaissance of the river.[161]

On 11 October, as the Pursuit was coming to a halt, the intelligence summary recorded that 'French civilians found in CAUDRY state that the enemy means to offer resistance along the River Selle' and that enemy prisoners 'stated that they had orders to withdraw to LE CATEAU, there to take up position'. Prisoners consistently referred, however, to further retirement to a line Bavai-Maubeuge-Namur. It was assumed, therefore, that the stand on the Selle would 'only be sufficiently prolonged to enable them to evacuate to the rear as much material as possible'. Air reconnaissance by now indicated a 'practically continuous trench' along the east bank of the river' 'which must have been very rapidly dug and implies considerable work by reserve troops'.[162] On 12 October, Fourth Army first used the term *Hermann Stellung*. Civilians in Maurois reported the Germans to be constructing trenches on the far side of the railway north of Le Cateau, 'to hold with machine guns', where it was alleged that there were also gas cylinders, a proposition that Fourth Army was disinclined to believe. Air reconnaissance confirmed further trenches and rifle pits being dug, and 'thin wire' erected. Some lines appeared to be 'thinly held' whereas lines further south were 'strongly held'. Two civilians in Bertry, however, claimed that they had been told by an officer on 30 September that the enemy realised they were not strong enough to sustain further allied assaults

158 Fourth Army Intelligence Summary No. 294, 8 October 1918, TNA WO157/199.
159 This and the following dates all refer to the date of the published intelligence summary, i.e. the intelligence had been gathered the day before.
160 Fourth Army Intelligence Summary No. 295, 9 October 1918, TNA WO157/199.
161 Fourth Army Intelligence Summary No. 296, 10 October 1918, TNA WO157/199.
162 Fourth Army Intelligence Summary No. 297, 11 October 1918, TNA WO157/199.

and were planning to retire in three stages to the Le Cateau line, the Maubeuge line, and finally the German frontier. Fourth Army again concluded that the enemy 'would oppose any further advance by our Army for the time being, with all the strength at their disposal, while retirements are being carried out elsewhere'.[163] By this time, of course, the decision had already been made to force the Selle position with a set-piece attack.

On 13 October, when Rawlinson was meeting with his corps commanders, prisoners of the *185th Division* captured by Third Army reported that they had been ordered to hold the *Hermann Stellung* 'at all cost'. Whilst this only reinforced Fourth Army's view that 'the enemy intend to resist any further advance by our troops for the present', these sorts of exhortations had been heard before. Reports, however, continued to arrive of the strengthening of the Selle defences. French citizens reported increased wiring and 'machine gun posts camouflaged with stones' being built into the embankments of the railway on the east side of the river. Frustratingly, there had been no confirmatory photographic evidence since 9 October.[164] Rawlinson noted in his journal that day that: 'The Boche has brought 4 fresh Div[isions] into line since the day before yesterday'.[165] By 14 October locals were reporting even more trenches and belts of wire on both sides of the river at St Souplet but air observation that day (at last) was able to shed further light. The Riquerval Wood – Vaux-Andigny line was shown not to be continuous, and what was in fact the *HWL II* to be made up of 'odd groups of rifle pits'. The route of the *HWL I* was confirmed and new wire was noted near Le Cateau Station and the Fassiaux bridge.[166] Whilst more trenches were confirmed by air observation on the following day, much transport was seen going east through the town of Wassigny on the plateau between the Selle and the Sambre-Oise Canal. It was concluded that 'preparations are being made by the Germans to withdraw across the OISE if attacked in strength'.[167] Third Army photographs similarly indicated strengthening of trenches across the river.[168] The intelligence summary issued on 17 October, the day of the opening of the Battle of the Selle, finally concluded that the 'the positions presently occupied by the enemy are only of a temporary nature, and that a progressive retirement will shortly be carried out'.[169] The Official History states that the *Hermann Stellung* 'existed for the most part only on paper'. It also refers to a map that had been captured on 13 October showing the position. This map is only noted in Fourth Army's intelligence summaries on the day of the battle,[170] and the Official History continues:

> Air photographs taken on the 14th did not show any Le Cateau-St Souplet position, except for a few lengths of trenches, protected in places by wire, which extended as far as Vaux-Andigny, and some rifle pits in pairs on the high ground west of the Selle.[171]

This statement is clearly not accurate, and underestimates the enemy position. 11th Essex and 2nd Durham Light Infantry had already found this out only too starkly, encountering thick belts of barbed wire near Regnicourt in their ill-fated attack of 12 October.

163 Fourth Army Intelligence Summary No. 298, 12 October 1918, TNA WO157/199.
164 Fourth Army Intelligence Summary No. 299, 13 October 1918, TNA WO157/199.
165 Sir H. Rawlinson, War Journal, 13 October 1918, Churchill College RWLN 1/11.
166 Fourth Army Intelligence Summary No. 300, 14 October 1918, TNA WO157/199.
167 Fourth Army Intelligence Summary No. 301, 15 October 1918, TNA WO157/199.
168 Fourth Army Intelligence Summary No. 302, 16 October 1918, TNA WO157/199.
169 Fourth Army Intelligence Summary No. 303, 17 October 1918, TNA WO157/199.
170 Adding that it had been captured by the French.
171 Edmonds & Maxwell-Hyslop, op. cit., pp.228-9.

Fourth Army thus had some knowledge of the position it would assault. What did it know of the strength and battle-freshness of the combatants who would attempt to use both topography and man-made defences to their advantage? On 9 October, the Fourth Army intelligence summary recorded that '69 different battalions of 31 regiments of 17 different divisions' had been captured in the recent fighting. This was taken to be a sign of 'disorganization'. Of these, three divisions would be encountered at the Selle.[172] Despite the paucity of reserves, German divisions were being rotated through the line. The arrival of the *204th Infantry Division* from Lorraine was noted on the day the Pursuit opened, but it was stated that 'none of the prisoners captured yesterday know of any fresh reserves in back areas'. It was predicted that the *27th Division* was 'now the only fresh division likely to reinforce this front'.[173] This in itself was a failure of global intelligence, and a hope which was soon proved groundless, as on 10 October, the *17th Reserve Division* 'fresh from reserve' was identified near Le Cateau. Fourth Army warned that 'increased resistance' must hence be expected in the area.[174] Similarly, on the following day, the *5th Reserve Division*, a 'good fighting division', was located at Mennevret beyond the Andigny Forest, and *54th Infantry Division* was found to have reinforced the Le Cateau area, although this was described as 'having suffered heavily and is of very poor moral'.[175] Further, on 12 October it was thought possible that the *243rd Infantry Division* might also now be on Fourth Army's front. Counterbalancing this at least three divisions were, however, (correctly) known to have been withdrawn into reserve.[176] On this day, in addition, the 'moderately fresh' *15th Reserve Division* was detected north of Riquerval Wood, prisoners stating that they had undergone recent training in 'the use of light machine guns' and that they 'had orders to stop any attempt at an advance by our troops'. Similarly, the fresh *44th Reserve Division* was located north of Le Cateau. On the two following days no new divisions were identified, but on 15 October there were indications that the *3rd Naval Division* had come into line between St. Benin and St Souplet.[177] On the day before the battle there were no new identifications. Fourth Army was, therefore, aware that contrary to initial expectations there had been a range of reinforcements both during the Pursuit and the pause that followed, a number of them relatively fresh.

As Table 3.3 shows, Fourth Army faced seven (position) divisions in line on 17 October, with four in reserve. Yet it had been estimated in the intelligence summary of the 13th that 'Fourth Army is now opposed by 3 fresh divisions, 1 moderately fresh, and elements of perhaps two tired divisions, reinforced by a Cyclist Brigade',[178] an assessment that did not change. Of the eleven actually present, four were believed incorrectly to have been withdrawn, and two were thought possibly present but unconfirmed. Even after years of perusal of the papers, the Official History still suggested that on the 17th, Fourth Army 'encountered initially … five fresh divisions and four fairly fresh divisions, and a tenth, (the *221st*) appeared during the morning in the IX Corps sector'.[179] This gave ten, rather than eleven divisions. The intelligence failure for Fourth Army was not that it did not know

172 *204th*, *24th* and *221st* Divisions. Fourth Army Intelligence Summary No. 295, 9 October 1918, TNA WO157/199.
173 Fourth Army Intelligence Summary No. 296, 10 October 1918, TNA WO157/199.
174 Fourth Army Intelligence Summary No. 297, 11 October 1918, TNA WO157/199.
175 Fourth Army Intelligence Summary No. 298, 12 October 1918, TNA WO157/199.
176 The *20th*, *119th* and *2nd* Guards Divisions.
177 Fourth Army Intelligence Summary No. 302, 16 October 1918, TNA WO157/199.
178 Fourth Army Intelligence Summary No. 299, 13 October 1918, TNA WO157/199.
179 Edmonds and Maxwell-Hyslop, op. cit., p.298. From north to south, the Official History suggests that the sequence 'seemed to have been *5th Reserve*, *15th Reserve*, *29th*, *3rd Naval* (at Molain), *54th*, *204th* (north of St Souplet), *243rd*, *17th Reserve*, *44th Reserve*'. This omits the *24th* and *221st Infantry Divisions*. The OH continues: 'Three more, the *34th*, *21st Reserve* and *119th* were close at hand'. The *34th* and *119th*

of the existence of any of the eleven divisions – it was even known that the *243rd Division* might be present. It was where they were expected to be on the morning of 17 October that represented the intelligence failure. The incorrect assumption of the four supposed withdrawals was the central problem. There were two principal reasons as to why this had happened. Firstly, Montgomery describes the 'distance which separated the forces' and the Selle being a 'bandage on the eyes' of both armies. This made it 'difficult to secure prisoners',[180] (not of course that reserve divisions could have been identified in this fashion). Secondly, the comparative absence of air observation, whilst it would not allow formation identification, also made recognition of troop movements difficult, and caused problems for identifying large bodies of troops held in close reserve.

Table 3.3 German divisions opposing Fourth Army on 17 October 1918 (north to south)[181]

Division	Type	Condition[1]	Date reported
17th Reserve	Position	1st Class (A)/well rested	11 Oct
44th Reserve	Reserve	1st Class (A)/strong/newly arrived	13 Oct
243rd Infantry	Position	3rd Class (D)/relatively high strength/well rested	(Possible) 12 Oct
204th Infantry	Position	3rd Class (C)/relatively high strength/well rested	9 Oct
54th Infantry	Intervention	2nd Class (B+)/exhausted	12 Oct (believed withdrawn)
3rd Naval	Position	2nd or 3rd Class (B/C)/exhausted/low strength	(Likely) 16 Oct
24th Infantry	Position	2nd or 3rd Class (C)/exhausted/low strength	9 Oct (believed withdrawn)
29th Infantry	Reserve	1st Class (A)/poor condition	14 Oct (believed withdrawn)
15th Reserve	Position	3rd Class (C)/reasonable condition	13 Oct
5th Reserve	Position	2nd Class (B)/status not clear	12 Oct
221st Infantry	Intervention	2nd Class (D-)/poor condition	13 Oct (believed withdrawn)

Note
1 German divisions were rated as 1st, 2nd, 3rd, or 4th Class by OHL. The Allies similarly rated opposing enemy formations as A, B, C, or D in capabilities. A: 'Superior and suitable for all attack and defensive fighting'. B: 'Good and suitable for all attack and defensive fighting'. C: 'Average divisions without special or remarkable combat characteristics'. D: 'Inferior, only suitable for calm front sectors'. (See http://www.agw14-18.de/formgesch/formatio_div.html).

Poor weather was the cause of the limited air reconnaissance. The 14th was the only day of unalloyed photographic success, with 31 photographic flights taking 763 pictures. This augmented the information gleaned from the 206 photographs taken on 9 October which initially confirmed the *HWL I* positions that would face IX Corps. During the Pursuit, as noted, the early mornings were

played no part 17-18 October, and the *21st* is an error and must in fact be the *121st* which intervened on the 18th. (Edmonds and Maxwell-Hyslop, op. cit., p.298).
180 Montgomery, op. cit., p.207; Edmonds & Maxwell-Hyslop, op. cit., p.298.
181 Descriptions of status from Whisler, op. cit.

dominated by mist. On the 12th, the day before active planning for the Battle of the Selle began, it was lamented that there had been no aerial photography for three days.[182] Again on 13 October 'rain and mist throughout the day prevented flying'.[183] II American Corps issued maps of the enemy defences believed to be in front of them that day, and noted 'bad weather has prevented verification by photographs; consequently locations can be considered as only approximate.[184] On the 14th, however, the weather was a good deal better, and 'several high-flying machines reconnoitred the forward areas and penetrated as far as RONSSOY – CHAULNES – MONCHY LAGACHE'.[185] The extent of the *HWL I* was confirmed. 35 Squadron RAF, attached to XIII Corps described how: 'Useful photographs had been taken during the day. Using a cellar as a dark-room the Photo Section worked throughout the night and furnished nearly 3,000 prints from 136 negatives'.[186] On 15 October there was 'much mist with rain later'. Observation was 'inconclusive, as flying was only possible for a short period of the morning'.[187] On the 16th, there was no flying, and hence no air reconnaissance at all.[188] The limited air observation had, therefore, confirmed the German defences, although some of the finer detail, particularly wiring, would remain unknown. Enemy movements during 15-16 October remained a complete mystery, and the absence of reconnaissance the day before the assault must have been a particular handicap.

Another aspect of air reconnaissance was the identification of enemy artillery positions, successful counter-battery fire (as Fourth Army hammered home) being essential prior to an attack. During the planning process 13-16 October, the RAF made 41 artillery patrols and sent down 35 zone calls, i.e. identifications of enemy batteries. According to RAF 5 Brigade records, eight enemy batteries were neutralised as a result of these.[189] Zone calls, therefore, resulted in a 23 per cent success rate, and it is notable that on the best day for flying (14 October) there were only four zone calls. As will be further examined in Chapter Eight, Fourth Army thus had limited knowledge of the location of the enemy artillery, and as a result had had little success in eliminating much of it with counterbattery fire.

Once the BEF had assumed its final position on the west bank of the Selle, the potential presented for reconnaissance on the ground. This, however, was nigh on impossible during the day under the noses of the German machine-guns. The divisions of IX Corps reported no organised raiding prior to 17 October. Only 71 Brigade gave an account of the activity of patrols, noting on 15 October that: 'A report received during the night that the enemy was withdrawing on our front was found by patrols to be without any foundation'.[190] No identification information was seemingly brought back. On 14 October the American 27th Division, being close to the river and having cover to mount an incursion from, raided the area between the river and the railway line south of the destroyed bridge at St Souplet, an operation supported by artillery. Prisoners amounting to one officer and 29 ORs were taken from *407 Infantry Brigade* of *204th Division* (already believed to be in line), company strength being estimated at 50 and morale as low. That night five patrols were sent out, and in the early evening of the following day the 27th Division sent out more patrols, encountering no enemy

182 Fourth Army Intelligence Summary No. 299, 13 October 1918, TNA WO157/199.
183 Fourth Army Intelligence Summary No. 300, 14 October 1918, TNA WO157/199.
184 II American Corps, Summary of Intelligence, 182-33.3 No.3, 14 October 1918, *USAWW Vol. 7*, p.568.
185 Fourth Army Intelligence Summary No. 301, 15 October 1918, TNA WO157/199.
186 Historical data concerning No. 35 Squadron Royal Air Force, TNA AIR1/173/15/164/1.
187 Fourth Army Intelligence Summary No. 302, 16 October 1918, TNA WO157/199.
188 Fourth Army Intelligence Summary No. 303, 17 October 1918, TNA WO157/199.
189 War Diary, 5 Brigade RAF, Operational Summaries 9-16 October 1918, TNA AIR1/2225/209/40.
190 War Diary, HQ 71 Infantry Brigade, 15 October 1918, TNA WO95/1620.

west of the river, and hence capturing no prisoners. Similarly, on 16 October the corps took no prisoners and made no identifications.[191] In XIII Corps, 50th Division recorded: 'Reconnaissance of R. SELLE being carried out nightly'.[192] 150 Brigade pushed daylight patrols into Le Cateau and found the town west of the river clear of enemy posts yet patrolled by the enemy. These patrols yielded no identifications.[193] 151 Brigade reported only that its Intelligence Officer carried out a reconnaissance of the Selle in the night of 14/15 October.[194] North of Le Cateau patrolling was even more difficult. 66th Division recorded: 'Patrols of enemy met with West of SELLE River night 15th/16th and prevented bridging'.[195] 1st South African Infantry attempted to get across the river on 12 October but were turned back by machine-gun fire, and the following day had one of its own posts captured by the enemy. Probings on 15 October revealed that the enemy was actually established on the west bank of the Selle, and the following evening these posts were cleared to allow bridging to take place.[196] Outside of the raid carried out by the American 27th Division, the two British corps seem to have limited their activities to patrolling, finding out where the enemy outpost zone was located rather than which enemy formations occupied them. The focus on the ground was on the defences and not the defenders. The reasons for the lack of information garnered are clear and indicate that the BEF was not to be blamed. Firstly, virtually everywhere (except in Le Cateau itself), patrolling was not possible in daylight due to observed approach. Secondly, even in darkness, there were barriers. The Americans, who raided, were close to a relatively narrow stretch of the river. Elsewhere a raid would have taken on the nature of a full assault. The result was that the BEF was as blind on the ground as it largely was from the air.

The final question concerned enemy morale and what sort of fight the Germans might be expected to make. On 9 October, an Alsatian soldier of *30th Division* stated that his company commander had 'told the rest of the company that they were to resist to the utmost and inflict as many casualties as possible', and then retire.[197] And on the 17th and 18th, exactly this would happen. Whilst it was impossible to judge the impact of such exhortations, undoubtedly such words were being spoken in encouragement up and down the German front. Given that the enemy had been turned out of any chosen defensive position to date, however, there was no doubt a degree of hubris. It was observed that the enemy resistance on 8 and 9 October was 'for the most part, slight', but that 'isolated cases have occurred where men fought well'. Germans captured in Gattigny Wood on 9 October, however, surrendered readily as they were 'under the impression that an armistice had been signed', whilst others 'offered no resistance' on the basis that they knew an armistice had been requested.[198] Rumours of armistice, therefore, appeared to be fuelling a growing disinclination to fight. What was evident to Fourth Army's intelligence gatherers was that the enemy knew that its own soldiers were in a state of exhaustion and low morale. A captured order of the *11th Division*, which must have dated from the first week in October, noted the 'present momentary physical and moral weakness of troops must be overcome by bringing home to the subordinate commanders and men by means of careful teaching the importance of the present fighting for the general welfare of our people'. The vain hope was expressed: 'Confidence in ultimate victory of the

191 II American Corps reports 14, 15 & 16 October, *USAWW Vol. 7*, pp.559-611.
192 War Diary, HQ 50th Infantry Division, 15 October 1918, TNA WO95/2812.
193 War Diary, HQ 150 Infantry Brigade, 13 October 1918, TNA WO95/2833.
194 War Diary, HQ 151 Infantry Brigade, 14 October 1918, TNA WO95/2839.
195 Wat Diary, HQ 66th Infantry Division, 15 October 1918, TNA WO95/3122.
196 War Diary, HQ South African Brigade, 12-16 October, TNA WO95/3146.
197 Fourth Army Intelligence Summary No. 295, 9 October 1918, TNA WO157/199.
198 Fourth Army Intelligence Summary No. 296, 10 October 1918, TNA WO157/199.

German cause must not be lost owing to temporary setbacks'.[199] Both writer and reader must have known this was nonsense. On 16 October Fourth Army published another captured order of a Bavarian infantry regiment from *12th Division*, dated 11 September noting false reports of enemy repulses and random instead of targetted firing, with men absenting themselves 'who only turn up again when the danger is over'. The commander declared: 'I call upon every single man to act more energetically. We must employ every possible means to inflict casualties on the enemy'.[200] Fourth Army had every reason to believe that enemy morale was particularly shaky and that this would progressively undermine resistance.

Conclusion

Fourth Army's preparations for the set-piece Battle of the Selle were in many ways remarkable. The army was determined to maintain tempo in its hammering at the enemy as far as was possible, and it was only logistical issues that frustrated this, and then only marginally. The efforts of the engineers to rebuild roads and railways were imbued with urgency and marked with success. The similar efforts of the transport services were dogged by delays caused by infrastructure issues, accidents, bad weather and a smattering of cap badge rivalry, yet they successfully delivered the matériel for battle. The problems that Rawlinson's forces faced were largely those outside its control, magnified slightly through overconfidence. Fourth Army was aware that the assault of 17 October would take place across some very difficult country, which would leave its troops exposed if enemy fire was not effectively suppressed. And the weather meant that the spotting of enemy batteries for elimination was very patchy. The route of the two lines of German defences to be attacked was known with clarity, even if some of the details, such as presence of or depth of wire had been missed (a miss that would indeed cause problems on the day). The nature of the German defence, based on extensive use of well-sited machine guns, was also anticipated. The plan of assault, taking the topographical obstacles into account, was sophisticated. It must also have been reassuring that the defences faced were relatively insignificant in comparison with those Fourth Army had so recently overcome. It was reasonable to assume that a set-piece attack would penetrate them without excessive difficulty. Fourth Army was over-optimistic, however, concerning the volume of the forces it would face, based on the incorrect perception that enemy divisions had been withdrawn. Weather and terrain had massively reduced effective intelligence gathering. The British may have also made a further wrong assumption about the extent of German disorganisation. Constantly reporting on the mixed nature of the prisoners captured, the German tendency to insert 'intervention units from one division into another divisional sector' was missed.[201] Fourth Army went into the assault of 17 October having certainly underestimated the degree of resistance that would be offered.

199 Fourth Army Intelligence Summary No. 297, 11 October 1918, TNA WO157/199.
200 Fourth Army Intelligence Summary No. 302, 16 October 1918, TNA WO157/199.
201 Whisler, op. cit., p.41.

Major-General H.K. Keppel-Bethell, GOC 66th (2nd East Lancashire) Division. (Private collection)

Major-General Gerald Farrell Boyd, GOC 46th (North Midland) Division. (Private collection)

Major-General George Windle Read, GOC US II American Corps. (Open source)

Major-General Walter Braithwaite, GOC 62nd (West Riding) Division. (Private collection)

Major-General Henry Cholmondeley Jackson, GOC 50th (Northumbrian) Division. (Private collection)

Lieutenant-General Sir Thomas Morland, GOC X Corps. (Private collection)

Major-General Peter Strickland, GOC 1st Division. (Private collection)

4

'A Pretty Heavy Fight Today'.[1] Forcing the Selle: 17 October 1918

> 'Everything is very simple in War, but the simplest thing is difficult'.[2]

The enemy was of course expecting an attack. Indeed, as the bombardment started, the German *Second Army* advised on 15 October that 'the large-scale enemy attack … seems about to be launched', and put its corps on 'increased combat alert' from 06.00 on 16 October.[3] Being well aware of the BEF's habit of attacking at 05.20, a 'heavy counter-preparation of H.E. and gas was put down … two hours before Zero'. The fog was thick that morning, and it was 'impossible to see 20 yards' in some places. In the IX Corps area, at least, 'the line of the barrage was completely hidden'.[4]

IX Corps

IX Corps, as observed, planned to use 46th, 6th and 1st Divisions in the attack. Mark Whisler estimates that that IX Corps and the 30th American Division fielded about 14,450-16,250 combatants in contrast to 8,700-9,400 German infantry and machine-gunners of the *I Bavarian Corps* on right wing of the German *Eighteenth Army* (which also faced the left of the French attack).[5] From right to left of the line as facing the BEF were the *3rd Naval Division* (rated as second/third class in 1918); *24th Infantry Division* (rated second/third class); *15th Reserve Division* (rated third class but in reasonable condition); and *5th Reserve Division* (rated second class). In reserve was the *29th Infantry Division* (rated first class but in poor condition) supporting the two divisions on the right, and the *221st Infantry Division* (rated second class but in poor condition) supporting the two on the left.[6]

1 Sir H. Rawlinson, War Journal, 16 October 1918, Churchill College RWLN 1/11.
2 C. von Clausewitz, *On War – Book One*, p.77.
3 Army Order, *German Second Army*, 15 October 1918, *United States Army in the World War Vol. 7*, p904.
4 IX Corps Narrative, 17 October 1918, IWM Docs 20537 Fourth Army Papers Vol. 63.
5 M. Whisler, 'Der Tommy Kommt', p.30. A detailed examination of the German opposition is contained in Whisler, op. cit., pp.251-266.
6 The class ratings are taken from General Staff AEF, *Histories of Two Hundred and Fifty-One Divisions of the German Army which Participated in the War (1914-1918)*, and in the two instances of divisions being rated as second/third class, the official rating was third, but this source suggests the rating should have been higher.

The *24th* and *3rd Naval Divisions* were 'exhausted and had very low infantry strengths'.[7] In addition to the total infantry and machine-gunner strength the corps possessed 260 field artillery pieces and 54 heavy guns.[8]

In 46th Division facing Riquerval Wood and the *5th Reserve Division*, 137 Brigade held a frontage of 5,000 yards. The previous attempt by 1/5th South Staffordshire to take the wood on the 12th had, of course, been fruitless. On the morning of 17 October, 1/6th North Staffords held the whole front. They were not, however, to attack with the rest of the army at 05.20. Rather, their frontage was to be used in a so-called 'Chinese' attack, drawing fire away from the main thrust. 46th Division's plan involved the left of 137 Brigade acting as a pivot point, the main attack of the other two brigades swinging south like a door to shut on the Regnicourt road creating a refused flank to the wood. To further the deception, three Royal Engineer carpenters constructed, at four hours' notice, 90 dummy figures and a mechanism for raising them.[9] These were placed in front of shell holes in which the men operating them could lie. One man could operate nine dummies, tying the line that raised them to a tree stump, and then retiring swiftly. Three dummy tanks were also provided, one a full-size replica of a Mark V, the other two profiles only. To add further conviction to the proceedings, 14th Brigade Royal Field Artillery provided a rolling barrage including gas supported by machine-guns, which came down in front of the bogus attack and proceeded through the wood.

The enemy was taken in by the ruse, bringing down a counter-barrage ten minutes later, hence dissipating the fire brought down on the real attack. At 07.30 the North Staffords, who had vacated their front line, returned. Strong patrols in gas helmets proceeded into the wood, opposed by some surviving snipers and machine-guns.[10] By 12.30, the wood that had resisted two previous assaults was free of the enemy, the Staffords having linked up with 1/8th Sherwood Foresters who were now at its far end. By 14.30 Hennechies Wood to the east had also been cleared. For the cost of three other ranks killed and eight wounded, not only had the woods been taken in an advance of 3,000 yards, but 20 prisoners, two field guns, four trench mortars and five machine-guns had also been bagged.[11] The success of the assault, however, showed how misguided had been the attempt to take the wood frontally five days earlier.

The area to be secured by the other two brigades of 46th Division roughly represented a triangle. One side, occupied by the British, was their front line, running south-west from Vaux-Andigny. The second side was the Bohain to Andigny-les-Fermes road (the refused flank), running roughly east; and the third was the Bellevue spur, running north-west (see Map 8). The first and third sides were on ridges, the centre of the triangle was the valley that Major Saunders of 11th Essex had been so concerned about being enfiladed along after the abortive attack of the 12th. The artillery

7 Whisler, op. cit., p.252. *I Bavarian Corps* had protested the weakness of these divisions and had stated that it could not guarantee holding the position if they were not replaced. Given that there were no fresh replacements to be had, OHL had released the corps 'from any responsibility in case a failure should result from the weak resistance of the two divisions'. (Whisler, op. cit., p.305).

8 Whisler, op. cit., p.253.

9 The BEF had, of course, used such a mechanism before, but these figures were constructed to a new design so that all could be packed in one lorry. (R.E. Priestley, *Breaking the Hindenburg Line*, p.144).

10 6th North Staffordshire were commanded by Lieutenant-Colonel Charles Child Dowding DSO MC, a retired ranker of the Worcestershire Regiment, who had served during the war in the Royal Lancaster and Welsh Regiments. The battalion began the month with a fighting strength of 11 officers and 356 ORs. During the month of October they sustained five officers killed/died of wounds and nine wounded. Fifty four ORs had been killed with 34 missing, and 265 wounded, i.e. over 100 per cent casualties, but reinforcements meant that their trench strength at the end of the month was 15 officers and 689 ORs.

11 War Diary, 1/6th Battalion North Staffordshire Regiment, 17 October 1918, TNA WO95/2685.

The shallow valley along which 138 and 139 brigades of 46th Division attacked Regnicourt on 17 October 1918 as seen from the shoulder of the Bellevue spur.

plan was rendered complex by the line of attack, i.e. down the valley in a south-easterly direction from the triangle's apex, across which the *HWL I* ran obliquely in a series of unconnected trenches. Given the placing of the artillery of both 1st and 6th Divisions and the American 30th Division, a normal frontal barrage was not possible, so 'it was decided to try the novel experiment of an oblique or "enfilade" barrage'.[12] Simon Peaple describes an artillery plan 'whose technical mastery is stunning', a triangular barrage firing 'in two parallel belts, which leapfrogged each other alternately',[13] individual batteries having 'a different number of lifts so that the advancing troops could advance behind a series of standing barrages'.[14] The guns were placed west and north-west of Bohain, providing 'a thick 18-pounder barrage with one round of "smoke" per lift, and a 4.5 [inch] How[itzer] barrage beyond the 18 pounders'. The field guns fired for three minutes on the opening line, and moved forward 100 yards every three minutes, resting on the edge of the Andigny Forest, firing for 30 minutes and ceasing. The howitzers fired until the infantry reached the road when they lifted to the northern edge of the Andigny Forest and fire smoke shell. Whilst the barrage may have been a technical triumph on paper, it caused the infantry, 'accustomed as they were to following a frontal barrage, to lose direction during their advance'.[15]

12 Priestley, op. cit., p.141.
13 J.E. Edmonds & R. Maxwell-Hyslop, *Military Operations France and Belgium 1918 Vol. V*, p.301
14 S. Peaple, *Mud, Blood and Determination*, p.189.
15 War Diary, HQ 46th Infantry Division, 'Attack of the 46th Division on Regnicourt – Andigny-les-Fermes, Oct 17th 1918', WO95/2666. As will be discussed in Chapter Eight, it may not have been as technically proficient as the plan required.

The machine-gun barrage was no less complex. Major George Wade had at his disposal 16 guns of C Company 46th Battalion Machine Gun Corps (MGC), all firing from different positions; 24 guns of 2nd Life Guards (No. 2 Battalion of the Guards Machine Gun Regiment); and 16 guns of the 6th Battalion MGC.[16] All three groups were in different locations and had their own barrage lines, a varying numbers of guns firing at different points during the barrage. C Company fired 250 rounds per minute to start with reducing to 100 rounds per minute for another 118 minutes. The barrage fired by the guns of the Life Guards mimicked the artillery barrage – 100 rounds per minutes in ten lifts. 6th Battalion fired at the same rate in four lifts. A prodigious amount of ammunition was therefore expended – 466,000 rounds in all.[17]

139 Brigade on the right, commanded by Brigadier-General J. Harington,[18] formed the hinge of the door that would swing against the woods. Their attack (and that of 138 Brigade to their left) would be made obliquely across the British front, along the length of the valley opening out between the spur running south-west from Vaux-Andigny and the Bellevue spur, a distance of some 3,000 yards on a front of 1,500 yards. 1/8th Sherwood Foresters, with two companies of the 1/5th Battalion in support,[19] would make the attack. Three sections of A Company 46th Battalion MGC were attached to the 8th Sherwoods, each with a specific task, one proceeding with the 5th. A section of Stokes mortars was also attached to the 8th for dealing with trenches of the *HWL I* on the left of the advance. A section of 18-pounder field guns followed. Lieutenant-Colonel Richard Currin and his company commanders had reconnoitred the ground the previous afternoon,[20] an activity interrupted by a fierce bombardment, during which to their amazement they watched 'an old lady moving her household effects on a wheelbarrow' down the road that was the objective for the attack of the morrow.[21] The battalion's action makes a good study of infantry practice and tactics that morning. The unit followed a tape laid by the Royal Engineers and formed up in the dark on another tape laid 70 yards south of the Bohain to Vaux-Andigny road. Replete with hot porridge, tea and rum, they advanced at 05.20, each of the three leading companies on a 400 yard frontage. One section of machine-guns stiffened A Company on the unit's right in their taking of the German outposts; another section accompanied the flank of C Company advancing on the

16 War Diary, 46th Battalion Machine Gun Corps, Fire Organization Orders, 16 October 1918, TNA WO95/2679. Major George Albert Wade MC, a private in the 5th North Staffordshire Regiment, was commissioned in November 1914 and was seconded as a lieutenant to the brigade Machine Gun Company in March 1916. Born in 1891, he left school to work in the family pottery business, becoming factory manager at the age of 19. Knighted in 1955 as chairman of Wade Ceramics, he died in 1986.

17 Simon Peaple points out that this is not a lot less than the 537,000 rounds of small arms ammunition issued by the Divisional Ammunition Column for the whole of April 1918. (Peaple, op. cit., p.191).

18 Brigadier-General John Harington had assumed command of 139 Brigade on 24 July 1918. A regular major of the Rifle Brigade in August 1914, he had commanded 11th Rifle Brigade from June to August 1916, 13th Cheshire from August to September 1917, 1/28th London from November 1917 to January 1918, and a battalion of the Machine Gun Corps from March to July 1918.

19 The trench strength of 1/5th Sherwood Foresters at the start of October was 22 officers and 450 ORs. They suffered two officers killed and 10 wounded during October, a period when 31 other ranks were killed and 182 wounded with 20 missing. They received reinforcements comprising 11 officers and 313 other ranks and ended the month with a trench strength of 23 officers and 513 ORs.

20 Lieutenant-Colonel Richard William Currin DSO and bar was a retired captain of the Cape Colonial Volunteers in August 1914. Commissioned in the York & Lancaster Regiment, he had commanded 1/5th Leicestershire between December 1917 and February 1918, commanding 1/8th Sherwood Foresters from 14 March 1918. Wounded on 5 September 1918 by a direct hit on battalion HQ, he returned on 12 October.

21 W.C.C. Weetman, *The Sherwood Foresters in the Great War 1914–1919 – 1/8th Battalion,* p.295.

left of the battalion, as did the section of trench mortars. The machine-gun section was also given a specific target, a copse to the north-west of Regnicourt, close to the spur on which the village and road lay. The remaining section followed the centre of the advance.[22] The battalion's attack first hit *III Battalion Reserve Infantry Regiment (RIR) 69* of *15th Reserve Division*, whose outposts were overcome. The thick mist made it extremely difficult to judge the barrage lifts which as noted were counterintuitive to previous experience, not being straight ahead, and the smoke shell signalling the lift completely lacked effectiveness in the fog. Direction was lost by all, but particularly so by C Company, who wandered left into 138 Brigade's area before correcting their error. A gap of 500 yards opened up in the battalion's centre. Whilst machine-gun nests encountered were overcome, others were thus missed. The right hand A Company pushed on towards the road,[23] overtaking the barrage and being caught by enemy machine-guns whilst reforming when the fog broke temporarily. They lost their commander, Lieutenant Hugh Toyne, wounded, and a further officer, Second-Lieutenant William Jacques, who was killed.[24] Lieutenant Morgan Thomas of the Royal Engineers took over command and stiffened the firing line with his sappers and elements of D Company, and took the objective.[25]

D Company was in support behind the wandering C Company. They advanced in a rectangle with a platoon at each corner, sections in blobs forming an arrowhead, company HQ in the centre. Their coherence soon fragmented in the mist, and company HQ ran into one of the missed machine-gun nests, putting the two guns out of action as well as capturing 11 of the enemy. The one platoon of D Company that had kept direction advanced towards Regnicourt and similarly ran up against machine-guns. 'Serg[ean]t Robinson and L[ance]-Corp[ora]l Harper went forward to reconnoitre the position, and finding it strongly held, went back for the rest of the platoon.' They outflanked and rushed the post. Harper, a few yards away, ill-advisedly stood to get a better aim, and was shot through the head. Lance-Corporal Coombes 'at once rushed forward, shot six Germans with his revolver, and finished off the last man who was trying to run away with his Lewis gun'.[26]

A similar example of the infantry tactics utilised was in response to the problem created by machine-guns in a clearing within the copse to the north-west of Regnicourt. As the mist lifted, B Company in the centre and A Company on the right came under heavy fire from this location, the commander of B Company, Captain Albert Gearey, being killed.[27] Colonel Currin, who had himself been lost and unable to find his advanced HQ, pushed his reserve company and straggler sections of the leading companies through higher ground to the north-east under the command of Major Victor Robinson to offer support.[28] They expelled ten of the enemy and a machine-gun from

22 War Diary, 1/5th Battalion Sherwood Foresters, Operation Order No. 84 16 October 1918, TNA WO95/2695.
23 A & B Companies each had half a section of Royal Engineers from 465 Field Company attached to assist in the forming of strongpoints and to repair road if necessary.
24 Hugh Miles Toyne was commissioned in May 1915. William Gladstone Jacques had been commissioned from private in June 1917. The unit began the month with 46 officers and 752 other ranks and ended it with 34 officers and 745 other ranks, having suffered 227 casualties.
25 Morgan Evan Thomas, a Cambridge student commissioned in July 1915, was awarded a bar to his MC.
26 Weetman, op. cit., p.298.
27 Captain Albert Edward Gearey MC was the youngest son of a sergeant-major of the West Yorkshire Regiment. He was training for the priesthood at Kelham Hall, Nottinghamshire, in August 1914 but enlisted to be commissioned from sergeant in January 1916. He was shot by a sniper bringing in a wounded man. (*De Ruvigny's Roll of Honour, Vol V*, p.67).
28 Major Victor Owen Robinson was one of 168 men who won the MC and two bars. He had commanded the battalion for three days at the start of October 1918. The citation for his MC related to this action

a trench on the ridge to the right front of the copse, and took cover. On the left, Sergeant Alfred Winson of C Company 'regardless of all risk … kept his Lewis gun trained on the enemy' whilst a party crawled over to the clearing and rushed the post.[29] The Germans realised that they were out-manoeuvred and shortly surrendered, yielding 140 men and no less than 27 machine-guns.

The retiring enemy then took up positions in 'strongly wired & entrenched positions along the road', where nine machine-guns were found in 100 yards of netted trench alone.[30] The CO of the 1/5th Sherwood Foresters, Lieutenant-Colonel Reginald Pratt,[31] realising the degree of resistance, pushed forward his two supporting companies. After a further flanking manoeuvre by A Company to the right, Regnicourt was finally taken at 10.15, with the unrequested assistance of a company of 11th Essex who had wandered off the Bellevue spur. Beyond the village they became aware of a broken-down tank which 'had a very rough time before its crew could be rescued'.[32] Under fire from a field gun in Hennechies Wood, which was forced by the following section of field artillery to withdraw,[33] the line was consolidated, and posts established by Lieutenant Thomas south of the road. At 11.00, *RIR 8* (*5th Reserve Division*) was seen massing for a counterattack about 1,500 yards away on the edge of the woods. Artillery fire was again quickly provided by the attached field guns, and 'the Boches were completely broken, only a half-hearted attempt being made, and only one man reaching our lines'.[34] At noon Major Robinson took a patrol forward into Hennechies Wood, dodging a few remaining machine-gun posts and emerging near Forester's House on the far side, encountering the French. 'The "poilus" were delighted to see them, and shewed their appreciation by giving our men the whole of the contents of their water bottles'.[35] A line was established north and south joining 138 Brigade on the left, with 137 Brigade moving up through the wood to join with the French.

The attack took up to 250 prisoners and 100 machine-guns. But losses had been heavy. In 1/8th Sherwood Foresters three officers had been killed and three wounded;[36] whilst 25 other ranks were dead and 54 wounded. Despite the success, the unit history concluded: 'In a way it was an unsatisfactory day'. The enemy was 'holding in much greater strength much more strongly fortified positions than had been anticipated', and the fighting had been 'extremely hard'. Although the battle for Regnicourt was a 'small matter' in the history of the Great War, for 1/8th Sherwood Foresters 'it was one of the most strenuously fought battles of the war'.[37] It also showed the British infantry

reads: 'On 17th October, after the attack on Regnicourt had been launched, finding the right being held up by heavy enemy machinegun fire, he gathered together all available men and pushed forward on the left. This action cleared the enemy from their strongly fortified positions, and enabled his right flank to push forward, enabling his battalion to gain its final objective. Throughout he showed great gallantry and able leadership'. (*London Gazette*, 4 October 1919, p.12235).

29 A Derbyshire coal miner who had joined up in October 1914, Winson won the Military Medal.

30 War Diary, 139 Infantry Brigade, 'Report on Operations Carried Out by 139 Infantry Brigade on 17/10/18', TNA WO95/2693.

31 Lieutenant-Colonel Reginald Stanley Pratt MC and two bars was a mining engineer commissioned into the Durham Light Infantry in January 1915. He had been in command for only 13 days.

32 Weetman, op. cit., p.300.

33 A section of C/231 Brigade Royal Field Artillery.

34 Weetman, op. cit., p.300.

35 Weetman, op. cit., p.301.

36 With a trench strength of 46 officers and 752 men at the start of the month, during October 1/8th Sherwood Foresters lost five officers killed and 10 wounded, with 50 other ranks killed/died of wounds, 171 wounded and 20 missing. With reinforcement, at the end of the month their strength was 34 officers and 745 men. (War Diary, 1/8th Battalion Sherwood Foresters, October 1918, TNS WO95/2695).

37 Weetman, op. cit., p.302.

of 1918 at their best. The battalion, which had been reasonably strong at the outset of the action, had shown dash and persistence. It proved itself highly adaptable on the ground, practising the best infantry tactics in outflanking points of resistance, and had been faced by an extraordinary number of machine-guns. Further, it showed effective leadership including to NCO level, whilst battalion COs showed initiative and inter-battalion cooperation.

On the left, 138 Brigade comprised the outer part of the swinging door that would slam shut at Andigny-les-Fermes on the end of the Bellevue spur. The brigade assembled on the ridge running south from Vaux-Andigny, shelled the while by high explosive and gas. 1/4th Leicestershire were on the right, 1/5th Lincolnshire on the left, each with a section of machine-guns and the Lincolns with a section of trench mortars, as they had the flank exposed to the Bellevue spur. 1/5th Leicestershire were in reserve. The fog created considerable difficulties for keeping direction and communication, the latter being problematic from platoon to corps level. Indeed, higher formations had little idea what was going on until late in the morning.[38] The degree of confusion was such that Major Beckett, commanding 1/4th Leicestershire, reported at 07.00 that he had elements of the Cameron Highlanders, Black Watch, and North Lancashire Regiment from 1st Division, and 1/8th Sherwood Foresters and 1/5th Lincolns intermingled with his unit. As Beckett's battalion started out, machine-guns were still firing from the German outposts on the right, unseen and untouched in the mist, as well as from Bellevue and Les Gobelets on the spur to the left. The Leicester advance ground to a halt in front of the trenches of the *HWL I*. At 09.00, when 1st Loyal North Lancashire on the ridge above had dealt with these last two positions, Beckett was able to move on. Whilst the Lancashire unit outflanked Andigny-les-Fermes to the north-east, 1/4th Leicesters became engaged in a 'very stiff fight' to take the village,[39] accompanied by 1/5th Lincolnshire. Outflanked, the defending *I Battalion RIR 69* retired, leaving behind 70 prisoners and two field guns.[40]

The 5th Lincolns, on the division's left in the foggy shadow of the Bellevue spur, had been led forward on compass bearings with two battalion scouts on each flank, but also suffered the same loss of direction. Close fighting took place for the trenches of the *HWL I, II Battalion RIR 69* being overrun. Three officers were wounded, but 'subordinate leaders, however, rose to the occasion'. Corporal A. Wilson, for instance, took charge of his section and captured two machine-guns and prisoners when his officer and sergeant were killed. Private Samson Meanwell behaved similarly faced with machine-guns when all his NCOs became casualties.[41] Losing the barrage in dealing with these obstructions, the attack stalled under fire in front of Andigny-les-Fermes, whilst the right flank wandered east to Regnicourt. However, when the former village was outflanked, the fight was successfully resumed with the 1/4th Leicesters, and the village taken.[42] The brigade pushed out strong patrols, but these met with heavy machine-gun fire, and no further progress was made. There had been significant cost in the advance. One officer from 1/5th Lincolnshire died of wounds and two were wounded,[43] whilst 17 other ranks were killed and 58 wounded. One

38 'IX Corps Narrative', 17 October 1918, IWM Docs 20537, Fourth Army Papers Vol. 63.
39 Priestley, op. cit., p.150.
40 Whisler, op. cit., p.272.
41 T.E Sandall, *A History of the 5th Batt. The Lincolnshire Regiment*, p.184. Samson George Edward Meanwell won the Military Medal. This unit history lists seven occasions where NCOs or privates used initiative and pressed on in the absence of officers.
42 1/4th Leicestershire did not record their casualties, but CWGC records list 14 fatalities amongst the other ranks.
43 Second-Lieutenant Frederick Pembroke Barton died of wounds on the 18th. He had been commissioned from the rank of corporal in February 1918. Second-Lieutenants J. Harris and W. Simpson were wounded.

hundred and fifty prisoners and 20 machine-guns had been captured. In an amusing coda to the action, Private Joseph Towers was conducting a party of these prisoners back when he ran into an enemy detachment of three machine-guns. On his own, Towers told the German officer he was surrounded, and in the ensuing argument (in English) kicked over the nearest machine-gun to make his point. The Germans submitted and Towers collected 40 more prisoners and the Military Medal for his coolness and confidence.[44]

46th Division made particular note of the support given by the artillery, especially the forward artillery placed under the command of infantry COs, the like of which had broken up the counterattack at Regnicourt.[45] The support given by tanks had been mixed. The tank battalion attached to IX Corps was the 16th, and its limitations were reflected in the number of machines allotted to divisions. From B Company three tanks were attached to 46th Division;[46] six to 6th Division;[47] and four to 1st Division.[48] The three attached to 46th Division had specific tasks. They were to head south along the German outpost line on the right of 139 Brigade, deal with a strong point near their start, then proceed to the road. Here, one was to advance down the line of a trench on the north side of Riquerval Wood, whilst the others were to turn left up the road to assist in mopping up Regnicourt and Andigny-les-Fermes. One machine, however, was knocked out soon after starting, and the other two suffered loss of direction in the fog. A second was hit by artillery fire near Regnicourt, the machine observed by 1/8th Sherwood Foresters, all the crew except one being killed or wounded.[49] The last tank survived to rally at Angin Farm beyond the Bellevue spur later that morning. Given their numbers, they were able to contribute little to 46th Division's success, which had been achieved with casualties that numbered seven officers and 200 other ranks. Fifteen German officers and 500 other ranks had been captured, and the *5th Reserve Division*, only one of whose regiments had been so disastrously engaged at Riquerval Wood, was forced by the threatened envelopment to withdraw some 3,000 yards.

6th Division's part in the 'very pretty tactical move' was not easy. Their front was narrow, only 1,500 yards, and five battalions were to debouche 'fan-wise from the village of Vaux-Andigny … advancing 2,500-3,000 yards to a front of 5,000 yards'.[50] The right of the advance would be astride the Bellevue spur, the left on the plain beyond, to the line of the *HWL II* west of la Vallée Mulâtre (the Angin farm ridge). 1st Division would then pass through. Like the 46th Division, it was proceeding obliquely to the British front. Eight brigades of field artillery were to fire a barrage, with 172 60-pounders and heavy howitzers. The artillery of 1st Division was superimposed on that of the 6th, and 80 machine-guns would complete the barrage.[51] It opened 200-300 yards in front of the infantry start line, lifting 100 yards every three minutes, and paused for half an hour 300 yards

44 Sandall, op. cit., p187
45 Priestley, op. cit., p.151.
46 Under Captain Alfred Viotti Rhodes.
47 Three machines with 18 Brigade under captain Arthur Stanley Lowe, and three with 16 Brigade under Captain Richard McCorry.
48 Under Captain Herbert Robert Chick.
49 Fatalities in tank 9146 included Corporal Charles George Drewett, Private William Fensome, Private Edwin Daniels, and Private James F. Doig. The officer had been wounded, and the tank commanded by an NCO, had lost direction in the fog. This clearing, the tank found itself opposite Regnicourt, and supported the infantry held up by wire to capture the village. Turning towards Andigny-les-Fermes, it was hit by a 77-mm gun at point blank range.
50 Marden, op. cit., p.70.
51 From 2nd Life Guards Machine Gun Battalion (two companies) and 6th Battalion Machine Gun Corps (three companies).

in front of the intermediate objective to allow 1st Division to catch up.[52] The IX Corps barrage maps show the two groups of artillery covering the advance firing two expanding fields of barrages, to match the fan-shaped advance, the group line being to the north-east of the Bellevue spur.[53] To the right was 46th Division's barrage – there were therefore three adjoining barrages all being fired at different angles up to the first objective. The plan was comprehensive and complex. The main opposition was the *15th Reserve Division*, occupying the *HWL I* in front of Vaux-Andigny covering the Bellevue spur, with the right of the weak *24th Infantry Division* confronting the left of 6th Division's advance to the *HWL II*.[54] The *221st Infantry Division*, in support, was concentrated around Wassigny. The *15th Reserve Division*, anticipating where the British attack would fall, concentrated its forces to the right, opposite Vaux-Andigny.[55] The front was held by *I* and *II Battalions RIR 25*, stiffened by anti-tank artillery, with *III Battalion* in close support, *RIR 17* being immediately to the rear. The rest of the front was held by *RIR 69* which was to be defeated by 46th Division's attack.

18 and 16 Brigades were in line, right and left. 16 Brigade, attacking along the Bellevue spur, suffered the misfortune of serious injury to their commander on the evening prior to the assault. Brigadier-General Henry Walker lost his left arm to a shell whilst standing behind brigade HQ. It was blown off 'so cleanly that his wrist watch was recovered by his orderly and was still going'.[56] Percy Brown, commanding the resting 71 Brigade took over until Brigadier-General William Braithwaite arrived on the 19th.[57] The brigade laid out long direction tapes pointing in the initial direction, necessary as their starting line 'faced east-south-east, while its direction of advance was south-east'.[58] Both brigades had three tanks attached. On the right, in 18 Brigade, strongpoints had been allotted as targets for the tanks on the inter-brigade boundary.

The forming up of all units was made difficult by the heavy enemy shelling with HE and phosgene gas which had begun two hours before zero. On the 600 yard frontage of 18 Brigade, expanding to 2,300 yards on the objective, two battalions advanced. 11th Essex were on the right, 2nd Durham Light Infantry on the left. The Essex unit advanced at 05.20 up the Bellevue spur on the right but soon met uncut wire and entrenchments, where they eventually captured 10 machine-guns and 50 prisoners. Uncut wire was a particular problem on 18 Brigade's front, and dealing with it caused the Essex unit to lose the barrage. The brigade later concluded: 'The rate of the barrage (100 yards in 3 minutes) was found to be much too quick for Infantry to keep up having regard to the inevitable

52 In terms of the 18-pounder barrage, for the first three minutes, fire was 'intense'; from 3-9 'rapid'; from 9-112 'normal rate; from 112-129 half a round a minute. From 129-132 minutes the fire would be intense, this being a signal to the infantry that the barrage was about to move on; from 132-180 the rate of fire was 'normal'; and from 185-190 it was 'slow'. Shrapnel was fired first and after 4-5,000 yards HE was fired. One gun in each battery fired 50 per cent smoke. Three hours after zero, two brigades of Field Artillery would move forward. (War Diary, 6th Infantry Division, 6th Division Artillery Instructions No. 5, 16 October 1918, TNA WO/95 1591).
53 War Diary, General Staff IX Corps October 1918, TNS WO95/837.
54 *24th Infantry Division* had been battered in Fourth Army's assault on the Beaurevoir-Fonsomme Line and Cambrai in the opening days of October.
55 Whisler, op. cit., p.256.
56 Marden, op. cit., p.70.
57 William Garnett Braithwaite CB CMG DSO (1870-1937), was a major of the Royal Welsh Fusiliers at the outbreak of war, serving with the New Zealand Forces. He had two spells commanding 2 New Zealand Brigade between November 1915 and November 1917, thereafter serving as BGGS XXIII Corps.
58 A. Montgomery, *The Story of the Fourth Army in the Battles of the Hundred Days*, p.212.

The broad shoulders of the Bellevue spur rising from Vaux-Andigny. The valley along which 46th Division advanced lies down to the right.

delays in passing obstacles even in slightly enclosed country'.[59] Further, the enemy were 'organised in depth and very cleverly arranged'. Despite advancing arm-in-arm because of the fog, direction was lost, and the right company of the Essex unit ended up well in 46th Division's area participating in the capture of Regnicourt.

The Bellevue spur commands the surrounding area. To the east it gives observation for miles over the plateau that eventually drops down to the Sambre-Oise canal. To the west it similarly gives good observation for a long distance over the undulating ground over which the Pursuit had been carried out. The opportunities for observation afforded by the spur were, of course, no use to its defenders on the morning of the 17th, the fog ensuring that the attack of IX Corps in the valley below was enshrouded. Had it not been, the casualty bill for the attacking troops would undoubtedly have been much higher. The shoulders of the spur are, however, broad. It was understandable that in the fog the relatively gentle slope did not provide sufficient warning to 11th Essex that they were being seduced into the valley below.

The attached tanks followed the right of the Essex assault off the spur, this depriving the infantry of support at Bellevue Farm. Here *III Battalion RIR 25* put up particularly stiff resistance, counterattacking and ejecting the elements of 11th Essex that had kept direction and secured a toehold. The company on the left shoulder of the spur also suffered misfortune when its company HQ was

59 War Diary, HQ 18 Infantry Brigade, 'Narrative of the Attack on the 17th October 1918', TNA WO95/1615.

wiped out by a shell, and it was some time before cohesion was regained.[60] Before this was achieved, however, they had wandered across the front of the 2nd Durham Light Infantry advancing on their left. The enemy was then encountered at the *HWL II* on the Angin Farm ridge, 'organised in depth', and with many machine-guns. This position would hold up a number of units that morning. Captain Charles Clayton, a staff officer with 2 Brigade, described how 'dislodging' the machine gun nests created problems for command and control in the advance. 'In the thick fog … they were hard to locate and after each had been located it had to be surrounded and separately rushed'. This was time consuming and 'through a series of these disconnected operations the platoons got out of touch with each other'. Whilst they would ultimately arrive on the objective, it would be 'some time before their positions were known to their Battalion Commanders'.[61] The stalled Essex battalion was, however, carried forward by leapfrogging units. The fog lifting, both the lost tanks and infantry regained the ridge at the group of farm buildings at Les Gobelets between Bellevue Farm and Andigny-les-Fermes. Suffering 73 casualties, they had captured 115 prisoners, three trench mortars, two 77-mm guns, and 33 machine-guns.[62]

On the left of the attack on the shoulder of the ridge, 2nd Durham Light Infantry were immediately met by the enemy counter-barrage and ran into both opposition on the ground and a good deal of uncut wire. With loss of direction and contact, company commanders found command and control impossible. As Clayton noted, 'it became a case of separate platoons fighting on their own'.[63] Considerable time was lost cutting wire at the *HWL I* trenches on the Bellevue spur, where under heavy machine-gun fire a vicious bombing action took place. Consequently, as elsewhere, the barrage was lost. Sustaining heavy casualties from *II Battalion RIR 25* as it drifted north, the attack completely lost steam, as it had for 11th Essex, on the Angin Farm ridge. The DLI were reinforced on the ridge by two companies of 1st West Yorkshire, but the attack was only carried forward by the impetus of 1st Division.

Immediately to the north, 16 Brigade, facing *24th Infantry Division*, attacked with 1st King's Shropshire Light Infantry leading despite having been subject to particularly heavy gas shelling.[64] Protected by the barrage and covered by the fire of 60 machine-guns they debouched from

60 The company commander Captain Herbert Vincent Corbett was killed. A Cambridge student commissioned in October 1914, he had been severely wounded at Ypres in April 1915, and during his convalescence had finished his degree, returning to the Western Front only in June 1918. CSM Percy Alfred Strait MM was also killed. Platoon commander Second-Lieutenant James Cecil Hubert Willett MC and bar (commissioned from lance-corporal in May 1917) restored the situation. The bar to his MC was won during this action. The citation reads: 'For conspicuous gallantry and devotion to duty during an attack south-east of Vaux-Andigny on 17th October, 1918. He was in command of the support company, and after his company had been used to reinforce the assaulting companies he spotted and charged an enemy post, capturing two machine-guns and twenty O.Rs. He did very excellent work during the whole operation'. (*London Gazette*, 4 October 1919, p.12257).

61 C.P.Clayton, *The Hungry One*, p.223.

62 War Diary, 11th Battalion Essex Regiment, 17 October 1918, TNA WO95/1616. In addition to Captain Corbett, 17 ORs were killed/died of wounds. Second-Lieutenant James McGrigor Groundwater (commissioned in January 1918) was wounded as were 40 ORs, 14 being missing.

63 War Diary, 2nd Battalion Durham Light Infantry, 17 October 1918, TNA WO95/1617. Lieutenant T. Shepherd was killed, as was Second-Lieutenant Louis Pollock (commissioned in August 1918). Second-Lieutenants Ernest William Gillard (commissioned August 1918), J.G. Evans, and L.J. Harvey were wounded. 61 ORs were wounded, 15 killed and 8 missing.

64 The battalion had been commanded since 10 October by Major Lyndon Henry Morris, a territorial captain of the 4th Battalion in August 1914. The unit's casualties were 'about 25 per cent, including 2nd Lieut. H.J. Taylor (The Buffs, attached) killed'. (W. de B. Wood, *The History of the King's Shropshire Light*

The Angin Farm ridge (*HWL II*) from Les Gobelets on the Bellvue spur. Behind it stretches the plateau that lies between the Selle and the Sambre-Oise canal.

Vaux-Andigny station. Both the attacking battalions had one gun of 16th Trench Mortar Battery attached. A special map made from photos had been issued to each unit to show probable points of resistance. Unfortunately, a 'large number of M.G.s opened at zero minus 3 minutes, which caused a certain amount of anxiety among the attacking troops'.[65] They found the wire to be 'practically uncut', and the enemy 'holding his line almost entirely with machine-guns'. Despite this, they successfully took their sub-objective, the trench system of the *HWL I* running along the railway line which cut immediately across their advance. The initial task of the three attached tanks was to assist the Shropshires with this capture. They recorded that 'stubborn resistance was offered by the enemy at VAUX-ANDIGNY Station' but that their tanks 'knocked out the machine-gunners here and at a quarry near the railway and at an isolated building S.E. of the Station and so allowed the Infantry to go forward'. By 06.30 the *HWL I* had been broken, *Battalion Selle Infantry Regiment (IR) 179* being crushed in the process. 1st Buffs passed through the Shropshires on the right,[66] their objective being the *HWL II*. The Buffs were aided in the poor visibility by having the railway

Infantry in the Great War, p.62). Harold James Taylor was commissioned in December 1917. Two officers were gassed, Captain C. R. Young MC (RAMC) and Lieutenant Frederick William Arthur Carter MC (commissioned in December 1915).

65 War Diary, HQ 16 Infantry Brigade, 17 October 1918, TNA WO95/1607.

66 The battalion was commanded that day by Major Lord Teynham, the CO Lieutenant-Colonel Roland Edward Power being on leave. Henry John Philip Sydney Roper-Curzon, 18th Baron Teynham, formerly a yeomanry officer, was commissioned captain in December 1914.

running to their left. They observed that the fog had its benefits, 'parties of the enemy being come upon unaware' to be either killed or made prisoner, and in at least one case an enemy machine-gun was outflanked unobserved.[67] Not being held up by uncut wire, they regarded the barrage as 'excellent', and had avoided the enemy counter-barrage by starting forward a few minutes before zero and keeping close to their own barrage start line. Using flanking movements to overcome the resistance of *I Battalion RIR 25*, a counterattack by elements of four different German units was swept away.[68] Their advance cost 56 casualties in reaching the Blue Line.[69] Following on the left were 2nd York and Lancaster. They were supported by the tanks who had been in action at Vaux-Andigny station, whose second task was to assist in the capture of the high ground between Molain and la Vallée Mulâtre north of the railway, and to provide enfilade fire across the valley up which the 1st Buffs were advancing. The battalion arrived on their objective at approximately the same time as the Buffs, 09.15.[70] 16 Brigade had advanced 2,500 yards and captured five officers and 568 prisoners from 17 different units. The fighting had been 'in some places severe, as the enemy … resisted with considerable determination'.[71]

The Chief of Staff of 30th American Division, Lieutenant-Colonel John Herr, made a serious allegation concerning 6th Division in an unpublished document.[72] He claimed to have contacted his counterpart in 6th Division, presumably Lieutenant-Colonel Thomas Grove the GSO1, to coordinate the jump-off. In this conversation he was allegedly told that 'the 6th would not jump off despite orders to do so'.[73] Herr asserted that he was told: 'There is no use in concealing from you the truth, we just can't do it. We can make a bluff at starting off and open up with artillery fire, but we simply cannot make a real attack'.[74] Herr states that he passed this information to his divisional commander, Major-General Lewis, who in turn relayed it to the corps commander, Major-General Read. Read, Herr wrote, would not take the matter up with Rawlinson, and suggested to his Chief of Staff, Colonel Simonds, that 30th Division form a defensive flank to its right. This did not happen. 6th Division, as has been seen, had a mixed experience that morning. 16 Brigade advanced in an exemplary fashion, but a difficult time was had on the front of 18 Brigade. Mark Whisler has commented that the published accounts, Montgomery's history of Fourth Army and

67 War Diary, 1st Battalion East Kent Regiment, 17 October 1918, TNA WO95/1608. The battalion's strength at the start of the month was 33 officers and 817 ORs, and during the month suffered 16 officer and 244 OR casualties.
68 Including one reserve company from *I Battalion* and two from *II Battalion RIR 25* and *Battalion Dressler (IR 133)* from the *24th Division* (Whisler, op. cit., p.273).
69 Second-Lieutenants Edward Crewdson Pitt-Pitts (commissioned in May 1918), Charles Vincent, Edward Henry Ronca (commissioned in June 1918) and Harold James Taylor (commissioned in December 1917) were killed; and Second-Lieutenant Noel Adair Harper (commissioned in June 1915) wounded. Five ORs were killed, 33 wounded and five gassed, with 13 missing.
70 The battalion war diary for the day of the attack is lost. The unit was commanded by Lieutenant-Colonel James Robert Robertson, who may well have been wounded that day as the unit was commanded two days later by the adjutant, Captain Ernest Edward Battle. Robertson had four battalion commands between July 1917 and 17 October 1918. CWGC records indicate one officer (Lieutenant Horace George Williams, commissioned from sergeant in August 1916) and eight other ranks killed, including CSM Herbert Yates, a time-expired regular private who had enlisted in 1907.
71 Montgomery, op. cit., p.213.
72 John K. Herr, 'My Personal Experiences and Observations in Connection with the Great War', John K. Herr Papers, United States Military Academy Archives, West Point, New York, cited in M. Yockelson, 'Brothers in Arms', p.312.
73 Yockelson, op. cit., p.302.
74 Herr, op. cit.

Marden's history of 6th Division, as well as the IX Corps Narrative of Operations, 'seem to gloss over the 18th Brigade's problems'.[75] This is not entirely fair, as Marden specifically noted that it had to be 'carried forward by the oncoming waves of the 1st Division'.[76] All three of its leading battalions met with uncut wire and stiff opposition, had lost the barrage, and had difficulty in keeping direction. This caused a complete loss of impetus on the brigade front, which had not happened for 46th Division in the valley below. The commentary in the war diary located the problems some way down the chain of command. It was thus suggested that the 'regrettable delay' on the part of 2nd DLI was occasioned by 'lack of experience' of company commanders 'who did not realise that with a fresh Division about to leap-frog through it was essential to push on without delay were it at all possible to do so'.[77] The same comment was not made about 11th Essex. As will be seen, 1st Cameron Highlanders similarly noted the 'stickiness' of the troops of the Essex companies who had remained on the ridge. The difficulties of 18 Brigade no doubt have a number of different roots. During the previous month, the formation had undergone an extremely hard time in the fighting for the Quadrilateral in front of the Hindenburg Line on 24 September. It had been rested during the heavy fighting of 8 October, coming into line again for the doomed small operation of the 12th. Peter Simkins concludes that 'the evidence … appears to suggest that the 18th Brigade <u>may</u> not have been as combat sharp as other formations in 6th Division and morale and leadership <u>may</u> have had something to do with this'.[78] However, it is similarly clear that if 18 Brigade had such problems, it did not extend across the whole division. It would indeed be highly surprising if the division's GSO1 had said that the whole division would fail to go forward. This would not just represent unthinkable lack of loyalty, there were also simply no general grounds in the division's previous performance for saying this. If anything, it was the 30th American Division who experienced difficulties on 17 October (as it had during the Pursuit and would again on the 18th and 19th), leaving the British flanks exposed rather than vice versa. In the American case, as will become clear, there were evident precursors. The credibility of the remarks attributed to Colonel Grove seems questionable.

Except at Vaux-Andigny station, tank support was of mixed value to the division, being of use on the left but suffering loss of direction on the right, despite navigation by compass. Five of the nine tanks allocated to 6th and 46th Divisions survived to rally near the Blue Line at Angin Farm 'one with the crew badly gassed and one with the sponson door blown off'.[79] One tank appeared to have been through Regnicourt and Andigny-les-Fermes in advance of the infantry, reaching the outskirts of Wassigny in the rear of the as then uncaptured *HWL II* before turning back. 16th Tank Battalion reckoned that three of their machines had been through Andigny-les-Fermes whilst it was still in enemy hands.[80]

I Bavarian Corps responded swiftly to the IX Corps attack by pushing forward its reserves. *15th Reserve Division's* own support asset, *RIR 17*, was deployed at 07.00, and of the two divisions held back to support the front line, *29th Infantry Division* was made ready to move and elements were

75 Whisler, op. cit., p.313.
76 Marden, op. cit., p.70.
77 War Diary, HQ 18 Infantry Brigade, 'Narrative of the Attack on the 17 October 1918', TNA WO95/1615.
78 Peter Simkins, personal communication, email 10 March 2016.
79 War Diary, 16th Tank Battalion, 'History of 16th Battalion Tank Corps, 17 October 1918', TNS WO95/115.
80 War Diary, 16th Tank Battalion, 'History of 16th Battalion Tank Corps, 17 October 1918', TNS WO95/115.

placed under the control of the *3rd Naval* and *24th Divisions*, whilst the *221st Infantry Division* actually began moving forward at 06.55.[81] These reinforcements would largely provide difficulties for the leapfrogging 1st Division, commanded by Major-General Edward Strickland.[82] The brigades of the division were to pass through those of 6th Division, and take the *HWL II*, pushing forward a further 1,500 yards to la Vallée Mulâtre. Here they would pause for three hours to allow field artillery and machine-gun battalions to move up. They would then push on a further 3,000 yards and take Wassigny, from whence patrols were to exploit to the Sambre-Oise Canal. 1 Brigade (Brigadier-General Leonard Wheatley)[83] and 2 Brigade (Brigadier-General George Kelly)[84] had a difficult assembly in an overcrowded position. They had to pass through the tail of both 46th and 6th Divisions, and avoid the tail of the 59th American Brigade and the head of the 60th, all though low scrubland. Both brigades had a section of Royal Engineers and a machine-gun company attached. Four tanks from 16th Tank Battalion had also been allotted to the division.

1 Brigade fielded the 1st Loyal North Lancashire on the right, with two sections of A Company 1st Battalion MGC attached to protect the right of the advance. On the road up the Bellevue spur, where so much had gone wrong for 11th Essex, they met heavy resistance from unsuppressed machine-guns at the shrine on the road at Bellevue Farm, which were holding the entire attack up.[85] The two leading companies and battalion HQ led by Lieutenant-Colonel Robert Berkeley outflanked the position and in a 'ferocious assault' smashed *III Battalion RIR 25*,[86] taking 170 of the enemy prisoner along with 10 machine-guns.[87] The two machine-gun sections came into action firing 6,000 rounds and 'many of the enemy were seen to fall.'[88] The two companies continued their advance and, straying slightly to the right under heavy fire, outflanked and participated in the capture of Andigny-les-Fermes, the objective of 46th Division. Here they captured a further 70 prisoners for the loss of five killed and five wounded. The two companies to the rear, which had lost touch, followed the correct direction and ended up north-east of Andigny les Fermes. When the mist suddenly cleared the enemy opened fire with two field guns and machine-guns,

81 Whisler, op. cit., p.273.

82 Major-General Edward Peter 'Hungry Face' Strickland KCB CMG KBE DSO (1869-1951) had been commanding 1st Manchester in August 1914. After commanding the Bareilly, Jullundur and 98 Brigades, he commanded 1st Division from 12 June 1916.

83 Brigadier-General Leonard Lane Wheatley DSO (1876-1954), was a regular captain of the Argyll & Sutherland Highlanders in August 1914. He successively commanded 1/4th London, 1st Royal Scots Fusiliers, and 2nd Argyll & Sutherland Highlanders between April 1916 and December 1917. He was promoted GOC 197 Brigade in April 1918, and moved to command 1 Brigade on 22 September.

84 Brigadier-General George Charles Kelly (1880-1938), was a regular captain of the King's Royal Rifle Corps in August 1914. He commanded 17th Middlesex and 2nd KRRC between April 1917 and March 1918, having served as a staff captain, brigade-major, and GSO2. He took over command of 2 Brigade on 23 March 1918. He was wounded on 26 September 1918, Lieutenant-Colonel Dudley Graham Johnson, 2nd Royal Sussex, taking over, and returned in October, but exactly when is not clear. 1st Division's order of battle gives him as in command on 17 October.

85 Even after both the leading battalions had passed through, 1st Black Watch in support met unsuppressed machine-guns, which had thus been passed over by battalions of both 6th and 1st Divisions.

86 Whisler, op. cit., p.271.

87 Lieutenant-Colonel Robert Esme Berkeley DSO MC, was a regular captain of the North Lancashire Regiment in August 1914, taking over command of the battalion six days before the opening of the Battle of the Selle. This attack cost 1st Loyal North Lancashire two killed and one officer and 15 ORs wounded. (War Diary, 1st Loyal North Lancashire Regiment, 'Report on part taken by the 1st Battalion Loyal North Lancashire 17 October 1918', TNA WO95/1266).

88 War Diary, 1st Battalion Machine Gun Corps, 'Summary of Operations from 17th to 27th October 1918', TNA WO95/1256.

which the Lancashire companies then rushed. Moving forward towards Blancs Fosses on the edge of the Andigny Forest, as the advance to the second objective demanded, they came under heavy machine-gun fire, HE and gas, and dug in.

To the left, in the valley, the 1st Cameron Highlanders found themselves under shellfire within minutes of moving off. They soon encountered a trench full of the 11th Essex, 'with a number of the enemy in the trench immediately to the front'. The Camerons passed through and 'rounded up the enemy'.[89] The Scots were, however, behind time, had lost the barrage, and themselves became stalled under machine-gun fire from the Bellevue spur. After the Loyal North Lancashires had cleared both the shrine and Bellevue Farm, the Camerons were able to mop up and push on with little opposition until they approached the Angin Farm ridge. As with the units of 6th Division, they became held up by both a line of machine-guns and enfilade fire from the right. Three of the tanks that rallied nearby were ordered to help them move forward, Lieutenant-Colonel John Bingham, the tank battalion commander,[90] arriving on horseback to sanction this. Although one of the tanks was knocked out, the resistance of *II Battalion RIR 25* was overcome, and the Camerons pushed on to join the North Lancashires west of la Vallée Mulâtre, digging in under heavy fire. They were, however, able to confidently introduce fire and movement tactics into the situation. Whilst the leading companies maintained covering fire, assisted by an attached section of guns of Royal Field Artillery, the Camerons' CO, Lieutenant-Colonel Henry Methuen, dispatched a platoon of the reserve D Company to work round by the railway on the left, coming up behind the enemy on the defended spur.[91] The manoeuvre was 'brilliantly carried out … with complete success'.[92] For absolutely no casualties they captured 42 prisoners, and 10 machine-guns.[93]

Forming up on 1st Division's left, 2 Brigade had carefully reconnoitred a route though gardens and hedges in Vaux-Andigny to avoid the road and any shelling directed upon it, but could not find it in the fog, ending up on the main thoroughfare it had sought to avoid.[94] The enemy was indeed shelling the town and the corps gun positions at Becquigny heavily. 1st Northamptonshire, commanded by Lieutenant-Colonel Guy Robinson,[95] advanced on the right, and the machine-gun

89 War Diary, HQ 1 Infantry Brigade, 'Summary of Operations October 17th-19th 1918', TNA WO95/1262.

90 The Honourable John Dennis Yelverton Bingham was a captain in the 15th Hussars in August 1914. He assumed command on 27 December 1917. It was appropriate that he arrived on horseback as he was a British Olympic polo player in 1924. Bingham's horse was one of the few in use on the battlefield that day – both 1 and 2 Brigades had a squadron of the Royal Scots Greys attached, but their use was not possible.

91 Lieutenant-Colonel Henry Charles Methuen DSO MOC, had been a regular lieutenant of Cameron Highlanders in August 1914, and had commanded the 1st Battalion since January 1917.

92 War Diary, 1st Infantry Division, 'Narrative of Operations of 1st Division on October 17th, 18th & 19th 1918', TNA WO95/1234.

93 War Diary, 1st Battalion Queen's Own Cameron Highlanders, 17 October 1918, TNA WO95/1264. During the two days of fighting 17-18 October the Camerons captured one 5.9-inch howitzer, five 4.2-inch howitzers, two 77-mm guns, three trench mortars and 60 machine-guns. Their casualties for the month included ten officers 196 other ranks.

94 The brigade group comprised B Company, 1st Battalion MGC, one section of 409 Field Company RE, a squadron of Royal Scots Greys, one section of 5th Cavalry Brigade Machine Gun Squadron, 6th Battalion Tank Corps and one section B Company 16th Battalion Tank Corps. (War Diary 2nd Battalion Royal Sussex Regiment, October 1918, 2 Brigade Order No, 232, TNA WO95/1269).

95 Guy St. George Robinson DSO had been a second-lieutenant commanding No. 16 Platoon of the battalion in August 1914. He commanded from 10 July 1917. Rising to the rank of major-general in the post-war period, he commanded 209th Independent Brigade in 1941.

nests passed unnoticed in the fog by 6th Division opened up on them. Overcoming these and advancing by compass, they formed up on the intermediate objective and when the barrage proceeded, moved off again, using the railway line to keep direction. 2nd King's Royal Rifle Corps on the far left of the division had set off through fog and smoke, and on leaving Vaux-Andigny Lieutenant-Colonel Herbert Smith and his adjutant 'found themselves alone in the mist with a handful of men, the rest of the battalion having disappeared'.[96] Reforming, the unit encountered elements of 16 Brigade apparently 'digging in some 800-1000 yards short of their objective' (a matter likely due to fog rather than stickiness). Meeting little opposition, albeit being shelled the while, they passed through them and arrived to the north of la Vallée Mulâtre. They had advanced for some four hours without knowledge of there being supporting units on either flank. Here they found that 'the enemy had a great number of well-concealed nests of MGs in hedges etc. which kept up a big volume of fire'.[97] The KRRC utilised the same tactics as had the Cameron Highlanders to deal with this block to their progress. D Company outflanked two machine-guns on the right, but the rest continued to hold up the advance. B and C Companies were ordered to conduct a similar manoeuvre to the left and encountered a well-held sunken road, uncleared as the neighbouring Americans had yet to appear.[98] After taking this, the American 117th Infantry arrived and together they rushed the Wassigny-St Souplet railway embankment to the north, where they were being fired on by no less than 51 machine-guns. The right of the battalion, however, could not progress.

La Vallée Mulâtre is an undistinguished village that was to see a back-and-forwards struggle that day. Situated on the outskirts of the tip of the Andigny Forest, it comprises three roads descending into the village centre, which lies in a shallow valley along which ran the Wassigny-Vaux-Andigny railway. *RIR 17* was pushed forward to protect it as the British approached. 1st Northamptonshire advanced towards it on a two company front. C Company, with two machine-guns of No. 1 Section B Company 1st Battalion MGC, were to occupy higher ground to the north of la Vallée Mulâtre, whilst A Company had been directed to take the village. The company advanced along the slope of the valley into the northern part round the right flank of *I Battalion RIR 17* who had entered the centre. The accompanying tanks headed into the railway cutting under a bridge in the south of the village, beyond which was a halt. The waiting enemy knocked out the first tank, but the second wiped out those defending the halt. After further fighting, the enemy unit was expelled. About half an hour later, however, a counterattack by *II Battalion RIR 17* and the remnants of *I Battalion* from the Andigny Forest in turn pushed the Northamptons back to the centre of the village. Fierce fighting ensued.

By the middle of the day, an impasse had been reached. *24th Division* ordered counterattacks by *IRs 142* and *113* in the early afternoon,[99] but these made little impact. The original barrage having long ceased, infantry weapons and the attached mobile artillery were proving insufficient to overcome an enemy who 'had fought well and were continuing to fight well'.[100] A new barrage was

96 Montgomery, op. cit., p.215. Lieutenant-Colonel Herbert Frederick Edgar Smith DSO was commissioned into 5th KRRC in September 1914. He commanded from 6 October 1918.

97 These were elements of the *24th Division*, *RIR 17*, and *IR 142* of *29th Division* which was in reserve at the junction of the British and American attacks. (Whisler, op. cit., p.275).

98 The role of the attached squadron of Royal Scots Greys had been to keep with the 30th American Division, and in the event of losing touch 'bridge a gap' or form a defensive flank. The squadron was under the effective control of the CO of 2nd KRRC. (War Diary 2nd Battalion Royal Sussex Regiment, October 1918, 2 Brigade Order No, 232, TNA WO95/1269).

99 Whisler, op. cit., p.282.

100 War Diary, 1st Infantry Division, 17 October 1918, TNA WO95/1234. The 1st Division captured prisoners from four divisions that day, the presence of the *24th Division* 'not being known to be in line'.

requested in order to renew the assault, and at 17.15 the attack resumed, although the shelling was 'only moderate'.[101] It fortuitously coincided with the counterattack of *221st Division*, *IR 45* pushing towards la Vallée Mulâtre, and *RIR 60* towards Andigny les Fermes.[102] *IR 45* were smashed by the barrage, and the village was once again re-occupied by the Northamptons with the capture of eight artillery pieces and some 30 machine-guns. The enemy again fled back into the Andigny Forest. The village now secured, the battalion established posts to the east, in front of the wood.[103] On the right, the Loyal North Lancashires and Camerons pushed back *RIR 60's* counterattack and reached the edge of the forest, but in a day of see-sawing action were in turn driven back by *221st Division's* barrage, which included gas.[104] Here they were sent two sections of B Company 1st Battalion MGC (three sections having been placed under the command of the CO of the reserve battalion, 2nd Royal Sussex) whose eight guns they organised for defensive work. This was typical of the way in which the heavy machine-guns were used that day, flexibly and opportunistically.

In addition to the heavy tanks which had already come into action, four Whippets of B Company 6th (Light) Tank Battalion had been ordered to la Vallée Mulâtre at 10.00. The Whippet operation had been in planning since 13 October, and B Company had received orders on the 15th that it would cooperate with 2nd KRRC, and C Company that it might be used in exploitation towards the canal. Preparation had been careful. The tank officers had visited both division and brigade HQs on 14, 15 and 16 October 'and personally saw officers commanding infantry units they were working with'.[105] They had proceeded north of the Wassigny-Vaux-Andigny railway liaising closely with the infantry. When 2nd KRRC became held up, the machines were summoned into action. Tank A.321 was ordered to deal with machine-guns in small copses to the north of la Vallée Mulâtre on the KRRC's right flank, but whilst it silenced a number of these guns, the infantry were still not able to advance. The other three machines were sent to the left flank in the direction of a small group of houses at Demi-lieue on the railway line,[106] with orders to work round the opposition from different directions, the infantry advancing behind the machines due to the heavy machine-gun fire. All the tanks were, however, knocked out in turn by a field gun, and the infantry had to retire some 200 yards. Tank A.321 then offered its services, but to spare it the fate of its fellows, Colonel Smith wisely declined.[107] The attempted advance came to a halt. KRRC's progress

101 War Diary, 1st Infantry Division, 'Narrative of Operations of 1st Division on October 17th, 18th & 19th 1918', TNA WO95/1234.

102 Whisler, op. cit., p.283.

103 Anonymous, *The Northamptonshire Regiment 1914-1918*, p.297. Second-Lieutenant Reginald Sydney Strange (commissioned from private in May 1918) was killed, as was Second-Lieutenant Frank Alfred George (commissioned from sergeant in July 1918). Lieutenant Alleyne St George Coldwell (commissioned in October 1914); and Second-Lieutenants Arthur Fullen MC (commissioned from CSM in July 1917), R. Lewis, J. T. Roberts and Bertram Lonsdale Keeshan (commissioned from private in 3rd Hussars June 1917) were wounded. 12 ORs were killed and 91 wounded. Keeshan was awarded the MC for his actions on the 17th. The citation reads: 'For conspicuous gallantry and good leadership while commanding a company during an attack on 17th October, 1918, near Vaux-Andigny. In spite of thick fog and machine-gun fire, he led his company on to the first objective. Later, he led his men to the attack and capture of La Vallée Mulâtre, capturing and killing many of the enemy. He has done consistent good service'. (*London Gazette*, 1 April 1919)

104 During the day 1st Loyal North Lancashire suffered five officers wounded, with 16 ORs killed, 16 missing and 90 wounded.

105 Anonymous, *The War History of The Sixth Tank Battalion*, p.184.

106 Tanks A.379, A.377 and A.347.

107 War Diary, 6th Tank Battalion, 17 October 1918, TNA WO95/107. C Company of Whippets (12 tanks) had followed B Company to near Angin Farm, being held for exploitation. One company of 4 tanks was

that day had been at considerable cost. Four officers were either killed or died of wounds,[108] with five wounded; and amongst the other ranks, 22 had been killed or died of wounds, whilst 135 were wounded and 16 missing.

2nd KRRC might have come to a halt, but this was not quite the end of 1st Division's advance. In reserve were 2nd Royal Sussex. They had proceeded to la Vallée Mulâtre behind the KRRC, in artillery formation of two lines of companies each in two lines of platoons. They dealt summarily with the remaining machine-gun nests they encountered en route. Seeing the KRRC were held up by machine-guns in a house on the north-west corner of la Vallée Mulâtre, Sergeant Albert Folwell on his own initiative placed two of the attached Vickers guns on high ground and engaged the enemy whilst a platoon encircled them.[109] A gap had opened up between the Northamptons and the KRRC and Lieutenant-Colonel Johnson pushed up a company to fill it, demonstrating the quick thinking of unit COs already evident in IX Corps that morning. The battalion was ordered to join the renewed attack at 17.15, and pass through the KRRC. This they did, but were the only unit to get much further forward uphill towards Bellevue (this other Bellevue being a farm on the rising ground between Demi-lieue and Ribeauville), finding themselves 1,000 yards in front of the KRRC and the Americans to their left, and enfiladed on both sides by the machine-guns of *IR 142*. They retired and formed up on the railway line at Demi-lieue, and threw out their flanks, having suffered four fatal casualties.[110] The day's advance for both 1st Division and IX Corps thus came to an end. In reviewing its progress on compass bearings alone in fog through opposition to arrive on the Red Line virtually on time, the division described a 'very great military achievement on the part of the units concerned'.[111] Given the problems, they were probably right.

In the air above the Fourth Army, 5 Brigade RAF described the weather as 'fine but very misty – clearing later – visibility poor'. There were no reconnaissance flights and balloon observation, with only eleven artillery patrols and 17 zone calls. Ground attack was carried out as and when possible. One hundred and sixty 25-pound bombs were dropped, one run being on trains and transport in Catillon, and just over 13,000 rounds of ammunition were fired. Patrols of 92 Squadron attacked three machine-gun pits near Wassigny; troops were attacked with machine-gun fire near Catillon, and patrols of 84 Squadron dropped 24 bombs and fired 1,200 rounds at enemy troops from low altitude. Similarly, patrols of 80 Squadron attacked an unspecified gun emplacement, and eight enemy field guns galloping into action. German air activity was described as 'very slight', and there were only three combats, each side losing one machine.[112] Overall, however, the RAF was able to

sent forward in support of B Company. Contact being lost, the company commander, Major William Otter Gibbs, went forward to get news of them and became a casualty. C Company did not see action. Gibbs had been an officer of the 10th Hussars, whom he commanded at several points during the war. He was seconded to the Tank Corps on 9 June 1918, and his wound on 17 October was his fourth of the war. 6th Tank Battalion had 12 casualties on the 17th, three fatal.

108 The four killed were Second-Lieutenants James MacMillan Hunter (commissioned from lance-corporal in September 1917); Alfred Claude Gant (commissioned from private in June 1918), Walter Septimus Gibbs (commissioned from private in March 1918); and Alan James Stephen (commissioned from lance-corporal in the South African infantry in August 1918).

109 Albert Folwell had enlisted in the Northamptonshire Regiment, transferring to the Machine Gun Corps.

110 War Diary, 2nd Battalion Royal Sussex, 17 October 1918, TNA WO95/1269. Ten machine-guns and a field gun were captured in Demi-lieue, and 215 prisoners taken.

111 War Diary, HQ 1st Infantry Division, 'Narrative of Operations October 17th, 18th & 19th 1918', TNA WO95/1234.

112 War Diary, 5 Brigade RAF, 17 October 1918, TNA AIR 1/2225/209/26.

add very little in support of the infantry on 17 October, much of the action described being beyond the front line established at the end of the afternoon, largely due to the fog early in the day.

The corps concluded its day significantly short of its optimistic objectives. In mitigation, the fighting had been 'very severe and confused in the fog, the enemy resisting with great determination'.[113] In particular, the accumulation of German reserve units had succeeded in bringing the advance to a halt at la Vallée Mulâtre by midday, and prevented much further progress late in the afternoon. The directional complexity of the attack and barrage reflected the ground. Even if morning mist was predictable given the weather of the previous days, nature confounded matters further with a particularly dense fog. Yet it was a double-edged sword. On one hand it was 'the cause of considerable delay and loss of direction', on the other 'it was undoubtedly of assistance in enabling the attack to be carried through against the strongly held enemy positions with comparatively light casualties'.[114] Homage was paid to the 'perseverance and gallantry' of the attacking troops.[115] The corps had advanced 4,500 yards, pushing though both the *HWL I* and *II*, and had 'firmly established itself on the crest of the water-shed which divided the Selle and the Sambre valleys, and was in an excellent position to continue its advance next day'.[116]

II American Corps

The American Corps had both its divisions, now weak in numbers, in line. The 27th Division which had been holding the line prior to the battle was on the left, the 30th was re-introduced on the right the day before having been out of the line for three days, resting. The official strength of an American division, over twice that of a British division, was 28,105 men. The 27th Division, however, had only a total rifle strength of 2,377 men, whilst the 30th Division was in slightly better condition with a strength of between 3,650 and 4,250.[117] The forces opposing the advance of the 30th Division were the weak *24th Infantry* and *3rd Naval Divisions*, whose estimated combined strength was about 1,300 combatants.[118] Although the time for stern exhortation had probably passed, the *Naval Division's* commander, Generalmajor Graf von Moltke, declared on the day before the battle that: 'Fear of the "Tommy" is not permitted'. Returning to the principles that had cost the German Army so dear on the Somme in 1916, he further ordered that any break in the *Hermann Stellung* 'must be levelled out through an immediate counterattack'. In a beseeching that must have rung particularly hollow, he continued that every counterattack 'of even the smallest detachment must drive forward with a Hurra and cold steel as the enemy flees back'. Although this may seem steeped in pathos in retrospect, von Moltke knew that he had little more to offer than words, for as he acknowledged to his corps commander, his entire force lay under the Fourth Army's guns, 'the troops lay in the few cellars in Molain, in small trench holes behind hedges … without protection against the weather or enemy fire'.[119] Despite this, the two formations put up a strong resistance which would cause the 30th Division to fall behind the British on the right and

113 'IX Corps Narrative', 17 October 1918, IWM Docs 20537 Fourth Army Papers Vol. 63.
114 'IX Corps Narrative', 17 October 1918, IWM Docs 20537 Fourth Army Papers Vol. 63.
115 'IX Corps Narrative', 17 October 1918, IWM Docs 20537 Fourth Army Papers Vol. 63.
116 Montgomery, op. cit., p.216.
117 The strength for 30th Division is an estimate as per Whisler, op. cit., p.242.
118 Whisler, p.277. The 3rd Naval Division's artillery comprised 44 77-millimetre guns, 21 10.5-centimetre field howitzers, seven 15-centimetre heavy howitzers, six 21-centimetre howitzers, and two naval guns (Whisler, p.259).
119 War Diary, *3rd Naval Division*, 15 & 16 October 1918, (quoted in Whisler, p.260).

the 27th Division on the left. Behind the two frontline German divisions stood the *29th Infantry Division,* its nearest elements just to the east of Mazinghien. Although Fourth Army intelligence rated it as first-class, by this point its strength was probably only 1,900.[120]

The barrage of 18-pounders began 200 yards in advance of the start line, firing 50 per cent shrapnel and six per cent smoke; with a 4.5-inch howitzer barrage a further 200 yards to the east. It moved forward 100 yards every three minutes to form a protector barrage on the Red Dotted Line, where it would remain until zero plus 132 minutes, during which time superimposed 18-pounder batteries would sweep the front, concentrating on specific areas. These included ground to the immediate east of l'Arbre de Guise (see Map 9), and, more optimistically, the gentle St Maurice River valley running across the line of advance between Jonc de Mer Farm and Catillon, a potential spot for artillery placement. This latter search and sweep was to be carried out by two brigades of artillery pushed forward when the infantry reached the first objective. The support battalions would leapfrog on the Red Dotted Line and continue the assault. Two minutes before the barrage moved on, its fire would be increased to rapid as a signal to the infantry. It would then progress at the same rate to the final objective, where at zero plus 222 minutes, it would cease. The heavy artillery meanwhile would put down a barrage on selected locations and points of assembly, its lifts coinciding with the barrage. Care was taken that there would be no heavy artillery fire within 600 yards of the infantry. After zero plus 222 minutes the heavy artillery was to target positions around Mazinghien, preparing the advance to the Brown Line. To support this exploitation, two brigades of field artillery, one brigade of mobile heavy artillery, and two mobile sections of 6-inch trench mortars were to be pushed across the river by both divisions as soon as bridges were up. Engineering would, therefore, be crucial to the advance. Tanks were fairly thin on the ground, but twenty machines of the 301st US Heavy Tank Battalion were to go into action, split equally between the two divisions. Officers of the battalion had not been able to survey the Selle by day, but night exploration had identified a suitable crossing point near Molain, to the south of which the river had its source and where it was less than 10 feet wide with no banks. Here it was deemed easily passable with the use of cribs (large and very strong hexagonal crates), which would be dropped into the river and which could bear the weight of a tank.[121] The American tank commander, Major Ralph Sasse, noted that the infantry 'were sceptical in the use of tanks with infantry since so many of the machines had proved a failure during the attack on the St Quentin Canal'.[122] Sasse ordered his officers to work with the infantry units to ensure that the orders were understood.

59 Brigade attacked with the 117th Infantry on the right, abutting IX Corps, and the 118th on the left. It was 'opposed by *1st, 2nd and 3rd Regiments German Saxon Marines*, who fought more desperately than any enemy we had yet encountered'.[123] They 'fought to the bitter end with no idea or thought of surrender'.[124] The brigade's start was compromised, however. The history of F Company 2nd Battalion of the 118th, which was in support to the leading 3rd Battalion, states that at five minutes before zero, a machine-gun barrage opened overhead. This over-eager start immediately drew counter-barrage fire, which included mustard gas, causing many American casualties. After this misfortune, the division's units had to cope with a second problem in that they had the longest distance of any unit that morning to travel, their starting point being 1,500 yards from

120 Whisler, op cit. p.262.

121 War Diary, Headquarters 4 Tank Brigade, 'Report on Operations 4th Tank Brigade September 27th to October 17th 1918', TNA WO95/108/5.

122 Yockelson, op. cit., p.296.

123 W.P. Sullivan & H. Tucker, *The History of the 105th Regiment of Engineers,* p.207.

124 E.A. Murphy & R.S. Thomas, *The Thirtieth Division in the World War,* p.122.

the enemy outposts in Molain. 59 Brigade set off downhill from their starting point to the east of la Haie Menneresse, struggling with direction in the fog, the enemy fire continuing to be heavy. Sergeant LeRoy Smith of F Company, badly affected by gas 'conducted the company by the aid of a compass … indicating the direction with his hands, being unable to speak'.[125] The 117th Regiment, which had lost its C Company two hours before zero due to ptomaine poisoning from eating rotten food, was not just affected by the artillery counter-barrage, but by machine-gun fire from the enemy outposts in Molain. The leading 1st Battalion missed machine-gun posts on the village outskirts in the fog, and these took their toll on the following 2nd Battalion, which by 07.00 had lost all its officers except one.[126] Whilst *Battalion Reichardt IR 139* of *24th Division*, defending the village, was almost completely destroyed in the fighting, Molain was only cleared by 09.00 with the help of tanks, and consequently the barrage was long lost. The remaining defenders from *Marine Infantry Regiments 2 and 3* retreated. After reorganising, the Americans pushed slowly up the slope, overrunning an artillery battery, the right of their advance catching up with the 2nd King's Royal Rifle Corps of 1st Division in whose company the railway embankment at Demi-lieue (at this point some 2,000 yards from the river) was jointly rushed. On the left, attempts to progress further met with intense machine-gun fire, and the 117th were only able to get forward a further 600-700 yards until they reached a track that ran south from l'Arbre de Guise, diagonally away from the Red Dotted Line on the Wassigny-Le cateau road towards where the right of the brigade had progressed to Demi-lieue. The 3rd Battalion of the 117th had attempted to outflank the opposing machine-gun nests, but either found that their advance was too exposed on the steep slope up to the road, or that there were two guns in a nest which could turn to either flank and defeat such a manoeuvre. In addition, the enemy brought up trench mortars and field artillery.[127] The unit could progress no further. Unfortunately, misunderstanding an artillery order, the 117th withdrew even further late in the afternoon, but managed to regain the ground vacated. That there was a command and control problem is not surprising – by noon, all the officers of the 1st and 2nd Battalions of the 117th had become casualties, and the whole regiment was under the command of the CO of the 3rd. The Americans were 900 yards short of the objective. Enemy fire from the direction of Ribeauville, which would cause similar problems the following day, had proved the sticking point.

On the left of the attack, hit by both the counter-barrage and the fog, the 118th Infantry advanced downhill to the south of St. Martin Rivière (actually on the east bank) but veered off to their right, some elements ending up in Molain before they had crossed the river. They were supported by tanks, but 'on account of the density of the fog' it was 'impossible' for the infantry to keep in touch with them. The troops of the 118th, therefore, fought a soldier's battle tackling 'machine-gun nests with automatic rifles, grenades, and rifles'.[128] The tanks made some impact at St Martin, but one was destroyed, according to German claims, by six bundled stick grenades, a feat which must have required perilously close proximity to the target.[129] At approximately 09.00 four tanks, probably strays from the 27th Division area, and the 2nd Battalion 106th Infantry from

125 P.H. Fike, *History of Co. F, 118th Infantry (Hampton Guards) 30th Division*, p.30. F Company had gone into action at the Hindenburg Line on 29 September with four officers and 185 other ranks, but by 20 October only 29 men remained.

126 'Report of Operations on October 17th 1918, Headquarters 2nd Battalion 117th Infantry, AEF', (cited in Whisler, op. cit., p.238).

127 'Report of Action, 3rd Btn. 117th Inf. AEF from Oct. 15 to Oct. 22 1918', cited in Whisler, op. cit., p.279.

128 S. Royall, *History of the 118th Infantry*, pp.39-40.

129 War Diary, *Stab/Marine Infantry Regiment*, 17 October 1918 (cited in Whisler op. cit., p.280).

The Selle near its source at Molain proved little obstacle to the 301st American Tank Battalion.

The Selle at St Souplet bridged by the 102nd American Engineers. The original bridge destroyed by the enemy was subject to reconstruction as an artillery bridge and was open by noon on 17 October.

the same division entered St Martin and hit the flank of the defenders, the battalion staff of the defending *I Battalion Marine IR 1* being captured. The arrival of these tanks was serendipitous, as they had struggled with direction in the fog. One tank commander had the added misfortune of a broken compass and, as a result, 'crossed the Selle three times, believing he was crossing different streams'.[130] The 118th pursued the retreating enemy up the 1,000 yard slope towards the railway, but struggled under heavy fire, arriving there only at 11.30. Overcoming the resistance, the 118th pushed on to join the 105th Infantry at l'Arbre de Guise on its left, and linked with the 117th at the road. 'The enemy was firing his artillery over open sights directly in front',[131] and no further advance was possible, the Germans having been reinforced by *IR 112* from the *29th Division*, which counterattacked to the unit's left.

On the left of the American attack the 27th Division, nicknamed 'O'Ryan's Roughnecks' after its commander, Major-General John O'Ryan,[132] faced the *204th Division* of the *LI Corps*. This division had seen recent heavy combat, was rated as third class, but its three infantry regiments had a trench strength of 3,531 troops.[133] In reserve was the *54th Division*, rated second class but badly battered, with a strength of only 575. The approach of 53 Brigade on the right had been subjected to heavy shelling both with high explosive and gas, and masks had to be worn continually.[134] The 27th had to effect a river crossing, and 'severe losses' were sustained by the 102nd Engineer Regiment 27th Division in placing footbridges across the Selle. Four of its sergeants were awarded 'well-merited commendation for their valour and determination in advancing and placing the heavy foot bridges'.[135] Major-General O'Ryan, however, in noting that 15 engineers were killed that day, with more than three times this number wounded, suggested that they suffered from 'the psychological effect of certain physical features of terrain'. Those carrying the ropes and bridges with the leading infantry units had stopped short in a sunken road parallel to St Souplet and had not proceeded over the open ground to the river, unable to judge how much further to advance. Here they were caught by the counter-barrage.[136] Why Ryan chose to invent a new psychological condition rather than simply to ascribe the faltering to the fog, is best known only to him.

Whilst the normal strength of an American infantry regiment was 3,770, the 105th Regiment, attacking on the right, only had a rifle strength of 732, each of its three battalions therefore comprising less than 250 men. The 1st Battalion led the assault.[137] The unit was to reach the Wassigny-Le Cateau road where they and the 108th Battalion of 54 Brigade to the left would be

130 R.B. Harrison, 'Famous Charges Told of the U.S. Tank Brigade', *The Army*, 1 (1919) p.15, cited in Yockelson op. cit., p.304.

131 Royall, op. cit., p.40.

132 John Francis O'Ryan (1874-1961), a lawyer, had been commissioned in the field artillery of the New York National Guard in 1900, and was commanding it as a major-general by 1912. He served in the Pancho Villa Expedition in Mexico in 1916. The New York National Guard became the 27th Division.

133 Whisler, op. cit., p.165. *Reserve Infantry Regiment 120* had 1,080 men, 30 heavy machine-guns and 62 light machine-guns; *Infantry Regiment 413* had 1,344 men, 32 heavy machine-guns and 48 light machine-guns; and *Infantry Regiment 414* had 1,107 men, 36 heavy machine-guns, and 65 light machine-guns.

134 53 Brigade was commanded by Brigadier-General Albert Hazen Blanding (1876-1970), a phosphate company executive, who was commissioned into the Florida National Guard in 1899, and had served as a colonel in the Pancho Villa Expedition. The brigade contained the 105th and 106th Infantry Regiments.

135 J.F. O'Ryan, *The Story of the 27th Division*, p.373.

136 O'Ryan to US Army Chief of Staff, cited in Yockelson, op. cit., p.300.

137 The 1st Battalion was commanded by Captain George F. Bradshaw; the 2nd, in support, by Captain Charles A. MacArthur. Lieutenant Charles R. Whipple commanded the 3rd Battalion. He was wounded during the morning, his place taken by Lieutenant Carl G.R. Ross.

leapfrogged. Like the 27th Division, their jump-off was dogged by misfortune. Captain Howard Bird, commanding the company of 105th Machine Gun Battalion attached,[138] confirmed that several minutes before zero the 30th Division opened up a machine-gun barrage, whereupon an enemy counter-barrage fell with accuracy on the right of the start line of the 27th Division, as it had done on the 30th. Three of the eight company commanders of the two leading infantry battalions became casualties, with many more amongst the other ranks. The machine-gun battalion had placed eight guns with the leading battalion, the rest with the 3rd Battalion. When the counter-barrage fell, three shells killed ten and wounded 45 of the machine-gunners alone. Despite this catastrophic start, the 2nd Battalion carried the 1st forward downhill into the fog and smoke. Progress was slow, and reaching the *HWL I,* which on this part of the front was only 200 yards beyond the river, at 06.00 *III Battalion IR 414* launched a counterattack. The Americans found themselves facing virtually the whole of this regiment, some 1,100 men strong. The delay brought about by the ensuing fighting resulted in the loss of the barrage, but the counterattack was defeated. Advancing uphill, l'Arbre de Guise was captured at 08.45. The 2nd Battalion had sent patrols out on both the north and southern flanks of the village, and had pressed it frontally, but the resistance was not strong, unsurprisingly as virtually the entire *IR 414* had been wiped out.[139]

As soon as it heard l'Arbre de Guise had been taken, 102nd Field Signal Battalion laid a wire up to the village under heavy fire, and good communication with the forward unit was established. Signaller George Morrice recorded his day with the unit in his diary, an account which indicates the intensity of the fighting:

> Lay on ground for 3/4 hour under whiz bang fire within 3 feet. Cpl. Crego 4 feet from me killed by direct hit. 4 direct hits and several wounded. Only God's will that I am still alive. Advanced thru St Souplet shelling. At railroad for 2 hours under shelling. Advanced to front line to Bat. HQ. In shell hole. Moved back to Jerry dig ins. Jerry saw us and strafed. Gas shell (read letters in shell hole) landed. Cleves paralyzed, Cunneen wounded. Sgt. Duble and myself gassed helping them. Went back to dressing station under shelling. Duble to hospital. Only absolutely necessary cases sent to hospital. Doc fixed me up and advised rest. Reported to Sgt. Sherman. He's a prince. Loaned me his shelter half and blanket. Reg. in town. Billeted in cellar at St Souplet.[140]

The machine-gunners attached to the 3rd Battalion had similarly pushed on through their demoralised comrades who had taken heavy casualties. Tasked with protecting the left flank of the advance, they assisted in the capture of Advantage Farm, a strongpoint on the road north of l'Arbre de Guise. After two hours of mopping up in the village, an attempt was made by the infantry to push on, with the initial assistance of a tank which was soon put out of action. The push met strong resistance and the American numbers were not sufficient for the task. They fell back and a line was formed around the eastern edges of the village, creating a small salient with a defensive right flank, which was eventually joined by the 118th Regiment which came up belatedly on the right, and by the early evening 21 machine-guns were organised to repel counterattacks.

138 O'Ryan, op. cit., p.368.
139 Whisler, op. cit., p.174.
140 Diary, Signaller George A. Morrice, 17 October 1918, http://www.oryansroughnecks.org/diary.html (accessed 10 February 2016).

The tank that had offered assistance at l'Arbre de Guise was in fact the only one of the ten allotted to the 27th that got into action to support the division that day. Both divisions' machines had crossed the Selle south of the inter-division boundary near to Molain, the Australian Flying Corps creating noise to mask the sound of the machines moving up. The tanks supporting the 27th Division were supposed to then turn north to assist the leading battalions. Most lost their way in the fog and smoke. Of the twenty that started, nineteen tanks crossed the river, and all made contact with the enemy, but only three reached the Wassigny-Le Cateau road. One had been put out of action at St Martin early on, a further two had burnt out, whilst three had ditched. Only half the number that started were fit for action at the end of the day.[141]

On the left of the American attack, 54 Brigade was essentially already on the river.[142] The 108th Regiment with a rifle strength of 592 attacked with the 1st Battalion in the lead.[143] Clearing the eastern part of St Souplet, the battalion waded across the Selle in the mist and carried on up the steep slope beyond to meet strong resistance at the *HWL I*. The following day, Private William Clarke would describe the aftermath of the assault on the railway embankment here.

> We roamed around the top of this embankment among the German dead and their machine guns. None of these German machine gunners had run, none had retreated. Some are still sitting at their guns, with their fingers frozen in death upon the triggers. Others had the vital lock mechanisms clutched in their fists in an attempt to prevent us from using their guns. These men must have suffered terrible punishment from the artillery and machine gun barrages our attack had played on them.[144]

In dealing with this resistance, essentially destroying the entire *III Battalion IR 413* in the process,[145] the 108th fell behind their barrage. Baudival Farm, half-way between the railway and the Wassigny-Le Cateau road, and part of the intermediate position, had been expected to give considerable resistance. It was situated at the head of a small valley that ran across the slope from St Benin up to the road, which developed at its head into a sharp Y-shaped ravine, providing good shelter for the enemy. The farm had received particular attention from the heavy guns, and the machine-gun barrage directed on it lifted only minutes before the infantry arrived at 06.30. Whilst the farm was captured quite easily, the Americans found that 'the most effective enemy machine-gun positions were those in the open',[146] part of the *HWL II*, away from locations that had been sought out by the artillery. They noted the utility of the enemy machine-gun posts, 'usually on the reverse slope of hillsides' which were mostly hidden from the front and 'effectively used for flanking fire'. Rifle pits, in contrast, were 'extremely shallow and had practically no parapet projecting to afford a target'. Ordinary infantry tactics had been 'scrapped, for German man-power had waned to

141 War Diary, Headquarters 4th Tank Brigade, 'Report on Operations 4th Tank Brigade September 27th to October 17th 1918', TNA WO95/108/5.

142 54 Brigade was commanded by Brigadier-General Palmer Eddy Pierce (1865-1940), a regular soldier commissioned in 1891. He had served in the Spanish-American War in 1898 and the Boxer Rebellion of 1900. Qualified as a staff officer, he had served as an aide to the Secretary of War and as Director of Purchases for the War Industries Board in 1917.

143 The 1st Battalion was commanded by Major Frederick S. Couchman; the 3rd, following, by Captain Samuel H. Merrill. The 2nd Battalion was in reserve.

144 W. Clarke quoted in D. Finlayson, *Crumps and Camouflets*, Chapter 12.

145 Whisler, op. cit., p.176.

146 O'Ryan, op. cit., p.359.

the point where a front could no longer adequately be manned – the rapidly-manoeuvred, desperately-fought machine-gun had to take the place of man-power'.[147]

The 108th took casualties from such positions as these in a sunken road to the north of the farm, but by 09.00 had reached the road. Under fire from higher ground in the direction of le Quennelet Farm (to the north-east) and from Jonc de Mer farm (on a ridge in front to the east), the 1st Battalion, with parties from the 2nd and 3rd, held the Red Dotted Line for some three hours. At 11.00 the German support battalions, *I Battalion RIR 120* and *II Battalion IR 413* counter-attacked at the American/British boundary. Reaching the road, the enemy established machine-guns which drove the British back several hundred yards, and the 108th ended up having to retreat themselves to avoid being enfiladed on an open flank. They dug in on a ridge some 250 yards west of the road, but maintained touch with the 105th in l'Arbre de Guise, under fire all the while from German positions at Jonc de Mer farm. The enemy also pushed up *I Battalion IR 413*, and further advance was impossible. 27th Division had advanced 2,500 yards and had captured a locomotive with 15 wagons, several motor trucks, numerous machine-guns and anti-tank rifles, together with minenwerfers and four field pieces. Twenty-three officers and 579 other ranks had also been taken prisoner.[148]

In the air over the Americans, 3 Squadron of the Australian Flying Corps made 25 flights. As soon as the fog cleared, Lieutenant William Palstra was the second plane in the air in an RE8 at 11.00, this time with Lieutenant Ernest Devlin-Hamilton.[149] The two pilots provided a fine example of how air observation assisted the infantry through cooperation with the artillery. Encountering enemy aircraft, they observed the American 'support troops advancing in open order and in small columns along the road from St Souplet to Arbre Guernon [l'Arbre de Guise]'. Subjected to anti-aircraft fire, they spotted the developing German counterattack that would drive back the British right and American left advancing in open order about two battalions strong. They dropped a flare to alert the artillery and a message at the relevant 18-pounder battery.[150]

The German resistance during the day had been strong, and during the afternoon no less than six counterattacks were made. *RIR 90* and *IR 112* counterattacked l'Arbre de Guise, as did *RIR 27*. *IR 84* attacked Advantage Farm, to the north of the same location, and *Fueselier Regiment (FR) 122* attacked through Quennelet Farm against the British 50th Division. *IR 478* attacked towards Baudival Farm.[151] Despite the effort, all the counterattacks caused little movement in the line. They were piecemeal, reflecting the developing disorder in the enemy's command and control, and thus dissipated their strength. *RIR 27*'s attack against l'Arbre de Guise found that 'the enemy had installed a great number of machine-guns in the windows of the house on the east side of the village'. The Germans reported that 'it was out of the question to take the village without a powerful artillery action and a simultaneous advance by adjacent troops'.[152] Given that the American accounts mention virtually nothing about these counterattacks, it is clear that they were easily repelled. They however prevented further forward movement that day.

The difficulties experienced by the 30th Division in both Molain and achieving the Wassigny-Le Cateau road should not necessarily be seen solely in the light of the comments made about it during the Pursuit by the British tanks and Australian artillery. The Division

147 Murphy & Thomas, op. cit., p.122.
148 O'Ryan, op. cit., pp.373-4.
149 Lieutenant Ernest Alexander Devlin-Hamilton DFC was previously with the Australian Light Horse.
150 3 Squadron Australian Flying Corps, Squadron Record Book, 17 October 1918, AWM4 8/6/22 PART2.
151 Whisler, op. cit., pp.184-5.
152 Report of *RIR 27*, quoted in Whisler, op. cit., p.188.

had the furthest to go of the two, and whilst the consequences of the premature machine-gun barrage, admittedly a self-inflicted wound, gave it a particularly uncomfortable start, it had fought hard in Molain against stiff opposition. Mark Whisler believes that the 'almost fanatical resistance' met from the machine gunners gave the 30th the most difficult task on 17 October of any division apart perhaps for the 66th.[153] However, the loss of the barrage and its undoubted tiredness, even if it was the numerically stronger of the two divisions, caused it to lose steam on the steep uphill slope beyond the river in the face of increasing opposition. The depletion of the division's officers particularly degraded command and control of inexperienced troops. The fact that the second barrage in the afternoon was arranged to enable it merely to progress to the Red Dotted Line is an interesting indication of the division's perception of what it could achieve, and the help it needed. The British 1st Division was, of course, itself stuck at Demi-lieue, where the American and British lines met. When 2nd Royal Sussex attempted to progress uphill at this juncture, the Americans could not assist. 30th Division was consequently left in a disadvantaged position for resuming the attack the following morning (although no more or less than 1st Division). All in all, II American Corps had fallen significantly short of Fourth Army's optimistic objectives, and the day's fighting had been hard. The same may be said, however, for all three corps of the BEF that day.

XIII Corps

The attack of XIII Corps (see Map 10) had been correctly anticipated by the enemy, and the opposing *LI Corps* of the German *Second Army* had 'deployed the strongest and most rested of the newly arriving divisions north and south of the town'.[154] Mark Whisler calculates that the *LI Corps* had a strength of approximately 11,750-12,200 infantry and machine-gunners compared to 10,000-10,500 in XIII Corps and the 27th American Division. The enemy therefore had 'at minimum parity and during the actual assault probably a superiority in battlefield manpower'.[155] *17th Reserve Division*, rated as first class and well rested, was the best division in *LI Corps* and would oppose 66th Division, with *IR 478* in reserve, a unit 1,300 men strong. It had a front of only 2,250 yards, and probably had a strength of 3,500. Not only was it the most formidable infantry division facing XIII Corps, it could also rely on further artillery support from neighbouring *IV Reserve Corps* to the north, whose *44th Reserve Division*, rated first class and both strong and newly arrived, was available. *243rd Infantry Division,* rated as third class but of relatively high strength and rested, held a 2,000 yard front from Le Cateau station (which it held jointly with the *17th Reserve Division*) to St Benin. Its two frontline regiments had a combined trench strength of 2,268.[156] In the south, the *204th Infantry Division*, rated third class, but of also relatively high strength and rested, faced the right of the British 50th Division (and the American 27th). Both divisions had the weak and exhausted second class *54th Division* in reserve.

XIII Corps would fire another complicated barrage.[157] Le Cateau itself would not be shelled, but a barrage fired by four brigades over a small area would cover the 66th Division attack. In 50th

153 Whisler, op. cit., p.298.
154 Whisler, op. cit., p.164.
155 Whisler, op. cit., p.27 and p.94.
156 Fourth Army was not positively aware of its presence until it captured prisoners from it on the 17th. It posessed over 70 heavy and 140 light machine-guns. *Machine-gun Sharpshooter Detachment 41*, with a further 36 heavy machine-guns, was also attached. Whisler, op. cit., p.167.
157 War Diary, Commander Royal Artillery XIII Corps, 17 October 1918, TNA WO95/902.

Division's area, the first stage up to the protector barrage line beyond the intermediate objective, the Wassigny-Le Cateau road (Red Dotted Line), would be fired by five brigades of field artillery from 25th Division, and comprised half shrapnel and half HE. The barrage began 100 yards east of the Selle, moving at a rate of 100 yards every three minutes. Ninety-six machine-guns were superimposed, (16 of the 18th Battalion MGC, 56 of the 100th, and 24 of the 50th), firing on specific targets. The 24 guns of No. 1 Group of the 100th Battalion MGC fired 92,000 rounds on the railway triangle alone.[158] The second stage of the barrage was to be fired by four brigades. On the right of the 50th Division front there was one field gun per 29 yards of front, on the left one gun per 15 yards. Eight brigades of heavy artillery would further support the assault with counter-battery work and the targeting of specific locations, lifts being in conformity with the field artillery barrage. The 4.5-inch howitzers and 60-pounders would shell the *HWL I* for six minutes, lifting to a road just beyond it for a further six minutes, then targeting 'sunken roads, tracks, trenches, railway, buildings, enclosures' 200 yards in advance of the 18-pounder barrage. The 6-inch howitzers shelled the railway yard.[159] The three northerly field artillery brigades (150, 104 & 86) all fired in a north-easterly direction, 150 Brigade, covering Le Cateau station, opening their barrage at zero + 35 minutes. The two southerly brigades (110 and 112) initially fired in an easterly direction, then east-north-east, the width of the barrage expanding as it progressed. Beyond the Red Dotted Line, the four brigades continued the barrage in unison in an east-north-easterly direction. Batteries would then be moved forward to cover the second stage of the advance. Companies of 50th Battalion MGC would be pushed across the river immediately 150 Brigade had crossed.[160]

50th Division, commanded by Major-General Henry Jackson,[161] attacked on a frontage of a mere 600 yards (see Map 11). The plan was complex, involving three phases. Firstly, 151 Brigade on the right (Brigadier-General Richard Sugden),[162] would cross the Selle just north of St Souplet on bridges, capture the *HWL I* and fan out, the right and centre battalions proceeding east-north-east to join the Americans on the Wassigny-Le Cateau road. The left battalion would roll up the *HWL I* moving due north to capture Le Cateau station. Secondly, in 149 Brigade (Brigadier-General Percy Robinson),[163] the centre and right battalions would use both the crossings created for 151 Brigade and less formal existing crossings further north. They would then pass through the tail of the battalion heading for the station and move uphill, leapfrogging the battalions who had secured the initial objective and cross the Wassigny-Le Cateau road to secure the first objective proper,

158 'Narrative of Machine Gun Operations – Fourth Army' Chapter VI, TNA WO158/332.

159 War Diary, Commander Royal Artillery 25th Division, 25th Divisional Artillery Instructions No. 2, 16 October 1918, TNA WO95/2230.

160 Due to congestion at the St Souplet crossings, their enterprising guide, Lieutenant Meredith, who had reconnoitred the river during the night, led them upstream and they used a damaged bridge further north.

161 Henry Cholmondeley 'Jacko' Jackson KCB CMG DSO (1879-1972) was a regular captain of the Bedfordshire Regiment in August 1914. He had commanded 8th Bedfordshire for three months January-April 1916, and had then commanded 175 Brigade from August 1916 to March 1918, when he was promoted to command 50th Division.

162 Richard Edgar Sugden DSO MC (1871-1951) was a territorial captain of the Duke of Wellington's Regiment in August 1914, and had commanded 3/4th West Riding then 1/4th West Riding from September 1916 to June 1918. He commanded 151 Brigade from 7 June 1918 to the Armistice.

163 Percy Morris Robinson CB CMG (1873-1949) was a regular major of 1st Royal West Kent in August 1914, and as depot commander was given command of the 6th Battalion in August 1914, but was sent to the Western Front to command the 1st Battalion until September 1915. He commanded 112 Brigade from September 1915 to November 1916, and 149 Brigade from 7 June 1918 to the Armistice.

the Mazinghien-la Jonquiere farm ridge (Red Line). The third battalion was to follow, crossing the *HWL I* and the tail of the two leading divisions, but then turn north to capture the railway triangle. This was a pre-war junction in the tracks north of Le Cateau station, both lines in cuttings to which the enemy had added a third track in a cutting enabling the westbound railway to turn north, creating a triangular moated fort. Here it would join up with the South African Brigade of 66th Division (see Map 12). Lastly, 150 Brigade (Brigadier-General George Rollo),[164] would push through in a north-easterly direction to capture Bazuel, whilst the South Africans moved on to the high ground above Richemont River to its north.

The tanks of 1st Tank Battalion supported 50th Division's attack. One section (four tanks) was to assist 151 and 149 Brigades on the right; a second section (three tanks) would be in the centre; and a third (four tanks) would support the left in its thrust towards Le Cateau station, pushing two tanks up each side of the railway embankment. The tanks were to 'proceed at top speed to overtake the infantry', passing through them on the Red Dotted Line to advance to the Red Line. Reconnaissance had been carried out over two nights by Captain Benjamin Bradbeer, Lieutenant Charles Thornback, and Major Maurice Miskin,[165] the latter unfortunately killed by a shell leading his section to the crossing on the morning of the 17th.[166] The group had discovered a location at St Souplet where the river was only eight feet wide and four deep, perfect for the deployment of two cribs which would ensure safe crossing.

All the attacking battalions of 151 Brigade were in position in the fog by 04.30. Thirty minutes before zero the enemy opened up a bombardment on all roads and tracks in the forward area, which caused numerous casualties, and the assembled troops were forced to don respirators. 4th King's Royal Rifle Corps, on the right, commanded by Lieutenant-Colonel John Brady,[167] had pushed patrols across the river just after midnight but encountered none of the German outposts. When the enemy shelling began, B Company had some 20 casualties including the company commander, Captain Arthur Nutting,[168] the first of five officer casualties that day. Unfortunately, the Americans

164 George Rollo DSO and bar (1881-1944) was a retired captain of volunteers (Lancashire RE) in August 1914. He commanded 19th Liverpool from July 1916 to December 1917, and 18th Liverpool for a matter of weeks before being promoted to command 150 Brigade from 29 September 1918.

165 Benjamin Frank John Bradbeer MC (commissioned in January 1917, and referred to in the *London Gazette* as Franz Benjamin John) was later assistant engineer of the boroughs of Lowestoft and Tunbridge Wells, chief assistant engineer of Surrey County Council, and assistant county surveyor for East Sussex. Charles Rodney Thornback MC, an Englishman living in Australia in August 1914, had been commissioned in the Cheshire Regiment in July 1916 and transferred to the Tank Corps in August 1917. He won an MC for his actions at the Selle: 'He carried out a highly important and difficult reconnaissance of the River Selle, in close proximity to the enemy, prior to the attack, on 17th October, 1918, and on the morning-of the attack, after his company commander had been killed, he led his company's Tanks across the river, and then, finding another company of Tanks lost in the mist, he guided them in turn. It was largely due to his courage and initiative at a critical time that the passage of the river was successfully effected by every Tank. (*London Gazette*, 3 October 1919, p.12342). Maurice James Miskin MC, an assistant master at Oundle School, had originally been commissioned in the North Staffordshire Regiment in December 1914.

166 War Diary, 1st Tank Battalion, 'Report on Operations October 17th 1918', TNA WO95/109/6.

167 Lieutenant-Colonel John Banks Brady DSO was a retired lieutenant of the South African Irregulars in August 1914. He had served as both brigade-major and GSO3, and had commanded the battalion only since 24 September 1918.

168 Arthur Forde Nutting MC (commissioned in December 1914) was wounded four times during the war. An indication of the severity of the October fighting, the battalion had 21 officer casualties (five fatal) and 330 amongst the other ranks (63 fatal).

The Selle in the northern outskirts of St Souplet where bridges were erected for the crossing of 4th King's Royal Rifle Corps on 17 October 1918.

to the right having to take ground on the west bank before they could cross the Selle, their barrage started 200 yards west of the river, i.e. behind and to the right of the KRRC's start line. They in turn could not advance under the protection of their own barrage until the *HWL I* had been reached and the American barrage had caught up. Crossing the footbridges they passed through the German wire, 30 yards deep,[169] and under heavy machine-gun fire were contesting the railway embankment with *II Battalion RIR 120* within 45 minutes, visibility being limited to 50 yards. Battalion HQ and B Company, crossing last, came under fire from the *HWL I* in the American area, as yet untaken. Sections went forward, locating the machine-gun nest by sound and silencing it by 08.30. Meanwhile, the leading companies pressed on over the spur, down into the ravine below Baudival Farm which awaited being dealt with by the Americans, and up the slope towards the road. They encountered obstinate resistance from the support companies of *II and III Battalions RIR 120* in the *HWL II* positions, taking two-and-a-half hours to cover some 300 yards.[170] The fog made it difficult to locate the enemy machine-guns, and the battalion required the support of the unit to its rear to achieve the Wassigny-Le Cateau road. This they finally reached at 10.00 and established a line 200 yards east of it, securing the crest of the ridge which gave excellent views over

169 Edmonds & Maxwell-Hyslop, op. cit., p.309.
170 Edmonds & Maxwell-Hyslop, op. cit., p.310.

The *HWL I* dominating the eastern bank of the Selle where 4th KRRC crossed.

the countryside beyond. Four more officers had become casualties,[171] but losses in the other ranks had been relatively small.[172]

1st King's Own Yorkshire Light Infantry, commanded by Lieutenant-Colonel Henry Mallinson,[173] were the centre battalion, and they effected their crossing a short distance north of the KRRC with little loss, although Mallinson and his Regimental Sergeant Major George Miller both fell in the river. Although both could swim, in Mallinson's case it subsequently resulted in a recurrence of malaria.[174] They met strong opposition from machine-guns and bombers in the *HWL I* but overcame this by 06.15, and moved along the eastern side of the railway and uphill towards their objective, keeping touch with the 4th KRRC despite the fog. Although they moved faster than their neighbours, they encountered heavy opposition in orchards near the road. Fruit growing was a significant occupation in the farms around Le Cateau on the east bank of the Selle, and this meant that there were many enclosed orchards that could conceal machine-guns. Touch with the 6th Royal Inniskilling Fusiliers who had crossed the river a few hundred yards to their left and were moving due north was lost, and a large gap had opened up on the Yorkshire unit's left flank by the time they reached the road at 10.00.[175]

Into this gap came the machine-guns of 50th Division which had been pushed across the river soon after zero. Their actions provide an example of the quality of junior officer leadership. Second-Lieutenant Leslie Fry took his section along the railway where he was held up by fire, which was dealt with through the employment of a passing tank. Totally isolated in the fog, he proceeded uphill and sited his guns in practice trenches to the east of St Benin. All the while the section was under constant heavy fire from machine-guns and trench mortars ahead and to the east, hidden in an orchard. Fry sent two NCOs to scout the locations of the fire,[176] and was joined by two officers and 16 other ranks of 1st KOYLI. A party of enemy emerged from the orchard under a white flag, but immediately opened fire. Fry moved two guns out into the open to enfilade a further set of practice trenches the enemy were attempting to reach, and despite losing his first two guns, tried again, moving a gun out to protect his right, and for some two hours beat off counterattacks.[177] Fry was awarded the Military Cross for his actions that morning, but would sadly be killed two days before the Armistice.[178]

171 Captains Maurice Edward Antrobus (commissioned in August 1914) and Gerald Balfour Eden (commissioned in November 1914), and Lieutenants W. M. Stewart (South African Defence Force, commissioned in July 1918) and Herbert Cecil Frederick Holgate, (commissioned September 1915).

172 War Diary, 4th Battalion King's Royal Rifle Corps, 17 October 1918, TNA WO95/2843. S. Hare, *The Annals of the King's Royal Rifle Corps, Vol 5*, pp.388-9.

173 Lieutenant-Colonel Henry Mallinson DSO, a regular captain of KOYLI in August 1914, had commanded the battalion since April 1916. George Miller DCM had arrived in France in January 1915.

174 R.C. Bond, *The King's Own Yorkshire Light Infantry in the Great War*, p.1009.

175 War Diary, 1st Battalion King's Own Yorkshire Light Infantry, 17 October 1918, WO95/2843.

176 Corporals William West Routledge and Charles McGurk. Routledge died of wounds on 25 October 1918.

177 War Diary, 50th Battalion Machine Gun Corps, 'Narrative of Operations Oct. 9th – 19th 1918', TNA WO95/2823.

178 Leslie Fry MC had been commissioned in March 1918. The citation for his MC reads: 'On the morning of the 17th October 1918, he was in command of a section of machine-guns detailed to cover a re-entrant on the intermediate objective of the Division east of St. Benin. He was held up by a hostile machine-gun nest, which, with the assistance of a tank, he put out of action. On arriving at his position he dug himself in under heavy fire, and shortly afterwards, together with a small party of infantry, beat off a strong counter-attack. He showed great courage and determination'. (*Edinburgh Gazette*, 11 December 1919, p.964).

149 Brigade followed 151 Brigade across the river. 13th Black Watch (Scottish Horse) and the 3rd Royal Fusiliers used both bridges and the logs that lay across the river at St Benin, suffering some 40 casualties in the process. Both battalions reached the *HWL I*, the Scottish Horse turning north following the Inniskilling Fusiliers, the Royal Fusiliers heading uphill. When it became apparent that the 4th KRRC were held up at the *HWL II* positions, the Royal Fusiliers' CO, Major William Trasenster, ordered his companies to assist them.[179] At 07.30 they advanced in the fog in diamond formation, each company 15-200 yards in depth, with 50-100 yards between companies. The two units pushed through, the Royal Fusiliers taking up a 400 yard front on the road to the right of the KRRC, forming a defensive flank to Baudival Farm, reinforced by two Vickers guns. Lieutenant Arthur Balding was awarded the MC as being the author of this manoeuvre: 'Although exposed to heavy machine-gun fire, he hung on to this position for nearly three hours until other troops came up on his right'.[180] By 11.00 some 100 Americans had come up to the road to secure Balding's position, but the joint action of both KRRC and Royal Fusiliers had caused their battalions to become intermingled.

Of the tanks supporting the right of the assault, one had developed mechanical trouble and had not crossed the river, but the remaining three reached the road. One company of the Royal Fusiliers penetrated to le Quennelet Farm several hundred yards on the east side of the road, which was cleared by the three machines taking 33 prisoners, very nearly capturing the headquarters of *III Battalion FR 122*. The tanks then jaunted about mopping up machine-gun nests ahead of the infantry, where they were joined by a disorientated tank of the left section which should have been proceeding north along the *HWL I*, and which was sent on its way. Despite the presence of the machines, the infantry had to withdraw after several hours in occupation of the farm as a German counterattack developed in the late morning. *III Battalion IR 479* of *243rd Infantry Division* attacked on the German right, *I & II Battalions FR 122* led personally by the regimental commander attacked in the centre, whilst *I Battalion RIR 120* on the right launched their assault from la Roux Farm to the east of le Quennelet Farm. German artillery fired in support over open sights. As noted previously, Lieutenant William Palstra of 3 Squadron AFC had observed the attack developing on the American left, and had called up artillery support. The Royal Fusiliers claimed to have attracted aircraft support, a number of planes machine-gunning le Quennelet farm and other locations for some 40 minutes. The infantry resisted and artillery and aircraft drove the counterattack back.[181] Two of the centre section of tanks, one machine late because its crew had become overcome by gas and fumes, arrived to help repel these attacks, engaging both machine-guns and artillery. One of the tanks under the command of Sergeant Leonard Pilcher received six direct hits well in front of the Red Dotted Line and he and all his crew became casualties.[182] The continued fire of the enemy machine-guns from the repelled counterattack, however, drove

179 William Augustus Trasenster was a Minor Counties cricket player (Lincolnshire) who was a second-lieutenant of the Royal Fusiliers in August 1914.

180 *London Gazette*, 4 October 1919, p.12269. Arthur Sydney Balding was commissioned in July 1916.

181 Untitled three page report of 3rd Royal Fusiliers misfiled with War Diary, 2nd Battalion Dublin Fusiliers, October 1918, TNA WO95/2832. There is no specific record of this in the 5 Brigade RAF records although it is noted that 85 Squadron fired 1,300 rounds at enemy troops in roughly this location. (War Diary, 5 Brigade RAF, 17 October 1918, TNA AIR 1/2225/209/40/26). The 4th KKRC were in no doubt that it was the action of the artillery that drove the Germans back. (War Diary, 4th Battalion King's Royal Rifle Corps, 17 October 1918, TNA WO95/2843).

182 War Diary, 1st Tank Battalion, 'Report on Operations October 17th 1918', TNA WO95/109/6. Leonard Cyril Pilcher had enlisted in the Oxfordshire & Buckinghamshire Regiment.

both the KRRC and Fusiliers a further 250-500 yards down the slope off the crest of the ridge, a retirement more marked on their left where the counterattack had made particular impact on 1st KOYLI. The Royal Fusiliers who began the day with only 11 officers and 308 other ranks lost nearly a third of their strength, 98 officers and men.

Meanwhile, the 2nd Royal Dublin Fusiliers, commanded by Lieutenant-Colonel Kenneth Weldon,[183] who had suffered 22 casualties simply approaching the river on the western bank, crossed the Selle at St Benin at 06.30 after waiting for the Scottish Horse to clear its front, one company using the bridges, the other three using fords. They immediately met heavy fire from a sunken road containing outposts and the *HWL I* on the railway at Fassiaux, and suffered casualties, including the commander of A Company, Lieutenant Charles Kidson, one of two officers killed that day.[184] Captain Gilbert Crawford won the MC reorganising the firing line and leading it forward.[185] It took two hours to overcome the *HWL I*, only 300 yards or so from the river at this location and which had already been crossed by other units. Pressing on beyond, the battalion was held up again after 100 yards. Due to the resistance met by the units of 151 Brigade ahead, the Dublin Fusiliers became embroiled in what was now a two brigade fight to take and hold the Red Dotted Line. The counterattack had driven the Yorkshire Light Infantry back towards the railway, pivoting on its right company in the orchards near the road, to become mingled with the advancing Dublin Fusiliers.[186] Here they were reinforced by a section of six Vickers guns, and held their line.[187]

At 10.00 the 150th Infantry Brigade crossed the river and took up positions on the railway embankment, and General Rollo gave orders for the advance to the Red Line to commence at 12.00 by 7th Wiltshire, 2nd Northumberland Fusiliers, and 2nd Munster Fusiliers. This advance was countermanded by division at 11.15, and Rollo was then summoned from his position on the *HWL I* for discussions with General Jackson. It was clear to both that the attack had not only stalled, but had been pushed back, and that all units were intermingled. At 16.00 Jackson and Rollo ordered the 7th Wiltshires, commanded by Lieutenant-Colonel Harold Hodgson,[188] up the slope in support of the KRRC and Royal Fusiliers; and 2nd Munster Fusiliers, commanded by Captain Charles Williams,[189] to the left in support of 1st KOYLI. The impetus of the Wiltshires' attack re-established the line at the road under the protection of a machine-gun barrage. The intermediate

183 Kenneth Charles Weldon DSO had been a regular captain of the Dublin Fusiliers in August 1914. He had commanded 7th Inniskilling Fusiliers for two months to October 1916, 7th Royal Irish Fusiliers from October 1917 to February 1918, and 2nd Dublin Fusiliers from mid-April 1918.

184 Charles Wilfrid Kidson, aged 24, was a Cambridge classics scholar who was commissioned in May 1915, (*De Ruvigny's Roll of Honour, Vol. 5*, p.100). The other officer killed was Second-Lieutenant Francis Ashton Walkey who had joined the Irish Rugby Volunteer Corps in August 1914 and the 7th Royal Dublin Fusiliers in March 1915. He was commissioned from the rank of private in April 1917.

185 The citation for Crawford's MC reads: 'On the 17th-18th October, 1918, northeast of St. Benin, he was in charge of the firing line. After the battalion had crossed the River Selle and lost heavily in doing so, he re-organised it under great difficulty and successfully led the firing line until the objective had been gained. It was due to his skill, courage, and power of command that the battalion was extricated from this dangerous situation'. (*London Gazette*, 4 October 1919, p.12282).

186 Despite being forced back, 2nd Royal Dublin Fusilers had captured seven officers and 347 men, nine trench mortars, 37 machine-guns and an artillery battery complete with teams. (H.C. Wylly, *Crown and Company 1911-1922*, p.119.)

187 War Diary, 1st Battalion King's Own Yorkshire Light Infantry, 17 October 1918, WO95/2843.

188 Harold John Hodgson DSO was a regular lieutenant of the Cheshire Regiment in August 1914. He commanded 7th Wiltshire from December 1917 to the Armistice.

189 Charles Reginald Williams DSO was a lieutenant of the Munster Fusiliers in August 1914. He took over command when Lieutenant-Colonel H.B. Tonson-Rye went sick on 13 October.

objective, which should have been taken by four battalions had, due to the enemy's resistance, required almost an entire division to take and hold it.

At 16.35 Jackson took extraordinary, if pragmatic, steps to re-establish command and control in his division. Rollo was given command of the units on the right, namely 7th Wiltshire (150 Brigade); 3rd Royal Fusiliers (149 Brigade); and 4th KRRC (151 Brigade). General Sugden was given command of the units in the centre, extending to the brickworks east of Le Cateau station, namely 1st KOYLI (151 Brigade); 2nd Munster Fusiliers (150 Brigade); and 2nd Dublin Fusiliers (149 Brigade). Lastly, General Robinson would take charge of the units fighting at the station, namely 2nd Northumberland Fusiliers (150 Brigade); 6th Inniskilling Fusiliers (151 Brigade); and 13th Scottish Horse (149 Brigade). They were ordered to establish their commands on the intermediate objective, i.e. literally with the action. Yet there was also a second step to this re-organisation, in that one battalion commanding officer was given command over two or three units, thus simplifying communication between a brigadier and a single CO. Rollo thus referred to Lieutenant-Colonel Hodgson of 7th Wiltshire in respect of his unit and 4th KRRC; Sugden would relate to Lieutenant-Colonel Mallinson of 1st KOYLI in respect of all three battalions; and Robinson would exercise command through Lieutenant-Colonel Blair of the Scottish Horse in respect of his unit and the 6th Inniskilling Fusiliers, maintaining direct command of 2nd Northumberland Fusiliers himself.

To the north the most confused and vicious fighting was taking place around Le Cateau station (see Map 13). It had been the task of the 6th Royal Inniskilling Fusiliers of 151 Brigade, commanded by Major Guy Greville,[190] to turn north once across the river and seize Le Cateau station. They would then establish a line from the brickworks to the east of the station to the sugar factory to its west, on the edge of the river. This was highly ambitious as it involved rolling up a considerable section of the *HWL I* and then facing the well-defended station with its array of buildings. Two trench mortars, each with 30 rounds, were to be attached, and four were to bombard the railway until 18 minutes after zero, but the officer in charge and several of his men were badly wounded by the German counter-barrage. The two promised mortars thus never joined the attack across the river. The battalion, despite finding its bridges too short, were soon across the river, the most northerly crossing of the three battalions of 151 Brigade. At zero + 36 they advanced astride the railway. They first hit *III Battalion RIR 120*, and then the left unit of *243rd Division*, *III Battalion FR 122*. Whilst the rolling up proceeded successfully, the latter unit put up a strong fight in the vicinity of the Fassiaux bridge, east of St Benin, where reinforcement from the supporting Scottish Horse of 149 Brigade was required at 07.30 to overcome it. The Scottish Horse, commanded by Lieutenant-Colonel Patrick Blair,[191] had crossed the river at 05.45, its task being to pass through the Inniskillings at Le Cateau Station and proceed to take the railway triangle. As with other units following battalions that had already passed the *HWL I*, they met considerable resistance there, indicating that the fog had prevented it being cleared fully.[192] Twenty machine-guns of A and C Companies 50th Battalion MGC crossed the Selle under the destroyed viaduct north of Fassiaux, making a bridge for themselves out of railway sleepers. They pushed on into what seemed a void, there being no apparent infantry. Eventually the Scottish Horse arrived, rolling up the *HWL I*,

190 Guy George Frederick Fulke Greville DSO MC became a regular lieutenant of the Leinster Regiment in August 1914. He had commanded since 3 October 1918. The battle strength of his battalion was 17 officers and 337 other ranks.

191 Patrick James Blair DSO was a lieutenant of 9th Royal Scots in August 1914. He commanded from 12 October 1918.

192 War Diary, 13th (Scottish Horse) Black Watch, 17 October 1918, TNA WO95/2831.

The exposed area on the eastern bank of the Selle where the 6th Inniskilling Fusiliers and Scottish Horse advanced towards Le Cateau station on 17 October 1918.

and Blair directed that two sections of machine-guns were to be placed where they stood, firing in north-easterly direction at the brickworks, and two sections just to their west, firing onto the detraining point ahead. The latter sections put two guns out of action that were firing from Chapel Bridge Mills, to the west of the detraining point, enfilading the left of the British advance.

Pushing on beyond St Benin, and hitting the left of *I Battalion IR 479*, ten minutes of 'sharp fighting' was required for the Inniskillings to reduce pockets of the enemy in the *HWL II*, in this case in rifle pits made out of shell holes on the rising ground to the east leading towards the brickworks. The Inniskillings' mode of assault was as other units that day – attacking the German flank by outmanoeuvring it to the rear. The Irish soldiers recorded how the enemy here 'came out to meet us but many were shot down and the remainder retired'.[193] At 08.15 the battalion arrived on the southern end of the detraining point at Le Cateau station. This had been considerably extended by the Germans from its pre-war state. To the east a range of buildings lay close to the old tracks, including the large Simons ceramics works, the yard being bounded on this side by a bank some 30 feet high. Extra lines for detraining had been installed to the west of the existing lines, creating an area some 200 yards wide and 500 yards long. It was also lined with buildings on the Le Cateau-St Benin road road on the western side which included a maltings. Although being at a lower level due to the slope, these structures had effectively been brought within the station yard by the extension of the tracks. A hundred yards to the north lay a petroleum refinery, and further down the slope towards the river 350 yards to the north lay a sugar refinery. As might have been expected, the advance of the Innsikilling Fusiliers ground to a halt in the face of stiff resistance emanating from

193 War Diary, 6th Battalion Inniskilling Fusiliers, 17 October 1918, WO95/2843.

good defensive positions. To make matters more difficult, although the station lay out of its sight, the brickworks uphill on the Wassigny-Le Cateau road to the east enfiladed the right of the British advance. Further, the enemy were in possession of a mound surrounded by trees some 50 yards east of the station in direct line with the brickworks above the southern end of the station buildings. This was not marked on British trench maps as trees had prevented its detection, and from it 'an exceptional command to the south was obtainable'.[194]

A tank of the centre section under Sergeant Walter Poulter had penetrated as far as the brickworks (although at what time is not clear), having previously signalled to unspecified infantry at the railway to 'come on'. It engaged machine-guns there, but being isolated, withdrew. The left section of tanks that had been directed to support the infantry at the station had ill luck, losing both a machine to mechanical trouble before crossing the river and the company commander, Captain Chaloner Robinson, to a shell splinter.[195] Further, of the three remaining tanks, two got bogged down shortly after crossing. Only one tank under Corporal Collins was, therefore, able to carry on, but he was immediately called upon to deal with two machine-guns on the boundary with the Americans, which he promptly did by crushing them. Having been drawn in the wrong direction, it was thus that his machine ended up going east rather than north and arriving at le Quennelet Farm. Setting off finally in the correct direction, Collins knocked out an enemy field gun, and then became embroiled in a struggle with a number of Germans who climbed on the top of his tank and were difficult to dislodge. He eventually ended up in the vicinity of the station, his correct destination, although again at what time is not clear. Here, he dealt with two trench mortars, but allegedly finding no infantry to support, and with his crew suffering from fumes, he returned from whence he had come. Of the ten tanks supporting 50th Division, six had reached the intermediate objective and made contact with the enemy, and in doing so fired 374 rounds of 6-pounder shells, and 11,700 rounds of small arms ammunition.[196]

The Inniskillings took on the German forces holding the station, employing the two Stokes mortars under the command of the CO of the Scottish Horse, but their resources were dwindling. The battalion's pack mules not having arrived, messages were sent back asking for ammunition and bombs, requests which continued at regular intervals. Small groups of troops began to infiltrate the station area, and by 09.15, a party under Lieutenant George Henderson was on the station platform,[197] 15 rifles strong but dwindling under machine-gun fire from virtually every location both right and left. Captain George Lyndon's group,[198] also in the station buildings and running low on ammunition and bombs, found at around 10.00 that the enemy were bombing their way

194 Montgomery, op. cit., p.205.

195 Chaloner Theodore Robinson, who had been on the Western Front since November 1914 had been commissioned from a ranker in the London Yeomanry in April 1916.

196 War Diary, 1st Tank Battalion, 'Report on Operations October 17th 1918', TNA WO95/109/6.

197 George Logan Henderson MC had been commissioned in March 1915. His MC was awarded for his actions at the Selle. 'At Le Cateau on 17/18th October, 1918, he showed great gallantry and determination throughout the attack. At one period he held on to a most isolated position, when his command had been reduced to some eight men, until reinforcements arrived. His cheerfulness and courage were a very fine example to his men. On 18th Oct. he materially assisted, by his skilful leading of his company, in the capture of a wood near Le Cateau'. (*London Gazette*, 8 October 1919, p.3270).

198 George Edward Beresford Lyndon MC (commissioned December 1914) was awarded his MC for actions at the Selle. 'For marked courage and ability, on 18th October, 1918, at Le Cateau, he, with his company succeeded in capturing a wood, with forty prisoners and three trench mortars. It was due entirely to his skilful handling of his company that the objective was taken and consolidated with the loss of only two men. He did most excellent work in action on 3rd October, near Gouy, and his coolness

The buildings of Le Cateau station fought over by 6th Inniskilling Fusiliers on 17 October 1918.

in at the southern end of the detraining point threatening to cut him off from the rest of the battalion. Another officer decorated that morning was Second-Lieutenant John Crawford whose party fought their way along the platform to locate the enemy machine-guns.[199] Finally, at 11.00, the pack mules arrived with rifle ammunition and Lewis gun magazines, followed by an artillery officer who was asked to organise a renewed bombardment. Tanks were also called for but none would reappear. At 12.00 Lyndon reported that he was now fending off a new round of bombers in the station buildings, and to compound matters at 12.30 German light machine-gunners advanced downhill from the brickworks, although they were forced to retire. By 12.45, the battalion had still received no bombs, and half an hour later news was received from Lyndon that he had been forced into different buildings and a nearby trench in the station. Both he and Henderson would remain exposed for some time. Their isolation increased as to their right, two companies of the Inniskillings in an advanced position uphill had to retire, unable to hold on, the battalion being pushed back onto the railway itself.

in action during the operations of 17th and 18th October, near Le Cateau, was very marked'. (*London Gazette*, 8 October 1919, p.3219).

199 John Crawford was commissioned in June 1918 from Warrant Officer Class II, having served overseas since July 1915. His MC citation reads: 'On 17th October, 1918, when the line was temporarily held up at Le Cateau Station, he gallantly led a small party of men right up to the platform of the station in order to obtain information of the enemy's position. He fought his way up and located the machine-guns, and fought his way back to reinforce his company as ordered. Throughout the day he behaved most gallantly and rendered excellent service'. (*London Gazette*, 4 October 1919, p.12282).

At 14.00, the barrage that had been requested three hours earlier was brought down, and the Scottish Horse attacked through the Inniskillings with the aim of taking the mound to the right and the petroleum refinery to the left at the north end of the station. C Company crossed the railway and assaulted, taking the mound under heavy machine-gun fire, covered by fire from B Company who had pushed into the southern station buildings where Henderson and Lyndon were lodged deeper in. A Company, to the west of the railway, took the buildings of Chapel Bridge Mills, the maltings, and possibly the petroleum refinery.[200] The Inniskillings followed close behind, pushing further into the complex of buildings, covering the Scottish Horse in their positions on both sides of the detraining point. From his vantage point, Henderson watched the Scottish unit become held up again. *IR 479*, defending to the north of the station, noted that *II Battalion* had been pushed back some 1,500 yards, leaving a gap of nearly 800 yards between itself and *IR 162* in the station itself.[201] The position of the morning, when British infantry were in a salient in the station with the enemy pressing them on either side was reversed. The Inniskillings remained in the station, with companies of the Scottish Horse in advance of them on either side, particularly so to the west, and the German defenders were now in a salient. By this time, however, units were intermixed and the fighting confused. The Irish battalion HQ had touch with not only the Scottish Horse, but companies of 1/6th Lancashire Fusiliers from 66th Division who had crossed the river close to the station, whilst the Royal Dublin Fusiliers were known to be in a sunken road some 500 yards to the rear. It was at this point that the reorganisation of command and control was pressed on the units, and Lieutenant-Colonel Blair of the Scottish Horse assumed responsibility on the ground for further operations to take the station complex.

At 17.00 a barrage for a further attack was put down by 104 and 150 Brigades RFA,[202] some 300 yards in front of a line between the sugar factory and the brickworks, and the apex of the railway triangle, which pointed directly at the station. The infantry were, however, still so disorganised that their attack was postponed until 21.00. Communication had meanwhile broken down between the infantry and the guns of A and C Companies MGC, and the section commanders 'were given no details of the attack by the infantry commanders on the spot'.[203] The heavy artillery again bombarded the railway triangle from 19.00 to 21.00, this being the main focus of the assault, i.e. the enemy remaining in the buildings west and north of the station would be outflanked.[204] In the hours between 17.00 and 21.00, however, the situation on the ground remained confused. At 20.00 the Scottish Horse, in the most forward exposed position on the mound where they were isolated, requested reinforcements of 20 men and two Lewis guns. These were dispatched by the Inniskilling Fusiliers but the officer commanding, Second-Lieutenant James Corscaden, was immediately killed, and another subaltern had to be found to take his place. Colonel Blair then ordered the Inniskillings to establish another post in between the mound and the detraining point in support.[205]

200 The Scottish Horse war diary only refers to 'the brewery'. (War Diary, 13th Black Watch, 17 October 1918, TNA WO95/2831). A range of other sources suggest that the petroleum refinery was also taken, and the distances the German units involved refer to being pushed back reinforces the likelihood.
201 War Diary, *Infantry Regiment 479*, cited in Whisler, op. cit., p.193.
202 War Diary, Commander Royal Artillery 25th Division, 17 October 1918, TNA WO95/2230. A protector barrage was put down by 110 and 112 Brigades RFA.
203 'Narrative of Machine Gun Operations – Fourth Army', Chapter VI, TNA WO158/332.
204 War Diary, Commander Royal Artillery XIII Corps, 17 October 1918, TNA WO95/902.
205 In terms of casualties, in the Inniskillings Captain Charles Geoffrey Barton MC (commissioned in September 1914) was killed, as were Second-Lieutenants James Noel Corscaden (commissioned

List of Maps

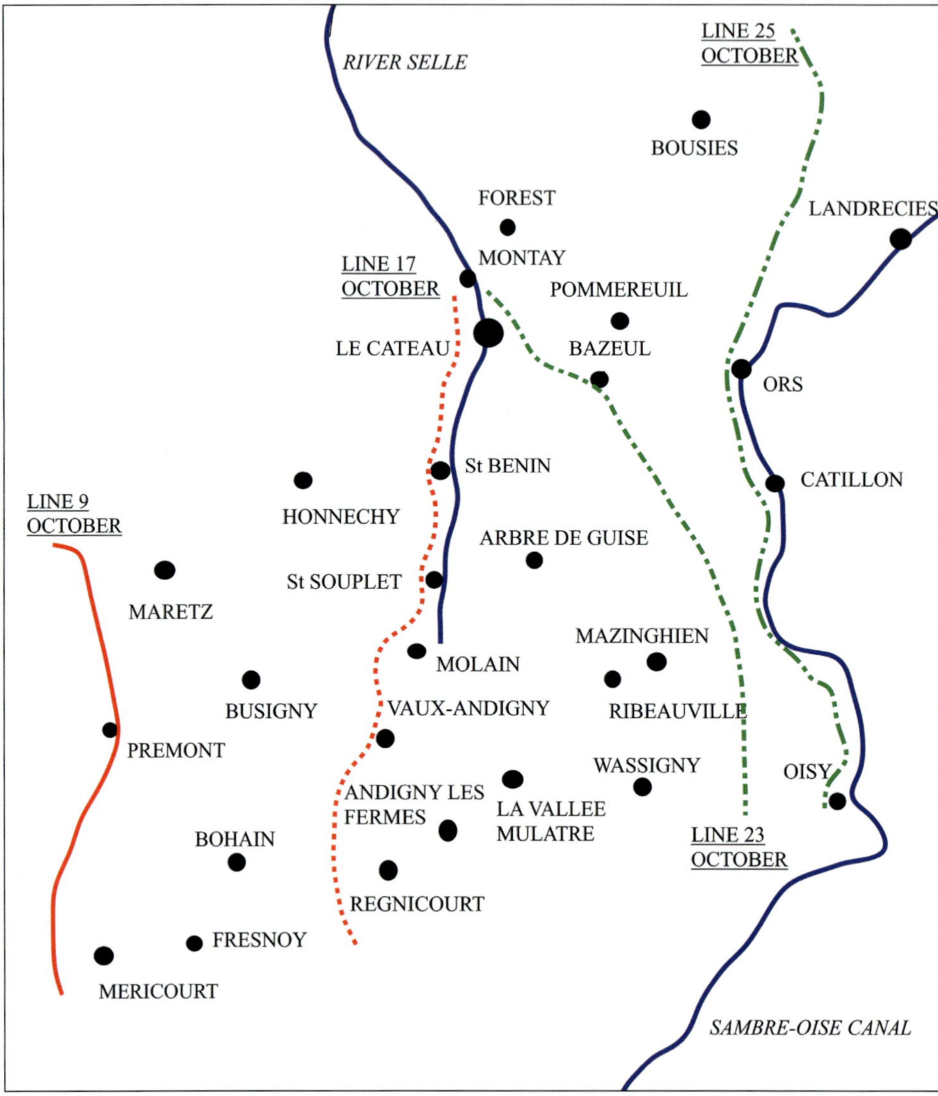

Map 1 Limits of advance during Selle operations 9-24 October 1918 and principal towns/villages.

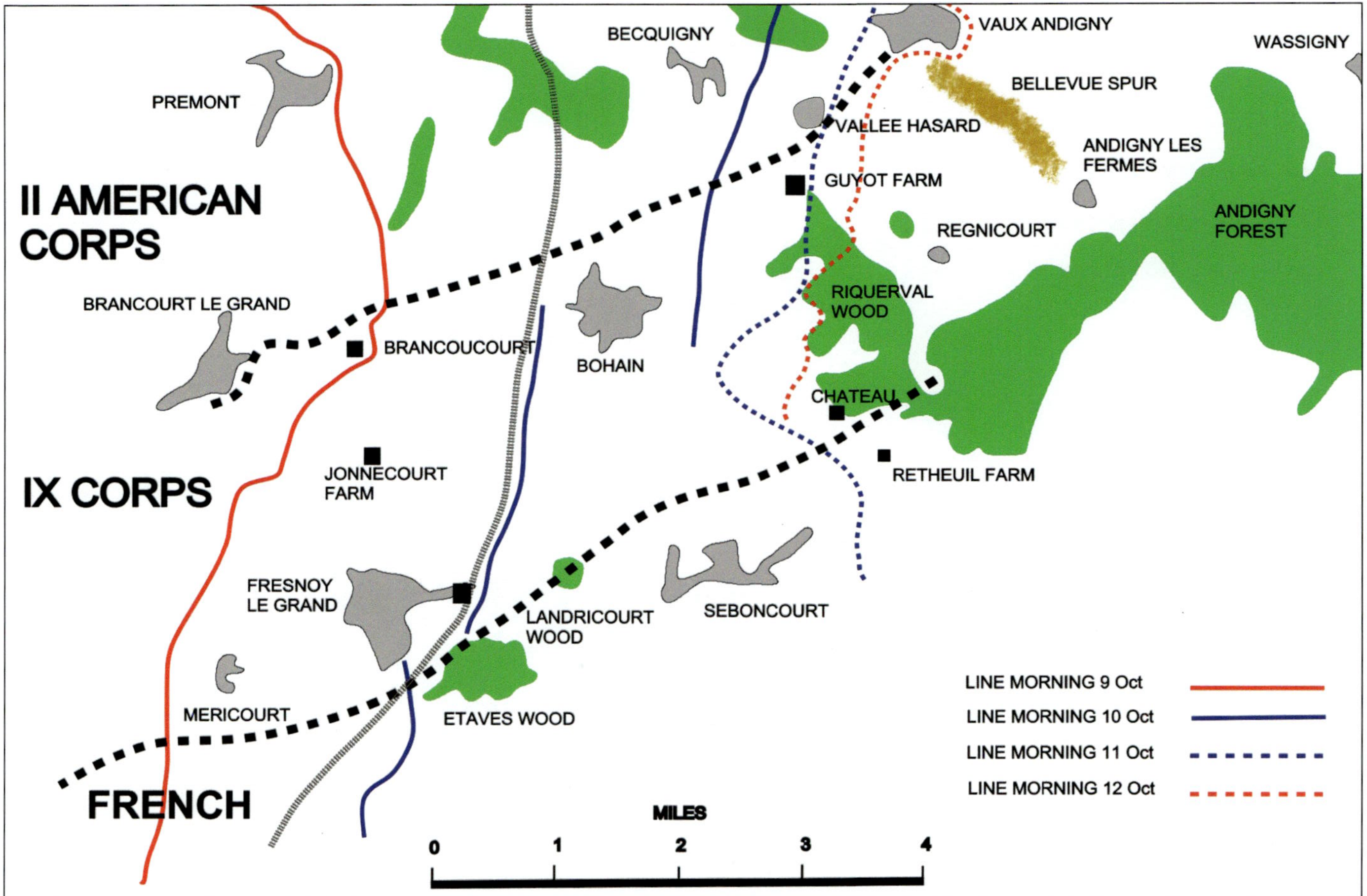

Map 2 IX Corps area of operations 9-12 October 1918.

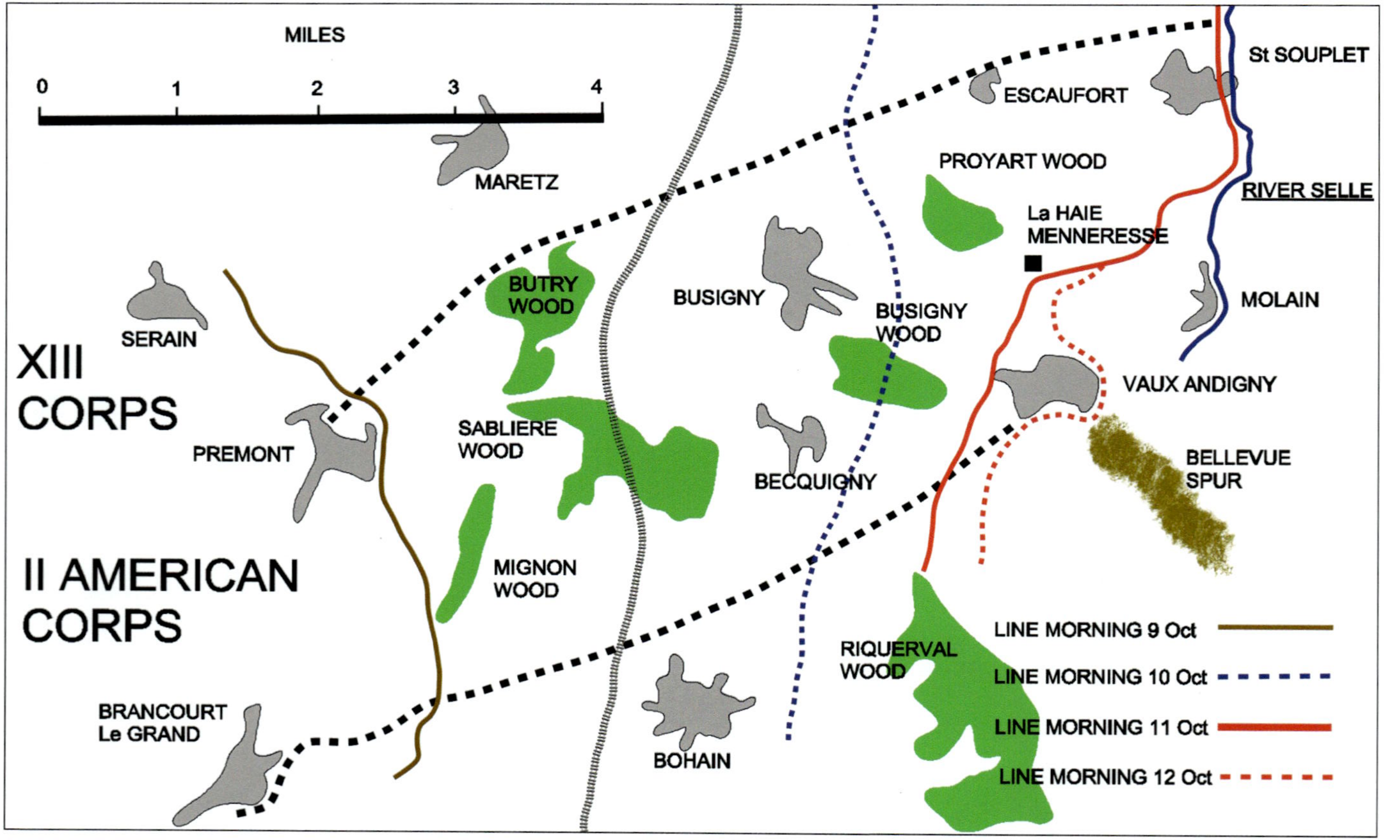

Map 3 II American Corps area of operations 9-12 October 1918.

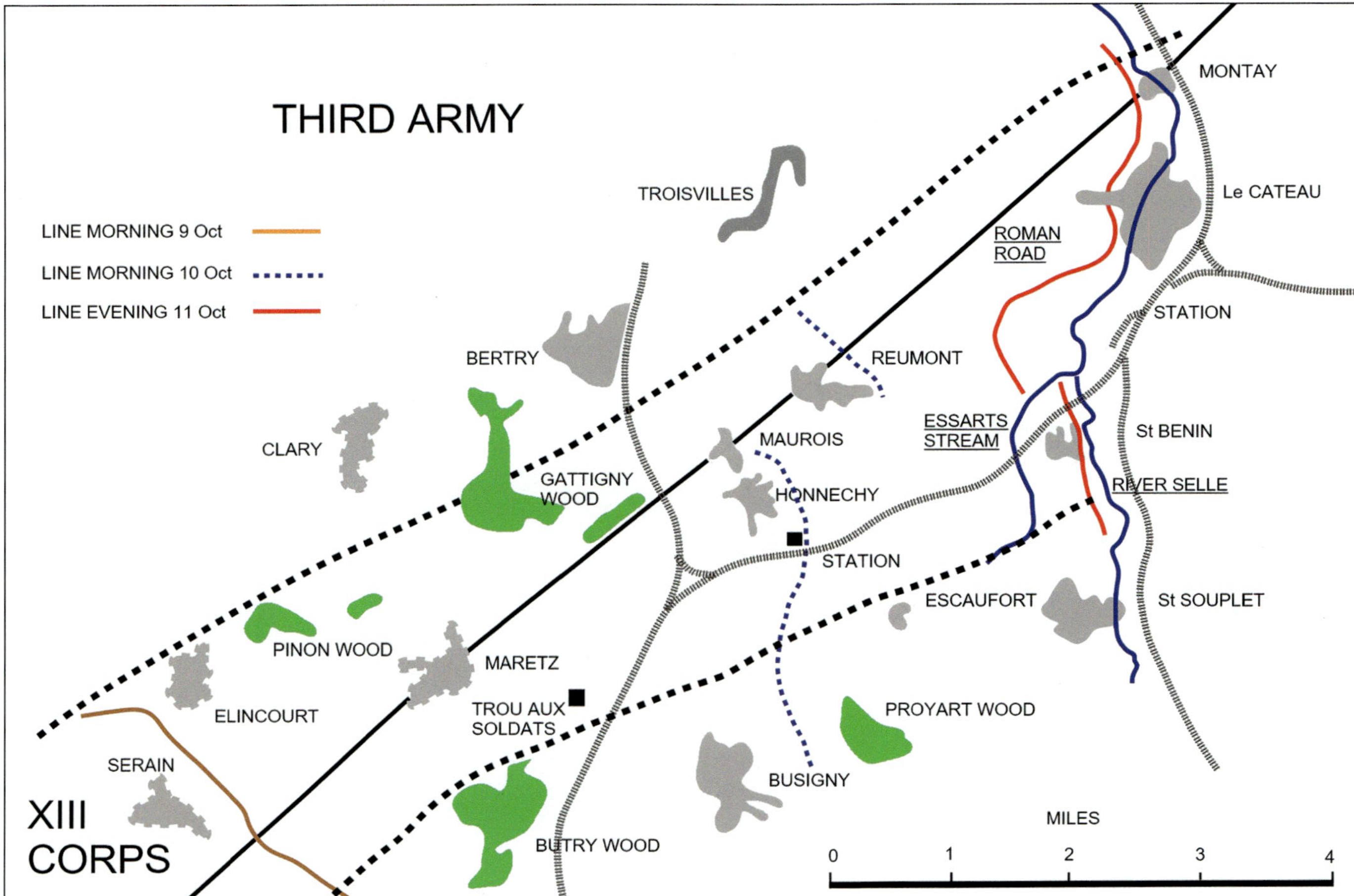

Map 4 XIII Corps area of operations 9-11 October 1918.

Map 5 Advance of Canadian and 6th Cavalry Brigades, 9 October 1918.

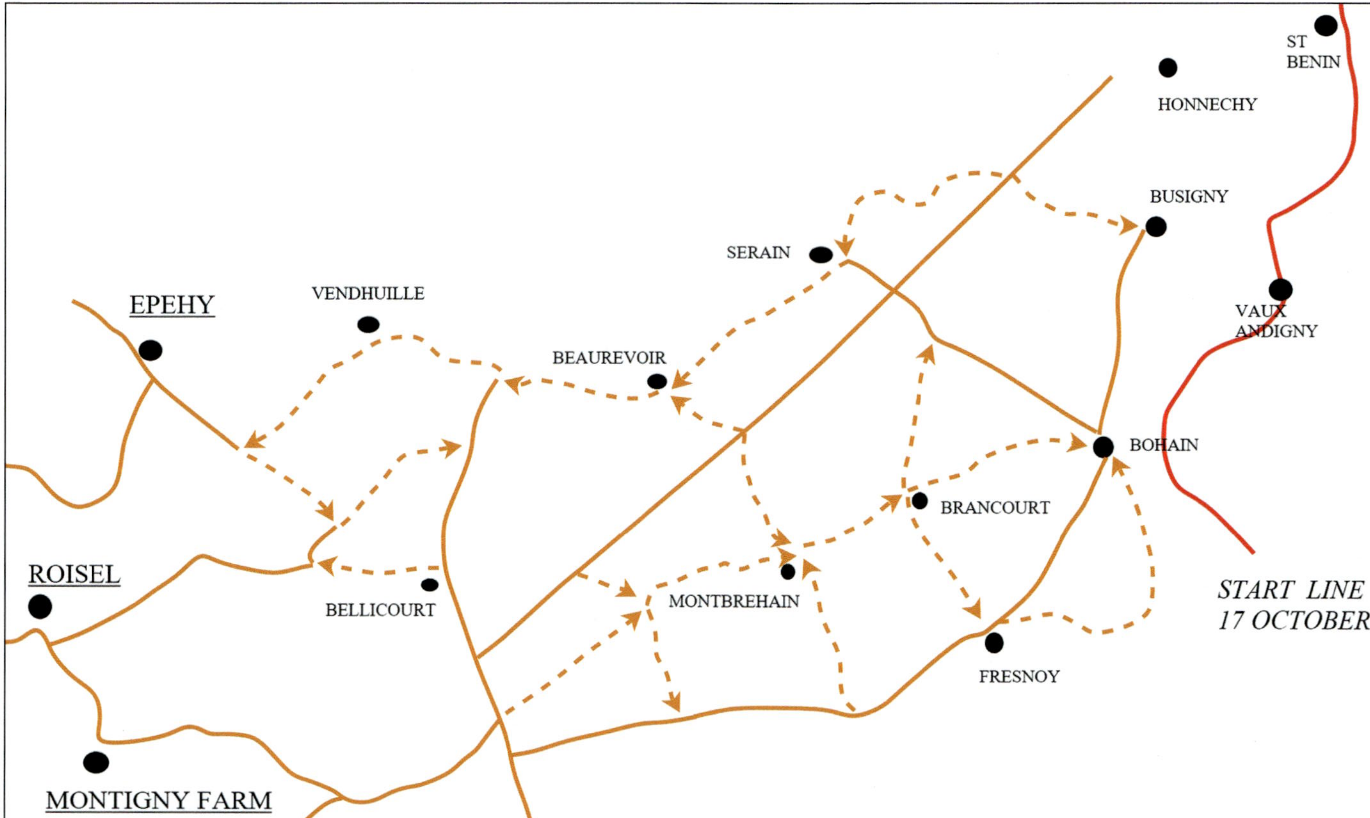

Map 6 Principal road routes opened by Fourth Army 16 October 1918 (one-way routes shown as broken lines).

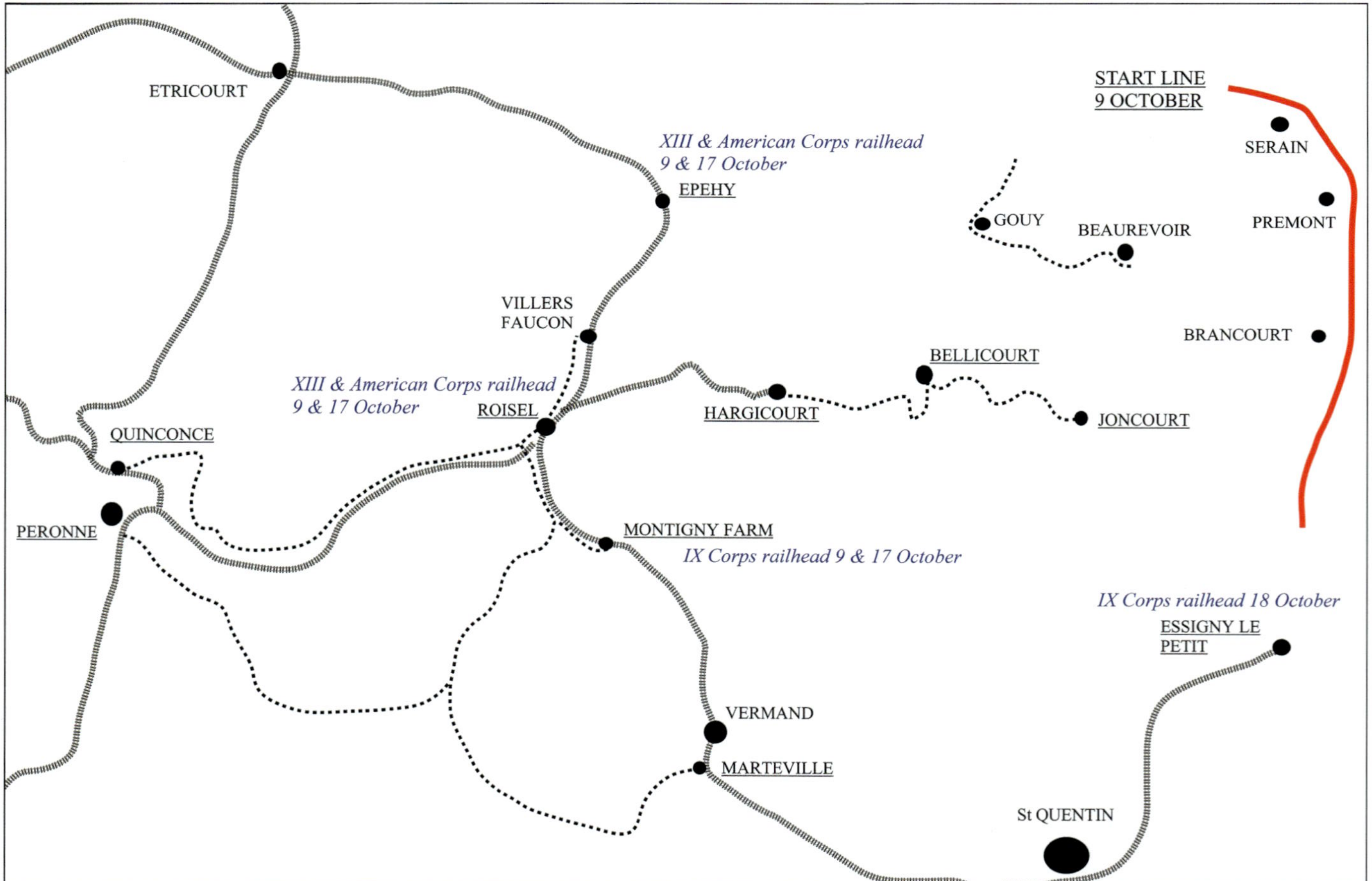

Map 7 Fourth Army railheads 9-23 October, with light railways (broken lines).

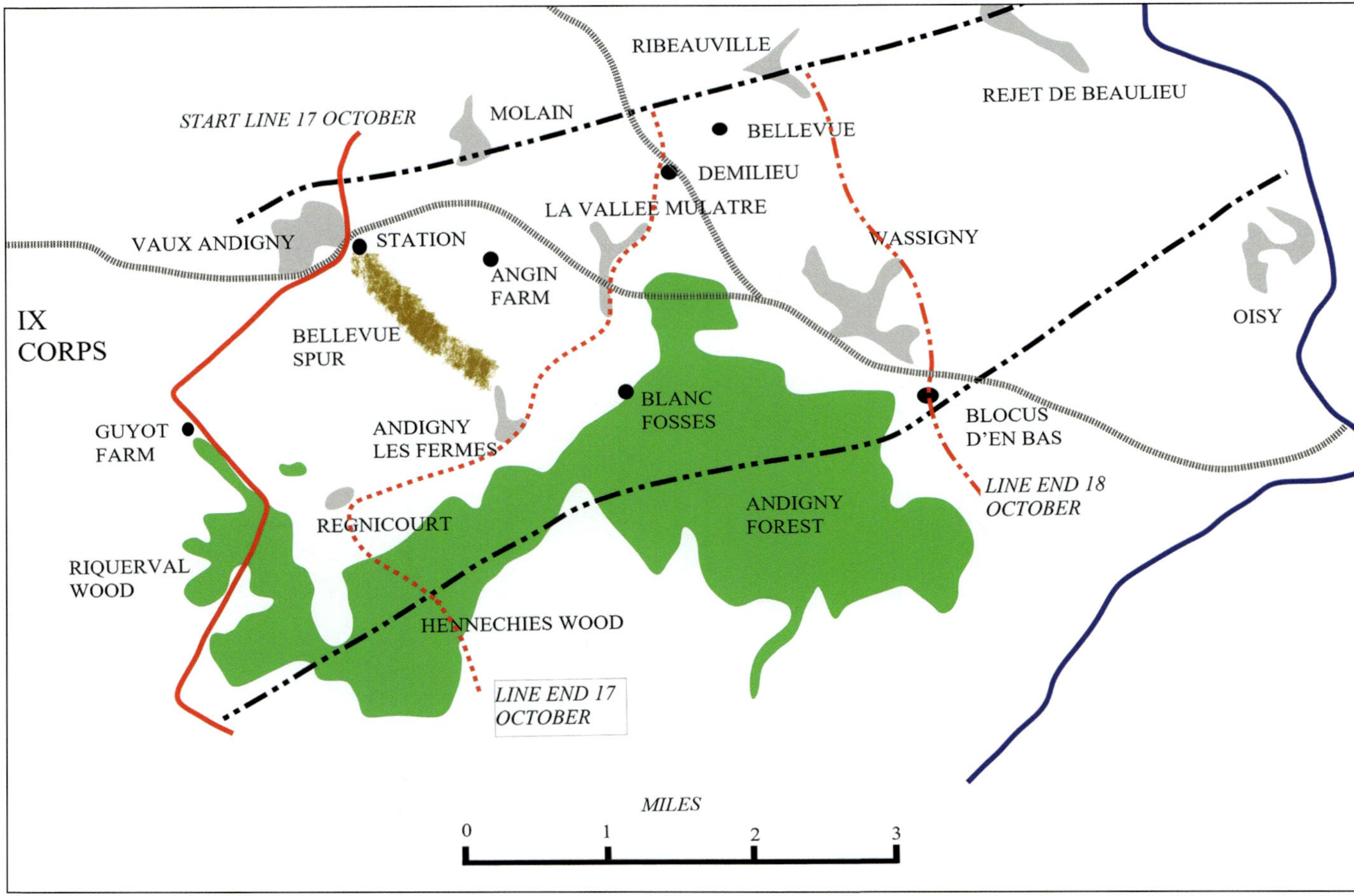

Map 8 Area of IX Corps operations 17-18 October 1918.

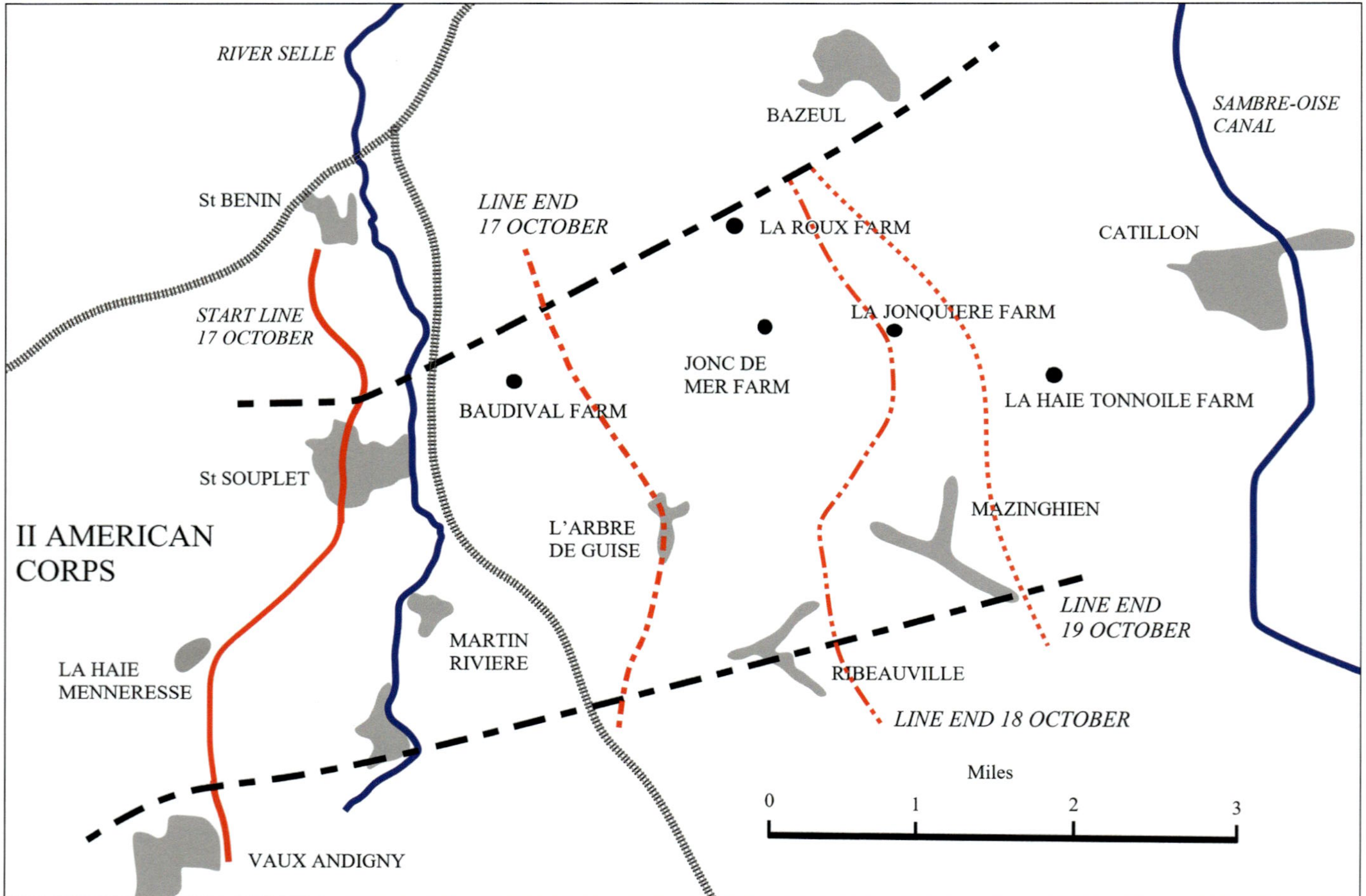

Map 9 Area of II American Corps operations 17-19 October 1918.

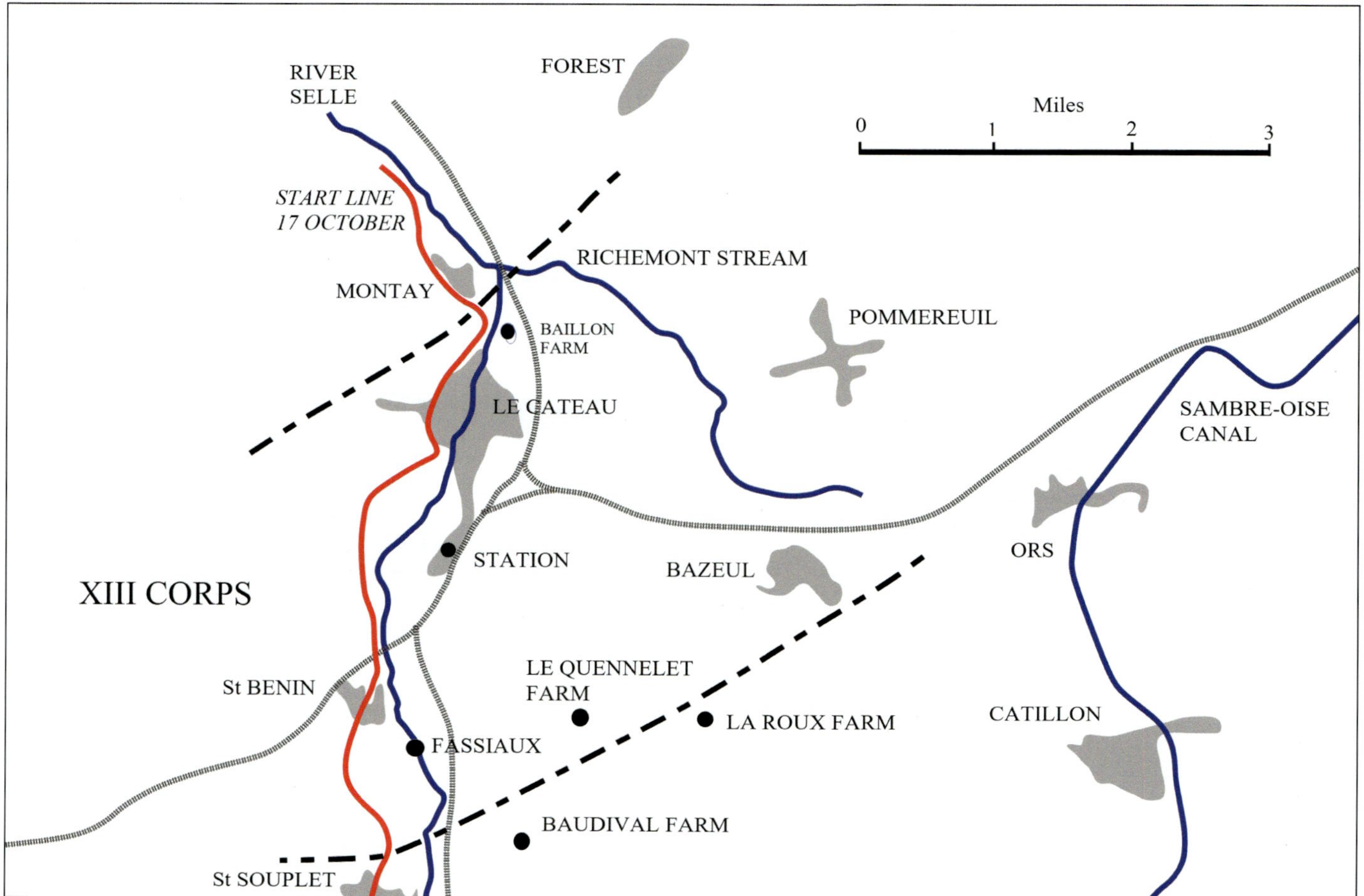

Map 10 Area of XIII Corps operations 17-18 October 1918.

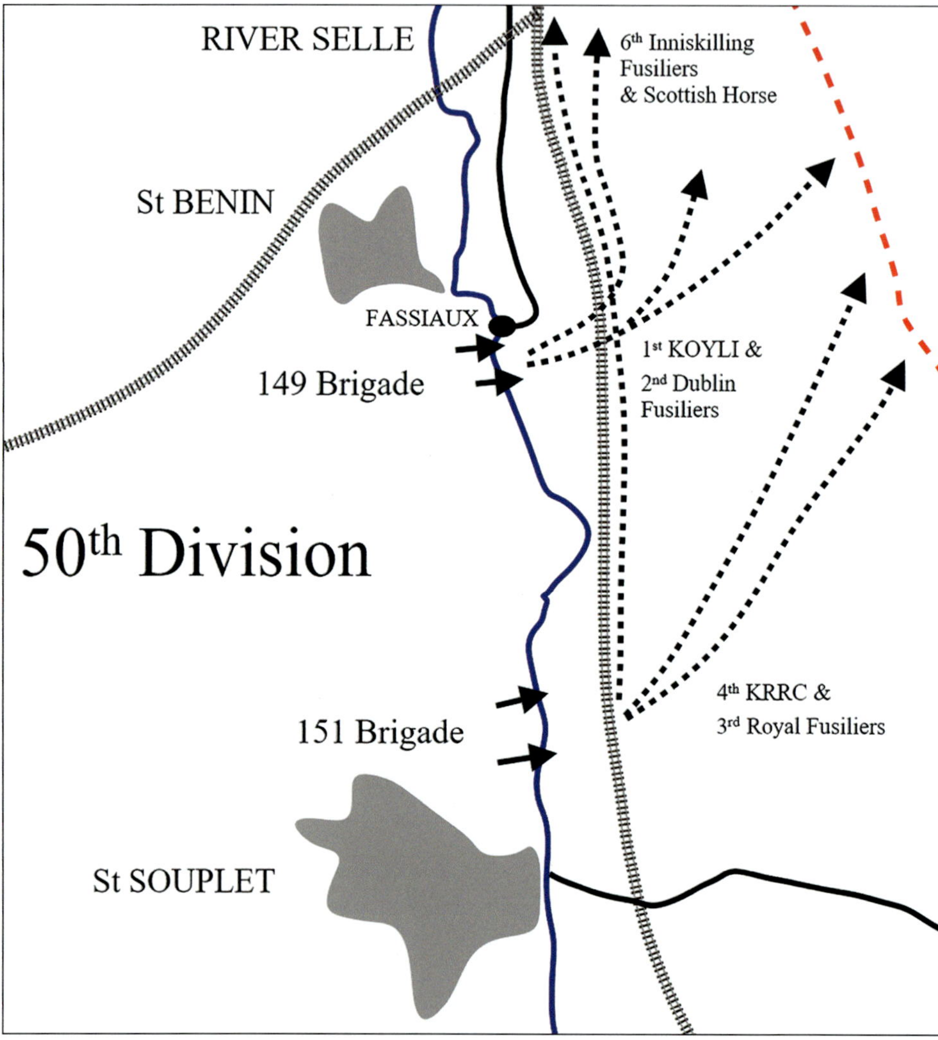

Map 11 50th Division's crossing of the River Selle 17 October 1918.

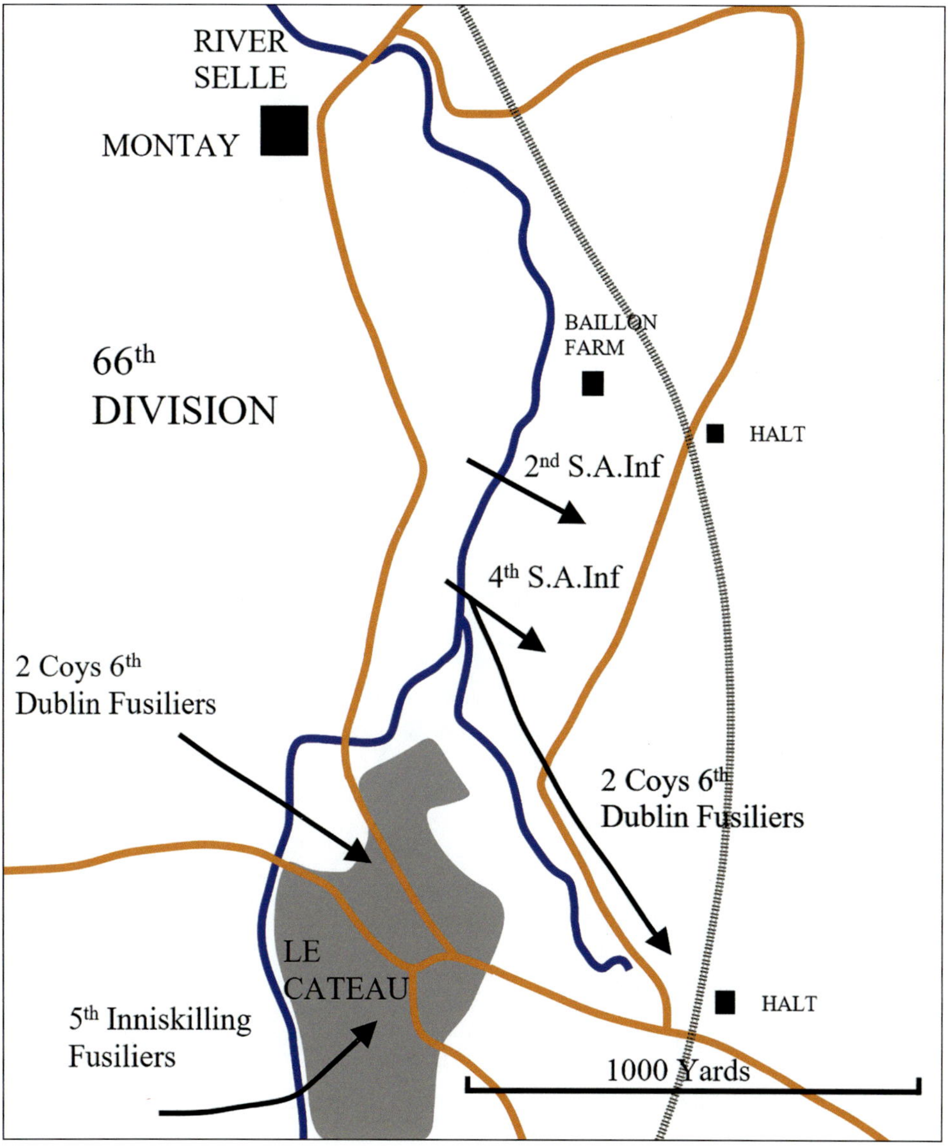

Map 12 66th Division's crossing of the River Selle and penetration of Le Cateau 17 October 1918.

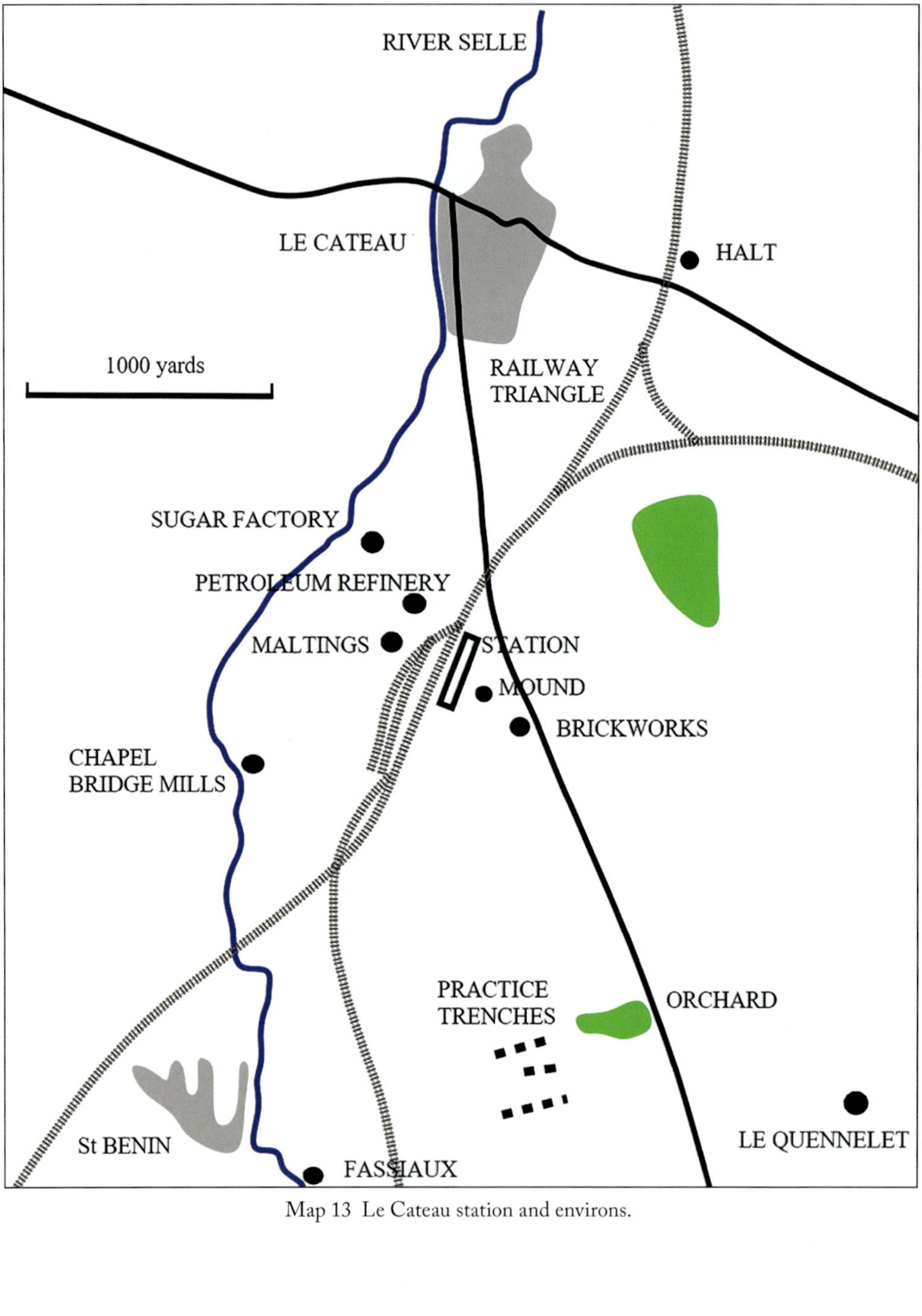

Map 13 Le Cateau station and environs.

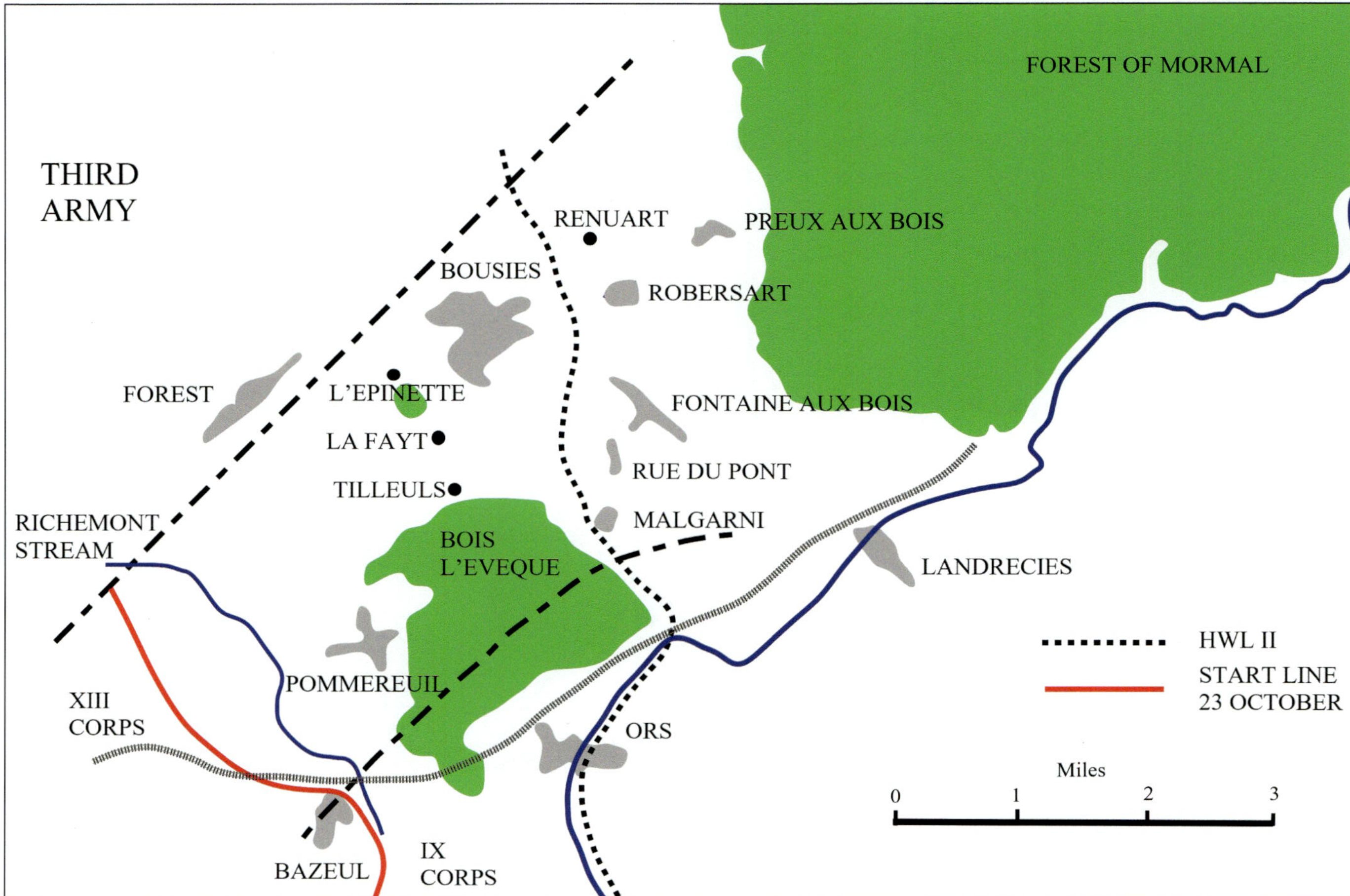

Map 14 Area of XIII Corps operations 23-24 October 1918.

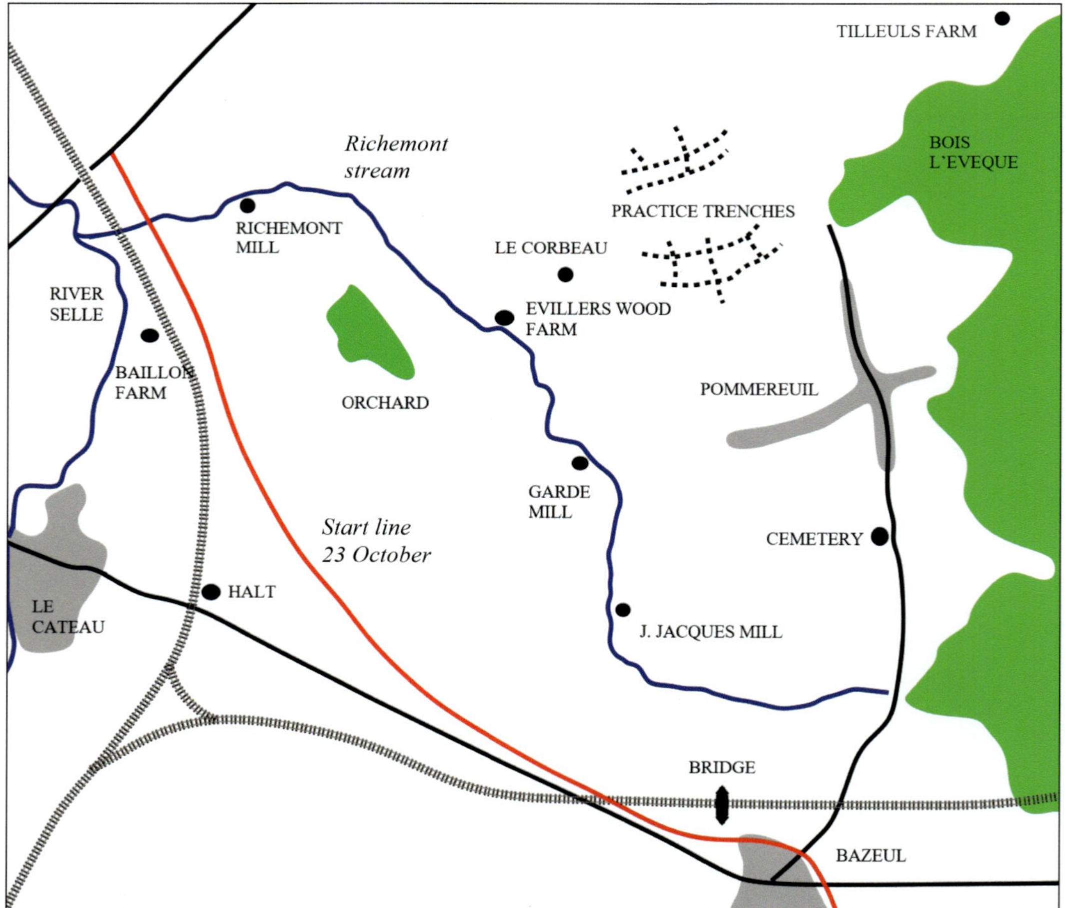

Map 15 18th Division's attack in the Richemont Valley, 23 October 1918.

The 2nd Northumberland Fusiliers, commanded by Lieutenant-Colonel Arthur Hardman-Jones,[206] who had moved up in support at 17.00 to the southern end of the detraining point, were to carry the burden of the evening assault on the railway triangle. They were ordered at 19.30 to pass through the Scottish Horse and attack at 21.00, but delays and the distance involved meant that the attack again did not take place. The Northumberland unit was ready to move off at 21.45, but again this further attack was aborted. There was to be no more offensive action that evening. The situation remained confused during the night. Some reports understood that the whole of the station had been occupied, others that the railway triangle had been attacked by infantry, but it seems that at midnight 17/18 October, the northern end of the station and the sugar refinery were both still in enemy hands, and the brickworks and railway triangle had been bombarded but never assaulted by infantry. Sir Henry Rawlinson would write four days later on visiting the scene: 'We should not have taken the station by direct assault'.[207]

North of Le Cateau, 66th Division, commanded by Major-General Hugh Bethell,[208] was to push the South African Brigade across the Selle, whilst 198 Brigade was to clear the town itself. They faced the strongest opposition of the day, namely *I & III Battalions RIR 76* of the *17th Reserve Division*, supported by elements of *RIR 206* of *44th Reserve Division* of *IV Reserve Corps* to the north, and their conjoint artillery resources. Feints at bridging in Le Cateau itself were carried out to confuse the enemy into thinking the main attack might come through the town itself.[209] The South African infantry would cross the river at zero on eight footbridges, and Third Army's artillery would lay down their 'Chinese attack' barrage to the left. The 18th Divisional artillery, however would perform the same deception in front of the South African infantry from zero to zero + 18 minutes. Until zero + 127 the ground in front of the infantry would be searched at a slow rate, at which point the barrage would resume on the start line for 15 minutes, moving forward at the rate of 100 yards every three minutes, the infantry now advancing behind it. Smoke was an important element of the barrage given the high ground to the east of the attack which would not be assaulted. The Forest spur was therefore enshrouded, as was the area in front of the *HWL I* north of Baillon farm, and the eastern suburbs of Le Cateau, screening both flanks of the attack from enfilade fire. Gas was put down in the Richemont valley around Richemont Mill, and to the west of Pommereuil. The 25th Battalion MGC and two companies of the 18th (96 guns in all) put down neutralising fire on the *HWL I*, roads and ravines, from the high ground north and west of Le Cateau. The delayed start was to enable the South Africans to arrive at the same time north of the railway triangle to shake hands with the attacking troops of 50th Division, who had much further

in January 1918), Victor John Frackelton Wilson (commissioned from private in April 1918), and Lieutenant J.J. Kennedy died of wounds. Second-Lieutenant Edward Richard McKenney (commissioned from private in the Canadian infantry in October 1917) was killed on the 18th. Lieutenant Herbert St George Stewart (commissioned November 1914), and Second-Lieutenants J. Crawford and Alfred Osmund Walter Buchanan were wounded. 11 ORs were killed, 67 wounded and 11 missing on the 17th; with one killed and five wounded on the 18th.

206 Arthur Cyril Langston Hardman-Jones was a regular captain of the Northumberland Fusiliers in August 1914, and commanded the 2nd Battalion from 29 October 1915 to the Armistice.

207 Sir H. Rawlinson, War Journal, 21 October 1918, Churchill College RWLN 1/11.

208 Hugh Keppel 'Beetle' Bethell CB CMG CVO DSO (1882-1947) began the war as a captain of 7th Hussars, and served as staff captain and brigade-major, commanding 1st Northamptonshire between December 1915 and October 1916. He was then promoted to command 74 Infantry Brigade between October 1916 and March 1918, at which point he took over the command of 66th Division. He was the youngest divisional commander of both world wars.

209 Montgomery, op. cit., p.222.

to go. It was a good plan, but like many such in both the Great War in general and the Battle of the Selle in particular, was doomed to frustration.

The South Africans proceeded down the open slope and crossed the river before zero, and were in place on the east bank by 05.00, right under the noses of the German machine-guns, the 2nd Infantry on the left and the 4th on the right. They were to encounter defences which their 1st Battalion, which had sent patrols onto the east bank the night before, had been unable to deal with. Enemy outposts had been very active, and the artillery had failed to seek them out because of proximity to the front line. On the left the 2nd Infantry had an unhappy start, losing the commander of D Company, Lieutenant Maurice Whelan, just prior to moving off.[210] Their assembly on the east bank took place within 40 yards of the enemy machine-guns, the body of Lieutenant Eustace James Brook, killed during the assembly, being later recovered riddled with bullets some five yards from the muzzle of the gun that may have killed him. The barrage opening, both battalions set off under heavy machine-gun fire up the slope towards the *HWL I* only to encounter a sunken road running across their front about thirty yards from the river. This was defended by a 'kind of brushwood palisade which in places had been reinforced with wire entanglements'.[211] Overcoming this obstacle, two hundred yards further on and at about 08.30 the two units met a second belt, 'several rows double apron with criss-cross wire between', uncut by artillery fire.[212] This hold-up generated a scenario which highlights the inherent communication difficulties that beset the fighting. At 09.30 General Tanner, commanding the South African Brigade, telephoned his divisional commander and informed him that none of his troops were through this wire. In fact, by the time he made his call both battalions were through and in the *HWL I.* He arranged for the barrage to come down again 100 yards east of the river at 10.30 to support the supposed intended progress through the wire, which would have proved very problematic, if not disastrous. Fortunately, messages returning via a very useful German communication trench alerted him to the altered position, and at 9.53 he telephoned again to cancel the barrage.

The South Africans set about dealing with the wire, cutting it partly by hand and partly by close range Lewis gun fire, but a shallow communication trench running under it and an enemy path through were discovered and used to reach the railway beyond at 09.25. Leading from the front, Major Edward George Clerk of the 4th Battalion emerged first and swiftly shot the two Germans guarding the entrance.[213] The South Africans swept over the embankment and dropped into the deep cutting, clearing the *HWL I* with bombing and Lewis gun fire, sections moving both north and south towards Le Cateau. After an hour dealing with resistance, both units pushed on some 200 yards beyond the railway uphill towards the crest of the ridge which gave access to the tactically important high ground that dominated the Richemont valley (Red Line). Opposition was such that they were unable to advance further, and posts had to be withdrawn due to sniping, machine-gun and trench mortar fire. One of the wounded of the 2nd Battalion who was left behind was passed by a German soldier who on learning he was South African 'rubbed his hands for him and gave him a drink of rum before passing on'.[214]

210 Maurice Esmond Whelan MC had been commissioned from sergeant in November 1916.
211 War Diary, 4th South African Infantry, 17 October 1918, TNA WO95/3147.
212 War Diary, HQ 66th Division, 'Narrative of Operations 66th Division 17th to 19th October 1918', TNA WO95/3122.
213 J. Buchan, *The History of the South African Forces in France*, p.245.
214 War Diary, 2nd South African Infantry, 'Report on Operations carried out by the Battalion 8.10.18 to 19.10.18', TNA WO95/3147.

The area of 2nd South African Infantry's crossing of the Selle at Baillon Farm on 17 October 1918.

The enemy, who were both in force and of good mettle, were relentless in their counter-attacks. There was a sunken road just east of the railway, and from here trench mortars and machine-guns attempted to cover small groups of the enemy pressing forward. Such efforts were repelled, but this was the least of the South Africans' problems. Although the railway ran on a slight curve, both battalions were under enfilade fire from each side where sections of the *HWL I* had not been taken. Machine-guns both at the halt east of Le Cateau and the signal box east of Baillon Farm needed constant suppressant fire. When the smoke cleared, the South Africans were even exposed to fire from houses in Le Cateau to the rear. Richemont Mill and the Forest spur to the left were further sources of constant machine-gun fire. The brigade had located its trench mortars and machine-guns on its left flank to attempt to deal with these problems, but even the artillery failed to silence the fire. The communication trench that the 4th Battalion had discovered became an important safe route for both units. The pressure did not remit as darkness fell, and the South Africans 'settled down to a most wearisome night, standing to almost the whole time' under bombing, machine-gun fire, trench mortar shelling and attention from both light and heavy guns and gas.[215] The cost was heavy – the 4th Infantry alone suffered 130 casualties, 23 fatal. D Company of the 1st Battalion, which came up in support to form a defensive flank on the left suffered no less, losing all its officers in a prolonged struggle with the counterattacks of *RIR 26*, and the 1st Battalion had to push up more reinforcements as the day went on. The South Africans had created a salient 1,000 yards wide

215 War Diary, 2nd South African Infantry, 'Report on Operations carried out by the Battalion 8.10.18 to 19.10.18', TNA WO95/3147.

and 500 deep, and had destroyed *III Battalion RIR 76* in the process.[216] Archibald Montgomery observed that the ground over which they attacked needed to be studied 'before the difficulties overcome by the initiative and leadership' of officers and NCOs and the 'gallantry of all ranks, can be fully realised'. He claimed that 'none but the very best troops' could have succeeded in crossing the Selle north of Le Cateau and fighting their way into the *HWL I*, which he likened to the titanic struggle at Delville Wood on the Somme in 1916.[217] However, the crucial ridge that was the objective remained tantalisingly out of reach, some 500 yards further on.

Le Cateau itself was not subject to a barrage, but it lay in the German outpost zone, and its houses and cellars promised resistance. Experience suggested that the clearing of even small villages at the Selle could take a number of hours. Relatively small groups of enemy could cause major difficulties, and the outposts of *I Battalion RIR 76* and a battalion of *IR 163* had to be expelled.[218] 198 Brigade, commanded by Brigadier-General Alan Hunter,[219] detailed two companies of the 6th Dublin Fusiliers, under the command of Lieutenant-Colonel William Little,[220] to follow the attack of the South African Brigade, crossing the southern bridges put across for their attack at zero + three hours. They were to mop-up Le Cateau from the north-east with the assistance of 198 Trench Mortar Battery, two mortars attached to each company. After progress had been made, the remaining two companies of the Dublins were to cross the Selle on the western edge of the town and begin to mop up from that direction, finally putting the eastern outskirts of the town in a state of defence.

B and C Companies thus crossed in the wake of the South Africans under heavy fire from HE and gas, fog and respirators making keeping touch very difficult, and some became involved in the fighting conducted by the South Africans. Elements of B Company under Captain Harold Shadforth kept direction and headed to the crossroads and railway halt to the east of the town that had been incorporated into the *HWL I*,[221] with the optimistic intent of cutting off the retreating enemy. They immediately became cut off themselves, however, and Shadforth and the men with him took refuge from bombing and machine-gun fire in a house near the halt, barricading themselves in with furniture and holding off the enemy until 13.00 when they had to escape through a shell hole in the rear of the building. They retired towards the Faubourg St Martin in the north-east of the town along the Tupigny stream that ran through the east of Le Cateau.[222] Company Sergeant Major Edward Synnot set off to alert Major John Luke of C Company who had taken charge of the mopping up. Luke sent a party to rescue Shadbolt, but they in turn became pinned down by machine-gun fire from the *HWL I* in an area of few houses. Meanwhile, A and C companies forded the river on the western side of the town to speed up the mopping up, but met considerable opposition in what developed into confused and disjointed fighting, finding the enemy 'a very brave and

216 Whisler, op. cit., p.182.
217 Montgomery, op. cit., pp.224-5.
218 Only 107 prisoners were taken in Le Cateau on 17 October.
219 Sir Alan John Hunter (1881-1942) had not commanded an infantry battalion during the war, having remained in staff posts. He commanded 198 Brigade from 17 April 1918.
220 William Benjamin Little DSO was a horticultural instructor at the outbreak of war and was commissioned on 30 September 1914 into the Durham Light Infantry. He commanded 4th Border Regiment from October 1917 to June 1918, and 6th Dublin Fusiliers from 28 August 1918.
221 Harold Anthony Shadforth OBE MC, a regular soldier, had been commissioned into the Dublin Fusiliers in February 1912, and had arrived on the Western Front in July 1915.
222 This stream originated in a valley between the station and Bazuel, joining the Selle at the point of the southern South African crossing.

stout lot of fellows and regret to say treacherous'.[223] Thus, Lieutenant William Hannin and a Lewis gun section had to proceed down a street in the town with two prisoners acting as a human shield to call upon an obstinate group of enemy holed up in a building to surrender.[224] Ten emerged with their hands up, but immediately opened up on the Dublins and their prisoners with a machine-gun. Taking cover, 'needless to say the prisoners in possession were promptly dispatched to another world'.[225] Erecting a barricade in front of the house, 'good street fighting began'. Another large body of the enemy was located and the German-speaking Lieutenant Andrew Whyte sent one of the prisoners along to them requesting surrender,[226] with the threat that if he did not return, his three comrades would be shot. In the face of the subsequent refusal, a platoon of the 5th Inniskilling Fusiliers, who were being pushed into the south of the town bit by bit by 198 Brigade, were sent to envelop them. By 12.30 the mopping up from the west had reached the church in the east of town, but the eastern outskirts remained under fire from the *HWL I* railway embankment which was situated on ground uphill from the town centre. A platoon of Inniskilling Fusiliers were dispatched to take the railway halt, where Shadbolt's Dubliners had failed only a few hours earlier, this being crucial to reduce the fire enfilading the South Africans. The Inniskillings in turn, predictably, also became pinned down, as were another platoon with two Vickers guns sent to assist Shadbolt, only three men arriving unwounded. By 17.30, however, the southern portion of the town had been cleared, and an hour later a post was established close the railway halt. Further progress could not really be made until the stalled attack of 50th Division had successfully restarted, however, as the *HWL I* could not be taken and held until fire from the railway triangle which dominated it from higher ground 300 yards to the south had been extinguished.[227] Equally frustrated, the remainder of the 5th Inniskillings,[228] who had crossed on logs to the south of Le Cateau, were by this time lodged on a light railway on the east bank, again under the eye of the railway triangle, but thus in the rear of the Germans to the north of the station. They could not attack either position. Despite this, at 19.00 the town centre was in British hands and the streets were being 'actively patrolled in case of lurkers coming out'.[229]

The position to the south of the 66th Division, on which their forward movement depended, remained very unclear towards the end of the day. In the early part of the afternoon, divisional HQ understood that 50th Division had taken both station and railway triangle, and ordered 198 Brigade to push 1/6th Lancashire Fusiliers across the river to secure the road running into Le

223 War Diary, 6th Royal Dublin Fusiliers, 'Operations 7-18 October 1918', TNA WO95/3140.

224 William Francis Hannin OBE MC was a sergeant in the Ceylon Planters Rifle Corps in August 1914, commissioned into the Dublin Fusiliers in July 1915. He won his MC in the Le Cateau fighting: 'During the mopping up of Le Cateau, on 17 October, 1918, when scouts had failed to get touch with platoons working in the opposite direction, he went forward himself under heavy machine-gun fire for the purpose. He also skilfully selected tactical points for his platoon with complete success. He set a fine example to his men by his utter disregard of personal safety, and was always ahead of his platoon in action'. (*London Gazette*, 3 October 1919, p.12296).

225 War Diary, 6th Royal Dublin Fusiliers, 'Operations 7-18 October 1918', TNA WO95/3140.

226 Andrew Ronald Whyte was commissioned in December 1914.

227 The casualties of 6th Dublin Fusiliers on 17-18 October were one officer killed and three wounded, and 12 other ranks killed with 73 wounded and seven missing.

228 5th Inniskilling Fusiliers were commanded by Arthur William Sibbald Paterson DSO, a first-class cricketer who played for Somerset, who was a regular captain of the Somerset Light Infantry in August 1914. He commanded 6th Royal Irish Fusiliers from January to November 1916, commanding 5th Inniskilling Fusiliers from that point until the Armistice.

229 War Diary, 6th Royal Dublin Fusiliers, 'Operations 7-18 October 1918', TNA WO95/3140.

Cateau from the south-west, on which the sugar refinery lay.[230] Whilst they were in the act of crossing the Selle opposite the station, it was discovered that 'the Station and Railway Triangle which dominate the valley entirely were NOT in our hands'.[231] The Lancashire unit was forced to cross back to the west bank late in the afternoon, the abortive crossing having cost it eleven casualties, victims of the fog of war.

Conclusion

17 October 1918 had been a day of extraordinarily hard fighting. For Carl von Clausewitz, the simplest thing was difficult in war, and 'these difficulties accumulate and produce a friction which no man can imagine exactly who has not seen War'.[232] And so it was on the 17th. Sir Douglas Haig noted in his diary that night: 'Fourth Army met with considerable opposition but made good progress'.[233] The Official Historians noted the 'strong German opposition', but that Fourth Army had 'broken well into the *Hermann Stellung I* and enabled a line to be established on the plateau … which separates the valleys of the Selle and the Sambre'.[234] Montgomery described that the fighting had 'broken the crust' of the *Hermann Stellung I*, and that 'the most difficult part of the task set to the three corps had been carried out with the same skill and dash which had been so noticeable in previous attacks'. He claimed, perhaps a little fancifully, that the army now believed 'no task was beyond their power'.[235] But as Montgomery continued, 'the resistance was even more obstinate than had been anticipated', and nowhere on the front had anything beyond the intermediate objective been taken, except in the south, where 1st Division lay just short of the first objective.

The cost ran beyond the two opposing armies. Gunner Alexander Caseby, crossing the river north of Le Cateau described how: 'The Huns before our bombardment had forced all the civilians into the railway embankment trenches and naturally this was one of our primary targets'. The reasons for this can only be guessed at – they could not have been seen. 'Boys, girls, old men and women lay mangled in heaps, and groaning children lay everywhere. In one sad case a woman lay dead and two small children were trying to make her speak'. Caseby concluded: 'Such awful sights would soften the hardest of hearts'.[236]

230 1/6th Lancashire Fusiliers were commanded by Lieutenant-Colonel Robert Ferguson Gross DSO and bar, a regular captain of the South Wales Borderers in August 1914. He served as GSOs 3, 2 & 1 before being given command of 12th Lancashire Fusiliers in January 1918, transferred to command the 1/6th Battalion in mid-August.
231 War Diary, HQ 198 Infantry Brigade, 17 October 1918, TNA WO95/3139.
232 Clausewitz, op. cit., p.77.
233 G. Sheffield & J Bourne (eds), *Douglas Haig: War Diaries and Letters 1914-1918*, 17 October 1918, p.474.
234 Edmonds & Maxwell-Hyslop, op. cit., p.314.
235 Montgomery, op. cit., p.225.
236 A. Caseby, 'War Memoirs of a Gunner in the Royal Field Artillery', IWM Docs 70861, pp.50-1.

5

'Same as First Objective of Today'.[1] Completing Victory: 18-19 October 1918

As 18 October dawned, Fourth Army's line stretched from the Andigny Forest in the south to Andigny-les-Fermes and then to la Vallée Mulâtre, from there to Demi-lieue to l'Arbre Guise and on to le Cateau station. Between there and the railway line north of le Cateau the situation was patchy, the line not continuously held, and it passed through the outskirts of the town where to the east a section of the *HWL I* remained untaken. Beyond Baillon Farm, the line reached back to the Selle south of Montay. Here the South Africans had experienced a torrid night, but there had been no offensive action since midday on the 17th. The clearing of Le Cateau had largely been completed by early evening that day, whilst fighting at Le Cateau station had ended mid-afternoon. 50th Division's line had stabilised on the Wassigny-Le Cateau road at around 16.30, whilst the Americans on the same position had ended their attempts to press on by midday. It was in the south where offensive efforts by 1st Division had continued well into the early evening.

At 19.30 on the 17th, Fourth Army issued brief orders that the attack by XIII and the left of II American Corps would recommence at 05.30 the following day, whilst '9 Corps will attack in conjunction with right of 2nd Amer[ican] Corps as early as possible at an hour which will be arranged between 9 and 2nd Amer[ican] Corps direct'.[2] The artillery instructions detailing 'First Objective' laconically stated: 'Same as First Objective of today'. Here there would be a halt for two hours before the army pressed on to the second objective, this again being much the same as on the first day, i.e. 1st Division taking Wassigny and exploiting towards the canal south of Rejet de Beaulieu, with II American Corps taking Ribeauville and advancing to a line from Mazinghien to la Haie Tonnoile farm to Bazuel. In the north, the railway triangle was to be taken (no operations in the east and north of Le Cateau being possible until it was), and a flank formed on the line of the ridge above the Richemont stream to Bazuel. Fourth Army emphasised exploitation from this position, the Brown Line.[3]

In the south, the German *Eighteenth Army* had tried the best it could during the evening of 17 October to prepare for the inevitable onslaught of the morrow. It toyed with the placement of the *19th Reserve Division* either strengthening *I Bavarian Corps* against the British or the neighbouring

1 War Diary, General Staff XIII Corps, XIII Corps Instructions No.9 Series 'B', 17 October 1918, TNA WO95/897.
2 War Diary, HQ Fourth Army, Message No. G 408, 17 October 1918, TNA WO95/439.
3 War Diary, HQ Fourth Army, Order G.408 issued 19.30 17 October 1918, TNA WO95/439.

XXVI Reserve Corps opposing the French. It even ordered an attack by units of these corps at 05.40 on the 18th but cancelled this, allocating the bulk of *19th Reserve Division* to the corps opposing the BEF, which gives good indication of the perceived threat. Meanwhile, *I Bavarian Corps* reorganized its front, reassembling the *221st Division* around Wassigny and giving the *29th Infantry Division* control over the battered *24th Infantry Division*'s sector. It placed much of the reinforcing *19th* behind the *15th Reserve Division*, which was probably now only 500-750 strong. The *29th Infantry Division* held its front with *IRs 142* and *113*, which were better off totalling between 900 and 1,000 troops. The *3rd Naval Division* was perhaps in the most dire position, numbering perhaps only 400 effectives.[4] In the north, German *Second Army* similarly pondered how to reinforce *LI Corps* for the battle of the 18th. In the end, it merely issued hollow bluster about a 'decisive action' to be fought along a new *HLW* (by which it meant the position of the various units on the night of 17/18 October), a defensive position the units would have absolutely no opportunity to establish, let alone defend. *204th Division* contained a wide mixture of units, and seemingly received no reinforcement; *243rd Division* received reinforcement of one regiment, *IR 478*; whilst *17th Reserve Division* had no reserves to call upon.[5] *Second Army*'s exhortations were completely empty without the offer of reinforcements.

Friday 18 October 1918

IX Corps

1st Division had fought on during the early evening of the previous day around la Vallée Mulâtre, and could not be ready for a 05.30 start. It needed to clarify the exact position of all its units in daylight and make 'reconnaissance of a definite kicking-off line'.[6] The division's own (post hoc) account first states that during the afternoon of 17 October 'it was decided that it would not be feasible to make a set piece attack with a barrage until a late hour the next morning'. Fourth Army's message of 19.30 authorised the British and American corps to agree a start time between themselves, although the IX Corps war diary makes no reference to any negotiation. A message timed at 19.25 sent to 1st Division on behalf of the IX Corps BGGS, Brigadier-General Archibald Cameron,[7] notes: 'Cooperation with 30th Amer[ican] Division to be arranged', but five minutes later the 'Corps Commander, the B.G.G.S. and G.S.O. II Operations returned to Corps Rear H.Qrs'.[8] The 1st Division war diary states that: 'The details for this attack were settled by the Div[isiona]l Commander at a Conference at B[riga]de H.Q. at 18.30 hours. The attack was to be launched at 11.30 hours'.[9] The chain of decision making was therefore upwards – the 'men on the spot' determined the start time and passed their decision up to corps, who were seemingly unaware of the time agreed on the ground at the moment of Cameron's message of 19.25. 1st

4 M. Whisler, 'Der Tommy Kommt', pp.287-289.
5 Whisler, op. cit., pp.196-198.
6 War Diary, HQ 1st Infantry Division, 'Narrative of Operations of 1st Division on October 17th, 18th & 19th 1918', TNA WO95/1234.
7 Archibald Rice Cameron GBE KCB CMG (1870-1944) served as BGGS X Corps from October 1915 to July 1918, and had taken over that role in IX Corps on 24 September 1918.
8 War Diary, HQ IX Corps, 17 October 1918 (and associated signal) TNA WO95/837.
9 War Diary, HQ 1st Infantry Division, 18 October 1918, TNA WO95/1234. Confusingly, the war diary of 1 Brigade states that this took place at '06.30 hours 18th October'. (War Diary, 1 Infantry Brigade, 'Summary of Operations, October 1918', TNA WO95/1262). The 3 Brigade war diary confirms that the conference between divisional and brigade commanders took place on the 17th, but does not state a time.

Division recorded: 'With the approval of the Corps the Div[ision] insisted that a set piece attack before late in the forenoon was impossible'.[10] The decision was therefore approved by IX Corps, but at what time is unknown. The 30th Division Summary of Operations, Mark Whisler notes, states that 'it was eventually settled that the earliest time the 1st Division could attack would be 11.30'. The assault would be joined by the right of 30th Division at that time, whilst the remainder of the American Corps would attack at 05.30 with 50th Division.[11] Whilst Lieutenant-General Braithwaite and his team were in transit, II American Corps sent out its orders at 20.00 to 30th Division for it to resume the attack at 05.30 the following morning. Details of the barrage were to be arranged direct with the divisional commander, who 'would arrange to keep in touch with IX Corps on his right during his advance, disposing troops in echelon on his right and flanks, if necessary'.[12] This message was, therefore, seemingly sent before the inter-corps discussion. 30th Division's Operations Report states, however, that at 21.00 on the 17th its regiments were ordered to 'hold line then occupied until 11.30, at which time British 3rd Brigade on right was attacking behind an artillery barrage, and for the attack to be renewed at that hour'.[13] This indicates that the American Corps learnt of and agreed the timing sometime between 20.00 and 21.00. It was a decision that would generate confusion and unfortunate consequences.

The morning was again foggy, though this cleared more quickly than on previous days, being largely gone by 09.00. The enemy was, of course, expecting the resumption of the attack, and the predictable British start time enabled the Germans to be ready to bring down a particularly heavy counter-barrage exactly when and where it would be most productive. The enemy also shelled St Souplet and St Benin, where they knew Fourth Army were bridging the river. 1st Division was therefore attacking without the benefit of the cloaking fog, but the later start meant that they 'escaped the enemy counter-barrage and reaped the advantage of surprise'.[14] 3 Brigade, the reserve infantry brigade of 1st Division, commanded by Brigadier-General Edward St Aubyn,[15] had moved forward during the night. It had been arranged that the RAF should smoke bomb the Wassigny-Ribeauville ridge so that their approach would not be observed, but the foggy morning prevented flying. Enough fog lingered, however, to at least partially achieve the same effect. Major-General Strickland came to St Aubyn's brigade HQ at 06.30 to finalise plans. 1st Cameron Highlanders would throw out a defensive flank to the Andigny Forest on the right, and 1st Gloucestershire of 3 Brigade would do the same on the left. It seems that Strickland did not have faith in the American 30th Division keeping up with his own. 3 Brigade would pass through 2 Brigade on the left of the division's front with 1st South Wales Borderers attacking on the left, 2nd Welsh in the centre, whilst the reserve unit of 1 Brigade, 1st Black Watch, would attack on the right.

At 05.30 1st Division's artillery carried out an hour's bombardment of the area south of Ribeauville in accordance with the rest of the army's start time. At 11.30 corps heavy artillery and 1st Division's

10 War Diary, HQ 1st Infantry Division, 'Narrative of Operations of 1st Division on October 17th, 18th & 19th 1918', TNA WO95/1234. These statements were copied word for word from the division's war diary for the 17th.
11 Whisler, op. cit., p.285, based on *30th Division Summary of Operations.*
12 Message from American II Corps to 30th Division, *United States Army in the World War Vol. 7*, p.638.
13 Operations Report, 30th Division AEF, 12 noon Oct 17 to 12 noon Oct 18 1918, *USAWW Vol. 7*, p.665.
14 J.E. Edmonds & R. Maxwell-Hyslop, *Military Operations France and Belgium, Vol. 5*, p.321.
15 Edward George St. Aubyn was a captain of the Special Reserve of the King's Royal Rifle Corps in August 1914. He had commanded 1/4th Battalion Duke of Wellington's West Riding Regiment from December 1915 to September 1916, then the 1/7th Battalion from November 1916 to May 1917, when he moved to staff posts, commanding 2nd Kings Royal Rifle Corps from April 1918, until being wounded on 29 September 1918, after which he assumed command of 3 Brigade on 6 October 1918.

field artillery opened their barrage, which proceeded at 100 yards every four minutes, i.e. it allowed more time for the infantry advance to keep in touch with it than the previous day. 1st Division was the only formation to shift from the seemingly standard 100 yards every three minutes. 1st Black Watch, commanded by Lieutenant-Colonel Francis Anderson,[16] set off with A and D companies in the lead following the barrage closely in artillery formation along the line of the railway through the tip of the Andigny Forest towards Wassigny. The machine-guns of 2nd Life Guards provided covering fire from near Vallée Mulâtre, eight guns of D Company 1st Battalion Machine Gun Corps (MGC) attached to the Cameron Highlanders covered their flank, firing 6,000 rounds of harassing fire on selected targets. Two sections of A Company followed to their rear firing 12,000 rounds over their heads in support of the initial advance, sometimes engaging targets with direct fire.[17] Forty guns fired 30,000 rounds.[18] Despite the fact that *RIR 17* of *15th Reserve Division* had spotted 3rd Brigade moving up, the attack seems to have been a surprise to the division's units and *IR 142* of the *29th Division*. Progressing rapidly – the Official Historians claim 'they carried all before them'[19] – they swept resistance away overrunning *I Battalion RIR 17* including one very active machine-gun nest where they captured five officers and 18 other ranks. Their impetus kept them close to the barrage, 'rendering mutual support by the concentration of L[ewis] G[un] fire on strong points of resistance'. Opposition stiffened on the railway spur west of the village, Wassigny station, and the western outskirts of the village itself, but this was 'quickly overwhelmed', and little opposition was offered in the village itself. The degree of the enemy's demoralisation is indicated by the fact that in one cellar five officers and 72 other ranks were captured by one Lewis gunner, who alone and without bombs, simply fired down the cellar steps. The degree of surprise achieved in the speedy advance is suggested by the capture of five officers at lunch in another cellar.[20] The eastern outskirts of the village were consolidated, and at 17.30 the battalion linked up with the French *126th Division* beyond the southern end of the village at Blocus d'en Bas. It had been a model attack. Establishing a defensive position, the attached machine-guns fired a further 11,000 rounds of harassing fire during the night on targets to the east.

Whilst the Black Watch were progressing round the tip of the Andigny Forest, units of 46th Division had been working their way north-east through the forest to meet them. On the morning of the 18th, 138 Brigade had established a line at 05.30 on the road between Andigny-les-Fermes and Mennevret, which the French had taken the previous evening. 137 Brigade then passed through to clear the forest during the afternoon, meeting little opposition. They kept touch with both the French and 1st Division, having a troop of Scots Greys and a platoon of cyclists attached for ease of communication. The Greys were ordered at 15.45 to seize high ground east of Wassigny but could not reach this due to heavy hostile machine-gun fire. When 1st Division made juncture with the French that evening, 46th Division were squeezed out of the line, and went into reserve to rest.[21] General Campbell noted of his brigade: "Having been in preparation for battle since the

16 Francis Anderson DSO was a regular lieutenant of the Black Watch in August 1914. He had served as a brigade-major from February 1917 until assuming command of 1st Black Watch on 10 June 1918.
17 War Diary, 1st Battalion Machine Gun Corps, 'Summary of Operations from 17th to 23rd October 1918', TNA WO95/1256.
18 Narrative of Machine Gun Operations – Fourth Army, Chapter VI, TNA WO158/332.
19 Edmonds & Maxwell-Hyslop, op. cit., p.321.
20 War Diary, 1st Black Watch, 18 October 1918, TNA WO95/1263.
21 Over the two days of fighting 46th Division captured some 15 officers and 500 ORs, two field guns, several trench mortars and 100 machine-guns. (War Diary, HQ 46th Infantry Division, 18 October 1918, TNA WO95/2666).

12th September … and after having fought three big battles, the strain of 8 days continuously in the line commenced to tell on all ranks'.[22]

1st Division were perhaps lucky in that *I Bavarian Corps* had re-routed five battalions arriving from the *19th Reserve Division* to support what they feared was the collapse of *204th Division* in the *LI Corps* sector. The one bit of ill luck that morning was experienced by 3 Brigade, whose approach had been observed by *RIR 17*, who called down a counter-barrage. 2nd Welsh, commanded by Lieutenant-Colonel John Badham,[23] attacked in the centre of 1st Division on a two company front of 1,000 yards. After initial resistance from *II* and *III Battalions RIR 17*, dealing with which Captain John Warren of the leading company won an MC,[24] they arrived on the Ribeauville-Wassigny road at 1.45. Their casualties amounted to one officer and 64 other ranks wounded, with six other ranks killed and two missing.[25] On the left, the mist was clearing as 1st South Wales Borderers, commanded by Lieutenant-Colonel Charles Taylor,[26] formed up. Astute 2nd Sussex had been busy identifying machine-gun positions prior to being leapfrogged and engaged them with Lewis guns as the Borderers came up behind. 'The finding of several of these enemy machine-guns knocked out and men of the teams lying killed near the guns' testified to the 'good shooting made by some of the Lewis Gun sections'.[27] Despite the smoke barrage being put down from 10.30, D Company was subject to heavy fire. A and D Companies led the attack uphill, hitting the boundary between *RIR 17* and *IR 142*, D Company being able to exact revenge for their earlier ordeal in the counter-barrage. They forced the surrender of some of *IR 142's* machine-gunners at Bellevue and dealt with those who would not when they 'got in with the bayonet killing 12'.[28] On the right, the resistance of *RIR 17* was weaker, and the objective, the road between Ribeauville and Wassigny was taken by 14.00. Another attached company of the Royal Greys attempted to reconnoitre, but were similarly turned back by heavy machine-gun fire. The two Welsh units had captured about 300 of the enemy, 50 machine-guns and five field guns and a team of horses.[29]

B Company of 1st Gloucestershire,[30] on the left of the division, meanwhile formed a defensive flank, a wise precaution given the failure of the Americans to advance. They pushed on uphill to

22 War Diary, 46th Infantry Brigade, 21 October 1918, TNA WO95/2666.

23 John Frederick Badham, a regular captain of the Worcestershire Regiment in August 1914, had commanded 2nd Royal Sussex for ten days in August 1918, and commanded 2nd Welsh from 17 September to 6 November, before leading 2nd Worcestershire for a few days prior to the Armistice.

24 The citation for Captain John East Lanfear Warren (commissioned in November 1914) reads: 'In the attack near Wassigny on 18th October, 1918, he was in command of the leading company. In spite of strong opposition from enemy posts, he pushed on with his company with great skill and fearless leadership. As a result of his gallantry and initiative his company succeeded in capturing 100 prisoners, five field guns, and twenty machine-guns. He did splendid work'. (*London Gazette*, 4 October 1919, p.12345).

25 War Diary, 2nd Battalion Welsh Regiment, 18 October 1918, TNA WO95/1281. The wounded officer, Lieutenant Ewart Aubrey David MC, had been commissioned in May 1917. The fatalities in the other ranks included 39 year-old CSM Henry Montague Millard who had joined up in 1897.

26 Charles Lancaster Taylor DSO was a regular captain of South Wales Borderers in August 1914. After serving in staff posts from January 1916, in December that year he was appointed to command the 1st Battalion.

27 War Diary, 2nd Battalion Royal Sussex Regiment, 18 October 1918, TNS WO95/1269.

28 War Diary, 1st Battalion South Wales Borderers, 18 October 1918, TNA WO95/1280.

29 Edmonds & Maxwell-Hyslop, op. cit., p.322. 2nd Welsh suffered one officer wounded (Lieutenant Ewart Aubrey David, commissioned in April 1017), with six ORs killed, 64 wounded, and two missing.

30 1st Gloucestershire were commanded by Lieutenant-Colonel John Lannoy Forbes Tweedie DSO. A regular captain of the Gloucestershire Regiment in August 1914 he had commanded 12th Lancashire

Bellevue meeting opposition all the way from machine-guns and artillery. B Company 1st Battalion MGC fired 20,000 rounds on targets in orchards to the left of Bellevue thus covering the flank of the advance.[31] At 18.00, the company was ordered to clear Ribeauville, which had been subject to 16,250 rounds of harassing fire from C Company 1st MGC, but met strong opposition, having either to knock machine-guns out, or force them back. Contact was only established at 23.30 with the American 119th Infantry on the left, who had finally begun to advance, and the South Wales Borderers on the right. Given the severity of the fighting in Ribeauville, it is perhaps surprising that only one officer and seven other ranks had been wounded, with three other ranks killed.[32]

1st Division's attack had gone well, but again there had been resistance, if not as strong as the previous day, and there was no exploitation beyond the first objective. This was largely due to the positioning of *221st Division* behind the crumbling *15th Reserve Division*, covering the canal. They had in fact been ordered to counter-attack, but the commander of *1st Reserve Ersatz Brigade* seems to have refused, and the order was cancelled.[33] Their presence, however, stopped 1st Division from reaching their further objectives.[34]

II American Corps

On the right of II American Corps, in 30th Division, 60 Brigade had relieved the 59th in their line trailing south down the slope from the Wassigny-Le Cateau road during the evening of 17 October. The 119th Regiment took over the line to the right, abutting 1st Division, the 120th the line on the left, adjoining the American 27th Division. In explaining the subsequent events, it was certainly problematic for 60 Brigade that it was operating with two different start times. Whilst the 120th would attack at 05.30, the 119th would go forward on its left but not on its right. The operations order from 30th Division to its two brigades, essentially ordering the formation of a defensive flank, issued at 23.30 on the 17th states:

> The British 1st Division will not move before 10 o'clock, therefore attacking line must be pivoted on right, keeping contact with British 1st Division on right, and 27th Division on left. This requires no movement on extreme right, but considerable movement on left in order to keep touch with 27th. When British 1st Division moves forward, our right will move with them.[35]

This order is curious because, as previously noted, 30th Division's operation report stated that it had informed its units that 1st Division would attack at 11.30 the following day at 21.00, i.e. two hours prior to the issuing of this order. The idea that 1st Division would arrange its jump-off on a 'not before' basis, given the need to coordinate barrages, is unthinkable.

Fusiliers from July 1916 to October 1917, and was given command of 1st Gloucestershire in March 1918.

31 War Diary, 1st Battalion Machine Gun Corps, 'Summary of Operations from 17th to 23rd October 1918', TNA WO95/1256.

32 War Diary 1st Battalion Gloucestershire Regiment, 18 October 1918, TNA WO95/1278. The wounded officer was Lieutenant Felix John Wilkinson Greene who had been commissioned in May 1916.

33 Whisler, op. cit., p.292.

34 During 17-18 October 1st Division captured 39 officers and 757 other ranks, as well as one 15-cm and one 10-cm guns, four 10-cm howitzers, 20 77-mm guns, eight trench mortars, 140 machine-guns, and a motor ambulance. (War Diary, HQ 1st Infantry Division, 18 October 1918, TNA WO95/1234).

35 Message No. G3/91, HQ 30th Division, *USAWW Vol. 7*, p.643.

The American advance was supported by five brigades of Australian field artillery operating in two groups, firing a creeping barrage at 05.30 with 100 yard lifts every three minutes.[36] At 05.30 the 120th Regiment, however, only advanced 'a few hundred yards',[37] even though the 30th Division summary of operations stated that this was achieved 'with little opposition'.[38] Here it allegedly paused to wait for the 119th to catch up,[39] thus losing the barrage. This was clearly in contradiction to their orders, which demanded 'considerable movement'. The events are redolent of inexperienced officers over-sensitive to an exposed flank. In the hour before zero the enemy had shelled the American front area with HE and mustard gas. It seems likely that the 60 Brigade advance, after the initial experience of the exceptionally heavy counter-preparation which had taken place all along Fourth Army's front that morning, were brought to a halt by the counter-barrage. At 07.45 the division requested heavy artillery to suppress hostile fire emanating from Ribeauville. It took an hour to identify the exact location of the American troops, but it was then agreed that Ribeauville would be bombarded until 10.00.[40] Whilst waiting, however, the fog cleared and well-targeted machine-gun and artillery fire forced the 120th back to the start line.

The left of the 119th Regiment, meanwhile, made some attempt to go forward when the 120th attacked at 05.30, but fell back more swiftly. The unit history states baldly that 'the attack could not be made', claiming lack of touch with units on either side,[41] whilst the 30th Division Summary of Operations makes no comment. The 30th Division history sets out that the British 1st Division 'remained stationary until late in the morning', leaving the 119th's flank 'up in the air'. This disingenuously fails to acknowledge both the agreed late start of the 1st Division and the unit's order to create a defensive flank. It further states that the advance 'was delayed until units on either side could come up abreast'.[42] This suggests that the 119th were the furthest advanced unit, which they were not. It also fails to acknowledge that the unit fell back. How far the 119th got that morning will remain unclear. Mark Whisler claims that 'the regiment had attempted to push forward without artillery preparation when the 120th had attacked at 5.30 am'.[43] On one hand, he is clear that the 119th went forward. On the other, the idea that they had no artillery support is not correct. The records of the Australian artillery show a creeping barrage was fired in front of the 119th Infantry at 05.30,[44] and 1st Division's artillery also bombarded the area to the right of the 119th's jump-off position for an hour at 05.30.[45] It is clear that both the 120th and 119th Regiments had perfectly adequate artillery cover for their attack. 13th Australian Field Artillery (AFA) Brigade notes that once the barrage had ended 'it was ascertained that the 30th American Division had not advanced'. This was of course not true on the left, and a whilst a contact patrol flown by Lieutenants Francis

36 War Diary, HQ 14th Australian Field Artillery Brigade, Left Group Operation Order No. 2, 18 October 1918, AWM4 Item no. 13/41/28.
37 General Staff, *Operations of the 2nd American Corps in the Somme Offensive*, p.33; Whisler (op. cit., p.293) suggests that the 120th advanced 'about 500-800 yards over the Arbre de Guise-Ribeauville road, probably occupying most of IR 112's outpost zone'.
38 American Battle Monuments Commission, *30th Division Summary of Operations in the World War*, p.32.
39 Edmonds & Maxwell-Hyslop, op. cit., p321.
40 War Diary, HQ 5th Australian Divisional Artillery, 'Summary of Operations on the Telephone 18/10/1918', AWM4 Item no. 13/14/33 Part 2.
41 Anonymous, *History 119th Infantry, 60th Brigade, 30th Division, U.S.A.*, p.53.
42 E.A. Murphy & R.S. Thomas, *The Thirtieth Division in the World War*, p.123
43 Whisler. op. cit., p.293.
44 War Diary, 7th Australian Field Artillery Brigade, Left Group Operation Order No.2, 18 October 1918, AWM4 Item no. 13/35/24 Part 2.
45 War Diary, HQ Commander Royal Artillery 1st Division, 18 October 1918, TNA WO95/1241.

Lock and Arthur Barrett between 09.00 and 10.50 appears to record the 119th in their jump-off positions, the flight noted 'seemed to show offensive spirit on left', although whether this simply refers to the neighbouring 27th Division is not clear.[46] 13th AFA recorded that: 'Arrangements were made with the 119th American Regiment's commander for a similar operation at 10 am. This Barrage was also carried out but the advance was also unsuccessful', stalled as has been observed, by unsuppressed fire from Ribeauville.[47] (The Americans described how the hedges and woods 'were literally bristling with machine-gun nests, so exceptionally well-emplaced that each nest had to be dealt with separately before our troops could advance'.)[48] Whatever elements of the 119th had attempted to get forward had clearly fallen back long before the 120th retired, and the barrage arranged specifically for the 119th at 10.00 was an attempt to get them up in line with the 120th. This fire may possibly have been arranged for 10.00 on the belief, as stated in the 30th Division order of 23.30 the night before, that the British 1st Division would jump-off after 10.00. When the British attack started at 11.30, the 119th went forward again, and Mark Whisler claims that the assault 'collapsed under short rounds from the creeping barrage – possibly because the artillery did not know the regiment had advanced earlier – and machine-gun fire'.[49] The 30th Division history, which does not mention the failed effort at 10.00, implies that the 119th were still in their slightly advanced position as when the further barrage arranged for 11.00 'fell short with some shots, our troops withdrew about 300 yards and aligned with the 120th Infantry on the line of departure'.[50] This withdrawal had, of course, happened some two hours earlier. If the 119th suffered from short rounds, they were in their start line of 05.30 when they did so.

All the Australian artillery brigade commanders had met the Commander Royal Artillery from midnight to 01.00, and clearly came away with the clear idea, as expressed in the 23.30 orders, the British would not jump-off before 10.00. The telephone records of 5th Australian Divisional Artillery show that both the last information that they had about the position of the 119th, and the first information they had that the British jump-off would be later than 10.00 was at 09.25. It was noted at this time: '119th Reg[imen]t will not advance till 10.00 but have heard that the British on the Right will not move until 11.00'.[51] HQ 5th Australian Divisional Artillery was getting its (still inaccurate) information from the regiment in the front line rather than II American Corps. 13th AFA noted that 'much difficulty was experienced in obtaining reliable information', and that any information had to be gleaned by them proactively: 'It was only by the excellent work of the F.O.O's and other Officers sent out that ultimately good and reliable information was received'.[52]

46 Squadron Record Book, 3rd Squadron AFC, 18 October 1918, AWM4 Item Number 8/6/22 Part 2. Twenty-three year-old pilot Francis Michael Lock was a postman and a pre-war volunteer infantryman. He was called up into the infantry in August 1916 but was commissioned into the AFC in April 1917. Suffering the misfortune of 'flying sickness' he had only re-joined from sick leave on 5 October. (NAA: B2455, Lock, Francis Michael). Lock's observer was 23 year-old Arthur George Barrett, a brewer who had also served as a pre-war volunteer infantryman. He was called up in September 1916, serving in the artillery, and was commissioned in the AFC in February 1918. (NAA: B2455 Barrett, A.G).

47 War Diary, HQ 13th Australian Field Artillery Brigade, 'Report on Operations 17-19 October 1918', AWM4 Item no. 13/40/32.

48 Elmer & Thomas, op. cit., p.123.

49 Whisler, op. cit., p.293.

50 Elmer & Thomas, op. cit., p.123.

51 War Diary, HQ 5th Australian Divisional Artillery, 'Summary of Operations on the Telephone 18/10/1918', AWM4 Item no. 13/14/33 Part 2.

52 War Diary, HQ 13th Australian Field Artillery Brigade, 'Report on Operations 17-19 October 1918', AWM4 Item no. 13/40/32.

They only learned after 10.00 that the 1st Division's jump-off was in fact 11.30. 'Timed area shoots on selected areas' were then arranged for 11.30, 'but this resulted in the position of the 119th American Reg[imen]t being unchanged'.[53] They did not therefore fire a creeping barrage which might have fallen short, although, certainly a creeper was fired by 1st Division commencing to the right of the 119th at 11.30. Crucially, in terms of understanding what happened when the 119th went forward for the third time, the 8th Australian Field Artillery Brigade who were directly supporting them received the message ordering the 11.30 shoot only at 11.25.[54] If there was any fire problem it is most likely that elements of the artillery may have started the shoot late due to the inaccurate and inadequate information from everyone from HQ II American Corps downwards. This shoot was targeted well ahead of the infantry, however. In any case, neither the 119th nor the 120th got forward, and another patrol flown between 12.10 and 13.35 noted the line to be the same as the previous contact patrol, and concluded: 'Our Corps front quiet'.[55] 30th Division Summary of Operations suggests that 'the fire from Ribeauville and Mazinghien was of such intensity' that the 119th was 'forced to withdraw'.[56] The unit history of the 119th Regiment acknowledged: 'Practically no advance had been made by this Regiment up to 5.00 o'clock that afternoon, nor by the units on either flank'.[57]

It is clear, therefore, that the artillery support for the American 30th Division, whilst intended to be as responsive as possible to the situation on the ground, was dogged by lack of certainty about the differential start times, and suffered considerable communication difficulties in obtaining up to date information. The fault lies entirely with II American Corps and 30th Division for not liaising accurately or properly with their artillery and infantry. But this does not account for the failure of the Americans to get forward behind their barrage at 05.30. The 120th Infantry did not follow their orders, halted, and lost their barrage, eventually falling back. The 119th made much less progress, retiring earlier than the 120th. The unit history makes little reference to the pre-11.30 debacle, except for noting that for the whole morning the 119th were subject to very heavy machine-gun fire from Ribeauville. Even though they were initially cloaked by fog, they were nevertheless subject to a heavy counter-barrage. It is clear that both units found the counter-barrage and unsuppressed fire demoralising, even when fog protected them. In their defence it is possible that the artillery may have been less than successful in supressing hostile fire that morning, as an hour's bombardment by heavy artillery on Ribeauville resulted in no slackening. The Australian artillery, unfortunately, had little intelligence to go on. The actions of both regiments, victims as they were of extremely poor staff work, also point to a leadership failure on the ground, officers being unable to get their men forward.

The success of 1st Division's attack had caused the *3rd Naval Division* to retire, and at 20.00 60 Brigade HQ finally ordered the 119th and 120th Regiments to advance.[58] In the leading 119th, 'the attack formation consisted of Combat Groups and Patrols joined by connecting files'. They made their way slowly over 'very rough country' by the use of compass, encountering little hostile fire until they reached the outskirts of Ribeauville, where a good number of mustard gas shells were

53 War Diary, HQ 13th Australian Field Artillery Brigade, 'Report on Operations 17-19 October 1918', AWM4 Item no. 13/40/32.
54 War Diary HQ 8th Australian Field Artillery Brigade, 18 October 1918, AWM4 Item no. 13/36/29 Part 2.
55 Squadron Record Book, 3rd Squadron AFC, 18 October 1918, AWM4 Item no. 8/6/22 Part 2.
56 *30th Division Summary of Operations,* p.33.
57 Anonymous, *History 119th Infantry,* p.54.
58 The 1st Battalion was commanded by Captain Robert J. Lamb, the 2nd by Major Graham K. Hobbs, and the 3rd by Major John Hall Manning.

falling. Enemy aircraft were 'very active flying low over our advancing infantry'.[59] II Corps claimed that Ribeauville 'was taken without firing a shot, the enemy having evacuated it',[60] whereas, of course, it had been cleared only with effort previously by 1st Glosters. The 30th Division continued its advance from Ribeauville under a heavy machine-gun barrage but was checked yet again by 'determined enemy opposition from Mazinghien'. In 'desperate night fighting a persistent assault was maintained on the German lines until midnight'.[61] At 01.30 the following morning the division reached Ecaillon, a hamlet between Ribeauville and Mazinghien.

On the left of the II Corps assault, 27th Division continued its attack on a two brigade front. In 54 Brigade, on the left, the 107th Regiment would go forward, in 53 Brigade it would be the 105th. The barrage line had been the subject of haggling in the night. 27th Division's line was not quite on the l'Arbre de Guise road, and the initial orders specified that the barrage would open 200 yards beyond it. Concerned about lack of suppression of the enemy dug in on the road's edge, General O'Ryan secured the agreement of Fourth Army's artillery commander, Major-General Charles Budworth,[62] that divisional commanders could dictate their own artillery start lines as long as adjustments were made in the barrage with the adjoining divisions. The barrage was therefore rearranged to start on the Wassigny-Le Cateau road, with the 105th and 106th Machine Gun Battalions firing on specifics targets.

Unfortunately, probably as a result of O'Ryan's late intervention generating uncertainty, the barrage fell 50 yards behind the 105th's front. Men 'huddled against the east bank of the road leading north from Arbre Guernon [l'Arbre de Guise]. Some commands, thoroughly disorganized remained here undecided, the victims of temporary fear, and for a while, uncontrollable'.[63] Going forward, the 105th immediately became entangled in heavy fighting with machine-gun nests sited by *204th Division* in the hedges to their front. The 30th Division having failed to progress to their right, they were also subjected to enfilade fire. In dealing with these problems, the 105th lost the barrage, and by 07.10 had only progressed some 700 yards. The 107th Regiment had less difficulty sticking close to the creeper, but had casualties all the same. Major Clinton Fisk of the 1st Battalion was giving his men the direction of the attack: 'Stick to the sun, boys', when he was killed by shell before even jumping-off.[64] The regiment's battalions pushed on behind the barrage, losing two more officers, Lieutenant Richard Raven commanding E Company of the 2nd Battalion, and Lieutenant Marsh Lockyear, the battalion intelligence officer. They however hit *I Battalion IR 413* of the *204th Division* with great force. Private Plato Demetriou of I Company 3rd Battalion described how he and his fellows moved through the counter-barrage without loss and getting amongst the enemy: 'Here there was good fighting and good off-shoulder shooting, for the Huns were hardly out of their dug-outs before our men were upon them. They went down in heaps and surrendered in bunches'.[65] The attack caused panic in *RR 120.* Men fled and the regimental commander reported to HQ *204th Division* at 08.20 that 'the situation is fully a rout, there is nothing more to do, no men

59 War Diary, HQ Fourth Army, Operation Message, HQ II American Corps timed 21.45, 18 October 1918, TNA WO95/439.
60 General Staff, *Operations of the 2nd American Corps in the Somme Offensive*, p.33
61 Elmer & Murphy, op. cit., p.123.
62 Charles Edward Dutton Budworth had been Fourth Army's chief artillery officer since May 1916.
63 History of M Company, RG 120, Entry 1241, Box 9, NARA II, quoted in Whisler, op. cit., p.229. The problem with the barrage is not mentioned in any official account.
64 G.F. Jacobson, *History of the 107th Infantry U.S.A*, p.319.
65 Jacobson, op. cit., p.384.

exist anymore … the situation west of the canal is fully lost and no longer tenable'.[66] All three regimental commanders in *204th Division* withdrew to *407 Infantry Brigade* HQ, thus 'undermining the will of the troops to make a stand'.[67]

At around 10.00, and with reinforcements from the *121st Infantry Division*, the German position stabilized. The 107th Infantry, moving across the plateau that lay beyond the Wassigny-Le Cateau road, approached la Roux and Jonc de Mer farms, about a thousand yards apart, which were heavily fortified. Here they were stopped by the weight of fire. The 3rd Battalion commander, Captain George Bradish was by this time also a casualty, and Private Demetriou's company found itself isolated and 'swept by hot fire from hedges to left and right'.[68] The 27th Division history suggests Brigadier-General Charles Debevoise, commanding the regiment,[69] decided to concentrate his forces on la Roux farm to his left first, defended by *IR 478* and *FR 122*, its buildings surrounded by hedges concealing machine-guns. In fact, the advance of the 107th had drifted north, in front of the progress of 4th King's Royal Rifle Corps on the extreme right of 50th Division's advance,[70] and Debevoise's force was concentrated here more by accident than choice. Two hours after being held up, the farm was taken. Attention was now turned to Jonc de Mer, defended by *IR 84*, *II Battalion IR 43*, and *Machine-Gun Sharpshooter Detachment 54*, which was successfully attacked by the 107th on the left and the 105th, who had now caught up, on the right. The degree of depletion of the American force is indicated by the fact that the 3rd Battalion of the 105th was commanded by Lieutenant Charles Whipple, and the attack on the right of Jonc de Mer farm was made by no more than 40 men. The 107th suffered five officers and 14 other ranks killed during the whole attack, with nine officers and 32 other ranks wounded, a further 21 being gassed. The strength of each of its companies averaged only 20 men. Although the two strongpoints had been overcome, the time expended in achieving this had, however, allowed *204th Division* to retire to another defensive position on the la Jonquière farm ridge 1,000 yards to the east.

One American Distinguished Service Cross was won by the 107th in these actions at the farms. Corporal Charles T. Stoll, after the advance had been stopped by machine-gun fire, 'with three companions, advanced far ahead of the front line' to attack a 'large farmhouse', (likely Jonc de Mer). 'By skilful manoeuvring in the broad daylight they covered all the entrances to the house and forced the surrender of the entire force of the enemy, numbering thirty-six men and two officers'.[71] Private James A. Lee was part of this initiative, and received a divisional citation when following the first part of the action he 'on his own initiative advanced to a near-by building and single-handed and

66 Quoted in Whisler op. cit., p.200 but source not given.
67 War Diary, *IR 84*, 17 & 18 October 1918, quoted in Whisler, op. cit., p.230.
68 Jacobson, op. cit., p.385.
69 Charles Isaac Debevoise had served as a sergeant in the 1898 Puerto Rico campaign, rising to command the 1st New York Cavalry, and had been acting as an instructor until brought to command the 107th. A capable commander, he was promoted to command 53rd Brigade after the Armistice, but had actually been promoted brigadier-general on 15 October.
70 S. Hare, *The Annals of the King's Royal Rifle Corps, Vol. 5*, p.390. On October 1 the battalion had numbered 47 officers and 952 ORs, whilst on the 31st the figures were 32 and 618 respectively. Their casualties 17-18 October numbered one officer killed with six wounded with 17 other ranks killed, 53 wounded and one missing. The officer killed was Second-Lieutenant Hugh Irving Williams, commissioned in September 1917. The battalion took 59 prisoners, 40 machine-guns, 18 grenade launchers, and two 77-mm field guns.
71 Jacobson, op. cit., p.173.

Jonc de Mer Farm.

The ruins of La Roux Farm.

alone captured a party of fifteen enemy soldiers'.[72] It was clearly not only British NCOs and other ranks who were capable of initiative and junior leadership.

To the right of the 105th, there was, of course, no support, the 30th American Division being long back on its start line. Patrols sent out into the void met heavy fire from unsubdued Mazinghien. A defensive flank was formed whilst the eastern edge of the Jonc de Mer ridge, marked by a sunken road, was secured. This was 'found to be very well organised with dugouts and shelters', where prisoners and large quantities of hand grenades and small arms ammunition were captured.[73] The prisoners were 'from numerous enemy regiments, including over 500 from two battalions of Marine Corps troops, with which the enemy attempted a counterattack'. Reflecting the degraded German morale, 'the prisoners far outnumbered the attacking forces that had captured them'.[74] The German resistance, as the Americans had previously noted, was 'dependent upon machine-gun groups, supported by infantry detachments, the whole in turn supported by enemy artillery fire from the heights of Catillon'. The Americans had found that the 'enemy machine-gunners were skilful and courageous. In most cases they fired their guns to the last.' In contrast, 'their supporting infantry detachments ... were lacking in morale and frequently sought an opportunity to surrender'.[75]

William Palstra, flying again with Ernest Devlin-Hamilton, was the last Australian pilot in the air above the Americans between 16.10 and 17.05. He reported: 'No enemy troops seen', although he noted machine-gun fire north-north-west of Mazinghien, and rifle fire in the south-east of Bazuel. He could see fires in l'Arbre de Guise, Mazinghien and Bazuel, and ever willing to help, his observer fired 50 Lewis gun rounds into a suspected post to the west of Mazinghien.[76] Perhaps as a result of his report of so little enemy activity, the Americans were not to have a restful night – they were ordered forward again in the early hours of the following morning. 27th Division set off into the gentle valley of the Jonc de Mer steam and up onto the la Jonquière farm ridge, which the *204th Division* had vacated by 20.00, and pushed patrols into the similarly gentle St Maurice valley, a target for the heavy artillery the previous day. Whilst this brought the Americans into line with the British in Bazuel to the north, the problems of 30th Division in getting forward had left the town of Mazinghien a threat to 27th Division's right.[77]

The poor staff work of II American Corps in general has already been explored. Given this applied to both divisions, it is difficult not to contrast the performance of the 27th and 30th. The 30th stalled after a couple of hundred yards under the counter-barrage, whilst the 27th stormed the strongpoints on the Jonc de Mer ridge. The 27th kept to the barrage and threw out a defensive flank to the right, the 30th were unable to do either. 14th Australian Field Artillery was part of a group positioned with the express intent of covering the attack of the 120th, and whose forward control station was established with its HQ.[78] The Australians were therefore close to the unfolding action, and in the aftermath proffered criticism of the American infantry. They attributed their difficul-

72 Jacobson, op. cit., p.211.
73 J. F. O'Ryan, *The Story of the 27th Division*, p.379.
74 Jacobson, op. cit., p.139.
75 O'Ryan, op. cit., p.380.
76 Squadron Record Book, 3rd Squadron AFC, 18 October 1918, AWM4 Item no. 8/6/22 Part 2. Of 10 flights that day, Palstra was the only pilot to effect a ground attack.
77 A. Montgomery, *The Story of the Fourth Army in the Battles of the Hundred Days*, p.227, states that 'Mazinghien was entered by the American troops later in the evening, its capture being completed during the night of the 18th', but this is not correct.
78 War Diary, HQ 14th Australian Field Artillery Brigade, 'Report on Operations from 13th–20th October 1918', AWM4 Item no. 13/41/28.

ties to five issues. 'In spite of adequate artillery covering fire', in their view, the failure resulted from 'inexperience of the individual infantry man, the absence of the officers and N.C.O's with which they were accustomed to work, and general disorganisation'. Fourthly, there was 'insufficient co-ordination with units on each flank.' In other words, the American lack of experience generated problems for effective command and control. Thus, the 120th halted contrary to orders, and thereby lost the protection of its barrage. Lastly, the Australians noted a 'disinclination to follow closely the artillery barrage'.[79] This further implies a lack of combat sharpness, and even, perhaps, a morale issue. Both the 119th and 120th Regiments were, as noted, demoralised by the fire that they encountered, and the 119th suffered a triple failure in getting forward under hostile fire. The Australians noted 'the absence of officers', and it will be remembered that both divisions were heavily depleted in numbers. The 30th, however, had more remaining personnel than the 27th.

It is also difficult not to wonder about the remarks of the Chief of Staff of 30th Division, Lieutenant-Colonel Herr, who years after the event cast aspersions on the British 6th Division. As observed, he allegedly attributed remarks to one of its senior staff officers that the 6th would not follow the barrage on 17 October. In reality, it was his own division who failed completely on the morning of 18 October, and it seems unlikely that he would not have been aware of any precariousness within it. The American histories were certainly reluctant to examine what happened in the 30th Division that morning. Whilst the events suggest a staff failure in a relatively inexperienced corps, it is impossible to ignore the division's simple degradation by combat. In its dilapidated state, weary and a shadow of its former self in terms of numbers, the 30th Division appears to have had staff-work, leadership and command and control issues, and morale problems impacting consequently on combat sharpness. Rawlinson wrote in his journal at the end of the day the Americans were 'tired, weak and much mixed up' and that he was intent on withdrawing them from the line.[80]

XIII Corps

To the south of Le Cateau, 50th Division advanced at 05.30 under a barrage fired by 25th Division's artillery. The Red and Brown line objectives were the same as the previous day, and the field and heavy artillery fired the same barrage plan starting from the Red Dotted Line which had been largely occupied the previous afternoon with the exception of the bitterly contested areas near Le Cateau station, namely the brickworks and railway triangle. Heavy artillery shelled the Richemont valley north-east of the town, and the railway triangle came in for particular attention during the night. There would be a halt for two hours on the Red Line, which involved an advance of 2,000 yards in the southern area of the division's attack to the ridge to the east of the Wassigny-Le Cateau road. The attack to the Red Line would be carried out by the three infantry groups which had been pragmatically formed the previous afternoon. 75 Brigade of 25th Division from corps reserve would carry out the second part of the attack, all of 50th Division's units being deployed already, starting at 05.30 under the command of 50th Division. Leapfrogging, 75 Brigade's attack would attain the Brown Line, namely Bazuel and the high ground above the Richemont stream. Because of the north-easterly direction of the attack, and the expanding nature of the ground to be covered, the barrage fired by the four brigades of field artillery was begun by the southernmost brigade at 05.30, the remaining three brigades joining in on different barrage lines at intervals as the area

79 War Diary, HQ 14th Australian Field Artillery Brigade, 18 October 1918, AWM4 Item no. 13/41/28.
80 Sir H. Rawlinson, War Journal, 18 October 1918, Churchill College RWLN 1/11.

to be shelled expanded, namely zero plus six, plus nine and plus 33.[81] Opposing the attack that morning, the German *243rd Division* was in better shape than might have been imagined. It had been reinforced by *IR 478* on 50th Division's right, but its line held by the battered *IR 479* south-east of the railway triangle was patchy. *17th Reserve Division* held the junction with *243rd Division* at the station, but was unable to reinforce *IR 162* holding this point.

On the right of the divisional attack, facing the road, 7th Wiltshire led General Rollo's group, with 3rd Royal Fusiliers in close support. The division, in company with most of the other BEF formations that morning, 'suffered considerably from the German counter-barrage'.[82] The Royal Fusiliers (whose strength only allowed a three company formation) fortuitously escaped it falling on them in the Y-shaped ravine by Baudival Farm where they had spent the night, by having formed up early behind the Wiltshires. Although Colonel Hodgson of the Wiltshires had been given overall command, the two COs controlled the advance by merging their battalions' HQs in a trench just west of the road. The Fusiliers observed that 'both Wilts[hires] and Americans appeared to run into the barrage', but this was likely the heavy German counter-barrage. In the difficult conditions of fog and bombardment, the Wiltshires failed to clear le Quennelet Farm properly, a task which fell to the Royal Fusiliers. Approaching a sunken road that ran between Le Cateau and la Roux Farm, the Wiltshires' attack faltered under fire from four battalions of *IR 478* and *FR 122* in the orchards around la Roux Farm.[83] The 4th King's Royal Rifle Corps were tasked with keeping up with the Wiltshires and maintaining contact with the American 27th Division to the right. They recorded that the 107th Infantry had lost direction in the fog and 'swung half-left across the battle front, hanging up our advance for several hours; this accounts for the delay in the capturing of the objective'.[84] As has been seen, the Americans took some two hours to master la Roux farm.

75 Brigade, who were to leapfrog, had some difficulty using the repaired Selle bridge at Fassiaux, which caused delay. Forming up on the railway embankment they were caught by the German counter-barrage. One HE shell alone caused 18 casualties in a platoon of A Company, 1/8th Worcestershire, advancing on the right with D Company 1/8th Royal Warwickshire attached. The leading companies lost touch with each other in the fog, but passed through the 50th Division units beyond le Quennelet Farm at about 08.45, under fire from the orchards of la Roux, as the Wiltshires had been. Exactly who captured la Roux Farm was the subject of erroneous British claims. The Official Historians claimed it was taken by the British 50th Division;[85] Montgomery in his history of Fourth Army believed that 75 Brigade participated in its fall.[86] The war diary of this brigade does not mention this, although it refers to the two right hand companies being held

81 War Diary, Commander Royal Artillery XIII Corps, XIII Corps Instructions No. 9 Series 'B' Artillery, TNA WO95/902.
82 Edmonds & Maxwell-Hyslop, op. cit., p.320.
83 During the period 11-18 October 7th Wiltshire's casualties included 6 officers and 99 ORs. CWGC records show that the battalion suffered 20 fatal casualties in the other ranks in the 18th. The wounded included Captains Charles Henry Sawtell (commissioned in September 1914) and Robert Archibald Fitzgerald Law MC (commissioned in September 1914 who would die of wounds on 31 October); Lieutenant Henry Percy Maskell (commissioned March 1917); and Second-Lieutenants Frank Henry Robins (commissioned from Corporal in March 1918), Edward Byrne (commissioned from sergeant in August 1918), and E.J. Stanford. Three of the four companies lost their CSMs. A Company lost CSM Arthur William Townsend MM, wounded; C Company lost CSM Charles Thorne DCM and bar, killed; and D Company lost CSM Albert Farrer DCM.
84 Hare, op. cit., p.390.
85 Edmonds & Maxwell-Hyslop, op. cit., p.319.
86 Montgomery, op. cit., p.228.

up by a 'village'.[87] The right hand unit of the brigade, 1/8th Worcestershire did not participate in attacking la Roux, nor did D Company 1/8th Royal Warwickshire. The war diary of 50th Infantry Division has it that General Rollo 'realised that LA ROUX farm was still held by the enemy and gave orders to have it cleared' at 15.00,[88] but the evidence of the units on the ground is that it was achieved well before this. 3rd Royal Fusiliers, who were in a good position to pass accurate judgement, were clear that the farm was 'not captured until about 2 p.m. by the Americans'.[89] Lieutenant James Oakleaf, Intelligence Officer of the 108th Regiment in support to the attacking battalions, may have left the clearest picture of what happened. He noted: 'Our patrols in conjunction with the British on our left cleared the woods west of LA ROUX Farm', i.e. elements of 1/8th Worcesters and 1/8th Warwicks likely dealt with resistance in the orchards to the west and north, pragmatically participating in clearing them as a matter of course.[90]

A gap had now opened up on the right of *FR 122* positioned to the rear of la Roux Farm, caused by the flight of *IR 479* as the railway triangle position unravelled to their right. Having dealt with the enfilade fire from the la Roux orchards, 75 Brigade drove into this opening. Increasing fire was directed on them as they approached Bazuel, from both machine-guns and 77-mm guns firing over open sights. Then, as now, the area to the south-west of Bazuel was honeycombed by hedges, orchards and small woods, ideal for sheltering defenders, more so than any area as yet encountered on the east bank. Lieutenant Walter Reynolds of the Worcesters succeeded in driving the enemy artillerymen off with his Lewis gun.[91] A Company pushed on towards the village, Lieutenant Watkinson agreeing with Lieutenant Fawke of the Warwicks that two of his platoons would protect their flank. A Company could not progress far, however, whilst C and D Companies were still held up north-east of le Quennelet farm. Colonel Clarke requested yet another company of Warwicks, and directed these reinforcements round to the north, in an outflanking manoeuvre.[92] Meanwhile, Captain John Walford commanding the held-up C Company made a personal reconnaissance towards Bazuel and decided to tackle the problem head-on, ordering his men to advance firing Lewis guns and rifles from the hips.[93] The commander of *FR 122*, Oberst von Alberti, perceived the danger of 75 Brigade's advance: 'The remnants of … two battalions and the corps reserve were in danger of being enveloped'. He therefore gave orders at 10.30 for the adoption of a 'delaying position at the east exit of Bazuel on both sides of the Bazuel-Ors road', whilst he pulled back

87 War Diary, HQ 75 Infantry Brigade, 18 October 1918, TNA WO95/2249.

88 War Diary, HQ 50th Infantry Division, 'Narrative of Operations October 18th -19th 1918', TNA WO95/2812.

89 Untitled three page report of 3rd Royal Fusiliers misfiled with 2nd Dublin Fusiliers War Diary, TNA WO95/2832. The battalion suffered one officer killed, Second-Lieutenant Benjamin Richard Corley Rogers (commissioned in February 1918), and four wounded. These included Lieutenant Forster, and Second-Lieutenants Laws, William Percival Caston (commissioned from private in January 1918), and Levers. Eight ORs had been killed, 67 wounded, eight gassed, and ten were missing.

90 J. F. Oakleaf, 'Notes on the Operations of the 108th Infantry Overseas', http://www.gwpda.org/memoir/Oakleaf/108th.htm , (accessed 15 March 1918).

91 Lieutenant Walter Hugh Reynolds, commissioned in September 1916, won an MC for this action. 'In the attack on Bazuel on 18th October 1918, he led his platoon with conspicuous dash and skill. When fired on by a 77 mm. gun at a range of 400 yards he brought his Lewis gun into action, drove the enemy gunners away and captured the gun. The initiative and leadership he displayed throughout the day contributed largely to the success of the operations'. (*London Gazette*, 9 December 1919, p.5364).

92 1/8th Warwickshire suffered one officer and 38 ORs wounded with two ORs killed.

93 John Osborn Walford MC had been commissioned into the Volunteers of the Warwickshire Regiment in 1899, but had retired. He was commissioned captain in the Worcestershire Regiment in September 1914.

units from near la Roux Farm.[94] The rearguard was still fighting with the British units at 12.00, and Bazuel was only finally secured by 15.00, C Company capturing an entire battery of 4.2-inch howitzers, complete with battery commander and 18 horses. 'Enemy aircraft were active, flying low and firing M.G.s',[95] but the Germans were evidently confused as to the situation as ammunition limbers pulled by six horses later drove into the village from Catillon only to be captured. One officer and 78 other ranks were taken prisoner, a bag reduced by Alberti's withdrawal. The Worcesters' casualties totalled one officer and 38 other ranks wounded, with two killed, a total surprisingly low given the severity of the struggle.[96] The unit's shortage of officers, however, is indicated in the divisional history by the comment: 'Sergt. Turner, M.M., Sergt. Faulkner, Sergt. Jones and Sergt. Hodgetts led their platoons with great courage and dash'.[97]

1/5th Gloucestershire had meanwhile advanced on the left after being caught by the counter-barrage whilst crossing the Selle. With 49 casualties, they leapfrogged 50th Division to capture the Le Cateau-Landrecies railway and the road to Le Cateau west of Bazuel.[98] Their progress during the day had been held up, as was that of the Worcesters, by machine-gun fire and sniping, particularly from buildings in the west of Bazuel and the orchards on this side of the town, which were dealt with in a turning movement attacking them to the flank and rear.[99] Platoon commander Second-Lieutenant Valentine Scroggie won the MC when on his own initiative he attacked the ridge in front of Bazuel 'under heavy fire, capturing it with 16 prisoners. Later, he beat off several enemy attempts to take the ridge'.[100] Officers were not the only ones to show initiative. Corporal William Peacey, clearing a hedge on the company flank, captured two machine-guns and four of the enemy; and later with his section rushed an enemy position, Peacey personally killing two of the enemy and capturing 14.[101] The two leading battalions of 75 Brigade had thus successfully occupied Bazuel itself and the railway line embankments and the cuttings to the north of the town. *243rd Infantry Division* ordered a counterattack to be made against Bazuel at 16.30, with a cobbled-together group of four units including two engineer companies, at the same time as counterattacks by *17th Reserve Division* on the German right and the newly arrived *121st Infantry Division* on the left. 75th Brigade were by this time well established. As the Germans advanced without artillery cover Alberti saw that 'the forward waves were ripped by such strong machine-gun fire that they could not come forward any more'.[102]

Brigadier-General Sugden's group in the centre of the 50th Division attack advanced with 2nd Dublin Fusiliers on the right. They had pushed out posts in the night but had to withdraw these at

94 Unit records, *FR 122*, October 1918, quoted in Whisler, op. cit., p.207.
95 War Diary, HQ 75 Infantry Brigade, 18 October 1918, TNA WO95/2249.
96 War Diary, 1/8th Battalion Worcestershire Regiment, 'Narrative of Operations, 18 October 1918', TNA WO95/2251.
97 M. Kincaid-Smith, *The 25th Division in France and Flanders*, p.354.
98 Second-Lieutenant Sydney Forest Woodward MM (commissioned from sergeant in July 1918) was mortally wounded and died the following day. He had been commissioned from sergeant in July 1918. Second-Lieutenant Herbert Haysham Searle (commissioned from lance-corporal in May 1918), was seriously wounded. During the three days of the battle the battalion suffered seven ORs killed, two officers and 64 wounded/missing.
99 War Diary, HQ 75 Infantry Brigade, 18 October 1918, TNA WO95/2249.
100 *Edinburgh Gazette*, 11 December 1919, p.3997.
101 William Peacey had been on the Western Front since March 1915. His DCM for this action was awarded on 10 January 1920.
102 Unit records, *FR 122*, October 1918, quoted in Whisler, op. cit., p.208.

05.30 because of the enemy counter-barrage.[103] They pushed on without difficulty across the railway to the Le Cateau-Bazuel road north of the railway triangle, where at 14.00 they had to clear enemy machine-gun posts out of the houses lining it, a task which took them some four hours. Elements of the unit over-ran their objective and entered Bazuel across the line of the Glosters' advance, and it was during this action that Sergeant Horace Augustus Curtis became one of three Victoria Cross recipients of the Selle operations:

> For most conspicuous bravery and devotion to duty East of Le Cateau on the morning of the 18th October, 1918, when in attack his platoon came unexpectedly under intense machine-gun fire. Realising that the attack would fail unless the enemy guns were silenced, Sjt. Curtis, without hesitation, rushed forward through our own barrage and the enemy fire, and killed and wounded the teams of two of the guns, whereupon the remaining four guns surrendered. Then, turning his attention to a train-load of reinforcements, he succeeded in capturing over 100 enemy before his comrades joined him. His valour and disregard of danger inspired all.[104]

The Dubliners, who were withdrawn from the line that evening, had gone into action on the Selle with 20 officers and 458 other ranks. Two officers and 35 other ranks had been killed, seven officers and 132 other ranks had been wounded with 24 gassed and five suffering 'shell-shock'. With five missing, they had lost 44 per cent of their numbers.[105]

2nd Munster Fusiliers were on the left of Sugden's group, the 1st King's Own Yorkshire Light Infantry being in support, although their CO, Colonel Mallinson, was in command of the whole group.[106] The Munsters had moved off at 21.30 the previous evening, and over unknown ground it

103 Whisler, op. cit., p.203, cites German unit accounts which suggest that at 01.00 there was a night attack which nearly destroyed three companies of *IR 479*. No primary source from Sugden's centre group mentions this.

104 *London Gazette*, 6 January 1919, p.307. Born in 1891, Curtis was a Cornish china clay worker who had enlisted in September 1914. He had been promoted sergeant in November 1916.

105 H.C. Wylly, *Crown and Company 1911-1922*, p.119. The wounded officers included Captain Arthur Bracton Bagley MC, ex-RFC (commissioned October 1910, who died on 29 October); Lieutenants William Humphrey MC (commissioned May 1917); Louis Campbell Byrne DSO MC (commissioned February 1915); Gilbert Malcolm Crawford MC (commissioned April 1915); Douglas Raymond Lambkin MC (commissioned October 1916); Bernard Glancy (commissioned December 1916); and John Vincent Staples MC (commissioned August 1917). Staples won his MC at the Selle: 'For marked gallantry and determined leadership, being with his platoon the first to cross the River Selle, east of St. Benin, on the 17th October, 1918, under heavy machine-gun fire, and to obtain a lodgement on the further bank, which enabled the remainder of his company to cross. Although wounded in the leg, he continued to command his platoon till he reached the final objective nearly twelve hours later.' (*London Gazette*, 4 October 1919, p.12337)

106 In the in the three days of the Selle operation the 1st King's Own Yorkshire Light Infantry had suffered 207 casualties. Three officers had been killed: Lieutenant Francis Scott; Lieutenant Ottley Tuke (commissioned from private in January 1915); and Lieutenant Charles Adolphus Row Bromham (commissioned in January 1916); with four wounded: Lieutenant Leslie Franklin (commissioned from lance-corporal in November 1915, who had been on the Western Front since October 1914); Lieutenant Frank Roebuck (commissioned from sergeant in October 1915); Lieutenant William Harrold (commissioned in March 1915), gassed; and Second-Lieutenant Charles William Gale (commissioned in March 1917, who would die in February 1919); whilst 14 other ranks were killed, 123 wounded, 40 missing and 3 gassed. In October the unit had a total 395 casualties with 68 sick. The balance had largely been maintained by five officer and 419 other rank reinforcements. (R.C. Bond, *The King's Own Yorkshire Light Infantry in the Great War*, p.1010)

had taken hours to get their companies into position. The orders for the attack had been received at 01.30 but it was 04.30, an hour prior to zero, before they were in the hands of company commanders. 'The true bearing of the advance and a brief outline of the operation was given to each company commander in turn by the light of an electric torch at the bottom of a small pit … the last order was given out by the company commanders a quarter of an hour before the barrage opened'.[107] At 05.35 there was a 'very heavy hostile counter barrage put down',[108] which caused significant casualties in the Munster's support company. At 06.30 'the fog gradually thinned and finally disappeared leaving the Battalion advancing over a rolling plain' littered with abandoned equipment and weapons'.[109] Like most units they ran into resistance from enclosed orchards, which two companies 'worked round', but despite this by 07.30 they were on their objective, pushing on towards the Le Cateau-Bazuel road. 'Owing to casualties amongst Co[mpan]y Officers and impossibility of fully explaining objectives to men prior to attack', they got in the way of the barrage put down for 75 Brigade's attack, and 'had to be withdrawn'.[110] The casualties had indeed been heavy. The Munsters had a battle strength of 11 officers and 316 ORs at the start of the engagement. Having had no casualties on the 17th, Lieutenant James Howe and 25 other ranks had been killed,[111] whilst a further four officers and 68 other ranks were wounded with 14 missing, reducing their numbers to a paltry 219.[112] By the end of the operation they could only immediately rally three officers and 70 men, but this group occupied a line running south from the Le Cateau-Pommereuil road at a point half way between Bazuel and the railway triangle. The troops of all three battalions of Sugden's group were again, however, badly intermixed.

On the left of the division's attack, General Robinson's group had a series of strongpoints to take – the remainder of the station that was in enemy hands, the brickworks, and the railway triangle. The 6th Inniskilling Fusiliers, who had fought long and hard the previous day, were on the right, tasked with taking the brickworks and woods in front of the railway triangle. Despite the 'intense barrage' put down by the enemy along the east of the railway and the station itself, the brickworks that had been out of reach the previous day were taken without a single casualty.[113] The wood, assaulted by one company on its western edge and one from the south, had fallen within 30 minutes of the jump-off at the cost of two casualties,[114] and over 40 prisoners were taken together with three trench mortars and three anti-tank rifles.[115] The Scottish Horse on the left swept through the station and assaulted the previously unreachable railway triangle, and by 07.00 troops from *IR*

107 H.S. Jervis, *The 2nd Munsters in France*, p.56.
108 War Diary 2nd Battalion Royal Munster Fusiliers, 18 October 1918, TNA WO95/2837.
109 Jervis, op. cit., pp.56-7.
110 War Diary, 2nd Battalion Royal Munster Fusiliers, 18 October 1918, TNS WO95/2837.
111 James Rowe Howe had been commissioned in July 1915.
112 The four officers were Captain Stephen William Whateley (commissioned in July 1910, who died of wounds on 25 October), Second-Lieutenant Daniel Minahan (who had served as a sergeant-major in the Australian Imperial Force and a sergeant in the Royal Irish Rifles, and who had been commissioned in February 1918); Second-Lieutenant H.W. Clarke; and Second-Lieutenant Horace George Canolin (commissioned in March 1917).
113 Whisler, op. cit., p.203, cites secondary sources to suggest the brickworks was taken the previous evening – primary sources contradict this view.
114 The two casualties included Second-Lieutenant Edward Richard McKenney, commissioned from a private in the 29th Canadian Infantry in November 1917.
115 War Diary, 6th Battalion Inniskilling Fusiliers, 'Report on Operations of 17/18th October 1918', TNA WO95/2843.

162 and *IR 479* defending the area were streaming back through Bazuel.[116] The unit then formed a defensive line on the railway facing north. The German resistance had melted away, 185 prisoners and 30 machine-guns being captured. The Scottish Horse had fought a formidable battle over two days. The battalion had had the advantage of being strong at the start of October, comprising 25 officers and 714 other ranks. It had sustained 108 casualties in the first half of the month and the two days' fighting 18-19 October had cost it one officer dead and five wounded;[117] with 31 other ranks killed and 126 wounded. It had lost a third of its strength in 19 days.

Finally, the 2nd Northumberland Fusiliers had been tasked with taking some 700 yards of railway to the north of the wood occupied by the Inniskillings and east of the railway triangle. They advanced 1,200 yards through 'heavy concentrations of 5.9 and 4.2 shells, which included a considerable amount of gas'. Despite the loss of Lieutenant James Wilson and five other ranks, killed as the railway was overwhelmed,[118] the whole position was taken by 08.30. One officer and 30 men with 29 machine-guns, were captured, Captain Urwin Dodd being awarded the MC for his part in leading two companies in the attack.[119] At the close of the day, despite their exertions, the Scottish Horse had largely sole possession of the front line, having linked up with the 66th Division in the eastern outskirts of Le Cateau, and had even relieved two companies of the Glosters to the west of Bazuel.

In 66th Division's area, covering Le Cateau and the area to the north as far as Baillon Farm, the artillery barrage fired by 18th Division's artillery started 200 yards in front of the infantry on the railway line at Zero plus 33, lifting at Zero plus 39, its lifts coordinating with those of 25th Division's artillery.[120] The infantry attack was to swing to its right on to the top of the high ground east of Le Cateau, and once the railway triangle had been captured it would be possible to clear the remainder of Le Cateau, Faubourg de Landrecies, that had remained in enemy hands overnight.

In the town itself, prior to jumping-off, 6th Dublin Fusiliers of 198 Brigade sent Lieutenant Harold Bruce of 5th Inniskilling Fusiliers under the cover of the barrage at 05.30 to a point in the eastern outskirts in front of the *HWL I* on reconnaissance.[121] He progressed to the town side of the railway cutting 'and crossed the Railway Line himself reaching many of the enemy, some

116 War Diary, *IR 479*, 18 October 1918, cited in Whisler, op. cit., p.204.

117 Amongst the wounded were Captain Archibald Noel Skelton (commissioned in September 1914); Lieutenant R. Watson; Lieutenant G. Robertson (commissioned in November 1916); Second-Lieutenant Leonard Samuel John Morgan (commissioned from corporal in September 1917); and Second-Lieutenant James Auchterlonie Keith (commissioned from corporal in May 1918).

118 28 other ranks were wounded. James Boyd Wilson was commissioned in November 1915.

119 H.R. Sandilands, *The Fifth in the Great War*, pp.286-7. Urwin Hunter Dodd MC was commissioned in October 1915. His MC citation reads: 'On 19th October, 1918, near Le Cateau railway station, he commanded two companies in the successful attack on the Triangle and railway east of the station. By his leading and skill he took his objective, including several machine-gun posts, with slight casualties. He started his attack in the dark and with no previous knowledge of the ground. Throughout the day he set a fine example by his coolness and courage'. (*London Gazette*, 4 October 1919, p.12286). Dodd, as chief engineer, went down on *SS Englishman* in January 1941.

120 War Diary, HQ Commander Royal Artillery XIII Corps, XIII Corps Instructions No. 9 Series "B" Artillery, TNA WO95/902.

121 Harold Easton Bruce MC had been commissioned in June 1915. His MC citation reads: 'For great courage and enterprise. On the 15th October, 1918, (sic) he was ordered to establish a post with his platoon in the eastern outskirts of Le Cateau. Finding all egress from the village barred by enemy machine-gun fire, he went out with a runner to reconnoitre. He succeeded in reaching the railway embankment, where he located eight machine-gun posts, and before withdrawing rushed one, shot two of the team, and caused further casualties by bombing. The information gained by his daring action

The River Selle passing through Le Cateau.

The bridge on the Le Cateau-Bazuel road in the western suburbs of Le Cateau where the *HWL I* dominated the British advance uphill from the town. To the left, the railway triangle enfiladed all approach to the bridge, the halt to the right at the same elevation as the railway line enfiladed the South African crossing for 1,000 yards.

establishing with M.G.s and other(s) digging in. He shot two with his revolver and threw a bomb amongst the remainder'. He then 'got back into the cutting and found what appeared to be an outlet of a big underground drain. Entering this he travelled along until he found an opening which brought him out in the centre of the town'.[122] Although the intelligence gleaned from his subterranean adventures was deemed very useful, it is unclear whether anyone used his route when at 8.30 the Dubliners seized the Bazuel road and railway crossing, with its high embankment, a position described as 'an extremely strong one'.[123] The railway triangle no longer proving a threat, 6th Dublin Fusiliers joined up with the Scottish Horse there. Their morning had not been without street fighting. 'The 4 trench mortars did useful work', two being used to clear machine-guns nests opposing the South Africans, and two being used in the town, also against machine-gun nests, 100 rounds being fired. A flavour of the struggle is given by the remark: 'Hand Grenades No. 36 and Smoke Grenades No. 27 were freely used in the mopping up of the Town'.[124] 1/6th Lancashire Fusiliers were ordered to relieve the Dublin Fusiliers and advanced to the high ground above the Richemont Valley, taking the Red Line there at 18.30 under heavy machine-gun fire.[125] The enemy machine-guns were, however, in the final stages of the advance, hampered by bad light. German prisoners stated that 'they were unable to see our men until they were right up to them'. 198 Brigade concluded after the capture of the nests on the high ground: 'This engagement furnished an interesting instance of the vulnerability of hostile machine-guns against infantry employing their own weapons skilfully and making the best use of ground'.[126] The brigade had captured five machine-guns and captured 35 prisoners, leaving 'severe casualties' amongst the enemy on the battlefield. Brigade however took the view that: 'More enemy could have undoubtedly been killed and captured had any Cavalry or fresh Infantry been available to exploit the success. Large numbers of enemy and some transport were seen retreating hurriedly Eastwards'.[127] When patrols were pushed out the following day to the Richemont stream, it was again the brigade's view that this line was easily achievable without artillery support, but such exploitation was countermanded to await a later set-piece assault. On the extreme left, the three South African battalions again spent the day under fire, and at 17.00 an order was issued for their relief. Whilst this was subsequently cancelled, B Company of the 1st Battalion, holding the flank, did not receive this news, and in returning suffered 13 killed, such was the intensity of the fire.[128] The South Africans eventually pushed forward in the early hours of the following morning across the ground that had been unachievable

turned out to -be of the greatest value'. (*London Gazette*, 4 October 1919, 12275). In the post-war period Bruce became Deputy Inspector General Indian Police.

122 War Diary, 6th Battalion Royal Dublin Fusiliers, 'Operation 7th-11th October 1918', TNA WO95/3140.

123 War Diary, HQ 198 Infantry Brigade, 18 October 1918, TNA WO95/3139.

124 War Diary, 6th Battalion Royal Dublin Fusiliers, 'Operation 7th-11th October 1918', TNA WO95/3140. In the operations 17-18 October the 6th Dublin Fusiliers lost two officers killed and 17 wounded, with 35 other ranks killed, 132 wounded and 5 missing. Twenty-four ORs were gassed and five suffered 'shell-shock'. Amongst the officers wounded were Second-Lieutenant Robert Frederick Hinson, commissioned in April 1917, and Second-Lieutenant Harold Ernest Atkins evacuated with 'shock'. Atkins had been on the Western Front since November 1915 and had been commissioned from private in the Army Cyclist Corps in August 1917.

125 This killed four other ranks and wounded 10, with two missing. (War Diary, 6th Battalion Lancashire Fusiliers, 18 October 1918, TNA WO95/3140).

126 War Diary, HQ 198 Infantry Brigade, 'The advance to the RED Line', TNA WO95/3139.

127 War Diary, HQ 198 Infantry Brigade, 18 October 1918, TNA WO95/3139.

128 J. Buchan, *The History of the South African Forces in France*, p.247.

the previous day, their left on the railway line, their right joining up with 1/6th Lancashire Fusiliers on the high ground to the north of the Le Cateau-Bazuel road.

The attacking divisions of Fourth Army had been devoid of tank support, but in the air, even though the weather had been very misty and visibility poor, 362 flying hours were undertaken by 233 pilots. Eleven artillery patrols were carried out, and 15 zone calls were sent down but without success. Five combats took place, only one of which was decisive, and both sides lost a machine during the day. Ground attack continued and 160 25-pound bombs were dropped, some on troops and trains in Catillon; and some 11,000 rounds were fired. Machine-gun pits to the west of Wassigny were targeted, as were troops retreating in the open, and eight field guns 'galloping into action were also attacked from a height of 100 feet and casualties caused to two teams'.[129] There was little enemy air activity reported (although the infantry would have disagreed with this, having been subject to attack from the air), but at 13.50 a group of low-flying enemy aircraft bombed the western outskirts of Le Cateau.

At the end of the day, XIII Corps was established on the Red Line, the first objective set for the previous day. It would remain stationary and take no further part in the Battle of the Selle itself, but its efforts had 'resulted in the capture, by six brigades of this corps, of a carefully prepared and strongly garrisoned position on a front of 7,000 yards, the greater part of which was protected by a difficult obstacle'.[130] On the right, IX Corps had secured its objectives but there had been no exploitation. In the centre the advance had been uneven. The left of the American Corps had taken its objective, although the right had not been able to take Mazinghien. Elsewhere, whilst Third Army had held its position, the French had also progressed, occupying a line east of the Andigny Forest and the villages of Aisonville and Grougis with 2,000 yards of the Sambre and Oise Canal. The resistance of the German infantry had diminished, particularly in the north, but their artillery had unleashed its most savage counter-barrage, Fourth Army noting that 'the enemy's artillery were very active and showed a considerable increase in comparison with yesterday'.[131]

Saturday 19 October 1918

Fourth Army, believing 'the resistance of the enemy having been broken',[132] directed at 22.15 on the 18th that on the following day the original line of exploitation of 17 October would be taken.[133] This involved advancing from where contact had been established with the French at Blocus d'en Bas to la Laurette on the Rejet de Beaulieu to Oisy road. An area of high ground overlooking the Sambre and Oise Canal would thus be occupied. A line would be established from there to Catillon, holding a flank from this point north-west to Bazuel, facing l'Eveque Wood, to await the advance of Third Army. It was also imagined that given the 'severe defeat' suffered on the 17th and the 18th,[134] the enemy would retire across the canal during the night. Indeed, *Eighteenth Army,* anticipating the inevitable following the early morning reverses, had given orders at 09.00 on 18 October for both *I Bavarian* and *XXVI Reserve Corps* (opposing the French) to withdraw across the Sambre and Oise Canal to the *Hermann Stellung II,* whose presence ranged from the partial to the

129 War Diary, HQ 5 Brigade RAF, 18 October 1918, TNA AIR1 2225/209/40/26.
130 Montgomery, op. cit., p.228.
131 War Diary, HQ Fourth Army, 18 October 1918, TNS WO95/439.
132 Montgomery, op. cit., p.228.
133 War Diary, HQ Fourth Army, Message No. G.420, 18 October 1918, TNA WO95/439.
134 Montgomery, op. cit., p.229.

non-existent.[135] It added, hopefully: 'The canal position must be held at all costs and with all means at our command. This order will speedily be made known to all troops'.[136] The *Eighteenth Army's* absolutely correct logic was that the 'situation west of the canal was untenable without reserves if additional heavy attacks were made'.[137] No army ever wishes to be trapped with its back to a river. *I Bavarian Corps* had issued its own withdrawal orders at 12.45 for the night of 18/19 October, 'the withdrawal being covered by rearguards holding woods and tactical features'.[138] In the north, whilst still maintaining the line of the Selle against Third Army, the German *Second Army* could not withdraw, and a flank was to be held stretched between the two watercourses. The orders for the withdrawal of the left of *Eighteenth Army*, abutting *Second Army*, had been given by the army group and then cancelled because of consideration of this issue, whilst the order for the removal of all the artillery would proceed.[139]

The withdrawal of *Eighteenth Army* proved momentarily controversial. Crown Prince Wilhelm, commanding the army group, frantically attempted to impress the importance of resistance in a message sent at 17.24 on the evening of the 18th: 'It is of far-reaching importance to the front of this group that the Canal Position be held'. Even though he was absolutely aware that the defences of the *Hermann Stellung II* were insubstantial, he gave 'explicit expression to the expectation that the army will hold its new position'. He asked 'all commanders to realize clearly that we can only force the enemy to terminate his attacks by holding out to the last'. To achieve this, despite the fact that his armies had been haemorrhaging machine-guns, he directed 'special attention to the necessity of liberally reinforcing the Canal Front with machine-gun organizations'. Lastly, hinting at his own sense of being out of control of what was happening, he stated baldly that 'my consent must be secured before any rearward movement is initiated'.[140] The Crown Prince would later write more openly: 'We must hold tight to the Hermann and the Gudrun positions! Good God! What have these positions to offer? They are incomplete and, in many places, only marked out!'[141] Hindenburg, up late that night, expressed his contempt for *Eighteenth Army's* withdrawal at 12.50 on the 19th. 'I regret that the direction was made today to withdraw the *Eighteenth Army* behind the Canal and was even carried out in the daytime'. Seemingly uncomprehending of the inexorable advance of Fourth Army he continued: 'The evening report of the *Eighteenth Army* shows that the enemy, in superior force, gained only a little ground in his attack'. And in a statement that surely infuriated those on the ground, he concluded: 'I request a check be made as to whether the responsible authorities maintained the proper composure in evaluating the reports received'.[142]

General von Hutier, commanding *Eighteenth Army*, who must have felt he had better things to do, was forced to respond at length to the Crown Prince. He reassured him that aggressive intent had always been in the mind of his army, hence the bringing up of the *19th Reserve Division* on the morning of the 18th for counterattack, even if this formation ended up simply bolstering the front. This counterattack, he suggested, relied on a similar attack by *Second Army* north of Le Cateau, which had replied to such request saying that it had not the strength to do so but would place the

135 Operations Section, German *Eighteenth Army*, no. 8529, 18 October 1918, *USAWW Vol. 7*, p.912.
136 Operations Section, German *Eighteenth Army*, no. 8542, 18 October 1918, *USAWW Vol. 7*, p.912.
137 Operations Section, German *Eighteenth Army*, no. 8568, 19 October 1918, *USAWW Vol. 7*, p.917.
138 War Diary, HQ Fourth Army, 19 October 1918, TNA WO95/439.
139 Operations Section, German *Eighteenth Army*, no. 8568, 19 October 1918, *USAWW Vol. 7*, p.917.
140 Operations Section, *Group of Armies German Crown Prince*, no. 7021, 1st Addendum, *USAWW Vol. 7* p.907.
141 *Memoirs of the Crown Prince of Germany*, p.271.
142 Operations Section, *Supreme Headquarters*, no. 10903, 19 October 1918, *USAWW Vol. 7*, pp.907-8.

54th Division on the army boundary. This division was only 400 rifles strong. Von Hutier tried to impress on the army group the weakness of his own formations. He reported that the *221st Infantry Division* was only 350 effectives strong, the *3rd Naval Division* 400, the *15th Infantry Division* a mere 205, whilst *24th Infantry Division* had the comparative riches of 500 men. He described how on the morning of the 18th 'the left wing of the *Second Army* was driven in and ... the *204th Infantry Division* to the *3rd Naval Division* fell back on Catillon'. Whilst seemingly trying to shift the focus of attention on to the shortcomings of *Second Army*, von Hutier was absolutely correct in emphasising the weakness of his units. The gap into which 75 Brigade had pushed had indeed been caused by the collapse of units from *Second Army*. Whether this threatened the envelopment of his forces on the east bank was an entirely different matter. 75 Brigade had come to a halt where it had been told to, and was in no position to conduct such an envelopment. Further, this supposed threat occurred in the very area where the withdrawal of *Eighteenth Army* that night was *not* made, and where II American Corps had been emphatically brought to a halt before reaching Catillon. It was however, such a fear that had caused *Second Army* to begin the retirement to the Selle after the breaking of the Beaurevoir-Fonsomme Line on 8 October. The Germans were determined not to leave a flank open to allow the turning and rolling up of any formation. Von Hutier concluded that:

> Looking back upon the events, this headquarters is firmly convinced that, if further attacks had been received by nightfall on the west bank of the canal, a breakthrough, which was to be avoided at all costs, would have taken place and the Canal Position would have become untenable.[143]

After perusing von Hutier's summary, Generalmajor Schulenburg responded on behalf of the Crown Prince,[144] reminding Hindenburg that Supreme Headquarters had sanctioned the withdrawal. He insisted that: 'Although at times the situation was judged too unfavourably on the part of the *Eighteenth Army*, the army cannot be reproached with having lost control of its nerves [or] of having acted too hastily'. Schulenburg continued: 'The army still holds to its opinion that the withdrawal of the artillery was ordered', and added that the Crown Prince's HQ was 'of the opinion that a powerful fire protection should not be taken away from the infantry as long as they are heavily engaged even at the risk of losing the artillery'.[145] In other words, Supreme Headquarters could not withdraw its artillery in the hope of keeping it in the event of a ceasefire yet leave its infantry cruelly exposed.

IX Corps

The last day of the battle again dawned with a heavy fog, and 1st Division moved off at 05.30 with the French *66th Division* on the right and 30th American Division on the left. The French division did not, in fact, move until 06.30, 'and a patrol of the Royal Scots Greys had, in consequence, to be sent to look for it'.[146] On the right, 1st Black Watch advanced from Wassigny on a one company front due east and by 08.00 were at Arrouaise Farm, half the way to Oisy on the canal. The fog

143 Operations Section, German *Eighteenth Army*, no. 8568, 19 October 1918, *USAWW Vol. 7*, p.917.
144 Generalmajor Friedrich Count von der Schulenburg was the Crown Prince's chief of staff from November 1916 until the end. An early Nazi supporter, he rose to the rank of *SS-Obergruppenführer*, and Adolf Hitler laid a wreath at his funeral in 1939.
145 Operations Section, *Group of German Armies Crown Prince*, No. 7021 Addendum No. 1, 21 October 1918, *USAWW Vol. 7*, pp.908-9.
146 Edmonds & Maxwell-Hyslop, op. cit., p.322.

rendered contact between the platoons very difficult, but the enemy had retired and the farm was occupied without opposition, and the company progressed to link up with the French north of Oisy. The battalion's last action in the battle had been a bloodless one, but over the days 17-19 October, 1st Black Watch had suffered three officers and 12 other ranks killed,[147] with four officers and 79 other ranks wounded with nine missing.

On their left, the 2nd Welsh moved off on a two company front at 05.30 under the cover of a rolling area shoot.[148] They were tasked with advancing 3,000 yards and occupying a 2,500 yard frontage, and this they did with little opposition, suffering only five other ranks wounded. A squadron of Royal Scots Greys went ahead to reconnoitre the canal crossings, but found them all blown. Coming under heavy shell fire, they retired.[149] 1st South Wales Borderers, also protected by the shoot, set off towards Rejet-de-Beaulieu and met no opposition until they reached the village, where a machine-gun crew of one officer and 11 men was encountered and taken prisoner. Capturing the village, a line was established 200 yards to the east at 11.30, but no further progress was able to be made due to the volume of machine-gun fire from the east bank of the canal. Over its days in the line, the battalion had lost one officer killed and four wounded, with 29 other ranks killed, and 60 wounded.[150]

One of the dead of the limited fighting of IX Corps on the 19th was 34 year-old Sergeant William J. Milton DCM MM, who had been a regular private in August 1914 and who had arrived on the Western Front on 13 August 1914. His Distinguished Conduct Medal was won over these two days, and the citation indicates the quality of the experienced British NCO:

> During the action near Wassigny on the 18th October, 1918, he pushed forward with a few men under heavy machine-gun fire, and working round a large party of the enemy, captured six and drove the remainder towards a Lewis gun section, which he knew were operating on his right, with the result that they surrendered. On the 19th October, when the company was temporarily held up, he at once reconnoitred the position, organised parties, and dealt with

147 The three officers killed were Second-Lieutenant Ernest Woods Gyle, a medical student from Edinburgh University (commissioned in March 1918); Lieutenant Herbert Henry Jalland, a classics scholar of Pembroke College Oxford, who went to work in the office of the King's Private Secretary and was commissioned in December 1915; and Second-Lieutenant David Smith MC DCM. A pre-war regular, Smith had gone to France in August 1914 and had been commissioned from the rank of sergeant. The fatalities amongst the other ranks included 39 year-old Sergeant Duncan Thomas who had enlisted in 1900.

148 These were provided by 1st Division's artillery according to the requests of individual brigades.

149 War Diary, Royal Scots Greys, 19 October 1918, TNA WO95/1139.

150 C.T. Atkinson, *The History of the South Wales Borderers 1914-1918*, p.467. Lieutenant Herbert Sydney Bennett, commissioned in May 1915 was killed, as was Private David Mason Macaulay DCM MM and bar (his DCM won at Loos, the bar on the Somme). Seventeen NCOs and men won the MM, and three of the battalion's second-lieutenants were awarded the MC. The first was John Joseph O'Neil, whose citation reads: 'On 18th October, 1918, near Wassigny, when all the other officers became casualties, he assumed command and led the company most gallantly, setting a splendid example to his men. Having gained his objective, he consolidated his position. Throughout the day he showed great energy and ability'. (*London Gazette*, 8 October 1919, p.3295). The second was Vivian John Lennox Napier, commissioned in April 1917, whose citation reads: 'He was in command of one of the leading companies during the attack near Wassigny on 18th October, 1918, and handled his company throughout the day, until wounded, with great ability and courage. There was heavy machine-gun fire, both from the direction of Belle Vue and immediately in front, but the attack ended in complete success'. (*London Gazette*, 3 October 1919, p.12,321). The third was T.C. Phillips.

> it. His fearless and able leadership had a marked influence on the success of the operations on both occasions.[151]

Over three days, 1st Division had advanced 9,000 yards on a 4,000 yard front, but further progress was not immediately possible. The enemy may have offered little resistance on the morning of the 19th, but as per instructions, was intending to hold the line of the canal. 'Every attempt … to occupy the western bank of the Sambre and Oise Canal was met with heavy machine-gun fire from the eastern bank, and hostile artillery fire considerably increased during the day'.[152]

II American Corps

The American 30th Division, after its very shaky day on the 18th, pushed off from its positions near Ecaillon at 05.15, the 60th Brigade supported by two battalions of the 59th. The Australian artillery did not fire a barrage, but 'put down bursts of fire for one hour to cover (the) advance'.[153] On the right, the 119th Regiment passed through abandoned Mazinghien without opposition at about 08.30 and established a line east of the village on the high ground overlooking the canal. 'Here very stout Machine-gun opposition was met' from *RIR 27* dug in at la Haie Tonnoile Farm, and 'supporting Machine-guns, Stokes Mortars and One Pounders' were sent up to establish the defensive position and were able to knock out a number of enemy machine-gun positions. Their front concluded on a line from Rejet de Beaulieu to the west of la Haie Tonnoile Farm. After three days of fighting the regiment was 'very, very tired, having advanced a distance of practically five miles'.[154] On the left of the division, the 120th Regiment had a much more difficult start. 'After several unsuccessful trials' (two earlier attacks) it pushed eastward north of Mazinghien later in the morning, similarly ending up on the line of a road west of la Haie Tonnoile, still some 1,000 yards short of the objective.[155] This farm and the surrounding fields and orchards were 'heavily manned with machine-guns', and had to be kept under constant fire by the artillery.[156] 30th Division described how 'every hedge sheltered enemy machine-gun nests, which with German trench mortars, poured murderous fire into our ranks'.[157] Mark Whisler has suggested that there was intense resistance to the American advance on the boundary between the *204th* and *3rd Naval Divisions*.[158] II American Corps, however, claimed that the resistance 'offered by the Germans could not have been great, as the total casualties in the brigade were 14 killed and 43 wounded and missing'.[159] It was clear from the performance of the 120th that the infantry of 30th Division had struggled again, the first two attacks of the 120th that day failing. In passing Mazinghien on the third attempt the 120th noted that the enemy withdrew without resistance, but this was not down to the offensive efforts of the 120th, but rather the appearance of a party of 100 or so from 27th Division from the north. II American Corps concluded that 'a little stronger push would have probably shoved them across the canal', clearly believing that the offensive effort was weaker than

151 *Edinburgh Gazette*, 4 December 1919, p.3807.
152 Montgomery, op. cit., p.229.
153 War Diary, HQ 14th Australian Field Artillery Brigade, 19 October 1918, AWM4 Item no. 13/41/28.
154 Anonymous, *History 119th Infantry*, p.55.
155 Neither the *30th Division Summary of Operations* nor the 30th Division history make any reference to the two abortive early attacks.
156 War Diary, HQ 14th Australian Field Artillery Brigade, 19 October 1918, AWM4 Item no. 13/41/28.
157 E.A. Murphy & R.S. Thomas, *The 30th Division in the World War*, quoted in Whisler op. cit., p.295.
158 Whisler, op. cit.p.295. There is no reference to the two early failures of the 120th.
159 General Staff, *Operations of the 2nd American Corps*, p.34.

it might have been. In defence of its infantry, however, II Corps pointed out, in truth, that they were 'tired out' and 'greatly depleted in numbers'.[160] Both regiments were well and truly stuck by 14.30, and plans were underway for a fresh push when, understanding the state of the American units as 'very weak and tired',[161] Fourth Army ordered that the Americans should not attempt to push on but should dig in and await relief by IX Corps. The 60th Brigade operational report over-optimistically suggested that 'another hour's fighting would have placed the Brigade squarely on its objective', blaming receipt of this order on the failure to get further.[162] It is clear the Fourth Army understood very well that this would not have been the case.

27th Division, which had pushed forward in the early hours of the morning, was busy establishing itself on the ridge between the Jonc de Mer and St. Maurice valleys. Their flank was exposed to Mazinghien, where the 120th Infantry was struggling to get forward. The two GOCs of the American divisions therefore arranged for reserve troops of the 27th to enter 30th Division's area and threaten the defenders, who must have been positioned just to its north, as the 119th had been through the town itself. As observed, this they did with success. One troop of 20th Hussars (three of whom were wounded), a platoon of infantry, a company of the 102nd Engineers, and a platoon of 104th Machine Gun Battalion moved from the orchard south of la Jonquiere Farm, and the simple presence of this motley crew was sufficient to force a German withdrawal.[163] That evening, the 108th Infantry crossed the Jonc de Mer stream and pushed on to the high ground overlooking Catillon and north of la Haie Tonnoile Farm, its line stretching to the north-west and joining that of XIII Corps near Bazuel. Forty-eight officers and 1,463 other ranks had passed as prisoners through the 27th Division's cages. However, over the three days the division had suffered 194 fatalities (including 12 officers), 866 wounded (including 33 officers), and 401 gassed (including 22 officers). It was now so understrength that it could not collect its booty, and had barely enough resources to evacuate its wounded and bury its dead. Rawlinson, who had been so critical in his journal of the Americans, and who had decided to withdraw them the previous day, wrote that night that he was 'pleased' with them, that they had 'done very well', but that 'their casualties have been twice what any other corps has suffered'.[164] This, of course, was down simply, if tragically, to inexperience.

The weather was yet again unfavourable for flying on 19 October, and the Australian Flying Corps did not get a single aircraft in the air over the Americans. 5 Brigade RAF recorded the mist and poor visibility for observation and only 190 hours were flown by 150 pilots. In terms of ground attack, only fifty-nine 25-pound bombs were dropped and 2,600 machine-gun rounds fired. The greatest excitement in the air was the bringing down of a Fokker biplane over Le Cateau by the American ace Lieutenant Emile Lussier.[165] This took place in the skies above XIII Corps, where 'noise of movement and other indications seemed to point to a general retirement of the German

160 General Staff, *Operations of the 2nd American Corps*, p.34.
161 War Diary, HQ Fourth Army, 19 October 1918, TNA WO95/439.
162 Elmer & Murphy, op. cit., p.126.
163 O'Ryan, op. cit., p.381.
164 Sir H. Rawlinson, War Journal, 19 October 1918, Churchill College RWLN 1/11.
165 War Diary, 5 Brigade RAF, 19 October 1918, TNA AIR1 2225/209/40/26. This was one of Emile John Lussier DFC's 11 confirmed kills, a run which only began on 25 July 1918. The citation for his DFC states: 'During recent operations this officer has driven down out of control or destroyed seven enemy machines, and, with the aid of two other pilots, has accounted for a further two. Three of these he destroyed in one day. In these combats he has proved himself an officer of very high courage, eager to attack without regard to the enemy's superiority in numbers'. (*London Gazette*, 2 November 1918, p.12,969).

line'.[166] Whilst 75 Brigade adjusted its line, clearing Bazuel and consolidating the high ground above the Richemont stream, it was evident on the ground that the enemy had not moved.

Conclusion

Fourth Army's Battle of the Selle was over. Von Hutier, commanding *Eighteenth Army*, was 'firmly convinced that, if further attacks had been received by nightfall on the west bank of the canal, a breakthrough, which was to be avoided at all costs, would have taken place, and the Canal Position would have become untenable'.[167] The Official Historians, too, suggested that the 'the opportunity to exploit the success of forcing the Selle was lost'. This, it was claimed, was due to the lack of an arm of pursuit, the absence of fresh troops, and 'too close adherence to a routine procedure, in this case dawn attacks under a creeping barrage'.[168] In response to the latter criticism, one might ask why Fourth Army should have abandoned what it understood to be a winning formula on the night of 19 October when it knew that pursuit had been largely devoid of operational gain when the enemy had a further geographical position to retire to, and its troops were tired. Further movement would depend on the advance of Third Army to the north coupled with reorganisation, notably the withdrawal of the exhausted Americans. The French *First Army* had similarly forced the enemy across the canal to the south, and Rawlinson was visited by General Debeney that afternoon. Always critical of his fellow army commander, Rawlinson must have been in expansive mood on the evening of the 19th, as he wrote somewhat patronisingly of Debeney: 'He has done much better lately'.[169] North of Rejet de Beaulieu, however, the enemy maintained a presence on the east bank running north-north-west towards Bazuel, and thence along the line of the Richemont valley back to the Selle near Montay. Over the three days of very hard fighting, the Fourth Army had advanced 9,000 yards and captured 143 officers and 4,996 other ranks from fourteen different divisions. This success 'had been achieved in the face of strong opposition, and in spite of the urgent appeals of the German High Command to its troops to prevent our passage of the Selle at all costs'. It was a hard won triumph.

166 Edmonds & Maxwell-Hyslop, op. cit., p.323.
167 *German Eighteenth Army*, Operations Section No. 8568, Report of Operations, 19 October 1918, USAWW Vol. 7, p.917.
168 Edmonds & Maxwell-Hyslop, op. cit., p.318.
169 Sir H. Rawlinson, War Journal, 19 October 1918, Churchill College RWLN 1/11.

6

Preparing for Battle: 19-22 October 1918

As the line settled after 19 October, Fourth Army found itself preparing for another set-piece attack, supporting the right flank of Third Army's Battle of the Selle.

Infrastructure and the Royal Engineers

If a central problem for the BEF in the Pursuit had been to make the roads usable in order to cross the river, the problem following forcing the Selle defences, at least in the north, was to cross the river and then repair the roads. As has been seen, the army's teeth crossed successfully. To get the tail across was a matter of heavier bridging. It was impossible to achieve this whilst the enemy was in possession of the immediate east bank. 66th Division had directed 430 Field Company RE to erect a bridge across the Selle south of Le Cateau on 11 October but the attempt ended in failure due to shelling and enemy proximity.[1] The company were returning to what was likely the same location on the 17th, but were intercepted by the Commander Royal Engineers (CRE) XIII Corps himself due to the lack of progress on the eastern bank. On 17 October, the CRE noted that 'practically no bridging' was possible 'owing to enemy M.G. fire', although during the night an attempt was made 'to prepare abutments for 2 bridges'.[2] It was thus only on 18 October that 430 Company were able to install their Weldon trestle structure to take first line transport. This was converted to take heavy traffic two days later.[3]

On 17 October, 25th Division's engineers had been ordered to erect four permanent bridges. 106 Field Company had been instructed to work on the bridge in the centre of Le Cateau that carried the Roman road from Cambrai, but they were unable to start this due to the urban fighting, and only managed two hours work the following day. 130 Field Company were to build two bridges, one in the south-western suburbs of Le Cateau and one further south. The first was to be constructed on the remains of an existing bridge made of cast iron, with two spans of 33 feet with a road width of over 16 feet, and the company had to adapt the surviving structure with trestles to take tanks. The second was at the site of an existing masonry bridge which carried the Le Cateau-Honnechy

1 War Diary, 430 Field Company Royal Engineers, 11 October 1918, TNA WO95/3129.
2 War Diary, Chief Engineer XIII Corps, 17 October 1918, TNA WO95/903.
3 The Mark IV Weldon Trestle comprised a deck secured on a height adjustable transom suspended by lever straps from four posts with steel feet, held at right angles by a ledger below the transom, i.e. in appearance it was like an 'H' with two crosspieces rather than one.

road across the river opposite the station and into the town. This was to be replaced by a 21 and a half foot span Class A bridge.[4] They attempted to work on this on 17 October, but like their fellows, were driven off by fire, although the work was completed in five hours the following day.[5] This bridge was capable of taking tanks, and its capacity was doubled on the 26th. The War Diary of CRE 50th Division notes that on 16 October the division's engineers constructed an artillery bridge to take 60 pounders at St Benin. 7 Field Company recorded that between 14-19 October a bridge for horse transport was erected 'west of St Benin' and a pontoon bridge 'in front of St Benin'.[6] The 60 pounder bridge was, therefore, over the Essart stream in the valley behind St Benin, hidden from the enemy, and it was the pontoon erected at Fassiaux that would get the guns across the Selle. The latter was finished by noon on 18 October. 105 Field Company were tasked with the building of a 30 foot Class A bridge at St Benin on the site of the Fassiaux bridge itself. They made three attempts to start on the 17th, all under fire, and the cost was 19 casualties. In the meantime, they made the dam to the south of the bridge passable for artillery three hours after zero. They finally began work on their main task at 10.00 on 18 October, alongside 7 Field Company, completing the structure by 18.00 the following day, by which time they had taken in hand a 22-foot span RSJ bridge half-a-mile further north, also completed on the 19th.[7]

The enemy was keenly aware that Fourth Army would seek to drive in the flank of their *Second Army* stretched between Montay and Catillon, the start line for which would partly rely on the British being able to use the Le Cateau-Catillon road. Although they blocked all the eastern exits from Le Cateau, they put particular effort into obstructing progress along this route, firstly blowing up the railway bridge over the part of the road running uphill out of Le Cateau. This bridge was on the line that had formed the *HWL I*, the halt next to it having dominated 66th Division's progress in the eastern suburbs 17-18 October. On the 20th, 430 and 432 Field Companies were at work clearing the debris. The pioneers, 9th Gloucestershire,[8] who had been clearing the road through Le Cateau, had moved the brick debris but the girder sections (three girders linked together) could not be shifted. The tunnellers had unsuccessfully attempted to blow them up with guncotton. A block and tackle was required.[9] By 21 October, however, this part of the route was open for two-way traffic. The second act of sabotage on this road had taken place 2,500 yards further east, where the railway which ran from Le Cateau station through Bazuel crossed on another bridge. This would not be open in time to allow passage for the attack on 23 October. 106 Field Company worked on this block from the 24th for five days, it being a much bigger job than anticipated.[10] Indeed, on the first day two men had to be sent with oxy-acetylene plant to cut the girders. A temporary road system had, therefore, to be created using two tracks to the south east of Le Cateau as a one-way system which turned north-east to reach Bazuel on a final two-way section. This was completed by 20 October but the Chief Engineer of XIII Corps dubbed it 'no good',[11] planks being needed. The

4 This was Military Load Classification 40 bridge, capable of taking tracked vehicles, i.e. tanks.
5 War Diary, 130 Field Company Royal Engineers, 17-18 October 1918 TNA WO95/2237.
6 War Diary, 7 Field Company Royal Engineers, 14-19 October 1918, TNA WO95/2821.
7 War Diary, 105 Field Company Royal Engineers, Narrative of Operations 3-31 October 1918, TNA WO95/2235.
8 The unit, commanded by Lieutenant-Colonel Eric Paytherus Nares, had 41 officers and 828 ORs at the end of October.
9 War Diary, 430 Field Company Royal Engineers TNA WO95/3129
10 War Diary, Chief Engineer 25th Division, 23 October 1918, TNA WO95/2232.
11 War Diary, Chief Engineer XIII Corps, 20 October 1918, TNA WO95/903.

The Selle at the present day Fassiaux bridge. The wide banks indicate why a 30 foot span bridge was required.

The mill at St Benin 100 yards south of the Fassiaux bridge. The Scottish Horse and 3rd Royal Fusiliers crossed the Selle here using logs and the mill's dam.

180th Tunnelling Company and 66th Divisional pioneers worked on this with assistance from 25th Division, and finished their corduroy construction just in time at 05.30 on the 22nd.

The 1st Battalion of the 105th Engineers, attached to the American 30th Division, was tasked with both the building of bridges for the artillery to cross the Selle on 17 October, and the establishment of water supply. The bridges were temporary, i.e. they were simply to be used in securing the initial crossing. Their instructions read: 'A one-way bridge, eight to ten feet wide, is all that should be attempted'.[12] The tasks proved difficult on the day. At 11.45 on the 17th Captain George of C Company reported: 'Am unable to get to St Souplet with lorry. Shell holes at V 7 d. 5.3'. Nor was this the only problem as the same officer reported: 'Am unable to get to Molain account shelling'.[13] At 14.45, Lieutenant Trescott of B Company reported: 'Have decided to put bridge at Marsh Mill. Will start as soon as artillery fire permits'.[14] More positively, Captain Brooks of A Company reported: 'Bridge at W16 a 6.0 will carry anything', this referring to a repair of the bridge at Molain. At 17.00 Lieutenant Trescott, who had been helped by finding a pile of suitable timber nearby, reported success from his efforts at Marsh Mill: 'Bridge capable of carrying eight-inch guns completed in one hour and 45 minutes', despite six men being gassed during the construction work. At 18.30 Lieutenant Hill of C Company reported that the bridge between Molain and St. Martin had been completed at 16.30. On account of heavy shelling it had been impossible to start before noon, and had taken four and a half hours. He detailed how: 'This bridge has five built up stringers of 3 inch x 10 inch, 3 planks thick and 24 feet long, supported in middle by one bent, and one bent at each bank. Decking is one layer of three-inch plank.' However, he can only have been speaking of the basic structure as at 19.00 he further reported that the bridge was being 'finished under heavy shell fire. Now open for 18 pounders; will complete for 6 inch howitzers'. [15] 102nd Engineers also had better luck than the British engineers of XIII Corps. Lieutenant Herbert Ross's detachment began an artillery bridge at St Souplet on 17 October and had it open for vehicular traffic by noon.[16] Only in the American sector, therefore, was heavier bridging achieved on the first day of battle. Bringing forward guns to support exploitation at zero + six hours even in this sector would clearly have been impossible.

In the days up to the attack of 23 October the efforts of the 1st Australian Tunnelling Company were directed at the roads closer to the river and at bridging. They erected a bridge at St Martin Rivière, and another in St Souplet adjacent to Lieutenant Ross's temporary bridge previously erected on the site of the original structure, removing this and preparing for a second bridge. In the days that followed they completed another bridge at Molain, and worked on unexploded charges on the railway as far as Wassigny, whilst on the west bank they continued to explore cellars at railway stations and large buildings for explosives. The American engineers, until the final relief of II American Corps on the morning of 21 October, continued work on the roads.[17] They also persevered with locating mines. On the 19th they removed explosives from the church steeple at St

12 W.P Sullivan & H. Tucker, *The History of the 105th Regiment of Engineers*, p.203.
13 Sullivan & Tucker, op. cit., p.208.
14 Sullivan & Tucker, op. cit., p.209.
15 Sullivan & Tucker, op. cit., p.211.
16 J.F. O'Ryan, *The Story of the 27th Division*, p.373.
17 They concentrated on opening up three principal road routes during the whole of the operations. The 'Red Road', La Haie Menneresse-St Martin Rivière-l'Arbre de Guise-Mazinghien-Catillon; the 'Black Road', Busigny-Vaux-Andigny-Molain- Ribeauville-Mazinghien-Rejet de Beaulieu-Catillon; and the 'Blue Roads', four in number, La Haie Mennerresse-Vaux-Andigny, the connecting road in Molain, l'Arbre de Guise to Ribeauville, and la Haie Tonnelle farm-Rejet de Beaulieu.

The Selle at Marsh Mill bridged by Lieutenant Trescott of the 105th American Engineers.

Martin, and 75 demolition charges along the railway east of the village, these generally placed at alternate joints so that one would blow in and the other out. To spot such charges, two men would walk along the inside of the rails, two on the outside, and two at the bottom of embankments. Identifying a demolition charge was sometimes a subtle business. Second-Lieutenant Albert Rust described the process. On a corduroy road: 'I noticed the guard rails had been pried loose at one point, and that the planks had been recently removed. This was shown by the absence of dirt in the crevices between the boards'. The guard rails had been moved just enough to slip the boards out to one side. Boxes of high explosive with a contact button on the top were placed with the plank lightly resting on it, 'so placed as to come directly under the place where the greatest weight of traffic would bear'. Dugouts were mined with the same device, the contact button and charge placed under a wooden step. Where roads were mined in villages, the enemy had often tunnelled from a nearby cellar to place a charge. Bridges had been mined by cutting 16 inch holes in the masonry, two holes on each side of the bridge; with girder bridges mined with explosives on the inside of the girders, or on the cross of lateral braces.[18] The examination of Le Cateau for mines by 66th Division took three days from 17 October. On the 18th the town hall, bank and tunnels and cellars were searched but nothing was found. It was only the next day that 1,700 pounds of explosive was discovered in the clock tower and church tower, electrically connected and with the explosive 'dry & in good condition'.[19] Le Cateau being in the river valley, these were the only points in the town that could have been useful for observation, as with the church at St Martin.

18 Sullivan & Tucker, op. cit., pp.233-4.
19 War Diary, Commander Royal Engineers 66th Division, 17-19 October 1918, TNA WO95/3125.

To the south in IX Corps area, the work largely consisted of road maintenance. On 18 October the Corps Chief Engineer recorded: 'Road work satisfactory; roads little damaged'.[20] On 22 October, however, when Fourth Army held much more of the eastern bank of the Selle, he was forced to note: 'Roads recently taken over are very bad'.[21] On the 17th, following up the attack, the pioneers of 46th Division, 1st Monmouthshire, immediately cleared the length of the Bohain-Regnicourt road as far as Andigny-les-Fermes. A central problem for transport was mud created by enemy shelling throwing earth onto the hard surface.[22] On the same day the adjacent 102nd American Engineers under Lieutenant Maxwell Gray crossed the river at St Souplet and started to clear the blown railway bridge that had formed the *HWL I* that was blocking the road uphill to l'Arbre de Guise. This area was a hive of activity over the next few days. On 19 October, 11th Leicestershire, the 6th Division pioneers were working on the road that ran up the Bellevue Spur, but by the 21st they were also working with the Australians on replacing the smashed bridge in St Souplet to carry heavier traffic than could be stood by 102nd Engineer's artillery bridge.[23] The following day 12 Field Company were working directly uphill from the bridge at St Souplet on roads in l'Arbre de Guise. On 21 October the RE Field Companies of 6th Division also began work on the roads on the eastern bank. 26 Field Company moved in the immediate rear of 1st Division's attack, and finding the source of the Selle to be reasonably dry, the following day brought two artillery bridges from the Bohain RE park and placed them over the stream. The railway bridge at Vaux-Andigny having been cleared of an unexploded mine so that horse transport could proceed to the newly installed bridges, more pontoons were brought up. On 20 October the company started work on the roads, as did 409 Field Company, and the following day 23 Field Company joined in work on the roads around la Vallée Mulâtre and Wassigny.[24]

By 24 October, Fourth Army and its corps had two areas of routes open. Firstly, on the east bank there were the routes to Bazuel, already described, serving XIII Corps, with two-way routes open along the Roman road north of Le Cateau, and from Honnechy into the south of Le Cateau on the west bank. Secondly, there was a series of one-way routes. Two-way routes from Bohain to Vaux-Andigny and Andigny-les-Fermes served XI Corps on the east bank, but from there the road along the east bank was open from Vaux-Andigny to St Souplet, and from this complex one-way routes were open from St Souplet through L'Arbre de Guise to Wassigny with return though Ribeauville, St Martin Rivière to Andigny-les-Fermes, and Wassigny to Molain. No Army or corps routes connected the two corps that attacked on 23 October.

As seen with the artillery bridging over the Essart, the Selle was not the only watercourse that needed engineering attention. The attack of XIII Corps on 23 October had to cross the Richemont stream and its marshy shoulders. Corps engineers were ordered to erect two trestle bridges near Evillers Wood Farm and at Richemont Mill. 130 Field Company were to lay nine out of 16 smaller bridges across the Richemont and would suffer 13 casualties in the process.[25] 106 Field Company were also tasked with creating bridges on the 23rd. They were organised into two forward bridging sections, each to construct artillery bridges at Garde Mill and Jean Jacques Mill. A third bridging

20 War Diary, HQ Chief Engineer IX Corps, 17 October 1918, TNA WO95/844.
21 War Diary, HQ Chief Engineer IX Corps, 22 October 1918, TNA WO95/844.
22 26 Field Company had to clear the same following the Pursuit which they reckoned was the spoil of infantry digging in on either side of the road during operations. War Diary, 26 Field Company Royal Engineers, 14-15 October 1918, TNA WO95/1253.
23 War Diary, 11th Battalion Leicestershire Regiment, 19-21 October, TNA WO95/1601.
24 War Diary, 23 Field Company Royal Engineers, 21-8 October 1918, TNA WO95/1252.
25 War Diary, 130 Field Company Royal Engineers, 23 October 1918, TNA WO95/2237.

The shallow ford across the Richemont at Jean Jacques Moulin discovered by 106 Field Company RE. Although the stream itself was never wide, the shoulders were marshy.

section was to erect a trestle bridge at Garde Mill for ordinary traffic, to be completed as quickly as possible. On the day, the machine-guns which had not been mopped up made progress impossible until daybreak at around 05.30. Lieutenant John Gurnhill, commanding the Jean Jacques Mill party, reconnoitred both locations. His first attempt was prevented by fire, the second at 04.30 resulted in his wounding as he attempted to 'round up' one of the machine-gun nests.[26] By 06.00 fire had been silenced, and the existing Garde Mill bridge was found intact but mined, and the artillery bridge was put in some distance from it, as was the trestle bridge. At Jean Jacques Mill a shallow ford was discovered, and it was decided that there was no need for a bridge. Establishing forward water supply was crucial, and over the next two days the company worked on this at Garde Mill, an old bricked-in spring being discovered and developed, and the roads in and out of the mill were improved.[27] On 24 October the work of the field companies moved to the roads captured the previous day and to establishing the water supply. A horse watering point for 1,200 animals was created at St Souplet, and another for 300 in Bazuel. On 24 October 509 Field Company were establishing water points in Bazuel and combing the railway for bombs, when their CO, Major Hugh Bambridge,[28] was wounded by a bomb from an enemy aircraft.

The reality of the difficulties caused for bridge building by the lack of progress on 17 October meant that artillery could not cross the Selle that day, but the limited progress itself made that irrelevant. The maximal effort of the engineers the following day opened a range of crossings for both artillery and supplies for finishing Fourth Army's Battle of the Selle. Over the next four days the engineers again completed herculean tasks to enable the prosecution of battle on the 23rd.

Logistics

The logistics situation for Fourth Army in the immediate wake of the forcing of the Selle did not get any easier. Sir Henry Rawlinson, as ever, was worrying on 20 October about the railways: 'Our railways are not getting on as fast as I should like'.[29] He was thus content that the attack had been put off until the 23rd because of Third Army's logistic problems. For the attack on 23 October the railhead for IX Corps remained at Essigny, with onward carry by motor transport except for the supplies of the infantry brigades of 6th and 46th Divisions, which were pulled by horse.[30] Manpower continued to be a problem: 'In most cases there is only one driver per lorry, and owing to the heavy pressure of work it is more than one man's capabilities to look after a 3-ton lorry'.[31] The railways were struggling as well. On the 20th the trains at Essigny were 'nearly 12 hours late, apparently great difficulty is being experienced by the French in operating the line which has only been opened a few days'.[32] Taking over the American front meant 'feeding strength of another 23,579 taken over', with responsibility for ammunition supply to the Australian guns, but the supply route for these was Roisel and the Montbrehain light railway.[33] On 21 October it was recorded with alarm that 'the congestion of traffic is increasing at Essigny'. The field ammunition train due on the

26 John Byron Gurnhill was commissioned from sergeant in February 1917.
27 War Diary, 105 Field Company Royal Engineers, 'Narrative of Operations 3-31 October 1918', TNA WO95/2235.
28 Hugh Gordon Bambridge was commissioned in October 1914.
29 Sir H. Rawlinson, War Journal, 20 October 1918, Churchill College RWLN 1/11.
30 War Diary, Assistant Quartermaster General IX Corps October 1918, TNA WO95/840.
31 War Diary, IX Corps Senior MT Officer, 19 October 1918, WO 95/846.
32 War Diary, IX Corps Senior MT Officer, 20 October 1918, WO 95/846.
33 War Diary, IX Corps Senior MT Officer, 20 October 1918, WO 95/846.

20th 'arrived at 6 a.m. to-day followed by two days' trains, and owing to the poor facilities at the railhead these will both have to be off-loaded before the supply packs can enter the yard'. In XIII Corps, the railhead for the 18th, 25th and 50th Divisions had advanced to Bellicourt, with light railway to Bohain. Onward transport was by lorry for 18th and 25th Division, and by horse for 50th and 66th Divisions, whose railhead was still at Roisel, with light railway to Montbrehain.[34] XIII Corps experienced similar railway miseries. The supply pack train for 25th Division due during the day on 20 October did not arrive at the railhead until 03.00 the following morning, and that due on the 22nd did not arrive until 11.00 on 23 October.[35] Onward transport had thereafter to use the bridges constructed across the Selle, with the exception of the Regnicourt route.

Field Artillery supporting IX Corps moved east of the Selle on 19 October as soon as the battle moved on and the bridges were up. The heavy artillery moved over the following two days, straddling the river with some units as far forward as Wassigny and Mazinghien.[36] The first units of field and heavy artillery of XIII Corps similarly began the move across to river as soon as possible on 19 October, the order for the remainder to move being given later that day, positioned further on the high ground on the east bank.[37] Ammunition was again the major issue. IX Corps Supply Column had 83 lorries carrying ammunition on 19 October, and 127 on the 20th, each doing two or three journeys. On 22 October 48 lorries were loaded with field ammunition and ordered to park on the Busigny-Vaux-Andigny road by 05.00 on the 23rd to replenish expended ammunition.[38] On the 19th, 150 Fourth Army lorries were engaged in moving ammunition from dumps at Tincourt and Epehy to forward dumps for the divisions of XIII Corps, and 93 lorries were shifting ammunition from the Bellicourt, Brancourt and Estrées railheads. The first ammunition trains arrived at Bellicourt on 20 October, and a new dump closer to the front line was opened near Honnechy on the 22nd, all available lorries being deployed to move ammunition there from Montbrehain.[39]

There were thus indications of increasing friction in the logistics system. Delays were increasing in the rail system and the onward transport suffered accordingly. However, whilst Fourth Army had its ammunition in place just in time for the attack of 23 October, logistics would henceforth increasingly interfere with tempo, not least due to the difficulty of pushing railways beyond the Selle. At the end of October the railheads would reach Honnechy, Busigny and Bohain,[40] but they would remain on the east bank of the Selle until the Armistice. The history of the Royal Engineers claimed that: 'The destroyed viaduct at St. Bénin held up any advance of rails. At the date of the Armistice the only reliable railheads for the Fourth Army were fifty miles behind the armistice line and, owing to the state of the roads, *horse transport* was being used to carry the loads forward.'[41] In reality there were ways around the destroyed viaduct, but the central problem was the rate of the German withdrawal. The speed of the enemy's backwards movement outstripped the engineers' ability to repair the roads. Railway could only be restored at a rate of one mile a day for single-track line if embankments, bridges etc. were intact. Yet Fourth Army needed double track if it was truly to maintain its supplies – even with the reduction to a mobile column spearhead, double-banking

34 War Diary, Assistant Quartermaster General XIII Corps, October 1918, TNA WO95/900.
35 War Diary, 25th Division Supply Column, 2-23 October 1918, TNA WO95/908.
36 War Diary, IX Corps Heavy Artillery, 21-22 October 1918, TNA WO95/842.
37 War Diary, Commander Royal Artillery XIII Corps, 19 October 1918, TNA WO95/902.
38 War Diary, IX Corps Supply Column, 19-22 October 1918, TNA WO95/847.
39 War Diary, XIII Corps 'N' Supply Column ASC, TNA WO95/907.
40 War Diary, Assistant Quartermaster General XIII Corps October 1918, TNA WO95/900.
41 H. L. Pritchard, *History of the Corps of Royal Engineers. Vol.5* p.660. Italics in original.

lorry supply could only be effective for so long.[42] As Rawlinson wrote: 'If the Bosche continues to destroy all railways we shall not be able to get to the German frontier before Feb[ruary]'.[43]

Intelligence

On 19 October, Fourth Army had in its possession captured sketch maps of the *Hermann Stellung II* as it ran along the east bank of the Sambre-Oise canal. From captured prisoners it was also aware that: 'The Germans have reinforced their front line opposite the Fourth Army, during the last two days, with one fresh and 6 tired divisions'. Prisoners indicated further defence lines, namely *Hagen Stellung* through Valenciennes, Hirson and Mezieres; and *Hundsruck Stellung*, on the German-Belgian frontier. If the defence of the Selle had been anything to go by, this must have given pause for thought. On 20 October it was concluded that: 'Any attempt made by us to gain ground towards Bois l'Evêque and the Forest of Mormal will meet with strenuous resistance'.[44] Direct information was hard to obtain, however, about the German defences. 'Repeated attempts were made to reconnoitre roads and railways behind the enemy's line, but the weather conditions were very bad'.[45] Information was obtained about minor field fortifications. By the following day prisoners described trenches being dug on the high ground to the north-east of the Richemont stream.[46] On the day before the attack of the 23rd strongly held shellholes were identified east of Montay, work on defences was spotted in progress south of Forest and at Pommereuil, and wire was known to be being placed north of Bazuel. It was also, yet again, difficult to obtain a picture of the defenders. It was estimated that the flank of *Second Army* which would be the main focus of the assault comprised three divisions (*17th Reserve*, *243rd* and *121st Divisions*), each holding a front of 3,000 yards.[47] This was again an underestimation. Whilst the *44th Division* had been previously identified, on the morning of 23 October the fresh *8th Division* was discovered in the Montay sector, as was the *44th*.[48] Indeed, prisoners from six different divisions were captured on 23/24 October.[49] Fourth Army's intelligence had yet again underestimated the strength of the enemy.

The reasons for the paucity of accurate intelligence were the same as had existed prior to the attack of 17 October. Prisoner identifications were limited, and aerial observation worse. On 19 October, although there had been flying, observation was 'practically impossible'.[50] On the following days, 20 and 21 October, there was virtually no flying at all, there being two low flying reconnaissances on the 20th and none at all on the 21st.[51] On the 22nd there was more flying as the mist was interspersed with clear intervals, but still only four reconnaissances were flown, with no zone calls.[52] Apart from its prisoner identifications, Fourth Army was possibly even more blind than it had been on 17 October, with only sketchy information about defences, inadequate information about the volume of opposition, and no information for accurate counter-battery work.

42 G. Clarke, personal communication, email dated 22 August 2016.
43 Sir H. Rawlinson, War Journal, 22 October 1918, Churchill College RWLN 1/11.
44 War Diary, HQ Fourth Army, Summaries of Information, 20 October 1918, TNA WO157/199.
45 War Diary, HQ Fourth Army, Summaries of Information, 19 October 1918, TNA WO157/199.
46 War Diary, HQ Fourth Army, Summaries of Information, 21 October 1918, TNA WO157/199.
47 War Diary, HQ Fourth Army, Summaries of Information, 22 October 1918, TNA WO157/199.
48 War Diary, HQ Fourth Army, Summaries of Information, 23 October 1918, TNA WO157/199.
49 War Diary, HQ Fourth Army, Summaries of Information, 24 October 1918, TNA WO157/199.
50 War Diary, 5 Brigade RAF, Operation Summary 19 October 1918, TNA AIR1/2225/209/40/26.
51 War Diary, HQ Fourth Army, Summary of Operations 20 & 21 October 1918, TNA WO95/439.
52 War Diary, 5 Brigade RAF, Operation Summary 19 October 1918, AIR1/2225/209/40/26.

Fourth Army Planning

On 17 October Sir Douglas Haig ordered that 'the Fourth, Third, and First Armies will … be ready to launch a general attack from positions on the east bank of the River SELLE on or about the 21st instant'.[53] In order to position themselves for this attack, the Third and First Armies advanced together to cross the Selle on 20 October. The assault was mounted as a surprise without a preliminary bombardment, and went in at 02.00 under a full moon. By the end of a day of hard fighting, both armies had established a bridgehead of varying depth across the river. There followed a pause of two days, two postponements being caused by 'the slow arrival of the ammunition trains in the Third Army area'.[54] The time was spent in those two armies in the familiar tasks of repairing bridges and dealing with mined roads in order to allow movement of guns and bring up supplies for the joint attack of all three armies on the 23rd. The purpose of the attack was to position the armies to 'stand opposite or beyond Hermann Position II'.[55] Whilst the French *First Army* promised cooperation, the Official Historians claim that 'it was soon evident … that no help was intended', and on 23-24 October the corps abutting the southern boundary of IX Corps did not move.[56]

On 19 October, Fourth Army ordered the relief of II American Corps, and issued orders on 20 October for the attack on the 23rd. These effectively cover no more than one side of paper. Intermediate, first and final objectives were set, marked on a map. There was to be 'no preliminary organized bombardment, but until zero corps were to 'maintain vigorous counter-battery work', harass the enemy's approaches, and bombard localities to be selected by corps. It was specified that the barrage would move at a rate of 100 yards in four minutes; tanks were allotted, and as before, 5 Brigade RAF was to liaise about covering the advance of the tanks to the start.[57] The following day Rawlinson met with his two corps commanders and the order of the 20th was cancelled. On the basis of arrangements with neighbouring Third Army, four lines of objectives were set with specific times of arrival and departure. Whilst the same barrage pattern as 17 October was set, the lifts were confirmed as every four minutes with the exception of the fire directed on the Bois l'Evêque. IX and XIII Corps were left to 'arrange mutually for such artillery action as they require', as they were in the matter of protective barrages.[58] This slower rate of lift reflected the countryside over which the attack would take place. Zero hour of 01.20, agreed in liaison with Third Army, was similarly ordered later on the 21st.[59] This was a break with Fourth Army tradition, but was agreed in recognition of there being a full moon. It was hoped that this unexpected timing would give some element of surprise, and that the enemy's machine guns would be disadvantaged in the 'uncertain light'.[60] There was, overall, more devolution in planning to corps than in the run-up to the operations of 17 October. IX Corps actually seems to have begun to issue orders on 19 October,[61] before General Braithwaite's meeting with his army commander, orders amended twice in the following days.[62] They are so brief that they imply staffs at corps and divisional level working

53 O.A.D 939, Adv. G.H.Q. 17 October 1918, IWM Docs 20537 Fourth Army Papers Vol.48.
54 Edmonds & Maxwell-Hyslop, *Military Operations France and Belgium 1918, Vol. V*, p.351.
55 Edmonds & Maxwell-Hyslop, op. cit., p.351.
56 Edmonds & Maxwell-Hyslop, op. cit., p.353.
57 War Diary, HQ Fourth Army, Order No. 20/44(G), 20 October 1918, TNA WO95/439.
58 War Diary, HQ Fourth Army, Order No. 20/45(G), 21 October 1918, TNA WO95/439.
59 War Diary, HQ Fourth Army, Order No. 20/46(G), 13 October 1918, TNA WO95/439.
60 Anonymous, Operations of XIII Corps between 3rd October and 11th November 1918, p.25.
61 The initial IX Corps order 147 has not survived.
62 War Diary, HQ IX Corps 19-21 October 1918, TNA WO95/837.

so well and closely that there was little need for the reams of paper that had accompanied operations earlier in the war. XIII Corps again issued a series of far more detailed orders than those of IX Corps. Those of 19 October particularly covered signals. Two wireless tanks were noted to be operating on the corps front, relaying messages to 2nd Tank Brigade HQ and thence onwards by telegraph/telephone.[63] The attack of XIII Corps was, however, much more complex than that of IX, and hence the greater volume of orders.

Fourth Army's line was strung out between the two waterways in a north-westerly direction from Oisy on the Sambre-Oise canal, to the high ground west of Catillon, and thence in a westerly direction towards Montay on the Selle, through Bazuel. The attack would be as a door pivoting on Oisy and swinging from Montay to shut north of Landrecies against the Forest of Mormal. IX Corps had, as noted, taken over the front from the exhausted II American Corps, a relief completed by 21 October. XIII Corps had in turn absorbed a further 1,000 yards of the line of V Corps of Third Army, as far as Montay. The dividing line between IX and XIII Corps began at Bazuel and during the attack would run through the centre of Bois l'Evêque and thence to north-west of Landrecies. IX Corps would push up to Catillon and Ors on the canal and establish a defensive flank on the railway line that ran from Ors to Landrecies to a point where Bois l'Evêque nearly touched a dog-leg in the course of the canal. XIII Corps, however, had a long distance to travel, some 11,000 yards, advancing on an expanding front in a north-easterly direction. Their attack abutted Third Army on the Roman road that passed through the village of Forest, on its ridge which overlooked the whole of the XIII Corps area of attack. The corps had to take the straggling villages of Pommereuil, Bousies, Fontaine au Bois and Robersart close to the edge of the Mormal Forest, to arrive on the Landrecies-Englefontaine road. IX Corps would not have to overcome the *Hermann Stellung II*, as in their area it ran on the eastern bank of the canal, but on the western bank it began beyond Ors. In the XIII Corps area it would have to be breached along the entire corps front, as it ran in front of Malgarni, and between Bousies and Robersart. The trenches of the position were hastily dug, but it had 'two lines of double apron wire, the hedges were wired, it was covered by an outpost zone, and where no defensible localities existed, strongpoints had been dug in the fields and orchards'.[64] However, details concerning it do not appear in intelligence reports and it is likely that it was something of an unknown quantity.

Whilst all the villages both in front of and beyond the *Hermann Stellung II* promised to be an obstacle, only Bousies had the sort of strong buildings suitable for sustained defence. All the villages and farms were, however, surrounded by an intricate network of orchards and small fields bounded by hedges and fences which had already proved ideal for concealment of the enemy, giving rise to delays. Indeed, the stout, high hedges were a worse obstacle here than any previously encountered on the east bank of the Selle. This had occasioned the change in barrage lifts from three to four minutes. On the right of the XIII Corps advance lay Bois l'Evêque which covered an area of some four square miles. Three-quarters of the trees had, however, been removed leaving brambles and undergrowth. It was incorrectly assumed by Fourth Army HQ that in the absence of trees this would present little difficulty to an infantry advance other than maintaining touch and direction, especially at night or in the now predictable fog. In practice, felled trees and swampy ground made the going very hard. Although the positioning of the armies was clearly to effect a crossing of the Sambre and Oise Canal, 'an essential strategical object in the operation was to secure artillery

63 War Diary, HQ XIII Corps 19-22 October 1918, TNA WO95/897.
64 Edmonds and Maxwell-Hyslop, op. cit., p.351

positions from which the important railway junction of Leval on the enemy's main lateral communications could be kept under fire of long range guns'.[65]

In terms of the general artillery scheme, the 18-pounder barrage would come down at zero 200 yards in front of the start line, the 4.5-inch howitzer barrage 200 yards in advance. The barrage would lift at zero plus four minutes and, as noted, advance at a rate of 100 yards every four minutes, except through Bois l'Evêque. Both corps would arrive on the Red Line (Catillon to Forest) at 03.40 and depart at 04.20. They would achieve the Red Dotted Line (Catillon to the south-west of Bousies but taking in the whole of l'Evêque Wood) at 05.20 and depart at 07.20, at which point IX Corps would have completely secured its objective. XIII Corps would then proceed to the Green Line for 08.00 (from the northern tip of l'Evêque Wood to the western edge of Bousies) and depart at 08.40. Finally, XIII Corps would achieve the Green Dotted Line (from the north-eastern corner of Bousies to eastern tip of l'Evêque Wood) at 10.12, and depart at 12.12, to take its final objectives, Fontaine au Bois and Robersart. Most of Fourth Army's plans at the Selle, were ambitious. These were exceedingly so, and were yet again doomed to frustration.

65 Anonymous, *Operations of XIII Corps*, p.24. Leval lay to the south of Aulnoye, some 12 miles from the start line.

7

'We Shall Have a Fight'.[1] Final Act at the Selle: 23-24 October 1918

In keeping with the strategy of alternate blows, but also governed by logistical constraints, in order to maintain tempo the Battle of the Selle was carried out in three stages. The first involved Fourth Army (17-19 October), the second concerned the First and Third Armies (20 October). The third involved the actions of all three armies. Fourth Army's final contribution would be the driving in of the flank of the German *Second Army*, in pace with the progress of Third Army to its left. The two armies would be brought face to face with the Sambre-Oise canal and the Forest of Mormal. In the north, First Army would continue its progress towards the enemy communications hub of Valenciennes.

Wednesday 23 October 1918

IX Corps

IX Corps attacked with 1st Division on a 6,000 yard frontage to the right and 6th Division on a frontage half that width to the left. The two divisions had very different tasks, 1st Division's longer frontage representing what was likely to be the easier operation. The barrage fired for the division by eight brigades of field artillery and one of heavy artillery was simple. So close was it to the canal that eight minutes of creeping intense fire (using 'as large a proportion of H.E. as possible') took it to the protector line, where one round per gun was to be fired for 107 minutes, mixed with smoke, allowing consolidation in the face of the enemy on the east bank. The heavy artillery was to pay special attention to la Haie Tonnoile Farm, whose defence had put an end to the advance of II American Corps four days earlier.[2] The barrage was augmented by fifty-two guns of 1st Battalion Machine Gun Corps (MGC) and 2nd Machine Gun Battalion Life Guards, also targeting la Haie Tonnoile and then moving forward to rain fire on Catillon.[3] The barrage fired by the Australian artillery protecting 6th Division, who had a much further distance to travel, was more complex.[4] The area covered was shaped like a wellington boot against the canal, its heel resting on Bazuel,

1 Sir H. Rawlinson, War Journal, 22 October 1918, Churchill College RWLN 1/11.
2 War Diary, HQ Commander Royal Artillery 1st Division, Artillery Instructions No. 14, 22 October 1918, TNA WO95/1241.
3 War Diary, 1st Battalion Machine Gun Corps, Order No. 57 22 October 1918, TNA WO95/1256.
4 The 3rd, 4th and 5th Australian Divisional Artillery, the 5th Division being withdrawn on the night 23/24 October.

its toe on Catillon, the leg stretching along the canal. The field guns fired shrapnel up to 4,000 yards and HE thereafter, the 4.5-inch howitzers firing 10 per cent CG (phosgene) shells mixed with smoke in equal rates, a formula dependant on the weather conditions.[5] The corps heavy artillery allotted seven brigades Royal Garrison Artillery to counter-battery work, and eight to the bombardment of specific targets.

Attached to IX Corps was the 301st American Tank Battalion organised in three sections of three Mark V tanks each, one further section being held in reserve. Two specific tasks involving dealing with strongpoints were allotted. Firstly, one section was attached to 1st Division to assist initially in the capture of la Haie Tonnoile and then drive due north to help 6th Division take Gimbremont Farm just to the north-west of Catillon. Secondly, two sections would assist the 6th in the taking of an area of enclosures at le Planty, further to the north-west along the Bazuel-Catillon road from Gimbremont. These machines would then proceed north to the eastern edge of Bois l'Evêque. 2nd Tank Brigade, to which the Americans were attached, had had only two to three days for reconnaissance, and the information as to what lay behind the enemy's front line was limited. 'The BOIS L'EVEQUE was expected from civilian statements and photographs to be almost impassable for tanks, and this proved to be the case'. Wisely, none of the machines strayed therein. The front line being somewhat fluid, tank reconnaissance officers 'in more than one case walked through the line unawares, and came under the fire of snipers or machine-guns'.[6] The 7,000 yard approach march of the tanks from Busigny to near Rejet-de-Beaulieu along taped routes from the west bank of the Selle over tank bridges passed without mechanical mishap.

In moonlight and thick mist, 1st Division attacked towards the canal with 3 Brigade on the right and 2 Brigade on the left. 3 Brigade in turn attacked with 2nd Welsh on the right. The enemy was evidently well prepared, and although 1st Division was spared the shelling prior to zero that was inflicted on the other divisions, a counter-barrage came down on both brigades 'practically at the same time our artillery opened'.[7] The brigade positioned four of its machine-guns covering the right of the assault with two Stokes mortars, with 16 machine-guns firing an enfilade barrage along the canal and six mortars targeting specific positions. Another four machine-guns moved forward with the 2nd Welsh, accompanied by two mortars.[8] The enemy's resistance relied solely on artillery – here, their infantry would not fight. In front of the Welsh, attacking with three companies with 50-60 yards visibility, the Germans vacated their positions as soon as the barrage opened. No machine-gun or rifle fire at all was encountered, and a line on the canal was established at 08.00. The ferocity of the counter-barrage, however, had led to over 140 casualties.[9] On the left, 1st Gloucestershire pushed forward successfully with 21 casualties,[10] but the 1st South Wales

5 War Diary, HQ 8th Australian Field Artillery Brigade, 6th Divisional Artillery Instructions No. 7, 22 October 1918, AWM4 Item No. 13/36/29 Part 2.

6 War Diary, HQ 2nd Tank Brigade, 'Report on Operations 23rd and 24th October 1918', TNA WO95/102/3.

7 War Diary, HQ 1st Infantry Division, 23 October 1918, TNA WO95/1234.

8 War Diary, HQ 3 Infantry Brigade, Battle Instructions Series 'D' No. 3, TNA WO95/1277.

9 Lieutenants William Henry Sutton (commissioned from private in December 1916) and Geoffrey Hubert Brown (commissioned December 1916) were killed, and Captain John East Lanfear Warren (commissioned November 1914) who had won his MC five days earlier at Wassigny, and Second-Lieutenant George Frederick Mears (commissioned into the Glamorgan Yeomanry in July 1917) were wounded. Amongst the casualties in the other ranks, Sergeant Benjamin Whitcombe, who had enlisted in 1900 and arrived on the Western Front as a lance-corporal on 20 September 1914 was killed, as was Sergeant Thomas Lawton who had arrived on the Western Front two days before Christmas in 1915.

10 Seven other ranks were killed and 14 wounded.

Borderers in support suffered particularly from the counter-barrage, incurring 25 casualties.[11] 2 Brigade attacked with 1st Northamptonshire on the right and 2nd Royal Sussex on the left. The brigade described the creeping barrage as 'one of the thickest the Brigade had followed for some time'.[12] The Northants, whose objective was high ground south-east of Catillon, were also caught by the counter-bombardment.[13] Captain Leslie Mackenzie,[14] commanding the leading D Company, lost his rear platoons in the fog, but pressed on with 30 men and two of the four machine-guns of D Company 1st Battalion MGC which were attached and arrived on the objective. Here he remained isolated until later in the day when he established contact with A Company to his south and the 2nd Sussex to his left.[15] The day had had its cost for the battalion – two officers and 12 other ranks had been killed and 67 wounded.[16] 2nd King's Royal Rifle Corps were in support and did not see action, but similarly suffered heavily from the counter-barrage.[17]

2nd Royal Sussex were to capture the high ground west of Catillon and the troublesome bastion of la Haie Tonnoile Farm. Two guns of D Company 1st Battalion MGC were attached to each of the two leading companies, under the direction of company commanders, as were two Stokes mortars which were attached to D Company whose objective was closest to Catillon. The attached tanks proved a disappointment. The section detailed to assist in the capture of la Haie Tonnoile had difficulties with terrain in the fog, and only one tank arrived on the objective some hours after it was taken. One machine had ditched in a small marsh within 400 yards of the farm whilst another lost direction in an orchard soon after moving off.[18] The forming up area had been shelled with mustard gas, and setting off in the heavy mists sections had to bunch together to keep touch. Under continuing shelled with HE and phosgene gas the leading companies pressed on to discover that the enemy infantry 'offered no resistance but ran as fast as they could before the barrage could catch them', abandoning everything including 20 of their number to be taken prisoner. By 03.30 the objective had been consolidated. Again, it was the barrage that exerted a toll on the unit, which had attacked with a strength of 17 officers and 353 other ranks, and suffered 56 casualties.[19] As a whole, however, 1st Division had had a successful morning, having advanced 2,000 yards. Once

11 Captain Edward Roy Taylor MC (commissioned September 1915) was killed with five other ranks and 19 wounded.

12 War Diary, HQ 2 Infantry Brigade, 23 October 1918, TNA WO95/1268.

13 Lieutenant Stables of C Company was killed during assembly. Leonard Theodore Drury Staples had been commissioned from lance-corporal in November 1916.

14 Leslie Henry Marc Mackenzie had been commissioned in May 1915.

15 Anonymous, *The Northamptonshire Regiment* 1914-1918, pp.300-301.

16 Second-Lieutenant George Oswald Timmins had been commissioned from private in February 1918 was killed, and Second-Lieutenant Cecil Henry Anscomb (commissioned January 1918) wounded.

17 2nd KRRC were commanded by Major Humphrey Butler, Colonel Smith having been wounded during line holding two days previously. Humphrey William Butler MC was mobilised as a second-lieutenant from the Special Reserve of the KRRC in August 1914 and had served in various staff posts until May 1918. Second-Lieutenant Andrew Campbell Dick (commissioned from the South African Infantry in September 1917) died of wounds. Fifteen other ranks were killed/died of wounds, including CSM Leonard Burt, who had enlisted in 1905 and arrived on the Western Front in August 1914, 36 were wounded and four gassed. (War Diary, 2nd Battalion King's Royal Rifle Corps, 23 October 1918, TNA WO95/1273).

18 War Diary, HQ 2nd Tank Brigade, 'Report on Operations 23rd and 24th October 1918', TNA WO95/102/3.

19 Captain Ernest Dolleymore MC (commissioned July 1915) was wounded, as were Lieutenant Cyril Leslie Michell MC (commissioned April 1915) and Second-Lieutenant Harold Henry Homewood (commissioned July 1917).

they had consolidated their objectives, 2nd Royal Sussex pushed out patrols towards Catillon, and 2nd Welsh reconnoitred Lock No. 1 at the canal, as did Corporal Claridge and Sapper Weeber of 26 Field Company Royal Engineers, who had gone ahead of the infantry, under rifle-fire.[20] There was no penetration of Catillon itself due to enemy rifle and machine-gun fire from the houses, although on the following day posts were established in the western outskirts.[21] Catillon would only be taken on 4 November when Fourth Army crossed the Sambre-Oise canal.

6th Division faced a somewhat more difficult prospect. The enemy had good artillery positions both in Bois l'Evêque and on the eastern bank of the Sambre and Oise Canal. The first opposed the left of the division's advance. Without suppression, the latter would enfilade their right. Indeed, the division shared the same experience as the 1st, that 'the hostile artillery fire was more than had been encountered since the fighting about St. Quentin'. In the days prior to the attack 'the shelling of roads, farms and villages in our rear area and of artillery positions was continuous'.[22] The division's assembly, in particular, was subject to damaging HE and gas shelling. A model of thoroughness, General Marden held a conference with his brigade commanders and battalion COs three hours before zero to ensure that the plans for the attack, supported by seven brigades of field artillery and one heavy, were completely understood by all. 18 Brigade comprised the right of the divisional assault, which would take the rest of the high ground to the west of Catillon, cross the Catillon-Bazuel road, and press on up the west bank of the canal towards Ors, brushing the edge of the Bois l'Evêque. The 2nd Durham Light Infantry abutted the attack of 1st Division. The Durhams assembled near la Jonquière Farm, where the heavy enemy shelling between midnight and 01.00 caused casualties and disorganisation in the two assaulting companies. Almost immediately on setting off, the two same companies and their support were caught by the counter-barrage, their commanders being wounded. The skill of the German artillery, hastily sited on the east bank of the canal, was evident: 'The enemy barrage crept back with our advance and rested in three places'.[23] The bombardment left only small groups of infantry advancing up the eastern slope of the valley of the St Maurice stream to meet the enemy on the high ground that overlooked Catillon. Topping the crest they met machine-gun fire and wired hedges. Despite the degradation of command and control, the opposition was overcome and the Durhams reached the Catillon-Bazuel road. Here they were held up by fire from houses north-east of Catillon, and the disorganisation began to have a negative effect. Small parties of infantry from the three companies, some under officers, some under NCOs, fell back out of touch with each other. None, on their own, were strong enough to deal with the opposition. Four hours beyond jump-off the British troops were still being shelled with a mixture of high explosive and gas. Lieutenant-Colonel Reginald Turner, essentially in the dark as to what had transpired, ordered A Company forward from reserve.[24] The first three companies having drifted to the right, A Company passed to their left, and their impetus overcame the opposition on the road. Thus, without the planned help of the tanks to take the stronghold at le Planty on their left, they had captured both the higher ground beyond the road and Gimbremont Farm itself by dawn. The day had ultimately been successful, but the Durhams had suffered 151

20 War Diary 26 Field Company Royal Engineers, 23 October 1918, TNA WO95/1253.
21 War Diary, HQ 1st Infantry Division 23-4 October 1918, TNS WO95/1234. During the month of October 1918 2nd Sussex had suffered four officers wounded. Six ORs had been killed, 214 wounded, and ten were missing.
22 T.O. Marden, *A Short History of the Sixth Division*, p.71.
23 War Diary, 2nd Battalion Durham Light Infantry, 23 October 1918, TNA WO95/1617.
24 Reginald Turner DSO was retired territorial officer of the Sherwood Foresters in August 1914. He was promoted to command 6th Northamptonshire in March 1917.

casualties.[25] Over the next two days posts were pushed forward to Malamison Farm and the Ors road, but Ors itself and a few remaining strongholds on the west bank of the canal would remain to be taken by 32nd Division on 4 November.

1st West Yorkshire attacked on the brigade's left, also having to proceed down into the shallow valley of the St Maurice stream and uphill again. 'Tapes had been laid previously to direct the attack and compass bearings carefully worked out',[26] the morning fog and obscured moon making this an absolute necessity. The battalion was supported by tanks, a section of machine-guns and a trench mortar. The country was more difficult in front of the West Yorkshires than in front of the Durhams, and the unit progressed more slowly, albeit with less casualties. The tanks cleared passages through the thick hedges in some places and in others the infantry went at them with bill-hooks. Unfortunately, the inevitable delays caused by forcing passage led to the loss of the barrage and exposed the battalion to unsuppressed enemy machine-gun fire. Around 08.30, however, brigade received reports that the West Yorkshires were on the Catillon-Bazuel road, and pushing forward with the co-operation of the tanks. One of the tanks had ditched within 200 yards of the road, but two progressed and 'an observer who saw these tanks in action reported that they practically cleared up the whole of the ground between R.10 and the BAZUEL-CATILLON road'. They thus cleared a distance nearly two-thirds of the way to Ors, abutting the southern tip of the Bois l'Evêque.[27] A defensive flank was put down to the left in the absence of contact with the adjacent battalion of 71 Brigade in the wood and by 15.00 the Yorkshire unit had advanced to the Red Line, the Durhams on their right being ahead on the Green Line. The fighting that day had, however, cost 1st West Yorkshire 107 casualties.[28] During the night they pushed their line out further and by 08.00 on the 24th were on the Green Line positioned around the west of Ors. That night they sent out patrols onto the canal banks to find the enemy, with the exception of a few machine-guns and sniper posts, gone.

The left of the division's assault, facing the scrubland and remaining trees of the Bois l'Evêque, was made by 71 Brigade, temporarily commanded by Lieutenant-Colonel Latham of 1st Leicestershire. On the right of the brigade, the 9th Norfolks formed up on a light railway running south-east from Bazuel on the eastern side of the Catillon road, fielding two companies each on a 300 yard frontage. Their Red Line objective lay some 300-400 yards beyond the south-east corner of the Bois l'Evêque. Despite the heavy shelling the battalion started well, but 'the first check occurred very soon, when many wired hedges and fences, in a close country of small fields, were met with and found to be

25 Second-Lieutenant Joseph Hunter Jeffrey was killed. Captain George Macaulay Garland (commissioned in February 1915) was wounded, as were Lieutenants William Osborne Pearson, (commissioned from private in August 1917) and W.N. Long; and Second-Lieutenants David Lawrie Shield (commissioned June 1918), Frederick Scarth Richardson (who had progressed from private in the Manchester Regiment to sergeant in the Yorkshire Regiment, to being commissioned in the DLI in July 1918), and A. Wilson. Twenty-four other ranks were killed with seven missing and 113 wounded.

26 E. Wyrall, *The West Yorkshire Regiment in the War 1914-1918*, p.377.

27 War Diary, HQ 2nd Tank Brigade, 'Report on Operations 23rd and 24th October 1918', TNA WO95/102/3.

28 Second-Lieutenants Robert William Jackson MC DCM (commissioned from sergeant in November 1917) and Reginald Pearson (commissioned from private in May 1918) were killed, and Second-Lieutenants Ernest Arthur Coope (commissioned from corporal in June 1918), J. Robson and Raymond Winn (commissioned in December 1917) wounded. Sixteen other ranks were killed, 70 wounded and 16 missing. Amongst the dead was Sergeant John Calder MM, who had enlisted in 1907 and arrived on the Western Front as a private in December 1914.

almost unpassable'.[29] At around 06.00 brigade learnt that the Norfolks had progressed no more than 400 yards. Opposition here was strong. The advanced troops were 'at one time surrounded by the enemy and after fierce hand to hand fighting some were able to get back'.[30] A party of about 50, however, eventually arrived in the corner of the wood, and the barrage having been lost, dug in and awaited support on both flanks. By now, the Norfolks had fallen behind the progress of 1st Leicestershire attacking on the brigade's left. The attached section of tanks had meanwhile reached the Red Line, but found themselves (not for the first time at the Selle) with no infantry to support. The 2nd Brigade Tank Corps later observed: 'The infantry was somewhat slow in following up the tanks, probably owing to the poor visibility and enclosed nature of the country'. Being under fire from machine-guns and a 77-mm gun, the tanks returned from whence they came. They had, however, 'reduced strong points and broke[n] paths through the hedges for the infantry'.[31] Two tanks were then ordered to report to Colonel Day of the Norfolks and deal with strong points in the orchards close to the wood that were holding progress up.

Bazuel being a centre for fruit-growing, immediately in front of 1st Leicestershire on the brigade's left 'were small orchards for a distance of 500 yards with thick hedges reinforced by wire, and although billhooks were used, the wire and the direction of the hedges soon caused the attacking lines to lose direction', and thus the barrage was again lost.[32] A machine-gun position in an outlying house north of Bazuel caused additional problems. By 05.00 the leading parties had only progressed 1,000 yards but had reached a ridge overlooking the wood. Communication proved a central problem across the division's front that morning. The Leicesters' CO, Major Herring-Cooper, had to go forward as the only information coming in about the progress of the attack was from the wounded proceeding to the rear. He was able to discern that his companies were on the Red Line, but was also clear that his right flank was in the air with no contact with the Norfolks. Referring matters to brigade, at 12.30 a company of 2nd Sherwood Foresters was ordered to push into the gap. Reports were received from HQ 6th Division of the Germans moving east with fires along the canal, and by 13.00 the enemy fire had slackened. During the afternoon the Leicesters were able to advance their line further into the wood which was 'very thick, a way having to be cut through it'.[33] The Sherwood Foresters pushed on to the second objective, their right resting on the railway line north-east of Ors adjacent to 6th Division.

The Leicesters and the company of Sherwood Foresters were now in front of the Norfolks, and the respite gave the latter battalion the chance to reform. General Marden and Colonel Latham, demonstrating the inventiveness of front-line commanders displayed during the Hundred Days, then decided to shift the Norfolks to the left round the rear of the Leicesters onto the Pommereuil road in 25th Division's area in order to attack the wood in a south-easterly direction. The line of this attack would follow paths and rides that ran across the previous line of advance rather than battling

29 F.L. Petre, *The History of the Norfolk Regiment*, p.207.
30 War Diary, HQ IX Corps, 23 October 1918, TNA WO95/837.
31 War Diary, HQ 2nd Tank Brigade, 'Report on Operations 23rd and 24th October 1918', TNA WO95/102/3. Across the whole of the 301st Tank Battalion there were only five casualties, all gassed.
32 War Diary, 1st Battalion Leicestershire Regiment, 23 October 1918, TNA WO95/1622. During the period 20-24 October 1st Leicestershire suffered five officers wounded, eight other ranks killed, 90 wounded and 33 missing, a total of 131. Less the battle nucleus their strength had been 14 officers and 362 other ranks – they had therefore lost a third of their numbers.
33 War Diary, HQ IX Corps, 23 October 1918, TNA WO95/837.

through the undergrowth. Darkness intervened before this inventive operation could be concluded, however. The 9th Norfolk were withdrawn that night, having suffered a hefty 136 casualties.[34]

At 17.00 a contact patrol was able to report that the IX Corps line held the southern part of Bois l'Evêque with its furthest reach at a point on the railway line to the north of Ors. The corps had taken nearly all of its objectives in a day of heavy fighting, especially in the area to the north-east of Bazuel where there was considerable opposition from the enemy's machine-gun nests. Fourth Army concluded that 6th Division's slow progress was 'due to the enemy's counter-preparation, which caused a certain amount of disorganisation resulting in the infantry being unable to keep up with the creeping barrage'.[35] The weight and skilled nature of the German counter-barrage had indeed caused significant casualties across the whole of the corps front. Although 6th Division experienced much more resistance than the 1st, the enemy's preparedness to withdraw was indicated by the fact that only 100 or so prisoners were taken. The Germans were bound to mount increased opposition facing 6th Division. Opposite 1st Division, they had largely withdrawn across the canal. Opposite the 6th, there was more of an imperative to protect *2nd Army*'s flank. In addition to artillery fire there was yet another clear reason for the army's failure to achieve its furthest objectives that day. The nature of the countryside had changed again. The enclosed fields which had been a feature of the fruit-growing east bank of the Selle in contrast to the west had become even more marked. 6th Division also faced the Bois l'Evêque, and it was in the undergrowth where the trees had been felled that the enemy machine-gun nests were concealed. The fact that the enemy had wired the hedges could not have been known (but might have been guessed). The nature of the countryside, however, was clear, and to a certain extent had been anticipated with the provision of billhooks. (On 24 October 500 billhooks were obtained for the 25th Division, and on the 26th Army HQ was asked for 2,000 more, a lorry being sent to Abbeville on the 28th for a further 450.)[36] Whereas 1st Division attacking towards the canal could easily keep up with the rate of 100 yards every four minutes of barrage progression, 6th Division, given these obstacles, could not. The artillery of Fourth Army had learnt from the experiences of 17-19 October, and had allowed for a slower rate of progress, 100 yards in four rather than three minutes (the barrage had even progressed at 100 yards every six minutes in Bois l'Evêque), but it was still too fast for the terrain. The universal loss of the protective barrage exposed 6th Division to the enemy machine-guns and progress slowed.

34 Second-Lieutenants Clifford Day Smith (commissioned from corporal in February 1918) and Reginald Boydon Bray (commissioned from lance-corporal in January 1918) were killed. Wounded officers included: Lieutenant Harold Garwood Palmer (commissioned in January 1917) and Second-Lieutenants Alfred Miller (commissioned from private in May 1918), Maurice Coates (commissioned in June 1918 and who had only arrived on the Western Front 14 days earlier), B. Campbell, Fred Whitely Teal (commissioned March 1918) and J.H. Clarke. Seven other ranks were known to have been killed, 61 were wounded, and 60 missing. During October 1918 9th Norfolk had 32 officer casualties and had 31 replacements, with 71 other ranks killed, 524 wounded, and seven missing. Lieutenant Frederick Henry Webber MC (commissioned from private in August 1917), wounded on the 15th, died on the 24th. Webber had won his MC during the Pursuit: 'During the operations near Bohain on the 8th, 9th and llth October, 1918, he showed great skill and gallantry whilst leading his platoon. Especially near Bohain, on the 9th, when he led them forward, under heavy machine-gun fire, and succeeded by his fire in silencing four, machine-guns, with the result that the town was reoccupied shortly after'. (*London Gazette*, 4 October 1919, p.12346).

35 War Diary, HQ Fourth Army, 23 October 1918, TNS WO95/439.

36 War Diary, Chief Engineer XIII Corps, 28-28 October 1918, TNA WO95/903.

XIII Corps

The attack of XIII Corps was more complex and challenging than that of IX Corps. It employed two divisions, the 25th on the right adjacent to 6th Division and the 18th on the left. The latter division was the fresher of the two having taken no previous part in the Selle operations. Both attacked on a frontage of 2,500 yards. The line held by the corps stretched from Montay across the high ground to the east of Le Cateau to Bazuel. The two divisions faced very different country. Both had to negotiate the Richemont stream, whose mills formed strongpoints. For 18th Division, from the high ground to the east of Le Cateau this involved a journey down the long exposed slope into the Richemont valley, on which there were a large number of enemy outpost machine-gun nests. In daylight, this would have involved a plethora of casualties. Bulging out above the opposite bank of the Richemont was a spur on which the enemy had dug a series of practice trenches. This dominated any approach to the northern end of the Bois l'Evêque. 25th Division had a shorter journey down the slope, but once the Richemont had been crossed, like 6th Division, it was faced by orchards, hedges and the undergrowth of the wood. The 18th Division, in contrast, could enjoy open countryside beyond the stream albeit where a string of villages had to be taken. Five objectives were identified. The first objective, to be taken by 7 Brigade of the 25th Division, was the Pommereuil-Forest road which cut across the head of both the practice-trench spur and the White Spring valley which led down to Richemont Mill, across whose northern end lay a further series of practice trenches. The only village that the division had to overcome was Pommereuil. In achieving this objective 7 Brigade would establish itself on the south-western edge of the Bois l'Evêque, whilst 6th Division took the southern and south-easterly part of the wood. The second objective was a target for 18th Division only, involving an advance from the Pommereuil-Forest road north of the Bois l'Evêque to capture the les Tilleuls Farm-Forest road which ran in a north-easterly direction from the northern edge of the wood. The third objective involved both divisions, the 25th clearing the western and northern part of the Bois l'Evêque, the 18th advancing to the western outskirts of Bousies. The fourth objective involved the taking of a ridge to the east of Bousies from the Jean Jacques Farm on the Forest road to Malgarni to the south; whilst the final objective consisted of the capture of the villages of Fontaine aux Bois and Robersart followed by an advance to the Landrecies-Englefontaine road. It was an extraordinarily tall order.

The complexity of the barrage halts and lifts was timed in relation to these series of objectives. 25th Division was covered by five brigades Royal Field Artillery, 18th Division by six. Two hundred and four 18-pounders and 60 4.5-inch howitzers were employed as were 156 pieces of heavy artillery. A barrage of considerable complexity was fired in two lanes, two brigades of field artillery firing in each. The general rate of creep was 100 yards every four minutes, but after the first protector barrage, only one brigade fired in each lane with a rate of creep of 100 yards every six minutes, this corresponding to the infantry's hoped-for progress through the Bois l'Evêque. Thereafter, the previous rate of creep resumed. Six-inch howitzers searched the wood, and 60-pounders enfiladed the rides. The rest of the heavy artillery laid down a barrage on specific lines ahead of the creeper. The barrage instructions covering 18th Division have not survived, but would have been of slightly less complexity as the division did not have to contend with the wood. The 18th Battalion MGC swept the ravines behind Richemont Mill with fire; the 100th Battalion concentrated its fire on Garde Mill and its surroundings. 25th Battalion MGC fired 150,000 rounds from 40 guns on selected targets in the Richemont valley and the outskirts of Pommereuil.[37] Field artillery brigades

37 'Narrative of Machine Gun Operations' – Fourth Army, Chapter VI, TNA WO158/332.

and sections of 6-inch guns were ready to move forward as the infantry progressed, three of the latter to be positioned to shell the Aulnoye railway junction.[38]

The 10th Tank Battalion was assigned to the corps for the attack. The 6,000 yard approach march was made without incident despite hostile shelling with HE and gas. The eight tanks of C Company were allotted to the 25th Division and 15 to the 18th. In the latter division B Company with eight machines attached one section to both 53 and 54 Brigades. These machines were committed to the initial attack, whilst A Company with seven machines was to operate with 55 Brigade in attaining the final objective. The smaller allocation to 25th Division was due to the tank-unfriendly obstacle represented by the Bois l'Evêque. Lieutenant-Colonel Justice Tilly,[39] commanding 10th Tank Battalion, had met with first the divisional commanders and then the brigade commanders to plan the operation. His company, section and sub-section commanders had subsequently visited the infantry battalions with whom they would be working. Only two days had been available for reconnaissance, but it was clear that the Richemont stream which had to be crossed by both divisions would prove an obstacle in places, especially near the mills. It had been reconnoitred by two officers, but aerial photographs proved inadequate to predict the degree of difficulty. Indeed, Colonel Tilly had some dispute with GOC 18th Division about the number of tanks to attempt the Richemont from Garde Mill west of Pommereuil up to Richemont Mill, where the machines would have to wait close to any enemy counter-barrage. Although he succeeded in reducing the number of tanks in this area to four, Tilly was proved right – none of the four tanks made it across the Richemont for the reasons he had predicted.[40] In retrospect, 18th Division noted that: 'On the aerial photographs this waterway looked a mere brook. Really it was wide swamp'.[41]

25th Division was depleted in numbers, but was receiving new drafts. After the fighting of 18-19 October the 25th Battalion MGC, for instance, had lost so many men to sickness and casualties that it could only operate 48 of its 64 guns, and then on minimum teams.[42] The division's rifle strength, despite reinforcement, was only 3,290. It mounted its attack employing all three battalions of 7 Brigade, commanded by Brigadier-General Carlos Hickie, to take the first objective.[43] The brigade's strength was correspondingly low, less than 700 rifles,[44] and 1/8th Warwickshire of 75 Brigade were attached and in close support. They were to be used if necessary to take the first objective. All participating wore white brassards made of RE tape to enable them to be distinguished in the dark. 7 Brigade's attack would take it to the western edge of the Bois l'Evêque, where, as the battle progressed, its units would clear the western portion, the second objective. Two sections of D Company 25th MGC followed the brigade using direct fire 'silencing enemy machine guns and

38 A. Montgomery, *The Story of the Fourth Army in the Battles of the Hundred Days,* p.233.

39 Justice Crosland Tilly DSO MC was a lieutenant in the West Yorkshire Regiment in August 1914, employed with the King's African Rifles. He served with the Machine Gun Corps before moving to the Tank Corps in July 1917. In WW2 he served as GOC 2nd Armoured Division from May 1940 until being killed in an accident in January 1941.

40 War Diary, 10th Tank Battalion, 'Report on Operations, 23rd & 24th October 1918', TNA WO95/103/3.

41 G.H.F. Nichols, *The 18th Division in the Great War*, p.438.

42 The 40 guns committed to the barrage on the 23rd fired 150,000 rounds.

43 Carlos Joseph Hickie CMG (1973-1959) was commissioned in the Gloucestershire Regiment in 1893 but progressed through both Yorkshire Light Infantry and Royal Fusiliers. In 1914 he was brigade-major to the East Lancashire Infantry Brigade, and served in this role until given command of 14th Hampshire from January 1916.He commanded 115 Brigade from August 1916 to March 1917, and 7 Brigade from May 1918 until the Armistice.

44 Montgomery, op. cit., p.232.

one field gun'.[45] As the 18th Division's advance to the north outflanked the wood, another battalion of 75 Brigade would advance further up the western and northern edges, establishing posts that would protect the flank of the 18th. The remaining unit would clear the north-eastern part of the wood, thus achieving the third objective. Two sections of A Company 25th Battalion MGC operated with these two brigades. Finally, 74 Brigade would establish themselves on the northern edge to take the final two objectives. The division, no doubt with deliberate understatement, viewed its objectives as 'somewhat ambitious'.[46]

The attached tanks got off to a poor start.[47] C Company 10th Tank Battalion lost two of its eight tanks to mechanical trouble before operations began,[48] and a third on the approach march. Of the remaining five, three ditched in the area of the Richemont stream, which was prone to marshiness in its wooded valley north of Bazuel. Of the three who ditched, tank 9066, commanded by Lieutenant Alexander Levy,[49] had been directed under a railway bridge in Bazuel. Here he found another tank of his section returning, but the intensity of the enemy barrage made it impossible for him to question this tank's commander. Levy took an alternative route, the other machine following, and crossed the steep railway embankment and engaged the enemy machine-guns which soon opened fire on him, dispersing them. In the course of this action he lost direction, but met a group of infantry who directed him towards more machine-gun nests. En route to these he encountered yet another tank of his section, also lost, lying up in orchard. The three machines proceeded on to the indicated nests, and the enemy fled. Pursuing, Levy's tank became ditched on unfriendly ground obscured by the dark and fog. Attempting to warn the two following machines, Levy was too late, and all three became stuck.[50] Another of the bogged down machines was 'female' tank 9433, commanded by Sergeant Esmond Redmill MM.[51] He had originally been following Levy, but lost contact. Like his leader he was fired on as soon as he crossed the railway embankment and although he scattered the machine-gunners he was unfortunate enough to have his left gun sponson blown off by shell fire. Disorientation was now so general that the infantry he encountered could not tell him in which direction the enemy lay. Waiting in the orchard, he was located by Levy, and during the subsequent action came round his left, breaking through a hedge only to ditch in the swampy ground. To make matters worse, a shell immediately burst overhead 'smashing my signalling apparatus and the bevil gear box as well as breaking an unditching rail. Efforts to unditch proved of no avail'.[52]

If the tanks found the area to the north of Bazuel boggy and difficult to cross, the infantry found it no less problematic but for different reasons. 21st Manchester were on the brigade's right, and attacked on a two company front, directly into an area on the northern outskirts of Bazuel thick

45 'Narrative of Machine Gun Operations – Fourth Army', Chapter VI, TNA WO158/332.
46 Kincaid-Smith, op. cit., p.356.
47 These tanks were commanded by Captain Richard Charles Snewing who was commissioned in October 1915 and seconded to the Tanks Corps in October 1917.
48 Broken Coventry chains, the mechanism which connected the secondary gearbox to an assembly at the rear of the hull which drove the tracks.
49 A private in the Warwickshire Regiment, Levy had been commissioned into the Tank Corps in January 1917.
50 War Diary, 10th Tank Battalion, Battle History Sheet, Tank No. 9066, 23 October 1918, TNA WO95/103/3. Levy had fired ten 6-pounder and 400 machine-gun rounds.
51 Esmond Redmill had entered France in December 1914, and had been previously attached to 32nd Divisional Cycle Company.
52 War Diary, 10th Tank Battalion, Battle History Sheet, Tank No. 9433, 23 October 1918, TNA WO95/103/3.

with hedges and orchards. Although there was bright moonlight, gas and fog made keeping direction and touch very difficult and for Major Donald Murray,[53] commanding that day, 'the progress of the attack was for a long time uncertain'.[54] At 02.40 Captain J.H. Miller commanding No. 1 Company on the right reported that they were held up by a large amount of wire and machine-gun fire. There were insufficient tanks left operational to deal with a local difficulty such as this. Of the surviving pair of machines, one successfully negotiated the eastern end of the Richemont, proceeded past where Miller was struggling, and up a sunken road towards Pommereuil. This was tank 9056, commanded by Second-Lieutenant Leonard Huddleston,[55] also carrying the section commander, Captain Cecil Shott.[56] It was actually due to support 74 Brigade who would perform the second leapfrog to the final objectives, making rendezvous with them near Tilleuls Farm on the northern edge of the Bois l'Evêque south of Bousies. En route, however, they reached Pommereuil, a village further up the slope based on a crossroads with four converging streets lined with houses over some distance. Huddleston and Shott 'found it to be full of the enemy, patrols, machine-gunners and snipers'. No British infantry were apparent, and Shott decided to set about clearing the village, doing 'great execution among the hostile machine-guns and enemy personnel'.[57]. The tank spent two and a half hours at this job, aided by infantry arriving in job lots.

Major Murray was ordered by his brigadier to follow the tank into Pommereuil. There he found confusion. In addition to 7 Brigade's units, 20th and 21st Manchester and 9th Devonshire, even A Company of 1/8th Worcestershire of the leapfrogging 75 Brigade, who were to progress up the western edge of the Bois l'Evêque, had become involved in the fight for the village. The Worcesters' progress into the village had been exciting. At its south-western corner they had come across an enemy post of ten men firing from a house. 'They were killed', it was summarily recorded. Pushing on, 'two enemy officers, one of high rank, and their orderlies met OC A Company on the Garde Mill road. These two officers put up a good fight but were killed'.[58] Their orderlies escaped back to Pommereuil, and soon after, 'a mob of about 30 Germans' came down the road. They were fired

53 Donald Murray DSO and bar was commissioned in January 1915. The bar to his DSO was awarded for his actions at the Selle. The citation reads: 'In the absence of his commanding officer he commanded his battalion throughout the operations from 22nd October to 28th October, 1918. In the attack on Pommereuil on 23rd October, when, owing to darkness and mist, units had lost direction and became intermixed, he went forward and reorganised the attack, which was then entirely successful. He showed great courage and ability to command'. (*Edinburgh Gazette*, 11 December 1919, p.3911).

54 War Diary, 21st Battalion Manchester Regiment, 31 October 1918, 'Narrative of Operations from 19th–24th October 1918', TNA WO95/2244.

55 Leonard David Huddleston had been commissioned from corporal into the Tank Corps in March 1918. He won an MC for his actions on the 23rd. The citation reads: 'For marked gallantry and dash on 23rd October, 1918. He rendered great service to the infantry in the initial stages of the attack in the neighbourhood of Pommereuil, overcoming considerable enemy resistance, and taking the infantry to their final objective. He then helped to break up an enemy counter-attack. He destroyed several machine-gun nests, and conducted the infantry who had been held up to the third objective, where his Tank received three direct hits. Though severely wounded, he got his crew back to the rallying point and gave valuable information'. (*London Gazette*, 3 October 1919, p.12302)

56 Cecil Douglas Shott enlisted in 2nd Company London Yeomanry and arrived on the Western Front in December 1917.

57 War Diary, 10th Tank Battalion, 'Report on Operations, 23rd & 24th October 1918', TNA WO95/103/3. Shott fired 30 6-pounder and 1,500 machine-gun rounds in Pommereuil, capturing three officers, 50 other ranks and a horse ambulance. (Battle History Sheet, Tank No. 9056, 23 October 1918, TNA WO95/103/3).

58 OC A Company was Captain George Lawrence Watkinson commissioned in May 1915. He was awarded a bar to his MC. Sergeant Arthur Thomas John Sherwood was awarded a bar to his DCM

on and retreated, the pursing patrol finding that Pommereuil was still strongly held.[59] A Company decided to await reinforcement, but then spotted Huddleston's tank and followed it into the village.

9th Devonshire were in the centre of the 7 Brigade attack and became badly disorganised after crossing the Richemont, having to pause to regroup in a sunken road 300 yards to the north before pressing on. General Hickie had already ridden forward to Pommereuil with his groom, capturing three Germans himself, and returned via the Devon's HQ, ordering Captain Reginald Pridham, who was temporarily commanding, forward to the village as well.[60] Here Pridham found a mixed group of Devons and 21st Manchesters, perhaps numbering no more than 45 men, attempting to clear the village having already nearly been set upon by Huddleston's tank. Major Murray then arrived, having been next on Hickie's visiting list, and took charge of the brigade front, withdrawing the Devons into a reserve at the cemetery to the south of the town.[61] This was not before Private Norman Courtney MM had won the DCM for rushing a machine-gun post alone and accounting for the whole crew with his fists and a revolver.[62] Other rankers had similarly shown their initiative, Lance-Corporal Charles Tuckerman collecting together a group and attacking a house to capture eight prisoners.[63] Pridham slowly reorganised his battalion amongst the gravestones.[64]

20th Manchester advanced on the left of 7 Brigade, starting on the Le Cateau-Bazuel road north of the village, facing the Richemont stream which was wider in their area. Thirty ORs had been detailed to help the Royal Engineers bridge this obstacle, but the two leading companies had not waited and had waded the stream. From this point their progress was lost to battalion HQ. What was clear, however, was that there was a good deal of unsuppressed machine-gun fire from both Garde Mill to the north and from orchards on the west bank further south. Colonel Pilkington detailed his reserve company to deal with these hazards, a tank going forward to Garde Mill, and at daybreak they worked forward surrounding the pockets of enemy who immediately surrendered. General Hickie, always in touch with the situation, prior to his mission to Pommereuil had ordered both 1/8th Warwickshire of the supporting 75 Brigade and the reserve of 21st Manchester to mop-up the machine-gun nests lying behind the brigade's advance. The resistance of the unsuppressed outposts had been a particular problem, causing the units of the leapfrogging 75 Brigade

'leading a party of 3 men to attack a defended building and capturing the house with its garrison'. (H. FitzM. Stacke, *Worcestershire Regiment in the Great War, Vol. 2*, p.471).

59 War Diary, 10th Tank Battalion, Battle History Sheet, Tank No. 9433, 23 October 1918, TNA WO95/103/3. Redmill fired 1,000 machine-gun rounds.

60 Reginald Poole Pridham MC was commissioned in September 1914. His MC was awarded for his actions at the Selle. The citation reads: 'For conspicuous gallantry and ability. In the absence of his commanding officer he commanded his battalion throughout the operations from 22nd October to 28th October, 1918. In the attack on Pommerueil on 23rd October, when owing to darkness and mist units had lost direction and became intermixed, he went forward and reorganised the attack, which was then entirelv successful'. (*London Gazette*, 10 December 1919, p.15305).

61 In the service of keeping Brigadier Hickie informed of what was happening in Pommereuil, Private Rutter of the Royal Engineers won a DCM 'for the courageous way in which he successfully mended 15 breaks along 800 yards of telephone cable at a time when it was very doubtful whether a runner could get through'. (M. Kincaid-Smith, *The 25th Division in France and Flanders*, p.358).

62 Norman Courtney had been on the Western Front since July 1915.

63 Charles Tuckerman was a pre-war regular ranker who had been on the Western Front since November 1914. His DCM was awarded on 10 January 1920.

64 In 9th Devons, three officers were killed/died of wounds: Lieutenant Bernard Joseph Pym Yeatman, a gunner in the Royal Navy commissioned in July 1915; Lieutenant William Joseph Hyatt, commissioned from sergeant in January 1916 and Second-Lieutenant Marcus Webb Higgs, commissioned from private in May 1918. Ten ORs were killed with 80 wounded and two missing.

to become intermingled with the leading 7 Brigade. Captain Harold Mortimore, commanding the Warwicks that day,[65] took direction of the mixed group, steadily clearing nests, after which the battalion proceeded. Meanwhile, the two leading companies of the 20th Manchesters had entered Pommereuil to join the mêlée of units there. Sergeant P.C. Wright in 'female' tank 9348 had also passed under the railway at Bazuel, and overtook the Manchesters held up by unsuppressed machine-guns to their left on the slope up to Pommereuil. These retired as Wright engaged them, and he pressed on, losing touch with the infantry, 'making deviations of several hundred yards on either side where the steepness of banks permitted, firing at flashes and any possible infantry cover'. He then encountered the Devons reforming at the cemetery south of the village. Entering Pommereuil, as yet not entirely in British hands, a valve spring on the engine broke. He 'started work on [the] engine finding it necessary to keep close watch on enemy snipers whom [he] engaged with machine-guns', in the process capturing several enemy patrols which he handed over to the infantry. Eventually he got his engine started and was able to rally with the other surviving tanks.[66] The 20th Manchesters, catching up, had also participated in consolidating the town, and dug in on the eastern outskirts. The majority of the battalion's significant casualties had occurred in orchards to the south-west of the village. Three officers had been killed and two wounded, with an unknown but considerable number of casualties in the other ranks.[67] Their sister battalion, 21st Manchester, had also suffered heavily. They had been low in numbers going into action with a strength of 9 officers and 308 other ranks, and had suffered 98 casualties, a third of their numbers.[68] Despite the hard fighting, 7 Brigade was established on the edge of the Bois l'Evêque by 07.20, and between 18.00 and 23.00 that night, its units advanced into the centre of the wood, achieving their second objective somewhat later than planned. It was an action in which tanks had demonstrated their tactical virtues, and where order had been restored to a potentially chaotic situation by a brigadier keeping close touch with both the progress of the action and his battalion COs and working hard to restore command and control.

It was the task of the two remaining units of 75 Brigade to leapfrog and achieve the third objective. In forming up on the railway at Bazuel they were subject to heavy shelling. 1/8th Worcestershire proceeded across the Richemont encountering unsuppressed machine-gun posts. A Company, as we have seen, became embroiled in the struggle for Pommereuil. C and D Companies

65 Harold Mortimore, who had enlisted in 1914 and commissioned from the rank of lance-serjeant in the Seaforth Highlanders in June 1916, won a bar to MC for his actions that day. 'For gallantry and skilful leadership of his battalion in the attack near Pommereuil on the 23rd October, 1918. In the darkness and fog many enemy machine-guns were passed and remained in action. The situation south-west of Pommereuil was dangerous, when he found himself in command of the battalion. By an attack from a flank he successfully cleared away enemy opposition and allowed the advance of troops who had been previously held up'. (*London Gazette*, 10 December 1919, p.15304).

66 War Diary, 10th Tank Battalion, Battle History Sheet, Tank No. 9348, 23 October 1918, TNA WO95/103/3. Wright fired 1,500 machine-gun rounds.

67 War Diary, 20th Battalion Manchester Regiment, 'Narrative of Events from 18th October to 30th October 1918', TNA WO95/2244. The casualties in the other ranks on that day is not stated but in the whole of October, 78 ORs were killed with 223 wounded, 27 missing and 60 evacuated sick, the total losses for the month being 405, during which time 375 replacements were received. Amongst the dead of the 23rd were Captain Gwynned William Llewellyn Pritchard MC, commissioned from a sapper in the Royal Engineers in November 1915; Second-Lieutenant Arthur Hulme, commissioned from company sergeant major in June 1918; and Second-Lieutenant George Stanley Walker, commissioned from private in June 1916.

68 Two officers were wounded, as were 69 other ranks. There had been 6 OR fatalities but 13 were missing, 8 being sick.

had meanwhile progressed well, keeping up with the stationary barrage and lifts, and bypassing the fighting in the village, they moved up the western edge of the wood and round its northern face. They had moved at such a pace that they were now between one and two miles behind the enemy's front. Rounding the north-east corner of the wood they were fired on by three 10.5 cm howitzers hidden behind a hedge near Tilleuls Farm. Despite machine-gun and rifle fire from the attached enemy infantry, D Company, under the command of Lieutenant Edmund Wedgebury MC DCM MM, and numbering only 17 men, attacked the howitzers with Lewis guns, killing or capturing all the teams. Wedgebury, demonstrating the courage to which his three decorations attested, killed the battery commander himself.[69] The rear platoons were brought up, and the farm was rushed resulting in the capture of 150 men and five machine-guns, an action for which the DSO became Wedgebury's fourth award. Holding the northern edge of Bois l'Evêque, the Worcesters had captured not only the howitzers but a replete signals wagon. They were, however, out on a limb. No other units were up on their flanks, and they could see 'the enemy's "S.O.S." rockets were still shooting upwards from posts over a mile behind'. As dawn broke, a large body of Germans retreated up the valley just to the north. The Worcesters opened fire upon them, and a further seven officers and 100 men surrendered, bringing the total captures to 15 officers and 371 men.[70] The unit's losses that day numbered 47 with only three fatalities. The attached section of 25th Battalion MGC, however, had three guns knocked out during the fighting with significant casualties.

1/5th Gloucestershire, following from Bazuel, advanced 300 yards but were then similarly held up by the machine-gun positions that had not been mopped up, and 'for five hours heavy & stubborn fighting ensued'. Private Francis Miles of C Company now won the second Victoria Cross of the Selle fighting:

> When his company was held up by a line of enemy machine-guns in the sunken road near the Moulin J. Jacques. Pte. Miles alone, and on his own initiative, went forward, under exceptionally heavy fire, located a machine-gun, shot the gunner, and put the gun out of action. Observing another gun nearby, he again advanced alone, shot the gunner, rushed the gun, and

69 Edmund Wedgbury DSO MC DCM MM was commissioned from sergeant in June 1917. He was awarded the DSO for his actions on the 23rd. The citation reads: 'For conspicuous gallantry and leadership in command of a company forming a defensive flank along north-west edge of Eveque Wood, on 25th October, 1918 (sic). He advanced three miles through country held by the enemy, picking up two platoons, which had lost direction, and reached Tilleuls Farm, two miles in rear of the enemy's main line of resistance. Here, with only 17 men, he charged and captured three 4.2 howitzers, killing the battery commander himself and capturing two other officers and the crews. Thanks to his determination and coolness, the defensive flank was successfully formed, with a total capture of five officers and 156 men'. (*London Gazette*, 10 December 1919, p.15291). The two second-lieutenants, Stephen Thomas Bateman MM (commissioned from lance-corporal in January 1918) and Dennis Gordon (commissioned from sergeant in May 1918) were awarded the MC. The citation for Bateman's award reads: 'During operations of 23rd and 24th October, 1918, near Pommereuil, he showed marked gallantry and ability to command. His guide was wounded soon after the attack started, but he pushed on through Pommereuil, which was still held, and achieved his objective, a mile behind the enemy main line, and held on to it after capturing many prisoners. On the 24th, during operation through Fontaine au Bois, he gained his objective after being wounded, again doing excellent work. (*Edinburgh Gazette*, 11 December 1919, p.3947). Gordon's citation reads: 'During operations of 23rd October, 1918, against Tilleuls Farm he became detached from his company. Collecting men of other units, he led them forward with great gallantry against machine-gun and rifle fire. In the attack on Landrecies on 4th November. 1918, he showed great ability in leading his company'. (London Gazette 10 December 1919, p.15336).

70 Stacke, op. cit., p.371.

> captured the team of eight. Finally, he stood up and beckoned to his company, who, acting on his signals, were enabled to work round the rear of the line and to capture sixteen machine-guns, one officer, and fifty other ranks. It was due to the courage, initiative, and entire disregard of personal safety shown by this very gallant soldier that the company was enabled to advance at a time when any delay would have jeopardised seriously the whole operation.[71]

Eventually leapfrogging 7 Brigade in Pommereuil, B and D companies began their sweep through the the wood at 16.45, moving towards the Worcesters established on its northern edge. In contrast to their experience of the morning they met little resistance and finished on a line on a road through the wood running north-east towards Malgarni, forming a defensive flank to the wood's eastern corner. The attached guns of two sections of A Company and one of B Company 25th Battalion MGC were positioned to command the rides through the wood. For all their heavy fighting, the Glosters had suffered only eight fatal losses and 39 wounded.[72] The tanks, meanwhile, had continued in their support of the advance beyond Pommereuil. Tank 9056 under Lieutenant Huddleston had arrived near Tilleuls Farm on time at 08.10, despite its diversion through Pommereuil, but for the second time that day found itself alone. It went on 500-600 yards and returned, but at 11.30 was ordered to the south of Bousies to break up a local counter-attack, and in helping the infantry forward engaged two machine-gun nests. Huddleston's machine was finally hit by a field gun which registered a fine shot as it was apparently positioned near Ors. Having already suffered two direct hits, Huddleston, who was by now badly wounded, was forced to give up his run.[73]

74 Brigade, with whom Huddleston was supposed to rendezvous, were similarly to move through the northern edge of the Bois l'Evêque behind 75 Brigade and press the attack on the fourth and fifth objectives. In the eventuality, its three battalions, 9th Yorkshire on the right, 11th Sherwood Foresters in the centre and 13th Durham Light Infantry on the left would struggle to arrive on the third objective, let alone pass beyond it. The battalions began moving forward at 11.15, having been held up first by the intermingled brigades in their path, and then by opposition in an area between 25th and 18th Division which had been missed by the barrage. 9th Yorkshire cleared this up with the assistance of Stokes mortars. Subject to these delays, the units only reached the Green Line, their supposed jumping-off position along the northern edge of the wood, at 16.00. Here the DLI on the brigade's right reported being held up by machine-gun fire and wire on the road west of Rue du Pont, a village just east of the wood's most northerly corner,[74] and the Sherwood Foresters dug

71 *London Gazette*, 3 January 1919, p.308. Francis George Miles (1896-1961) left school at 13 and worked in the Princes Royal Company mines in Gloucestershire. He enlisted in 9th Gloucestershire with his stepfather on 28 December 1914. He arrived on the Western Front in September 1915, but after treatment for a foot infection, his battalion having been sent to Salonika, he joined the 8th Battalion and then served with the Royal Engineers as a tunneller. He was wounded a second time in July 1917 when he was buried alive by an exploding shell and was the sole survivor out of 50 men. After service in Italy he returned to the Western Front. He returned to work as a collier, and during WW2 served in the Pioneer Corps. http://www.glosters.org/milesvc.htm (accessed 10 April 2016).

72 War Diary, 1/5th Battalion Gloucestershire Regiment, 23 October 1918, TNS WO95/2251. The wounded included Lieutenant Frederick James Lovell (commissioned in September 1916 from private in the Lancashire Hussars Yeomanry) and Second-Lieutenant Hugh Busby (commissioned in May 1918 from private in the Wiltshire Yeomanry). The battalion numbered 564 men at the end of the week.

73 War Diary, 10th Tank Battalion, Battle History Sheet, Tank No. 9056, 23 October 1918, TNA WO95/103/3. Shott fired 30 6-pounder and 1,500 machine-gun rounds in Pommereuil.

74 War Diary, 13th Battalion Durham Light Infantry, 23 October 1918, TNA WO95/2247. Second-Lieutenant Charles Harold Bishop MC was killed, as were 25 ORs. Bishop had been commissioned

in to their left. The progress of 9th Yorkshire, however, had been held up by fire from the wood itself and they were ordered to take a roundabout route around the edges to be in position on the brigade's left to continue the attack the following day. These orders were issued by Major-General Charles himself, who had come forward to 74 Brigade HQ.[75] Both Hickie and Charles clearly had a belief in being close to the action to speed effective decision-making. 25th Division had only secured its first three objectives, but nearly the whole of Bois l'Evêque was in British hands, and the flank of 18th Division's advance was ensured. The central hindrances to progress had been the German outpost zone machine guns on the western bank of the Richemont, and the unexpectedly long time taken to clear Pommereuil. The first was a problem created by an advance conducted at night. The same protection offered to the advancing British by darkness was also of advantage to the German defenders. The second problem reflects the fact that the time taken and effort involved in subduing resistance in village clearance was always seemingly underestimated at the Selle.

On the left of the XIII Corps area, 18th Division, commanded by Major-General Richard Lee,[76] was attacking across relatively open country, where 'the enemy defence appeared to collapse under the excellent barrage'.[77] To the north, the boundary between the division and Third Army lay along the Roman road, whilst the boundary between the 18th and 25th Divisions lay through Garde Mill, skirted Pommereuil, and ran along the western edge of Bois l'Evêque. The division would attack with two brigades, the 53rd on the right, the 54th on the left. The 55th would follow close behind to pass through them and take the final objectives. 53 Brigade, commanded by Brigadier-General Michael Barker,[78] advanced with 7th Royal West Kent on the right and 10th Essex on the left, with 8th Royal Berkshire in support. The whole division had difficulties in forming up in a relatively small area, and the Berkshires were eventually sited in the old *HWL I*, which unhappily coincided with the German counter-barrage line. The West Kents had experienced a close encounter with losing their Battalion HQ. Colonel Hickson and his other officers were sitting down to breakfast in a shop basement in Le Cateau prior to the attack. 'There was a white tablecloth, some good quality borrowed crockery, eggs and bacon, and the first pot of marmalade that the expectant party had seen for weeks'. The direct hit that occurred claimed only one casualty, however – 'the breakfast had vanished'.[79] Setting off down the long exposed slope through the machine-gun outposts, the West Kents had two objectives on the Richemont, namely Ervillers Wood Farm and Garde Mill, on a front of 900 yards.[80] They then had to move up a steep exposed slope, cross the series of practice trenches on the dominating spur above the Richemont valley and

from private in June 1917.

75 J.E. Edmonds & R. Maxwell-Hyslop, *Military Operations – France and Belgium 1918, Vol V*, p.359. During the month of October, 9th Yorkshire suffered 6 officers killed and 15 wounded, with 63 ORs killed, 356 wounded and 47 missing. CWGC records indicate that Major Gerald Norman Hunnybun MC (commissioned in September 1914) was killed on the 23rd.

76 Richard Phillips Lee (1865-1953) was a colonel of the Royal Engineers in August 1914. He served as Chief Engineer to I Corps from September 1915 to May 1916, and Chief Engineer of Fifth Army from May 1916 to January 1917. He commanded 18th Division from that point until the end of the war.

77 War Diary, HQ 18th Infantry Division, 23 October 1918, TNA WO95/2017. Fifty-six machine-guns of 18th and 100th Battalions MGC fired in contribution to this barrage.

78 Michael George Henry Barker CB DSO (1884-1960) was a captain in the Lincolnshire Regiment in August 1914. He commanded 11th West Yorkshire from February 1916 to April 1918, being promoted to the command of 53 Brigade in April 1918. He commanded I Corps in 1940, unsuccessfully.

79 Nichols, op. cit., p.436.

80 7th Queen's Own Royal West Kent were commanded by Lieutenant-Colonel Lionel Henry Hickson, a regular captain of the regiment in August 1914, who had commanded since 23 August 1918.

The Richemont valley where 7th Royal West Kent attacked Ervillers Wood Farm. The downhill slope was heavily covered with machine gun nests.

reach the Forest-Pommereuil road. Here, the two tanks of B Company 10th Tank Battalion who would help clearing the outposts on the downhill slope would meet them.[81]

Unfortunately, 'owing to the difficulty experienced in finding battery positions' only half of 53 Brigade's front was covered by the 18-pounder barrage, although further ahead a 4.5-inch howitzer barrage could be laid down.[82] Whether due to this or not, in crossing the Richemont, the battalion suffered most of its casualties at the hands of trench mortars at Corbeau, a small set of houses higher up the slope beyond Ervillers Wood Farm on the left of their advance, where 'the gunners who fought them were admirable in their skill and fortitude'.[83] Here Lieutenant West and a small group cleared 60 of the enemy from cellars at the cost of only one casualty. This was Sergeant John Douglas Aitchison, who had scouted the enemy positions, crawling to one of the machine-gun nests and shooting the crew, before carrying on to the final objective even though seriously wounded in the neck.[84] Sergeant Alfred Gregory showed similar courage and initiative. He had not only carried out a number of daring reconnaissance patrols before the attack, but during it he rushed a machine-gun nest singlehanded, killing all the crew. After the final objective was reached, Gregory 'established two posts and proceeded to mop up a sunken road and the ground on his right flank, killing many of the enemy himself and capturing many prisoners'.[85] On their right, Garde

81 The machines were to cross the Richemont stream at Jean Jacques Mill.
82 Edmonds & Maxwell-Hyslop, op. cit., p.359.
83 Nichols, op. cit., p.439.
84 His DCM was awarded 10 January 1920.
85 *London Gazette*, 2 December 1919, p.14845.

Mill was taken by Captain Macdonald of B Company, isolated with 65 men, who killed many of the enemy, capturing 75, for the cost of 13 casualties. Before they had dealt with these strongholds, however, the West Kents had lost the support of the two tanks that had tackled machine-gun nests on the western bank of the Richemont where both were knocked out, as Justice Tilly had feared.[86] Despite this, the West Kents' progress over the spur was without major difficulties and by 05.00 had reached the objective on the road having taken some 400 prisoners.[87] 10th Essex, commanded by Major Alexander Churchill,[88] meanwhile had advanced from Baillon Farm. They were able to keep close to the barrage, despite having difficulties forming up due to harassing fire, and at the orchard to their front on the slope down to the valley bottom 'came into close contact with the enemy before he had an opportunity to man his machine-guns'. The remaining two tanks of B Company were due to assist with this, but the crew of one had been gassed at the starting point and the other was knocked out very quickly. The latter was No. 9072, commanded by Second-Lieutenant Lawes. In a sunken road in front of the railway, 700 yards from the start, the driver was hit by fire from one of the enemy outposts and the tank engine stopped. 'While the tank was stationary the enemy threw bombs tied in bunches of 3 at the tracks', not the first time that this happened to a tank in the Selle operations, and again a feat requiring courage. That the enemy had been successful in their mission was discovered when the engine was restarted. Not daunted by immobility, 'the crew fought the tank for 3 h[ou]rs before evacuating it', firing 53 6-pounder rounds and 275 machine-gun rounds.[89] The Essex unit cleared the orchard on their own. Having kept close to the barrage this was an easier task than for some other units facing the enclosed orchards that morning. C Company, mopping up, took 20 prisoners, five machine-guns and an anti-tank gun. Machine-guns at Ervillers Wood Farm enfiladed the right of the Essex unit as it crossed the Richemont, and a platoon of D Company helped silence these by crossing the stream and attacking the farm from the rear. Sweeping up the practice trench spur, D Company did not have the luck of the West Kent's, who had passed between the practice trenches to their left and the fighting in Pommereuil to their right. The Essex unit met with machine-gun fire, and became held up in a sunken road.

That tank 9072 spent three hours in immobile action on the western valley slope is a testament to the resistance of the unsuppressed enemy outposts, the like of which had created many problems for 25th Division. 8th Royal Berkshire,[90] advancing in support, had run into heavy fire from them. Indeed, one strong machine-gun nest killed Second-Lieutenant James Grant, commanding B Company, and rendered most of his company HQ casualties. Despite this, the Berkshires crossed the stream and pushed on up the spur until they came to the stalled Essex unit. After several

86 Tank 9848 commanded by Sergeant Wilson had fired 46 rounds of 6-pounder ammunition and 347 machine-gun rounds at these nests before it took a direct hit on the top and the crew had to evacuate. War Diary, 10th Tank Battalion, Battle History Sheet, Tank No. 9848, 23 October 1918, TNA WO95/103/3.

87 War Diary, 7th Battalion Royal West Kent Regiment, 'Battle Narrative', TNA WO95/2040. Second-Lieutenant Alan Baird Cullerne MC (commissioned from the rank of private in July 1917) was killed getting his men across the stream, the only officer fatality of the day. Second-Lieutenant Robert Bernard Lewin Hill MC (commissioned in January 1918) was wounded. In addition during October the battalion suffered 12 ORs killed, and a further two officers and 62 ORs wounded, with three missing.

88 Alexander Phayre Churchill had been commissioned into the Essex Regiment in 1896. He had served as a brigade-major between January 1916 and March 1918.

89 Unfortunately, whilst evacuating, Lawes and four of the crew were wounded. War Diary, 10th Tank Battalion, Battle History Sheet, Tank No. 9072, 23 October 1918, TNA WO95/103/3.

90 Commanded by Major Arthur Frederick Northcote, a regular lieutenant of the Devonshire Regiment in August 1914.

attempts, the obstructing machine-gun nests were taken by both units approaching under the cover of a fold in the ground and rushing the entrenched guns under covering fire as dawn broke. 'The enemy garrison immediately ceased fire and ran but the majority were either killed or wounded by Lewis Gun or rifle fire'. Over 30 heavy and light machine-guns were taken, which indicates the strength of the position.[91] 10th Essex reached their objective on the Forest-Pommereuil road at 04.15, having skilfully used classic fire and movement tactics to overcome all their opposition.[92] The Berkshires then pushed on to occupy the road from la Fayt Farm, south west of Bousies, to Tilleuls Farm, where they linked up with Lieutenant Wedgebury and his party of Worcesters on the north side of the wood.[93]

54 Brigade, commanded by Brigadier-General Oswald Borrett,[94] attacked on the left of the division, 2nd Bedfordshire leading. The brigade had a 'parapet strength' of only 48 officers and 1,197 ORs.[95] Tapes had been laid out, but assembly had been interrupted by heavy bursts of fire at 23.15 and 00.15. As soon as the infantry advance from the railway line began, the attached mobile field guns came under the control of Colonel Arthur Percival of the Bedfords, who were also accompanied by one section of B Company 18th Battalion MGC.[96] The ground was particularly convoluted immediately in front of their attack. The Richemont stream, which lay parallel to the starting line of the advance of the other formations of XIII Corps, followed the base of the Forest spur which rose to the battalion's left and ran due east bisecting their line, to join the Selle to their rear. Further, there were three small gullies on the northern bank running into the Richemont valley, which lay parallel to the Bedford's advance. The stronghold of Richemont Mill nestled in the valley opposite these gullies, and just to its north lay a much longer gully, White Spring. This contained another small stream in its bottom, and the gully ran in a north-easterly direction, the left bank

91 War Diary, 8th Battalion Royal Berkshire Regiment, 23 October 1918, TNA WO95/2037. The battalion's strength on 19 October was 39 officers and 765 ORs.

92 War Diary, 10th Battalion Essex Regiment, 'Narrative of Operations on October 23rd near LE CATEAU', TNA WO95/2038. 10th Essex had a trench strength of 19 officers and 563 ORs at the start of October. The battalion had four officers wounded that day, Lieutenants James Valentine Jacklin (commissioned in June 1915) and Bernard Alfred Morrow (commissioned in March 1915 from private in the 15th London Regiment), and Second-Lieutenants William Herbert Dean (commissioned in March 1917) and Ernest George Ovenden (commissioned in November 1917 from the rank of sergeant-major in the ASC). In the month of October 20 ORs were killed and 139 wounded. CWGC records do not list any fatalities on the 23rd.

93 In addition to Second-Lieutenant James Grant, Second-Lieutenant Norman Henry Gershorn Blackburn (commissioned from private in October 1917) was also killed. Second-Lieutenants Francis Winton Beeny (commissioned in February 1918), William Deans (commissioned from sergeant in the RAMC in March 1918) and William Alexander McConnell (commissioned in May 1918) were wounded as was the medical officer, Captain William Haig Ferguson MC. Twenty ORs were killed/died of wounds, and 67 were wounded with two missing. Among the dead was Company Sergeant Major Arthur Beaufoy who had arrived on the Western Front in August 1915 as a private.

94 Oswald Cuthbert Borrett KCB CMG CBE DSO (1878-1950) was a regular captain of the Royal Lancaster Regiment in August 1914. He commanded 5th Shropshire Light Infantry from August 1915 to July 1916, transferred to command 1st Royal Lancaster until July 1917 when he was promoted to command 197 Brigade until April 1918, commanding 54 Brigade from 12 October 1918.

95 11th Royal Fusiliers numbered 365; 2nd Bedfordshire 468; and 6th Northamptonshire 412. Over the two days 23-4 October the brigade lost a third of its strength, 446 effectives. War Diary, HQ 54 Infantry Brigade, October 1917, TNA WO95/2042.

96 Arthur Ernest Percival CB DSO and bar OBE MC was a clerk in August 1914. He commanded 7th Bedfordshire from January to May 1918, and 2nd Bedfordshire from the end of July to the Armistice. As a lieutenant-general he was forced to surrender Singapore to the Japanese in February 1942.

Richemont Mill. The gullies attacked by 2nd Bedfordshire lie to the rear of the mill, running down from the Forest Spur.

being part of the Forest spur, the right bank forming the slope up to the practice trench spur on which the Essex and Berkshire units would be fighting together. Indeed, at the head of the gully, there were further practice trenches.

Two tanks from B Company 10th Tank Battalion were allocated to the first objective and two to the second. One machine broke down with track trouble and never reached the starting point. The other, 'female' tank 9331 commanded by Second-Lieutenant Powell, set off on a six mile odyssey during which it expended 1,000 machine-gun rounds. Whilst it cleared a number of machine-gun posts it was clearly unsure of direction, and ended its report, somewhat defensively: 'It did not desert the infantry'.[97] C Company of the Bedfords had first to take the three gullies and then Richemont Mill, which had been subjected to the enfilade fire of forty machine-guns from a position east of Le Cateau.[98] As the Bedfords would discover, the areas north and south of the mill were heavily defended by many machine-guns. The first two gullies north of the mill were taken easily, but progressing over the spur to the third exposed C Company to heavy machine-gun fire. Progress stalled, but 'good leading by Lieut. H.D. Chester and 2nd Lieut. W. Ashton M.C. got the company going again'.[99] A Company passed north of the gullies, further up the slope, but lost Lieutenant Clarence Hart before they hit their most strenuous opposition near White Spring.[100] D

97 War Diary, 10th Tank Battalion, Battle History Sheet, Tank No. 9331, 23 October 1918, TNA WO95/103/3.
98 Montgomery, op. cit., p.235.
99 Henry Dibble Chester was commissioned in October 1915 and William Ashton MC, who was wounded in this action, was commissioned from corporal in June 1917.
100 Clarence Herbert Hart was commissioned in March 1915.

Company also became involved in the fighting around the Richemont gullies, but Captain Philip Reiss sent a platoon on after Lieutenant Powell's tank and they managed to keep up with the barrage.[101] B Company on the right of the attack ran into further unsuppressed machine-guns located within the barrage start line, and 'it was entirely due to the splendid leadership displayed by 2nd Lieut[enant] H.B. Lang and other officers and N.C.O.s who led the men forward in the face of intense machine-gun fire and bayonetted the gunners, that the company was got going again'.[102] The barrage had been lost, but the company fought its way forward. The Bedfords achieved their objective on the Forest-Pommereuil road, which ran across the head of the White Spring gully, but the fighting had been heavy. Many Germans had been killed, and 'their dead were numerous all over the battlefield'. A hundred prisoners, over 60 machine-guns, three artillery pieces and three trench mortars, as well as two anti-tank rifles had been captured, but the Bedfords had suffered 129 wounded and 32 killed.[103]

11th Royal Fusiliers, commanded by Lieutenant-Colonel Kingsmill Gwynn,[104] were to pass through 2nd Bedfordshire. Unsuppressed machine-guns and artillery caused them trouble from the outset. Captain Wilfred Hornfeck's company were to move in single file across a narrow foot-bridge across the Richemont, but the enemy immediately put down a heavy barrage on it. His men faltering, Hornfeck pushed to the front and encouraged his men across, remaining under fire throughout.[105] The battalion then ran into further machine-gun fire on the slope north-east of Richemont Mill.[106] Passing through the Bedfords they began to take more casualties, being held up by field guns near the cemetery east of Forest which crowned the spur to their left. They had been assigned two tanks, but only one met them on the Montay-Forest road. This was tank 9326 commanded by Second-Lieutenant Leonard Pulley.[107] The Fusiliers were pleased with the support it gave: 'This tank did remarkably fine work … in spite of the fact that it was fired on at close range

101 Philip Julius Reiss MC and bar MM had been commissioned from CSM in the 18th Royal Fusiliers in August 1916.

102 Harry Beckett Lang MC was a Canadian medical student who enlisted as a private in 6th Canadian Field Ambulance. He was commissioned in June 1917. He won his MC during the Selle fighting: 'During the operations on the 22nd October 1918, near Le Cateau, he was in command of one of the leading companies. When his company was held up by machine-gun fire he organised local encircling movements which were entirely successful in dealing with the machine-guns and enabled the advance to be continued to the final objective. During this and the following day he behaved most gallantly'. (*London Gazette*, 8 October 1919, p.3281).

103 War Diary, 2nd Battalion Bedfordshire Regiment, 'Narrative of Operations N.E. of Le Cateau 23rd/24th October 1918', TNA WO95/2042. In addition to Lieutenant Hart, Second-Lieutenant William Frederick Shirley Wilford MM (commissioned from private in May 1918) died of wounds two days later. Lieutenant Charles James Vowles (commissioned in April 1918) was also wounded.

104 Kingsmill Douglas Hoseason Gwynn DSO and bar was a retired lieutenant of the South Wales Borderers in August 1914.

105 Wilfred Hornfeck MC had been commissioned from private in June 1917. He had performed a similar act of leading from the front at Ronssoy on 18 September, and was awarded the MC. (Nichols, op. cit., p.442).

106 They lost Second-Lieutenant Lawrence to this, killed. John James Lawrence was commissioned from sergeant in June 1917.

107 Leonard John Pulley was commissioned from sergeant in the Machine Gun Corps in March 1918. He was awarded the MC for his actions on the 23rd. The citation reads: 'For marked gallantry and energy on 23rd October, 1918, in the neighbourhood of Forest, and Bousies. Owing to the darkness he immediately got out of the Tank and directed it on foot, pointing out targets to his gunners under heavy machine-gun fire. Later, he cleared enemy machine-guns for an infantry company, and personally led the company to their final objective'. (*London Gazette*, 4 October 1919, p.12328)

by 2 field guns and had to engage several machine-gun nests which should have been already dealt with by the preceding tanks and infantry'. It advanced with the infantry to within 200 yards of the final objective before it had to return being low on petrol. Pulley 'shewed great determination, and although his tank was pierced in several places by armour-piercing bullets, rendered the greatest assistance throughout the attack'.[108] A further five 77-mm guns in an orchard east of Croix, a thousand yards further on the road through Forest, had been captured by Lieutenant Leslie Willis, leading his company with 'remarkable skill and daring'.[109] Despite a period when both flanks were in the air, and the leading company had to withdraw, the Royal Fusiliers secured their objective, capturing eleven artillery pieces in all.

55 Brigade, commanded by Lieutenant-Colonel Alfred Irwin from the day of the attack as Brigadier-General Edward Wood had reported sick,[110] followed the two leading brigades. 8th East Surrey followed the 53rd and 7th Buffs the 54th. The brigade's battalions had one section of machine-guns and one of trench mortars attached.[111] Seven tanks had been allocated to the brigade, but forming up north of Montay they were caught by the enemy's counter-preparation and one tank had a track blown off. The battalions of 55 Brigade had followed the lead formations so closely that 'there was considerable risk of their becoming involved in the fighting prematurely'.[112] They did not, however, meet opposition until 07.20 about 1,000 yards west of the second objective, the road running north-west from Tilleuls Farm to Forest, where they were to perform their leapfrog. The East Surreys, commanded by Major Walter Baddeley,[113] had thus to fight simply to achieve their jumping-off position on the road. From here, they pushed on towards Bousies across open country 'described by several officers who took part as a "CODFORD Field Day"'.[114] In practice, field day it was not. The unit had arrived on its jump-off line forty minutes after the barrage had moved on, and they advanced without artillery cover. Although the East Surreys captured la Fayt Farm at about the same time that Epinette to their left was taken, both were 'formidable enemy strongholds',[115] and the Germans resisted with all means at hand. Epinette had in fact fallen

108 War Diary, 11th Battalion Royal Fusiliers, 'Report on Operations carried out by the 11th Bn. The Royal Fusiliers from Oct. 23rd to Nov. 4th 1918', TNA WO95/2045.

109 Leslie Charles Willis had been commissioned in May 1915. He was awarded the MC: 'During the operations on 23rd October 1918 east of Le Cateau. He led his company with remarkable skill and daring, and was instrumental in capturing a battery of enemy 77 m.m. guns, together with a large number of machine-guns. Throughout the day he set a very fine example to his men'. (*Edinburgh Gazette*, 8 October 1919, p.3320).

110 Alfred Percy Bulteel Irwin DSO was a regular lieutenant of the East Surrey Regiment in August 1914. He commanded 8th East Surrey from June 1916. Wood accompanied the leading battalion on its march to get into position, and then returned to divisional HQ, sent four days later for six months rest in the UK.

111 The orders to the attached machine-gun sections stated: 'During the advance, M.G. Section Commanders will make every endeavour to engage all suitable targets and to co-operate generally with the "fire and movement" tactics of the infantry'. They were also to 'suggest suitable defensive positions for his guns to take up to cover the lines of final objective on the usual principle of disposing them in echelon to a depth of 1500 yards from the front line'. War Diary, HQ 55 Infantry Brigade, Order No. 225, 22 October 1918, TNA WO95/2048.

112 War Diary, HQ 55 Brigade, 'Narrative No. 6 – The Capture of Bousies and Robersart', TNA WO95/2048.

113 Walter Hubert Baddeley was a divinity student in August 1914. He commanded 8th East Surrey from 18 September 1918 to the Armistice. During WW2 he was Bishop of Melanesia. The battalion had one section of machine-guns and one trench mortar attached.

114 War Diary, HQ 55 Brigade, 'Narrative No. 6 – The Capture of Bousies and Robersart', TNA WO95/2048. Codford Camp was in Wiltshire on the rolling Salisbury Plain training area.

115 Nichols, op. cit., p.445.

to the 7th Buffs. They had suffered 15 casualties simply forming up behind the railway line, and as with the East Surreys, they were fired on whilst approaching their start line. Their main trouble, emanating from a set of machine-gun nests, 'was settled by an aeroplane dropping 4 bombs on the position',[116] a feat which is rightly described as precision bombing. They started from the line of the second objective at 08.00, and to the south-east of Forest D Company on the left outmanoeuvred and captured a group of enemy artillery although shortly after this the company commander, Captain Eric Morse, was killed.[117] C Company on the right performed a similar feat. Having mastered Epinette farm, by 10.00 the battalion had established a line on the edge of woods where the farm lay, to the south-west of Bousies, these having been cleared by Second-Lieutenant Henry White's tank. Battalion HQ moved up into the farm, a few yards behind the front line in the trees, and Lieutenant-Colonel Hubert Curtis placed both front line companies under the unified command of Captain Arthur Whitmarsh.[118] Here they attempted to fathom what was occurring in Bousies, a thousand yards away to the north-east.

Bousies covered about a square mile and was surrounded by the typical orchards with their thick hedges, on the east side of which the enemy had dug machine-gun nests as well as fortifying houses and barns. The Official Historians described Bousies as a 'labyrinth',[119] and 'in all these posts throughout the day the enemy fought most desperately', the British infantry fighting on 'with determination'.[120] The buildings of the village were strongly built, ideal for defence, and there was a large Renault factory. Curtis ordered Whitmarsh to push on. The colonel then found himself in the unusual position of being bombarded by intelligence from a range of sources. Tank 9440 commanded by Corporal W.A. Taylor operating just north of the wood that sheltered the Buffs 'captured a small enemy field gun with a map showing enemy organisation', which Taylor delivered to Colonel Curtis.[121] Soon after, an aircraft dropped a message: 'Huns still in BOUSIES – our boys in eastern part mopping up. Hun transport just galloped from village'. At 12.30 tank 9145 commanded by Lieutenant James Gray reported to Curtis that A Company, the right support company under Lieutenant Philip Greig, was in the village mopping up, and on this news the rest of the battalion proceeded.[122] Gray's tank had been in action well before reaching Bousies, dealing with a series of machine-gun nests with his 6-pounder guns. 'Several times (Gray) reconnoitred forward in front of the infantry and dealt with many machine-guns shewing absolute disregard of

116 War Diary, 7th Battalion East Kent Regiment, 'Report on Operations 22nd – 26th October 1918', TNA WO95/2049.

117 Eric Victor Morse MC was commissioned in September 1914, and had been on the Western Front since December 1915.

118 Hubert Montagu Cotton Curtis was a retired captain of the Imperial Yeomanry in August 1914. He commanded 2/6th South Staffordshire from April 1917 to July 1918 and 7th Buffs from September to November 1918. Arthur John Whitmarsh DSO was commissioned in November 1914.

119 Edmonds & Maxwell-Hyslop, op. cit., p.361.

120 War Diary, HQ 55 Brigade, 'Narrative No. 6 – The Capture of Bousies and Robersart', TNA WO95/2048.

121 War Diary, 10th Tank Battalion, Battle History Sheet, Tank No. 9440, 23 October 1918, TNA WO95/103/3.

122 Philip Humphreys Greig was commissioned in November 1915. He was awarded the MC for his actions on the 23rd. The citation reads: 'East of Le Cateau, on 23rd October, 1918, he showed great skill and tact in the handling of his company, and was an example of courage, cheerfulness and determination to his men. When wounded in the leg, he refused to relinquish command, and only consented to do so when compelled by a second and more serious wound in the chest. His work throughout was admirable'. (*London Gazette*, 4 October 1919, p.12294).

danger and his own personal safety'.[123] Gray, in his own words, 'assisted in organising and carrying out an advance on both sides of the Croix-Bousies road'.[124] Noting that he had received permission to retire at 15.00 the modest Canadian did not mention in his report that with all his crew casualties, he had taken over driving the tank himself and promptly dealt with a troublesome machine-gun nest solo by running it over.

Advancing on Bousies from la Fayt Farm, field guns and machine-guns had enfiladed the approach of the East Surreys. They fought their way into the village, supported by the attached section of tanks, mopping up resistance around the factory in the south-eastern outskirts. Tank 9164 commanded by Second-Lieutenant Henry White, which had cleared the woods at Epinette, was told by the infantry company commander in the vicinity that 'he was being badly sniped from the factory and houses near', so White promptly 'went and fired several rounds of 6 p[ounde]r A.P. into these'.[125] The road leading south-east out of Bousies was being heavily shelled, and enemy machine-guns were very active firing from a ridge to the north-east. 'Two flashes' caught White's attention on the road leading out of the centre of the town running north-west. These made him 'break through the hedge and I found 2 field guns. I put these out of action and then proceeded across the brook in direction of the ridge.' Unfortunately 'the M.G.s here offered strong resistance and an anti-tank bullet penetrated my engine cover and wounded one of the crew'.[126] White had to retire, but by 15.00 a line of posts had been established on the east of the town with supporting companies in cellars behind.[127] The East Surreys had by this time suffered 87 casualties.[128] The Buffs were also established on the road on the far side of Bousies, but were held up by machine-gun fire from the north.[129] 55 Brigade stated that it was not before 20.00 that the village was fully

123 War Diary, 7th Battalion East Kent Regiment, 'Report on Operations 22nd – 26th October 1918', TNA WO95/2049. James Roy Gray, a Canadian student, had enlisted in November 1914 as a private in the Canadian Motor Machine Gun Brigade, and had arrived in France in December 1915. He had been commissioned in February 1917 second-lieutenant in the Machine Gun Corps, and subsequently transferred to the Tank Corps. Gray was awarded the MC for his actions. 'For great gallantry and good work on 24th October, 1918, north-east of Bousies. He went into action with his Tank and knocked out machine-gun posts, thus enabling the infantry to advance without casualties. Later, he ran into a nest of machine-guns, his tank was riddled with armour-piercing bullets, wounding four of his gunners and his driver. He promptly drove the Tank himself, and although his guns were out of action, he succeeded in putting out the nest of machine-guns by running over them and dispersing their crews'. (*London Gazette*, 4 October 1919, p.12294).

124 War Diary, 10th Tank Battalion, Battle History Sheet, Tank No. 9145, 23 October 1918, TNA WO95/103/3. Gray used 20 rounds of 6-pounder ammunition and 250 machine-gun rounds.

125 AP = armour piercing. Henry James White had been commissioned in February 1918.

126 War Diary, 10th Tank Battalion, Battle History Sheet, Tank No. 9164, 23 October 1918, TNA WO95/103/3. This tank fired 115 rounds of 6-pounder ammunition and 600 machine-gun rounds.

127 War Diary, 8th Battalion East Surrey Regiment, 'Report on Operations carried out by the 8th East Surrey Regiment at Bousies and Robersart', TNA WO95/2050.

128 On 21 October the strength of the battalion was 22 officers and 640 ORs. Second-Lieutenants Alfred Herbert Osborn (commissioned from private June 1918), Charles Bernard Marks (commissioned in April 1918), and Frederick Alexander Staley (commissioned from private in April 1917) had been killed, and Second-Lieutenants Archibald James Bone (commissioned December 1917) and Reginald Herbert Warren (commissioned from private in May 1918) wounded. Eleven ORs had been killed with 58 wounded and 16 missing.

129 No record of the 7th Buffs' casualties that day exists, but CWGC records indicate 20 fatalities, including Captain Morse and Sergeant William Joseph Miles. Miles, a shipwright, had been serving in the 3rd Battalion in August 1914, having enlisted in 1905, and he had served on the Western Front since January 1915.

cleared by its two battalions, and did not hold back on explicit criticism of the over-optimistic expectations of Fourth Army: 'The systematic clearance of such a large village could not proceed at the pace laid down for the advance'.[130] The GSO I of 18th Division, Lieutenant-Colonel Guy Blewitt,[131] who was right at the front, postponed any further advance, and Major-General Lee approved this decision.[132]

18th Division had experienced a day of hard fighting, and although it had advanced 8,000 yards, by its end it was not established on the fourth objective. 55 Brigade, despite its reservations concerning the objectives, however, regarded it as a 'most successful day'. It recorded that: 'Great credit is due to the leadership shown by all officers and NCOs', and praised the supporting artillery for 'the rapidity with which requests were complied with'. There was 'an excellent co-operation of all arms'.[133] The tanks, in particular, had had a very active day, demonstrating their tactical worth. In the air above Fourth Army there had been a great deal of activity, 602 flying hours being clocked up by 275 pilots. Six successful reconnaissances were carried out and 17 artillery patrols made 26 zone calls as a result of which five hostile batteries were put out of action. Enemy aircraft were very active over 18th and 25th Divisions, however, two-thirds of the German machines operating in this area. Two strong patrols were seen, but 'the general tendency was not aggressive, most of the flying being behind the enemy's lines', the Germans clearly attempting to prevent observation over their *Second Army*. Fourth Army records note that 50 combats took place, claiming that four enemy aircraft were downed, although six British machines were lost.[134] Two of the successful combats occurred over Englefontaine, on the border between Third and Fourth Armies. Captain Malcolm McGregor of 35 Squadron attacked a DFW two-seater enemy aircraft at close range,[135] bringing it down; and Captain William Reed of 92 Squadron attacked another DFW two-seater out of the sun and from the front, watching it crash into a hedge.[136] Just to the west over Third Army, Captain James Robb of 92 Squadron dived on yet another DFW two-seater and brought it down over Poix du Nord. Lieutenants Horace Fenwick and Jack Holmes also brought down a Fokker Biplane whilst on a photographic mission.[137] Another decisive combat belonged to Captain Walter Southey on offensive patrol who spotted 9 Fokker bi-planes and with two flights of S.E.5's above him attacked with his flight.[138] 'We had a short dog-fight lasting about ten minutes during which I had several indecisive combats'. Towards the end of this: 'I got on the tail of one Fokker and within about 50 feet. I then fired about 200 rounds into the E.A. and saw him go down in … an uncontrollable spin',

130 War Diary, HQ 55 Brigade, 'Narrative No. 6 – The Capture of Bousies and Robersart', TNA WO95/2048.
131 Guy Blewitt DSO MC was a captain of the Oxford & Buckinghamshire Light Infantry in August 1914 and served in staff posts from July 1915, being appointed the GSO1 of 18th Division on 29 June 1918.
132 Edmonds & Maxwell-Hyslop, op. cit., p.361.
133 War Diary, HQ 55 Brigade, 'Narrative No. 6 – The Capture of Bousies and Robersart', TNA WO95/2048. The 53 guns captured that day was a record for the division.
134 War Diary, HQ Fourth Army, 23 October 1918, TNA WO95/439.
135 Malcom Charles McGregor DFC was a New Zealander commissioned into the RFC in January 1917 and credited with 11 victories. He was killed in an air accident in 1936.
136 William Ernest Reed DFC was commissioned from the Tyne Electrical Engineers into the Durham Fortress Engineers in June 1915, and seconded into the RFC in September 1916. He was credited with nine victories.
137 Horace Edgar Fenwick was commissioned in September 1916 and transferred to the RAF in April 1918. He was killed crash-landing at Kenley Aerodrome on 4 November 1920 in fog. Jack Armitage Holmes was commissioned from private in October 1917.
138 Walter Alfred Southey was commissioned from private into the RFC in Novemeber 1916. With 20 aerial victories including five balloons, he was the second most successful ace in 84 Squadron. He died in 1920 in a motorcycle accident.

to crash near Fontaine.[139] Typical of an indecisive combat that day was that involving Lieutenants William Amery and Francis Nottingham. On a counter-attack patrol at 09.30 they were dived on by three Fokkers. Nottingham fired 70 Lewis gun rounds and a red Very light and the enemy aircraft flew away. They then encountered 'many Halberstadts and Fokkers coming back from [a] bombing raid' which dived and fired on them. Nottingham again fired 50 Lewis gun rounds and the enemy machines flew off. Similarly, Lieutenant A. Glen was over Bousies at 14.50 watching 'many low flying E.A.' when he was suddenly attacked by two Fokker bi-planes, the first burst hitting his observer in the back. This unnamed flyer, although badly wounded, fired 100 rounds at close range and drove the Fokkers off. The sheer number of enemy aircraft is noted by Captain James Pearson who encountered ten enemy aircraft 'who were reinforced by 10 others, and proceeded to attack them. We were joined by some S.E.5's and a running fight took place'. Despite firing 300 rounds, Pearson could not record a hit.[140] In terms of ground attack, Fourth Army recorded that only 72 25-pound bombs were dropped. 3rd Squadron Australian Flying Corps however made 14 offensive flights, and of these half were bombing runs. William Palstra made two such flights that day. The first was at 07.30 when he dropped three phosphorous bombs on the Happegarbes Spur to the front of 6th Division's advance, and at 12.25 he went up again and dropped six 25-pound bombs on the east side of the canal opposite Catillon from whence the British advance was being enfiladed. In one of three ground attacks, Lieutenant Jack Pengilley dropped five 25-pound bombs on limbers (at whom his observer Lieutenant Christopher Fenwicke fired 180 Lewis gun rounds) and an ammunition dump. For their pains their RE8 was shot down on the way back near Fontaine.[141]

The fighting on 23 October 'was the biggest successful moonlight operation undertaken in France during the course of the war'. The history of 10th Essex expressed the belief that the tactic saved a large number of lives, and 'gave a sense of confidence in the capable handling of affairs by our higher commanders'.[142] Even using a night attack, however, heavy casualties had been sustained due to machine guns nests in the Richemont Valley, and a highly accurate and heavy enemy counter-barrage. At the end of the day, Fourth Army had again not secured its objectives. To the east, in the IX Corps area, the villages of Catillon and Ors had not been taken and would remain in enemy hands until 4 November. In XIII Corps area to the north, the fourth objective had not been achieved. On the other side of the Roman road, V Corps of Third Army had similarly not obtained all its objectives, but had broadly kept up, having taken the village of Vendegies-aux-Bois to the north-west of Bousies. During the day over 849 prisoners and 40 guns had been captured, the majority of these by XIII Corps.[143] There had been a balance for the enemy between withdrawal beyond the canal in the south and the need to protect the flank of the German forces in the north. Many of the enemy close to the waterway, however, had 'simply bolted'. 2 Brigade noted that: 'In one place preparations for breakfast showed the haste with which they had evacuated the cellar', whilst one wag had tarried 'to chalk up "GOOD-BYE" on the side of a house'.[144]

139 Southey also brought down an enemy observation balloon.
140 James William Pearson was commissioned in November 1917.
141 Squadron Record Book, 3 Squadron Australian Flying Corps, 23 October 1918, AWM4 Item No. 8/6/22 Part 2. Jack Joseph Pengilley transferred from the Australian Light Horse to the Royal Flying Corps in November 1916, as did Christopher Rupert Fenwicke.
142 T.M. Banks and R.A. Chell, *With the 10th Essex in France*, p.311.
143 The prisoners were from 'the *8th*, *17th Reserve*, *44th Reserve*, *121st*, *204th* and *243rd Divisions*, and the *2nd Cyclist Brigade*. Of these Divisions the *8th* and the *204th* were in the act of relieving the *44th Reserve* and *121st Divisions* in the Bousies and Catillon areas respectively'. Montgomery, op. cit., p.236.
144 War Diary, HQ 2 Infantry Brigade, 23 October 1918, TNA WO95/1268.

Thursday 24 October 1918

On the 24th, Fourth Army tasked its two corps with taking the objectives that had not been achieved the previous day. In IX Corps, 71 Brigade of 6th Division had reached a line by night about half-way through the eastern corner of the Bois l'Evêque, and was relieved by 16 Brigade which resumed the assault under a creeping barrage at 09.30. Generals Braithwaite and Marden, again models of thoroughness, visited the adjacent 25th Division the previous afternoon and returned to hold a conference with their own battalion commanders to ensure that the adjacent brigades of both divisions understood the attack.[145] A machine-gun barrage was put down on the south-east edge of the wood and the ground between the wood and the canal. The two attacking battalions formed up on the defensive flank maintained by XIII Corps through the centre of the wood during the night, and attacked in a south-easterly direction. On the right, 2nd York and Lancaster met less opposition than had been offered the previous day, and were on their objective by 11.30. 1st Shropshire Light Infantry attacked on the left. Barrage lifts that morning were 100 yards every six minutes due to the expected thickness of the scrub in Bois l'Evêque, but in fact progress proved relatively easy, and the advancing troops for once had to halt and wait for the barrage to move on. The unit's line was established on the objective on the right, but not on the left where 25th Division were struggling.[146] Elsewhere on their front, IX Corps patrolled the canal. By the following day, the corps was on the canal south of Catillon and established in the western outskirts of the village itself, and was able to exploit Ors with patrols, but not occupy it. A small area of the eastern tip of Bois l'Evêque remained outside the British grasp, due to machine-gun fire from high ground to the east.

XIII Corps had a more strenuous day, attacking at 04.00 with 25th Division fielding 74 Brigade and 18th Division attacking with 55 and 54 Brigades. 10th Tank Battalion believed that they would have eight machines available, four from A Company to work with 55 Brigade; and four tanks to work with the 25th Division, two supporting 74 Brigade.[147] On the day, however, two machines broke down and only six arrived on the start line.[148] In the 25th Division area, 74 Brigade had positioned itself at the end of the previous afternoon on the northern edge of the Bois l'Evêque and all three battalions attacked under a creeping barrage with 1/8th Worcestershire operating on the left flank. The division found itself attacking the largely uncut barbed wire of the hastily prepared *Hermann Stellung II,* which had been encountered the previous afternoon. The division stated that 'nothing had been previously known of this line', which reflects the restriction on air reconnaissance.[149] Immediately on leaving the wood to commence the assault, therefore, 'the troops came under heavy Machine-gun and Rifle Fire from behind two thick belts of wire which had escaped the attention of the Artillery'.[150] This line was forced by 07.30, Lieutenant

145 War Diary, HQ 16 Infantry Brigade, 23 October 1918, TNA WO95/1607.

146 War Diary 1st King's Shropshire Light Infantry, 24 October 1918, TNA WO95/1609. During the day Lieutenant George Wildig DCM (commissioned from sergeant in September 1916, having been on the Western Front since September 1914) was wounded, dying on 6 November 1918) and there were 30 casualties in the ranks.

147 The 10th Tank Battalion operational summary suggests that two were allocated to 7 Brigade, which had in fact been withdrawn from the line on the evening of 23rd and would not participate in operations on the 24th.

148 War Diary, HQ 10th Tank Battalion, 'Report on Operations 23rd & 24th October 1918', TNA WO95/103/3.

149 Kincaid-Smith, op.cit. p.362.

150 War Diary HQ 74 Brigade, 'Narrative of Operations of 74th Infantry Brigade from October 23rd to November 7th 1918', TNA WO95/2245.

Roderick Mitchell of the 13th Durham Light Infantry, who attacked in the centre, winning a bar to his Military Cross leading his company 'with great dash through the German wire' at Rue de Pont, and later being 'prominent in directing the consolidation of the captured position'.[151] The fourth objective was secured by 10.00. Lieutenant-Colonel Percy Hone became one of three infantry battalion commander casualties of the Selle operations here, wounded by a sniper whilst making a personal reconnaissance.[152] Having secured Rue de Pont, the attack restarted at 14.00 under a second creeping barrage, and Hone being down, the acting adjutant, Second-Lieutenant John Willey, played a key in preparing for the resumption of the assault, for which he was also awarded the MC.[153] The Durhams consolidated into two companies for the renewed attack,[154] driving through le Faux to high ground south east of Fontaine aux Bois above the Happegarbes spur. Second-Lieutenant Harold Gardner commanded one of these two companies, the third MC winner of the action.[155] The DLI were now in 'enclosed country ... movement forward was difficult, for the German machine-gunners commanded roads, paths and gaps in hedges from vantage points in houses',[156] especially from the high ground to the east of Malgarni. The battalion pushed patrols out and established a Lewis gun position which gave opportunity for retaliation. Troops learned quickly to keep clear of gaps in hedges which would have machine-guns trained on them, cutting their own instead. 9th Yorkshire meanwhile established themselves on the right of the Durhams, having penetrated the barbed wire to take Malgarni, sustaining 17 fatal casualties, some during hand-to-hand fighting in the village. Captain William Knott was awarded the MC for leading his company though a 'belt of 20 yards of wire, capturing several machine-guns'.[157]

On the left, 11th Sherwood Foresters were disappointed in the non-arrival of the supporting tank. Indeed, the tank support for 74 Brigade proved very limited. Of the two machines, one

151 W. Miles, *The Durham Forces in the Field 1914-18*, p.335. Roderick Sutherland Forbes Mitchell MC and bar was commissioned in January 1916 from Gunner in the Royal Field Artillery.

152 Percy Frederick Hone DSO MC and bar was a retired colonial volunteer who was farming in Rhodesia in August 1914. He commanded 21st Middlesex from May 1918, and 13th DLI only from 13 October. Hone won a bar to his MC over 23-24 October. 'He commanded his battalion during the attack north-east of Le Cateau on 23rd and 24th October, 1918. He personally led his battalion in the attack south-east of Fontaine au Bois, having previously gone forward to reconnoitre. On the 24th October 1918, when reconnoitring in advance of his battalion, he was wounded. His fine example of courage and determination contributed in a large measure to the success of the operations'. (*London Gazette*, 10 December 1919, p.15281).

153 John William Willey MC was commissioned from private in March 1915. His MC citation reads: 'At Rue du Pont and south-east of Fontaine au Bois on the 24th October, 1918, as acting adjutant when his C.O. was wounded, he rendered invaluable assistance in reorganising the battalion. It was largely due to his energy and coolness that the attack continued and was successful'. (*London Gazette*, 10 December 1919, p.15376).

154 Before the action the ration strength of 13th Durham Light Infantry was 17 officers and 606 ORs. They suffered a further 13 fatalities that day, including Second-Lieutenant Andrew Holmes. Second-Lieutenant Henry Cecil Geipel (who was commissioned in January 1918) was wounded. By 8 November 1918 unit strength had increased to 21 officers and 786 ORs.

155 Harold Gardner was commissioned in February 1918. His MC citation reads: 'For conspicuous gallantry and able leadership on 24th October, 1918, during the attack at Rue du Pont. He led his company with great skill through the belts of wire in face of very heavy machine-gun fire, and finally overcame the enemy resistance. After the objective had been reached he personally supervised the consolidation of the position'. (*London Gazette*, 10 December 1918, p.15334).

156 Miles, op. cit., pp.335-6.

157 *Edinburgh Gazette*, 11 December 1919, p.3978. William Robert Knott was commissioned in September 1914.

broke down on the front line, and was only able to give covering fire as the infantry jumped off. The second machine was delayed in starting with clutch trouble, but caught the infantry up, and whilst it came under heavy shellfire sustained no damage, but broke down, finally, for a second time.[158] Most of the Sherwood Foresters' casualties occurred attempting to negotiate the barbed wire, an operation in which the tanks would have been best placed to help. Snipers and machine-guns opened up on the advancing infantry. Lewis gun sections on the right of the Sherwoods and left of the Durhams cooperated in moving along the Fontaine road 'and succeeding in silencing the enemy machine-guns and snipers by enfilade fire'. They then moved on swiftly into Fontaine-au-Bois although on arrival they were shelled by a field gun firing over open sights. Establishing a line curving round the village to the east, they dug in whilst the village was 'bombarded & filled with gas' by the enemy. At 14.00 they moved forward under cover of a barrage to join up with the 1/8th Worcesters who had passed through them earlier.[159] Moving into Fontaine the following day, the commanding officer, Lieutenant-Colonel Herbert Young was killed by a shell and his adjutant, Captain Basil Bird, wounded. Young thus became the most senior infantry fatality of the Selle fighting.[160]

1/8th Worcestershire had pushed on to take Les Grandes Chênes, a group of houses north of Fontaine, capturing some 375 prisoners. The 18th Division were struggling to the north, and the Worcesters maintained a defensive flank. Ordered at 13.00 to attack again at 14.00, it was not possible to warn the two forward companies who suffered five casualties from their own barrage.[161] By 18.00, however, all the objectives had been secured. The depletion of 74 Brigade was such, however, that on coming out of action 9th Yorkshire had a trench strength of 9 officers and 360 other ranks,[162] 13th DLI had only five officers and 221 other ranks, whilst 11th Sherwood Foresters had 10 officers but only 194 other ranks. During the period 23-31 October the brigade suffered casualties amounting to 18 officers and 517 ORs, a third of its strength.[163] The degree of Fourth

158 War Diary, HQ 10th Tank Battalion, 'Report on Operations 23rd & 24th October 1918', TNA WO95/103/3.

159 There were eleven fatal casualties amongst the other ranks of 24 October, including Sergeant Ralph Bagshaw, twice mentioned in despatches, who had joined up September 1914 after previous service with the Volunteers and arrived on the Western Front September 1915. Captain William Arthur Clifton MC and bar (commissioned from CSM in October 1917), and Captain Joseph Hill Spicer MC, (commissioned in March 1917), were wounded. Clifton won the bar to his MC in the Selle operations: 'During the advance east of Le Cateau, on the 23rd and 24th October, 1918, he showed marked courage and able leadership of a company. During the attack on Fontaine au Bois, when the advance was checked, he pushed forward with a small party and succeeded in cutting a gap in the face of heavy artillery and machine-gun fire. During this operation he was wounded, but continued to lead his men forward, materially helping the capture and consolidation of the final objective'. (*Edinburgh Gazette*, 11 December 1919, p.3928). Second-Lieutenant Joseph Pickard (commissioned from sergeant in April 1918) was also wounded.

160 Basil William Bird MC was commissioned in July 1915.

161 During 18 October 1/8th Worcestershire suffered three officers killed (one in the operations of 23-24 October, Lieutenant Cleveland Alexander Connor, commissioned in September 1915), and 12 wounded, and 51 ORs killed and 313 wounded with four missing. They had captured 16 officers and 657 ORs, 13 machine-guns, 11 artillery pieces, 25 horses, 40 railway trucks, four limbers, two baggage wagons, 1 signal wagon and 25 bicycles. (War Diary, 1/8th Battalion Worcestershire Regiment, Appendix W, October 1918, TNA WO95/2251).

162 During the month they had suffered six officers killed and 15 wounded, and 63 ORs killed with 356 wounded and 47 missing.

163 War Diary, HQ 74 Infantry Brigade, 'Narrative of Operations from October 23rd to November 7th 1918', TNA WO95/2245. In action from the 23rd 11th Sherwood Foresters suffered 25 ORs killed/died of wounds, and 89 wounded/missing.

Army's ability to reinforce its units, however, is indicated by the fact that by 8 November 1918 the ration strength of 13th DLI was up from 11 officers and 365 ORs to 21 officers and 786 ORs.[164]

In the north of XIII Corps, 18th Division again deployed 55 Brigade on the right and 54 Brigade on the left of the attack. 55 Brigade decided to rest the battered 7th Buffs and 8th East Surreys and as 'the enemy was known to be in a fairly tired condition', optimistically decided to attempt to take the fifth objective using only the 7th Queen's Own Royal West Surrey. They formed up south-east of Bousies, with one section of 18th Battalion MGC and one section of 55th Trench Mortar Battery attached. The creeping barrage fired by two brigades of field artillery remained on its opening line for 12 minutes to allow the infantry to catch up, thereafter proceeding at 100 yards every four minutes, halting for an hour half-way to the final objective. Brigade orders recognized that the battalion had been 'given a very large area to clear', but optimistically believed that 'the enemy appears to be in such a demoralized condition that the task should be easy'.[165] This was tempting fate. As was later noted with understatement: 'The advance did not proceed according to plan'.[166] The Germans offered 'stout resistance' in the thick orchards between Bousies and Robersart, the line of the *Hermann Stellung II*, where hedges and trees provided good cover. In addition the double apron wire that had held up the units of the 25th Division was encountered. B Company of the Queen's reached the western outskirts of Robersart at 06.30, but had to withdraw under heavy machine-gun fire. Shelling made it impossible for the companies to keep in touch. Just before 09.00 a tank officer reported that his tank had been in Robersart and that he had 'seen nobody in the village'.[167] This was machine number 9102, commanded by Sergeant Christopher McEune.[168] It had hit a tree on the way up and lost the left 6-pounder sponson door, which rendered it less safe for the crew. McEune nevertheless went into action south of Bousies in support of the Queen's and going ahead of the infantry, met machine-gun fire which he rated 'not especially troublesome'. He had approached Robersart, but whilst he did not actually enter the village, he could indeed see no infantry.[169] The village was occupied soon after. The 7th Queen's had, however, suffered sufficient casualties amongst officers and NCOs not to be able to conduct the advance further. Late in the afternoon the 8th East Surreys took over the front line and attempted to take the final objective. Resistance was such that even the following day this could not be achieved, one of the few areas in Fourth Army's attack where this was not possible. The line remained just to the east of Robersart.

Brigadier-General Borrett of 54 Brigade, who that day would be the second brigadier of 18th Division to go sick during this episode of fighting,[170] communicated his orders to 6th

164 War Diary, 13th Battalion Durham Light Infantry, 23 October 1918, TNA WO95/2247.

165 War Diary, 7th Battalion Queen's Own Royal West Surrey Regiment, 55th Brigade Order No. 227, 23 October 1918, TNA WO95/2051.

166 War Diary, HQ 55th Infantry Brigade, 'Narrative No. 6 – The Capture of Bousies and Robersart', TNA WO95/2048.

167 War Diary, 7th Battalion Queen's Own Royal West Surrey Regiment, 23 October 1918, TNA WO95/2051. 7th West Surrey began October with 31 officers and 697 other ranks. There were seven officer and 105 OR casualties during this period. The battalion was commanded by Lieutenant-Colonel George Lee Harrison DSO, a territorial second-lieutenant in August 1914, who had commanded since 15 August 1918.

168 Christopher Stanley McEune MM, a ship's steward, enlisted in the 6th Dragoon Guards in August 1914, rising to corporal before transferring to the Tank Corp, and had arrived on the Western Front in October 1915.

169 War Diary, 10th Tank Battalion, Battle History Sheet, Tank No. 9102, 24 October 1918, TNA WO95/103/3.

170 To be replaced by Lieutenant-Colonel Turner of 6th Northamptonshire.

Northamptonshire, who were to head the advance, at 01.40 by motor car. The battalion would lead with A and B Companies who would advance 500 yards from Bousies and consolidate. As soon as they reached this line, they were to open rapid fire with every Lewis gun and rifle to allow C & D Companies to leapfrog them. These two companies would maintain rapid fire until 2nd Bedfordshire to the south, and 11th Royal Fusiliers to the north, who received their orders verbally, had passed through them as well. The details for the barrage were unknown at the time of issuing the orders, although the start time was known, and it came down 'ragged and short', causing casualties to the Northamptons. Indeed, the artillery support for 18th Division would be problematic all day. Despite this, A and B Companies advanced from their positions east of Bousies and achieved their line, but the two companies following ran into the *Hermann Stellung II*, meeting both heavy machine-gun fire and wire. The barrage was lost and the opposition caused the infantry to fall back from the flat, open ground a short distance into Bousies Wood, some 1,500 yards north of the village. One of the sticking points was the presence of machine-guns in a sunken lane stretching across their front some 750 yards away, and another set of nests at a strongpoint at Renuart Farm, on a ridge beyond the sunken lane. There were also more machine-guns behind these positions on higher ground to the north-west of Preux-aux-Bois. Further, an enemy counter-attack at 06.00 had to be repelled.

The two following battalions were tasked with taking the fourth and fifth objectives, ending their advance on the Englefontaine-Landrecies road. Despite the short notice and great difficulty in the enclosed countryside in forming up, 2nd Bedfordshire were ready with 15 minutes to spare. 11th Royal Fusiliers also set off, describing how 'our barrage was weak and short and inflicted several casualties on us' but that the enemy artillery response 'was also weak and scattered, but he was using a fair amount of gas'.[171] In forming up, they lost Captain Wilfred Hornfeck, hero of the Richemont crossing the previous day, who had one foot virtually cut off by shell fire. Despite this, he continued to supervise the assembly 'and again cheered his men on as they went forward'.[172] Hornfeck subsequently had his leg amputated. At Zero plus 70 minutes both battalions leapfrogged the Northamptons but were immediately and predictably pinned down by the phalanx of machine-guns that had caused the Nothamptonshire unit to fall back. Arriving behind his battalion, Colonel Percival of the Bedfords found a disorganised group of men of all the brigade's three battalions in the road running along the edge of Bousies Wood. He spent some time reorganising the front and decided that any further advance in daylight would be impossible without heavy casualties. To make matters worse: 'At about 9.15 a.m. a most regrettable incident occurred, an organised shoot by our heavy artillery falling short and causing two companies to evacuate their positions, besides inflicting a number of casualties'. The Royal Fusiliers noted that this friendly fire fell right on the front line and was 'extraordinarily accurate'.[173] Percival reported this, 'but at 12.15 p.m. an exactly similar thing occurred again and further casualties were reported'.[174] 54 Brigade were under fire

171 War Diary, 11th Battalion Royal Fusiliers, 'Report on Operations carried out by the 11th Bn. The Royal Fusiliers from Oct. 23rd to Nov. 4th 1918', TNA WO95/2045.

172 Nichols, op. cit., pp.442-3.

173 11th Royal Fusiliers had only four fatalities in the other ranks, but amongst their officers, in addition to Hornfeck, Captain Bernard Percy Webster (commissioned September 1916); Lieutenant G. Tyler; and Second-Lieutenants Charles Francis Macklin (commissioned from private in May 1918), F. Lyons (commissioned from sergeant in August 1918) and Francis Alexander Garner (commissioned from private in July 1918) were wounded.

174 War Diary, 2nd Battalion Bedfordshire Regiment, 'Narrative of Operations N.E. of Le Cateau – 23rd/24th October 1918', TNA WO95/2042.

from both friend and foe alike. The friendly fire problem was caused by two 6-inch howitzer and two 60-pounder batteries situated west of Pommereuil who were tasked with shelling positions east of the Renuart Farm ridge. They were making use of an aerial photograph to identify the line of the front of the wood, and in attempting to shell the wire to its east, fell short.[175]

The stalled brigade's problem was eventually solved by Lieutenant Frederick Hedges, commanding C Company of the Northamptons, who would win the third Victoria Cross of the Selle operations.[176] The citation reads:

> He led his company with great skill towards the final objective, maintaining direction under the most difficult conditions. When the advance was held up by machine-gun posts, accompanied by one Serjeant and followed at some considerable distance by a Lewis-gun section, he again advanced and displayed the greatest determination, capturing six machine-guns and 14 prisoners. His gallantry and initiative enabled the whole line to advance, and tended largely to the success of subsequent operations.[177]

Hedges, accompanied by Sergeant Frederick Gibson and the Lewis guns, had gone out to reconnoitre, and located 16 machine-gun nests. In taking the first, Hedges lost his rifle 'but rushed on unarmed with the sergeant, who had a revolver, a few shots from which caused the enemy to throw up their hands'. Hedges was wounded in the head and shoulder, and Gibson (awarded the DCM), although unscathed, was wounded a fortnight later.[178] The group, however, successfully outflanked the opposing machine gun nests.

Major-General Lee had appeared at 54 Brigade HQ at 11.30 with the news that Third Army on the left had pushed on, and were several thousand yards ahead near Englefontaine. With the flank thus known to be secure, three companies of the Northants were extricated from the stalled units and sent north towards the Roman road to turn the enemy's flank.[179] Again, senior commanders keeping close to the action were able to make prompt decisions, effectively realigning their units to free a stuck attack. As the flanking movement proceeded, 2nd Bedfordshire, the machine-gun defence in front of Renuart Farm largely eliminated, mounted an attack on the farm itself with the assistance of a tank commanded by Lieutenant Charles Thomson which 'continued circling round and making straight for German M.G. emplacements'.[180] Although the machine had been 'riddled with armour piercing bullets and all the crew except the officer and driver were wounded it went back and continued to give assistance to the infantry'.[181] The four tanks attached to 18th Division worked hard. They 'remained behind the Infantry under cover for the greater part of the day, clearing up various nests of machine-guns when called upon'. Thomson's tank, number 9004,

175 Edmonds & Maxwell-Hyslop, op. cit., p.374.

176 Born in India in 1896, Frederick William Hedges VC was commissioned in July 1915 into the Bedfordshire Regiment from private in the 1/9th Battalion London Regiment and had arrived on the Western Front in November 1914. He had suffered frostbite at First Ypres in 1914 whilst serving in the other ranks, and had been wounded during the Battle of Arras in 1917. During World War II he became a Civil Defence Coordinator. Following the accidental death of his only son from drowning in 1941, he became severely depressed and an alcoholic, finally committing suicide at his home in Harrogate, North Yorkshire, in 1954 at the age of 57.

177 *London Gazette*, 28 January 1919, p.1503.

178 Anonymous, *The Northamptonshire Regiment*, p.308.

179 Edmonds & Maxwell-Hyslop, op. cit., p.374-5.

180 Charles Abernethy Thomson was commissioned in December 1917.

181 War Diary, 6th Battalion Northamptonshire Regiment, 24 October 1918, TNA WO95/2044.

covered seven and a half miles, firing 20 rounds of 6-pounder and 400 rounds of machine-gun ammunition, and 'also blew up an enemy dump and inflicted very severe casualties'.[182] Thomson had not had an easy journey to get into action. He had started off at 03.45, but the fan belt broke after an hour. A crew member was sent to find another from any nearby machines, and got lost, only returning at 06.20. Getting going again, the split pin sheared on two cylinders, and replacements had to be sought. Starting again, the tank developed autovac (fuel feed) trouble, and conked out once more. Finally functioning, Thomson described with remarkable understatement how he 'did a small show for 16.30 hours'.[183] His subjugation of the machine-guns at Renuart Farm allowed the infantry forward beyond the line cleared by Lieutenant Hedges. Although Thomson's role ended here as he ran out of petrol, the fall of the farm opened the way for yet further progress, and by 22.00 the final objective on the Engelfontaine-Landrecies road had been reached.[184] The 11th Fusiliers formed themselves into three 'battle patrols' and pushed forward at 19.00, achieving the same objective with little further problem.[185]

18th Division had experienced yet another hard day of fighting. They suffered from five problems. The first was self-inflicted – 'the weight of the attack was not heavy'[186] – and again reflected the British tendency to underestimate enemy opposition. Secondly, the division had to cover a good deal of ground; and thirdly, the artillery barrage was weak and inaccurate. Fourthly, lines of defence were encountered about which little was known, with the enemy offering unexpectedly firm resistance in the hedges and orchards that covered the landscape. Lastly, the loss of two brigade commanders due to sickness during the day cannot have helped command and control, even if did not materially affect the fighting at the sharp end. For the second day, the tanks had proved their ability to make tactical gains and move stalled infantry attacks on. Meanwhile in the air, 535 flying hours were clocked up by 244 pilots. Five successful reconnaissances were carried out and 20 artillery patrols made 23 zone calls although, significantly, no enemy batteries were put out of action. The enemy artillery response, in comparison with the previous day, had been weak, no doubt reflecting the fact that guns were being pulled back. In terms of ground attack, 227 25-pound bombs were dropped and 16 112-pound bombs targeted the important Aulnoye rail junction.[187] The RAF still had the notion of 'deep battle' in mind. Enemy aircraft activity, in contrast to the previous day was very slight, although there were five decisive combats for the loss of one British machine. The successful combats of the day which resulted in the downing of five enemy aircraft occurred in one action. Captain Horace Lale was leading an offensive patrol of 14 Bristol Fighters which had been bombing the Aulnoye railway tracks,[188] and whilst taking photographs sighted 15 Fokker bi-planes. Lale attacked, and his observer, Second-Lieutenant Clement

182 War Diary, HQ 10th Tank Battalion, 'Report on Operations 23rd & 24th October 1918', TNA WO95/103/3.
183 War Diary, 10th Tank Battalion, Battle History Sheet, Tank No. 9004, 24 October 1918, TNA WO95/103/3.
184 2nd Bedfordshire suffered 45 ORs killed/died of wounds, 177 wounded and eight missing 20-24 October. Captain Philip Julius Reiss and Second-Lieutenants W.D. Hall and H. Dysart were wounded on the 24th.
185 War Diary, 11th Battalion Royal Fusiliers, 24 October 1918, TNA WO95/2045.
186 Edmonds & Maxwell-Hyslop, op. cit., P.373.
187 War Diary, HQ Fourth Army, 24 October 1918, TNA WO95/439.
188 Horace Percy Lale DSO DFC and bar had 23 kills to his name. His victory was in June 1917, but a run of 20 victories began only in June 1918. He rose to the rank of wing-commander in the 1930s.

Boothroyd,[189] was able to fire at one of the Fokkers below him during the dog-fight and bring it down. Re-engaging, Lale fired 300 rounds at between 50 and 150 yards into another, and watched it crash into the Mormal Forest. Lieutenants R.B Trapp and Alan Perkins both brought enemy machines down,[190] as did Captain Leslie Burbidge,[191] observer to Captain Thomas Traill.[192] Traill's flight back to his airfield did not go smoothly. He 'collided with another machine in the haze and had part of his right hand wings taken away'. Traill was unable to stop his machine spinning so Burbidge 'climbed out on to the lower plane and stayed there until the machine side-slipped into the ground'. In the crash, Traill was unhurt but Burbidge, perhaps unsurprisingly, broke his nose and bit through his tongue.[193]

Over the following days both XIII and IX Corps carried out very minor adjustments to their lines, and the enemy carried out a dutiful harassing fire. Fourth Army's major operations on the Selle were, however, at an end. The Official Historians summarised that during these final two days of fighting, Fourth Army had 'defeated eight German divisions and a cyclist brigade, and captured 27 officers, 1,213 other ranks and 66 guns'.[194] In the south, over the following days, the French pushed up to the Sambre-Oise Canal, and approached Guise, whilst Third and First Armies pushed on to the north and east of the Vallenciennes-Le Quesnoy railway. The enemy was, however, making another stand on the west of the Mormal Forest and the canal. In contemplating this, Fourth Army took the view that the German troops 'were depressed by continuous defeat and exhausted by incessant fighting, while the morale of our own men was magnificent'.[195] The BEF did not know, however, that one more shove would drive the Germans into capitulation.

189 Clement Graham Boothroyd was commissioned in May 1918. Boothroyd was awarded the DFC: 'An officer of high courage. On 23rd October, after attacking with bombs a railway station, the formation with which this officer was flying was engaged with about fifteen enemy scouts; of these, he destroyed one and his pilot accounted for a second. In all he has to his credit eight enemy aircraft and one kite balloon'. (*London Gazette*, 8 February 1919, p.2035).

190 Alan Christopher Temple Perkins was commissioned in November 1915

191 Leslie Williams Burbidge was commissioned in October 1914.

192 Thomas Cathcart Traill had been a midshipman in the Royal Navy. He transferred to the Royal Flying Corps in 1917 and notched up eight aerial victories. He served in staff posts during WW2 and ended his career as air vice-marshall.

193 War Diary, 5 Brigade RAF, Combat Reports 24 October 1918, TNA AIR1 2225/209/40/26.

194 Edmonds & Maxwell-Hyslop, op. cit., p.375.

195 Edmonds & Maxwell-Hyslop, op. cit., p.237.

8

Lions Led by Tigers?[1] Fourth Army at the Selle

The concept of the 'learning curve' was only ever at best a shorthand description of operational and tactical improvement in the BEF. There was never a smooth ascending curve of increasing competence – there was, rather, a rollercoaster of ups and downs. This uneven progress, as William Philpott has pointed out, was the result of a 'dynamic process of adjustment to new technologies, more sophisticated and flexible tactics, novel operational doctrines, complex logistics and fundamental change in the systems of command, control, communications and intelligence'. During the Hundred Days, the British army was not practising an improved version of the warfare of 1914, it was executing an entirely new form.[2] It possessed enough of the right sort of weapons, some hardly dreamed of in 1914; had an evolved concept of using them within industrial, attritional war conducted on a vast scale under the direction of a largely confident and experienced senior command; and possessed a raft of junior leaders who were well-trained and seasoned in battle.

Robin Prior and Trevor Wilson, in their study of the career of Sir Henry Rawlinson on the Western Front, crystallised the concept of the 'weapons system'. This image encompassed a largely invincible interlocking set of weapons, based primarily on the 'god of war', the artillery,[3] but including 'light and heavy machine-guns, rifle grenades and trench mortars, tanks and armoured cars, gas, smoke and wireless telegraphy'. These were coupled with sophisticated tactics for their use, blended together 'to produce a strike force against which the enemy ultimately could provide no resistance'.[4] This hyperbole falls victim to the friction of war that was inevitable during a campaign such as the Hundred Days, where the supposedly infallible system could indeed stutter. Paul Harris suggests that: 'To think in terms of the constant application of a set formula would be

1 This phrase of John Bourne's parodies the supposed 1914 description of the BEF as 'lions led by donkeys', a phrase impossible to attribute clearly to any German if indeed it was ever used. The original epithet likely dates to the Crimean War, where Russians supposedly used it to describe the British at Sebastopol; the Franco-Prussian War where the British may have used it to describe the French, or even Sir James Grierson (the original commander of II Corps in August 1914), to describe the Russians during the Boxer Rebellion.
2 https://rusi.org/commentary/beyond-learning-curve-british-armys-military-transformation-first-world-war (accessed 5 September 1918).
3 The phrase 'god of war' to describe the artillery was coined by Josef Stalin in 1944.
4 R. Prior & T. Wilson, *Command on the Western Front*, p.394.

to underestimate the dynamism and complexity of the campaign'.[5] The high point of the deployment of the full 'weapons system' was the Battle of Amiens. The Battle of the Selle, in contrast, involved no surprise, a preliminary bombardment lasting several days, inadequate counter-battery fire, partially ineffective barrages, poor intelligence, a diminished contribution from the RAF, and the deployment of only a handful of tanks. As Harris concludes, to see the Battle of the Selle 'as just another overwhelming triumph for the BEF's weapons system seems particularly misleading'.[6]

The 'Weapons System'

What then were the limitations of the 'weapons system' of Fourth Army in October 1918?

Artillery

By 1918 the BEF was fighting a rich man's war in respect to artillery. Mark Whisler has estimated that on the left of the BEF's attack on 17 October (XIII Corps and American 27th Division) the advantage in guns was about 1.8-2.00 to one; and on the right (IX Corps and the American 30th Division) an advantage of 1.7-1.00 in field artillery and 5:1 in heavy.[7] The enemy had approximately 688 guns of all types,[8] whilst Fourth Army brought up 1,320.[9] Despite this advantage, the 'god of war' proved less than all powerful at the Selle in a variety of respects.

As noted in the introduction, the Official History states that the brigade commanders were unwilling to proceed further on 8 October in the absence of artillery support. Artillery was the key element of support of the infantry advance in the combined arms attack, and the OH comment suggests an overreliance on barrage. Highly successful in getting infantry forward, the monolithic progress of a barrage had its limitations. Firstly, the creeping barrages fired at the standard rate of 100 yards in three minutes moved too quickly for the infantry in the set-piece attacks at the Selle.[10] The company commanders of 2nd Dublin Fusiliers specifically noted: 'Barrage too quick to allow mopping up of farms'.[11] The time spent overcoming enemy outposts, resistance in fortified positions such as the *HWL I*, dealing with uncut wire, or mastering even small groups of houses meant that barrages were almost invariably lost by the troops whose advance they were supposed to be protecting. On 17 October this exposed them to the machine-gun nests of the *HWL II*. The effect was to make progress slow. Further, despite their lack of cover the enemy infantry had survived the artillery preparation leading up to the 17th remarkably well, and fought back ably.[12]

5 J.P. Harris & N. Barr, *Amiens to the Armistice*, p.298.
6 Harris & Barr, op. cit., p.299.
7 Whisler, 'Der Tommy Kommt', pp.27, 30.
8 See Appendix II.
9 Prior and Wilson, op. cit., p.383, taking figures from 'Fourth Army Summary of Operations 17 October 1918'.
10 The artillery had experimented in 1916 with lifts of 50 yards per minute and settled on 100 yards in three minutes, an artillery officer claiming that: 'There was no doubt that a barrage at this rate fired by shrapnel was effective. The machine gunners were killed in their shell holes'. (A.F. Becke, 'The Coming of the Creeping Barrage'.)
11 War Diary, 2nd Battalion Royal Dublin Fusiliers, 'Company Commander Points October 1918', TNA WO95/2831.
12 The army's artillery would make an allied mistake at the Battle of the Sambre, where it had been observed that machine guns, batteries and single artillery pieces were located in hedges close to the canal, yet the barrage stood on the canal for five minutes before lifting 300 yards to stand for thirty minutes. N. Barr, 'The Last Battle of the BEF', in G. Sheffield & P. Gray, *Changing War*, p.77.

Occasionally, however, the barrage moved too slowly for the infantry's liking. The artillery had taken good note of the Selle bocage and on 23 October adopted a 100 yards every six minutes barrage rate around the Bois l'Evêque. When 1st Shropshire Light Infantry attacked in its north-west corner the following day, supported by the same rate of lifts, progress was quick and the troops found themselves waiting. The Official Historian offered the opinion that this rate was, 'in view of the poor resistance, too slow'.[13] On balance, the situation must have been preferable to losing the barrage and advancing without protection.

On 9 October 25th Division set off under the apparently standard creeping barrage, one which was noted in Chapter Two not to have been strictly necessary. The reality was, however, that the barrage that day may not have been sophisticated – Colonel Frederick Rice of 82 Brigade RFA described his brigade's artillery support for the division as 'short and simple'. They 'merely fired concentrations on three small areas, beginning with the nearest, at a certain time and for a certain definite period. This was to save ammunition'. (The BEF had plenty of ammunition, but when guns were constantly moving forward, shells often had to be left at abandoned gun positions for collection later). He confessed that the exact position of the enemy's 'forward troops was not known accurately, so the most likely spots were selected'. It may have been exactly this uncertainty and hurried preparation that caused the friendly fire incident on troops of 25th and 66th Division that morning. Indeed, there are further question marks which hang over the artillery's performance in respect of the complex barrage plans that had been drawn up for the set-piece attacks. Thus on 17 October, when the guns of 1st Division were superimposed on those of the 6th, the artillery warned that due to 'hastily occupied positions an accurate creeping barrage will not be possible'. Rather, a 'heavy area shoot' was promised, the front edge of which might be 'somewhat irregular'. The infantry were warned not to 'follow too closely'.[14] Thus what looked an impressive barrage on paper was more ragged in practice. In reviewing the days of the Pursuit 16 Brigade noted: 'The Artillery barrages were not up to the high standard to which we have been accustomed'.[15] The survival of so much wire encountered on the morning of 17 October indicates either lack of knowledge, inaccuracy, or both.

The frequent moves of artillery into new positions were undoubtedly highly disruptive to providing swift and accurate indirect fire. On the afternoon of 17 October a renewed barrage was requested in order for the infantry to renew the assault on La Vallée Mulâtre, but the two and a half hours' notice granted the artillery, 'was not really sufficient in view of the fact that all the guns had moved during the morning and communications were slow'. The barrage was therefore 'only moderate'.[16] Slow communications created a problem for gleaning exactly where the infantry were. As noted in Chapter Five, on 18 October the Australian artillery had great difficulty in establishing where the 30th American Division had advanced or retired to in order to provide a supplementary barrage after the early morning failure. Similarly, the opening barrage for 27th American Division fired that morning fell behind the American front line as a result of attempting to comply with the divisional commander's late intervention the previous evening concerning a change in the barrage line for his division. Accurate mapping was also an issue. Commanders noted that the maps of the Selle area lacked many of the features they found on the

13 J.E. Edmonds & R. Maxwell-Hyslop, *Military Operations France and Belgium Vol. 5*, p.373.
14 War Diary, HQ 1st Infantry Division, 1st Division Battle Instructions Series D No. 8, 19 Oct 1918, TNA WO95/1234.
15 War Diary, HQ 16 Infantry Brigade, G.O. 530, 14 October 1918, TNA WO95/1607.
16 War Diary, 1st Infantry Division, 'Narrative of Operations of 1st Division on October 17th, 18th & 19th 1918', TNA WO95/1234.

ground. The artillery supporting 18th Division on 24 October repeatedly shelled its front-line troops drawn up along the edge of a wood that was a late addition to the trench map issued on 10 October, attempting to work from an aerial photograph. It is surprising, therefore, that there was not more inaccurate shooting. It is remarkable that during 50th Division's desperate fighting for Le Cateau station on 17 October there was no report of friendly artillery fire causing casualties in the supplementary barrages that were organised later that day.

The two geographical issues, the artillery being in hastily occupied positions and the problems of knowing exactly where the infantry were, interacted with a third and uncontrollable factor, the weather. The weather was probably the dominant factor in many of the artillery problems at the Selle. Thus IX Corps produced its novel oblique barrage plan for 17 October, only to find that the infantry advancing in fog had extreme difficulty in following it, when, to be precise, they were not to follow its exact direction. Smoke, intended to indicate barrage lifts, was both invisible and complicated the picture rather than eased it. The fog created problems for identifying and overcoming machine-guns outposts and this slowed the infantry from the start, leading them to fall behind the barrage from the start. Further, there appears to have been a minimum of effective counter-battery work, another matter related to the weather. Mark Whisler's examination of German records suggests that whilst there was much mention of fire on battery positions, few were knocked out. Indeed, his view is that the constant artillery fire had more of a psychologically wearing effect than anything else.[17] By this stage in the war, 90 per cent of counter-battery observation was achieved by aircraft. Hence, 'the success of the artillery battle had come to depend on the weather being suitable for flying'.[18] Given the importance of the artillery/air-power axis in the new warfare, the October weather was a considerable handicap, rendering the RAF ineffective in terms of observation for a significant part of the time. Fourth Army's sound-ranging sections were present at the Selle, at Joncourt on 11 October, and Prémont and Bohain on 19 October, but have left no record of the detail of their work.[19] Only XIII Corps artillery made a single reference to sound-ranging during the Selle operations, noting on 17 October: 'Sound Rangers gave the only 3 locations during the day, accuracy doubtful owing to lines being cut in places'.[20] In a war of movement the complications of sound-ranging based on triangulation were more in evidence. Flash-spotting, given the nature of the terrain and the state of the weather, was an even less useful proposition.

During the Selle operations, as Table 8.1 shows, 235 zone calls were sent down by aircraft, resulting in 50 successful battery neutralizations, a 21 per cent success rate. The success rate in the four days planning the operations of 17 October was 23 percent, but in the three days planning the operations of 23 October only four zone calls were made, albeit with the same neutralization success rate. This was inevitable given that there were days when the RAF essentially could not fly at all. Jonathan Boff notes that in neighbouring Third Army counter-battery work was 'almost impossible' during the week ending 24 October, with the guns of VI Corps engaging only eleven targets in support of the 23 October assault.[21]

17 Whisler. op. cit., p.39.
18 S. Bidwell & D. Graham, *Fire-Power*, p.143.
19 War Diary, 5 Field Survey Company Royal Engineers, October 1918, TNA WO95/492.
20 War Diary, Commander Royal Artillery XIII Corps, 17 October 1918, TNA WO95/902.
21 J. Boff, *Winning and Losing on the Western Front*, Kindle edition location 4531.

Table 8.1 Artillery patrols and zone calls during the Selle operations 9-24 October 1918

Date	Artillery Patrols	Zone Calls	Neutralizations
9	19	49	11
10	5	29	2
11	16	25	15
12	8	11	8
13	5	4	3
14	14	4	3
15	18	27	2
16	4	0	0
17	7	2	0
18	11	15	0
19	12	16	0
20	0	0	0
21	0	0	0
22	2	4	1
23	17	26	0
24	20	23	0

Continued emphasis, however, rightly continued to be placed on counter-battery work throughout operations. On 23 October, Fourth Army HQ asserted again that:

> Counter battery work will be pursued with vigour, long range howitzers being pushed forward for the purpose. A free use will be made of gas shells. Additional aeroplanes should be demanded if necessary. Failing aeroplane observation, shoots will be carried out by switching from datum points, by co-operation with sound rangers and by all other possible means. Direct observation will always be employed where possible.[22]

And this is essentially what Fourth Army's artillery did. The gunners shelled areas where it was *likely* that enemy artillery might be, rather than where they were *known* to be. The list of counter-battery targets for the artillery of IX Corps for the attack of 23 October, to be hit with a mixture of HE and gas, survives. There were 58 targets of which 22 were 'definite locations', the remainder being 'possible battery areas'. Only just less than a third of the counter-battery targets had therefore been clearly identified.[23] 18th Division circulated a list of located hostile batteries in the divisional area on 21 October. There were seven such, and three contained one gun only.[24] The reports of the German units noted by Whisler indicates that in a number of cases they got the locations right, but were insufficiently effective. The enemy artillery was thus often able to maintain effective harassing fire on the BEF's rear areas. In the week 12-19 October they were able to achieve 'very heavy' gas shelling (some 20,000 shells) with four heavy bombardments

22 War Diary, HQ Fourth Army, Order No. 20/47(G), 23 October 1918, TNA WO95/439.
23 War Diary, HQ IX Corps Heavy Artillery, Operation Order No. 12, 22 October 1918, TNA WO95/842.
24 War Diary, 18th Infantry Division, Order No. G.940 Appendix B, 21 October 1918, TNA WO95/2048.

with Yellow Cross (mustard gas) and a 'considerable amount of double yellow cross' (mustard gas shells with HE). This caused 1,894 casualties, particularly in the area of II American Corps which received the greater part of the shelling.[25] They were also able to bring down counter-barrage, and did so particularly effectively on 23 October, virtually at the same time as the British barrage. The units of IX Corps noted how sophisticated the use of this counter-barrage was. Fourth Army concluded that 'this counter-preparation was undoubtedly the result of insufficient counter-battery work', but acknowledged the obvious: 'During the few days prior to October 23rd the weather was unsuitable for flying, and observation was difficult, consequently few hostile batteries were located and counter-battery work was restricted'.[26] Overall, Fourth Army seemed unimpressed with its heavy artillery in particular:

> Insufficient use of heavy howitzer fire is being made. Corps will ensure that strong points immediately on the front of Divisions are adequately dealt with by heavy howitzer fire. The fire of field guns for the purpose is insufficient. The difficulties connected with moving forward ammunition are fully realised, but ample ammunition is available and very little of it is being used. Strong points from which machine gun fire is reported will be dealt with by putting on at least one or two hundred heavy howitzer shells.[27]

There was, of course, a major effort at harassing fire on the road network in the enemy's rear to disrupt their retreat, and on the Sambre-Oise canal. The success of this is difficult to assess.

Robin Prior and Trevor Wilson note that: 'Almost all the attacking divisions ascribe their success to the key element of the British weapons system, artillery. Once more the counter-battery fire had accomplished its purpose'.[28] This is incorrect on nearly all counts. It is true that some divisions were happy with their artillery cover, but on much of the battlefront, as described, the artillery barrage lacked its usual effectiveness, and counter-battery fire certainly did not accomplish its purpose.

As can be seen from Table 8.2, the weight of the barrages fired on the opening days of the set-piece attacks of 17 and 23 October were far less powerful than the barrages fired at the battle of Amiens or the storming of the Hindenburg Line. That a strong position such as that overcome on 29 September did not face the Fourth Army on 17 October is a partial explanation, and whilst the defences at the Selle presented a stronger proposition than those at Amiens, a good proportion of the shells fired on 8 August were directed at neutralising the 95 per cent of enemy guns that had been identified. Fourth Army therefore fired a considerable weight of shell on 17 October with results less positive than might have been hoped. As the Official Historians noted, the main effect of the barrage was to 'induce the enemy to take cover' and 'a large number of his machine guns remained untouched'.[29]

25 War Diary, HQ Fourth Army, 'Enemy Gas Shell Activity on Fourth Army Front for Week Ending October 19th 1918', TNA WO95/439.
26 War Diary, HQ Fourth Army, 23 October 1918, TNA WO95/439.
27 War Diary, HQ Fourth Army, Order No. 20/47(G), 23 October 1918, TNA WO95/439.
28 Prior & Wilson, op. cit., p.383.
29 Edmonds & Maxwell-Hyslop, op. cit., p.574.

Table 8.2 Comparative barrages on day of opening of set-piece attacks September/October 1918

	Amiens	Hindenburg Line	Selle	
	8 August 1918	29 September 1918	17 October	23 October
Guns				
13 pdr. AA	305	534	60	138
13 pdr. RHA		6,231	3,245	5,400
18 pdr.	281,697	244,502	149,675	111,671
60 pdr.	27,627	23,801	11,020	9,753
6 inch	3,936	2,404	1,176	445
12 inch	26	42		
14 inch		26		
Howitzers				
4.5 inch	60,500	67,656	28,527	29,232
6 inch	57,329	63,271	28,368	20,033
8 inch	10,576	9,764	2,711	1,757
9.2 inch	6,553	7,768	2,522	1,506
12 inch	369	805		

Artillery still, however, had the power to mount an effective intervention on request during battle. Thus, the artillery of XIII Corps broke up the counter-attack mounted around Le Quennelet Farm late morning on 17 October, indicating that once the weather improved, aircraft and artillery could work effectively in cooperation. However, on other occasions, disorganisation of the infantry on the ground made such swiftly arranged barrages ineffective. Thus, in the late afternoon that day, the infantry were unable to take advantage of those arranged on the area around Le Cateau station as they were simply unable to get in place to follow them.

Air-power

As its Official History stated, the RAF's 'first duty was reconnaissance. All its other and later uses were consequences of this central purpose'.[30]

(i) Reconnaissance

Simon Coningham states that in 'fast-moving mobile warfare, aerial co-operation, even at the sophisticated level of 1918, often failed to perform its fundamental tasks' weather being the 'major hindrance to all forms of reconnaissance'.[31] Nowhere is this more the case than in the Selle operations. As Table 8.3 shows, there were only three days where more than ten reconnaissance flights were made. On the day when most reconnaissance reports were achieved (18 reports on 9 October) the twelve logged for 24 Squadron by 5 Brigade RAF included six reports of train movements, five of troop movements, one of a 'flaming onion' battery (but none of artillery), one report of enemy hangers and another of a fuel dump. There were two days of less fettered reconnaissance during the planning process for 17 October. Walter Longton's two flights along the route of the

30 W. Raleigh, *The War in the Air, Vol 1*, p.213.
31 S. Coningham, 'The Battle of Amiens', in Sheffield and Gray, op. cit., p.211.

HWL I probably had most relevance to operations that day. Of the seven reconnaissance reports of the squadron on the good flying day, 14 October, five concern train movements, and they again contained little intelligence crucial to front-line operations. Reconnaissance during the planning of the operations of 23 October was virtually zero. The second aspect of reconnaissance, the identification of enemy artillery batteries followed the same problematic pattern, as noted. On the days of action, the RAF kept a counter-attack patrol in the air continuously, and these certainly were effective, e.g. identifying the counter-attack against 50th Division on 17 October. On spotting this developing, the patrol dropped white parachute lights immediately over the counter-attacking troops and artillery came into action.

Table 8.3 Reconnaissance and photographic flights during the Selle operations

Date	Flying hours	Recons	Photo flights	Plates	Weather
9	778	18	8	206	Fair but misty
10	321	8	2	20	Low cloud, rain, clearing later
11	448	7	3	0	Low cloud, rain
12	174	3	?	49	Low cloud, mist, rain, poor visibility
13	101	8	?	?	Low cloud, mist, rain
14	657	13	31	763	Fine, mist developing
15	253	11	2	38	Fine early, much mist/rain later
16	54	2	0	0	Low cloud, mist
17	252	3	9	0	Low cloud, mist
18	362	0	6	35	Fine, very misty
19	190	3	2	21	Very misty all day
20	30	0	0	0	Low cloud, rain, mist
21	56	0	0	0	Low clouds, thick mist
22	176	4	0	0	Rain and mist
23	602	6	19	265	Fine with mist
24	535	5	1	3	Fine, poor visibility

The third broad reconnaissance task, filling in the gaps in communication that the fog of war generated, was the contact patrol. This was a difficult task requiring low flying. As Simon Coningham describes, the forward position of friendly troops was often found only 'by a dangerous process of elimination, first being fired upon from German-held positions and then circling back until' friendly forces could be located.[32] As the instructions issued by 66th Division on 6 October made clear, the reply of troops to contact patrols was of 'urgent importance', not least because failing to do so made them vulnerable to friendly fire. Contact patrols would fly along each objective calling for flares by 'sounding a succession of As on the Klaxon Horn, and by firing a White Very Light'.[33] Troops could further identify a contact patrol machine as it had rectangular panels measuring two foot by one on both lower wings about three feet from the fuselage and a streamer

32 Coningham, op. cit., p.212.
33 War Diary, South African Brigade, Instruction No. 2 Issued under Divl. Order No. 97, 6 October 1918, TNA WO95/3146.

on the tail. Every NCO and section commander carried three red ground flares, which were to be lit in response, and three Very lights were to be similarly fired in succession. Stocks of these were easily exhausted, however, and troops were reluctant to use them as their position was thereby given away.[34] Additional signalling methods were therefore detailed. Pocket torches were to be flashed in a westerly direction, reflectors were to be flashed and ground sheets or helmets were to be waved. The days on which most contact patrols were flown, logically enough, were the first two days of the Pursuit – 39 were flown on 9 October, and 23 on the 10th. On the days of set-piece operations, 19 were flown on 17 October, 10 on the 18th, and 15 on the 23rd. Here, the flyers were aided by the fact that as the mornings progressed the fog lifted and they had more chance of fulfilling their task. It is unclear how many planes had radios, but each division and brigade had a message dropping ground – that for the South African Brigade, for instance, was on the reverse slope of high ground to the west of Le Cateau, about 1,500 yards from the Selle.[35]

(ii) Ground support

Hugh Trenchard, the long-serving commander of the RFC on the Western Front, had always believed that the main thrust of air-power should be offensive action in support of the army's general aims.[36] Ground attack had proved a significant feature of the Battle of Amiens, and the three days of the Pursuit saw by far the most significant period of ground attack of the Selle operations, both with machine-gun and 25-pound bombs. Thereafter, there was less evidence of ground-attack in front of the infantry – even on the best day of weather prior to the first set-piece action, there were only 157 bombs dropped and just over 4,000 rounds fired. Ground attack was, therefore, associated mainly with helping the infantry get forward, and targets were serendipitous. The fog on the days of set-piece action, 17-18 October, was most dense at the times infantry attacks jumped-off, and ground attack was not a strong feature of those days. 3rd Squadron AFC would, however, record on the 19th that 'our planes attacked with M.G. fire enemy infantry and strong points, inflicting casualties'.[37] 8 Squadron had been trained to work on co-operation with tanks, identifiable to the infantry due to their low flying activity by a black band at the tail, working to their front to take out anti-tank weapons, but the same problems applied in terms of weather at the times the tanks were deployed.

The RAF's heavier bombs 'could not be said to have been more than moderately effective against railways, blast furnaces, aerodromes and industrial centres',[38] and in addition to poor aiming, in 'most raids, a quarter, and sometimes as much as two thirds, had failed to explode'.[39] Their use at Amiens in trying to cut off the German army by attacking the Somme bridges had not been successful, and the distraction had allowed the concentration of enemy aircraft later in the day. In one week in March 1918, during the German spring offensives, 12,000 25-pound (86 per cent) and

34 Coningham, op. cit., p.213.
35 War Diary, 66th Infantry Division, 66th Divisional Instructions No.6 16 October 1918, TNA WO95/3122.
36 Rather than strategic bombing. D. Jordan, 'The Genesis of Modern Air Power: The RAF in 1918', in Sheffield & Gray op. cit., pp.192-3.
37 182-20.1: Summary of Intelligence, Aerial Annexe – American II Corps Intelligence Summary, 18 October 1918, *United States Army in the World War Vol. 7*, p.660.
38 P. Dye, 'RFC Bombs and Bombing 1912-1918', p.13.
39 RAF Museum B401, 'Report on the Effect of the Bombing by 8th Brigade and Independent Force – Bombs, March 1919', quoted in Dye, op. cit., p.13.

2,000 112-pound bombs (14 per cent) were dropped,[40] the percentage of 25-pound bombs used in the three days of the Pursuit being higher, 97 per cent. The view was taken that the 25-pound bomb in particular was 'useless' against structures – 'the damage done has been nothing.'[41] In the Pursuit its use was higher than previously because it was largely used tactically against personnel and transport, against whom it would clearly have some effect, if only in respect of morale. Forty pound phosphorous bombs were also used to create smoke to shield attacks. In terms of heavier bombs, on 9 October all of the 28 112-pound bombs were dropped on Wassigny, but on the 14th the target had switched to Aulnoye station, ten such bombs being dropped from a height of 1,800 to 2,000 feet, where bombers returned on the 24th, dropping another 10 112-pound bombs. With the exception of the attacks on the Aulnoye railway, the one example of deep battle,[42] all of the bombing was local and tactical, and did not reach far beyond the eastern bank of the Sambre-Oise Canal.

Table 8.4 Ground attack by bomb and machine-gun during the Selle operations[43]

Date	25-pound	40-pound phosphorous	112-pound	Rounds
9th	501		28	30,670
10th	618		7	48,370
11th	404		9	29,705
12th	54		0	1,350
13th	80	1	0	1,550
14th	157		10	4,280
15th	71		0	?
16th	3		0	?
17th	86	32	0	8,975
18th	140		0	4,760
19th	175		0	2,608
20th	0		0	500
21st	0		0	0
22nd	32		0	2,310
23rd	246	22	3	300
24th	227		10	?

The RAF evidently did not achieve air supremacy at the Selle. The enemy, for instance, bombed the immediate rear of XIII Corps area on the night of 8/9 October, and their machines were able

40 Dye, op. cit., p.12.
41 RAF Museum B401, 'Report on the Effect of the Bombing by 8th Brigade and Independent Force – Bombs, March 1919', http://www.da.mod.uk/Publications/category/516/The-Independent-Force, (accessed 26 September 2016).
42 A 'reliable prisoner' stated that a raid on Aulnoye in the early part of October 'caused an ammunition train to blow up in the neighbourhood of a leave train. The station was wrecked, and 900 casualties are said to have been caused'. Fourth Army Summary of Information, No. 302 13 October 1918, TNA WO157/199.
43 Taken From 5 Brigade RAF Operational Summaries, 9-24 October 1918, AIR1 2225/209/40/26; and War Diary, HQ Fourth Army, 9-24 October, TNA WO95/439.

to attack the advancing cavalry on the 9th (the RAF dubbed the enemy air activity as 'slight' that day). The enemy were keen to cover their retreat from the air, attempting to disrupt the inevitable morning thrust of the 9th, including the action against the cavalry. The following day a flight of 31 enemy machines was reported operating just behind the British front-line at Reumont.[44] The enemy did not fly on 17 October, but the following day bombed the western outskirts of Le Cateau, again attempting disruption in front of the collapsing left wing of their army.[45] The enemy was largely using its aircraft defensively, in minor disruptive actions just behind the front of the British advance. Although British flyers largely achieved a local air superiority, and thereby deterred deeper enemy reconnaissance, there were combats on each day that flying was possible. On 23 October enemy aircraft were 'very active', and 35 combats took place. On this day, however, the main enemy activity was in the northern sector, and the combats took place behind the enemy's lines. The Germans were yet again using their aircraft defensively, attempting to prevent RAF oversight of the retreating flank of *Second Army*.

It is clear that, like the artillery, the RAF was less effective than it would have wished to have been in the Selle operations. This was entirely due to the weather, rather than any error on the RAF's part. It was the failure of its main task, reconnaissance, so limited by fog, which had the result of reducing the effectiveness of Fourth Army's artillery. The RAF employed ground attack during the Pursuit, but this was almost certainly at most a significant irritation in terms of disturbing morale, rather than representing a powerful adjunct to the degradation of enemy forces. Thus, a captured German order emanating from *38th Division* of 12 September stated that the participation of low-flying machines in fighting on the ground 'has on many occasions had decisive effect on the battle', this due to the 'bad effect which the element of the unknown in such low-flying surprise attacks exercises on the battle discipline of the troops'.[46] Whilst such an effect was to be welcomed, it is important not to over-value the effectiveness of ground-attack during these days.

Tanks

The tank, as was observed in Chapter Two, was self-evidently not a weapon of pursuit. The Tank Corps urged their use sparingly. They deemed it unwise 'to put 12 tanks where 4 would do', nor was it 'sound to use Tanks just because they were allotted – better to keep them till really wanted'.[47] The Tank Corps was highly aware that in the Hundred Days infantry corps commanders (under whose control their battalions were) wanted to make full use of their available machines. In the Pursuit, however, it is notable that both IX and XIII Corps declined to use their allotted tanks on occasions. During the set-piece Selle operations they were a relatively scarce resource. *SS 204* (along with *SS 214*), the closest the army had to a tank doctrine, recommended one tank to every 100 to 200 yards of frontage, and the frontage attacked on 17 October was some 10,000 yards (expanding to some 15,000 yards), with 44 tanks (plus 16 Whippets).[48] They were also an unreliable resource. The mechanical problems of the machines on approach marches during both the Pursuit and the battles of 17 and 23 October are evident. The rate of Fourth Army's advance had a direct bearing on reliability. As Bryn Hammond remarks: 'The influence of logistical factors on tank employment in

44 War Diary, HQ Fourth Army, 10 October 1918, TNA WO95/439.
45 War Diary, HQ Fourth Army, 17 October 1918, TNA WO95/439.
46 Fourth Army Summary of Information, No. 302 13 October 1918, TNA WO157/199.
47 War Diary, HQ 4th Tank Brigade, 'Report on Operations 4th Tank Brigade September 27th to October 17th 1918', TNA WO95/108/5.
48 General Staff *SS 204 Infantry and Tank Co-Operation and Training. SS 214 Tanks and their Employment in Co-Operation with Other Arms.*

the war's last months cannot be overstated'.[49] The endurance of a heavy tank was three days or 200 miles, that of a Whippet being 400 miles.[50] An army moving forward, therefore, wore out the life of its machines simply by advancing beyond its railheads. Spare parts were at a premium and there was a great demand on workshop hours. Men who might have been gainfully employed in fixing machines had to be put to work salvaging parts from abandoned tanks.[51] Given their unreliability, tank crews were trained in maintenance. Thus Sergeant P.C. Wright was able to mend the broken valve spring on his machine, under fire, in Pommereuil on 23 October. Wright was lucky that his assailants were apparently poor shots – crew casualties were generally high, some 41 per cent during the Hundred Days.[52] Lastly, as was well recognised, they were vulnerable to well-aimed artillery. The destruction of the Whippets north-east of Vallée Mulâtre on 17 October, is instructive.

The term 'penny-packeting' has been used disparagingly to describe the use of tanks in the aftermath of the Battle of Amiens. The Tank Corps itself opposed this model of useage, 'which disrupted command and control arrangements'.[53] It was, however, the only pragmatic choice given available numbers, and not the only such choice made in relation to tanks. The Whippets, which were viewed as tools of exploitation (if not of pursuit), were pushed into breaking lines of enemy defence. This is how they were deployed on 17 October when they almost universally came to grief. As has been seen, during the set piece actions, tanks were allotted specific tactical objectives, namely the reduction of known strongpoints, in accordance with the 'doctrine' of *SS 204*. But the fact that tanks were not available, either by numbers or mishap, to work together in a section as intended meant that they were also drawn into serendipitous action. This often led to a breakdown in tank-infantry co-operation, as is clearly demonstrated in the roaming tanks in 50th Division area at the brickworks and detraining point near Le Cateau on the 17th. If there was a point on the battlefield that morning that weight of machines might have made a tactical difference given the opposition, it was here. Yet the tanks left the scene before the infantry arrived. In IX Corps area, a single tank passed through Andigny les Fermes, where German resistance appeared to be over, only for the enemy to reoccupy the village once the tank had passed. 4th Tank Brigade was unstinting in its criticism of the infantry: 'Infantry should be better informed as to the use, misuse, role and scope of tanks'. This lack of understanding, they believed, gave rise to 'neglected opportunities by Infantry to take advantage of the frequent openings secured by Tanks'.[54] In terms of the Selle operations, this criticism seems unfair – there were very few 'openings' created by the tanks. The attack on Le Quennelet Grange is a good example of an initiative by tanks in taking a major strongpoint in co-operation with infantry, yet one that was not feasible to hold in the face of the enemy counter-attack. The operations to the west of Catillon on 23 October showed tanks traversing ground ahead in the infantry, but infantry moving much more slowly to the rear having to deal with opposing forces that had been bypassed by tanks. It was German resistance that was the key, not simply a failure by the infantry to take advantage of supposed openings created by armour.

49 B. Hammond, 'Practical Considerations in British Tank Operations on the Western Front, 1916-1918', in A. Searle (ed.), *Genesis, Employment, Aftermath*, p.54.
50 Tank Corps: Tank Board, agenda and minutes, TNA WO158/867. 'Notes on Fourth Army Operations', 11 August 1918; and letter from H. Elles 11 October 1918.
51 Hammond, 'Practical Considerations', p.53.
52 See R. Blaber, 'Tanks in the "Hundred Days" 1918'.
53 B. Hammond, 'After Amiens', in Sheffield & Gray, op. cit., p.59.
54 War Diary, HQ 4th Tank Brigade, 'Report on Operations September 27th to October 17th 1918', TNA WO95/108/5.

The demand for maintaining tempo created significant problems for tanks. A successful tank action relied on good reconnaissance of the ground to be crossed, and organisation of infantry co-operation in relation to the objectives identified. As *SS 204* stated: 'Tank and Infantry Commanders must get to know each other, reconnoitre the ground together and so plan success'.[55] This was patently impossible in the semi-mobile warfare of the pursuit. Whilst liaison was achieved to a certain extent on 17 October, the short time in which operations were planned (a good indication of Fourth Army's staff efficiency) created problems for tank-infantry cooperation. There were also operational decisions that did not favour the tanks. The attack of 23 October was made at the early hour of 01.20 to achieve surprise, take advantage of the full moon, and disadvantage enemy machine-gunners. General Lee of 18th Division and Lieutenant-Colonel Irwin temporarily commanding 55 Brigade that day stated that 10th Tank Battalion 'had rendered great service to the Infantry' and that infantry-tank co-operation 'had been eminently satisfactory. Many machine gun emplacements were knocked out and very severe casualties inflicted'. The Tank Battalion itself, however, deprecated its use 'in a night attack over unknown ground, especially when no aeroplane photographs are available beforehand'.[56]

There were influences on effective tank operations beyond simple liaison with infantry. For instance, aircraft-tank cooperation at first relied on tank officers and flyers sitting down over a map and identifying potential anti-tank gun positions. A captured German document revealed the enemy principles for siting these, and the task became easier. An aircraft would thereafter be allotted 2,000 yards of front and would bomb and machine-gun likely sites regularly, and if a gun was actually seen firing, to attack with vigour. Trafford Leigh-Mallory of 8 Squadron reckoned that at the height of practice fifty per cent of sites anticipated for anti-tank guns would be correct.[57] The work of aircraft in this role in the two set-piece attacks was hampered by the choice of both a night assault and early morning jump-offs that took place in fog. The infantry were unable and the RAF absent to prevent the wholesale loss of the Whippets to anti-tank fire at la Vallée Mulâtre. 10th Tank Battalion bemoaned the fact that on 23/24 October the infantry had not 'sufficiently understood that Infantry can protect the Tank against a Battery in much the same way as a Tank will protect infantry against machine guns'.[58] The loss rate of tanks was significant – the fewer the tanks deployed, the more likely was a higher casualty rate, some 40 per cent at this point of the Hundred Days.[59] Those that were not put out of action by enemy fire could fall foul of unknown hostile terrain. The Richemont marshes provide a clear example, as the tanks supporting 25th Division found out. The utility of tanks was also degraded by another hazard, fog. Keeping direction to locate the allotted objective often proved difficult at the Selle. Corporal Collins' tank in XIII Corps area on 17 October should have been heading north, but got distracted whilst turning briefly south in an act of tank-infantry cooperation, and ended up heading east, and having to be redirected north again. Tanks wandered off the Bellevue spur, as did the infantry, on 17 October.

55 *S.S. 204*, p.6.
56 War Diary, HQ 10th Tank Battalion, 'Report on Operations 23th & 24th October 1918', TNA WO95/103/3.
57 'History of Tank and Aeroplane Co-Operation', 31 January 1919, TNA AIR 1/1671/204.
58 War Diary, HQ 10th Tank Battalion, 'Report on Operations 23rd & 24th October 1918', TNA WO95/103/3.
59 As distinct from a knock-out rate of 25 per cent in August 1918. BTM E1949.127- Weekly Tank Notes No. 21, Appendix A, Summary of Casualties 8 August to 24 October 1918, quoted in Blaber, op. cit., p.118.

When on objective, however, they could be of considerable local tactical use – the clearing of Molain on 17 October and Pommereuil on 23 October demonstrates this.

Tanks were not simply used in action. A wireless tank was deployed on the Bellevue spur on 17 October, and there is an account of the journey of a supply tank in the war diary of 7th Queen's.[60] Loaded with such items as water and small arms ammunition, this tank travelled from Maurois at night on 21/22 October using the valley north of the Roman road to Montay, where the following night it moved through Le Cateau to an assembly point in the Richement valley, proceeding on the 23rd to La Fayt Farm, north of Bois l'Evêque. In terms of fighting tanks, however, there was probably no field of action at the Selle where the tank made a clear or crucial difference. This is attributable to two factors. Firstly, limitations of the machines themselves meant that they 'were not of sufficient importance to determine the pace at which the advance progressed'.[61] Secondly, the independent will of the enemy – the 'resilience and rugged adaptability' of the German army, which meant that 'there was never going to be a simple formula guaranteeing British success in operations – whether they involved tanks or not'.[62] As Bryn Hammond concludes: 'Tanks were inefficient in ergonomic terms and their means to effect co-operation with other arms remained primitive and unsatisfactory throughout the war'.[63] The tank could not make a difference at the Selle in anything other than local tactical situations by virtue of their paucity of number, their mechanical vulnerability, and their problems with unknown terrain and the vagaries of meteorological conditions.

Mobile weaponry

Given the difficulties presented to artillery, airpower, and tanks, the infantry had the potential to rely on the weapons that could be made mobile to support them. As noted in Chapter Two, mobile field artillery could and did make a difference during the Pursuit, but could not operate in quite the same way during the set-piece actions. The infantry here had to rely more on automated fire and trench mortar support.

(i) Heavy machine guns

The Vickers machine-gun was used in two ways, both in barrage and pushed forward with the infantry. Of the 256 machine guns available to IX Corps on 17 October, half were deployed in barrage work. In 46th Division, three companies of the 46th Battalion Machine Gun Corps went forward with the attack. Fourth Army's 'Narrative of Machine Gun Operations' describes a strong machine gun nest in the outpost zone in front of Regnicourt which was engaged by eight guns at distance of 1,300 yards, 'whose fire enabled the infantry to advance with slight loss'. The infantry failed to mop it up, however, so when the eight machine guns in their limbers moved forward to the spot to bring fire on Andigny les Fermes, they were fired on at 50 yards distance, although 'the limbers got away undamaged'.[64] This little vignette provides a reminder, apart from indicating the interdependence of arms, of the practical issues of transporting a heavy machine gun across a battlefield under fire. A Vickers gun, which required a six to eight man team, could be transported

60 War Diary, 7th Battalion Queen's Royal West Surrey, 'Brief Summary of Journey of Supply Tank to 7th Queens and 6th Northants Regt. October 1918', TNA WO95/2051.
61 Blaber, op. cit., p.120.
62 Hammond, 'Practical Considerations', op. cit., p.56.
63 B. Hammond, 'The Theory and Practice of Tank Co-Operation with Other Arms on the Western Front During the First World War', p.406.
64 Infantry then mopped up the position, taking 12 machine guns and 200 prisoners. 'Narrative of Machine Gun Operations – Fourth Army', Chapter VI, TNA WO158/332.

strapped to a horse, but spare parts and ammunition also had to accompany. A limber was a two-part affair drawn by two horses. Vulnerability was high.

It is worthwhile to examine the tactical deployment of a MGC battalion, which would be organised into groups and batteries. On 17 October the 50th Battalion MGC, commanded by Lieutenant-Colonel Charles Hoare,[65] had an advanced battalion report centre in a quarry 2,500 yards west of St Benin, connected to three group report centres by telephone, and also laterally to the battalion report centre of adjacent 100th Battalion MGC to the south. All were at a distance of 1,000 to 1,500 yards from each other. As soon as the guns providing the barrage had completed their tasks, they consolidated in depth close to their battery positions. Companies then moved forward. Twenty guns of D and C Companies crossed the river immediately in the rear of 150 Brigade to take up position on the *HWL I* at St Crepin, south of Fassiaux, to cover the right flank of 149 Brigade, detaching one section to cover a re-entrant 700 yards north-west of Le Quennelet Grange. Twenty-four guns of B and C companies moved forward behind 150 Brigade to support its advance, sending two sections forward to assist in consolidation. Lastly, 20 guns of A and C Company, which had fired in the barrage, moved forward at zero plus 60 minutes towards Le Cateau station to cover the left flank of 151 Brigade. These companies had to move forward through fog, gas, and the counter-barrage, but one of their main problems was manoeuvring through the congested river crossings. The 20 guns of D and C Companies followed Lieutenant Philip Meredith who located a crossing utilising the demolished remains of an existing bridge. Eight guns were established on the *HWL I*, but most of the remainder were temporarily lost, although Lieutenant Fry, as seen in Chapter Four, pursued an independent adventure to the north. When the counter-attack drove the 4th King's Royal Rifle Corps back later in the morning, the CO liaised with Meredith, and two guns were pushed forward 1,000 yards. When a second counter-attack developed at 1.45, these guns 'had good targets'.[66] On a third counter-attack at 17.30, Meredith was ordered verbally to withdraw his guns but disobeyed his orders, and assisted the 7th Wiltshires in re-establishing the line. In conjunction with their CO, Lieutenant-Colonel Hodgson, now commanding the brigade front, Meredith arranged a flanking barrage.[67] The 50th Battalion MGC therefore directed its mobile support primarily to provide cover to brigade flanks, enabling units to push forward without concern to the progress of units to their sides which might discourage their forward momentum. Secondly, they engaged targets directly. Further, in deference to the knowledge of the 'man on the spot', section commanders clearly had a certain freedom over the placement of their guns responding directly to the needs of the infantry, some sections being placed directly under the command of infantry COs. The friction of war could make this cooperation less than perfect. As illustrated in Chapter Four, after initial good liaison and coopera-

65 Lieutenant-Colonel Charles Hervey Hoare (later Grey) DSO, an Oxford educated solicitor, was a captain in the TF Reserve (Yeomanry) in 1914. He commanded 2/6th West Yorkshire from July 1917 to January 1918, transferring to the MGC in March 1918. In the post-war years he gained a reputation as a distinguished horticulturalist.

66 'Narrative of Machine Gun Operations – Fourth Army', Chapter VI, TNA WO158/332.

67 22 year-old Philip Russell Meredith was commissioned from Oxford University OTC into the 1/7th Royal Scots in April 1915, and had served on Gallipoli. Meredith was awarded the MC for this action: 'On the night of 16/17th October, 1918, previous to our attack, he was in command of a section of machine guns detailed to take up a position east of the River Selle, near St Souplet. With his orderly he found a way across the stream and reconnoitred almost as far forward as his battery position, some 500 yards behind the enemy's line, with the result that his guns arrived in position in time to carry out their task. Throughout the day he did splendid work, especially during a heavy hostile counter-attack'. *London Gazette*, 10 December 1919, p.15355.

tion, the communications between A & C Companies and the infantry fighting at the detraining point on 17 October broke down rendering machine-gun support impossible in the planned late afternoon attack on the brickworks.

Overnight 17/18 October, 50th Battalion MGC devised a further barrage on specific targets, and again directed its companies to move forward with the infantry. Two sections of D Company quickly advanced with 75 Brigade on the 18th to put down covering fire on the Richemont valley. Two sections of B Company moved to help consolidate a line running south from Bazuel to La Roux Farm and protect the right flank of the advance. Indeed, Second-Lieutenant Harry Brandrick pressed two German machine guns into service to augment just this when the American advance lagged behind.[68] Two sections of A Company advanced similarly to consolidate a line from Bazuel to the high ground north-east of Le Cateau, and protect the left flank. Guns moved forward to the sugar factory and petroleum refinery to protect the advance of the Scottish Horse, liaising closely with its CO; and two guns were placed on the east side of the detraining point to fire into the railway triangle, with two guns by the small wood in front of the triangle to fire over it. Again, the Machine Gun Corps was clearly well integrated into the infantry advance, elements placing themselves under the direct command of Lieutenant-Colonel Blair of the Scottish Horse who was in control of the brigade front.

Colonel Hoare was, however, critical of infantry brigadiers and battalion commanders. He believed that both were 'apt to forget in the stress of battle, the fire-power of machine guns and their great value for the protection of a flank with fire', continuing that this did not necessarily mean that the guns had to be 'on the extreme edge of that flank'. He further took the view that 'sections placed at the disposal of B[attalio]n Commanders without tasks previously allotted are hardly ever used to the best advantage'.[69] His detailed orders and dispositions on 17-18 October clearly reflect his determination that his guns would be put to best effective use. An interesting footnote to machine-gun/infantry co-operation appears in the narrative of Fourth Army's machine-gun operations. An officer from the Northumberland Fusiliers whose troops were crossing the ridge that ran south-east from the Le Cateau-Bazuel road allegedly 'asked that the machine guns overhead covering fire should not open till his men were over the ridge and down the other side'. This would evidently have defeated the object of the protective fire. After reassurance, they crossed the crest of the ridge safely. The narrative continues that 'several of the infantry' later described how 'at first the sound of the bullets over head rather frightened them, it very soon gave them confidence and helped them forward'.[70] As it is inconceivable that the infantry in general was unfamiliar with advancing under a machine-gun barrage, it seems the battalion in question had a considerable number of fresh recruits.

(ii) Light trench mortars

The standard mobile mortar, the 3-inch Stokes mortar of 1918, weighed 113 pounds, and could potentially fire 20-30 rounds a minute (though more usually eight) over a distance of a maximum 800 yards.[71] Distance affected accuracy, as did the stability of the base plate. It was broken down into its three constituent parts for transport, accompanied by a team of five. A Stokes battery

68 Harry Brandrick was commissioned in September 1917.
69 War Diary, 50th Battalion Machine Gun Corps, 'Report on Recent Operations, 21 October 1918', TNA WO95/2823.
70 'Narrative of Machine Gun Operations – Fourth Army', Chapter VI, TNA WO158/332.
71 There were 1,636 in service on the Western Front in November 1918. (M. Farndale, *History of the Royal Regiment of Artillery: Western Front 1914-1918*, p.342.

(attached to brigade) comprised eight mortars, two per section. Its use at the Selle is shrouded in some mystery – brigade Trench Mortar Battery (TMB) war diaries for this period are few and far between, most references appearing in divisional orders and occasional infantry battalion war diaries. In general, its first tactical use was fire suppression after the main barrage had lifted. Secondly it was used as a mobile weapon, one section going forward with each battalion. 'Doctrine' advised that this would normally be in the centre of the advance,[72] but at the Selle the section was often placed on the flank. The actual position taken up by detachments in the course of the advance 'was determined by the nature of the opposition expected, the condition of the ground, and the distance to be covered'. The mortar was well integrated into fire and movement tactics of the infantry: 'Generally a short hurricane bombardment was begun, during which the attacking party advanced as near their objective as possible'. Thirdly, like the Vickers gun, it was used in consolidation, and the interdiction of counter-attacks. In reality, in mobile deployment the 'battery personnel and attached carrying parties carried heavy loads and could not advance as rapidly as the infantry'.[73] Indeed, one of its most significant limitations was how much ammunition a gun team could carry – the bomb weighed 10.7 pounds. The two mortars attached to the left of 151 Brigade's advance towards Le Cateau station on 17 October carried only thirty rounds each. Lieutenant-Colonel Day of 9th Norfolk, whose battalion was very low in rifle strength, was forced to find four men to help carry mortar ammunition for each gun taken forward on the 23rd.

During the pursuit, there is record of 1st Leicestershire advancing with a section of Stokes mortars attached on 11 October. 2nd Sherwood Foresters attacked the same day under their covering fire. Despite the lack of progress by both battalions, 71 Brigade were of the opinion that the mortars 'proved their utility as an Infantry weapon', describing how that day they 'engaged several hostile M.G.s with two direct hits. Living targets were also engaged with good effects and casualties inflicted'.[74] On 17 October 1/8th Sherwood Foresters advanced with a section of mortars on their left flank tasked specifically with dealing with the *HWL I* positions. (1/5th Leicestershire had to provide two platoons to carry ammunition for 138th TMB).[75] 1/5th Lincolnshire similarly advanced that morning using their attached mortars to protect their flank. The attachment of a whole section was not always the rule. Both 1st Buffs and 2nd York & Lancaster of 6th Division advance against the *HWL I* on the 17th with only one mortar from 16th TMB attached to deal with strongpoints. Similarly, 1st West Yorkshire went forward on 23 October with only one. Whilst the trench mortars attached to the Inniskilling Fusiliers advancing on Le Cateau Station on the 17th never made it beyond the river due to their sections being hit by a shell, those under command of the CO of the Scottish Horse came into action there. Town fighting was certainly assumed to require the use of light mortars, as 6th Dublin Fusiliers had all the guns of 198th TMB attached in clearing Le Cateau, one section with each company. They were used against machine-gun posts and fired about 100 rounds that day,[76] just over twelve rounds per gun – undoubtedly the limitations of ammunition carrying made their use sparing. The use of trench mortars was not universal. 1 Brigade's TMB moved No. 1 Section up to join 1st Black Watch on 17 October, but it appears

72 General Staff, *SS 169 Employment of 3-in Stokes Mortars in Recent Fighting*.
73 W.E.L. Napier, *With the Trench Mortars in France*, Chapter IX.
74 War Diary, HQ 71 Infantry Brigade, 'Narrative of Operations – 8th to 11th October 1918', TNA WO95/1620.
75 War Diary, 138 Infantry Brigade, Order NO. 254, 15 October 1918, TNA WO95/2689.
76 War Diary, 6th Inniskilling Fusiliers, 'Account of Operations Part IV 12-18 October 1918', TNA WO95/3140.

they did not go forward with the attack the following day. On the 23rd, Nos. 1 and 3 Sections put down a barrage in support of 3 Brigade, but again, did not go forward with the infantry.[77]

It will be clear from the account of the tactical employment of heavy machine guns that both machine guns and mortars were used in tandem. On 23 October, 3 Brigade positioned four machine-guns covering its right flank along with two Stokes mortars, with 16 machine-guns firing an enfilade barrage along the canal and the remaining six mortars targeting specific positions. In addition to the artillery barrage, 54 Brigade's TMB put down a 'hurricane bombardment' that morning, two mortars firing on a trench just in front of the start line, and four firing on Richemont Mill and the sunken road running north from it.[78] When 1st Shropshire Light Infantry attacked on the morning of the 24th, a machine-gun nest in close proximity to their front caused difficulty in forming up. In a good example of how an infantry battalion used such attached resources, a section of 16th TMB engaged the post for half an hour before zero, stepping up its rate of fire at jump-off. The utility of *ad hoc* use is demonstrated by the use of the mortars with 9th Yorkshire in clearing up machine-gun nests on 23 October in an area missed by the barrage between 25th and 18th Divisions on the Richemont stream.

Arnold Harvey, in his review of the light trench mortar and its use, abstracts a quote from the history of 2/4th Oxfordshire and Buckinghamshire Light Infantry to the effect that: 'Though sometimes supplied, cooperation of this arm was never asked for'.[79] Asked for by whom is not specified, but traditionally in trench warfare the appearance for a quick shoot and subsequent disappearance of a mortar in the front line had never been welcome at battalion level because of the retribution it called down. It is clear at the Selle, even though the evidence is limited, that brigades integrated TMBs into both barrage and advancing units. What is not clear is how effective they actually were. As Harvey notes: 'The contribution of mobile light mortars to successful infantry advances is rarely alluded to in the War Diaries of Infantry Battalions',[80] and this is certainly true at the Selle. Anthony Saunders asserts that the capabilities of the Stokes mortar 'allowed the development of an entirely novel form of infantry warfare'.[81] This claim is over-enthusiastic. It was the cover provided by artillery which allowed this continuing development as a range of new weapons came into use by the infantry. Harvey is probably nearer the mark when he suggests that the weapon 'certainly cannot be said to have triumphantly vindicated its potential in the way that the Vickers machine gun and the Lewis Gun had'.[82]

(iii) The Lewis Gun

Both heavy machine guns and trench mortars presented problems in speed of movement in the wake of an infantry attack. The infantry's integrated weaponry included, of course, rifle, bomb and Lewis gun. In a period where the units of the BEF were depleted in numbers, the Lewis gun became crucial in maintaining unit firepower. There is no more telling reflection of the importance place on automated fire at this time than the response to a message sent two days before the attack of 23 October by Lieutenant-Colonel Day of 9th Norfolk, to 71 Brigade. Day had written that he did not believe that his unit was 'fit to take part in an offensive operation owing to the lack of bayonet and rifle power'. He asked that 'permission be given to carry fewer Lewis Guns or that

77 War Diary, 1st Division Trench Mortar Battery, 17 & 23 October 1918, TNA WO95/1251.
78 War Diary, HQ 54 Infantry Brigade, 23 October 1918, TNA WO95/2042.
79 G.R. Rose, *The Story of the 2/4th Oxfordshire and Buckinghamshire Light Infantry*, p.12.
80 A.D. Harvey, 'Trench Mortars in the First World War', p.88.
81 A.J. Saunders, 'A Muse of Fire', p.270.
82 Harvey, op. cit., p.90.

reinforcements be sent me without delay'.[83] His companies had strengths of 39, 49, 40 and 46, with either five or six Lewis guns per company (the establishment per battalion was 36 in late 1918, two with each platoon and four with battalion HQ for use in anti-aircraft fire). A Lewis gun team was normally eight men plus an NCO – Day was evidently assuming five men per team which would have both limited the ammunition carry and left him with virtually no riflemen. The response from brigade HQ was that he should deploy his full complement of Lewis guns, as 235 reinforcements were on their way and carriers could also deploy rifle and bayonet. Whether Day was satisfied with this response is unclear.

The Mk II Lewis gun could fire 550 rounds a minute, fed by a 97 round pan magazine, each Lewis gun team being normally issued with a total of 44 magazines. In their advance on 17 October it was noted in Chapter Four how 9th Yorkshire were unable to harass the retreating enemy as their Lewis guns were on a cart to the rear. Hand-drawn carts had supposedly been phased out in 1917, but it is clear that such were still in use in 1918. They had supposedly been replaced by a horse-drawn limber which would carry four guns, spare parts, 176 filled magazines, 22 metal ammunition boxes, and nine 1,000 round boxes.[84] As with the heavy machine-gun and trench mortar, the key issue was transport of ammunition. Thus even this weapon presented a movement issue. The Lewis gun itself had long since been well-integrated into the infantry attack. Indeed, it has been claimed that 'British machine-gun doctrine was probably the most advanced of any army'.[85] As will be seen later in this chapter, even in October 1918 great stress was being placed on training in the use and tactical deployment of the weapon. *SS 197 The Tactical Employment of Lewis Guns*, issued in January 1918, set out two main tactical roles of the use of the weapon in the support of infantry. Firstly, the gun would provide supporting fire for advancing infantry. Whereas in trench warfare it had been advised that Lewis gunners should not be in the first wave of infantry because of the provision of targets, in the open warfare of 1918 it was recommended that for maximal utility they should not only be in the first wave but in front of the first wave to establish 'offensive points' to cover the advance. The weapon could be fired from a prone position, where on its bipod greatest accuracy could be achieved; or, more rarely, from the hip. Indeed, in Chapter Five Captain John Walford and his company of 1/8th Warwickshire were encountered entering Bazuel and overcoming opposition advancing firing Lewis Guns from the hip (this was recommended tactically when encountering an 'invisible enemy firing through undergrowth'). If the platoon was caught by fire, the Lewis gun would engage it head on, whilst the infantry rushed it; if the Lewis gun team identified the position before the infantry arrived it would work round to a flank and engage it as the infantry approached, cutting off the possibility of the enemy escaping. Woods and villages were to be enveloped, positioning the Lewis guns to sweep clearings, or firing down streets and covering exits. Secondly, the weapon had a role in consolidating captured positions, established in outposts and supporting patrols.[86] The accounts in the foregoing chapters testify to many of these uses – given the heavy reliance of the enemy on machine-guns, the Battle of the Selle was often a battle of infantry-borne automated fire on both sides.

83 War Diary, 9th Battalion Norfolk Regiment, Message to HQ 71 Infantry Brigade 21 October 1918, TNA WO95/1623.
84 General Staff, *SS 197 Tactical Employment of Lewis Guns*.
85 N. Grant, *The Lewis Gun*, p.46.
86 *Tactical Employment of Lewis Guns*, pp.10-17.

The British Infantry

At its heart the Selle fighting was a soldier's battle *par excellence*, and a main focus of our attention should be the 'queen of the battlefield', the infantry. 'Resurgam' might well have been the motto of Fourth Army and a number of its formations.[87] After its efforts on the Somme in 1916, it had been sent to the coast for operations associated with the Third Battle of Ypres which were subsequently aborted. It languished there from June to November 1917, taking over the Second Army front when Sir Herbert Plumer went to Italy. In February 1918, Sir Henry Rawlinson was sent to Versailles as British Representative on the Supreme War Council, and when Plumer returned in mid-March, Fourth Army became Second Army. After the sacking of Sir Hubert Gough in March, Rawlinson returned to take command of Fifth Army, which was renamed Fourth Army. His new command comprised five under-strength divisions, and numbered around 9,000 effectives – rebuilding was the order of the day, as was subsequent change. The three corps that fought at Amiens that August – Australian, Canadian and III Corps – were not constituents of Fourth Army at the Selle. In response to Rawlinson's September pleas for fresh formations, IX Corps, having been without troops since the end of July, was reconstituted, and arrived in Fourth Army on 4 September 1918. The 1st Division moved from First Army at the same time, 6th Division having made the transition from Second Army on 1 September. 46th Division was the last of the new arrivals, beginning its move from First Army on 12 September. The 32nd Division had been with Fourth Army since the start of the Hundred Days campaign, but played no part in the Selle operations. XIII Corps left Fifth Army on 25 September and took over the line from Fourth Army's III Corps. Of its four divisions, the 18th had been present since Rawlinson's arrival. The other three divisions in the corps had undergone very hard times. The 25th and 50th Divisions had been hit by the German offensives of 21 March on the Somme, on 9 April on the Lys, the *coup de grace* finally being administered at the Chemin des Dames on 27 May. The 25th was reduced to cadre and only fully reconstituted on 17 September. The 50th Division was reconstituted earlier, on 15 July, and joined Fourth Army on 22 September with 25th and 66th Divisions. The latter had been smashed by the offensive of 21 March and reduced to cadre in late April, being reconstituted in a much more lengthy process which only settled when the South African Brigade joined on 22 September. The Fourth Army that fought at the Selle was, therefore, an agglomeration of formations with little history of working with each other. Their success suggests a high level of ingrained skill at mounting operations both at corps and divisional level which could function beyond the comfort of lengthy inter-formation contact. The almost completely untried American Corps was, however, a different matter.

Mark Whisler was of the opinion that Fourth Army's infantry at the Selle 'did not comprise a particularly select elite – such as the Australian or Canadian Corps – and can be considered representative of most British corps and divisions'.[88] As it happens, Whisler is not entirely correct on either count. Table 8.5 shows the rankings of the battle performance of British divisions in the Hundred Days as identified by the SHLM Project. There were 50 British divisions on the Western Front during the campaign, and as can be seen three of the four divisions of XIII Corps, (66th, 25th and 18th) fall in the top ten, and all except the 46th Division fall in the top half. The 66th and 25th Divisions keep their rankings when the ten Australian, New Zealand and Canadian divisions are included, the 18th Division being displaced one position by the 4th Australian Division. Three of the British divisions at the Selle were, according to this calculation, as effective as the top

87 Resurgam translates as 'I shall rise again'.
88 Whisler, op. cit., p.36.

Dominion division. Such an analysis is open to criticism that a perfect algorithm for quantifying success may be unobtainable, and there is inevitably loss of sophistication of detail. Nowhere is this more evident than in the performance of 46th Division, which had enjoyed spectacular success crossing the St Quentin Canal, and again did well on 17 October.

Table 8.5 Rankings of success rates of Fourth Army's infantry divisions in the Hundred Days (*excluding American divisions)[89]

Division	Attacks	Success in opposed attacks	Failures	Ranking in British divisions in BEF	Ranking of all divisions in BEF*
66th	10	100%	0%	Joint 1st	Joint 1st
25th	20	85%	10%	4th	4th
18th	37	78%	19%	6th	7th
1st	16	69%	0%	14th	21st
50th	17	65%	12%	20th	27th
6th	16	62.5%	25%	23rd	32nd
46th	17	54%	31%	33rd	43rd

An analysis of the daily activities of the 63 battalions of IX and XIII Corps that fought between 9 and 24 October reveals that 17 per cent of their time was spent in action, the same proportion involving moving between locations. Six per cent of their time was spent reorganising between actions or preparing for action, whilst 18 per cent involved line holding or being in immediate reserve. Nineteen per cent of their time was concerned with rest in billets or bivouacs. Perhaps most importantly, 23 per cent of time was spent in training. It may seem surprising that the highest proportion of the infantry's time in a mobile campaign was spent thus. This reflects both the importance placed upon training for all, and the need for it given the influx of drafts into the ranks, the degree of training that these newcomers had received being very variable. Four training programmes from this period survive. The programme of 1/5th South Staffordshire, spread over nine days 21-31 October 1918, placed emphasis on physical training (five sessions) and drill (eight sessions); attack formations (eight sessions), and handling arms (four sessions). There were five sessions of Lewis gun training and five of musketry. Amongst other sessions of interest were six 'young officer' and NCO classes, and one concerning wood fighting. There was thus an emphasis on raising physical fitness, infantry having to cover distance on foot; infantry tactics and weapon skills; and junior leadership.[90] In terms of physical fitness and endurance, 66th Division carried out three ten or eleven mile route marches between 23 and 28 October, firstly without arms or equipment, next in drill order, and finally in battle order, following this with 'attack schemes'.[91] General Boyd of 46th Division wrote training notes on 20 October which stated that 'the best men are of little value unless they are physically and mentally fit', prescribing a mix of physical drill, marching,

89 P. Simkins, personal communication of data concerning all BEF divisions in the Hundred Days from the work of the SHLM Project. See also P. Simkins, 'Co-stars or Supporting cast?' in P. Griffith (ed.), *British Fighting Methods in the Great War*, pp.50-69; and J. Lee, 'The SHLM Project', in Griffith, op. cit., pp.175-181.

90 War Diary, 1/5th Battalion South Staffordshire Regiment, 'Training Programme 21-31 October 1918', TNA WO95/2686.

91 War Diary, 66th Infantry Division, 23-30 October 1918, TNA WO95/3122.

bayonet training, games, football, as well as recreation. Boyd's longest set of instructions was for the 'training of leaders' (as reflected in the South Staffords' programme). These covered both the importance of paternal care for the other ranks, and tactical issues, namely 'the leading of companies and platoons in attack on M.G. nests: the value of outflanking movements; covering fire; fire combined with moves to a flank'. He made no condemnatory references to the qualities of drafts, merely referring to them needing being given a 'valuable final polish'.[92] 8th Royal Berkshire held a ten day programme between 7 and 17 October 1918, intended to be 'as intensive as possible'. This was split into two periods, the first for sections and platoons, the second for platoons and companies. There was an eight day Lewis gun course ('the greatest stress will be laid on the tactical use of Lewis Guns'), and a seven day musketry course, with a six day rifle grenade course. Emphasis was to be placed on 'correct extended order and artillery formation' and 'fire and movement'. In addition to the emphasis on combat effectiveness, there was similar premium placed upon junior leadership in the shape of a seven day 'Junior NCO's' course. There was, however, only a single lecture to subalterns.[93] This is a clear reflection of the reality that NCOs (and even privates, as the examples given in the foregoing chapters indicate) were expected to be able to offer tactical leadership. 55 Infantry Brigade set out training programmes for 7th Queen's, 7th Buffs, 8th East Surrey and 55th TMB (which reflected how they were expected to be integrated with the infantry in advance) between 14-19 October 1918. Each programme was slightly different. Lewis gunners and scouts had instruction every day, as well as training in using captured German machine guns. 8th East Surrey noted having formed a battalion Lewis gun school. Many battalions whose training schemes have not survived make extensive reference to Lewis gun training in their war diaries. Musketry practice was carried out every day within 7th Buffs. 7th Queen's spent a day on 'attack formations', another on 'outpost schemes', and yet another on 'advance guards' – 8th East Surrey held a conference at battalion HQ which included discussion of the use of advanced guards.[94] 6th Lancashire Fusiliers carried out a two week training programme at the end of September 1918, but the notes on their 'field firing practices' are of interest. These included exercises in applying fire to a pill box, quickly obtaining superiority of fire, section rushes, and platoon attacks with Lewis guns. This battalion, too, held classes for junior NCOs.[95]

The BEF at the Selle, with the war almost won, therefore did not sit on its laurels. It devoted the highest proportion of its infantry's time to ensuring that its men were fit, skilled in the 'fire and movement' tactics of open warfare, and particularly skilled in the deployment of automatic weapons. Secondly, it was concerned with junior leadership, indicating the commitment to devolved command and initiative. The Official Historians, with their focus on the Regular soldier, stated that: 'Very few officers and men who had received training in open warfare were in the field in 1918'. They describe the army of 1918 as 'practically devoid of real tactical sense'.[96] This, as these pages bear testimony, was far from the truth.

92 War Diary, 46th Infantry Division, 'Notes by the Divisional Commander on Training', 20 October 1918, TNA WO95/2666.
93 War Diary, 8th Battalion Royal Berkshire Regiment, 'Training Programme 7-17 October 1918', TNA WO95/2037.
94 War Diary, 55 Infantry Brigade, 'Training Programme 14-19 October 1918', TNA WO95/2048.
95 War Diary, 6th Battalion Lancashire Fusiliers, 'Notes on Training' and 'Field Firing Practices', September 1918, TNA WO95/3140.
96 Edmonds & Maxwell-Hyslop, op. cit., p.575.

Generals

John Bourne has described the key features of generalship in the First World War as: 'The capacity to take infinite care with planning and preparation; to respond effectively to battlefield emergencies; and to maintain the initiative by constant harassing of the enemy'. He continues how on 29 September 1918, when all the five British armies were in action, these qualities 'were widespread at battalion, brigade and divisional command levels throughout the BEF and were increasingly to be found at corps level'.[97] He thus describes a bottom-up progression of able men, evolving through infantry battalion command or staff experience, and honed by the experience of the new warfare.

Sir Henry Rawlinson, the army commander, was of a different ilk. Robin Prior and Trevor Wilson describe him in 1914 as 'well equipped to exercise command in battle'.[98] Progressing from divisional command in 1914 to corps and then to army command, Rawlinson was very far from fault-free: 'There was no undeviating advance towards wisdom, and no certain demonstration that at the end of the day Rawlinson was master of his job'. Prior and Wilson suggest that in the final analysis, in 1918 this mattered less because 'expertise in the technical aspects of conducting battles had become so widespread' throughout the army, and supplies of artillery and other weaponry that this expertise could call on had become so extensive, that 'the importance of command in accomplishing victory had diminished absolutely'.[99] This last statement is correct if one assumes that it is army command which is meant. Responsibility for planning operations, however, had long been centred at corps and divisional level. In 1918 Rawlinson was far from a majestic figure driving the progress of Fourth Army; rather, he 'presided' over events 'shaped by many forces and many individuals in addition to himself'.[100] Rawlinson's staff team had been together for over two years, notably Archibald 'Archie' Montgomery, Major-General General Staff, and Charles 'Buddy' Budworth, General Officer Commanding Royal Artillery. Prior & Wilson, without performing a close analysis of how the Fourth Army team worked, state that Rawlinson had been 'able to assemble a team equipped … to administer battles thoroughly and level-headedly on most occasions'.[101] Montgomery (a gunner by trade) had been BGGS from August 1915 to February 1916 and MGGS with Fourth Army from that point. If he had had been over-enthusiastic in terms of planning regards the length of line to be assaulted on 1 July 1916, he had learnt from this, and had always been (with Rawlinson) a proponent of limited objective attacks. He recognised the value of training, and whilst a champion of new technologies, was well aware of their limitations. Rawlinson was able to devolve planning to Montgomery who liaised closely with corps commanders – Fourth Army's reputation for good staff work became well recognised. Whilst the Fourth Army orders at the Selle were brief, reflecting greater confidence and devolution to corps, Montgomery's eye was always upon it, and his influence was no doubt exerted in Army meetings with corps commanders. If Budworth did not 'invent' the creeping barrage, he certainly fostered its proliferation. He had served a Brigadier General Royal Artillery with both IV and X Corps before becoming General Officer Commanding Royal Artillery Fourth Army in May 1916, although he had less control over corps artillery than his job title implied. He was a relentless producer of artillery tactical notes, and

97 J.M. Bourne, 'The BEFs Generals on 29 September 1918', p.113, in P. Dennis & J. Grey, *1918 Defining Victory*.
98 R. Prior & T. Wilson, *Command on the Western Front*, p.10.
99 Prior & Wilson, op. cit., p.397.
100 Prior & Wilson, op. cit., p.396.
101 Prior & Wilson, op. cit., p.397.

Shelford Bidwell and Dominic Graham describe him as an 'all-rounder' who 'learned the intricacies of the heavy artillery game'.[102] It was a competent team.

By this stage of the war corps and division had assumed a key role in planning. Andy Simpson summarises that: 'By September 1917 … Army merely passed to corps the outline of what it had to do, and corps organised the whole operation, delegating to divisions as necessary'. By the Hundred Days, there was sufficient flexibility in command 'for corps to leave divisions to get on with attacks with minimal supervision, unless a co-ordinated approach was especially required'.[103] The complexity of the artillery arrangements of 17 October, the very factor that had brought corps to organisational prominence, required this level of co-ordination. The two corps commanders were Sir Walter Pipon Braithwaite and Sir Thomas Lethbridge Napier Morland. Braithwaite, 53 years old, had commanded 62nd Division from December 1915 to August 1918, and had only been appointed to command IX Corps on 13 September 1918. He had born a good deal of the criticism for the failure of operations during the Gallipoli campaign, where he was Chief of Staff to Sir Ian Hamilton. John Gellibrand, a future Australian general did not mince his words in his 1906 diary entry: 'Imagination is as foreign to him as independence. To sum up, a good regimental officer, fair office man and Brigade Major but a mind like a waiter's and the independence of a tick. Besides, he appears over anxious to please those he thinks influential and this again betrays his waiter's mind'.[104] This was certainly an outdated and likely unfair assessment. Sir Douglas Haig always thought well of him, ensuring his rehabilitation through appointment to divisional command. After a difficult baptism at Bullecourt in May 1917, the division performed well at Cambrai, and again in checking the German Spring Offensive at Bucquoy, 'where Braithwaite's personal leadership was conspicuous'.[105] Although it is perhaps 'difficult to make out a case for his deserving the appointment', there being 'many more experienced and distinguished divisional commanders',[106] Braithwaite's elevation to command IX Corps revealed him as 'open to new ideas and sympathetic to technological solutions to tactical problems',[107] and his command of the corps is difficult to fault. John Bourne and Peter Simkins judge him to be a more able corps commander than his counterpart.[108] Sir Henry Rawlinson agreed – by 21 September he was writing: 'Braith doing well',[109] and the plan that Braithwaite and his staff concocted for 17 October was creative and effective.

Thomas Morland, also aged 53, commanded 5th Division from October 1914 and X Corps from July 1915. He was transferred to command XIII Corps on 14 April 1918, thus being one of the longest-serving corps commanders. He had been notorious for climbing a tree on 1 July 1916 some two miles from his corps HQ (albeit connected by telephone), not a logical place for a corps commander to be, to get a better view of the fighting. Hubert Gough did not 'think very much of him', finding him 'not sufficiently decisive'. Although Haig agreed to replace him on 22 July, he

102 Bidwell & Graham, op. cit., p.101.
103 A. Simpson, 'The Operational Role of British Corps Command on the Western Front, 1914-18', pp.9-10.
104 E & J. Gellibrand, Diary, 10 March 1906, quoted in J. Walker, *The Blood Tub*, p.4.
105 http://www.westernfrontassociation.com/great-war-people/the-british-generals-biographies/3405-lieutenant-general-sir-walter-pipon-braithwaite-kcb.html (accessed 1 August 2016).
106 J. Bourne, personal communication, email dated 7 July 2016.
107 http://www.westernfrontassociation.com/great-war-people/the-british-generals-biographies/3405-lieutenant-general-sir-walter-pipon-braithwaite-kcb.html (accessed 1 August 2016).
108 J. Bourne, personal communication, email dated 7 June 2016.
109 Sir H. Rawlinson, War Journal, 21 September 1918, Churchill College RWLN 1/11.

wrote that he 'personally found Morland one of our best brigadiers at Aldershot'.[110] He was soon rehabilitated with temporary command of XIV Corps in Fourth Army, and by 22 May 1917 Haig would write, probably accurately: 'Sir T. Morland seems greatly improved since July last year on the Somme. He has now more knowledge and more confidence'.[111] Rawlinson commented on 21 October 1918, however, that 'XIII Corps do not work as well nor are they as far-sighted as the IX Corps … Morland is inclined to be extravagant with troops'.[112] The corps was also more prescriptive in its orders than were IX Corps, perhaps indicating slightly more concern in directing divisional commanders. Andy Simpson, writing of the year 1917, notes that 'corps commanders were less likely to be sacked than their divisional counterparts, for it was harder to find even half-competent corps commanders than new divisional GOsC'.[113] A Corps commander had to interpret the ideas of the Army commander, assess the detailed all-arms plans of divisional commanders, and supervise the work of his own staff. They did not do all of this this alone, of course – whatever their deficiencies, these two men were surrounded by staff well used to planning. As Mark Whisler comments: 'The ability of the staffs to assemble the formations at the right places and times is clear'.[114]

The operational plans produced for 17 October indicate competent corps commanders and staff. In IX Corps, the BGGS, Archibald Rice Cameron, had spent 985 days in the same role with X Corps before being moved to IX Corps 11 days after Braithwaite's arrival. Whilst he was, therefore, more used to working with Morland, he was richly experienced. When Haig had met with Morland and Cameron on 22 May 1917, spending an hour with them going through their plans for Messines, he described them as 'carefully thought out and sound'.[115] Braithwaite's BGRA, Gardiner Humphreys, had served as CRA of 6th Division for 872 days before being promoted to IX Corps on 22 June 1916, and Haig found him on 23 May 1917 'fully alive to his work'.[116] Braithwaite therefore possessed two key staff officers who had lengthy experience of operational planning at corps level. In XIII Corps, Morland's BGGS, Ian Stewart, had been in that role since 16 November 1916; and the BGRA, Richard Ashmore Colley Wellesley, had been CRA of 21st Division for 584 days before being promoted to XIII Corps on 13 May 1917. Again, both were very experienced staff officers. It could be suggested that a long tenure of a specific role might lead to atrophy of innovative thinking, but there is no evidence of this in the plans for 17 October.

The seven major-generals who commanded British divisions at the Selle had an average age of 44 years and eight months. All were regulars, but they were an eclectic mix.[117] Hugh Keppel Bethell (66th Division) had been commissioned into the Royal Artillery, transferring to the Indian Army and again to the 7th Hussars in February 1914, afterwards commanding an infantry battalion. Aged only 36 he was the youngest divisional commander of either world war. Bethell, 'a thruster in a class of his own', was 'distinguished, or notorious, for flouting regulations or higher authorities'. Walter Guinness, GSO2 to 66th Division, described him as 'like quicksilver', but 'frightfully impa-

110 D. Haig, diary entry 22 July 1916, G. Sheffield & J. Bourne, *Douglas Haig: War Diaries and Letters 1914–1918*, p.208.
111 Sheffield & Bourne, op. cit., p.295.
112 Sir H. Rawlinson, War Journal, 21 October 1918, Churchill College RWLN 1/11.
113 Simpson, op. cit., p.103.
114 Whisler, op. cit., p102.
115 Sheffield & Bourne, op. cit., p.295.
116 Sheffield & Bourne, op. cit., p.295.
117 Of the 72 men commanding divisions at the Armistice, 65.3 per cent were infantrymen, 12.5 per cent cavalrymen, 13.9 per cent were artillerymen and 9.7 per cent engineers. J. Bourne, 'British Divisional Commanders During the Great War'.

tient and unreasonable when things don't go right', when: 'Vesuvius in eruption couldn't compete'. Brian Bond states that: 'Bethell's infantile behaviour when out of action should not be allowed to obscure his outstanding record as a commander in battle'.[118] Personality disorder or not, he took over and rehabilitated a shattered division at the end of March 1918. Indeed, he has been portrayed as 'touched by genius'.[119] Richard Phillips Lee (18th Division) had been commissioned into the Royal Engineers and was a sapper through and through, having served as Chief Engineer of both I Corps and Fifth Army, and was the oldest of the group at 53. Peter Simkins has described him as 'a sound and practical officer' as a sapper, but 'perhaps not an obvious choice' as the illustrious Ivor Maxse's successor.[120] According to the divisional history: 'He displayed infinite knowledge, quick grip and decision. His opinion was considered and not easily changed, as indeed it rarely had need to be'. In terms of operations: 'He had a great gift for map-reading, and consequently never failed in his battle dispositions to make full use of ground' having 'a settled distaste for frontal attacks'.[121] Lee 'achieved very notable results with young, untried and frequently exhausted troops. His dispositions for the moving battles that concluded the campaign were masterly'.[122] 10th Essex paid tribute with similar words to his 'masterly conduct' of these final operations, but also to 'his inspiring right-hand man, Guy Blewitt'.[123] James Ronald Edmonston Charles (25th Division) was also a sapper who had served as BGGS with the Indian and XVII Corps. 'Charles's finest hour as a staff officer probably came during the German spring offensive'. XVII Corps was the only corps whose HQ was not compelled to retreat in March 1918 and 'this owed much to the highly efficient staff team that Charles had created, but perhaps more to the practical application of his under-used skill as a sapper'. He had organised a 'system of defence in depth that the Germans failed to penetrate'.[124] He then took over and completely reconstituted 25th Division in the summer of 1918 and quickly turned it into 'an innovative and efficient formation'.[125] Gerald Farrell Boyd (46th Division) was a commissioned ranker in the infantry, from which branch of the army the remaining three also came. Boyd's confidential report at the end of the war describes him as 'a disciplinarian, a tremendous worker, at all times cheerful and optimistic' and that he 'can and does breathe his own indomitable spirit into his men'.[126] Certainly he brought some tactical innovation and tighter planning into a division that had previously had a lacklustre reputation. Edward Peter Strickland (1st Division) was the only one of the group who did not have staff experience, but by the Armistice he was the sixth longest serving commander of an infantry division and the longest serving commander of a Regular division in the BEF. Regarded as a martinet, Haig described Strickland as 'a hard and capable soldier'.[127] He possessed a 'violent temper' and was 'unpleasantly

118 B. Bond & S. Robbins (eds), *Staff Officer: The Diaries of Walter Guinness (First Lord Moyne) 1914-1918*, pp.16-17.
119 J. Bourne, personal communication, email dated 14 June 2016.
120 P Simkins, personal communication, email dated 7 June 2016.
121 G.H.F. Nichols, *The 18th Division in the Great War*, p.138.
122 Nichols, op. cit., p.6. Nichols particularly mentions his turning movements at Combles on 1st September 1918, and his clearing of the Forest of Mormal on 4 November. Peter Simkins similarly rates highly his defensive battle at Villers-Bretonneux in April 1918.
123 T.M. Banks and R.A. Chell, *With the 10th Essex in France*, p.311. GSO1 Lieutenant-Colonel Guy Blewitt DSO MC had been in staff posts since July 1915.
124 J. Bourne, unpublished biographical notes on J.R.E. Charles.
125 J. Bourne, personal communication, email dated 14 June 2016.
126 Cited in S. Peaple, *Mud, Blood and Determination*, p.447.
127 Diary entry 2 March 1915, Sheffield & Bourne, op. cit., p.105.

rude' but was 'an ambitious fighting man with any amount of energy'.[128] Both Strickland and Thomas Owen Marden (6th Division) had been commanding infantry battalions in August 1914. Marden's 648 days of brigade and 416 days of divisional command speak to a man who steadily grew in organisational competence. When Sir Henry Rawlinson met Marden on 9 September he noted: 'He is all right – I rather liked the look of him'.[129] His division, however, had its problems on 17 October, although the source of these may have rested below the level of divisional command. Lastly, Henry Cholmondeley Jackson, who had previously commanded a service battalion, took over 50th Division two days into the March Offensive and had a very difficult time on the Somme, Lys and Aisne. That this testifies to his solidity is indicated by John Bourne's observation: 'This might have broken a lesser man or even an older one (Jackson was only 38)'.[130] It was Jackson who, when the units of his brigades became hopelessly intermingled on 17 October, swiftly stepped in and pragmatically imposed a temporary command solution. Similarly, Major-Generals Lee and Charles pushed forward to the HQs of their leading brigades on 23 October to ensure effective decisions were made.

In terms of command experience prior to elevation to divisional level, the two sappers had not commanded infantry brigades; whilst of the remaining five, Strickland had notched up three brigade commands. They had an average of 550 days of brigade command. Whilst the organisational changes in the army in the opening months of the year and the heavy casualties of the Spring offensive had generated a lack of continuity for many divisions across the BEF, the seven had been in post with for an average 342 days before the Selle operations commenced. Boyd was the relative newcomer having had only 51 days of brigade command and 31 days of divisional command, and Charles had been in post with his division for only 67 days. John Bourne concludes that 'the "learning curve" is apparent at this level of command',[131] i.e. the officers commanding divisions at the Selle were, by and large, an outstanding group who had learnt their craft and demonstrated their skill. Sir Douglas Haig wrote after meeting with the senior officers of II Corps on 20 July 1917: 'Looking round the faces opposite to me, I felt what fine hard looking determined men the war had brought to the front'.[132] This is absolutely true of Fourth Army's divisional commanders at the Selle.

Twenty-two individuals commanded brigades during the Selle operations. Of the 21 British brigadiers,[133] their average age was a month over 43, the oldest being Frank George Mathias Rowley at 52, the youngest being Charles William Frizzell at 30. Seventeen were Regulars, one was from the Special Reserve and two from the Territorial Force. This represents a third of the Territorial officers who by the start of the month had achieved infantry brigade command.[134] All but four had commanded infantry battalions, Percy Wilson Brown having commanded five, and four had commanded three. Of the four who had not, Guy Charles Williams had been serving with the Royal Engineers, and the other three had long histories of staff service, nine of the group having served in staff posts. For two, William Garnett Braithwaite and Frank Rowley, their brigade command at the Selle was their third, and for another four it was their second. They had an average

128 TNA CAB 45/132, Pearson Choate to Sir James Edmonds, 6 April 1936.
129 Sir H. Rawlinson, War Journal, 9 September 1918, Churchill College RWLN 1/11.
130 J. Bourne, personal communication, email dated 14 June 2016.
131 J. Bourne, personal communication, email dated 14 June 2016.
132 Sheffield & Bourne, op. cit., p.304.
133 W.E.C. Tanner of the South African Brigade is omitted from this analysis.
134 Bourne, op. cit., p.102. 'By 29 September 1918 there were only 11 Territorials holding general officer rank … six infantry brigade commanders … and five BGRAs'.

of 292 days of experience of brigade command, 207 with the formations they commanded at the Selle. There was, unsurprisingly, more evidence of change and potential discontinuity at brigade than at divisional level. Frank Rowley had 737, John Vaughan Campbell had 690 and William Braithwaite 624 previous days of command. The majority were therefore highly experienced. Three, however, were relative newcomers. Edward St Aubyn had been in command for only three days at the start of the Pursuit, Charles Frizzell for nine days, and George Rollo for ten. Oswald Cuthbert Borrett took up post during the operations themselves.

In reviewing brigade command at the Battle of Arras in 1917, Trevor Harvey has asserted that 'the most significant contribution of brigadier-generals was not on the field'. Rather, their role was in preparation, being 'on a treadmill to recreate the capability of their brigades to fight'.[135] Peter Simkins makes a case, however, that 'by mid-1918, the BEF's senior commanders were much happier than hitherto to leave basic tactical decision-making and leadership to the "man on the spot", as pre-war Field Service Regulations emphasised. 'Since there was no longer any *one* tactical formula that could be applied in the majority of operations, much more flexibility was allowed to, and required of, divisional and brigade commanders and their staffs'.[136] The formation commander who was the 'man on the spot', or as Simkins delightfully terms it, 'up the sharp end', was the brigadier-general, one of a group of men 'schooled to accept personal danger and discomfort'.[137] In the Selle operations we have indications of brigadiers up the sharp end with their battalion commanders. Thus Frank Rowley on 9 October was on horseback in Maricourt under shellfire directing the advance, and on 23 October Carlos Hickie was capturing German prisoners whilst on personal reconnaissance of his front line's progress in Pommereuil, returning to marshal his battalion commanders. On the 17th, George Rollo was recalled from the railway embankment opposite St Benin to agree a scheme whereby he, Richard Sugden and Percy Robinson would base their commands very close to the front line controlling different units to their own brigades through one battalion commander. Simon Justice notes Sugden's 'experiences through 1916 and 1917 proved he was definitely a fighter and a leader of men in combat'.[138] Rollo had been a captain of 1st Lancashire Engineers (Volunteers), but had not converted to the TF in 1908. He therefore rose from civilian via a service battalion to brigadier-general in four years, collecting two wounds and a DSO and bar on the way. His promotion shows both indications of a remarkable talent and the BEF's openness to promotion based on merit.[139] In contrast, 16 Brigade clearly viewed the fighting of the period as up to the battalion commanders on the spot. The role of their brigade HQ concentrated on reorganising mixed-up units, relieving the most tired troops, organising a reserve, ordering consolidation, and ascertaining and informing units as to the positions on flanks.[140]

It must not be assumed that all brigadiers were military polymaths. Walter Guinness recorded the following comments about Hugh Craigie-Halkett, GOC 74 Brigade: 'He is a very nice person to work with but knows nothing whatever about Regimental work and he used to get me to set him problems of the kind we used to do at Hesdin to work out, never having in his life before even drawn up a marching table'.[141] He added that: 'Halkett is a very nice person and a dashing leader of men,

135 T. Harvey, 'An Army of Brigadiers', p.336.
136 P. Simkins, 'A Man on the Spot – Brigadier-General R.E. Sugden', unpublished paper.
137 P. Simkins, *From the Somme to Victory*, p.193.
138 S.M. Justice, 'Means to and End', p.34.
139 William Tanner, the commander of the South African Brigade had previously been given command of 8 Brigade in 3rd Division, a clear indication of his perceived quality.
140 War Diary, HQ 16 Infantry Brigade, G.O. 38/310 14 October 1918, TNA WO95/1607.
141 Bond & Robbins, op. cit., p.178.

but completely ignorant about all Staff work and the detail of running a Brigade. During Bethell's leave he used to keep me busy setting him march tables and other routine orders etc. to practise on, and always ended by getting me to do them while he looked on',[142] continuing that he 'leaves the Brigade much more to run itself'. He was barely more complimentary of Standish Craufurd, stating on 21 March 1918 that he 'seemed much relieved to have someone [Bethell] so violently sure of his own mind and what ought to be done. He is a nice little man, an oriental scholar and linguist, but by this time was very tired'.[143] In Chapter Four it was observed that it was Craufurd's 18th Brigade that struggled 17 October and may have had combat sharpness and leadership issues. Yet there were clearly tiger luminaries amongst the brigadiers. John Vaughan Campbell VC was one such. The 'Tally-Ho VC', commanding 3rd Coldstream Guards at Ginchy on 15 September 1916, had rallied his men under fire by blowing a hunting horn and giving the traditional hunting cry of the Shropshire Harriers leading the third line forward to capture the machine gun that had decimated the first two waves. He was rewarded with the command of 137 Brigade on 17 November 1916 and on 29 September 1918 it spearheaded 46th Division's breaking of the Hindenburg Line at Bellenglise. His achievement was recognised a matter of days before the war ended by his transfer to command of 3 (Guards) Brigade. Major Charles Clayton similarly described George Kelly of 2 Brigade as a man who 'wastes no time. Capturing villages and pushing on seems his only field of thought. He spares no one and he certainly does not spare himself'.[144]

Another true warrior was Edward Allen Wood. John Bourne points out that in addition to being an alcoholic, he was also 'a liar, a fantasist and an embezzler'. He commanded 55 Brigade for almost a year in heavy fighting, 'won four DSOs, claimed to have been recommended for the Victoria Cross twice, was wounded five times, gassed twice, buried once and mentioned in despatches seven times'. A retired 49 year-old captain of British South Africa Police, he evidently had 'war in his bones'.[145] He commanded 6th King's Shropshire Light Infantry for almost two years, winning the first two of his DSOs. One of his soldiers, Private Robert Cude (7th Buffs), declared that he would 'serve in Hell, so long as General Wood was in command of the Brigade'.[146] Bourne suggests that: 'One of a commander's most difficult tasks is to rally broken troops'. Wood achieved this at a crucial moment of the German spring offensive, near Monument Farm, re-organising three companies of 7th Queen's after they had been caught in an intense enemy barrage while forming up for an important counter-attack. Instead of disintegrating, Wood succeeded in getting the unit to move forward. Bourne concludes: 'His extraordinary career perhaps culminated on 20 September 1918 when, alone and unarmed, he captured more than twenty Germans by pelting them with lumps of chalk and old boots!'[147] Adrift in civilian life, without his beloved fighting, Wood drifted into bankruptcy and died of cirrhosis of the liver in 1930.

Battalion Commanders

62 British officers at the rank of lieutenant-colonel commanded infantry battalions during the Selle operations. They had an average age of 36 years six months (the average age across the whole

142 Bond & Robbins, op. cit., pp.198-9.
143 Bond & Robbins, op. cit., p.191.
144 C.P. Clayton, *The Hungry One*, p.222. Charles Pritchard Clayton, a teacher in August 1914, commanded 2nd Welsh on several occasions in 1918.
145 A phrase John Reith used to describe himself. J. Reith, *Wearing Spurs,* p.15.
146 R. Cude, Private Papers, IWM Docs 129.
147 J. Bourne, unpublished biographical notes on E.A.Wood.

army on 29 September 1918 being 34 years 11 months), the two youngest being 25. [148] These two COs were Dudley Lewis of 1/5th Gloucestershire and Noel Baring Hudson of 8th Berkshire, both civilians in August 1914 with no previous military experience – the first an articled clerk, the latter later taking holy orders, becoming bishop of Labuan and Sarawak, Newcastle and Ely. Fifty-two per cent were Regulars (the average for the army on 29 September being 40 per cent). This higher figure was at the expense of the Territorial Force, COs with a TF background totalling 18 per cent (against an overall 31 per cent on 29 September); and to a lesser extent citizens of August 1914, who similarly totalled 18 per cent (against 22 per cent overall on 29 September).[149] Fourth Army therefore seems to have had a bias towards Regular officers in battalion command. They were, in addition, a more experienced group than the army as a whole, having an average 317 days experience of battalion command, whereas the average across all five armies on 29 September was 185.[150] The longest-serving CO at the Selle was Arthur Hardman-Jones of 2nd Northumberland Fusiliers, who had 1,109 days of command beneath his belt. It would be unwise to assume that either length of battalion command or the higher proportion of Regulars was necessarily connected to success – many factors would have contributed beyond the influence of an individual CO. However, in a period of devolved command, there were circumstances in which experience and skill certainly did count. In 139 Brigade's advance up the valley under the Bellevue spur towards Regnicourt on 17 October, Lieutenant-Colonel Richard Currin of 1/8th Sherwood Foresters (a retired captain of the Cape Colonial Volunteers with 255 days of command experience) reconnoitred his ground, pushed his own unit reserves forward at the right moment, and promptly brought his attached artillery into play to break up an enemy counterattack. But it was Lieutenant-Colonel Reginald Stanley Pratt (a civilian mining engineer in August 1914 with only five days of command experience), leading the two following companies of 1/5th Sherwood Foresters, who realised the degree of resistance and brought his two companies into action at exactly the right moment to maintain the brigade's impetus. 'Archie' Montgomery credited the success of the IX Corps attack on 17 October to both efficient staff work and 'exceptional leadership from battalion and company commanders'.[151]

To give a flavour of the mix of experience and innate skill in the battalion commanders of Fourth Army, it is interesting to consider Richard Owen Wynne, who on the evening of the second day of the Pursuit, between Le Cateau and Montay commanding 18th Liverpool, would report to brigade: 'Everything here seems very obscure'. Wynne had commanded both a regular and a new army battalion. He was born at Moss Vale, New South Wales, in 1892, but left Australia ten years later, attending Marlborough College, and at the outbreak of war was at Clare College, Cambridge. At Marlborough he played rugby for the school, and was a member of the school shooting eight, competing for the Ashburton Shield at Bisley between 1907 and 1910. He rowed for his college in 1913 and 1914. He was commissioned second-lieutenant in 3rd Bedfordshire on 15 August 1914, and arrived on the Western Front in March 1915, joining 2nd Bedfordshire as a lieutenant in June 1915, in which battalion he served until May 1918. It was whilst commanding both B and C companies on 31 July 1916 that he was awarded the DSO, consolidating a trench on the Maltzhorn Ridge. He first commanded the battalion from 8 to 17 November 1916, and from 25 November to 5 December he was in temporary command of 17th Liverpool. In January 1917 he was sent to Senior

148 P. Hodgkinson, *British Infantry Battalion Commanders in the First World War*, p.63. The youngest CO on 29 September 1918 was 21 years and 5 months old.
149 Hodgkinson, op. cit., p.53.
150 Hodgkinson, op. cit., p.56.
151 A. Montgomery, *The Story of Fourth Army in the Battles of the Hundred Days*, p.209.

Officer School, Aldershot, returning on 6 April. He did not have to wait long, for on 8 April, Lieutenant-Colonel H.S. Poyntz went sick and Wynne took over until 15 June, thus commanding the battalion during its operations at Arras. On 10 July he was sent to command 19th Liverpool for six days. He assumed command of his battalion again for brief periods in August and November 1917. On 22 February 1918, he took command again, this time as lieutenant-colonel, commanding virtually continuously until 22 May, when he went to train American units.[152] He was awarded a bar to his DSO as commanding officer for 'great skill and bravery', when he personally led an attack against machine guns that had been worked up close to his front line, himself killing the German officer in charge of them. He was given command of 18th Liverpool in August 1918 and remained in this role at the armistice, being wounded at Le Cateau, but remaining at duty. After the war, Wynne returned to his home town in Australia, where he described himself as 'a worker among workers'.[153] The nature of the award of the bar to his DSO suggests this was not an empty claim.

Did the COs of the Selle operations represent a meritocracy? Undoubtedly Richard Wynne's promotion was based on merit. The community of COs do not, however, represent a meritocracy in terms of a modern definition as a group 'selected competitively according to merit'.[154] Selection was not made against explicitly stated and mutually agreed criteria, even if there was a commonly held, if unwritten, view on what characteristics constituted the best sort of commanding officer. Selection was also always at the mercy of personal recommendation which could be influenced by a variety of factors. Not least of all, the bias towards the regular soldier, particularly evident in Fourth Army, and away from the pre-war amateur meant that promotion to CO was always a weighted process, but one in which the unstructured assessment of merit always and increasingly played a part, and, in a temporary sea-change for the British army, seniority did not.[155]

Junior regimental officers and other ranks

A popular folk-myth concerning 1918 is that the British army during the second half of that year was largely composed of 18 year-old conscripts led by officers similarly new to their craft. This would be the result of the attrition of the previous years, the losses suffered in the German spring offensives, and the high casualty rate of the Hundred Days. Whilst this view does contain elements of truth, it is certainly not the whole story. In terms of the officer group, the myth of the 'six-week subaltern' has been long exploded. The life expectation of officers in the Royal Warwickshire Regiment at the front, for instance, has been shown to be one year two months.[156] Jonathan Boff in his study of Third Army notes both that there was a shortage of experienced officers but that 'some divisions at least were able to maintain a core of regular veterans right through to the end of the war'.[157] In a group of over 400 officers with the rank of captain and below known to have served in Fourth Army during the Selle operations,[158] the average age of second-lieutenants was exactly 26, that of lieutenants was 26 years four months, and that of captains was 27 years three months. In terms of the length of time since they were commissioned, for second-lieutenants this was 11.3

152 TNA WO95/1658 War Diary, 2nd Battalion Bedfordshire Regiment.
153 http://www.mtwilson.com.au/mt-wilsonmt-irvine-historical-society/miscellaneous-articles/215-2005-remembrance-day-transcript.html (accessed 29 November 2016)
154 Definition of meritocracy as per the *Oxford English Reference Dictionary* 2nd Edition.
155 Hodgkinson, op. cit., p.206.
156 C. Kang, 'The British Regimental Officer on the Western Front in the Great War, with Special Reference to the Royal Warwickshire Regiment', p.42.
157 Boff, op. cit., location 1833.
158 These were identified from those, killed, wounded, decorated or otherwise mentioned in unit war diaries.

months; for lieutenants the period was 33.6 months; and for captains it was 41.4 months. Although there is no yardstick to measure how long it took an officer to become 'experienced' in the Great War, they were therefore, by and large, a reasonably experienced group. Further, 44 per cent are known to have been other ranks prior to commission, and thus their knowledge of war was deeper still. Of the 243 second-lieutenants in the group, 45 per cent were commissioned in 1918, yet of these at least 61 per cent were commissioned from the other ranks. It is therefore the case that at most around a third of subalterns commissioned in 1918 and serving at the Selle were young men without much previous experience of the war. The picture is, therefore, still of the majority of junior officer group being a group with relevant and recent knowledge of fighting modern war.

Mark Whisler promotes the view that: 'The enlisted personnel in all of the British divisions were predominantly 18 and 19 year old conscripts fresh out from Britain'.[159] Gary Sheffield has written that: 'Most of the replacements that arrived at the front during the latter part of 1918 were extremely youthful and lacking in military experience'.[160] The Official Historian similarly claimed that in Third Army '50 per cent of … infantry were said to be "boys"',[161] and even Richard Holmes asserted that 'half the infantrymen in France were eighteen years old'.[162] In 'Reflections' on the Hundred Days, the Official Historians further stated: 'The drafts consisted of very young officers and men who had little useful training of any kind'.[163] Whilst these drafts almost certainly contained officers returning from recovery from wounds and commissioned NCOs, there is a certain amount of truth in the statement. In terms of the other ranks, in a group of 3,000 other ranks killed in action or died of wounds and buried in the cemeteries within the area of Fourth Army's operations at the Selle, 17 per cent were aged 18-19.[164] The average age of a private was, however, 24 years eight months; that of a lance-corporal 25 years one month; that of a corporal 25 years six months; that of a sergeant 27 years eight months; and that of company or regimental sergeant-major 30 years one month. These figures hardly indicate a juvenile group, and again suggest experience. Whilst some officers were disparaging about their drafts, Lieutenant-Colonel William Fraser of 1st Gordon Highlanders, 3rd Division, stating: 'Although perhaps 10 per cent of these boys might do quite well the remainder are quite useless',[165] lacking in stamina, some Fourth Army units were complimentary about the quality of their reinforcements. On 15 October 1st Monmouthshire received a draft of 38 ORs, and described them as 'likely looking men' who 'appear intelligent and are mostly from the land'. A further draft of 52 on the 19th were regarded as 'a particularly good looking lot'. 25th Division had been particularly depleted after the Pursuit, but 'large numbers of reinforcements, of exceptionally good material, were arriving daily'. These were 'young men of the best fighting age, from the coal mines and agricultural life, who had only recently been withdrawn from their civil employment'.[166]

The chapters of this book that concern the fighting at the Selle certainly demonstrate that there was a significant casualty rate amongst officers and senior NCOs. Had this continued, a picture may have indeed emerged in 1919 that corresponded more to the myth of youthfulness.

159 Whisler, op. cit., p.36.
160 G. Sheffield, *Command and Morale*, Chapter 8.
161 J.E. Edmonds, *Military Operations France and Belgium, 1918, Vol. 4*, p.181
162 R. Holmes, *Tommy*, p.367.
163 Edmonds & Maxwell-Hyslop, op. cit., p.575.
164 Jonathan Boff calculates that in Third Army, 36 per cent of men were 21 or under during the Hundred Days, as against 28 per cent for the whole war as a whole. (J. Boff, *Winning and Losing on the Western Front*, Kindle edition location 1750).
165 War Diary, 1st Battalion Gordon Highlanders, 23-4 October 1918, TNA WO95/1435.
166 M. Kincaid-Smith, *The 25th Division in France and Flanders*, p.330.

Operational planning and command and control

The cascading process of operational planning has been evident. By 1918, the BEF had enshrined this in *The Division in Attack – 1918 (SS135)*.[167] After army had issued its limited instructions, corps would issue tasks and a general outline of the artillery plan to divisions. The divisional commander would form his own plan of disposition of his troops, their tasks, and plans for his reserves. Once approved by the corps commander, a memorandum would be submitted to subordinate commanders, divisional staff working out the details of the plans set out in the memorandum, and issuing divisional instructions. Brigade commanders would flesh out any further local detail and issue the relevant portions of these instructions to units. It is a testament to the practised skill of staff officers that the set-piece attack of 17 October was organised in four days and the attack of 23 October in three days.

In the discussion of semi-open warfare, it was observed that devolved command was an enforced solution to the problems of both communications and tempo. Jonathan Boff's study of Third Army suggests that delegation was never consistent.[168] It is difficult to draw conclusions about consistency of delegation during the Selle operations. As noted in Chapter Two, command of mobile weapons was often devolved down as far as the battalion commander. Brigade commanders were typically close to the action, up with their battalion commanders, with brigade HQs repeatedly pushed forward. In the case of Carlos Hickie on 23 October the brigadier was actually in front of his COs, returning to give them effective direction. These individuals clearly understood that they had devolved responsibility. Perhaps the most striking example of the interplay of communications, command and control, and delegation is Henry Jackson's reorganisation of his command on 17 October. The commander of 150 Brigade, George Rollo, had crossed the Selle with his brigade to perform the planned manoeuvre of passing through the two leading brigades. He was at the advanced brigade report centre on the railway embankment 1,000 yards north of St Souplet station and about 1,500 yards in the rear of the front line. He was then recalled to meet Jackson on the Busigny-Le Cateau road exactly 3,000 yards to the west of Rollo's position and 6,000 yards in front of 50th Division HQ at Le Trou Aux Soldats.[169] This implies that communications were effective – Jackson knew his two leading brigades were stalled and was able to recall Rollo. 150 Brigade's advanced brigade report centre was in touch with the brigade HQ at Honnechy station by telephone, this also being the advanced divisional report centre. (This line to the railway embankment was swiftly laid by 50th Division Signal Company RE that morning, and enabled 150 Brigade HQ to move along its route to just over 1,000 yards west of the advanced brigade HQ).[170] Jackson was likely at his advanced divisional HQ and only had to travel a further 2,000 yards to meet Rollo. He was, therefore, in as advanced a position as he could usefully be, just as was Rollo for the planned leap-frog manoeuvre. The two roughly split the distance they had to travel to confer. Almost certainly presuming devolved responsibility, and without reference to corps, Jackson then devolved command via Rollo to his three brigadiers of groups that were different to their normal brigades, and they in turn devolved command to one lieutenant-colonel in each group. This series

167 J. Beach, *The Division in Attack – SS135*, Section 4.

168 J. Boff, 'Command Culture and Complexity', in Sheffield & Gray, op. cit., p.23; see also J. Boff, *Winning and Losing on the Western Front*.

169 War Diary, 150 Infantry Brigade, 'Narrative of Operations 16th October 1918', TNA WO95/2833.

170 150 Brigade had been allotted a trench set wireless, but heavy shellfire prevented the erection of both mast and station 1,500 yards west of the Selle. A loop wireless was able to work from this location, however. (War Diary, 50th Division Signal Company RE, 'Operations From 16th to 19th October 1918', TNA WO95/2822).

of events is a model of effective command and control and devolution of responsibility. Occurring within the context of a set-piece attack, it is interesting to note Boff's conclusion for Third Army, that as the campaign went on the exercise of initiative seems to have become rarer: 'The more open the warfare, the less delegation seems to have contributed to the tempo'.[171] In many ways, whilst there was clear devolution of command at the Selle, the opportunities for reaping real benefit in terms of tempo from devolved command were quite limited as relatively little open warfare was achieved after the first few days of operations.

The Americans at the Selle

The two American divisions had only begun their training with British units in June 1918. That of 30th Division had been especially problematic. Brigadier-General Faison, the acting divisional commander, advised General Read in July 1918 that: 'The infantry brigades were "badly handicapped by the lack of suitable and well-trained officers" and that "under present conditions this division is not capable of manoeuvres and the prospects are not bright for this state of affairs to come about"'.[172] Read never responded. The very first taste of battle was at Hamel on 4 July 1918. Four American companies took part, despite General Pershing's objections. Rawlinson noted: 'The Americans … fought like tigers'.[173] Their courage was never in question – it was a matter of skill in leadership and staff work. When Pershing removed American divisions from II Corps in the British sector in mid-August 1918, he of course left the 27th and 30th behind. Mitchell Yockelson notes: 'One explanation might be that Read recently had rated them deficient' – interestingly he rated 30th Division particularly poorly. 'Pershing may have felt they needed more specialised training and were not ready for the operation in the St. Mihiel salient which was in the planning stages'.[174] Both divisions had a difficult time in the front line at Ypres during the last two weeks of August, particularly for officers – indeed, Major-General Lewis of 30th Division expressed particular concern about his officers' training.[175] It was not an auspicious prelude to the operations at the Hindenburg Line. Rawlinson was wary of II American Corps even before they came into action with Fourth Army. Discussing the plans for the attack of 29 September, he visited both divisions and described their plans as 'backward'. II Corps, he confided to his diary, 'cannot possibly function as a corps without much assistance in their staff work'.[176] Sir Douglas Haig also visited General Read on the day before the assault at his HQ close to that of the Australian Corps whom Haig described as 'nursing the 2 American Divisions'. He thought Read 'a good honest fellow, but all this class of warfare is quite new to him, and he was genuinely very anxious'.[177] Rawlinson viewed their participation in the attack as a 'bit of a lottery'.[178] The Americans were set a very difficult task on 29 September, and struggled with it. Criticisms have since been levelled at the planning of Lieutenant-General Sir John Monash, the Australian Corps commander, and the lack of effectiveness of the British counter-battery fire. Read, however agreed that 'lack of experience was the chief failing of

171 Boff, *Command Culture*, p.27.
172 Commanding General, 30th Division to Commanding General, II Corps, AEF, 9 July 1918, Status of Training of 30th Division, File 353, Folder 36, Entry 267, RG 120. NARA, quoted in M. Yockelson, 'Brothers in Arms?' p.154.
173 Sir H. Rawlinson, 'Notes on today's attack', 4 July 1918, Churchill College RWLN 1/12.
174 Yockelson, op. cit., p.178.
175 Yockelson, op. cit., p.228.
176 Sir H. Rawlinson, War Journal, 25 September 1918, Churchill College RWLN 1/11.
177 Sheffield & Bourne, op. cit., diary entry 28 September 1918, p.466.
178 Sir H. Rawlinson, War Journal, 28 September 1918, Churchill College RWLN 1/11.

the regimental and higher command'. Rawlinson believed simply that the Americans were 'in a state of hopeless confusion', and that they were 'short of officers and know nothing about fighting'. He concluded, rather cruelly, that their heavy casualties were 'their own fault'.[179] Haig, looking over Rawlinson's comments, concluded: 'These two divisions are quite unfit to operate as a corps under an American Corps Staff'.[180] If the remarks seem patronising, it is perhaps because both overlooked the difficult task the Americans were set and had forgotten their own army's learning process. In the attack of 8 October, however, the Army commander was more complimentary: 'The Amer[ican] Corps did quite well and sent in information quickly and accurately'.[181]

Mitchell Yockelson claims that during the operations the contribution of II American Corps was 'more than average … they had done extraordinarily well'.[182] Detailed examination shows this assessment to be over-optimistic. The American performance at the Selle has been analysed above as it unfolded – the comments of high command were echoed by both tank and artillery commanders on the ground. British tank commanders found their performance 'sticky' at Butry Wood on 9 October, and the Australian artillery believed that the same issue prevented them from effecting a crossing of the Selle on the 10th, although the second comment may be less fair than the first. Major-General Read was warning on 11 October that 'troops of the 30th Division have become tired due to the difficulties of continued fighting over ruined country during inclement weather'.[183] On 17-18 October they struggled, 30th Division particularly. II Corps may have issued competent orders, as previously noted, but both corps and divisions lacked competent staff work in follow-up. The debacle over the start time for 30th American Division and 1st Division on 19 October demonstrates this only too well. Similarly, the quality of officering at unit level also seems open to criticism. To take one brief example, Lieutenant-Colonel Hoare of 50th MGC made personal reconnaissance of his front adjacent to II American Corps on 12 October and found that the 'American dispositions were none too good, and had no depth at all'. Clearly worried about penetration in the event of counterattack, he pushed more guns to his right flank to protect 50th Division.[184] It was this inexperience that lay behind Rawlinson's observation that their casualties were twice as high as those of the other two corps.[185] The Americans paid in blood for their lack of combat experience. Their performance might be likened to the immensely brave but ill-fated performances of Kitchener units at Loos in September 1915. The doughboys could not be blamed for having such a short time to accrue combat wisdom, a discrepancy which was bound to be magnified by the performances of the 'tiger' units of IX and XIII Corps.

In December 1918, Major-General Read compiled his report on the operations of II Corps. He took the view that the British troops 'had neither the dash nor initiative of the Americans'. This was clearly neither particularly fair nor accurate. Both forces showed initiative amongst the infantry, and dash and death were never far apart, Read admitting the problem of excessive loss of American lives. He only acknowledged superiority in combat of the British infantry, based on experience, in the area of mopping-up. The area in which he accepted that the British, 'whose extensive experience kept units well in hand', had a true advantage was in command and control, although he

179 Sir H. Rawlinson, War Journal, 29 September 1918, Churchill College RWLN 1/11.
180 Sheffield & Bourne, op. cit., diary entry 29 September, p.467.
181 Sir H. Rawlinson, War Journal, 8 October 1918, Churchill College RWLN 1/11.
182 Yockelson, op. cit., p.304.
183 182-33.3: Operations Report II Corps AEF 11 October 1918, *USAWW Vol. 7* p.511.
184 War Diary, 50th Battalion Machine Gun Corps, 'Narrative of Operations Oct. 9th-19th 1918', TNA WO95/2823.
185 Sir H. Rawlinson, War Journal, 19 October 1918, Churchill College RWLN 1/11.

blamed this (reasonably) partly on shortage of officers and partly on experience. Yet the problems of command and control stemmed from the top. Mark Whisler quietly observes of II American Corps HQ that 'it does not appear to have intervened frequently in the battle'.[186] This was not, of course, an insignificant matter. Read acknowledged this issue too, believing on one hand that staffs 'as a rule functioned efficiently', but that on the other there was a 'tendency for them to lose the remarkably close touch with the combatant units that all British Headquarters had'.[187]

The German Army at the Selle

Clausewitz states in *On War* that 'the defensive form of war is in itself stronger than the offensive'. He acknowledged that the former left initiative in the hands of the latter, but suggested that the defensive had the advantages of both waiting for the enemy to declare their hand and being able to choose ground. He also acknowledged, however, that the defensive has a 'negative object', attempting only to hold what one has, and is a sign of 'weakness'.[188] The overwhelming reality for the German army was exactly that – it was fatally weak, and would never be able to resume the offensive. The toll of the Selle operations is indicated in the order of *Eighteenth Army* of 21 October: 'All recruits fit for assignment to unit must be brought up with dispatch and put in line. All men trained to use arms, regardless of whether they are fit for garrison duty and for labour in the field, belong at the front'.[189] German theatre strategy on the Western Front during the Hundred Days was to attempt to hold the Allied thrust as far to the West as possible, fight defensively to create a stalemate, and negotiate a compromise peace. Max Schwarte describes the decision to 'yield ground bit by bit and defend every yard, in the expectation that the enemy's losses and German political proposals would gradually cause the hostile attacks to weaken'.[190] Ludendorff wrote in his order of 4 August: 'Commanders and men must be imbued with a bitter determination to conquer, both in the defensive as well as in the offensive'. In this he echoed Clausewitz, yet he recognised the problems of the defensive: 'The organized defensive is the more difficult. It … imposes the greatest test upon the spirit of the troops'.[191] It is clear that senior German commanders were uncomfortable with the defensive. *Bavarian I Army Corps* acknowledged on 10 October that: 'For the most part our opponents owe their present successes to the fact that we are constantly on the defensive',[192] which allowed the British to assemble the elements of the weapons-system and bring it to bear. Von Hutier of *Eighteenth Army* responded, opining that a counter attack that captured, forced back or destroyed British artillery (thus giving a clear opinion as to what his army's biggest problem was) would 'raise the morale of the troops to a marked degree'.[193] Whatever the mixed feelings, the German defence at the Selle largely corresponded to *OHL*'s memorandum of 24 November 1917 'Principles for the Conduct of Defensive Battle in Trench Warfare', with a forward/outpost zone,

186 Whisler, op. cit., p154.
187 II Corps Gen. File: Fldr, 7: Operations, Operations II Corps, 18 December 1918, *USAWW Vol. 7*, pp.793-4.
188 C. von Clausewitz, *On War*, Book 6, Chapter1.
189 *German Eighteenth Army*, Operations Section No. 8651, All Men Suitable for the Front to be Employed at the Front, 21 October 1918, *USAWW Vol. 7*, p.920.
190 M. Schwarte, *Der Grosse Krieg*, Vol. 3 p.577.
191 OHL Order Ia. No. 9670. Op. Sir H. Rawlinson, War Journal, Churchill College RWLN 1/11.
192 HS Ger. File: Group Armies Ger. Crown Prince: 810-33.5: Fldr. VII: Reports, Estimate of Successful Defensive Action, *USAWW Vol. 7*, p.899.
193 Operations Section No. 8313 German *Eighteenth Army*, 11 October 1918, *USAWW Vol. 7*, p900.

and a Main Line of Resistance (*Hauptwiderstandlinie – HWL*). The *HWL* would form the Battle Zone, with reserves pushed forward.[194] The outpost zone was to be 500-600 metres deep, although at the Selle geography shaped its variable depth. Further, an *HWL II* was added, comprising only rifle pits and machine gun nests, a nod no doubt to the reality of limited reserves. *54 Corps* ordered on 19 October that: 'The Army Group will accept the decisive battle on the Hermann Line. The Hermann Line must be held at any price'. The artillery of the *79th Reserve Division* was similarly informed that all troops must understand that 'the Hermann Stellung must be held at all cost' as it was held 'there are good prospects of carrying peace negotiations'.[195]

As Mark Whisler notes: 'The British victory ... was not achieved against a disintegrating German opponent, but one that fought hard and skilfully using defence in depth doctrine'.[196] Fourth Army's casualties are a testimony to the power of enemy resistance. In XIII Corps on 17-18 October 66th Division's two brigades had a casualty rate of 37 per cent;[197] and 50th Division a 35 per cent rate.[198] The 27th American Division suffer a 52 per cent casualty rate;[199] and the 30th a rate over 30 per cent.[200] The losses for IX Corps were less. 6th Division had an approximate casualty rate of just over 20 per cent;[201] 1st Division had a 25 per cent rate;[202] whilst 46th Division, which only fought on 17 October, had a 15 per cent rate.[203] The steadily and fatally weakening German army was still able, even in defeat on 8 October, to retreat, reform and cause the Allies to mount yet another costly set-piece attack at the Selle. The infantry resisted tenaciously on 17 October, at least, and the German artillery remained a threat because of the widespread short-comings of counter-battery fire. Despite the artillery of Fourth Army providing harassing fire continually, there was little German artillery fire (except over open sights) on 9 October. It was still in a process of withdrawal. From then on enemy artillery was constantly striking Fourth Army's rear areas and front lines. On 15 and 16 October, as the British bombardment proceeded: 'Hostile artillery activity showed a marked increase during the night and continued throughout the day',[204] despite supposed counter-battery fire. The enemy artillery was, however, well back, ready to be withdrawn across the Sambre-Oise canal.

Historians have generally sought to explain the German collapse rather than the resistance. The observation of *221st Division*, fighting at the Selle, probably spoke for the entire German Army: 'The heavy exertion of two months unbroken defensive fighting have consumed the physical and mental forces of leaders and men'.[205] Exhaustion was very probably the overriding feature of the German army. The pattern of Allied attacks had absorbed all the available reserves, and divisions were spending far longer in the front lines than they otherwise would. The German army had begun the offensive of 21 March 1918 in a state of good morale, expecting success, even if that

194 Boff, *Winning and Losing*, location 5325.
195 War Diary, 66th Infantry Division, 'Narrative of Operations 17-19 October 1918', TNA WO95/3122.
196 Whisler, op. cit., p.40.
197 889 infantry casualties. War Diary, AA & QMG 66th Infantry Division, October 1918, TNA WO95/3123.
198 Approximately 1,200 casualties. Whisler op. cit., p.112.
199 Approximately 1,500 casualties. *27th Division Summary of Operations*, p.36.
200 1,262 casualties. *30th Division Summary of Operations*, cited in Whisler op. cit., p.112.
201 509 casualties. War Diary AA & QMG 6th Division, October 1918, TNA WO 95/1587.
202 Approximately 1,000 casualties. Whisler, op. cit., p.112.
203 Approximately 400 casualties. Whisler, op. cit., p.112.
204 HS Brit. File: Fldr. IV B. II Corps: Summary of Operations, 16 October 1918, *USAWW Vol. 7*, p.627.
205 *221 Infantry Division* records 16 October 1918, cited in Whisler, op. cit., p.307.

willingness to fight was 'highly conditional' on promised victory.[206] Morale had slowly begun to ebb as no breakthrough was achieved, a decline made rapid following the French attack on the Marne on 18 July. At the front, the clearest indication of this decline is taken to be surrender. Alexander Watson notes a contradiction in this area. Fourth Army's intelligence summary of 23 September recorded that prisoners reported that officers could still make soldiers resist: 'The officers' word "MUST" is still the driving force'.[207] Yet on the other hand Watson concludes that 'many front officers were leading their men into surrender'.[208] Following the Peace Note of 3 October, German fighting on must have seemed pointless to many. Fourth Army report on 10 October that XIII had taken prisoners who offered no resistance 'in view of a telegram received from the Kaiser on the 9th inst. referring to an armistice having been asked for'.[209] Fourth Army similarly publicised a letter written on 12 October from a resident of Hamburg to his combatant brother, taken prisoner: 'My Dear Ludwig: – The war is going to end now … we cannot oppose such a number of enemies'.[210] In line with this, Watson suggests: 'Exhausted German soldiers simply waited for the advancing allies to roll over them'. Yet exactly the reverse of this happened on 17 October.

What, therefore, was the German resistance at the Selle based on? Senior command was full of exhortation to the front-line troops from the beginning of the Hundred Days. Crown Prince Rupprecht's *Army Group* issued an order on 22 August claiming to have 'strong reserves in readiness everywhere', and that battle was awaited with 'complete confidence'. Unfavourable ground would be yielded here and there, but that the army must 'defend to the last' then 'will victory rest with our arms'.[211] A captured order of *11th Division* from 24 August read: 'The present momentary physical and moral weakness of the troops must be overcome' (thus demonstrating the awareness of the vulnerability of the front line), this 'by bringing home to the subordinate commanders and the men by means of careful teaching, the importance of the present fighting for the general welfare of our people'.[212] Some three weeks later, *1st Reserve Division* was issuing an order that acknowledged that 'the enemy has gained the initiative', and that there was 'no doubt he possesses the means to overcome the difficulties which confront him' (namely the *Siegfried Stellung*). Yet such an attack 'must be completely repulsed', 'utmost exertions are required', and 'energetic measures are necessary'.[213] It is unlikely that these exhortations from on high, with all their dissonance in relation to the reality on the ground, had much effect in themselves.

At a personal level, the German soldier began the war believing he was defending his homeland. Even at the end of the gruelling defensive campaigns 1917, 'men continued to recognise the necessity of protecting their families and homes'.[214] As the soldier went back towards his country's border, the imperative of protection can only, for some, have increased. Secondly, just as in the British army, there was still loyalty to comrades and officers.[215] Men would fight for each other. The strength of this

206 A. Watson, *Ring of Steel*, p.519.
207 Fourth Army Summary of Information, No. 279 23 September 1918, TNA WO157/199.
208 A. Watson, *Enduring the Great War*, p.224.
209 Fourth Army Summary of Information, No. 296 10 October 1918, TNA WO157/199.
210 Fourth Army Summary of Information, No. 308 22 October 1918, TNA WO157/199.
211 Annex to Fourth Army Summary, 16 October 1918, *USAWW Vol. 7*, p.606.
212 Annexe to Fourth Army Summary, dated October 11 1918, *USAWW Vol 7* p.494
213 Memo from Count von Waldersee, *1st Reserve Division*, 16 September 1918, Extracts from GHQ Summary No. 652, 14 October 1918, *USAWW Vol. 7*, pp.607-8.
214 Watson, *Enduring*, p.172.
215 Watson, *Ring*, p.529.

imperative no doubt varied from formation to formation. At an organisational level, the quality of German units naturally varied. Of the 11 German divisions fighting at the Selle on 17 October, only three were rated 1st Class/A (see Chapter Three, Table 3.3). Of these *17th and 44th Reserve Divisions* held 66th Division north of Le Cateau; and *29th Infantry Division* held the junction of the XIII and American Corps attacks. These elite divisions (only 20 per cent of German Divisions were rated as A/A+) likely had higher morale, and their officers may well have had more influence in encouraging resistance. Less highly rated divisions, however, also had their elite elements – as Jack Sheldon has stated: 'The men manning the machine guns were the elite of their units, specially picked and trained'.[216] Thus it was often noted that the machine gunners offered the greatest resistance. Indeed, Mark Whisler, as noted in Chapter Four, described the 'almost fanatical resistance' met by the 30th American Division on 17 October at Molain from the machine gunners.[217] Whilst German unit strengths were plummeting, machine-gun strengths held up much better than those of riflemen,[218] and it was on automated fire that the defence at the Selle was predicated. 50th Division noted that in the operations 17-19 October 'machine gun prisoners and gunners captured in BASEUL were of much better quality and the machine gunners particularly put up a good fight'.[219]

The fact that Fourth Army underestimated the enemy's resistance at the Selle may have been not only to do with failing to identify all the units in line, but in misinterpretation of its intelligence. Jim Beach has noted that GHQ relied on both captured documents and prisoner/deserter testimony to assess morale. In the case of the latter, prisoners, and in particular deserters (and in the later stages of the Hundred Days, if Watson is right, many prisoners were *de facto* deserters) 'could tell their interrogators what they thought the latter wanted to hear'.[220] Whilst GHQ probably moved away from reliance on this after 1916, it is more than probable that more weight came to be placed upon this again with the influx of prisoners after August 1918. Secondly, there may have been a confusion of the Clausewitzian distinction between 'spirit' and 'mood'.[221] The spirit of an army is manifest when 'proud of its victories' it 'will not lose the strength to obey orders and its respect and trust for its officers even in defeat'.[222] Mood is a temporary matter, brought about by particular circumstances, and changeable. The mood of the German Army on the Selle was poor, but its spirit was not entirely broken yet. Boff observes that in front of Third Army, German soldiers actually became more likely to be killed and less likely to be taken prisoner in October than in August.[223] If those with the poorest morale were able to desert on lines of communication, as Alexander Watson has demonstrated, this left a distilled group at the front, whose 'spirit' was more intact. It may well have been this group that demonstrated heroic resistance on 17 October, but whose defence would fail though sheer weakness. The German Army had organised for defence in depth at the Selle, but had not the numbers to make it effective.

216 http://1914-1918.invisionzone.com/forums/index.php?/topic/46667-german-soldiers-chained-to-machine-gun/ (accessed 29 November 2016)
217 Whisler, op. cit., p.298.
218 Boff, *Winning and Losing*, Kindle edition location 1571.
219 War Diary, 7th Battalion Wiltshire Regiment, 'Note on German Troops Opposite the Divisional Front October 17th-19th 1918', TNA WO95/2836.
220 J. Beach, *Haig's Intelligence*, p.187.
221 Boff, *Winning and Losing*, location 3568.
222 Clausewitz, op. cit., Chapter Five, Book Three, p.187.
223 Boff, *Winning and Losing*, location 3637.

Conclusion

Fourth Army in October 1918 was an efficient operational planning machine. Its senior officers were a largely battle-hardened and tactically skilled group. Its junior leaders, despite dilution by a certain number of youngsters, included a majority with experience and initiative. Hugh Keppel Bethell attributed the success of the forcing of the Selle to 'the drive, marching and staying power of the men', the 'foresight and initiative displayed by junior officers and N.C.O.s', and 'the quickness with which all commanders adapted themselves the constantly changing situation'.[224] Peter Simkins has suggested that however proficient were the BEF's logistics, technology and combined-arms tactics, 'the doggedness and resilience of the British front-line soldier remained as important – and perhaps even more important – than the methods he employed'.[225] Indeed, the second would have been less than useful without the first. Clearly, any view of Fourth Army having a 'weapons system' repeatedly and invincibly deployed, is not born out at the Selle. Weather, availability, intelligence failure, and the Selle terrain all served to degrade its utility. Nor is there any evidence that Fourth Army attempted to deploy a modified version of its weapons system to suit circumstances, as per the model of Paul Harris. Fourth Army attempted to throw everything it had at the enemy on 17 October, was frustrated in its efforts by matters outside its control, yet won all the same. Jonothan Boff takes the view that there is no evidence that Third Army in the Hundred Days consistently used 'fire and movement' tactics.[226] There is plenty of evidence in Fourth Army that they did, but on 17 October, for example, in the fighting around Le Cateau station or during the South African Brigade attack, there was little opportunity, and relentless slog took the place of tactical finesse. This impels us towards having to consider Simkins' view of the British infantry as having substance. Within the limitations of their mobile arms and the degraded support of artillery and air-power, they were the key factor in victory whether they deployed greater or lesser tactical sophistication. Whilst Major Christopher Stone would write on 3 October: 'These are great days for all of us and I pity anyone who isn't on the spot … Everyone is in fine form and confident to a degree not known hitherto',[227] it would be incorrect to be carried away with the idea that the British morale was universally elevated. Yet the 'spirit' of the BEF, in its true Clausewitzian meaning, was by far the higher of the two armies, however tenacious the German resistance might temporarily have been. They may not have exactly been 'lions led by tigers', but they were close.

224 War Diary, 6th Battalion Lancashire Fusiliers, Special Order 24 October 1918, TNA WO95/3140.
225 Simkins, *Somme to Victory*, p.205.
226 Boff, *Winning and Losing*, location 4113.
227 G.D. Sheffield & G.I.S. Inglis (eds), *From Vimy Ridge to the Rhine*, p.138.

Conclusion

'Allemande buggered now!'[1]

As Peter Simkins reminds us, it is mistaken to believe that simply because the Hundred Days represent the finest string of victories in the history of any British Army that it was a 'period of unqualified success'.[2] It is clear, however, that the Fourth Army during the Selle operations achieved a high level of operational sophistication in terms of swift planning and execution. The attack of 17 October was far more sophisticated than other operations that had taken much longer to plan. Fourth Army was also able to maintain its tempo reasonably well in the three stages of the operations, the main brake on this, given the necessity to mount two set-piece attacks, being logistics. The effort of both engineers and transport to make battle possible as soon as practicable was not without flaws, but was extraordinary none the less. The three-dimensional combined-arms approach, however, was compromised at the Selle. Artillery and air-power were frustrated by weather, which in turn both hampered and bestowed certain benefits upon the infantry. Within the bounds of the limited objective attack, the all-arms tactics deployed by the infantry were able to overcome enemy divisions who were using topography to their advantage, and repel counter-attacks. During the month of October 1918, Fourth Army took some 489 officers and 20,191 other ranks prisoner whilst capturing 3,500 machine guns, 305 field guns and 49 heavy guns.[3] If the BEF was able at the Selle to make 'the German armies dance to its operational tune',[4] the enemy in return was able tactically to make the British victory a far from easy matter. This was partly due to its remaining ability to resist, and partly due to failure of elements of the British 'weapons system'. The so-called Pursuit to the Selle was, essentially, no such thing – it proceeded at a pace largely determined by the enemy rearguards. The fighting was universally heavy. Fourth Army's experience was not unique – 50th Brigade in Third Army described the fighting from 11 to 20 October as 'probably the fiercest [it had] ever fought'.[5] The German resistance on 17 October may well have been a factor in Sir Douglas Haig's suddenly downbeat assessment in Downing Street two days later. He concluded: 'The German Army is capable of retiring to its own frontier and holding that line if there should be any attempt to touch the honour of the German people and make them fight

1 Comment of German prisoner captured near Cambrai in October 1918. R.G. Dixon, 'The Wheels of Darkness', IWM Docs 2001, p.134.
2 P. Simkins, 'Building Blocks', in G. Sheffield and D. Todman (eds), *Command and Control on the Western Front*, p.165.
3 'Captures by Fourth Army During the Months of August, September, October 1918', Rawlinson Papers, Churchill College RWLN 1/11.
4 M. Whisler, 'Der Tommy Kommt', p.34.
5 Anon, *History of the 50th Infantry Brigade 1914–1919*, published privately 1919, p.105.

with the courage of despair'.[6] Paul Harris states that the originator of this pessimism was Herbert 'Lorenzo' Lawrence, Haig's Chief of Staff.[7] Lawrence was convinced that the German army could not be beaten into complete submission in 1918, a view which Haig had previously rejected. The resistance at the Selle seems to have tipped him towards Lawrence's pessimism.[8]

The British commanders at the Selle, and their teams, were men who were well-versed in the new warfare. A majority of junior regimental officers had a bedrock of experience, so many of them having risen from the ranks, ranks which were not as extensively populated by 18 and 19 year-olds as has been believed. Command was often, if not universally, decentralised, although perhaps partly only in response to necessity rather than in any profound change in army attitude. Initiative was broadly valued. Yet the Hundred Days contain their share of faulty command decisions and sloppy work by tired staff. Fourth Army for all of its operational sophistication was not beyond these as the abortive attacks of 12 October show. The attempt to take Riquerval Wood with one battalion was absurdly optimistic, when the exact same attack had failed the previous day. Just further north the attempt to take ground in front of the Bellevue spur failed because of a hastily arranged and misplaced barrage, whilst the infantry attempted to funnel through an enemy opening in the wire, which any veteran of trench warfare would have assumed would have machine-guns trained on it. There were thus errors of ambition overtaking military common sense; errors caused by hasty arrangements and lack of information, and occasional basic errors of infantry tactics. Indeed, Fourth Army always demonstrated a tendency to underestimate likely opposition.

Despite Sir Douglas Haig's eternal hope that the cavalry would achieve a breakthrough on the Selle, British operations in the Hundred Days were never truly geared to achieving such. The attacks were always limited in objective, and closed down relatively quickly, shifting the locus of thrust to another army. Even in October 1918, as the Selle operations demonstrated, the Germans were well able to 'rapidly reconstitute a defensive position that would still require a set-piece attack'.[9] Yet such an ability was partly self-defeating. The weight of the attack meant that reserves would have to be found to relieve the threat (reserves arrived at the Selle on 18 October as the main attack closed down), and as soon as they had arrived a threat would appear elsewhere (in this case First and Third Armies' attacks across the Selle), and reserves would be needed elsewhere.

In individual operations, Fourth Army's aims as expressed in orders were never fully achieved on the ground. In September 1916, when Thiepval was finally taken, the history of 10th Essex records Ivor Maxse (then commanding 18th Division) as saying 'something like this: "If you take and hold your first objective you do well; if you take and hold your second objective you do just about as much as is humanly possible; and higher command sets a third objective in case of possible break-down of the enemy's morale"'.[10] This betrays a desirable 'planning in hope' element. The history of II American Corps comments with the benefit of hindsight on the planned 9,000 yard advance that the artillery orders did 'not indicate that the army and corps commanders really expected an advance beyond the first objective on October 17'.[11] Whilst this probably represents a justification for lack of progress, Rawlinson's private comments indicate that he believed his army would be

6 G. Sheffield & J. Bourne (eds), *Douglas Haig – War Diaries and Letters 1914-1918*, 19 October 1918, p.475.
7 Sir Herbert Alexander Lawrence KCB (1861-1943) had commanded 66th Division from February 1917, and a year later succeeded Launcelot Kiggell as Haig's Chief of Staff.
8 J.P. Harris, *Douglas Haig and the First World War*, p.508. See also G. Sheffield, *The Chief*, p.330.
9 Whisler, op. cit., p.35.
10 T.M Banks & R.A. Chell, *With the 10th Essex in France*, pp.154-5.
11 General Staff, *Operations of the 2nd American Corps in the Somme Offensive*, p.30.

lucky to secure its furthest objectives. At the Selle, some of the objectives are redolent of hubris, born on 9 October both of lack of knowledge of the defences that lay ahead and the enemy's intent; and later in assumption that enemy resistance would crumple.

Just as the German forces were weak, so British units were weak, if to varying degrees. 9th Norfolk had a dismal rifle strength of 174 across four companies on 21 October. At the end of that month, 11th Essex had a rifle strength of only 271. The units of 151 Infantry Brigade (50th Division), however, had an average strength of 29 officers and 708 ORs during October 1918, although this figure hides a drop from 38 officers and 835 ORS in the first week of the month to 25 officers and 686 ORs in the last week.[12] 150 Brigade had similar average levels at the end of the month, 25 officers and 656 ORs, but unit strengths varied. Thus, 2nd Northumberland Fusiliers had 31 Officers and 730 ORs, whilst 2nd Munster Fusiliers had 23 officers and 541 ORs.[13] The picture of variability in strength is reinforced by the very low numbers in brigades of XIII Corps during the attacks of 23/24 October. Weak units often found themselves attacking on broad fronts. The company commanders of 2nd Royal Dublin Fusiliers, who had the comparative riches of 612 ORs at the end of September stated that on 17 October: 'In view of the strength of the Battalion the frontage given them was much too great'.[14] 50th Division acknowledged that for a depleted battalion attacking on affront of 800 yards with 300 rifles or less, 'the principles of attack in depth ... have to be abandoned'.[15]

Fourth Army's 'wastage' at the Selle from 9 to 15 October, i.e. during the Pursuit, was 505 officers and 12,637 other ranks. This figure includes both the American Corps and sickness across all three corps. For the period 16 to 22 October, i.e. covering the period of the forcing of the Selle, the figures were 503 officers and 11,882 other ranks. Total 'wastage' during the Pursuit and the forcing of the *Hermann Stellung I* therefore numbered 25,527, and if the figures for 1st Division are representative, 22 per cent of 'wastage' was sickness. Reinforcements numbered 16,221 during the same period. These figures are distorted by the apparent non-reinforcement of II American Corps – if only British formations are considered, the numbers of wastage over reinforcement amounted to 1,213. Fourth Army was therefore keeping itself almost up to strength, albeit with a very slow dwindling. In terms of British battle casualties alone, between 15 October and 3 November, i.e. the period covering the two set-piece attacks, IX Corps lost 156 infantry officers killed wounded and missing, and 3,382 ORs; whilst XIII Corps lost 253 officers and 5,264 ORs. This roughly equates to a British casualty rate of 2,200 per day over the four main days of fighting.[16]

Undoubtedly the British infantry fought tenaciously. What is perhaps most extraordinary is that in these final days of the war, troops did not become 'combat shy'. XIII Corps noted that: 'It might have been anticipated ... that a certain reluctance to take unnecessary risks would have manifested itself among troops'. Yet the determination of the British infantry remained – 'the very reverse was the case'.[17] All wanted to play their part in beating the enemy. The 'will to battle' was almost universally present. The German defences at the Battle of the Sambre, fought on 4 November,

12 War Diary, 151 Infantry Brigade, October 1918, TNA WO95/2839.
13 War Diary, 150 Infantry Brigade, October 1918, TNA WO95/2833.
14 War Diary, 2nd Battalion Royal Dublin Fusiliers, 'Company Commander Points October 1918', TNA WO95/2832.
15 War Diary, HQ 50th Infantry Division, 'Lessons Learnt During Recent Operations, October 1918', TNA WO95/2812.
16 Various casualty tables, Rawlinson Papers, Churchill College RWLN 1/11.
17 War Diary, HQ XIII Corps, November 1918, 'Report on XIII Corps Engineer Work During Operations 1 October 1918-11 November 1918', TNA WO95/897, cited in Barr, op. cit., p.89.

were not as solid as at the Selle. Of the 13 divisions on the whole British front that day, only five reached or exceeded their objectives, but all the German forward defences were overrun. The risk of counter-attack was virtually non-existent, and 'the Germans, knowing they were beaten, mostly melted away during the hours of darkness'.[18] The enemy resistance at the Sambre was not token, but it did not match that offered at the Selle. The Battle of the Sambre was 'decisive',[19] in that it was the final battle of the war, but it was the intensity of the Selle operations that finally made it decisive, the last stage of semi-mobile attrition. Whether the Selle was 'one of the greatest military victories in the nation's history' is a point that would no doubt generate debate without conclusion.[20] The battle was certainly a triumph of tenacity for the infantry of possibly the finest army Great Britain has ever fielded.

18 J.D. Clayton, 'The Battle of the Sambre, 4 November 1918', p.345.
19 Clayton, op. cit., p.350.
20 J.P. Harris & N. Barr, *Amiens to the Armistice*, p.262.

Appendix I

Order of Battle – Fourth Army – from 9 October 1918 during the Selle Operations[1]

1. Fourth Army Headquarters

General Officer Commanding	General Sir H.S. Rawlinson
Major-General General Staff	Major-General A.A. Montgomery
Deputy Adjutant & Quartermaster General	Major-General H.C. Holman
General Officer Commanding Royal Artillery	Major-General C.E.D. Budworth
Chief Engineer	Major-General R.U.H. Buckland
Director of Medical Services	Major-General Sir M.W. O'Keefe
Deputy Director of Supplies and Transport	Brigadier-General E.C.F. Gillespie
Chief Signal Officer	Colonel R.G. Earle
Labour Commandant	Colonel T. Ogilvie
Deputy Director of Ordnance Services	Colonel R.S. Hamilton
Deputy Director Remounts	Colonel J.W. Yardley
Deputy Director Veterinary Services	Colonel W.J. Tatam

Army Troops

5th Brigade RAF	Brigadier-General L.E.O. Charlton
15th Corps Wing 8 & 73 Squadrons	Lieutenant-Colonel J.A. Chamier
22nd Army Wing 20, 23, 24, 46, 80, 84, 85, 92, 205 & 208 Squadrons	Lieutenant-Colonel T.A.E. Cairnes
5th Balloon Wing	Lieutenant-Colonel F.F.M. Roxby

4th Aircraft Park
4th Air Ammunition Column
4th Reserve Lorry Park
4th Army Troops Motor Transport Company

Artillery
Half 456 Siege Battery, RGA (9.2 inch railway mounted)
Half 471 Siege Battery, RGA (14 inch railway mounted)
Half 543 Siege Battery, RGA (12 inch railway mounted)

1 Augmented from A. Montgomery, *The Story of the Fourth Army in the Battles of the Hundred Days*, pp.301-27; S.M. Justice, 'Means to and End: The Experience of 1918 and its Influence on the British Fourth Army's Performance on the Selle'; and General Staff, *Operations of the 2nd American Corps in the Somme Offensive*, p.39.

Anti-Aircraft Defence	Lieutenant-Colonel R. Bruce Hay
F, G, P & Q Batteries	
50 Field Searchlight Company Royal Engineers	
1, 7, 16, 17, 36, 69, 3 & 4 Canadian Searchlight Sections RE	
66 AA Company	

5th Field Survey Battalion	Lieutenant-Colonel F.C. Legh
2, 3, 14 & 24 Observation Groups	
A, B, G, K, O & R Sound Ranging Sections	

Fourth Army Signals Company
43, 45, 48 & 53 (Motor) Airline Sections
BL, BM & BR Cable Sections
4 Telegraph Construction Company RE
4 Signal Construction Company RE

Other Royal Engineers
574 & 213 Army Tramways Companies RE
353 Electrical and Mechanical Company RE
B & Z Special (Poison Gas) Companies RE
3 Water Boring Section RE
8 & 11 Pontoon Parks RE
648 Field Company RE
224 Transportation Works Company RE

2. IX Corps

General Officer Commanding	Lieutenant-General Sir. W.P. Braithwaite
Brigadier-General General Staff	Brigadier-General A.R. Cameron
Deputy Adjutant & Quartermaster General	Brigadier-General J.C. Harding-Newman
General Officer Commanding Royal Artillery	Brigadier-General G. Humphreys
Chief Engineer	Brigadier-General R.A. Gillam

Corps Cavalry & Cyclists	
5th Cavalry Brigade	Brigadier-General N.W. Haig
9th Cyclist Battalion	

Corps Heavy Artillery	Brigadier-General G.B. Mackenzie
5, 12 & 14 Brigades RGA (8 inch howitzer)	
69 & 98 Brigades RGA (9.2 inch howitzer)	
79 & 83 Brigades RGA (Mixed)	
9, 21 & 41 Brigades RGA (Mobile)	
50, 222, 498 & 499 Siege Batteries RGA (6 inch gun)	
1 Siege Battery RMA (12 inch howitzer)	
80 Siege Battery RGA (12 inch howitzer)	
V/IX Heavy Trench Mortar Battery, RGA	

Field Artillery
5 & 16 Brigade RHA
5, 14, 23, 232 & 298 Brigades RFA

Royal Air Force
9 Squadron

Tank Corps	
3rd Tank Brigade	Brigadier-General J. Hardress-Lloyd
1 Company 6th (Light) Tank Battalion	
5th & 16th Tank Battalions	

Corps Signals
E Corps Signal Company
11 & 81 (Motor) Airline Sections
AA, BT & SV Cable Sections

Other
1 Advanced Section, 353 Electrical and Mechanical Company RE
4 Siege Company Royal Anglesey RE
216, 221 & 567 Army Tramways Companies RE
253, 254 & 256 Tunnelling Companies RE

IX Corps Troops Motor Transport Companies ASC

1st Division

General Officer Commanding	Major-General E.P. Strickland
GSO1	Lieutenant-Colonel E.N. Tandy
Assistant Adjutant & Quartermaster General	Lieutenant-Colonal H.H. Spender Clay
1 Infantry Brigade	Brigadier-General L.L. Wheatley
1st Black Watch	Lieutenant-Colonel F. Anderson
1st Loyal North Lancashire	Lieutenant-Colonel T.R. Forsyth-Forrest (to 11 October 1918) Lieutenant-Colonel R.E. Berkeley (from 11 October 1918)
1st Cameron Highlanders	Lieutenant-Colonel R.L. McCall (to 12 October 1918) Lieutenant-Colonel H.C. Methuen (from 14 October 1918)
1st Trench Mortar Battery	
2 Infantry Brigade	Brigadier-General G.C. Kelly
2nd Royal Sussex	Lieutenant-Colonel D.G. Johnson
1st Northamptonshire	Lieutenant-Colonel G. St. G. Robinson
2nd King's Royal Rifle Corps	Lieutenant-Colonel H.F.E. Smith
2nd Trench Mortar Battery	
3 Infantry Brigade	Brigadier-General E.G. St Aubyn
1st South Wales Borderers	Lieutenant-Colonel C.L. Taylor
1st Gloucestershire	Lieutenant-Colonel J.L.F. Tweedie (to 25 October) Lieutenant-Colonel J.R. Guild (from 25 October)

2nd Welsh	Lieutenant-Colonel J.F. Badham
3rd Trench Mortar Battery	
1 Battalion Machine Gun Corps	
Divisional Artillery	Brigadier-General H.F.E. Lewin
15 & 29 Brigade RFA	
X/1 & Y/1 Trench Mortar Batteries RA	
1st Divisional Ammunition Column	
Divisional Engineers	Lieutenant-Colonel C.E.P. Sankey
23, 26 & 409 Field Companies RE	
1st Divisional Signalling Company RE	
1/6th Welsh Regiment (Pioneers)	Lieutenant-Colonel L.C. Frisby
1st Divisional Train ASC	
1st Divisional Motor Transport Company ASC	
Other	
1, 2 & 141 Field Ambulances	
2nd Mobile Veterinary Section	
6th Division	
General Officer Commanding	Major-General T.O. Marden
GSO1	Lieutenant-Colonel T.T. Grove
Assistant-Adjutant & Quartermaster General	Lieutenant-Colonel P. Hudson
16 Infantry Brigade	Brigadier-General H.A. Walker (to 16 October 1918) Brigadier-General W.G. Braithwaite (from 19 October 1918)
1st Buffs	Lieutenant-Colonel R.E. Power (to 13 October 1918) Major Lord Teynham (from 13 October 1918)
1st Shropshire Light Infantry	Lieutenant-Colonel G. Meynell (to 9 October 1918) Lieutenant-Colonel L.H. Morris (from 10 October 1918)
2nd York & Lancaster	Lieutenant-Colonel J.R. Robertson (to ?17 October 1918) Captain E.E. Battle (18-21 October 1918) Major P.H.C. Collins (from 21 October 1918)
16th Trench Mortar Battery	
18 Infantry Brigade	Brigadier-General G.S.G. Craufurd
1st West Yorkshire	Lieutenant-Colonel D.L. Weir
11th Essex	Major A.G. Saunders
2nd Durham Light Infantry	Lieutenant-Colonel R.V. Turner

18th Trench Mortar Battery

71 Infantry Brigade	Brigadier-General P.W. Brown
9th Norfolk	Lieutenant-Colonel F.R. Day
1st Leicestershire	Lieutenant-Colonel F. Latham
2nd Sherwood Foresters	Lieutenant-Colonel C.E. Hudson

71st Trench Mortar Battery

6th Battalion Machine Gun Corps

Divisional Artillery	Brigadier-General E.F. Delaforce
2 & 24 Brigades RFA	
X/6 & Y/6 Trench Mortar Batteries RA	

6th Divisional Ammunition Column

Divisional Engineers	Lieutenant-Colonel H.A.L. Hall
12, 459 & 509 Field Companies RE	
6th Divisional Signal Company RE	
11th Leicestershire (Pioneers)	Lieutenant-Colonel R.H. Radford

6th Divisional Train ASC
6th Divisional Motor Transport Company ASC

16, 17 & 18 Field Ambulances
6th Mobile Veterinary Section

32nd Division (resting during Selle operations)

General Officer Commanding	Major-General T.S. Lambert
GSO1	Lieutenant-Colonel E.F.G. Dillon
Assistant-Adjutant & Quartermaster General	Lieutenant-Colonel J.P.B. Robinson

14 Infantry Brigade	Brigadier-General L.P. Evans
5/6th Royal Scots	Lieutenant-Colonel J.A. Fraser
1st Dorset	Lieutenant-Colonel H.D. Thwaytes
15th Highland Light Infantry	Lieutenant-Colonel V.B. Ramsden

14th Trench Mortar Battery

96 Infantry Brigade	Brigadier-General A.C. Girdwood
15th Lancashire Fusiliers	Lieutenant-Colonel C.E.R.G. Alban
16th Lancashire Fusiliers	Major P.E.Robathan (to 12 October 1918) Lieutenant-Colonel J.N. Marshall (from 12 October 1918)
2nd Manchester	Major J.L. Murphy

96th Trench Mortar Battery

97 Infantry Brigade	Brigadier-General Sir G. Armytage
1/5th Border	Lieutenant-Colonel H.N. Vinen
2nd Yorkshire Light Infantry	Lieutenant-Colonel L. Lamotte (to 11 October 1918) Major A.W. Robinson (from 11 October 1918)
10th Argyll & Sutherland Highlanders	Lieutenant-Colonel H.G. Sotheby
97th Trench Mortar Battery	
32nd Battalion Machine Gun Corps	
Divisional Artillery	Brigadier-General J.A. Tyler
161 & 168 Brigades RFA	
X/32 & Y/32 Trench Mortar Batteries RA	
32nd Division Ammunition Column	
Divisional Engineers	Lieutenant-Colonel G.C. Pollard
206, 218 & 219 Field Companies RE	
32nd Divisional Signal Company RE	
16th Highland Light Infantry (Pioneers)	Lieutenant-Colonel R. Kyle
32nd Divisional Train ASC	
32nd Divisional Motor Transport Company ASC	
90. 91 & 92 Field Ambulances	
42nd Mobile Veterinary Section	

46th Division

General Officer Commanding	Major-General G.F. Boyd
GSO1	Lieutenant-Colonel C.F. Jerran
Assistant-Adjutant & Quartermaster General	Lieutenant-Colonel R. Duckworth
137 Infantry Brigade	Brigadier-General J.V. Campbell
1/5th South Staffordshire	Lieutenant-Colonel A. White
1/6th South Staffordshire	Lieutenant-Colonel C. Lister
1/6th North Staffordshire	Lieutenant-Colonel C.C. Dowding
137th Trench Mortar Battery	
138 Infantry Brigade	Brigadier-General F.G.M. Rowley
1/5th Lincolnshire	Lieutenant-Colonel H.G. Wilson
1/4th Leicestershire	Major G.R.A. Beckett (to 11 October 1918) Lieutenant-Colonel F.H. Edwards (from 11 October 1918)
1/5th Leicestershire	Captain J.D. Hills (to 9 October 1918) Major R.S. Dyer-Bennett (9 October 1918 to 19 October 1918) Lieutenant-Colonel A.J. Dignan (from 19 October 1918)
138th Trench Mortar Battery	
139th Infantry Brigade	Brigadier-General J. Harington
1/5th Sherwood Foresters	Lieutenant-Colonel R.S. Pratt

1/6th Sherwood Foresters	Lieutenant-Colonel G.S. Clayton
1/8th Sherwood Foresters	Lieutenant-Colonel J.F. Dempster (9-12 October 1918) Lieutenant-Colonel R.W. Currin (from 12 October)

139th Trench Mortar Battery

46th Battalion Machine Gun Corps

Divisional Artillery 230 & 231 Brigades RFA X/46 & Y/46 Trench Mortar Batteries	Brigadier-General Sir S. Hill Child

46th Divisional Ammunition Column

Divisional Engineers 465, 466 & 468 Field Companies RE 46th Divisional Signal Company	Lieutenant-Colonel H.T. Morshead
1/1st Monmouthshire (Pioneers)	Lieutenant-Colonel F.G. Philips

46th Divisional Train ASC
46th Divisional Motor Transport Company ASC

1/1st, 1/2nd & 1/3rd (North Midland) Field Ambulances
1/1st (North Midland) Mobile Veterinary Section

3. XIII Corps

General Officer Commanding	Lieutenant-General Sir T.L.N. Morland
Brigadier-General General Staff	Brigadier-General I. Stewart
Deputy-Adjutant & Quartermaster General	Brigadier-General S.W. Robinson
General Officer Commanding Royal Artillery	Brigadier-General R.A.C. Wellesley
Chief Engineer	Brigadier-General C.A. Elliott
Corps Heavy Artillery 47 & 89 Brigades RGA (8 inch howitzer) 23 Brigade RGA (9.2 inch howitzer) 27 & 76 Brigades RGA (mixed) 85 Brigade RGA (mobile) 189, 312 & 545 Siege Batteries RGA (6 inch gun) 243 Siege Battery RGA (12 inch howitzer)	Brigadier-General J.D. Sherer

Field Artillery
65, 84, 86, 104, 108 & 150 Brigades RFA

Royal Air Force
35 Squadron

Tank Corps

4th Tank Brigade 3rd (Light) Tank Battalion	Brigadier-General E.B. Hankey

1st Tank Battalion

Corps Signals Troops
N Corps Signal Company
35 & 95 (Motor) Airline Sections
HH & VV Cable Sections

Other
2 Advanced Section 353 Electrical and Mechanical Company RE
1 Siege Company Royal Anglesey RE
144, 283 &288 Army Tramways Companies RE
180 & 182 Tunnelling Companies RE
XIII Corps Troops Motor Transport Company ASC

18th Division

General Officer Commanding	Major-General R.P. Lee
GSO1	Lieutenant-Colonel G. Blewitt
Assistant-Adjutant & Quartermaster General	Lieutenant-Colonel R.H.L. Cuthill
53 Infantry Brigade	Brigadier-General M.G.H. Barker
10th Essex	Lieutenant-Colonel R. Forbes
8th Royal Berkshire	Major A.F. Northcote (to 24 October 1918) Lieutenant-Colonel N.B. Hudson (from 24 October 1918)
7th West Kent	Lieutenant-Colonel L.H. Hickson
53rd Trench Mortar Battery	
54 Infantry Brigade	Lieutenant-Colonel R. Turner (to 12 October 1918) Brigadier-General O.C. Borrett (from 12 October 1918) Lieutenant-Colonel R. Turner (24 October 1918) Lieutenant-Colonel K.C. Weldon (from 25 October 1918)
11th Royal Fusiliers	Lieutenant-Colonel K.D.H. Gwynn
2nd Bedfordshire	Lieutenant-Colonel A.E. Percival
6th Northamptonshire	Lieutenant-Colonel R. Turner
54th Trench Mortar Battery	
55 Infantry Brigade	Brigadier-General E.A. Wood (to 24 October 1918) Lieutenant-Colonel A.P.B. Irwin (from 24 October 1918)
7th Queens' Own Royal West Surrey	Lieutenant-Colonel G.L. Harrison
7th Buffs	Lieutenant-Colonel H.M.C Curtis (to ? October 1918) Major H.C.T. Stronge (from ? October 1918)
8th East Surrey	Lieutenant-Colonel W.H. Baddeley
55th Trench Mortar Battery	

18th Battalion Machine Gun Corps	
Divisional Artillery	Lieutenant-Colonel T.O. Seagram
82 & 83 Brigades RFA	
X/18 & Y/18 Trench Mortar Batteries RA	
18th Divisional Ammunition Column	
Divisional Engineers	Lieutenant-Colonel C.B.O. Symons
79, 80 & 82 Field Companies RE	
18th Divisional Signal Company RE	
8th Royal Sussex (Pioneers)	Lieutenant-Colonel B.J. Walker
18th Divisional Train ASC	
18th Divisional Motor Transport Company ASC	
54, 55 & 56 Field Ambulances	
30th Mobile Veterinary Section	
25th Division	
General Officer Commanding	Major-General J.R.E. Charles
GSO1	Lieutenant-Colonel D.F. Anderson
Assistant-Adjutant & Quartermaster General	Lieutenant-Colonel E.P.J. Stourton
7 Infantry Brigade	Brigadier-General C.J. Hickie
9th Devonshire	Lieutenant-Colonel H.I. Storey
20th Manchester	Major J.S. Gemmell (to 12 October 1918)
	Lieutenant-Colonel C.R. Pilkington (from 12 October 1918)
21st Manchester	Lieutenant-Colonel C.E.N. Lomax
7th Trench Mortar Battery	
74 Infantry Brigade	Brigadier-General H.M. Craigie-Halkett
9th Yorkshire	Lieutenant-Colonel R.S. Hart
11th Sherwood Foresters	Lieutenant-Colonel H.N. Young (to 25 October 1918)
	Lieutenant-Colonel W.R. Corrall (from 28 October 1918)
13th Durham Light Infantry 1918)	Major L.M. Greenwood (to 13 October
	Lieutenant-Colonel P.F. Hone (to 23 October 1918)
	Major H.G. Faber (from 24 October 1918)
74th Trench Mortar Battery	
75 Infantry Brigade	Brigadier-General C.W. Frizzell
1/8th Royal Warwickshire	Lieutenant-Colonel P.H. Whitehouse
1/5th Gloucestershire	Lieutenant-Colonel D. Lewis
1/8th Worcestershire	Lieutenant-Colonel H.T. Clarke

75th Trench Mortar Battery	
100th Machine Gun Battalion (2-19 October) 25th Machine Gun Battalion (from 19 October)	
Divisional Artillery	Brigadier-General K.J. Kincaid-Smith
110 & 112 Brigades RFA X/25 & Y/25 Trench Mortar Batteries RA	
25th Divisional Ammunition Column	
Divisional Engineers	Lieutenant-Colonel R.J. Done
105, 106, 130 Field Companies RE 25th Divisional Signal Company RE	
11th South Lancashire (Pioneers)	Lieutenant-Colonel C.C. Champion
25th Divisional Train ASC 25th Divisional Motor Transport Company	
75, 76 & 77 Field Ambulances 37th Mobile Veterinary Section	
50th Division	
General Officer Commanding	Major-General H.C. Jackson
GSO1	Lieutenant-Colonel E.C. Anstey
Assistant-Adjutant & Quartermaster General	Lieutenant-Colonel A.C.H. Duke
149 Infantry Brigade	Brigadier-General P.M. Robinson
3rd Royal Fusiliers	Major W.A. Trasenster
13th Black Watch	Lieutenant-Colonel P.J. Blair (from 13 October 1918)
2nd Royal Dublin Fusiliers	Lieutenant-Colonel K.C. Weldon (to 25 October) Major J. Luke (from 25 October)
149th Trench Mortar Battery	
150 Infantry Brigade	Brigadier-General G. Rollo
2nd Northumberland Fusiliers	Lieutenant-Colonel A.C.L. Hardman-Jones
7th Wiltshire	Lieutenant-Colonel H.J. Hodgson
2nd Royal Munster Fusiliers	Lieutenant-Colonel H.B. Tonson-Rye (to 13 October 1918) Captain C.R. Williams (from 13 October 1918)
150th Trench Mortar Battery	
151 Infantry Brigade	Brigadier-General R.E. Sugden
6th Royal Inniskilling Fusiliers	Lieutenant-Colonel G.G.F.F. Greville
1st King's Own Yorkshire Light Infantry	Lieutenant-Colonel H. Mallinson

4th King's Royal Rifle Corps	Lieutenant-Colonel J.B. Brady
151st Trench Mortar Battery	
50th Battalion Machine Gun Corps	
Divisional Artillery (detached – with Second Army)	Brigadier-General W. Stirling
Divisional Engineers	Lieutenant-Colonel P. de H. Hall
7, 446 & 447 Field Companies RE	
50th Divisional Signal Company RE	
5th Royal Irish Regiment (Pioneers)	Lieutenant-Colonel G.H. Hawkes
50th Divisional Train ASC	
50th Divisional Motor Transport Company ASC	
1/1st, 1/3rd & 2/2nd Northumbrian Field Ambulances	
1/1st Northumbrian Mobile Veterinary Section	

66th Division

General Officer Commanding	Major-General H.K. Bethell
GSO1	Lieutenant-Colonel F.P. Nosworthy
Assistant-Adjutant & Quartermaster General	Lieutenant-Colonel F.J. Lemon
198 Infantry Brigade	Brigadier-General A.J. Hunter
1/6th Lancashire Fusiliers	Lieutenant-Colonel R.F. Gross
5th Royal Inniskilling Fusiliers	Lieutenant-Colonel A.W.S. Paterson
6th Royal Dublin Fusiliers	Lieutenant-Colonel W.B. Little
198th Trench Mortar Battery	
199 Infantry Brigade	Brigadier-General G.C. Williams
18th King's Liverpool	Lieutenant-Colonel R.O. Wynne
9th Manchester	Lieutenant-Colonel J.F.B. Morrell
5th Connaught Rangers	Lieutenant-Colonel V.M.B. Scully
199th Trench Mortar Battery	
South African Infantry Brigade	Brigadier-General W.E.C. Tanner
1st South African Infantry	Lieutenant-Colonel H.H. Jenkins
2nd South African Infantry	Lieutenant-Colonel L.F. Sprenger
4th South African Infantry	Lieutenant-Colonel D. MacL. Macleod
South African Trench Mortar Battery	
100th Battalion Machine Gun Corps (from 19 October 1918)	
Divisional Artillery (detached – with Second Army)	Brigadier-General A. Birtwistle

Divisional Engineers	Major S.H. Morgan
430, 431 & 432 Field Companies RE	
66th Divisional Signal Company RE	
9th Gloucestershire (Pioneers)	Lieutenant-Colonel E.P. Nares

2/2nd & 2/3rd (East Lancashire) and South African Field Ambulances
1/1st East Lancashire Mobile Veterinary Section

4. II American Corps

General Officer Commanding	Major-General G.W. Read
Chief of Staff	Colonel G.S. Simonds
General Officer Commanding Royal Artillery	Brigadier-General K.K. Knapp
Assistant Chief of Staff G-1	Lieutenant-Colonel R.K. Hale
Assistant Chief of Staff G-2	Lieutenant-Colonel K.T. Riggs
Assistant Chief of Staff G-3	Colonel F.E. Buchan
Assistant Chief of Staff G-4	Lieutenant-Colonel J.P. Terrill

Corps Heavy Artillery	Brigadier-General F.H. Metcalfe
68 & 71 Brigades RGA (8-inch howitzer)	
18 Brigade RGA (9.2-inch howitzer)	
51 & 93 Brigades RGA (mixed)	
9 & 41 (Mobile) Brigades RGA	
222, 440 & 504 Siege Batteries RGA (6-inch gun)	
494 Siege Battery RGA (12-inch howitzer)	

Army Troops Field Artillery
6 & 12 Australian Brigades

Divisional Artillery

2nd Australian	Brigadier-General O.F. Phillips
4 & 5 Brigades AFA (attached 27th Division)	
X/2A and Y/2A Trench Mortar Batteries AFA	
3rd Australian	Brigadier-General H.W. Grimwade
7 Brigade AFA (attached 27th Division)	
8 Brigade AFA (attached 30th Division)	
X/3A & Y/3A Trench Mortar Batteries AFA	
4th Australian	Brigadier-General W.L.H. Burgess
10 & 11 Brigades AFA (attached 30th Division)	
X/4A & Y/4A Trench Mortar Batteries AFA	
5th Australian	Brigadier-General A.J. Bessell-Browne
13 Brigade AFA (attached 30th Division)	
14 Brigade AFA (attached 27th Division)	
X/5A & Y/5A Trench Mortar Batteries AFA	

Australian Flying Corps
3 Squadron

Tank Corps

4th Tank Brigade	Brigadier-General E.B. Hankey
6th (Light) Tank Battalion	
4th Tank Battalion	
301st American Tank Battalion	

Royal Engineers
146 & 288 Army Tramways Companies RE
1 Australian Army Tramways Company RE
1 & 2 Australian Tunnelling Companies RE
Detachment Australian Electrical & Mechanical Company RE

27th American Division

General Officer Commanding	Major-General F. O'Ryan
Chief of Staff	Lieutenant-Colonel S.H. Ford
Assistant Chief of Staff G1	Lieutenant-Colonel E. Olmstead
Assistant Chief of Staff G2	Major W.T. Starr
Assistant Chief of Staff G3	Colonel T.B. Taylor
53 Infantry Brigade	Brigadier-General A.H. Blanding
105th Regiment (3 battalions)	Colonel J.M. Andrews
106th Regiment (3 battalions)	Colonel W.A. Taylor
105th Machine Gun Battalion	Major K. Gardner
54 Infantry Brigade	Brigadier-General P.D. Pierce
107th Regiment (3 battalions)	Colonel C.I. Debevoise
108th Regiment (3 battalions)	Colonel E.S. Jennings
106th Machine Gun Battalion	Major M.D. Bryant
Divisional Troops	
102nd Engineer Regiment	Colonel A.H. Acker
102nd Field Signal Battalion	Major A.L. Howe
104th Machine Gun Battalion	Major C.H. King
102nd Divisional Train	
106 & 107 Ambulance Sections	
105 & 106 Field Hospital Sections	

30th American Division

General Officer Commanding	Major-General E.M. Lewis
Chief of Staff	Lieutenant-Colonel J.K. Herr
Assistant Chief of Staff G1	Lieutenant-Colonel A.M. Pope
Assistant Chief of Staff G2	Captain C.C. Rutledge
Assistant Chief of Staff G3	Lieutenant-Colonel C. Burnett
59 Infantry Brigade	Brigadier-General L.D. Tyson
117th Regiment (3 battalions)	Colonel C.F. Spence

118th Regiment (3 battalions)	Colonel O.R. Wolfe
114th Machine Gun Battalion	Major E.B. Cantey
60 Infantry Brigade	Brigadier-General S.L. Faison
119th Regiment (3 battalions)	Colonel J. Van B. Metts
120th Regiment (3 battalions)	Colonel S.W. Minor
115th Machine Gun Battalion	Major W.W. Pierce
Divisional Troops	
105th Engineer Regiment	Lieutenant-Colonel J.M. Pratt
105th Field Signal Battalion	Major F.A. Montrose
113th Machine Gun Battalion	Major W.H. Hyde
105th Divisional Train	
118 & 119 Ambulance Sections	
118 & 119 Field Hospital Sections	

5. Australian Corps (in Army Reserve)

6. Cavalry Corps

General Officer Commanding	Lieutenant-General C.T. McM. Kavanagh
Brigadier General General Staff	Brigadier-General A.F. Home
Deputy Adjutant & Quartermaster General	Brigadier-General J.C.G. Longmore
General Officer Commanding Royal Artillery	Brigadier-General H.S. Seligman
Commander Royal Engineers	Lieutenant-Colonel W.H. Evans

Corps Cyclists

Royal Air Force

6 Squadron
Tank Corps

17th (Armoured Car) Tank Battalion

Corps Signal Troops
Cavalry Corps Signal Squadron RE
Cavalry Corps Wireless Squadron RE
AD & GG Cable Sections RE

Other Royal Engineer and Army Service Corps
Cavalry Corps Bridging Park RE
Cavalry Corps Troops Motor Transport Company ASC

4 Guards Brigade	Brigadier-General Hon. L.J.P Butler
4th Grenadier Guards	Lieutenant-Colonel W.S. Pilcher
3rd Coldstream Guards	Lieutenant-Colonel R.B.J. Crawfurd
1/st Honourable Artillery Company	Lieutenant-Colonel P.C. Cooper

Household Machine Gun Brigade
1st (1st Life Guards) Battalion, Guards Machine Gun Regiment
3rd (Royal Horse Guards) Battalion, Guards Machine Gun Regiment

1st Cavalry Division

General Officer Commanding	Major-General R.L. Mullins
GSO1	Lieutenant-Colonel R.E. Cecil
Assistant-Adjutant and Quartermaster	Lieutenant-Colonel J. Blakiston-Houston

1 Cavalry Brigade	Brigadier-General H.S. Sewell
2nd Dragoon Guards	Major R.M. Stewart-Richardson
5th Dragoon Guards	Lieutenant-Colonel J. Van der Byl
11th Hussars	Lieutenant-Colonel R.J.P Anderson

I battery RHA (13-pounder)
1st Cavalry Machine Gun Squadron
1 Signal Troop

2 Cavalry Brigade	Brigadier-General A. Lawson
4th Dragoon Guards	Lieutenant-Colonel E.M. Dorman
9th Lancers	Lieutenant-Colonel R.H.R. Brocklebank
18th Hussars	Lieutenant-Colonel W. Holdsworth

H battery RHA (13-pounder)
2nd Cavalry Machine Gun Squadron
2 Signal Troop

9th Cavalry Brigade	Brigadier-General D'A. Legard
8th Hussars	Lieutenant-Colonel G.M. Mort
15th Hussars	Lieutenant-Colonel H. Combe
19th Hussars	Lieutenant-Colonel A.W. Parsons

Y battery RHA (13-pounder)
9th Cavalry Machine Gun Squadron
9 Signal Troop

7 Brigade RHA & Ammunition Column
1st Field Squadron RE
1st Signal Squadron
HQ 1st Cavalry Divisional ASC
1st Cavalry Divisional Motor Transport Company ASC
1st Cavalry Divisional Auxiliary (Horse) Company
1, 3 & 9 Cavalry Field Ambulances
1, 10 & 39 Mobile Veterinary Sections

3rd Cavalry Division

General Officer Commanding	Major-General A.E.W. Harman
GSO1	Lieutenant-Colonel G.P.L. Cosens
Assistant-Adjutant and Quartermaster	Lieutenant-Colonel T.W. Pragnell

6 Cavalry Brigade	Brigadier-General E. Paterson
3rd Dragoon Guards	Lieutenant-Colonel C.L. Rome (to 9 October 1918) Major J.T. Gibbs (from 9 October 1918)
1st Royal Dragoons	Lieutenant-Colonel F.W. Wormald
10th Hussars	Lieutenant-Colonel F.H.O.C. Whitmore

C Battery RHA (13-pounder)
6th Cavalry Machine Gun Squadron
6th Signal Troop

7 Cavalry Brigade	Brigadier-General A. Burt
7th Dragoon Guards	Lieutenant-Colonel R. Sparrow
6th (Inniskilling) Dragoons	Lieutenant-Colonel C.R. Terrot
17th Lancers	Lieutenant-Colonel T.P. Melvill

K Battery RHA (13-pounder)
7th Cavalry Machine Gun Squadron
7th Signal Troop

Canadian Cavalry Brigade	Brigadier-General R.W. Paterson
Royal Canadian Dragoons	Lieutenant-Colonel C.T. van Straubenzee (to 9 October 1918) Lieutenant-Colonel T Newcomen (from 10 October 1918)
Lord Strathcona's Horse	Lieutenant-Colonel D.G. MacDonald
Fort Garry Horse	Lieutenant-Colonel H.I. Stevenson

Royal Canadian Horse Artillery Brigade (13-pounder)
Canadian Cavalry Machine Gun Squadron
Canadian Signal Troop
4 Brigade RHA & Ammunition Column
3rd Field Squadron RE
3rd Signal Squadron
HQ 3rd Cavalry Divisional ASC
3rd Cavalry Divisional Motor Transport Company ASC
3rd Cavalry Divisional Auxiliary (Horse) Company
6, 7 & Canadian Cavalry Field Ambulances
13, 14 & A Canadian Mobile Veterinary Sections

Appendix II

Skeleton Order of Battle – German Army opposing Fourth Army during the Battle of the Selle[1]

Second Army – General von Carlowitz

IV Reserve Corps General von Conta

44th Reserve Division Generalmajor Haas

87th Reserve Infantry Brigade
Reserve Infantry Regiments 205, 206 & 208
Pioneer Battalion 344

Artillery Command 44
Reserve Field Artillery Regiment 44
2nd Battalions Foot Artillery Regiments 2 & 21
Field Artillery Regiment 183
1st Battalion Reserve Foot Artillery Regiment 1
Actual artillery totals: 72 field artillery and 33 medium heavy artillery
Up to 48 7.7 cm field guns
Up to 24 10.5 cm light field howitzers
Up to 11 10 cm field guns
Up to 22 15 cm heavy field howitzers

8th Infantry Division Generalleutnant Hamann

16th Infantry Brigade
Infantry Regiments 72, 93, 153 & 118
Pioneer Battalion 118

Artillery Command 8
Field Artillery Regiment 74
Actual artillery total: Up to 36 field artillery

1 Adapted from M. Whisler, 'Der Tommy Kommt', pp.59-80.; and General Staff AEF, *Histories of Two Hundred and Fifty-One Divisions of the German Army which Participated in the War (1914-1918).*

LI Corps Generallleutnant von Below

17th Reserve Division Generalleutnant von Mutius

81st Infantry Brigade
Infantry Regiments 162, 163 & 478
Reserve Infantry Regiment 76
Machine Gun Sharpshooter Detachment 54
Pioneer Battalion 317

Artillery Command 110
2nd Battalion/Field Artillery Regiment 238
Reserve Field Artillery Regiment 17
3rd Battalion Foot Artillery Regiment 26
1st & 2nd Battalions Reserve Foot Artillery Regiment 2
2nd Battalion Landwehr Foot Artillery Regiment 22
2nd Battalion Field Artillery Regiment 72
Actual artillery totals: 48 field artillery and 34 medium and heavy artillery
Up to 36 7.7 cm field guns
Up to 12 10.5 cm light field howitzers
Up to 7 10 cm field guns
Up to 14 15 cm heavy field howitzers
Up to 5 15 cm field guns
Up to 8 21 cm Moerser heavy howitzers

243rd Infantry Division Genelalleutnant von Schippert

247th Infantry Brigade
Fuesilier Regiment 122
Infantry Regiment 479
Machine Gun Sharpshooter Detachment 41
Pioneer Battalion 243

Artillery Command 235
Field Artillery Regiment 238
Foot Artillery Battalion 36
1st & 2nd Battalions Bavarian Field Artillery Regiment 23
3rd Battalion Reserve Foot Artillery Regiment 2
Foot Artillery Battalion 54
Actual artillery totals: 60 field artillery and 26 medium and heavy artillery
Up to 36 7.7 cm field guns
Up to 24 10.5 cm light field howitzers
Up to 17 15 cm heavy field howitzers
Up to 6 21 cm Moerser heavy howitzers
Up to 3 10 cm field guns

204th Infantry Division Generalleutnant von Stein

407th Infantry Brigade
Infantry Regiment 413
Infantry Regiment 414

Reserve Infantry Regiment 120
1 company Machine Gun Sharpshooter Detachment 54

121st Infantry Division

HQ Reserve Infantry Regiment 7
Combat Battalion Infantry Regiment 60
Combat Battalion Reserve Infantry Regiment 7
Combat Battalion Reserve Infantry Regiment 56
Pioneer Company 247
Pioneer Company 260
Pioneer Battalion 204

Artillery Command 204
Reserve Field Artillery Regiment 27
Foot Artillery Battalion 101
3rd Battalion Bavarian Field Artillery Regiment 23
2nd Battalion Bavarian Foot Artillery Regiment 4
Actual artillery totals: 48 field artillery and 21 medium and heavy artillery
Up to 32 7.7 cm field guns
Up to 16 10.5 cm light field howitzers
Up to 7 10 cm field guns
Up to 14 15 cm heavy field howitzers

54th Infantry (Intervention) Division Generalmajor Ernst Kabisch

108th Infantry Brigade
Infantry Regiment 84
Reserve Infantry Regiment 27
Reserve Infantry Regiment 90
Pioneer Battalion 138

Artillery Command 55
Field Artillery Regiment 108
Actual artillery total: 19 field artillery

2nd Infantry (Cyclist) Brigade
Reserve (Cyclist) Regiment 26
1st, 2nd, 4th, 5th, 6th & 7th Cyclist Battalions
Cuirassier Regiment 8

Corps Artillery Group
Foot Artillery Battalion 170
10th Battery Landwehr Foot Artillery Regiment 22
9th Battery Reserve Foot Artillery Regiment 2
Actual artillery totals: 8 field artillery and 14 heavy artillery
Up to 3 13cm and 5 15 cm field guns
3 21 cm Moerser heavy howitzers
Up to 11 heavy artillery

Eighteenth Army – General der Infanterie von Hutier

1 Bavarian Corps Generalleutnant Ritter von Endres

3rd Naval Division Generalmajor Graf von Moltke

Marine Infantry Brigade
Marine Infantry Regiments 1, 2 & 3
Boat Cannon Battery
Machine Gun Sharpshooter Detachment 63
2nd Machine Gun Company/Landsturm Battalion Tilsit 1
Pioneer Battalion 115

Artillery Command 146
Field Artillery Regiments 9 &78
Foot Artillery Battalions 47 & 110
3rd Battery Foot Artillery Regiment 77
Actual artillery totals: 51 field artillery and 13 heavy artillery
44 7.7 cm field guns
21 10.5 cm light field howitzers
7 15 cm heavy field howitzers
6 21 cm Moerser heavy howitzers

24th Infantry Division Generalleutnant Hammer

89th Infantry Brigade
Battalion Dressler (Infantry Regiment 133)
Battalion Reichardt (Infantry Regiment 139)
Battalion Selie (Infantry Regiment 179)
Machine Gun Sharpshooter Detachment 74
Pioneer Battalion 22

Artillery Command 24
Field Artillery Regiment 77
Foot Artillery Battalion 96
1st Battalions Field Artillery Regiments 4 & 504
Actual artillery totals: 38 field artillery and 12 heavy artillery
30 7.7 cm field guns
8 10.5 cm light field howitzers
2 10 cm field guns
10 15 cm heavy field howitzers

15th Reserve Division Generalmajor Hucke

30th Reserve Infantry Brigade
Reserve Infantry Regiments 17, 25 & 69
Pioneer Battalion 315

Artillery Command 104
Reserve Field Artillery Regiment 15
Foot Artillery Battalion 125

2nd Battalion Field Artillery Regiment 504
3rd Battalion Foot Artillery Regiment 4
Actual artillery totals: 45 field artillery, 7 heavy artillery
28 7.7 cm field guns
17 10.5 cm light field howitzers
3 10 cm field guns
3 15 cm heavy field howitzers
2 21 cm Moerser heavy howitzer

5th Reserve Division Generalleutnant von Auwaerter

9th Reserve Infantry Brigade
Reserve Infantry Regiments 8, 12 & 48
Bavarian Machine Gun Sharpshooter Detachment 1
Pioneer Battalion 305

Artillery Command 90
Reserve Field Artillery Regiment 5
4th Battalion Reserve Foot Artillery Regiment 17
2 battalions Field Artillery Regiment 70
Foot Artillery Battalion 134
2nd Battery Foot Artillery Battalion 145
Actual artillery totals: 49 field artillery, 14 heavy artillery
41 7.7 cm field guns
8 10.5 cm light field howitzers
3 10 cm field guns
4 15 cm heavy field howitzers
7 21 cm Moerser heavy howitzers

Corps Heavy Artillery Group
3rd Battery Foot Artillery Battalion 39
3rd Battery Foot Artillery Battalion 134
3rd Battalion Foot Artillery Battalion 145
Totals:
3 10 cm field guns
6 15 cm field guns
9 heavy artillery

29th Infantry Division Generalmajor von Berendt

58th Infantry Brigade
Infantry Regiments 112, 113 & 142
Pioneer Battalion 130

Artillery Command 67
Field Artillery Regiment 30
2nd Battalion Reserve Foot Artillery Regiment 9
Actual artillery totals:
27 field artillery, 5 heavy artillery

221st Infantry Division Generalmajor von La Chevellerie

1st Reserve Ersatz Brigade
Infantry Regiments 41 & 45
Reserve Infantry Regiment 60
Pioneer Battalion 221

Artillery Command 221
273 Field Artillery Regiment
3 batteries 40 Foot Artillery Regiment
Actual artillery totals: not known

Bibliography

I. ARCHIVE SOURCES

The National Archives of the United Kingdom

TNA AIR 1/173/15/164/1	Historical data concerning No. 35 Squadron Royal Air Force.
TNA AIR 1/1671/204.	History of Tank and Aeroplane Co-Operation.
TNA AIR 1/2225/209/26	War Diary, 5 Brigade RAF.
TNA CAB45/132	Committee of Imperial Defence, Historical Branch and Cabinet Office, Historical Section: Official War Histories Correspondence and papers.
TNA WO95/39	War Diary, GHQ Quartermaster General Branch.
TNA WO95/102	War Diary, HQ 2 Tank Brigade.
TNA WO95/103	War Diary, 10th Tank Battalion.
TNA WO95/105	War Diary, HQ 3 Tank Brigade.
TNA WO95/107	War Diary, 6th Battalion Tank Corps.
TNA WO95/108	War Diary, HQ 4 Tank Brigade.
TNA WO95/109	War Diary, 1st Battalion Tank Corps.
TNA WO95/110	War Diary, 4th Battalion Tank Corps.
TNA WO95/111	War Diary, 5th Battalion Tank Corps.
TNA WO95/115	War Diary, 16th Battalion Tank Corps.
TNA WO95/439	War Diary, HQ Fourth Army.
TNA WO95/445	War Diary, Assistant Quartermaster General Fourth Army.
TNA WO95/452	War Diary, Deputy Director Ordnance Service Fourth Army.
TNA WO95/492	War Diary, 5 Field Survey Company Royal Engineers.
TNA WO95/575	War Diary, HQ Cavalry Corps.
TNA WO95/837	War Diary, HQ IX Corps.
TNA WO95/840	War Diary, Assistant Quartermaster General IX Corps.
TNA WO95/842	War Diary, HQ IX Corps Heavy Artillery.
TNA WO95/844	War Diary, Chief Engineer IX Corps.
TNA WO95/844	War Diary, Assistant Director Ordnance Services IX Corps
TNA WO95/846	War Diary, IX Corps Senior Motor Transport Officer.
TNA WO95/847	War Diary, 1st Division Supply Column.

TNA WO95/848	War Diary, 6th Division Supply Column.
TNA WO95/897	War Diary, HQ XIII Corps.
TNA WO95/900	War Diary, Assistant Quartermaster General XIII Corps.
TNA WO95/902	War Diary, Commander Royal Artillery XIII Corps.
TNA WO95/903	War Diary, Chief Engineer XIII Corps.
TNA WO95/907	War Diary, XIII Corps 'N' Supply Column ASC.
TNA WO95/908	War Diary, 25th Division Supply Column.
TNA WO95/936	War Diary, HQ XVII Corps.
TNA WO95/1138	War Diary, HQ 5th Cavalry Brigade.
TNA WO95/1139	War Diary, Royal Scots Greys.
TNA WO95/1142	War Diary, HQ 3rd Cavalry Division.
TNA WO95/1152	War Diary, 6th Machine Gun Squadron.
TNA WO95/1154	War Diary, HQ 7th Cavalry Brigade.
TNA WO95/1234	War Diary, HQ 1st Infantry Division.
TNA WO95/1241	War Diary, HQ Commander Royal Artillery 1st Division.
TNA WO95/1251	War Diary, 1st Division Trench Mortar Battery.
TNS WO95/1252	War Diary, 23 Field Company Royal Engineers.
TNA WO95/1253	War Diary, 26 Field Company Royal Engineers.
TNA WO95/1254	War Diary 409 Field Company Royal Engineers.
TNA WO95/1256	War Diary, 1st Battalion Machine Gun Corps.
TNA WO95/1262	War Diary, HQ 1 Infantry Brigade.
TNA WO95/1263	War Diary 1st Battalion Black Watch.
TNA WO95/1264	War Diary, 1st Battalion Queen's Own Cameron Highlanders.
TNA WO95/1266	War Diary, 1st Battalion Loyal North Lancashire.
TNA WO95/1268	War Diary, HQ 2 Infantry Brigade.
TNA WO95/1269	War Diary, 2nd Battalion Royal Sussex Regiment.
TNA WO95/1273	War Diary, 2nd Battalion King's Royal Rifle Corps.
TNA WO95/1277	War Diary, HQ 3 Infantry Brigade.
TNA WO95/1278	War Diary, 1st Battalion Gloucestershire Regiment.
TNA WO95/1280	War Diary, 1st Battalion South Wales Borderers.
TNA WO95/1281	War Diary, 2nd Battalion Welsh Regiment.
TNA WO95/1435	War Diary, 1st Battalion Gordon Highlanders.
TNA WO95/1587	War Diary, AA & QMG 6th Division.
TNA WO95/1591	War Diary, 6th Division Royal Field Artillery.
TNA WO95/1599	War Diary, 12 Field Company Royal Engineers.
TNA WO95/1599	War Diary, 459 Field Company Royal Engineers.
TNA WO95/1600	War Diary, 509 Field Company Royal Engineers.
TNA WO95/1601	War Diary, 11th Battalion Leicestershire Regiment.
TNA WO95/1607	War Diary, HQ 16 Infantry Brigade.
TNA WO95/1608	War Diary, 1st Battalion East Kent Regiment.
TNA WO95/1609	War Diary, 1st King's Shropshire Light Infantry.
TNA WO95/1615	War Diary, HQ 18 Infantry Brigade.

TNA WO95/1616	War Diary, 11th Battalion Essex Regiment.
TNA WO95/1617	War Diary, 2nd Battalion Durham Light Infantry.
TNA WO95/1620	War Diary, HQ 71 Infantry Brigade.
TNA WO95/1622	War Diary, 1st Battalion Leicestershire Regiment.
TNA WO95/1623	War Diary, 9th Battalion Norfolk Regiment.
TNA WO95/1624	War Diary, 2nd Battalion Sherwood Foresters.
TNA WO95/1918	War Diary, HQ 66th Infantry Division.
TNA WO95/2017	War Diary, HQ 18th Infantry Division.
TNA WO95/2026	War Diary, 18th Division Ammunition Column.
TNA WO95/2037	War Diary, 8th Battalion Royal Berkshire Regiment.
TNA WO95/2038	War Diary, 10th Battalion Essex Regiment.
TNA WO95/2042	War Diary, HQ 54 Infantry Brigade.
TNA WO95/2042	War Diary, 2nd Battalion Bedfordshire Regiment.
TNA WO95/2044	War Diary, 6th Battalion Northamptonshire Regiment.
TNA WO95/2045	War Diary, 11th Battalion Royal Fusiliers.
TNA WO95/2048	War Diary, HQ 55 Infantry Brigade.
TNA WO95/2049	War Diary, 7th Battalion East Kent Regiment.
TNA WO95/2050	War Diary, 8th Battalion East Surrey Regiment.
TNA WO95/2051	War Diary, 7th Battalion Queen's Own Royal West Surrey Regiment.
TNA WO95/2227	War Diary, HQ 25 Infantry Brigade.
TNA WO95/2230	War Diary, Commander Royal Artillery 25th Division.
TNA WO95/2232	War Diary, Chief Engineer 25th Division.
TNA WO95/2235	War Diary, 105 Field Company Royal Engineers.
TNA WO95/2237	War Diary, 130 Field Company Royal Engineers.
TNA WO95/2244	War Diary, 20th Battalion Manchester Regiment.
TNA WO95/2244	War Diary, 21st Battalion Manchester Regiment.
TNA WO95/2245	War Diary, HQ 74 Infantry Brigade.
TNA WO95/2247	War Diary, 13th Battalion Durham Light Infantry.
TNA WO95/2247	War Diary, 11th Battalion Sherwood Foresters.
TNA WO95/2247	War Diary, 9th Battalion Yorkshire Regiment.
TNA WO95/2247	War Diary, 13th Battalion Durham Light Infantry.
TNA WO95/2249	War Diary, HQ 75 Infantry Brigade.
TNA WO95/2251	War Diary, 1/8th Battalion Worcestershire Regiment.
TNA WO95/2251	War Diary, 1/5th Battalion Gloucestershire Regiment.
TNA WO95/2422	War Diary, 1st Battalion Scottish Rifles.
TNA WO95/2665	War Diary, HQ 46th Infantry Division.
TNA WO95/2666	War Diary, HQ 46th Infantry Division.
TNA WO95/2669	War Diary, HQ 46th Division Royal Horse Artillery and Royal Field Artillery.
TNA WO95/2676	War Diary, 465 Field Company Royal Engineers.
TNA WO95/2678	War Diary, 468 Field Company Royal Engineers.
TNA WO95/2685	War Diary, 1/6th Battalion North Staffordshire Regiment.

TNA WO95/2679 War Diary, 46 Battalion Machine Gun Corps.
TNA WO95/2679 War Diary, 1st Battalion Monmouthshire Regiment.
TNA WO95/2686 War Diary, 1/5th Battalion South Staffordshire Regiment.
TNA WO95/2689 War Diary, HQ 138 Infantry Brigade.
TNA WO95/2690 War Diary, 1/5th Battalion Leicestershire Regiment.
TNA WO95/2693 War Diary, HQ 139 Infantry Brigade.
TNA WO95/2695 War Diary, 1/5th Battalion Sherwood Foresters.
TNA WO95/2812 War Diary, HQ 50th Infantry Division.
TNA WO95/2816 War Diary, Commander Royal Engineers 50th Division.
TNA WO95/2816 War Diary, Deputy Assistant Director Ordnance Service 50th Division.
TNA WO95/2821 War Diary, 7 Field Company Royal Engineers.
TNA WO95/2822 War Diary, 50th Division Signal Company Royal Engineers.
TNA WO95/2823 War Diary, 50th Battalion Machine Gun Corps.
TNA WO95/2831 War Diary, 13th Battalion (Scottish Horse) Black Watch.
TNA WO95/2832 War Diary, 2nd Battalion Dublin Fusiliers.
TNA WO95/2833 War Diary, HQ 150 Infantry Brigade.
TNA WO95/2837 War Diary, 2nd Battalion Royal Munster Fusiliers.
TNA WO95/2839 War Diary, HQ 151 Infantry Brigade.
TNA WO95/2842 War Diary, 4th Battalion King's Royal Rifle Corps.
TNA WO95/2843 War Diary, 1st Battalion King's Own Yorkshire Light Infantry.
TNA WO95/2843 War Diary, 6th Battalion Inniskilling Fusiliers.
TNA WO95/3122 War Diary, HQ 66th Infantry Division.
TNA WO95/3123 War Diary, AA & QMG 66th Infantry Division.
TNA WO95/3125 War Diary, HQ Commander Royal Engineers 66th Division.
TNA WO95/3128 War Diary, 66th Division Ammunition Column.
TNA WO95/3129 War Diary, 430 Field Company Royal Engineers.
TNA WO95/3129 War Diary, 431 Field Company Royal Engineers.
TNA WO95/3130 War Diary, 432 Field Company Royal Engineers.
TNA WO95/3133 War Diary, 66th Divisional Train Army Service Corps.
TNA WO95/3139 War Diary, HQ 198 Infantry Brigade.
TNA WO95/3140 War Diary, 1/6th Battalion Lancashire Fusiliers.
TNA WO95/3140 War Diary, 6th Battalion Royal Dublin Fusiliers.
TNA WO95/3140 War Diary, 5th Battalion Royal Inniskilling Fusiliers
TNA WO95/3140 War Diary, 6th Battalion Royal Dublin Fusiliers.
TNA WO95/3143 War Diary, HQ 199 Infantry Brigade.
TNA WO95/3146 War Diary, HQ South African Brigade.
TNA WO95/3147 War Diary, 2nd South African Infantry.
TNA WO95/3147 War Diary, 4th South African Infantry.
TNA WO157/199 Fourth Army Intelligence Summaries, October 1918.
TNA WO158/867 Tank Corps: Tank Board, agenda and minutes.
TNA WO158/241 Fourth Army Operations.

TNA WO158/332	Narrative of Machine Gun Operations – Fourth Army.
TNA WO158/191	First Army Operations.

Library and Archives Canada

RG 9 III-D-1, vol. 4686, folder 36, file 6	War Diary, Machine Gun Squadron, Canadian Cavalry Brigade.
RG9 III-D-3, Volume 5012, Reel T-10861.	War Diary, 2nd Battalion Canadian Railway Troops.
RG 9 III-D-3, vol. 4955, folder 494	War Diary, Lord Strathcona's Horse.
RG 9 III-D-3, vol. 4956, folder 496	War Diary, Fort Garry Horse.
RG 9 III-D-3, vol. 4956, folder 495	War Diary, Royal Canadian Dragoons.

Imperial War Museum

Docs 2001	R.G. Dixon, Private Papers.
Docs 3233	K. Earle, Private Papers.
Docs 7197	F.J. Rice, Private Papers
Docs 10076	'War Experiences and Tactical Notes of the 17th Armoured Car Tank Battalion'.
Docs 70861	A. Caseby, 'War Memoirs of a Gunner in the Royal Field Artillery'.
Docs 20537	Fourth Army Papers
	Vol. 48 General Headquarters' Letters, July 1918 to February 1919.
	Vol. 51 Operation Orders & Instructions, 23 September 1918 to 11 November 1918.
	Vol. 63 III and XI Corps Narratives, August 1918 to October 1918.
	Vol. 64 XIII Corps Narratives, October 1918 to November 1918.

Australian War Memorial

AWM4 Item No. 8/6/22	Squadron Record Book, 3rd Squadron AFC.
AWM4 Item No. 13/4/17	War Diary, HQ GOCRA 1st Anzac Corps.
AWM4 Item No. 13/11/32	War Diary, HQ 2nd Australian Divisional Artillery.
AWM4 Item No. 13/14/33	War Diary, HQ 5th Australian Divisional Artillery.
AWM4 Item No. 13/33/35	War Diary, HQ 5th Brigade Australian Field Artillery.
AWM4 Item No. 13/35/24	War Diary, HQ 7th Brigade Australian Field Artillery.
AWM4 Item No. 13/36/29	War Diary, HQ 8th Brigade Australian Field Artillery.
AWM4 Item No. 13/38/33	War Diary, HQ 11th Brigade Australian Field Artillery.
AWM4 Item No. 13/38/33	War Diary, HQ 5th Brigade Australian Field Artillery.
AWM4 Item No. 13/40/32	War Diary, HQ 13th Brigade Australian Field Artillery.
AWM4 Item No. 13/41/28	War Diary, HQ 14th Brigade Australian Field Artillery.
AWM4 RCDIG1006531	War Diary, 1st Australian Tunnelling Company.

National Archives of Australia

Series B2455
Barrett, A.G
Lock, Francis Michael.
Palstra, William.
Macdougall, W.A.

Churchill College, Cambridge

Sir Henry Rawlinson, War Journal, RWLN 1/11 & 1/12.

II. OFFICIAL PUBLICATIONS

American Battle Monuments Commission, *30th Division Summary of Operations in the World War*, Washington, Government Printing Office, 1944.
American Battle Monuments Commission, *27th Division Summary of Operations in the World War*, Washington, Government Printing Office, 1944.
Anonymous, *The Work of the Royal Engineers in the European War 1914-19 – Bridging*, Chatham, Mackay, 1921.
J. Beach, *The Division in Attack – 1918 (SS 135 T/1635 40/WO/7036)*, The Strategic and Combat Studies Institute, 2008, (originally published 1918).
J. Beach, *Haig's Intelligence – GHQ and the German Army, 1916-1918*, Cambridge, Cambridge University Press, 2013.
S. Bidwell & D. Graham, *Fire-Power – The British Army Weapons & Theories of War 1904-1945*, Barnsley, Pen & Sword, 2004, (originally published 1982).
J.E. Edmonds, *Military Operations France and Belgium, 1918, Vol. 4*, London & Nashville, Imperial War Museum & Battery Press, (originally published 1947).
J.E. Edmonds & R. Maxwell-Hyslop, *Military Operations – France and Belgium 1918, Vol V*, London & Nashville, Imperial War Museum & Battery Press, (originally published 1947).
Center of Military History, *United States Army in the World War 1917-1919, Military Operations of the American Expeditionary Forces, Vol VII*, Washington, United States Army, 1990.
General Staff, *Operations of the 2d American Corps in the Somme Offensive*, Washington, Government Printing Office, 1921.
General Staff, *[SS 143] The Training and Employment of Platoons 1918*, London, HMSO.
General Staff, *[SS 169] Employment of 3-in Stokes Mortars in Recent Fighting*, London, HMSO, 1917.
General Staff, *[SS 197] Tactical Employment of Lewis Guns*, London, HMSO, 1918.
General Staff, *[SS 204] Infantry and Tank Co-Operation and Training*, London, HMSO, 1918.
General Staff, *[SS 214] Tanks and their Employment in Co-Operation with Other Arms*, London, HMSO, 1918.
General Staff, *[SS 169] Employment of 3-in Stokes Mortars in Recent Fighting*, London, HMSO, 1917.
General Staff American Expeditionary Forces, *Histories of Two Hundred and Fifty-One Divisions of the German Army which Participated in the War (1914-1918)*, Washington, Government Printing Office, 1920.
A.M. Henniker, *Transportation on the Western Front*, London, HMSO, 1937.

War Office, *Field Service Regulations, Part I, Operations 1909* (amendments 1912), London, HMSO.
War Office, *Statistics of the Military Effort of the British Empire During the Great War 1914-1920*, London HMSO, 1922.

III. PRINTED SOURCES

Anonymous, *History 119th Infantry, 60th Brigade, 30th Division, U.S.A.*, Wilmington Chamber of Commerce, n.d.
Anonymous, *History of the 50th Infantry Brigade 1914-1919*, published privately, 1919.
Anonymous, *The Northamptonshire Regiment 1914-1918*, Uckfield, Naval & Military, 2005.
Anonymous, *The War History of The Sixth Tank Battalion,* privately printed, 1919.
Anonymous, *Operations of XIII Corps Between 3rd October and 11th November 1918*, Stoke, Hill & Ainsworth, n.d.
Anonymous, *Operations of the 17th (Armoured Car) Tank Battalion during the Battle of 1918*, Aldershot, Gale and Polden, 1920.
C.T. Atkinson, *The History of the South Wales Borderers 1914-1918*, London, Medici Society, 1931.
S. Badsey, *Doctrine and Reform in the British Cavalry 1880-1918,* Aldershot, Ashgate, 2008.
T.M. Banks and R.A. Chell, *With the 10th Essex in France*, London, Burt, 1921.
J. Bickersteth, *The Bickersteth Diaries*, London, Leo Cooper, 1995.
J.B. Bickersteth, *History of the 6th Cavalry Brigade*, London, Sanders Phillips, n.d.
G. Blaxland, *Amiens 1918*, London, W.H. Allen 1981.
J. Boff, *Winning and Losing on the Western Front,* Cambridge, Cambridge University Press, 2012.
B. Bond & S.Robbins (eds), *Staff Officer: The Diaries of Walter Guinness (First Lord Moyne) 1914-1918*, London Leo Cooper, 1987.
R.C. Bond, *The King's Own Yorkshire Light Infantry in the Great War*, London, Lund Humphries, 1920.
I. M. Brown, *British Logistics on the Western Front 1914-1919*; London, Praeger, 1998.
J. Buchan, *The History of the South African Forces in France,* London, Thomas Nelson, 1920.
C. von Clausewitz (translated by J.J. Graham), *On War – Volume One*, London, Kegan Paul, Trench Trubner & Co, 1908 (originally published 1832).
A. Clayton, *Paths of Glory – The French Army 1914-18*, London, Cassell, 2003.
C.P. Clayton (M. Clayton ed.), *The Hungry One*, Llandysul, Gomer Press, 1978.
G. Chapman, *A Passionate Prodigality*, London, Mayflower-Dell, 1967 (originally published 1933).
H. Cron (translated C.F. Colton), *Imperial German Army 1914-18: Organisation, Structure, Orders of Battle,* Solihull, Helion, 2002.
Crown Prince William, *Memoirs of the Crown Prince of Germany*, New York, Charles Scribner's Sons, 1922.
W.J.K. Davies, *Light Railways of the First World War: A History of Tactical Rail Communications on the British Fronts, 1914-18*, Newton Abbot, David & Charles, 1967.
P. Dennis & J. Grey, *1918 Defining Victory,* Canberra, Department of Defence, 1999.
M. Farndale, *History of the Royal Regiment of Artillery: Western Front 1914-1918,* Woolwich, Royal Artillery Institution, 1986.
P.H. Fike, *History of Co. F, 118th Infantry (Hampton Guards) 30th Division,* Spartanburg, Band & White, 1919.
D. Finlayson, *Crumps and Camouflets – Australian Tunneling Companies on the Western Front*, Newport, Big Sky, 2010.
H. FitzM. Stacke, *Worcestershire Regiment in the Great War,* Privately published, 1928.

F. Foch, (translated by T.B. Mott), *The Memoirs of Marshal Foch*, New York, Doubleday Doran, 1931.
N. Grant, *The Lewis Gun*, Oxford, Osprey, 2014.
P. Griffith (ed.), *British Fighting Methods in the Great War*, London, Frank Cass, 1996.
W. Griffith, *Up to Mametz*, London: Severn House, 1981 (originally published 1931).
S. Hare, *The Annals of the King's Royal Rifle Corps, Vol 5*, London, John Murray, 1932.
J.P. Harris, *Douglas Haig and the First World War*, Cambridge, Cambridge University Press, 2008.
J.P. Harris and N. Barr, *Amiens to the Armistice*, London, Brassey's, 1998.
J. D. Hills, *The Fifth Leicestershire,* Loughborough, Echo Press, 1919.
P. Hodgkinson, *Glum Heroes – Hardship, Fear and Death – Resilience and Coping in the British Army on the Western Front 1914-1918*, Solihull, Helion, 2016.
P.E. Hodgkinson, *British Infantry Battalion Commanders in the First World War*, Farnham, Ashgate, 2015.
R. Holmes, *Tommy: The British Soldier on the Western Front*, London, Harper Collins, 2004.
D. Hughes, *Moltke on the Art of War: Selected Writings,* Novato, Presidio, 1993.
G.F. Jacobson, *History of the 107th Infantry U.S.A*, New York, Seventh Regiment Armory, 1920.
H.S. Jervis, *The 2nd Munsters in France*, Aldershot, Gale & Polden, 1922.
M. Kincaid-Smith, *The 25th Division in France and Flanders*, London, Harrison & Sons, 1918.
N. Lloyd, *Hundred Days – The End of the Great War*, London, Penguin, 2014.
T.O. Marden, *A Short History of the Sixth Division*, London, Hugh Rees, 1920.
C. Messenger, *The Day We Won The War – Turning Point at Amiens 8th August 1918*, London, Weidenfeld & Nicolson, 2008.
W. Miles, *The Durham Forces in the Field 1914-18*, Uckfield, Naval & Military (originally published 1920).
A. Montgomery, *The Story of the Fourth Army in the Battles of the Hundred Days*, London, Hodder & Stoughton, 1919.
E.A. Murphy and R.S. Thomas, *The Thirtieth Division in the World War*, US Government Printing Office, 1944.
W.E.L. Napier, *With the Trench Mortars in France*, Auckland, Alpe, 1923.
G.H.F. Nichols, *The 18th Division in the Great War*, London, W. Blackwood & Sons, 1922.
V. Orange, *Coningham – A Biography of Air Marshal Sir Arthur Coningham*, London, Methuen, 1990.
J.F. O'Ryan, *The Story of the 27th Division*, New York, Wynkoop Hallenbeck Crawford, 1921.
Oxford English Reference Dictionary (2nd Edition), Oxford, Oxford University Press, 1996.
S. Peaple, *Mud Blood and Determination – The History of the 46th (North Midland) Division in the Great War*, Solihull, Helion, 2015.
F.L. Petre, *The History of the Norfolk Regiment*, Norwich, Jarrold & Sons, 1924.
R.E. Priestley, *Breaking the Hindenburg Line – The Story of the 46th (North Midland) Division*, London, Fisher Unwin, 1919.
R. Prior and T. Wilson, *Command on the Western Front – The Military Career of Sir Henry Rawlinson 1914-1918*, Barnsley, Pen & Sword, 2004 (originally published 1992).
H. L. Pritchard, *History of the Corps of Royal Engineers. Vol. 5, The Home Front, France, Flanders and Italy in the First World War,* Chatham, Institution of Royal Engineers, 1952.
W. A. Raleigh, *The War in the Air; Being the Story of the Part Played by the Royal Air Force, Vol. 1*, Oxford, Clarendon, 1922.
J. Reith, *Wearing Spurs*, London, Hutchinson, 1966.

G.R. Rose, *The Story of the 2/4th Oxfordshire and Buckinghamshire Light Infantry*, Oxford, Blackwell, 1920.

S. Royall, *History of the 118th Infantry, American Expeditionary Force, France*, Columbia, State Company, 1919.

Marquis de Ruvigny, *De Ruvigny's Roll of Honour 1914-1918*, 5 Vols, Uckfield, Naval & Military, 2001.

T.E Sandall, *A History of the 5th Batt. The Lincolnshire Regiment*, Oxford, Blackwell, 1922.

H.R. Sandilands, *The Fifth in the Great War*, Dover, G.W. Grigg & Son, 1938.

M. Schwarte, *Der Grosse Krieg*, Barth, 1923.

A. Searle (ed.), *Genesis, Employment, Aftermath: First World War Tanks and the New Warfare, 1900-1945*, Solihull, Helion, 2015.

G. D. Sheffield, *Forgotten Victory : The First World War: Myths and Realities*, London Headline, 2001.

G.D. Sheffield, *Command and Morale: The British Army on the Western Front 1914-1918,* Barnsley, Pen & Sword, 2014.

G. Sheffield, *The Chief: Douglas Haig and the British Army*, London, Aurum, 2011.

G. Sheffield & J. Bourne (eds), *Douglas Haig: War Diaries and Letters 1914-1918*, London, Weidenfeld & Nicolson, 2005.

G. Sheffield & P. Gray (eds), *Changing War: The British Army, The Hundred Days Campaign and the Birth of the Royal Air Force, 1918,* London, Bloomsbury, 2015.

G.D. Sheffield & G.I.S. Inglis (eds), *From Vimy Ridge to the Rhine: The Great War Letters of Christopher Stone DSO MC,* Crowood, Ramsbury, 1989.

G. Sheffield and D. Todman (eds), *Command and Control on the Western Front – The British Army's Experience 1914-18*, Staplehurst, Spellmount, 2004.

P. Simkins, *From the Somme to Victory – The British Army's Experience on the Western Front 1916-1918,* Barnsley, Pen & Sword, 2014.

A. Simpson, *Directing Operations: British Corps Command on the Western Front 1914-18*, Stroud, Spellmount, 2005.

P. Strong & S. Marble, *Artillery in the Great War,* Barnsley, Pen & Sword, 2011.

W.P. Sullivan & H. Tucker, *The History of the 105th Regiment of Engineers,* New York, George Doran, 1919.

D.F. Trask. *The AEF & Coalition Warmaking*, Lawrence, University Press of Kansas, 1993.

J. Walker, *The Blood Tub: General Gough and the Battle of Bullecourt,* Staplehurst, Spellmount, 1998.

J.O. Walker, W.A. Graham & T. Fauntleroy, *Official History the 120th Infantry, '3rd North Carolina', 30th Division,* Lynchburg, J.P. Bell, n.d.

A. Watson, *Enduring the Great War: Combat, Morale and Collapse in the German and British Armies 1914-1918*, Cambridge, Cambridge University Press, 2008.

A. Watson, *Ring of Steel: Germany and Austria-Hungary at War 1914-1918*, New York Basic, 2014.

W.C.C. Weetman, *The Sherwood Foresters in the Great War 1914-1919 – 1/8th Battalion*, Nottingham, Thomas Forman, 1920.

W. de B. Wood, *The History of the King's Shropshire Light Infantry in the Great War*, London, Medici Society, 1925.

G.C. Wynn, *If Germany Attacks: The Battle in Depth in the West*, London, Faber & Faber, 1940.

H.C. Wylly, *Crown and Company 1911-1922,* Aldershot, Gale & Polden, 1923.

H.C. Wylly, *The First and Second Battalions The Sherwood Foresters (Nottinghamshire and Derbyshire Regiment) in the Great War,* Aldershot, Gale & Polden, 1936.

E. Wyrall, *The West Yorkshire Regiment in the War 1914-1918*, London, Bodley Head, 1923.

IV. JOURNAL ARTICLES

E.P. Anderson, 'The Railway Organization of an Army in War', *Journal of the Royal United Services Institution*, (72) 1927, pp.503-511.
A.F. Becke, 'The Coming of the Creeping Barrage'. *Journal of the Royal Artillery*, (58) 1931, pp.19-42.
D.J.C.K. Bernard, 'The Crossing of Rivers in Warfare', *Journal of the Royal United Services Institution*, (70) 1925, pp.416-430.
R. Blaber, 'Tanks in the "Hundred Days" 1918 – A Diminishing Resource', *British Journal for Military History*, (2) 2015, pp.104-122.
R. Bonham-Smith, 'Railway Transport Arrangements in France', *Journal of the Royal United Services Institution,* (61) 1916, pp.47-62.
J. Bourne, 'British Divisional Commanders during the Great War: First Thoughts', *Gun Fire: A Journal of First World War History*, 29, n.d. p.29.
J.M. Diehl, 'Germany in Defeat, 1918 and 1945: Some Comparisons and Contrasts', *The History Teacher*, (22) 1999, pp.397-409.
P. Dye, 'RFC Bombs and Bombing 1912-1918', *Royal Air Force Historical Society Journal*, (45) 2009, pp.8-14.
R.B. Harrison, 'Famous Charges Told of the U.S. Tank Brigade', *The Army*, (1) 1919.
A.D. Harvey, 'Trench Mortars in the First World War', *Journal of the Royal United Services Institution,* (157) 2012, pp.86-92.
G. Sheffield, 'A Once in a Century Opportunity? Some Personal Reflections on the Centenary of the First World War', *British Journal for Military History*, (1) 2014, pp. 1-11.
M.G Taylor, 'Land Transportation in the Late War', *Journal of the Royal United Services Institution*, (66) 1921, pp.699-722.

V. THESES/UNPUBLISHED PAPERS

J.D. Clayton, 'The Battle of the Sambre, 4 November 1918', PhD University of Birmingham, 2015.
B.N. Hall, 'The British Expeditionary Force and Communications on the Western Front 1914-1918', PhD University of Salford, 2009.
B. Hammond, 'The Theory and Practice of Tank Co-Operation with Other Arms on the Western Front During the First World War', PhD University of Birmingham, 2005.
T. G. Harvey, '"An Army of Brigadiers" British Brigade Commanders at the Battle of Arras 1917', PhD University of Birmingham, 2015.
S. M. Justice, 'Means to an End: The Experience of 1918 and its Influence on the British Fourth Army's Performance on the Selle', MA University of Birmingham, 2009.
C. Kang, 'The British Regimental Officer on the Western Front in the Great War, with Special Reference to the Royal Warwickshire Regiment', PhD University of Birmingham, 2007.
D. Kenyon, 'British Cavalry on the Western Front, 1916-1918', PhD Cranfield University, 2008.
A.J. Saunders, 'A Muse of Fire – British Trench Warfare Munitions, their Invention, Manufacture and Tactical Employment on the Western Front, 1914–18', PhD Exeter University, 2008.
P. Simkins, 'A Man on the Spot – Brigadier-General R.E. Sugden'.
A. Simpson, 'The Operational Role of British Corps Command on the Western Front', PhD University College, London, 2001.
M. Whisler, '"Der Tommy Kommt" – British Expeditionary Force Campaign Orchestration and Fourth Army Operational Execution at the battle of the Selle River, October 1918: A Case

Study in British Offensive Operations against the Imperial German Army'. Master of Military Studies, United States Marine Corps Command and Staff College, 2001.
M. Yockelson, '"Brothers in Arms?" The American and British Coalition on the Western Front 1918', PhD Cranfield University, 2006.

VI. THE INTERNET

http://bef-battles.org.uk (accessed 28 January 2016).
http://www.glosters.org/milesvc.htm (accessed 10 April 2016).
The Guardian, http://www.theguardian.com/world/2013/may/21/remembering-war-to-promote-peace 21 May 2013 (accessed 02 January 2016).
http://1914-1918.invisionzone.com/forums/index.php?/topic/46667-german-soldiers-chained-to-machine-gun/ (accessed 29 November 2016)
Jessica Meyer, http://armsandthemedicalman.wordpress.com/2013/05/22/possibly-an-angry-post/ 22 May 2013, (accessed 02 January 2016).
http://www.da.mod.uk/Publications/category/516/The-Independent-Force, (accessed 26 September 2016).
G.A. Morrice, Diary, http://www.oryansroughnecks.org/diary.html (accessed 10 February 2016).
J.F. Oakleaf, 'Notes on the Operations of the 108th Infantry Overseas', http://www.gwpda.org/memoir/Oakleaf/108th.htm (accessed 15 March 2016).
http://parkt-scheisse.de/formgesch/formatio_div.html Interessen und Arbeitsgemeinschaft Weltkrieg 1914-1918 (AGW14-18) (accessed 17 November 2016).
W. Philpott, https://rusi.org/commentary/beyond-learning-curve-british-armys-military-transformation-first-world-war (accessed 5 September 2016).
K.R. Thrower, 'Army Radio Communication in the Great War', http://blogs.mhs.ox.ac.uk/innovatingincombat/files/2013/03/Army-radio-communication-in-the-Great-War_V2.pdf (accessed 15 September 2016).
http://www.mtwilson.com.au/mt-wilsonmt-irvine-historical-society/miscellaneous-articles/215-2005-remembrance-day-transcript.html (accessed 29 November 2016).
http://parkt-scheisse.de/formgesch/formatio_div.html Interessen und Arbeitsgemeinschaft Weltkrieg 1914-1918 (AGW14-18) (accessed 17 November 1918).
http://www.westernfrontassociation.com/great-war-people/the-british-generals-biographies/3405-lieutenant-general-sir-walter-pipon-braithwaite-kcb.html (accessed 1 August 2016).

Index

Index of People

Index of Places

Index of Military Formations & Units